State of Emergency

*Never Had It So Good: A History of Britain from
Suez to the Beatles*

White Heat: A History of Britain in the Swinging Sixties

DOMINIC SANDBROOK

State of Emergency

The Way We Were: Britain, 1970–1974

ALLEN LANE
an imprint of
PENGUIN BOOKS

ALLEN LANE

Published by the Penguin Group
Penguin Books Ltd, 80 Strand, London WC2R ORL, England
Penguin Group (USA) Inc., 375 Hudson Street, New York, New York 10014, USA
Penguin Group (Canada), 90 Eglinton Avenue East, Suite 700, Toronto, Ontario, Canada M4P 2Y3
(a division of Pearson Canada Inc.)
Penguin Ireland, 25 St Stephen's Green, Dublin 2, Ireland (a division of Penguin Books Ltd)
Penguin Group (Australia), 250 Camberwell Road, Camberwell, Victoria 3124, Australia
(a division of Pearson Australia Group Pty Ltd)
Penguin Books India Pvt Ltd, 11 Community Centre, Panchsheel Park, New Dehli – 110 017, India
Penguin Group (NZ), 67 Apollo Drive, North Shore 0632, New Zealand (a division of Pearson New Zealand Ltd)
Penguin Books (South Africa) (Pty) Ltd, 24 Sturdee Avenue, Rosebank 2196, South Africa

Penguin Books Ltd, Registered Offices: 80 Strand, London WC2R ORL, England

www.penguin.com

First published 2010
1

Set in 10.2/13.87 pt Linotype Sabon
Typeset by Ellipsis Books Limited, Glasgow
Printed in Great Britain by Clays Ltd, St Ives plc

ISBN: 978–1–846–14031–0

www.greenpenguin.co.uk

*For my great-aunt Muriel Wilcox
and my wife Catherine Morley, with love*

All over the nation, families who had listened to the news looked at one another and said 'Goodness me' or 'Whatever next' or 'I give up' or 'Well, fuck that', before embarking on an evening's viewing of colour television, or a large hot meal, or a trip to the pub, or a choral society evening. All over the country people blamed other people for all the things that were going wrong – the trades unions, the present government, the miners, the car workers, the seamen, the Arabs, the Irish, their own husbands, their own wives, their own idle good-for-nothing offspring, comprehensive education. Nobody knew whose fault it really was, but most people managed to complain fairly forcefully about somebody: only a few were stunned into honourable silence.

Margaret Drabble, *The Ice Age* (1977)

We look back on past ages with condescension, as a mere preparation for us . . . but what if we're only an after-glow of them?

J. G. Farrell, *The Siege of Krishnapur* (1973)

Michael Cummings in the *Daily Express*, 9 February 1972

Contents

List of Illustrations

List of Cartoons

All cartoons supplied by the British Cartoon Archive.

State of Emergency

Preface: A State of Emergency

But now here it is, the day of beginning again, the day that is written down in so many diaries, and it is raining, and dreary, and bleak.

– Malcolm Bradbury, *The History Man* (1975)

It was, everyone agreed, a lovely morning for a wedding. After days of rain, the clouds had cleared and London's newly scrubbed streets sparkled in the unseasonal November sunlight. Along the route from the Palace to the Abbey, the roads had been closed to traffic, making room for tens of thousands of onlookers, many groggily shaking themselves awake after a cold night under the stars. Even as the early spectators brewed their cups of tea, the coachmen in the Royal Mews were finishing their exercises and the troops were marching smartly into position along the processional route. Hundreds of little flags fluttered in the brisk morning breeze, testament to the hard work of the staff of the Department of the Environment, who had spent the last few days decorating the streets with Union Jacks, monograms of 'A' and 'M', and decorations in what one official described as 'coral pink and what used to be called nigger brown'. Everywhere there was a palpable sense of anticipation, 'an atmosphere of festivity and expectation'. And as the sun climbed in the sky and the crowds swelled from hundreds to thousands, as the Boy Scouts in their green uniforms trudged down the lines with their souvenir programmes, as the hawkers moved in with their hot dogs and drinks and their 'Mark and Anne' souvenir T-shirts, the first guests began to arrive at the Abbey, filing solemnly in beneath the bright television lights, the grand chandeliers and the softer, dimmer glow of the candles in the flower-decked sacrarium.[1]

The wedding of Princess Anne and Captain Mark Phillips on 14

November 1973 was the first major royal event in London since the Coronation, twenty years previously. And in some ways, whether watching from among the crowds or listening to the BBC's reverential commentary, it was possible to imagine that nothing had changed since that rainy June day two decades before – except that this time the weather was better. As the Blues and Royals escorted the Queen's carriage through the central arch of Buckingham Palace and along the Mall, their horses' hooves clattering on the tarmac and their finery glittering in the sunlight, the spectators seemed just as respectful and enthusiastic as their predecessors had been back in 1953. It was 'one of those stately pageants that the British remain best in the world at producing', said *The Times* the next day, lovingly describing the shining silver of the Abbey plate, the sapphire blue of the Queen's outfit, the lobster, the partridge and the peppermint ice cream of the wedding breakfast. It was a celebration of history and tradition, in which the Princess and her Captain used 'the same old vows and blessings and the same old beautifully simple language of the sixteenth-century Prayer Book that is used at all Church of England weddings'. And it was a glamorous fairy-tale wedding, an old-fashioned romantic fable with a dashing bridegroom in the scarlet and blue of the Dragoon Guards and a 23-year-old bride in virginal white, who 'smiled so gaily', one reporter wrote, 'that the adjective radiant trembled even on hard-bitten lips'.[2]

Like the Coronation, the wedding was a genuinely national event. In the Wiltshire village of Great Somerford, where Captain Phillips's parents lived, all the residents over 60 were invited to the village school so that they could follow the occasion live on colour television, followed by a buffet lunch with a replica of the wedding cake. There was a tea party for local children, a fireworks display and a barbecue of suckling pig. Across the country, schools had devoted hours to telling their pupils about the significance of the day, while retailers had slashed their prices to induce viewers to invest in new televisions so that they could appreciate the spectacle in glorious colour. And when the BBC collated its viewing figures afterwards, it emerged that a staggering 28 million people had tuned in to watch the wedding live, the third biggest television audience of the decade after the Apollo 13 splashdown and the FA Cup Final replay between Chelsea and Leeds three years before. Indeed, thanks to the wonders of technology, it was not merely a national event but an international one. In the Republic of Ireland, bitterness at recent events

4

in Belfast and Londonderry did not stop so many people tuning in that Dublin's electricity board struggled to cope with the demand. In France, an estimated 10 million people gathered around their televisions; in West Germany, many British servicemen were given time off to watch the wedding, and army wives held parties around their glowing sets. And in the United States and Canada, where live coverage began at five in the morning on the East Coast, the wedding dominated the breakfast bulletins. So many Americans were glued to their televisions, reports said later, that they ended up being late for work.[3]

Yet although American viewers loved the royal wedding for its patina of tradition, the very fact of the television coverage reflected the extraordinary changes that had overtaken British life since London's last major royal occasion. In 1953, when the Coronation had been the first such event shown live on television, most people had not owned a set. Even though ownership doubled to 3 million in the run-up to the big day, the vast majority of Britons had watched the ceremony with family, friends and neighbours, gathered in awe around a popping, crackling black-and-white box. By 1973, however, almost every family in the country had a set of their own. Watching television, once a relative luxury, was now by far the most popular form of entertainment in the country, so deeply embedded in national cultural life that the Dean of Westminster agreed to share his viewing recommendations for the week with the readers of the *Radio Times*. (He would be watching *Dad's Army* the night before the wedding, he admitted, but not *Match of the Day*, which was on a bit late.) And although some people held parties or invited relatives for lunch, most watched in the privacy of their own homes. The collective solidarity exemplified by the Coronation street parties was now an increasingly distant memory; by 1973, even working-class families were used to spending their evenings, weekends and holidays on their own, basking in the benefits of the affluent society.[4]

If a Londoner from the cheering Coronation crowds had been catapulted forward twenty years to the wedding of the Queen's daughter, what would he have made of Britain in 1973? No doubt he would have been amused by the new fashions: the jeans and sweaters that many spectators wore that cool November morning, the flares and high heels, the parka anoraks and flowing maxi-dresses, the sheepskin coats and corduroy jackets, the mini-skirts left over from the late 1960s, the long sideburns and shaggy beards, the long-haired men and the women in trousers. But he would surely have been more struck by the general air of prosperity and comfort, by the fact that so many people had cars of their own, by the central heating, the indoor toilets, the gleaming new kitchens and bathrooms, by the appliances – telephones, fridges, washing machines – that families now took for granted. Casting his eyes across the skyline, he would have been startled by the slim cylindrical intrusion of the Post Office Tower, that supreme symbol of the technological modernity of the 1960s, but he would have been even more stunned by the vast concrete monoliths along the horizon, the glowering council tower blocks and faceless office buildings that had utterly transformed the urban landscape.

And if, as the royal carriages rolled past, he had broken away from the crowds and turned towards the West End, he would surely have rubbed his eyes in wonder at the high-street fashion stores overflowing with new designs, the bookshops groaning under their weight of stock, the Italian pizzerias, the Indian curry houses, the Chinese takeaways. If he had opened a newspaper, he would have been taken aback by the complacent assumptions of abundance – the classified offers of second-hand cars and old appliances, the endless promises of bargain-bonanza sales, the features on gardening, motoring and DIY, the glossy advertisements for cigars, liqueurs and foreign holidays. But if he had looked at a map, he would have been stunned to see so many new countries, and probably horrified by the apparent extinction of the British Empire. And if he had plucked up the courage to go into a pub, to buy a drink – perhaps lager or keg beer, not the bitter or mild he usually drank – he would have recognized some of his neighbours' conversation, but not all of it. He might remember the name of Harold Wilson, a youthful President of the Board of Trade back in Mr Attlee's day, but the names of Edward Heath and Enoch Powell, Jeremy Thorpe and Jim Callaghan, would be entirely unfamiliar to him. He would never have heard of Torremolinos or Benidorm, of Bruce Forsyth or Michael Parkinson, of David Bowie or James Bond. What was a comprehensive school? What on earth was the sexual revolution? And why was everything so expensive?

But while our time traveller would have spent his first hours in the future rubbing his eyes in disbelief at the affluence of the early 1970s, if he had stayed a little longer he would have found a very different side to life on 14 November 1973. That morning, as the upper-class diarist James Lees-Milne caustically observed, 'the public were determined to enjoy the Princess, who is ugly, marrying a handsome boy who is barely a gentleman'. But as Lees-Milne also noted, 'the newspaper posters on the other hand contained the gloomiest portents in their headings, fuel crises, more strikes, Bank Rate rising to unprecedented heights, the stock market falling to the plumbiest depths'. Another acerbic observer, *Private Eye*'s Auberon Waugh, told *Time* magazine that Britain had become 'something between Nkrumah's Ghana and Anthony Hope's Ruritania'. 'Many of us here are more or less permanently on strike,' Waugh explained. 'We are all paid far too much and expect to be paid much more. It is true that the public services in London are breaking down even while Mr Heath pursues his grandiose schemes to build supersonic airliners and dig railway tunnels under the Channel to France. It is true that electricity supplies are more or less permanently threatened by industrial action, and urban violence is just beginning.' And yet it seemed that most people were far more interested in 'the spectacle of two totally absurd young people being driven around London in a glass coach'. The obvious conclusion, Waugh admitted, was that Britain was suffering from a 'mild attack of schizophrenia'. Yet he thought that Britain was 'as united as any nation can be – in a gigantic effort to be entertained. That is the essence of the new Britain: the show goes on, but now it is played as farce. We are citizens of the world's first satirical Ruritania.'[5]

The truth was that the royal wedding could hardly have unfolded against a more depressing backdrop. Just over a month before, Egypt and Syria had launched a stunning surprise attack on Israel, prompting the Arab-dominated OPEC cartel to impose a devastating 70 per cent increase in the cost of oil. Almost overnight, the Western economy had lurched into a nightmarish combination of recession and inflation: 'stagflation'. And with oil prices soaring, the Conservative government's opponents in the National Union of Mineworkers had seen their chance, quite literally, to strike. On Monday, 12 November, just two days before the royal wedding, Britain's 260,000 miners had begun an overtime ban in pursuit of higher pay, in clear defiance of the nationwide wage limits that Edward Heath had imposed only weeks before. By that evening, the Electricity Board was already warning that snap power cuts were likely to affect much of the country, plunging homes and offices, schools and hospitals into darkness. And on Tuesday afternoon, even as Princess Anne was making the final preparations for her big day, the government took drastic action, announcing an immediate state of emergency, outlawing electric advertising and floodlighting, and ordering public buildings to cut fuel consumption by a tenth. The looming energy crisis, the Home Secretary told the Commons, was 'a threat to the essentials of life in the community', leaving the government no choice but to assume 'immediate emergency powers'. It spoke volumes about Britain's political and economic situation in the early 1970s that this was the fifth State of Emergency in three years.[6]

On Wednesday morning, the front page of *The Times* featured a photograph of the Queen being driven back from the wedding rehearsal at Westminster Abbey, her face pale with the nerves of any bride's mother before the big day. By her side, the Duke of Edinburgh was grinning broadly for the photographers. But the headlines made for cheerless reading. 'Lights Go Out As Emergency Powers Bite', declared the title of the paper's main story. 'Urgent Action To Meet Energy Crisis: Triple Threat To The Nation'. Along the left-hand side of the page ran a series of equally depressing subheadings: 'Bank Lending Rate Soars / Bank Curbs / Equities Down / Wall Street Losses / Dearer Overdrafts / Sterling Unsteady / Power Plea Rejected / Floodlights Off / Fuel Cut Order / Ambulance Ban / Hospitals Face Threat'. And that was not all. The previous day, the government had announced a monthly trade deficit of what the paper's economics editor Peter Jay called 'epithet-defying' proportions. In a desperate attempt to preserve international confidence in the British economy, the Bank of England had been forced into the tightest credit squeeze imaginable, raising its lending rate to a record 13 per cent and urging banks to raise their overdraft interest rates to 18 per cent. Inside, the paper's lead editorial made no mention of the royal wedding. Instead, it bluntly warned that 'a fight to the death between the Government and the miners' would have brutal consequences. 'The nation knows very well', it concluded, 'that this is a critical winter.' The stark title said it all: 'A State of Emergency'.[7]

In this book's predecessors, *Never Had It So Good* and *White Heat*, I told the story of the British experience from 1956 to 1970 – the period often loosely described as 'the Sixties' – showing how the onset of mass affluence, the dismemberment of the colonial empire, the arrival of thousands of Asian and Caribbean immigrants, the rise of television and youth culture, and the revolution in the expectations of women affected the lives of Britain's 50 million people. *State of Emergency* takes the story from the summer of 1970, when the Conservative leader Edward Heath unexpectedly unseated Harold Wilson in one of the biggest election surprises of the century, to the spring of 1974, when Heath's modernizing ambitions collapsed in ruins amid the most terrifying economic crisis since the Second World War. It re-creates perhaps the most maligned moment in our recent experience, a period marked not just by outlandish fashions, cosy sitcoms, long-haired footballers and women in dungarees, but by a pervasive sense of crisis and discontent with few parallels in our modern history. It traces Heath's political journey from triumph to disaster, but it also explores the birth of the women's liberation movement, the explosion of pornography, the rise of package holidays and the spread of football hooliganism. It is a story with more than its fair share of strikes, car bombs and men in donkey jackets. But it is also a book about *Cosmopolitan* and *Men Only*, the Campaign for Real Ale and Friends of the Earth, George Best's sacking from Manchester United and Slade's quest for the Christmas number one, reflecting both the grim calamities and the gaudy pleasures of life in Britain at the dawn of the 1970s.

The 1970s have not had a good press. In the first account of the decade, published in 1980, the columnist Christopher Booker wrote that they had been 'a kind of long, rather dispiriting interlude: a time when, in politics, in the arts or in almost any other field one considers, the pre-vailing mood was one of a somewhat weary, increasingly conservative, increasingly apprehensive disenchantment'. And within just a few years, the image of the 1970s as a uniquely drab, depressing period in modern British history had become deeply embedded in the popular imagination. Conservatives were particularly keen on bashing the 1970s, often con-veniently forgetting that they themselves had presided over some of the worst episodes of monetary incontinence and industrial unrest. And by the end of the century, the leadership of the Labour Party, too, had found in the 1970s a convenient rhetorical target and a way of proclaiming their own reasonableness and moderation. It was during the Heath years that Gordon Brown cut his teeth in Scottish student politics; but when, as Prime Minister, he held talks with the unions to discuss new labour legislation, he took care to assure reporters that there would be 'no return to the 1970s'. And so it is little wonder that during the financial crisis of 2007–10, it was to the 1970s that commentators turned for parallels. 'The defining characteristics of the Seventies were economic disaster, terrorist threats, corruption in high places, prophecies of ecological doom and fear of the surveillance state's suffocating embrace,' Francis Wheen told the readers of the *Daily Mail*. The 1970s had never really gone away, he added. 'They have merely been lurking, like a madwoman in the attic, waiting for a suitable moment when they can re-emerge and scare us out of our wits all over again.'[8]

Of course this view of the 1970s is a bit of a caricature, just like the common vision of Britain in the 1960s as a country of dope-smoking, Beatles-loving free-love addicts. And although television producers love to slice modern history into precise ten-year units, each with its own flavour and personality, there was much more continuity between the 1960s and 1970s – and between the 1970s and 1980s – than we commonly remember. We often think of the Heath years as the inevitable hangover after the wild party of the 1960s, a 'prolonged "morning after"', in Booker's words. Yet many of the things we associate with the 1960s only gathered momentum in the first half of the following decade. It was in the early 1970s, not the 1960s, that young single women began taking the Pill, the feminist movement really got off the ground, gay liberation first made the headlines and progressive education took hold in many schools. And to complicate matters further, many of the things we habitually associate with the 1970s actually had much deeper roots. Strikes had been a major political issue since the late 1950s, while inflation was already running out of control in the late 1960s. The conflict in Northern Ireland, which dominated the headlines in the Heath years, actually claimed its first victim in 1966, while the environmentalist movement, apparently steeped in the values of the early 1970s, drew inspiration from books published by Rachel Carson and Barbara Ward in 1962 and 1966. Even Thatcherism, supposedly such a radical response to the traumas of the three-day week and the Winter of Discontent, built on a long prehistory of Conservative antipathy to the welfare state and the post-war consensus.

Not surprisingly, historians have often been quick to challenge the exaggerated arch-Thatcherite vision of the 1970s as a period of unprecedented gloom and decline. It is certainly true that for many people living standards stagnated, and middle-class families in particular felt trapped between high taxes and soaring inflation. But we often forget that most Britons, whether young or old, were not very interested in politics and continued to lead happy, prosperous lives indifferent to the great public affairs of the day. Even the writer Richard Clutterbuck, whose book *Britain in Agony* (1978) was a classic example of the doom-laden introspection of the day, admitted that most people wanted 'stability and confidence in the future more than they want radical political change'. So on Thursday, 28 February 1974, a day that marked the end of one of the most tumultuous election campaigns in modern history, an Essex teenager noted in her diary that it was 'voting day today', predicting that 'Labour will be the party to get in'. But she devoted far more space to recording the guest artists on that evening's *Top of the Pops*, who included Ringo Starr, David Bowie, Suzi Quatro and the Wombles. And when, after several days of unprecedented stalemate and agonizing negotiations, Labour eventually regained power, she did not even bother to record it. Instead she devoted her attention to Colin, 'the greatest boy ever', who had asked to borrow her biro in class.[9]

What this teenager's diary reminds us is that, for most people, daily life never approached the extremes often commemorated in histories of the 1970s. Even though the language of British politics was becoming increasingly aggressive, most voters were much more interested in the new series of *On the Buses*, the supermarket opening down the road and their forthcoming holiday on the Costa del Sol. And even during the dreadful economic crisis of 1973–4, most still led relatively comfortable, affluent lives. Despite all the fuss about rising unemployment under Edward Heath, it was actually much lower in the early 1970s than it ever would be again. As a Labour activist reminded Clutterbuck during the final months of 1974, Britain was 'more prosperous in real terms than ever before in our history', and most people 'had the highest standard of living we had ever had'. And what is more, it is worth remembering that for every loser there was often a winner. While working-class teenagers struggled to get jobs and felt abandoned by society, their parents, if they were in steady employment, enjoyed living standards they could hardly have imagined a few decades before. And while middle-class homeowners felt threatened by strikes and squeezed by inflation, their university-educated children had few such worries. 'With higher wages for the working classes, access to affordable housing, free health care, free higher education and low levels of crime, all in a much less unequal society, life then was superior to life as experienced by most of us today,' one Ayrshire man wrote to the *New Statesman* in April 2009. 'In 1976, I was a fully funded sociology undergraduate on a new parkland campus. I had a lovely girlfriend, a motorbike, hair down to my armpits, Neil

Young on the stereo. And it was a glorious summer. Bleak? It was bloody marvellous!'[10]

To call the 1970s 'bloody marvellous', though, is going much too far. The Heath years were indeed a period of extraordinary cultural and social flux, when immigrants were transforming the cultural landscape of Britain's cities, feminists and homosexuals were testing the boundaries of conventional morality, teenagers were growing their hair and defying their parents, and environmental campaigners were questioning the assumptions behind the great post-war boom. But they also represented something of a reckoning for a country and a consensus that had been living on borrowed time – a reckoning reflected in the fact that the Heath government was forced to declare five states of emergency in barely four years. And at a very basic level, the power cuts and strikes of the 1970s, the hysterical headlines and predictions of disaster, were rooted in profound international challenges, from the collapse of the old colonial empires to the surging tide of globalization. For more than a decade, as Britain's imperial possessions disappeared, its economic lead evaporated and its manufacturers struggled to compete with foreign rivals, politicians of both parties had talked of sweeping modernization and structural reform, from decimalization to European integration. In general, however, they had shrunk from radical economic change, frightened that it would undermine full employment and alienate the voters, content merely to keep muddling through. Perhaps this was not surprising: for twenty years, thanks to its soft Commonwealth markets and the weakness of its rivals, Britain had been protected from the harsh winds of global competition. But by the early 1970s, as Edward Heath was to discover, the kaleidoscope was shifting. Not only were foreign consumers less inclined to buy expensive British goods, but international investors were much less disposed to prop up an economy that had become slack and self-indulgent. And when war broke out in the Middle East in 1973, prompting the Arab oil nations to hike up their prices to unprecedented levels, Britain found itself facing the worst economic crisis since the war, its pretensions to greatness exposed as hollow fantasies, its complacent assumptions scattered to the winds.

In many ways the period from 1970 to 1974 is reminiscent of another turbulent four-year episode in modern British history, described most colourfully by the journalist George Dangerfield in his classic book *The Strange Death of Liberal England*. Between 1910 and 1914, Dangerfield argued, H. H. Asquith's Liberal order was radically undermined by four challenges: the Conservative Party's revolt against the People's Budget; the threat of armed rebellion in Ulster; the protests of the suffragettes; and a crippling wave of strikes orchestrated by militant trade unionists. Dangerfield's story was one of political ferment and economic turmoil, of challenges to the moral order and rebellions against traditional gender roles, of utopian socialism and Irish sectarianism – all rooted, like the challenges of the early 1970s, in profound historical trends that no government could possibly control. And although historians have taken issue with his thesis, the parallels with the 1970s are irresistible, from the Balliol-educated technocratic reformer in Number 10 to the contending nationalist passions in Northern Ireland. Heath's Britain, like Asquith's, stood on the brink of a profound transformation, caught between past and present: its political consensus fragmenting under the pressure of social change, its economy struggling to cope with overseas competitors, its culture torn between the comforts of nostalgia and the excitement of change, its leaders groping to understand a landscape transformed by consumerism and social mobility. An old world was dying; a new was struggling to be born.

This book takes the story of Heath's Britain from a warm June morning in 1970 to a gloomy February evening in 1974. As in my previous books, I have not felt constrained by the chronology: where it makes sense to look back to the 1960s, I have done so, while broader chapters – on the rise of feminism, say, or the new suburban lifestyles – look forward to the end of the decade. Of course no book can be entirely comprehensive, and there is always bound to be an element of picking and choosing. There is naturally a lot about politics and economics in *State of Emergency*, and there is also a lot about sex, television, enviromentalism, race relations, feminism and football. Some topics, however, such as education or rock music, will be covered more fully in this book's sequel, *Seasons of Discontent*, which will take the story from 1974 to 1979. Perhaps the most notable omission is coverage of the growing nationalist movements in Wales and Scotland. In the preface to *White Heat* I promised that I would write about them in my next book, but in the end I rather shamefacedly decided that it would make more sense to discuss them in the build-up to the devolution votes of 1979. I am also conscious that my books betray a marked bias towards England, particularly its more populous areas. There is a lot here about London, but Birmingham, Belfast, Leeds, Nottingham, St Helens and even Milton Keynes get a look-in, too, as do the miners of the Rhondda and the shipbuilders of the Upper Clyde. Still, even in quite a long book like this, I am painfully aware of everything – and everybody – I have had to leave out.

As before, politics drives the narrative, which is hardly surprising given that this was an intensely politicized period. We see Edward Heath banging away at his piano after securing British entry into the EEC, and Harold Wilson knocking back the whisky as his political career apparently slipped away; we follow the Yorkshire miners onto the picket lines, and the British army into the killing grounds of Belfast. But as I argued in both *Never Had It So Good* and *White Heat*, there is more to contemporary history than politics and government. And so *State of Emergency*, too, tries to capture the experience of millions of people who spent the early 1970s drinking Watney's Red Barrel and Blue Nun, listening to Elton John and Emerson, Lake and Palmer, laughing at *Morecambe and Wise* and *Bless This House*, and cheering on Kevin Keegan, Jackie Stewart and Red Rum; the kind of people who spent their evenings glued to *Crossroads* and *Upstairs, Downstairs*, their weekends in the supermarket and the garden centre, and their holidays in Malta and Majorca; the kind of people, indeed, who lined the streets with their flags and banners at the wedding of Princess Anne.

Their lives and experiences, their anxieties and expectations, are just as much part of this story as any of the major events of the day. They began the decade full of hope, looking forward to the technological innovations that would surely transform their daily lives, to the new possibilities of an orderly, peaceful world, to the new prosperity that their leaders promised them. And when they went to bed on the balmy summer's evening of 17 June 1970, most of them expected that Harold Wilson would comfortably beat Ted Heath in the next day's election. In this, as in so much else, they were in for a shock.

I

A Better Tomorrow

This is an exhilarating moment. Britain is alive again. The people have chosen a new Government and a new direction.

– Daily Mail, 20 June 1970

As the first voters gathered outside the polling stations, it was already obvious that it was going to be a beautiful day. There seemed almost a party atmosphere, a mood of rare communal good humour as Britain's 39 million eligible voters queued in the June sunshine. For the first time in history, 18-year-olds were eligible to vote, and outside almost every polling station photographers competed for pictures of the youngest and most attractive teenage voters. In Edinburgh, they sang 'Happy Birthday' to Janis Weir, a typist, who arrived to vote at exactly 8.09 a.m., eighteen years to the minute after she had been born. In Lowestoft, they wished good luck to Robert Farman, another birthday boy, who was facing a Maths A-level exam that afternoon. In Surbiton, officials had to turn away 4-year-old Nicholas Old, who had been sent voting papers by mistake. 'I'm sorry, Mr Old,' one official said, chuckling at his own joke, 'but you're not old enough to vote.' But at Westcliffe-on-Sea, there was a warm welcome for Britain's oldest voter, William Chapman, aged 107, who arrived at the polls with his Boer War medals clinking on his chest. The only voter who could vividly remember the days of William Gladstone and Joe Chamberlain, Mr Chapman remained a man of firm opinions. 'I've been a working man all my life,' he said, 'and there is only one party to vote for.'[1]

Young and old, rich and poor, north and south, almost everyone agreed that William Chapman's party was going to win. In Huyton, where the Prime Minister, Harold Wilson, ate a hearty lunch of steak and chips before visiting his local polling stations, there was a mood of calm, of confidence, even of complacency. And hundreds of miles to the south, where his Tory rival Edward Heath toured the polls in his shirtsleeves, his tanned, heavy features fixed in a rictus grin, reporters were already preparing their obituaries. *The Times* thought that Heath had shown 'great strength of character' and inspired 'real affection' in his brave but futile fight against the odds, but few doubted that after two defeats under his brusque, awkward leadership, the Conservative Party would call for a fresh start. In secret, his senior colleagues had already made arrangements for his predecessor, Sir Alec Douglas-Home, to take over as interim leader after the election. And as Heath was snatching a quick lunch, his friend Peter Carrington arrived with the equivalent of the loaded revolver. Once the result was certain, he said gently, it would be time to go.[2]

At six, as the sun was beginning to dip, Heath arrived at Bexley's Conservative headquarters, sipped a cup of tea, and began making the ritual calls to Tory election agents around the country. If he was nervous, he did not show it, and Carrington felt a surge of admiration for his chief's bravery in the face of defeat. Heath had already lost one election in 1966, outsmarted by the wily Wilson, and this time, too, he had struggled to catch the attention of an electorate distracted by the World Cup and the gorgeous weather. While Wilson, buoyed by polls showing him 7 or 8 per cent ahead, had laughed and joked with the crowds in the sunshine, Heath had never been able to relax. 'Do you want a better tomorrow?' he had kept asking, but it was clear that nobody was listening. Ted Heath was yesterday's man; tomorrow belonged to Wilson.

Heath was sitting in the bar of the Crook Log Hotel, quietly nursing a drink, when everything changed. The first result was in from Guildford, a swing of more than 5 per cent to the Conservatives, and at that moment, just after eleven on the night of Thursday, 18 June, he knew he had done it. Quite suddenly, all the predictions were turned on their heads. The undecided voters, the housewives whom everybody had said would decide the election, had lost patience with Wilson's endless twisting and turning, his broken promises, his excuses for devaluing the pound, his failure to keep prices down, and at the last moment they had changed their minds. In Huyton, where Wilson's entourage were gathered around the screen, the room fell silent. In London, the Downing Street secretaries started packing. And in Bexley, Heath's election agent gleefully dug out a bottle of Glenlivet, and the mood turned from inevitable disappointment to incredulous delight. At two, as the Labour seats were still falling, Heath phoned his 81-year-old father. 'Things seem to be going well,' he said, almost as though he could not believe it himself.[3]

Heath did not make it back to his flat in the elegant London enclave of the Albany, off Piccadilly, until almost three in the morning, his ears still ringing with the congratulations of his supporters. When one of his closest colleagues, Willie Whitelaw, called a few moments later, the emotion that Heath usually kept in such tight check finally rose to the surface: as Whitelaw offered his congratulations, he said nothing, choked with feeling. He did not fall asleep until five, and by the time he awoke, at midday, a large and boisterous crowd was waiting outside on Piccadilly. The Queen was at Ascot, enjoying a day's racing, so he had to wait until seven for the long-anticipated call to the Palace. But at last it came, and as the Queen smiled encouragingly ('in the most delightful way', he remembered), the Broadstairs boy accepted her invitation to form a government.*

'There were wild scenes as Mr Heath arrived at Downing Street,' reported *The Times* the next day. With no security barriers to keep back the crowds, the narrow Georgian street was packed with more than a thousand well-wishers, and as Heath's blue Rover limousine eased to a stop they pushed through the thin line of policemen to serenade their new leader with 'For he's a jolly good fellow'. But as Heath began to speak, the singing subsided a little, and the tones that had become so familiar to voters across the country rang round the little street. 'To govern is to serve,' Heath said, his voice straining above the noise of the crowd. 'This government will be at the service of all the people – the whole nation. Our purpose is not to divide but to unite, and where there are difficulties, to bring about reconciliation. To create one nation.' And then he turned, and the black door closed behind him.[4]

While few people later remembered what Edward Heath said to the nation during those first moments of his turbulent premiership, few would ever forget his curiously strangulated way of saying it. He had an accent all his own, the vowels oddly stretched, as though his voice had been very slightly slowed down by some technical trickery: 'Heath As It

* The Tories won 322 seats, Labour 287, the Liberals 6, the Ulster Unionists 8, the Scottish National Party 1 and smaller parties 5, giving Heath a 31-seat majority.

Is Spoken', as the *Monty Python* comedian Eric Idle mockingly called it. And yet Heath's accent not only reflected his social insecurity, it also marked how far he had come. The artificial vowel sounds were the sign of unstinting self-improvement, the mark of a man who had remade himself from the son of a Kentish craftsman into an organ scholar at Balliol, Oxford's most prestigious college, a rising star in the party of the rich and powerful, and ultimately the leader of his country. For the new Prime Minister was the embodiment of what Anthony Sampson called the 'cult of the self-made meritocrats', the bright grammar school boys who had come to dominate British life in the 1950s and 1960s, the pioneers of the affluent society.[5]

On the surface, with his bachelor lifestyle, his fondness for classical music and ocean racing, his total lack of interest in sex and his old-fashioned emotional awkwardness, Heath made a supremely inappropriate representative of British society at the beginning of the 1970s. And yet the Tories had elected him their leader in 1965 precisely because he seemed a breath of fresh air, a man of the age who had risen from a humble background through brains and hard work. His paternal grand-father, back in Britain's late Victorian imperial heyday, had been a Kentish dairyman, railway porter and greengrocer; his father began work at 13 as a carpenter's apprentice and eventually became a successful builder. Yet Heath never exploited his background for political purposes, as later politicians tried to do; instead, he seems to have been very sensitive about it. His strange accent, for example, dated from his Oxford days, when his original provincial intonation must have made him stand out among his upper-class contemporaries, while his hobbies were those of someone anxiously imitating the tastes of the rich. Yet despite his sensitivity, Heath was indelibly a son of the Kentish coast and a symbol of Britain's increasingly fluid society. He was 'a new kind of Tory leader – a classless professional politician who has fought his way to the top by guts, ability and political skill', said the *Mirror*. 'Do you appreciate', one interviewer once asked him, 'that you are the first Tory leader with wall-to-wall carpeting?'[6]

Heath's constituency, Bexley, itself embodied the changes that had come over Britain in little over half a century since his birth. In his grandfather's day, even his father's, it had been a quiet rural backwater. Now it was a typical section of the south London commuter belt, a world of identical semi-detached houses and brick council estates, inhabited by skilled workers, clerks and technicians. In 1945 it had been a safe Labour seat; now it was classic aspirational upper-working-class and middle-class Conservative. It was a place transformed by light industry, rising wages and full employment, a place where farms had been replaced by shopping centres and labourers had given way to pharmacists. It seemed a long way from the sensationalist high jinks that later dominated popular memories of the post-war years – the Profumo scandal, Swinging London, the Beatles and the Rolling Stones – and yet, better than any of those things, it symbolized the subterranean economic and social trends that had changed the lives of Britain's 55 million people. And as Heath tramped the streets of Bexley, shaking hands and exchanging banter with his familiar shoulder-shaking laugh, the signs of change were everywhere, from the cars on the roads to the short skirts of the teenagers in the parks. Even to knock on a random front door was to be reminded of the new opportunities that affluence had brought.[7]

By the early 1970s, just over half the population owned their own homes, almost twice the proportion two decades before. But these were not just places to eat and sleep. They were markers of affluence, status, identity and independence, decorated in styles – garish patterned wall-paper, thick carpets, Formica surfaces, synthetic tiles – that were sup-posed to denote luxury and elegance. They were places to relax and socialize, perhaps by watching the new colour television, or by mulling over the collection of faux-leather encyclopedias or *Reader's Digest* abridgements, or by sharing a bottle of wine from the streamlined drinks cabinet. And of course Bexley's little semi-detached homes were temples to consumerism, typified by the electric appliances that had dominated people's daydreams in the 1950s and 1960s. By 1971, 64 per cent of families owned their own washing machine, 69 per cent had a fridge, and more than 90 per cent had a television. Even in poor working-class areas, affluence had left a deep imprint, thanks to the availability of hire purchase: researchers visiting Nottingham's deprived St Ann's district in the late 1960s found that four out of five people owned a television, while two out of five had a washing machine or vacuum cleaner. 'The domestic servants of the twentieth century', a middle-class character calls them in Piers Paul Read's novel *A Married Man* (1979). Totting them up, he puts his staff at two dozen, including a washing machine, a tumble drier, a dishwasher, two lawnmowers, a chainsaw, a vacuum cleaner, a liquidizer, an egg-beater, a coffee-grinder and a lemon-squeezer, not to mention televisions, record players and tape decks. Of course not many Bexley families could afford all of these things, especially at the beginning of the decade. But almost every household had at least one or two of them, and almost everybody could reasonably expect to buy more.[8]

The affluent society had always had its critics. It was 'an ugly society still', the socialist firebrand Aneurin Bevan had thundered in 1960, calling it 'a vulgar society ... a meretricious society ... a society in which priorities have gone all wrong'. The cultural critic Richard Hoggart even thought it had produced a mass culture of 'corrupt brightness, of improper appeals and moral evasions': slick, shallow, materialistic, empty. A decade on, however, the people of Bexley, like their counterparts elsewhere, showed no sign of having taken any notice. For all but the poorest, the oldest and the unluckiest, the 1960s had been a decade of abundance and comfort on a level unimaginable a few years previously. 'The golden age had come at last,' reflects a character looking back on the 1960s in Margaret Drabble's novel *The Ice Age* (1977). After toiling through 'years of austerity ... suddenly here it all was, the world of *Penthouse* and the Beatles, the world of large steaks and double cream on real gateaux, the world of girls and nightclubs and expense account champagne'.[9]

And even though millions of people never went to nightclubs or quaffed champagne, they still enjoyed their slice of the ever-expanding cake. By 1973, one in three people told researchers they had gone out for a meal in the previous month, a luxury few of their parents could have imagined. And despite all the economic turmoil of the early 1970s, the strikes and inflation, the oil shock and the power cuts, most of Bexley's voters remained far more prosperous than they could have expected twenty years before. Three years after Edward Heath had walked into 10 Downing Street, there were more cars on the roads than ever, more products on the supermarket shelves, more colour televisions in suburban homes, more planes taking off for the beaches of Spain.[10]

As a relatively affluent, Conservative-voting slice of London suburbia, Bexley was not exactly representative of the national experience at the dawn of the 1970s. Yet very different social landscapes, hundreds of miles away, reflected similar trends. During his Balliol days, Heath had become friends with an ebullient, bushy-browed, highly intelligent young man from the West Riding of Yorkshire. Like Heath, Denis Healey was an ambitious grammar school boy; his politics, though, were rather different, and as Defence Secretary he had been one of the few real stars of the Wilson government in the 1960s. His constituency, on the east side of Leeds, had been solid Labour territory for sixty years, a classic Northern working-class landscape of long red-brick terraces, neighbourhood pubs and Methodist churches. When Healey became the area's MP in 1952, it had changed little since the Industrial Revolution. His party members were garment workers, engineers, railwaymen and miners, men of firm principles and distinctly traditional attitudes. They lived as their parents had done: 'the housing was appalling,' he wrote later, 'the dirt indescribable.' Smoke hung over the city's rooftops; soot stained its great Victorian town hall. Healey's very first campaign headquarters was 'a condemned terraced house of unimaginable squalor, with a lavatory outside which was full of filth and would not flush'. The contrast with Bexley's neat, upwardly mobile suburban estates was stark indeed.[11]

By 1970, however, Leeds bore the imprint of the affluent society just as deeply as the suburbs of the South. The clothing and engineering industries responsible for so many local jobs were already suffering from inadequate investment and global competition, their travails symptomatic of the growing problems of the British economy. Montague Burton's, once the world's biggest tailor, was struggling to adapt to the more casual look that had taken over in the early 1960s: as Healey recalled, Burton's 'went on making three-piece suits long after people stopped wearing waistcoats'. But while the old industries were dying, others were expanding. By 1970, more people worked in new offices – in insurance, banking, accountancy, law, health, education, hotels, retailing – than in the clothing industry for which Leeds had been famous. Once synonymous with the muck and brass of industry, the city was slowly becoming a richer, more white-collar place: as early as the beginning of the 1960s, three out of four households owned a television. The city fathers dreamed of turning the centre into a 'Shoppers' Paradise'. By the mid-1970s, it even had a theme pub: the Hofbrauhaus in the Merrion Centre, selling German beer for 32p a pint.

Not everything about Leeds had changed since the 1950s. It remained a hard, unforgiving town, fiercely masculine and suspicious of outsiders, as anyone who went to Elland Road to watch Don Revie's Leeds United, the country's best but least-loved football team, would readily testify. But as the football coaches thundered into the city along the new M1 and M62, their passengers could see that its landscape had fundamentally changed. Like so many other Northern cities, Leeds had keenly embraced the new era of concrete and tarmac. Its Victorian skyline had given way to 'motorways, pedestrian precincts, shopping centres, multi-storey car parks, high-rise flats': buildings like the glass and concrete City House, glowering with menace over the railway station, the brainchild of the corrupt West Yorkshire architect John Poulson; or the bleak Hunslet Grange flats, a gigantic pebble-dashed concrete complex opened in 1973, poorly maintained and abysmally heated; or the new Merrion Centre, a statement of brutal, uncompromising utilitarianism in the heart of the city. For their critics, such as the poet Sir John Betjeman, these were ugly abominations, reminiscent of nothing so much as the totalitarian cityscapes of Communist Eastern Europe. The sound of Leeds, Betjeman remarked in a BBC film made in 1968, was that of 'Victorian buildings crashing to the ground'. To the city fathers, however, they were welcome symbols of modernity. They even adopted the slogan 'Leeds: Motorway City of the Seventies', which was franked on all envelopes sent from the city to sum up its new identity as a place of 'exciting flyovers and splendid roads'.[12]

For some observers, Britain's new urban landscape was merely the outward symptom of deeper social and cultural changes that had radically altered the texture of life for millions of people. It was more than a question of washing the laundry in a machine instead of by hand, or of drinking Nescafé at breakfast instead of leaf tea, or of spending Sunday at a National Trust property instead of in church, or of going out for a curry instead of making shepherd's pie, or even of going on holiday to Majorca rather than to Morecambe. It was deeper than that, epitomized by the plight of the Bingley Musical Union, a mainstay of male working-class culture in the West Yorkshire mill town for more than eighty years, which in the mid-1970s began to struggle badly for young recruits, because, a visitor reported, 'young men were no longer following their fathers into the choir'.[13]

When the former social worker and radical journalist Jeremy Seabrook went to another traditional working-class town, Blackburn, Lancashire, at the dawn of the 1970s, he found a world of 'derelict streets and decayed mills', in which older residents were often full of misery and anger at the changes that had overtaken their home town during the supposed golden age of the 1950s and 1960s. Listening to their laments for the 'predictability and discipline' of the old days, he concluded that 'since the time when two thirds of the working population were employed in textiles and life was dominated by the immutable realities of mill, school, and chapel, the town has been in decline'. Seabrook did not necessarily mean that it was becoming poorer – although parts of it were – because most people led lives of unprecedented material comfort. What he meant was that the old, reliable working-class culture, the culture of hard work at the mill, pints at the local pub, Saturdays cheering the Rovers and Sundays singing hymns, was gone, and nothing had replaced it. It was this, he thought, that explained the ubiquitous racism towards the town's Pakistani immigrants: a cry of 'anguish and fear' based on 'the decline of their dwindling culture'.[14]

When Seabrook returned to the North of England five years later for his book *What Went Wrong?*, he was even more pessimistic. No amount of affluence, he argued, could compensate for the death of the old culture. In Wigan, a 'new denim bazaar and a delicatessen' took pride of place in the 'shopping arcades full of consolations', yet they could not make up for the death of the mines and mills on which the town had once depended. Echoing Richard Hoggart's warnings twenty years earlier, he diagnosed the town's youngsters as 'passive and purposeless', preoccupied by 'image and fashion, the endless spool of excitement and novelty that has been unwound before their eyes since they were born'. They were 'anchored in a sea of commodities', he said grimly, their lives governed by the logic of the marketplace, deprived of the culture that had nourished their forefathers. It was barely ten years since the Kinks, in 'Autumn Almanac', had paid tribute to the rituals of football on a Saturday, roast beef on Sundays and holidays in Blackpool. But they might have been singing about a different century.[15]

In an odd way, this was the mirror image of what fashionable young celebrities like Mick Jagger and Terence Stamp had boasted back in the mid-1960s: that an old world had died, giving way to a new one in which the guiding lights were spectacle, shopping and sensation. Clearly there was some truth in it: the churches, for example, were in deep and apparently unstoppable decline. By 1970, fewer than half of all newborn babies were baptized in the Church of England, while confirmations fell by half between 1960 and 1977. Methodist membership was in free fall: in Manchester, it fell by a staggering 44 per cent in just twenty years. It was hardly surprising that, by 1976, a church was being pulled down somewhere every nine days.[16]

To many of the elderly churchgoers who increasingly dominated Sunday congregations, Edward Heath's Britain did seem a distressingly alien place: a world of new town centres, new tower blocks, new housing estates, new road signs, new telephone numbers, new county names, even the new postcodes. Even that most basic staple of everyday British life, the pound sterling, the symbol of everything solid and reliable in national life, underwent radical change. For centuries, generations had grown up with the system of pounds, shillings, and pence: 12 pence to the shilling, 20 shillings to the pound. But in 1961, during a spasm of self-flagellation in which commentators lined up to blame the nation's economic problems on its supposedly anachronistic Establishment, Harold Macmillan had set up a committee to examine the possibility of switching to a decimal currency, in imitation of Britain's European competitors. By 1966, Harold Wilson had embraced the issue as a sign of progressive modernization, and five years later, on 15 February 1971, the currency was formally decimalized. This was not quite the overnight operation that is sometimes imagined. Three of the six new coins – the 5p, 10p and 50p pieces – had been legal tender for more than a year, while the halfpenny and half-crown had disappeared in 1969. The government organized a massive publicity blitz to alert people to the new coinage, and prices were displayed for months in both currencies – something worth a shilling, for example, being sold at '1s.(5p)'. The BBC broadcast a series of five-minute programmes on decimal themes, while the singer Max Bygraves even recorded a mildly excruciating single, 'Decimalisation'.[17]

'It's terrible!' a grim-faced elderly Scotswoman, her hair tightly bound in a headscarf, told the BBC evening news on the much-anticipated 'Decimal Day'. In fact, polls put support for decimalization at barely 46 per cent, and in the West End 'anti-decimal terrorists' distributed leaflets denouncing the government's 'failure to consult public opinion' and begging shoppers to boycott the new currency. Yet despite predictions of disaster in the popular press, 'D Day' passed off without a serious hitch. Most major stores were well prepared: Harrods had an army of 'decimal pennies', girls in 'rakish boaters and blue sashes', to help confused shoppers, while Selfridges boasted a troop of 'girls dressed in shorts and midi split skirts and other suitably mathematical costumes'. British Rail and London Transport even went decimal a day early. 'There were no riots, no queues, and only a mercifully few facetious comments about the new toy-shop money,' reported *The Times* the following day.

Even the surly and suspicious newspaper sellers on the Strand 'did not take their eyes off them or refuse to accept them'.[18]

The group least impressed by the new currency, not surprisingly, was the elderly. Conversion from old to new pence was not always easy: the government recommended the rough and ready trick of doubling the figure in new pence and adding a slash between the digits, so that 17p became 3/4 or 3s. 4d. Canny entrepreneurs, meanwhile, sold 'Decimal Adders' that people could carry around the shops, although by the standards of later calculators these were inconveniently clunky and cumbersome. But many older people remained distrustful: according to an internal Conservative report a year later, some even blamed the new currency for the inflation that was beginning to cripple the British economy. It was merely another symptom of a world that seemed to have cast out all tradition, all familiarity, all reassurance, all order: a frightening world beset by inflation, terrorism, crime and delinquency. And for those who vividly remembered the world before the war, nothing seemed impervious to the mania for change. There is a lovely scene in Peter Nichols's television play *Hearts and Flowers* (1970), when old Uncle Will, at a funeral service for his brother, stands to recite Psalm 23 with the congregation, only to find that the words have changed. 'These aren't the proper words!' he whispers in horror as his family read aloud from the new prayer book, but nobody is listening. Even something as fixed and unmoveable as the Old Testament, it turns out, has changed, and Will has been robbed of the traditional words of consolation that have sustained him all his life. The world has left him behind.[19]

Young people, the group most enthusiastic about the new decimal currency, were a particular source of worry to the old. 'They have it too easy today. They don't care about anything or anybody,' said John Johnson, an elderly Blackburn man. 'They're answerable to nobody. There's ninety-nine percent of the parents step beside, our John can't do any wrong, our Mary can't do any wrong.' Mr Johnson remembered his own younger days: one of eight children, he had scrubbed his father's clogs clean every night before bed, and left school at 14 to work in the mill. Only during the First World War, when his father was away at the front, did he 'get a bit of liberty' from his mother. But the liberty of the young, with their loud music and outrageous fashions, astonished and disturbed him. A friend of his, walking his dog in Blackburn's Corporation Park, had recently come across two teenagers on the steps of a pavilion, the girl with her knickers around her ankles. 'What's going on up there?' the man had burst out in shock, to which the boy replied 'with a four-letter word'. So the man, who knew where the boy lived, went off to complain to his father. 'Did my lad say that to thee?' the father said. 'Well, I'll say it to thee an' all, mind thee own eff. business.' Mr Johnson shook his head in disbelief. 'Now that's God's true word of honour, if I should choke when I have a cup of tea.'[20]

To people who vividly remembered the days of the General Strike and the Depression, whose memories were full of tin baths, empty stomachs and Stanley Baldwin on the radio, the Britain of George Best, Marc Bolan and *Confessions of a Window Cleaner* must indeed have been a shock. And yet, although Jeremy Seabrook was right to note the ways in which traditional working-class culture was dying, it was too simplistic, and too pessimistic, to say that everything had changed. Take the gangster film *Get Carter*, which was shot in the winter of 1970 and released the following year. Not only was the film's violence, and especially its brutality towards women, shocking for critics and audiences alike, but its themes – gambling, pornography, local government corruption – reflected the new concerns of the late 1960s. Its very settings, the grim concrete fastness of Newcastle, the Brutalist Trinity Square car park in Gateshead, seemed to represent the radical modernization of British life. Indeed, Newcastle's council boss T. Dan Smith, who had promised to turn his city into the concrete 'Brasilia of the North', turned out to be up to his neck in the Poulson corruption scandal, having pocketed generous kickbacks in return for approving miles of tower blocks. Even the film's star, Michael Caine, the son of a Billingsgate porter and a charlady, a Camberwell grammar school boy turned Hollywood celebrity, liked to be seen as the champion of the new generation. 'We are here, this is our society and we are not going away,' the erstwhile Maurice Micklewhite told an interviewer. 'Join us, stay away, hate us – do as you like. We don't care about your opinion any more.'[21]

And yet in many ways *Get Carter* reflected a world that had changed surprisingly little. Behind the gangsters' violence, as one critic observes, the film shows 'another world entirely, a city that remains remarkably untouched by their activities; we see pubs, a dance hall, a bingo hall, a kids' marching band in the streets, a whole community going about its everyday business'. When Caine's character steps off the train from London and into the North-eastern bar, it is as though he has stepped back in time, to a world of gnarled working-class men grimly supping their pints and glaring at outsiders. And the pub as an institution nicely reflects the way in which Heath's Britain felt uneasily poised between two worlds. In affluent suburbs like Bexley, many pubs had closed down, victims of the new trend for family- and home-centred leisure. Others were becoming much more upmarket, whether by installing thick carpets and televisions, or by remodelling themselves as Beefeaters and Berni Inns (for example the Mitre in Oxford, or the New Inn in Gloucester), dispensing prawn cocktails, steak and chips and Black Forest gateau to aspirational young couples. 'The regular users of street-corner locals find to their horror that their pub has been re-designed as a large pineapple, a sputnik or a Wild West saloon to attract the gin-and-tonic and lager-and-lime trade,' lamented Roger Protz, one of the founding fathers of the Campaign for Real Ale, in 1978. 'Public bars are ripped out and replaced with lounges with soft lights, soft carpets, wet-look mock leather – and several pennies on the price of a pint.'[22]

Yet many pubs remained defiantly traditional. In Nottingham, pubs in the poor St Ann's district still displayed the Queen's portrait behind the bar. In Blackburn, Seabrook drank in a pub with 'yellow distemper, frosted glass, dark brown paint', where conversations were punctuated by 'the sound of darts as they struck the board, and the squeak of chalk on slate, as well as the sounds of *Coronation Street* from the next room'. And when Colin Dexter's detective Inspector Morse goes for a drink in the novel *Last Seen Wearing* (1977), he finds a public bar barely touched by change, the only innovation a solitary fruit machine in the corner. Cigarette smoke hangs in the air 'like morning mist'; the chatter is 'raucous and interminable'; the atmosphere is one of 'cribbage, dominoes and darts, and every available surface cluttered with glasses'.[23]

The survival of the old-fashioned pub, albeit in slightly modified form and reduced numbers, was indicative of a working-class culture that had changed much less, or at least was changing more slowly, than pessimists like Seabrook feared. Although most people in St Ann's had televisions, for example, they lived in conditions that would have seemed distinctly familiar to residents in the 1930s: tight row upon row of damp, decaying brick back-to-backs, fewer than one in ten with inside toilets, fewer than two in ten with an inside bathroom, only half of them with hot running water. Theirs was a life of 'damp, rot, decrepitude', wrote researchers from the local university, in a world of 'dingy buildings and bleak factories and . . . functionally austere chapels, a host of second-hand shops stacked out with shabby, cast-off goods; overhung throughout the winter by a damp pall of smoke'. It was a similar story elsewhere. In Bingley, it was not unusual well into the 1970s to see a pony tethered outside one of the pubs, or rabbit-skins hanging from washing lines on the council estates. In Sunderland, nine out of ten families in privately owned houses had no indoor toilet, three-quarters had no bath, and half did not even have *cold* running water. As late as 1973, more than 2 million people in England and Wales lived without either an inside toilet, a bathtub or hot running water.[24]

This is not to say, of course, that nothing changed: for instance, the merciless decline of British manufacturing had a drastic effect on the lives of millions who lost their jobs, while rising wages for the rest inevitably brought lifestyle changes, from domestic gadgets to foreign holidays. Yet most families led strikingly conservative lives. In 1970, an extensive survey of habits and values found that by far the most popular leisure activity was watching television (97 per cent), followed by gardening (64 per cent), playing with children (62 per cent), listening to music (57 per cent), home decoration or repairs (53 per cent) and cleaning the car (48 per cent). Outside the home, meanwhile, the preferred activities were going for a drive (58 per cent), to the pub (52 per cent), for a walk (47 per cent) and for a meal (32 per cent), with darts and church close behind. And this picture changed little over the course of the decade. An official household survey in 1977 found that apart from watching television, the most popular leisure activities were going for a meal or a drink, listening to records, reading, walking, DIY, gardening, needlework and knitting. Clearly some of these things reflected growing affluence: wealthier families were more likely to go out for meals or to have a car to clean. But few of these activities would have shocked or surprised the respondents' parents or grandparents.[25]

If these figures represented any great change, it was simply that collective leisure was giving way to more individualistic, family-centred activities, as couples elected to spend more time together rather than with relatives, friends and colleagues. This fits with the common interpretation of life in the 1970s, epitomized by Seabrook's book *What Went Wrong?*, which holds that Britain was becoming an increasingly individualistic society even before Mrs Thatcher had been given the keys to Number 10. And yet this picture of selfish proto-Thatcherites turning their backs on society feels far too simplistic. For this was also a period in which union membership – for many people, the ultimate expression of collective solidarity – reached its peak, and in which the number of charities and voluntary associations more than doubled. By 1984 one survey found that more than half the population had joined voluntary organizations and one in five people regularly did voluntary work – a stunning rebuke to the caricature of a selfish, introverted society.[26]

Indeed, in many ways Britain still conformed to the stereotype of a nation obsessed with collective membership. One survey estimated that at the dawn of the 1970s, more than half of all adult men and a third of all women belonged to clubs of various kinds. In Birmingham, more than 4,000 active associations – sporting, dancing, educational, social – were recorded during the course of the decade. In Milton Keynes, which had fewer than 100,000 people, there were around 500; in Kingswood, Bristol, with a population of just 85,000, there were some 300. These spanned a wide range, from pony clubs to traditional working men's clubs. The latter, which really should have died out completely if working-class culture was in such desperate straits, commanded the allegiance of 2 million people at the beginning of the 1970s. In Huddersfield alone, there were seventy working men's clubs. They had gently changed with the times, admitting women and children, offering billiards, bingo and weekly concerts, and even organizing holidays and trips abroad. But they remained an excellent example of the way in which gradual change could comfortably coexist with reassuring, traditional values. So did the town's thirty-three bowling clubs, making Crown Green Bowls comfortably Huddersfield's most popular participatory sport – although because the players tended to be elderly and working-class, many people barely knew it existed.[27]

It was not just in working-class areas, of course, that the old ways survived into the world of Brian Clough, Noel Edmonds and *The Liver Birds*. The diaries of the architectural historian James Lees-Milne, for instance, are famously saturated with anger at social and cultural change. Britain had reverted to a 'jungle society', he wrote in the autumn of 1971, which he blamed on the working classes: 'no loyalties, no gratitude, no morality, no decency.' Yet his diaries also record a lifestyle that had changed surprisingly little, a world of country-house parties in which women retired from the table while the men lit up and began to complain about Denis Healey's tax plans. And while Lees-Milne complained that the old values had disappeared, polls do not bear this out. A major Gallup survey of moral attitudes in January 1973 found that two out of three people favoured the death penalty, one out of two believed that the Bible was literally true, one out of two believed that chastity was a virtue, three out of five backed school uniforms, and one in four still believed in innate white superiority. A few months later, marking the thirty-fifth anniversary of its first newspaper poll, Gallup asked people a range of questions from the late 1930s, and found that the answers – on everything from belief in life after death to visiting a dentist, pet ownership, and the desirability of living by the seaside – showed remarkably little change.[28]

The point is not that Britain was a stagnant or unchanging society, but that the overall picture was so messy, diverse and variegated that any generalization is bound to be risky. Continuity and change were like two tightly interwoven threads; sometimes one predominated, sometimes the other, usually depending on the viewpoint of the beholder. This was a society that had supposedly thrown off the chains of deference and hierarchy, yet it was also one that voted the Queen the nation's most admired individual in 1970, tuned in every year for her Christmas message and celebrated her Jubilee in overwhelming numbers. It was the society with the highest divorce rate in Europe, yet it was also one in which couples married earlier than ever and half of all divorcees remarried within five years. It was a society in which a black man captained Britain's rugby league team to the World Cup and millions enjoyed seeing Muhammad Ali verbally sparring with Michael Parkinson, yet it was one in which Enoch Powell was easily the most popular politician in the country, thanks largely to his position on immigration. It was a society in which only a tiny minority went to church every week, yet it was also one in which almost nine out of ten families had a household Bible.[29]

The complications and contradictions of the early 1970s were well illustrated by an article in *The Times* on 2 January 1973, the day after Britain's formal accession to the European Economic Community, the outstanding accomplishment of Heath's premiership. Britain was not what it was, wrote Tom Stacey: 'Our leaders have for some time done their best to unpick the only context of allegiance in which they can appeal to us – by flooding us with exotic immigrants [and] emasculating us with welfare and taxes.' As a result, Britain presented 'an image today of unprecedented sloth, selfishness, envy, greed, insularity and presumption', quite a charge sheet. And yet Stacey thought that people still talked

about 'our nation' and 'know what they mean'. National identity
still depended on 'our inherited characteristics, our shared heroes, our
victories and our defeats. Drake, Wellington, Churchill. The defeat of
the Armada, Waterloo, Dunkirk, Shakespeare, Dickens, Hardy.' And
people still responded to qualities that George Orwell would have recognized: 'our sense of fair play, and a very high grade of humour, law,
government, horticulture and breakfast'.[30]

And since any account of the 1970s is necessarily dominated by everything that went wrong – bombs, strikes, riots, disasters – it is worth
emphasizing that for most people, these things happened offstage. For the
typical family, if there really was such a thing, there was much to lament
but also much to enjoy in the everyday experience of 1970s life, from
colour television and foreign holidays to the pleasures of the garden and
the enjoyment of a good wine. One survey in 1972 found that almost nine
out of ten were either 'satisfied' or 'very satisfied' with their jobs, while
eight out of ten were satisfied with their living conditions. Asked in 1975
whether Britain was a good country to grow up in, 84 per cent agreed that
it was, a verdict often borne out by the rose-tinted recollections of twenty-
first-century adults trembling with nostalgic delight at the thought of
chopper bikes and *Bagpuss*. And even people now remembered as the
victims of history, like the Durham miners interviewed by *New Society* in
1978, regarded themselves as fortunate to be enjoying such expanded
opportunities and new horizons. 'There's more money through our hands,'
one explained. 'A miner's nowadays got a car, a caravan, a garden, things
like that. We're beginning to enjoy ourselves and get about.'[31]

At a time when most American correspondents were gleefully wallowing
in the miserable condition of Britain's economy, the corruption of its leaders
and the greed of its workers, the *Washington Post*'s Bernard Nossiter
sounded a salutary dissenting note. Despite all the fuss about strikes and
violence, he wrote that same year, Britain remained a remarkably stable,
polite and tolerant society, marked by its strong sense of 'fair play and
justice'. True, it was a long way from being the New Jerusalem: its inflation
and unemployment figures were appalling, the political consensus seemed
to have collapsed, and there was a sense of growing tension between
working-class whites and their immigrant neighbours. But it was far from
the 'sinking, chaotic, miserable swamp' of American caricatures, Nossiter
wrote. 'Britain is a solid, healthy society, bursting with creative vigour.'[32]

*

As historians often point out, many of the things popularly associated with the 1960s, from feminism and pornography to gay rights and flared trousers, did not become familiar elements of British life until the following decade. There was far more continuity between these two supposedly so different episodes in post-war history than we often remember; it is not as though, as the clock tolled midnight on New Year's Eve 1969, people everywhere threw away their silver lipstick, ditched their copies of *With the Beatles*, dug out their donkey jackets and headed to the nearest brazier to hurl abuse at passing lorry drivers.

One very marked difference, however, was the almost total disappearance of that supremely fashionable media catchphrase of the mid-1960s, the classless society. At the height of the Swinging London boom – which was merely an embarrassing memory by the time Edward Heath arrived at Number 10 – no self-respecting newspaper had failed to enthuse about the classless Britain spearheaded by the Beatles and the Rolling Stones. 'People like me, we're the moderns,' the actor Terence Stamp modestly explained. 'We have no class and no prejudice.' Journalists were quick to endorse the idea: the young Jonathan Aitken, for instance, wrote in 1967 that Britain had seen the appearance of a new 'talent class', in which birth and breeding were irrelevant and only ability mattered – although since some of his examples included the young Norman Lamont and Michael Winner, this was surely a bit dubious. The 'ancient partitions' had been 'swept away', agreed David Frost and Antony Jay that same year: 'Mr Edward Heath takes over from the fourteenth Earl of Home: the clubs of St. James's yield to the coffee houses of Chelsea; Carnaby Street usurps Savile Row; Liverpudlian pop stars weekend at ducal castles; dukes go out to work; ancient universities welcome upstart sons of hobnailed workmen. The bad old system is smashed . . . The three great classes melt and mingle. And a new Britain is born.'[33]

This was utter nonsense, of course. British politics and culture in the 1970s were saturated in class-consciousness; indeed, it is astonishing to reflect how little the affluent society had affected people's sense of their own place within a social and economic hierarchy. Edward Heath, supposedly a representative of the new classlessness, was actually an excellent example of the survival of class distinctions. When he was hailed as the first Tory leader with wall-to-wall carpeting, the message was *not* that he was classless, but that his class background – modest, provincial, not gilded by money or family connections – made him different from other senior Conservatives. Indeed, Heath's palpable insecurity about his background was a sign of how much class distinctions still mattered. As his biographer remarks, one reason his leadership of the party in the late 1960s had been such a nightmare was that the landed interests who dominated rural Tory associations were not impressed by his awkward manner and odd accent, so he never enjoyed the automatic respect given to his predecessors.[34]

'The class system is alive and well and living in people's minds in England,' wrote Jilly Cooper in her humorous investigation into class at the end of the 1970s. It was a messy and confusing concept, she admitted, but it pervaded everything: family, homes, religion, sex, food, drink, dress, language, the arts, even death and gardening. What nobody could agree, however, was what it really meant. During the 1950s, a popular formula had been to divide people into 'U' and 'Non-U', but by the 1970s this had rather fallen out of vogue. Many analysts now used the National Readership Study's social grading system, which in 1976 put 16 per cent in the A and B categories (upper-middle- and middle-class), 21 per cent in the C1 category (lower-middle-class), 35 per cent in the C2 bracket (skilled working-class), and 28 per cent in the D and E categories (un-skilled workers and the very poorest). This was an attractive formula, making allowances for the pronounced gaps between different kinds of middle-class or working-class families, but it did not exactly catch on with the public at large; nobody ever referred to himself as a C2. Instead, people continued to shift between different models of class: the rich versus the rest, or middle-class versus working-class. In 1966, one survey found that 67 per cent called themselves working-class and 30 per cent middle-class, the rest denying they belonged anywhere. But in October 1974, Gallup produced very different results: 0.3 per cent upper-class, 2.3 per cent upper-middle-class, 30.9 per cent middle-class, 11.9 per cent lower-middle-class, and 49 per cent working-class. It is hard to believe that people's identities could have changed so much in just eight years; more plausibly, their answers simply depended on what they were asked.[35]

Class was not static, of course, and there were plenty of examples of mobility and change. Pop and rock stars who bought country houses and lived like eighteenth-century lords of the manor defied easy classi-fication; so too did the affluent Tottenham Hotspur footballers, all from working-class backgrounds, whom Hunter Davies observed 'dripping with rings and jewellery' in their flashy evening suits ('brocade lapels,

satin collars, embroidered jackets and shirts in every colour and material')
at a club dinner in 1972. To make things more confusing, from the early
1960s onwards middle-class youngsters often adopted regional accents
or proletarian idioms as a way of annoying their parents and proclaiming
their own progressive credentials, following in the footsteps of rock stars
like Mick (formerly Mike) Jagger or Jimmy Page, whose accents moved
suspiciously down the social ladder after their boyhood appearances on
television. Welcoming his great-nephews to lunch in 1972, James Lees-
Milne was shocked to find that they had 'that fashionable cockney accent
which is so odd in children of their upbringing. Winchester of all correct
schools too.' Wondering why 'upper-class boys have to speak like the
lower classes', he concluded that 'they hear it spoken all around them,
and imitate it like parrots'.[36]

Despite what had been claimed in the mid-1960s, birth, accent and
education still mattered enormously. 'Class-based inequality persists,'
reported the eminent sociologist A. H. Halsey in 1981, with 'the top half
of the population receiving three quarters of all personal income, the
bottom half one quarter', and the richest 20 per cent owning three-
quarters of all the nation's personal wealth. But of course class was about
more than just money. In the 1971 edition of his bestselling *Anatomy of
Britain* series, Anthony Sampson noted that there were 65 Old Etonians
in the House of Commons, accounting for 22 per cent of Heath's new
government. Oxbridge, meanwhile, maintained its 'special hold' over
Westminster, Whitehall, Fleet Street and the BBC, providing 26 of the
civil service's 30 permanent secretaries, and 250 out of 630 members of
Parliament. Of Heath's seventeen-person Cabinet, all but three had been
to Oxford or Cambridge. Indeed, one college alone dominated political
life in the 1970s: not only had Heath and Healey been Balliol under-
graduates, but so had Labour's deputy leader Roy Jenkins, the former
Liberal leader Jo Grimond, the liberal Tory grandee Sir Ian Gilmour, the
leading Labour moderate Dick Taverne, and the editor of *The Times*,
William Rees-Mogg. Sampson thought it seemed 'more like a cult than
a college'. Reflecting on the late Lord Samuel's quip that life was 'one
Balliol man after another', he concluded: 'It still is.'[37]

On the streets of West Yorkshire, a long way from the quadrangles of
Oxford, class was no less powerful a force. In his book on working-class
Huddersfield, Brian Jackson found it in the 'wage structure and the chain
of authority' in the mills and the pompous letters sent by council officials

to working men's clubs. 'Just about everything,' agreed the *Financial Times*'s Joe Rogaly ten years later, 'from the newspapers we read through the food we eat to the holiday we take is differentiated by class.' Every government statistic was steeped in it: the lower down the scale people were, the more likely they were to have long-standing illnesses, to suffer accidents at work, to die young, even to smoke. Researchers in Nottingham found that even at 4, the middle-class child was much more likely to be talked to at mealtimes and read to at bedtime. At 7, he was much more likely to be taken to the cinema, the library, museums and concerts, to read, paint and draw at home, and to be helped with his homework. And he was much less likely to be smacked; middle-class parents were more likely to reason with him, rather than threaten or beat him. Perhaps it was hardly surprising that youth culture, just like that of adults, was deeply divided by class. A teenager who wore his hair cropped short, spent his Saturdays cheering on Kevin Keegan and John Toshack, and spent his earnings on Slade and Black Sabbath records, probably had very little in common with one who grew his hair, affected vaguely countercultural fashions, and spent his days listening to *In the Court of the Crimson King* or *Tales from Topographical Oceans*.[38]

In the late 1950s, Richard Hoggart had colourfully evoked Britain's deep class resentment in a passage describing 'them' from the perspective of 'us'. 'They' were 'the people at the top', the 'higher-ups', the people who handed out doles and National Service call-ups: they 'aren't really to be trusted', 'talk posh', 'are all twisters really', 'never tell yer owt', 'clap yer in clink', 'will do y' down if they can', 'summons yer', 'are all in a click together', 'treat y' like muck'. At the time, this sounded outdated: surely all this was being swept away by the great tides of state education, social mobility and consumer spending? Quite the reverse, in fact, for as the promise of full employment and rising wages turned sour, people fell back on the language and concepts of class conflict. The obvious contrast was with the United States, where political vocabulary in the 1970s reverted to an almost classless anti-Washington populism that had no real British equivalent. The Britain of Edward Heath and Denis Healey was one in which the language and concepts of class came quickly to the tongue. And just as James Lees-Milne was quick to blame the working classes when things went wrong, so many Labour MPs keenly embraced the rhetoric of class warfare.[39]

Few readers could have been surprised, for example, by the guest column one Labour MP wrote for *The Times* in December 1976, entitled 'Why there must be no truce in the class war'. A former politics lecturer and author of *Socialism Since Marx*, he explained that the Labour Party was unashamedly a 'class party', founded 'by and for the working class to protect and advance its interests'. Radical redistribution of wealth and power, he said, was not 'the politics of envy' but 'the politics of justice', for class distinctions 'poison every aspect of our lives, and it is a class war we are fighting'. And blaming Labour for dividing society was wrong, for 'it is divided already. Nowhere is this more clear than in the factories where manual workers enter by one gate, eat in segregated canteens and work longer hours in worse conditions than their "betters".' It was for them that he was fighting, 'and only if we win shall we have a civilized society'. Reading such stirring words, few people could then have imagined that Robert Kilroy-Silk would end up smothering himself with cockroaches to amuse the viewers of ITV.[40]

Yet Kilroy-Silk's analysis certainly resonated with millions of his countrymen, men such as Doug Peach, a 57-year-old shop steward at the Black Country car-parts plant of Rubery Owen. Like so many firms in the mid-1970s, Rubery Owen was plagued by strikes, and in September 1975 its tribulations were the basis for a special feature in the American magazine *Time*. A family business founded in 1893, Rubery Owen now comprised seven different companies in twenty countries, but had never lost its paternalistic ethos. What fascinated *Time*, though, was the deep contrast between the lives and values of Doug Peach, representing the workers, and John Owen, the 35-year-old son and grandson of directors, and now managing director in his turn.

On a typical morning, John Owen left his 16-acre estate at around 8.30 for the short drive to work. He lived in the village of Knowle, 25 miles from the plant, in a rambling, rose-covered sixteenth-century house surrounded by spacious lawns, well-tended flower beds, a small pond and a paddock for Granby, the family pony. Owen, who had played rugby for England and would later become a senior figure in the Rugby Football Union, had three children; on the day *Time*'s reporter visited, his daughters were looking forward to their morning's riding lessons from their 'handsome blonde mother', while Owen dropped his son off at his private day school on the way to work. With a salary of around £14,200 a year (perhaps £175,000 today), a stylish red Jaguar convertible, an enviable home life in unspoilt countryside and a senior position in his beloved family firm, he was a handsome, confident man, wanting for very little, sure of his place near the top of the social pyramid.

Doug Peach's typical day began rather differently, with a cup of tea in his two-bedroom terraced house in Bloxwich, close to the factory. His four sons all worked for Rubery Owen; his wife Hilda ran a textile stall in Wednesfield market. The son and grandson of Black Country welders, Peach had been invalided out of Dunkirk and worked as a welder before becoming shop steward, for which he earned some £4,000 a year. 'Barrel-chested and brisk-gaited', giving his height as 'five foot bugger all', he was a man of traditional tastes. In the evenings, after work, he liked to feed his chickens and inspect his tomatoes, cucumbers and onions. 'They are my pride and joy,' he explained. 'I look after them like my union members.' Later, he would eat a cold tea in front of the television, and then perhaps go to the working men's club for cribbage or the little pub next door for dominoes and a pint of mild. He was no firebrand, no extremist: when far-left militants tried to win over the workers, he recalled, 'I crushed the bastards.' But Doug Peach believed that Britain was two nations, not one, and was determined to fight to the last for the interest of the workers. 'This battle will continue when I have finished. This will always be the case,' he insisted. 'There has got to be us and them. There has always got to be us and them.'[41]

One very obvious difference between John Owen and Doug Peach was the kind of newspapers they read; indeed, in Britain in the 1970s there were few more instantly recognizable badges of social and political identity. By far the bestselling paper in 1970 was the *Daily Mirror*, the voice of working-class Labour traditionalism, owned by the gigantic IPC group and read by an estimated 15 million people every day. Perhaps 10 and 5 million people respectively furrowed their brows over the middle-market *Daily Express* and *Daily Mail*, more than 3 million read the middle-class Tory *Daily Telegraph*, 1.3 million read *The Times*, the self-proclaimed paper for 'top people,' and around 900,000 'Herbivores', as Michael Frayn called them – 'the do-gooders, the signers of petitions, the backbone of the BBC' – sighed righteously over the pages of the *Guardian*.[42]

Despite its financial woes, the 1970s were good years for the *Guardian*: many of its innovations, from lifestyle features to a women's page, soon caught on with its competitors. But the real success story of the decade was a newspaper so utterly different in ethos and content as to come from a different planet. Originally founded in 1964 as the mouthpiece of the affluent society, calling itself 'a radical newspaper . . . championing progressive ideas', the *Sun* had been a disaster, and was quietly sold five years later to an obscure Australian businessman. Under the ownership of Rupert Murdoch and editorial control of Larry Lamb, however, the *Sun* was transformed into the tabloid voice of cheeky, hedonistic working-class populism. Lamb maintained that it was still a 'radical' paper, and in 1970 he urged readers to vote Labour. But the *Sun*'s eye-catching mixture of sex, sport and sensation was something new on Fleet Street, and although many old hands were horrified, the public clearly loved it. By 1970, it was already selling 1.5 million copies a day; by 1975, thanks to aggressive advertising, the innovation of Page Three girls and a relentless emphasis on sex and humour, it was selling almost 4 million. And three years later, Murdoch achieved what had once been unthinkable, deposing the *Mirror* from its throne as Fleet Street's sales king.[43]

Although the *Sun*'s critics shook their heads in horror at what they saw as its prurient philistinism, there is a case that it represented a welcome blast of irreverence in the rather staid world of British newspapers. And while its rise looks like a foretaste of the aggressive individualism of the 1980s, it was also the heir to a long tradition, from the scurrilous pamphlets of the seventeenth century to the lurid popular papers of the Victorians. Above all, though, its success reiterated a point of national pride: the fact that the British were some of the most avid readers in the world. No other English-speaking country, and certainly not the United States, devoured so many newspapers, sold so many magazines, or produced so many books per head. As always, there were gloomy reports of crisis and looming illiteracy: surging printing and wage costs meant that many publishers cut back on the production of experimental or 'niche' books, while in 1978 the *Bookseller* mourned London's 'dearth of bookshops' and complained that 'boutiques, hairdressers, betting shops (now 8,000 of them), shoe shops, hamburger bars' were forcing booksellers 'out of the High Street'.[44]

But this was excessively pessimistic. Heath's Britain remained an immensely literate, reader-friendly culture; there were even complaints of a 'surfeit' or 'suffocation' of books. The *Bookseller* recorded 24,000 new titles in 1970 alone, rising to 36,000 in 1980. Library lending reached an all-time peak, while book clubs like BCA and the Literary Guild were stunningly successful, boasting more than a million members by 1978. Older publishers sometimes complained that retailers wanted to sell books like records: in 1975 WH Smith pioneered the 'top ten paperbacks' list, making household names of such wordsmiths as Wilbur Smith and Jeffrey Archer. But nobody could possibly deny that Britain was a nation of readers.[45]

In the 1970s, as afterwards, it was very common to hear that British fiction was in terminal decline. Not only did literary critics, picking up on the latest Continental ideas, wax lyrical about the 'Death of Literature', 'Death of the Author' and 'End of Liberal Culture', but they often argued that British writing, usually as opposed to American, was in a particularly wretched condition. It was 'in crisis', wrote Bernard Bergonzi in 1970, characterized by 'neurotic symptoms of withdrawal and disengagement'. British literature was 'poorer, more cost-conscious and less outgoing', agreed Brian Aldiss in a *New Review* symposium in 1978. Other contributors sounded similar notes: A. S. Byatt thought that British fiction had fallen well behind American writing, Emma Tennant thought that Commonwealth writing was much better, while Nicolas Freeling argued that 'in a decadent society . . . weeds flourish'. Literature had been 'the main underpinning of English culture for the last couple of centuries', J. G. Ballard claimed in 1981. 'Now this underpinning has completely gone.'[46]

What seems neurotic now, of course, is the exaggerated diagnosis of decline. After all, Aldiss, Byatt and Ballard themselves produced fine books during this period, *The Malacia Tapestry*, *The Virgin in the Garden* and *High Rise*, to name but three. It is true that no particular trend or movement dominated: as David Lodge perceptively noted in 1971, there was now a sense 'of unprecedented cultural pluralism which allows, in all the arts, an astonishing variety of styles to flourish simultaneously'. But the sheer diversity and richness of British literature in the 1970s remains astonishingly impressive. Among established literary novelists, Anthony Powell, Graham Greene, V. S. Naipaul, Angus Wilson, William Golding, Anthony Burgess, Kingsley Amis, Malcolm Bradbury, John Fowles, John le Carré and Lodge himself published new work, while Ian McEwan, Salman Rushdie and Martin Amis (widely seen as the champion of the new generation), came of age in the mid-to-late 1970s. Fiction by women was arguably even more impressive: Doris Lessing, Muriel Spark,

Margaret Drabble and Iris Murdoch were all on top form during these years, while the works of Angela Carter – *The Infernal Desire Machines of Doctor Hoffman* (1972), *The Passion of New Eve* (1977) – were not only milestones in feminist fiction but proof that British writers were not immune to major international developments such as postmodernism and magic realism. And this is merely to stick to fiction; for poetry lovers, the publication of Ted Hughes's *Crow* (1970), Geoffrey Hill's *Mercian Hymns* (1971), Philip Larkin's *High Windows* (1974) and Seamus Heaney's *North* (1975), as well as the emergence of younger talents such as James Fenton, Craig Raine and Carol Ann Duffy, made the decade something of a golden age. Indeed, although poetry remained a minority interest compared with fiction, sales were extraordinarily good: *Crow* sold 50,000 copies and *North* 30,000, while the Poet Laureate, Sir John Betjeman, was one of the nation's most familiar faces, loved as much for his conservation campaigns and television documentaries as for his deceptively accessible verse.[47]

To many ordinary readers, of course, most of the above names re-mained either obscure or irrelevant. Popular taste was increasingly tolerant of explicit sex, violence and horror, as illustrated by the success of, say, Jackie Collins's *Lovehead* (1974) and *The Bitch* (1979), or James Herbert's *The Rats* (1974) and *The Fog* (1975), which surely would have been far too shocking for previous generations. But while the decade produced bestsellers that reflected the new political and cultural concerns of the day, such as Richard Adams's *Watership Down* or Alex Comfort's *The Joy of Sex* (both 1972), most readers had markedly conservative tastes. These were boom years, for example, for the romance publishers Mills & Boon, who produced more than twenty books a year and saw sales increase by 33 per cent between 1972 and 1974 alone. They were also good years for writers like Alistair MacLean, Wilbur Smith and Dick Francis, whose stories of rugged masculine heroes under extreme stress offered reliable, reassuring escapism from the depressing headlines of the day. And it is notable that two of the most conservative and endur-ingly popular twentieth-century writers of all, Agatha Christie and J. R. R. Tolkien, enjoyed huge commercial success with books published after their deaths: *Sleeping Murder* (1976) and *The Silmarillion* (1977). Neither of these books fared very well with critics, and neither could be said to reflect the themes and interests of the 1970s – though this was hardly surprising given that Christie had written her book during the

Second World War, while Tolkien had begun work on his myth cycle in 1914. All the same, their enormous appeal makes a mockery of the idea that Britain had experienced some kind of cultural revolution, and is another reminder that despite the headline-grabbing innovations of the day, most people's tastes changed only gradually, if at all.[48]

Across the cultural landscape of the 1970s, in fact, the same pattern repeated itself: enormous richness and diversity, yet also an intense popular thirst for nostalgic escapism. For the critic Christopher Booker, the 1970s was an age of 'cultural collapse' and the 'most dramatic dead end in the history of mankind'. But this was certainly not how millions of people saw it at the time. Although the Heath government horrified the arts world by introducing gallery charges – with the result that admissions to the National Gallery dropped by a third in just twelve months – these were generally fine and fertile years for the arts. The Tate's blockbuster exhibitions on landscape painting (1974), Turner (1975) and Constable (1976) drew enormous crowds, while the British Museum's Tutankhamun show in 1972 attracted a staggering 1.7 million people, many queuing for up to eight hours and taking home T-shirts, wall-charts and postcards, like latter-day Grand Tourists carrying off their booty. At a time when the headlines were dominated by terrorism, strikes and political unrest, the queues were a sign of the underlying civility and intellectual curiosity of British life. One man queued for fourteen hours to get a ticket on the exhibition's first day, while Londoners soon got used to the sight of people camping outside the museum overnight. And since hundreds of thousands of tickets were reserved for school groups, the charges of rampant commercialism were not entirely fair. The show was 'smashing', one schoolboy told *The Times*'s reporter, who judged that the word 'summed up the day to most children as they emerged, eyes popping, after an hour amid all that gold'.[49]

But the nation's artistic life was not confined to the major galleries of the capital. From Scotland to the south coast, as the *Observer*'s Richard Findlater noted in 1975, mass enthusiasm was the hallmark of British cultural life. 'Never before in British history', he wrote, had the arts 'been so accessible to so many people: the evidence is there in the record-breaking attendance figures at major exhibitions; the sale of LPs, prints and paperbacks; the viewing statistics for opera, ballet and drama on television'. Never before, either, had 'there been so much do-it-yourself art – amateur acting, music-making, Sunday painting', and never had there been 'so much money' in 'institutions, objects and events'. Indeed, despite the economic troubles of the period, business patronage for the arts reached a record £6 million by 1979, while Arts Council funding for regional arts associations more than trebled during the decade. Between 1967 and 1981, the number of local arts centres in England and Wales grew from 34 to 174, while there were also innumerable new theatre groups, dance troupes, art workshops, newsletters, magazines, bookshops and presses.[50]

With public interest booming, theatres and concert halls did particularly good business, enabling them to keep afloat when many people feared inflation would finish them off. It was in this period that Benjamin Britten wrote his last two operas, that Michael Tippett reached his peak, that Harrison Birtwistle and Peter Maxwell Davies came of age. It was also in this period that the London Symphony Orchestra faced perhaps the greatest trial in its history, when Edward Heath appeared on the platform in November 1971, baton in hand, to conduct Elgar's *Cockaigne* overture. In fairness, he acquitted himself pretty well, and afterwards, by his own account, 'found myself laughing with delight', which seems a bit unlikely. But the critics seemed to like it: *The Times* quipped that 'we could well hear more of this Mr Edward Heath'. Sadly, not all of his musical ventures were quite so successful. Passing through Paris in the late 1970s, where Heath had just conducted the European Youth Orchestra, the journalist Alexander Chancellor claimed to have seen the banner headline 'Heath a massacré Mozart'. Years later, when Heath agreed to conduct a professional orchestra in Salisbury Cathedral, his dictatorial manner drove them to the brink of mutiny. Eventually the leader could no longer restrain himself. 'If you don't stop being so rude to us, Sir Edward,' he burst out, 'we may start obeying your instructions.'[51]

As the victim of a court assassination plotted by a strong woman, Heath might not have appreciated Trevor Nunn's intense version of *Macbeth* (1976) with Ian McKellen and Judi Dench, perhaps the most acclaimed production in the Royal Shakespeare Company's history. But these were golden years for the RSC, for whom Patrick Stewart, Janet Suzman, Ian Richardson, Francesca Annis and Ian Holm gave a succession of mesmerizing performances. Indeed, with the emergence of radical young playwrights such as David Hare, David Edgar, Howard Brenton and Trevor Griffiths, with Harold Pinter, Michael Frayn, Alan Ayckbourn and Peter Shaffer continuing to delight audiences, and with an enormous proliferation of fringe and radical theatre groups, these were golden years for British theatre as a whole. Only the West End, with its feeble diet of farces and revivals, stood out as a disappointment. Even there, though, change was coming. 'I can think of no other modern score that does more to reawaken one to what musical theatre is for,' *The Times*'s critic wrote of Andrew Lloyd Webber's music for *Joseph and the Amazing Technicolor Dreamcoat* in February 1973. Not everyone was so impressed: after going to see *Evita* five years later, the National Theatre supremo Peter Hall returned home depressed at the 'cult of kitsch . . . inert, calculating, camp, and morally questionable'. But even he admitted that he was 'out of step with popular taste', for that very month, *Jesus Christ Superstar* became the longest-running musical in theatrical history, having taken more than £6 million and been seen by almost 2 million people – another victory for the conservatism of popular taste.[52]

In the years of Heath's first steps up the political ladder, by far the most popular form of popular entertainment had been the cinema. By the time he became Prime Minister, however, the days when millions of people went to the pictures every week seemed a distant memory. The late 1960s had been terrible years for the British film industry, which, as the critic Alexander Walker put it, had been reduced to the status of Hollywood's kept woman, dependent on handouts and burning with resentment. Disastrously, however, few of the British-made block-busters – *Doctor Dolittle*, *Battle of Britain*, a musical remake of *Goodbye, Mr Chips* – made any money, and when Hollywood understandably decided to call off the affair, the domestic industry was left high and dry. In 1968, American studios had invested £31 million in Britain; by 1974, they were investing less than £3 million. Production collapsed dramatically: in 1970, Britain made 84 films; by 1979, it made just 41, most of them feeble low-budget 'comedies', using the term very loosely. All in all, it was a woeful picture.[53]

Contemporary verdicts on British cinema were not complimentary. For Walker, it was 'dull, drained, debilitated, infected by a run-down feeling becoming characteristic of British life'; for the director Lindsay Anderson, it mirrored 'a nation that has ceased to believe in itself, is confused and fatigued, divided and without imagination'. And although academics have struggled manfully to rehabilitate the horror films and sex comedies of the era, the truth is that most were simply atrocious both in design and execution. Horror, for instance, was easily the biggest adult genre of the day, second only to children's films in terms of production. Yet with producers vainly hoping to win back audiences with nudity, sex and sensationalism, most horror films were wildly overblown, lurid, incoherent affairs, unfit to stand comparison with the products of Hammer's heyday. *Frankenstein Must Be Destroyed* (1969), for instance, boasted a gratuitous rape scene added over the objections of the director and actors, while *Dracula AD 1972* was little better, transposing the Count and Van Helsing to the streets of Swinging London (albeit five years behind the times). It was hardly surprising that audiences stayed away; by the late 1970s, horror production had tailed off, and when Hammer went bankrupt in 1979 it marked a miserable end to what had once been the model of a successful small studio.[54]

Hammer's fate makes a perfect metaphor for what happened to the rest of the British film industry. The second biggest genre of the day, for example, was made up of sex comedies such as *Confessions of a Window Cleaner* (1974) and *Come Play with Me* (1976). Again, some critics have done their best to speak up for them; unfortunately, not only were they not sexy, they were not even very funny. Perhaps the only really remarkable thing about them, in fact, was that by the standards of the time they were astonishingly popular. Eight came out in 1973, ten in 1974 and twelve in 1975, from *Penelope Pulls It Off* and *I'm Not Feeling Myself Tonight* to *The Amorous Milkman* and *Ups and Downs of a Handyman*. 'They said British cinema was dead. Maybe it is,' lamented *Films and Filming*'s review of *Confessions of a Window Cleaner*. 'There's nothing in this sorry tale of the pathetic sexual activities of window-cleaning folk that resembles living matter.' Indeed, that the adventures of Robin Askwith – the classic working-class hedonist, half-cocking a snook at authority – managed to attract audiences at all was a testament to the rigidity of the censorship laws and the prurience of popular attitudes. By comparison, the *Carry On* series, which had been emblematic of working-class humour during the 1960s, now seemed tired and tame, and its mid-1970s entries were comfortably the worst of the sequence. *Carry On England* (1976) effectively sounded the death knell for the series: many cinemas removed it from the schedules within days of the premiere, and it struggled even to cover its filming costs. 'The *Carry On* series is in a worse state than the economy,' remarked the *Daily Mirror*'s reviewer – and in 1976, that was saying something.[55]

Given the fare on offer, it is hardly surprising that most people preferred either to watch American films like *Jaws* and *Star Wars*, or just to stay away altogether. By 1970, only 2 per cent of the population went to the cinema once a week, compared with a third in the late 1940s. During the next ten years, audiences continued to collapse: by 1980, total admissions had fallen by half, dipping below 100 million for the first time since the early years of moving pictures. Cinemas themselves were miserable, run-down places, the erstwhile elegance of the art deco façades rather undermined by the holes in the faux-velvet upholstery. By 1980, there were fewer than 950 cinemas left; many had been transformed into bingo halls and nightclubs, shoddily converted into uncomfortable multi-screen complexes, or simply demolished entirely. By this point, it seemed a reasonable assumption that cinema-going would die out entirely in Britain as anything other than a mildly eccentric minority pursuit, like wearing a bowler hat or following West Bromwich Albion.[56]

There was, of course, one other popular adult film genre, perhaps the most reliable money-spinner of all. At the end of 1971, the box-office chart showed that the most popular film of the year had been Disney's *The Aristocats*, but in second place was a very different kind of picture: the cinematic version of Thames Television's *On the Buses*. The adventures of Stan, Jack and Blakey, the stuff of working-class situation comedy, might seem bizarre material for the big screen. But it was not the only spin-off to do well that year; in eighth place was the film version of *Up Pompeii*, with *Dad's Army* in tenth. More sitcom spin-offs followed a year later, and *Steptoe and Son*, *Mutiny on the Buses*, *Please Sir!* and *Up the Chastity Belt* all ranked among the twenty most popular films of 1972. In fact, few series escaped adaptation for the cinema: 1973 brought *Love Thy Neighbour*, 1976 *The Likely Lads*, and 1979 *Porridge*. A year later there was even a version of *Rising Damp*, Richard Beckinsale's untimely death having failed to deter the producers – although, like almost all of these films, it was a pale shadow of the original.[57]

That the British film industry had been reduced to making feeble spin-offs of *Love Thy Neighbour* spoke volumes about the balance of power between cinema and television. 'We don't go to the cinema very often,' remarked a Sutton warehouseman. 'All they have nowadays is sex and Walt Disney and I can get both of those at home.' Instead, like the vast majority of Britons in the 1970s, he preferred to stay in and watch the box. Watching television was by far the most popular leisure activity of the day, and the one that people said they most enjoyed. Viewing figures were pretty consistent: most people watched for about sixteen hours a week in summer and twenty in winter, far more than in any other European country, and double the rates in Belgium, Italy or Sweden. It seems unlikely that Britons were much lazier than their counterparts: the obvious explanation is that television had spread earlier and more quickly in Britain and was more tightly woven into the fabric of national life and culture. Almost everybody, barring eccentrics, owned a set; by now, people were even buying portable sets for their bedrooms or bathrooms. And more than other institutions, it was the BBC and ITV that defined and disseminated the national experience in the 1970s. Television was everywhere, the stuff of everyday conversations from the playground to the pub: a 'common cultural skin for the nation', as one account puts it. For many people, indeed, the fact that television had to close down at 10.30 was the most shocking thing about the economic emergency of January 1974, and the supreme symbol of Britain's political crisis.[58]

In hindsight, one of the remarkable things about television in the 1970s was how ordered and unchanging it was. Viewers could choose from three channels, each with its own familiar and well-defined identity, and the schedules rarely held shocks or surprises. The one great innovation of the decade was colour, which had first appeared in July 1967 but did not become widespread until the early 1970s. By 1972, 1.5 million households had a colour set; by 1978, more than 11 million. This was faster than many people had initially expected, but slower than is often recalled today; it is a shock to reflect that in 1974, there were still more than twice as many black-and-white households as colour ones. Interestingly, take-up was much quicker among working-class families. Having a good television clearly mattered more to people who did not have the money for alternative entertainment, and there was still a strong streak of middle-class snobbery towards television, usually manifested as a deep distrust of ITV. But colour did make one very big difference to the television landscape: it transformed the broadcasting of sport. Football had always been popular, of course, so the gigantic audience for the Chelsea–Leeds Cup Final replay in 1970, watched by 28 million people, was no surprise. But nobody could have anticipated the enormous appeal of sports like darts and snooker, which would have been almost inconceivable in a black-and-white age.[59]

Since the 1970s are almost universally regarded as the high point of

British television, it is amusing to note that the newspapers were full of doom and gloom about its abysmal quality. Television's biggest critic, of course, was the former schoolteacher, moral campaigner and president of the National Viewers' and Listeners' Association, Mary Whitehouse, from whose Shropshire home there issued a stream of condemnation aimed at the supposedly Communist-dominated BBC. People watched its programmes, she believed, 'at the risk of serious damage to their morals, their patriotism, their discipline and their family life'. Since her organization boasted more than 30,000 members by 1975, this was not an entirely isolated opinion. Watching *Panorama*'s review of the year at the end of 1971, Kenneth Williams fumed that its vision of 'smoke-filled cities and slag heaps and utter devastation' was clearly politically motivated. 'The BBC must be absolutely full of socialistic or communistic sympathisers,' he wrote in anguish. 'The organisation is rotten to the core.'[60]

A more reasoned version of the same argument came from the conservative writer Antony Jay, the future co-creator of *Yes, Minister*, who thought that the BBC was run by 'a small educated left-wing minority' whose 'social, political and moral assumptions are opposed to the majority of the country'. There may have been a small element of truth in this: the tiny Workers' Revolutionary Party did have a significant presence in the BBC's Plays Department, and counted influential figures such as Colin Welland, Frances de la Tour (*Rising Damp*'s incomparable Miss Jones) and Vanessa and Corin Redgrave among its members. The head of Equity admitted that he had 'more members involved in ultra-left activities than in most unions', but put it down to their histrionic temperament, explaining that 'there is an air of drama to a life based on a belief in imminent revolution'. At times it certainly seemed that *Play for Today* had become a branch of some Marxist sect's public education department. In 1975 alone it presented the story of an inner-city teenage delinquent working on a farm, a harrowing portrait of a day in the life of a mental health nurse, a violent evocation of sectarian prejudice in Northern Ireland, a searing play about a woman facing a mastectomy on the NHS and the four-part story of the betrayal of socialism and workers' rights in the 1920s.* In this context, *Private Eye*'s parody – 'Joe

---

* The plays in question were *The Death of a Young, Young Man* by Willy Russell, *Funny Farm* by Roy Minton, *Just Another Saturday* by Peter McDougall, *Through the Night* by Trevor Griffiths and *Days of Hope* by Jim Allen, which was directed by Ken Loach. Perhaps the biggest success was Griffiths' play, which attracted 11 million viewers and launched a national debate about the treatment of women with breast cancer.

Hartlepool's Last Fling', a 'realistic account of a 60-year-old Rotherham rivet-welder's mate, Stan Hornipants (sensitively portrayed by Reginald Maudling)' – was not far wide of the mark. But perhaps we should not overplay this. *Play for Today* did not *entirely* conform to the stereotype of single mothers sobbing in council flats and mustachioed Trotskyites on picket lines. In any case, it was hardly representative of the BBC's total output, and long-running series like *Upstairs, Downstairs, The Brothers* and *Terry and June* were not exactly models of left-wing propaganda.[61]

The other common complaint about British television was that it was simply no good. As early as 1972, the *Daily Telegraph*'s Sean Day-Lewis complained that the 'old peaks of creative writing' were no longer being scaled and that comedy was 'almost extinct', while the same paper's Marsland Gander (who had first written about broadcasting for the *Telegraph* in 1926!) complained that much of it was 'ugly and objection-able ... a nightly torment of convention and violence, nudity, bed-hopping and coarse language'. Future generations, however, would not judge the television of the 1970s in quite the same way. Of course there was some dreadful stuff: the BBC drama *Churchill's People*, which tried to tell the nation's history in twenty-six weekly plays, was widely regarded as an all-time low. But not only were viewers offered an extraordinary range of one-off dramas (for many editions of *Play for Today* were extremely good), the quality of series like *I, Claudius, Tinker Tailor Soldier Spy, The Pallisers* and *The Onedin Line* was exceptional by any standards. And in Dennis Potter Britain boasted probably the greatest television playwright in the world, whose series *Pennies from Heaven* (1978), challenging naturalistic conventions, broke new ground for a mainstream drama.[62]

There was more to television in the 1970s, of course, than serious drama. What many people loved most was the sheer escapism of light entertainment, from Michael Parkinson's chat show and Mike Yarwood's impersonations to the performances of comedians such as Tommy Cooper and Les Dawson, who represented a glorious final flowering of the traditions of the music hall. Above all, there were the double acts: the Two Ronnies, whose show first appeared in April 1971, and the supreme exponents of the genre, Eric Morecambe and Ernie Wise. Morecambe and Wise were steeped in the old traditions of song and dance and Northern working-class comedy, and had paid their dues in seaside resorts, on radio and in occasional appearances on other people's shows. In many ways their success was down to the public appetite for conservative, even familiar material, harking back to the kind of jokes that had made their parents and grandparents laugh on piers and promenades before the war. But it was also down to the fact that they were enormously likeable, imaginative and well drilled, and their appearances were woven into the fabric of contemporary cultural life in a way that would be impossible today. At their peak, in the Christmas Day specials of 1976 and 1977, their comic dance routines were watched by almost 30 million people. At those moments, perhaps more than ever before or since, Britain came closest to Heath's dream of one nation united by a common culture.[63]

Perhaps the emblematic genre of British television in the 1970s, though, was the sitcom. Sean Day-Lewis's claim that comedy was almost extinct seems particularly bizarre given that the schedules were so packed with situation comedies. In 1973 alone, for example, keen viewers could see the first episodes of *Last of the Summer Wine*, *Whatever Happened to the Likely Lads?*, *Some Mothers Do 'Ave 'Em*, *Open All Hours*, *Porridge* and *Man About the House*, while *It Ain't Half Hot Mum* and *Rising Damp* followed in 1974, *The Good Life* and *Fawlty Towers* in 1975, and *George and Mildred* and *The Fall and Rise of Reginald Perrin* in 1976. The work of a single author (or writing duo), unlike their team-written equivalents on American television, their quality was often underrated. 'How that ever became accepted for television is beyond me,' recorded Kenneth Williams after watching the prison comedy *Porridge* in December 1975, calling it 'sickening and disgusting', a bit rich from someone who was soon to make *Carry On Emmannuelle*. Even at the time, however, some critics recognized that they offered unparalleled glimpses of the values and attitudes of ordinary British families. Writing in *The Times* in 1973, Stanley Reynolds argued that *Whatever Happened to the Likely Lads?* had 'built up a better picture of sociological and structural change in the regions than a hundred hours of straight documentary'. Even the much-derided *On the Buses*, he thought, offered 'a window on to the real working-class world where worries about jobs and the colour of your neighbours and the price of a loaf or the slightest deviation from the sexual norm are matters of great significance'.[64]

Although sitcoms were often derided as formulaic and predictable, the half-hour format actually permitted tremendous variety. BBC sitcoms, for example, ran the gamut from the nostalgic character comedy of *Dad's Army* and the thinly veiled political commentary of *Till Death Us Do Part* to the smutty historical parody of *Up Pompeii* and the out-and-out farce of *Fawlty Towers*. The stereotype of sitcoms being filled with middle-class reactionaries in nasty trousers arguing about the summer fête, too, is not quite fair: both *The Good Life* and *Reginald Perrin* poked considerable fun at suburban conservatism, while *On the Buses* revelled in anti-establishment populism, mocked middle-class prudishness, and made its lead character a proud shop steward. Almost all of these shows, in fact, were steeped in class anxieties: many presented a lead character desperate to rise above his social situation, from Basil Fawlty and Rupert Rigsby to Bob Ferris and Captain Mainwaring. A classic example is the second run of *Steptoe and Son* (1970–74): while Albert, the father, is comfortable in his working-class rag-and-bone world, his son Harold hates his dirty environment, reads voraciously to improve his mind, and is desperate to get out and mix with more middle-class people. Like so many of these shows, the series glories in his frustration: many episodes end with Albert triumphant, and Harold dragged back into the bosom of his working-class home.[65]

One sitcom character who does manage to clamber up the social ladder, though, is Bob Ferris, the awkward Northern product of a secondary modern school, played by Rodney Bewes in *Whatever Happened to the Likely Lads?* Better than any other series of the day, Dick Clement and Ian La Frenais's show captured the changes that affluence had brought to working-class life. In its predecessor, *The Likely Lads* (1964–6), Bob was an electrician; when we see him again in January 1973, however, he has become a surveyor for a wealthy builder and, thanks to his engagement to the librarian Thelma, is moving into higher social circles. He has bought a semi-detached house on a brand-new estate, is a proud member of the local badminton club, takes skiing holidays in Norway and fancies himself as a wine buff, with comically disastrous results. But like Edward Heath, Bob occupies an uncertain position in the class structure. A dinner party with a middle-class family goes horribly wrong when they start arguing about their working-class roots, while his best friend Terry Collier (James Bolam), just back after serving in the army in West Germany, makes no secret of his contempt for what Bob has become. Terry is the epitome of the old, 'rough', defiantly masculine working-class culture: he loves nothing more than an honest pint, a glance at the racing paper and a trip to the bookies. 'I love Andy Capp,' he snaps when Bob teases him. 'Just because you're flirting with the lower-lower-middle classes, just because you've got yourself an office job and your fiancée lives in a Tudor estate with a monkey-puzzle tree . . . I'm working-class and proud of it.' 'So am I,' Bob insists, passionately but not very convincingly. 'I'm no less working-class than you. I went to the same school, grew up on the same streets, lived in the same draughty houses. But that's my point: you still want to live like that, you like the old working-class struggle against the odds. What you won't realise is that some of us won the struggle and it's nothing to be ashamed of.' But faced with the evidence of Bob's brand-new suburban house, his sharp suits and his pronounced views on dole recipients, Terry is having none of it. 'You still lost something in the process,' he says firmly.[66]

The most common class theme of 1970s sitcoms, though, was not the tension between working class old and new, or even between middle class and working class, but between two different kinds of middle-class identity: the difference between the conservative Leadbetters and the enviromentalist Goods in *The Good Life*, for instance, or between the aspirational Rigsby and the student Alan in *Rising Damp*, or even between old and new money in *To the Manor Born*. But the best example, albeit one transposed to the 1940s, is the rivalry between Captain Mainwaring and Sergeant Wilson in *Dad's Army*. One is a fiercely patriotic and no doubt unerringly Conservative bank manager, a self-made man impatient with privilege, his pomposity a cover for his social insecurities. The other is a languid upper-middle-class patrician, educated at public school, with no appetite for hard work and a slightly disreputable love life. And when Mainwaring loses his temper – 'You know where *I* went, don't you? Eastbourne Grammar! . . . I had to fight like hell to go there . . . *You* never fought for anything in your life! Brought up by a nanny, father in the City – all *you* had to do is just sit back and let everything come to you!' – it is not difficult to imagine Margaret Thatcher nodding with appreciation.[67]

By far the most celebrated sitcom of the decade, voted the best programme in television history by the British Film Industry in 2000, was *Fawlty Towers*, which was written by John Cleese and Connie Booth and ran for two series in 1975 and 1979. At the time, many critics saw it as an unadventurous hotel farce: the *Evening Standard* called it 'thin and obvious', the *Listener* thought it 'pretty hollow', and the *Mirror*'s verdict, infamously, was 'Long John Short on Jokes'. But of course the coincidences and misunderstandings so familiar from traditional farces were only one element in the show's charm. Few programmes captured so well the nuances of the class system, from the lower-middle-class, highly ambitious Sybil, with her elaborate hairdos, golfing habit and machine-gun laugh, to the snobbish, tweedy Basil, with his military moustache, Korean War wound, fondness for Brahms and atrocious grasp of foreign languages. And in Basil's determination to 'build up a higher class of clientele', his fawning attitude towards the fraudulent 'Lord Melbury', and his distaste for foreigners, the young and the working classes, Cleese and Booth brilliantly captured the neurotic mood of Middle England at a time of economic and political crisis. 'It sits there for months, and when you actually have a fire, when you actually *need* the bloody thing, it blows your head off!' Basil explodes after a fire extinguisher goes off in his face. 'I mean, what is happening to this country? It's *bloody Wilson!*'[68]

But it was not just in the character of the frenetic, frustrated Basil that *Fawlty Towers* seemed to capture the national experience in the mid-1970s. The hotel itself, with its genteel façade, peeling wallpaper and underheated rooms, could hardly have been a better metaphor for Britain's economy and industry during the Wilson and Heath years. Its only reliable guests are two dotty old ladies and a retired major with pronounced views on strikes, foreigners and immigrants ('No, no, the niggers are the *West* Indians. These people are *wogs*'); the food is barely fit for human consumption ('I assure you, they were absolutely fresh when they were frozen'); and the service culture is almost non-existent ('Dinner? Well, it *is* after nine o'clock'). Almost unbelievably, however, it was based on a real hotel, the Gleneagles in Torquay, where Cleese had stayed while filming *Monty Python*. But it was not the only terrible fictional accommodation of the 1970s. There is Rigsby's freezing, decrepit boarding house in *Rising Damp*, which his local Tory candidate calls 'the unacceptable face of capitalism' and threatens with demolition. There is the seedy Paddington hotel where Smiley stays in John le Carré's *Tinker Tailor Soldier Spy* (1974), a 'firebowl of clashing wallpapers and copper lampshades'; or there is the noisy motel he visits later in the same novel, with its yellow chairs, yellow pictures and yellow carpet, its orange paintwork and 'candlewick bedspread'. And as for bad food, there is the Oxford college breakfast consumed by the hero in Kingsley Amis's novel

Jake's Thing (1978) – 'sausages that went to coarse powder in your mouth, electric-toaster toast charred round the edges but still bread in the middle, railway butter and jam, and coffee tasting of dog fur' – or his meal in an 'authentic old-fashioned' hotel later in the book, where 'all the dishes were firmly in the English tradition: packet soup with added flour, roast chicken so overcooked that each chunk immediately absorbed every drop of saliva in your mouth . . . soggy tinned gooseberry flan and coffee tasting of old coffee-pots.' By these standards, perhaps Fawlty Towers was not such a bad place to stay after all.[69]

In an unguarded moment, Ted Heath once confided that he had 'a hidden wish, a frustrated desire to run a hotel'. The mind boggles at the prospect of Heath the hotelier: while he might have run a tight ship, surely even Basil Fawlty would have seemed warm and gregarious by comparison. But as Number 10's black door closed noiselessly behind him on his first night as Prime Minister, he was soon to find that not even Downing Street rose very far above Fawlty Towers' standards of service.[70]

After meeting his new staff, Heath closeted himself with his lieutenants Willie Whitelaw and Francis Pym in the Cabinet Room, where they began to sketch out the new administration. At eight, Heath suggested that they should break for supper, and pressed the bell to summon his Principal Private Secretary, Sandy Isserlis. But when Isserlis finally appeared, he brought bad news. 'There's no food here,' he said, 'and no staff, so it's impossible to get you anything to eat. Everyone left with Mr Wilson and there are no supplies here.' Heath impatiently suggested that Isserlis go out and find some sandwiches, and the civil servant duly disappeared. Twenty minutes later there was a knock on the half-open door and Isserlis stuck his head through the gap. 'Grub's up!' he shouted cheerfully, indicating a pile of sandwiches, pork pies and beer bottles – good ploughman's fare, no doubt, but hardly the ideal sustenance for a con-quering national leader. Willie Whitelaw could hardly believe his ears. 'How can anyone behave like that?' he burst out to Heath. 'He must be sacked at once.'[71]

As it happened, Isserlis was indeed sacked a few weeks later, although the fact that he had been Harold Wilson's appointee probably mattered more than the unveiling of the pork pies. His replacement was Robert Armstrong, a talented young Treasury official, whose father Sir Thomas, the former principal of the Royal Academy of Music, had known and conducted the young Heath during his Oxford days. As a music lover himself, Robert Armstrong was expected to get on well with the nation's bachelor leader, and eventually did so. But when he arrived for his first day at Number 10, it was to a frosty welcome. 'Oh. You're here,' Heath said, when he walked in. 'It's going to be very hard work, you know.' He meant it just as the usual gruff masculine banter. But not even the new Prime Minister could have guessed just how hard it would be.[72]

2

Heathco

When someone remarked [that] the new Prime Minister's Steinway had already been installed in the drawing room, Heath sat down at the keyboard and began to play. After he had completed an entire Beethoven sonata, he stood up. 'I'm sorry,' he said, 'but, gentlemen, when I start something, I always finish it.'
                                        – Time, 9 November 1970

The stark truth now appears. Grocer the waxwork, like Franken-stein's monster before him, has run amok.
                        – Auberon Waugh, in Private Eye, 30 July 1971*

On Edward Heath's first full day as Prime Minister, a woman threw red paint at him. He could hardly have known it at the time, but the incident was an uncanny preview of what was coming in the next few years. But he did not allow it to distract him from his immediate priority: banishing all memories of the hated Harold Wilson. He wasted no time in cancelling Wilson's Downing Street television rental, and arranged for a removal firm to bring over the furniture from his flat in the Albany, the trappings of his rich bachelor lifestyle: the black leather chairs, the marble tables, the oriental carpets, the collections of old glass and porcelain, the gleaming stereo equipment, the specially built clavichord and, of course, the piano. Meanwhile, he had already made plans for Number 10 to be completely renovated. Out went the chintzy patterns installed by Dorothy Macmillan; in came supposedly 'masculine' gold, brown and beige. In the corridors, the dark red carpets were ripped up and replaced with old

---

* The *Eye* had referred to Heath as 'Grocer' since 1962, a reference to his role negotiating food prices during Britain's abortive Common Market application under Macmillan.

gold ones; on the walls, workmen put up sheets of white and silver patterned paper. In the Cabinet Room, the dark green leather blotters, the worn leather of the chairs, the patchy green felt on the Cabinet table, were all torn out and replaced with 'a symphony of muted browns': fawn baize on the table, light brown leather for the blotters, new brown leather for the chairs. Even the paintings of great old statesmen were taken down, with French pastoral scenes mounted in their place. Admirers told Heath that it looked modern and masculine. But when the former Labour minister Barbara Castle laid eyes on it four years later, she was horrified. 'Gone was the familiar functional shabbiness,' she wrote. 'Instead someone with appalling taste had tarted it up . . . It looked like a boudoir.'[1]

Banishing the memory of Harold Wilson, even down to the Downing Street wallpaper, was something of an obsession for Heath. To the new Prime Minister, his rival was a trickster and a cheat, the incarnation of the cheap, squalid compromises and half-measures that were holding Britain back. Even when they met socially, colleagues remembered, Heath would freeze with ostentatious distaste. But now that Wilson was yesterday's man, the new Prime Minister could apply himself to the task of which he long dreamed, dragging Britain into the brave new world of the 1970s. His had been a very personal victory; and his, he determined, would be a very personal government, a far cry from the feuding and faction-fighting that had blighted Wilson's years in office. From the very first meeting of his new Cabinet, at eleven o'clock on Tuesday, 22 June, it was obvious that Heath intended to be the boss, the clipped and businesslike captain running a tight, well-disciplined ship. Far more than any of his predecessors, he saw himself as a dynamic, modernizing chief executive, hired to turn around a vast but struggling corporation.[2]

At that first meeting, Heath told his assembled ministers that he expected 'a new style of administration' and 'changes in the machinery of government'. That was classic Heath; having briefly been a civil servant after the war, he was an unrepentant machinery man. Colleagues often thought that he would have made an excellent civil service mandarin, such was his obsession with efficiency, rationalization and problem-solving. A taciturn and withdrawn man himself, he had never seemed comfortable with political passion or emotion; what mattered was the application of reason to sort out difficult issues. If the committee structure worked properly, 'with the help of dispassionate and largely apolitical policy analysis,' wrote his aide William Waldegrave, 'previously intractable problems could be rationally solved.' At Heath's very first Tuesday evening audience with the Queen, his agenda began with 'the formation of the government, civil service matters and the place of businessmen in the work of government'. But even his aide Douglas Hurd, one of his most loyal admirers, reflected that they had placed rather too much emphasis on how the government worked, on endless boards and commissions and councils, rather that what it was actually going to do. Heath, he thought, 'tended to exaggerate what could be achieved by new official machinery'. But if the chief executive of Heathco, as *Private Eye* dubbed him, thought that Britain's problems could be solved merely with the creation of another board or two, he was heading for disappointment.[3]

In that first Cabinet meeting of Heath's premiership, there were already signs of some of the troubles that would define his era. The third item on the agenda concerned Heath's plan to apply for British membership of the Common Market, which had long been an obsession for him. Within days, he told his ministers, his representatives would be meeting European officials to launch the application. Meanwhile, the new Home Secretary, Reginald Maudling, reported that the chief military commander in Northern Ireland had asked for five more battalions to help contain the demonstrations expected during the July marching season. This met with general agreement, although Heath added that 'a fresh political approach to the problem of Northern Ireland was urgently needed'. And there were problems closer to home, too. The new Chancellor, Iain Macleod, reported that while Britain's balance of payments was in a decent state, inflation was a growing concern, thanks to recent 'sharp increases in earnings and prices'. And the new Employment Secretary, Robert Carr, warned that trouble loomed in the docks, where the unions had threatened to walk out in pursuit of a higher minimum wage. Carr hoped to persuade the employers to 'conduct the negotiations as far as possible on their own responsibility, without leaning too heavily on Government assistance'. Unfortunately for Heath, however, the strike quickly got so far out of hand that just two weeks later, he was forced to declare a state of emergency – the first of a record five in less than four years.[4]

In the hot summer of 1970, many people expected the new government to take a radical right-wing approach to public affairs. After all, when the Tories had picked Heath as their new leader five years before, he had been the candidate of change: 'thrusting, pugnacious, aggressive', as

Panorama had called him, 'the man for those Conservatives who think the party needs "a tiger in its tank"'. Since then, grass-roots activists had been disappointed by his moderation, especially over issues such as immigration, on which he had been outflanked to the right by Enoch Powell, the tribune of white working-class resentment and free-market prophet in the wilderness. But in January 1970, Heath had apparently decided on a genuinely radical approach after a Shadow Cabinet strategy meeting in the magnificent Selsdon Park country hotel, near Croydon. Harold Wilson had even nicknamed him 'Selsdon Man' (after 'Piltdown Man'), warning that the meeting heralded 'not just a lurch to the right' but 'a wanton, calculated and deliberate return to greater inequality', while *The Economist* hailed the new 'Stainless Steel Tories'. In fact, Wilson's phrase rather backfired, giving the Selsdon meeting a sense of coherence and a public impact it never deserved. Much of the discussion had been vague and inconclusive: far from lurching to the right, Heath's economic policy remained a bit of a fudge, especially where inflation and incomes policies, the two burning issues of the moment, were concerned. But Heath went along with the Selsdon Man image. Even though it gave a misleading impression, it at least made him look decisive and coherent, a tough leader promising radical free-market solutions. And if nothing else, it bought him some credit with the right wing of his party, who now thought that the Messiah had come at last. The only problem, of course, was that he had aroused expectations on which he could not possibly deliver.[5]

With Selsdon Man in mind, many commentators interpreted Heath's victory as the end of the consensus that had governed British politics since the late 1940s. Even though the consensus is often exaggerated – the two parties had very different aims, often talked different political languages, and enjoyed a bitter rivalry – there was still a sense in which political and economic life in the 1950s and 1960s fell between universally accepted limits. Both parties, for instance, were committed to the Cold War and retreat from empire; both agreed that the government had a responsibility to ensure social welfare, based on the structures created in the 1940s; both believed in full employment; both recognized and respected the role of the trade unions; and, crucially, both believed that it was the role of government to ensure steady economic growth through managing demand, taking inspiration from the arguments of the great inter-war economist John Maynard Keynes. Unfortunately, although the economy had boomed during the 1950s and 1960s, allowing Tory and Labour governments alike to push through vast increases in social spending, the consensus felt distinctly tired, even threadbare by the time Heath came to power. Even in the early 1960s, there had been a torrent of criticism that Britain had failed to modernize, and that, beneath the superficial prosperity, the rot was setting in. In 1964, Harold Wilson had come to power promising to build a 'New Britain' in the 'white heat' of the technological revolution. But he had been sucked into a long, debilitating and ultimately misguided attempt to prop up the pound, which ended in defeat with devaluation in November 1967. Even Wilson's keenest admirers, of whom there were very few, could not disguise the fact that his administration had been a disappointment. Between 1964 and 1970, inflation had doubled, while unemployment rose from 1.6 to 2.5 per cent (small by future standards, of course, but seen as distressingly high at the time). Above all, despite Wilson's promise of 'planned, purposive growth', the oxygen had gone out of the economic boom. From a healthy 5.4 per cent in 1964, growth was down to just 1.8 per cent in 1970. It was no wonder that there was such a pervasive sense of disillusionment and betrayal: as the Labour MP David Marquand later put it, 'few governments have disappointed their supporters more thoroughly'.[6]

Behind this, however, lay a deeper problem. For while Britain was clearly much more affluent than in the days when Heath had been growing up, there was also an increasing sense that the country was falling behind its overseas rivals. Some of this showed symptoms of what the historian Jim Tomlinson calls 'declinism', a morbid obsession with economic decline that was often politically motivated and overlooked the fact that for most people, life was getting considerably better, not worse. And yet, even though it was inevitable that Britain would eventually lose the competitive lead it had established after the Second World War, there was an overwhelming sense of alarm at the speed with which it seemed to be slipping. In 1950, Britain had commanded a share of about 25 per cent of the world trade in manufactures. By 1960, this had slipped to less than 17 per cent, and, by 1970, barely 10 per cent, just half that of West Germany. In the league table of GDP growth, meanwhile, Britain fell from ninth in 1961 to thirteenth in 1966 and fifteenth in 1971, on its way to a miserable eighteenth in 1976. What was particularly striking was the gulf between Britain and the countries of Europe's

Common Market, which made rather a mockery of the government's arrogant decision to stay out in the 1950s. By almost every measure, from investment and productivity to the rate of GDP growth per head and the growth of average real earnings, the Common Market countries were ahead. It was no wonder that in the early 1960s, critics had asked 'What's Wrong with Britain?' 'For the past 25 years or more the United Kingdom has been in a state of chronic crisis . . . a British disease,' wrote Lord Shawcross in July 1970. The public needed to face facts: 'this country is not, and for a long time has not been, sufficiently competitive in world markets.'[7]

Entire books have been written about what went wrong with British industry. What is clear, however, is that the rot had set in during the 1950s, although it took the global shocks of the late 1960s and 1970s to expose all the weaknesses to public view. At a time when Britain still enjoyed enormous advantages, with many of its competitors busy re-building their war-shattered economies, managers and executives were far too complacent, allowing their access to soft colonial markets to blind them to the need for modernization. If Britain had joined the Common Market, its manufacturers might have been exposed to the bracing winds of proper competition, with beneficial consequences in the long run. But it did not. And on top of that, the attachment to full employment (perfectly understandable given the trauma of the 1930s), as well as the power of the unions, meant that politicians shrank from the job losses that would inevitably come in a radical shakeout. So British industry coasted along through the 1950s, only to find the waters getting progressively choppier as foreign rivals caught up. By the early 1960s, the problems were there for all to see: high prices and uncompetitive goods; conservative management; a financial sector obsessed with short-term profits rather than long-term growth; and, of course, short-sighted, defensive unions that did not cause the problems (contrary to what some on the right claimed) but made it almost impossible to take worthwhile measures to resolve them.

Indeed, when the government did intervene, it generally only made matters worse. In a sense, the very idea that the government had a responsibility to manage the affairs of industry was part of the problem. Since it would inevitably be attacked for every rise in unemployment or inflation, no sensible government was ever likely to take radical measures, even though they might be the right ones. Instead, governments of both parties kept intervening to prop up struggling industries like cotton and shipbuilding, although any clear-sighted analyst could see that they were doomed. The Wilson administration was particularly culpable because it was convinced that the way out of the mess was to select 'national champions', often huge, unwieldy conglomerates formed after government pressure. But by and large, the 'merger mania' of the late 1960s was a disaster. None of the Wilson government's beloved industrial leviathans, from the gigantic shipbuilding groups in Scotland and the North-east to the ICL computer giant, really worked, while the words 'British Leyland' should surely be etched on the tombstone of the man who oversaw its creation, the supreme champion of merger mania, who then called himself Anthony Wedgwood Benn. The problem was not that government intervention in industry was automatically a bad thing; when the French intervened, it often worked, although it is notable that the West Germans, who intervened least, had the best economic record. The problem was that British governments did it so badly, making the wrong choices time after time. And by the time Heath moved his piano into Downing Street, some industries – cars, textiles and shipbuilding, to name but three – were already in desperate trouble.[8]

In the early days of the Heath government, some predicted that he would bring the radical approach necessary to turn Britain around. Ten days after the election, *The Times* told its readers that the Tory victory would 'produce greater changes in the way Britain is run than in any administration since the Attlee government', a 'revolution of the generations' in which 'most of the pre-1970 assumptions' would inevitably be discarded. With its promises to cut taxes and to roll back the power of the state, Heath's manifesto certainly promised something new, and he talked a great deal about setting industry free to stand on its own two feet. And yet the truth was that Heath remained a creature of the post-war consensus. For all his talk of change, he had been a loyal, dependable insider all his political life, and, as Harold Macmillan's Chief Whip, he had been at the right hand of perhaps the most moderate, collectivist Conservative leader of the century. He was a technocrat, not a radical, a good staff officer who was never comfortable with ideas. His rival Enoch Powell even remarked that 'if you showed Ted an idea he immediately became angry and would go red in the face'. What people wanted to know, Heath once said, was '*how* we are going to do things rather than what needs to be done'. And like Macmillan and Wilson before him, he hoped that somehow faster economic growth would be the answer to all Britain's problems. 'No one will ever understand the Heath government,' said his friend Robert Carr, 'unless they understand the degree of our commitment to economic growth.'[9]

Despite his antipathy to Wilson, Heath and his rival had much more in common than people realized. Both were former civil servants, doers rather than thinkers, who talked a lot about modernizing Britain without quite explaining how they were going to do it. Crucially, both took power with distinctly vague economic plans. For all the nonsense about Selsdon Man, Heath came into office with a yawning policy vacuum concerning the most urgent economic issue of all: the incessant pressure on prices and incomes, which was driving up inflation. Both Macmillan and Wilson had tried to hold down wage increases with statutory freezes – 'incomes policies', according to the jargon of the time – but these invariably only postponed and exacerbated the inflationary pressures. The problem for Heath was that the Tory high command was split over the issue. Most senior figures, led by Reginald Maudling, who had been Chancellor in the early 1960s, believed that although incomes policies were blunt and unpopular, they were among the regrettable necessities of life. On the right, however, there was a growing movement to drop them entirely, spearheaded by free-marketeers like Enoch Powell, who thought the government had no business telling people what they should earn. Faced with a crucial choice, Heath's answer was a fudge: 'ringing condemnations of compulsory controls qualified by meaningless reservations', as his biographer puts it. Almost unbelievably, therefore, his five years as Leader of the Opposition had failed to produce a clear sense of how his government would tackle inflation, which was to prove the defining issue of the 1970s. But the public had no way of knowing this, because Iain Macleod had persuaded him that for the campaign it was better to look decisive than to say nothing. 'Manifestos had to be black or white,' one colleague remembered Macleod saying. 'Either we said we were going to have an incomes policy and it would be superb, or that we were not going to have one at all. We should say that we were not going to have one and if in a few years we changed our minds we would have to explain there were special circumstances.' It was pure cynicism, but Heath went along with it. 'We utterly reject the philosophy of compulsory wage control', declared the manifesto – words that even Heath probably did not believe at the time.[10]

Of all Heath's ministers, it was Macleod, the D-Day veteran and former bridge prodigy whose mixture of Yorkshire cynicism and Highland romanticism had made him one of the most colourful figures on the Tory front bench, who was expected to set the tone for the 1970s. A brilliant orator whose liberal views on the death penalty, abortion and homosexuality horrified the Conservative rank and file, Macleod had presided over British withdrawal from Africa between 1959 and 1961, but resigned from the government two years later in protest at Sir Alec Douglas-Home's elevation to the leadership. Everybody agreed that he was Heath's most brilliant asset; it was said he was the only opponent in debate whom Harold Wilson really feared. As Shadow Chancellor, he was a bit like Denis Healey, a fellow Yorkshireman with a sharp mind and biting wit, in that he prided himself on not reading about economic theory, but cared only about the practical nuts and bolts. Macleod was certainly no fan of laissez-faire, which he thought was 'a Whig rather than Tory doctrine', and remarked that setting the market free was 'an excellent policy for the strong, but we are concerned also with the weak'. As Chancellor, he planned to be a radical reformer, slashing taxes and spending, but not a reckless or uncaring one; in many ways, he was the soul of One Nation Toryism. The only cloud on the horizon was his health. In 1940 he had sustained a severe thigh wound which still affected him, and he also suffered from kidney failure and chronic spondylitis, a spinal disease, which meant that he walked with a pronounced limp, his body hunched and twisted.[11]

At the beginning of July, Macleod went into hospital for what seemed like appendicitis, but was in fact a benign abdominal condition. On Sunday, 19 July he was back in 11 Downing Street, watching the Commonwealth Games on television, when the heart attack struck. Within an hour, aged just 56, having been Chancellor for exactly a month, he was dead. For Heath, who immediately came over from Number 10 and sat up for the rest of the night trying to comfort Macleod's wife Eve, it was a terrible blow. 'I felt numb and sick,' he later recalled. 'I was shattered by the news.' Quite apart from the human tragedy, it was an enormous loss to the government. None of Heath's ministers had comparable wit, charisma or rhetorical skill, and certainly none had Macleod's tactical instinct. 'He was our trumpeter,' said Robert Carr, 'and any party, any government, needs a great trumpeter.' What was more, he was the one colleague Heath really respected and who could stand up to him, the first mate the captain could not do without. With Macleod gone, the government lost its balance. In his place, Heath appointed his protégé Anthony Barber, who had been an RAF pilot in the war, was imprisoned by the Nazis after his plane crashed, and once escaped as far as Denmark before being recaptured. But as Heath's new Chancellor, Barber cut a much less colourful figure than one might expect from a man who had broken out of Stalag Luft 3, looking more like a balding provincial accountant than a war hero. He had a high voice and hesitant manner, and John Kent's *Private Eye* cartoons always showed him addressing Heath as 'Sir'. To put it bluntly, he was a lightweight; from now on, it was Heath who ran economic policy.[12]

During the 1970 election, Harold Wilson's advertising men had come up with a famously negative poster campaign, showing a set of evil-looking clay figurines of Heath, Macleod, Douglas-Home, Quintin Hogg, Reginald Maudling and Enoch Powell, with the caption 'YESTERDAY'S MEN (They failed before!)'. In fact, yesterday's men played much less weighty parts in Heath's government than anyone had anticipated. Macleod was dead, Powell was in exile after speaking out against immigration, and Hogg had been moved upstairs to become Lord Chancellor as Lord Hailsham. Douglas-Home, a former Prime Minister now running the Foreign Office, had too much on his plate already to worry about domestic issues (which had never interested him greatly anyway). The one man who might have been most help to Heath was Reginald Maudling, the Home Secretary, who had been a contender for the Tory leadership in 1965. Maudling was in many ways an enormously appealing politician: clever, affable and fun-loving, a man with a Rolls-Royce intellect who thought nothing of spending the morning tasting vintage port with his officials, and said that his favourite kind of whiskies were 'large ones'. He might have been a great liberal Home Secretary, a kind of Tory Roy Jenkins. But he was not on good form in the early 1970s. Losing the leadership had brought out his worst characteristics: laziness, greed and self-indulgence. By 1966 he was beginning every day with brandy at breakfast and gin throughout the morning, and while never completely drunk, he was rarely entirely sober either. His wife Beryl, who always liked a drink or several, loved the good life too, and by 1970 they had been sucked into a nether world of flagrant corruption to pay for their extravagant lifestyles. Maudling was turning into a Westminster joke: as Robin Day told a friend in 1969, he was increasingly 'bone-lazy and quite useless after lunch'. The large Scotches and day-long lunches were taking their toll, and 'there was an air of shabbiness and disorder in his appearance', as his biographer puts it. Maudling's features had thickened; his suits were crumpled; his shoulders were dusted with dandruff; his hair was lank and oily. But these were merely the superficial manifestations of his deeper moral decline.[13]

From the start, therefore, Heath relied on an inner circle of advisers and officials, the court of a President rather than a Prime Minister. Unlike Wilson's faction-ridden 'Kitchen Cabinet', this was a tight, professional team, albeit a very introverted and technocratic one, including Heath's political secretary Douglas Hurd, his press officer Donald Maitland, his Principal Private Secretary Robert Armstrong, who soon established an exceptionally close, even filial relationship with Heath, and above all, his Permanent Secretary, Sir William Armstrong, the head of the Civil Service, who became virtually deputy Prime Minister. Beyond them, Heath relied upon a small group of ministers nicknamed the 'Heathmen' by the press, who were supposed to be a new breed of thrusting Tory modernizers, united by their modest origins, managerial style and loyalty to their master. This was a bit of an exaggeration, since most came from distinctly wealthy backgrounds, but the press loved the idea of a new generation of ruthless go-getters. Anthony Sampson, an inveterate trend-spotter, thought that they represented the rise of a 'New Toryism': 'men who actually sounded interested in industry; and who were dedicated to making the capitalist system work, with tougher competition, greater incentives and the injection of eager management methods into govern-ment'. Among them he singled out the new Education Secretary, Margaret Thatcher, a grammar-school-educated research chemist with a 'quick mind' and 'a scientist's interest in teaching machines and aids', and the new Environment Secretary, Peter Walker, a grocer's son from Gloucester who had become a self-made City millionaire and the ultimate 'manager-minister', running his department 'as if it were a giant corporation'. Walker was not popular inside his own party: at only 38, he was too young, too arrogant, too ambitious and too liberal for many older backbenchers. It was as though an old family firm had been 'suddenly invaded by icy time-and-motion experts', one Conservative MP com-plained. But Heath liked Walker's emphasis on efficiency, and nobody could deny that he got results.[14]

In later years, Heath became famous for his hilarious, world-class grumpiness, whether manifested in glacial silences, withering put-downs or selfishness of the most outrageous kind. Stories of his rudeness are legion: the time his campaign bus crashed and threw a middle-aged lady passenger to the floor, prompting Heath to call immediately for a glass of brandy which he then drank himself; or the occasion in the 1970 campaign when a man in a pub asked him whether he would get a tax cut because he was a family man and a home-loving man, to which Heath snapped: 'Well, you had better go home now, I think.' Much of this can be traced back to his Kentish boyhood, when he was a spoiled prodigy, smothered with maternal affection: not only did he have his own armchair, he was spared washing-up duty (unlike his brother) because it would interfere with his music practice. Even then, visitors thought him a self-centred little boy, and there was an extraordinary solipsism in the fact that he called his dog 'Erg', after his own initials. He did not change as he got older; if anything, as the historian John Ramsden observes, he had a 'decreasing fund of small talk and a reluctance to spend those diminishing reserves on political colleagues'. His ministers had to get used to long, frosty silences punctuated by flashes of brutally dry humour: after summoning one official away from his wedding anniversary, he greeted him with the words, 'You're well out of that.' 'The outrageous statement in a deadpan voice, the sardonic question, the long quizzical silence,' wrote Douglas Hurd, 'were hard for a newcomer to handle.' And perhaps only Heath could have attended a dinner of Tory agents before the party conference, organized to show his human side, and sat in silence for so long that his friend Sara Morrison passed him a napkin on which she had scribbled, 'For God's sake, say something.' Without saying a word, Heath slowly unfolded the napkin, read the message, wrote something, folded it, and passed it back. When Morrison opened it, she saw the words 'I have.'[15]

And yet there is no denying that Heath inspired exceptional loyalty among his closest colleagues. He was 'very shy, very reserved', one civil servant later said, but 'every so often the clouds would roll back and you saw that he liked you and depended on you. And those moments were worth much more than more frequent signs of friendship from other people.' Heath's friend Jim Prior, who was first Agriculture Minister and then Leader of the Commons, agreed that his rudeness was born of shyness and boredom, and that he had a softer side that the public never saw. Other close colleagues, such as Hurd, Whitelaw and Carr, similarly felt a tremendous sense of affection for their chief. Whitelaw even made the extraordinary statement that if Heath told him to become ambassador to Iceland, he would be on the first flight to Reykjavik. 'I trust his judgement absolutely,' he said. 'It's not because he has charm, because he hasn't any charm. It's not because he's easy to work for, because he isn't easy to work for. I don't know what it is – it's a mystery to me. I only know I trust him more than I've ever trusted anybody.'[16]

Having won such a personal victory in June 1970, Heath had good reason to feel pleased with himself as he looked forward to remaking his country. He had arrived in Downing Street as the 'master of Britain's fate for the immediate future', said *The Times*, 'full of authority and command as the leader who was doubted and who conquered against the most daunting psychological odds'. But this carried a profound danger. Always a solitary, proud man, Heath felt no humility in victory, only the confirmation of his enormous self-belief, which his biographer summarizes as an attitude of 'Bugger them all – I won'. Although he had won on the back of a slick, professional advertising campaign, he increasingly disdained the media and refused to listen to his public-relations men, preferring instead to communicate by giving long, austere television lectures, like some Soviet commissar reading out tractor statistics. And as time went on, so he withdrew deeper into the Downing Street bunker, a lonely man with no family to relieve the pressure, no wife to act as a confidante, just his beloved music to keep him company in the long evenings, as one by one his dreams of modernizing Britain turned inexorably to dust.[17]

As Heath's administration got under way in the summer of 1970, there was a palpable sense of anticipation at the radical departure to come. With four early announcements – the application to join the EEC, a plan to reform local government, an initiative to allow tenants to buy their council houses, and the withdrawal of Labour's attempt to compel education authorities to scrap their grammar schools – the Conservative grass roots were immediately delighted. On the first day of the new parliamentary session, Heath told the Commons that he meant to rebuild Britain as 'one nation', with national unity as the theme in everything from education to the economy. But when he rose to speak in Blackpool a few months later at a celebratory Conservative Party conference, his message was rather more pointed. To the delight of his audience, Heath promised 'to reorganise the functions of Government, to leave more to individual or to corporate effort, to make savings in Government expenditure, to provide room for greater incentives to men and women and to firms and businesses', encouraging them 'to take their own decisions, to stand on their own two feet, to accept responsibility for themselves and their families'. This was Heath the radical modernizer, not Heath the consensual compromiser. He wanted 'to permanently change the outlook of the British people', he said grandly, for 'to cling desperately to the present will be to find ourselves embracing only the past'. And finally there came the phrase for which he hoped his premiership would be remembered. 'If we are to achieve this task,' he concluded, 'we will have to embark on a change so radical, a revolution so quiet and yet so total, that it will go far beyond the programme for a Parliament to which we are committed and on which we have already embarked: far beyond this decade and way into the 1980s. We are laying the foundations, but they are the foundations for a generation.'[18]

At the time, the phrase 'the quiet revolution' seemed likely to capture the mood of the historical moment, just like Wilson's talk of white heat or Macmillan's boast about people never having had it so good. In the *Evening Standard*, one reporter wrote that Heath was 'pulling down the [Rab] Butler boarding house' and replacing it with 'a skyscraper with self-operating lifts,' while in the *New Statesman*, Paul Johnson wrote that exchanging Wilson for Heath was like swapping 'an India-rubber-ball for a spanner'. And at least as far as the machinery of government was concerned, Heath seemed to be delivering on his boasts of a 'radical reforming government'. In the middle of October, he reorganized White-hall by creating two new 'super-ministries': a gigantic new Department of Trade and Industry, and an even bigger Department of the Environment, run by his protégé Peter Walker, which swallowed up Transport, Housing, Local Government, and Public Building and Works. Meanwhile, he had also set up a new Central Policy Review Staff under the biologist, MI5 agent and mandarin Victor Rothschild, which for the first time would supply disinterested advice to the Cabinet. Known as the Think Tank, it was much mocked by Heath's critics but had considerable influence, not only in urging his U-turns over incomes policy in 1972, but also in predicting the OPEC oil shock. It also had the unusual distinction of being the only Whitehall unit parodied in *Doctor Who*: in Tom Baker's debut story, 'Robot', in 1974, the Doctor has to foil an evil plot to hold the world to ransom, hatched in the National Institute for Advanced Scientific Research, or 'Think Tank'. Fortunately, none of Rothschild's schemes were so nefarious, or involved giant robots.[19]

The modernization drive did not end there. By early 1971, the government had edged towards a policy of privatization, selling off some of its more eccentric holdings, from the Thomas Cook and Lunn Poly travel agents, which had been nationalized by the Attlee government for no very good reason, to the state-owned pubs in Carlisle, which had been taken over as an experiment in limiting drinking during the First World War. Even this minor divestment provoked fury on the Labour benches. Harold Wilson even warned that the once 'respected' firm of Thomas Cook would be turned into one of the 'crook organizations in the travel industry who are not too squeamish about their safety level', adding that his own sister had recently had the misfortune to be 'fleeced' by a package company. And there were also, in due course, tentative moves towards reforming council housing, thanks to Walker's Housing Finance Act, which redirected subsidies from all tenants to those in most need. Since this meant that more affluent tenants' rents promptly went up, it caused an enormous outcry: in Clay Cross, Derbyshire, the Labour authority refused point-blank to implement it, and eleven councillors were personally surcharged. Meanwhile, Walker tried to persuade local authorities to sell council houses to their tenants, but this did not catch on at all. By 1974 just 7 per cent of eligible houses had changed hands, and the next government immediately changed course.[20]

There were two obvious problems with Heath's 'quiet revolution'. The first was that it was not terribly popular. Although most people had read in their newspapers about Britain's competitive decline, and were certainly aware that the country had lost power and prestige since the Second World War, their own lives, by and large, had been marked by greater affluence and opportunity. They had not yet realized the penalties – in higher prices, falling living standards, pay freezes and strikes – they would have to pay for Britain's economic problems, and there was little sense that they wanted radical change. What was more, Heath's bloodless brand of time-and-motion modernization was not always very attractive, a classic example being Walker's reform of local government. The historian John Campbell argues that since the existing system was such a messy, disorganized patchwork of counties, county boroughs, non-county boroughs, district councils and parish councils, 'reform was long overdue'. The Redcliffe-Maud Report, commissioned under Labour and published in 1969, had advocated taking a chainsaw to the old counties and creating eight large provinces, which was too radical even for Walker. But his solution, enshrined in the Local Government Act of 1972, horrified most ordinary taxpayers, who felt a vague but powerful sense of attachment to the historic county system. Rutland, which had been fighting a desperate battle for survival for years, was abolished, as were the much-loved Yorkshire ridings. Herefordshire and Worcestershire were combined; Shropshire was unaccountably renamed Salop; and entirely invented bodies such as 'Avon', 'Cleveland' and 'Humberside' were foisted upon their residents, almost all of whom loathed them. In Wales, the situation was even worse: the old counties disappeared entirely, replaced by made-up entities like Clwyd and Dyfed. It was Heathite modernization at its worst: unresponsive, high-handed and entirely insensitive to history. In some areas, such as doomed Rutland, or Berkshire, which lost its beloved White Horse of Uffington, there were even protests and marches against the scheme, and most people saw it as a symbol of everything least attractive about Heath's government, a 'monstrous bureaucratic abortion derived from a misplaced belief in institutional change for its own sake'. And the one thing it was not, of course, was conservative.[21]

The other problem with the 'quiet revolution' was that behind the sweeping rhetoric and the superficial changes to county councils and Whitehall departments, it was much less radical than it seemed. Heath and Barber talked a lot, for example, about slashing government spending, much to the horror of the Labour Party and the unions. And yet despite the accusations that Heath was a callous, flint-eyed reactionary, filled with loathing for the poor, this was a myth. As Jim Prior later recalled, they were committed to the 'social consensus', and planned 'an improved Welfare State . . . in which the social services should be expanded and more should be done about housing'. In fact, social spending, both in real terms and as a proportion of GDP, increased more under Heath than under any other post-war government since Attlee. There was a strange irony in the fact that, even as Wilson was denouncing his successor for cold-hearted cruelty, Heath was approving spending increases that went well beyond anything in the 1960s, including small acts of generosity such as giving pensions to people who had retired before 1948 and thus had not qualified for a state pension, or giving

Christmas bonuses to the elderly, or giving pensions to widows over 40, or allowances to the disabled. A senior civil servant who worked for Keith Joseph, the new Secretary of State for Social Services, recalled that at the beginning 'there was a little Selsdon Man phase'. But that lasted no more than three months, and then Joseph settled down to behaving just like his predecessor, Labour's Richard Crossman. 'For all practical purposes,' the official reflected, 'the Heath government was exactly like working for the Wilson government.'[22]

Despite his subsequent reputation as the founding father of Thatcherism, Joseph was one of the Heath government's two biggest spenders. Born into the wealthy Jewish family that was behind the Bovis housing giant, he was an introverted, tortured personality, afflicted both by terrible medical problems (plagued by ulcers, he had had half his stomach removed in 1968), and by a burning though unfocused social conscience. In the late 1960s he had been a keen supporter of the Child Poverty Action Group, and even his Labour opponents conceded that he was 'a compassionate man who cares about the problems of the underprivileged'. He even had the courage to tell his party conference that there were far fewer 'shirkers and scroungers' than they thought, and that he would never inflict poverty and starvation on the children of those 'who cannot manage their lives effectively'. As head of the DHSS, he presided over a steady expansion of the welfare state, from higher disability benefits to higher child allowances; and while his attempt to reorganize the NHS ended up as yet another bureaucratic nightmare, he spent more money at a faster rate on the health service than had ever happened under Labour.[23]

As a spender, Joseph had only one Cabinet rival: the Education Secretary, Margaret Thatcher. Derided as the 'Milk Snatcher' in 1971 because she had to carry out Macleod's plan to scrap free school milk for children aged between 8 and 11, Mrs Thatcher was actually a big-spending education chief who secured the funds to raise the leaving age to 16 and to invest £48 million in new buildings. In December 1972, she even published a White Paper envisaging a massive £1 billion a year for education by 1981, with teaching staff almost doubling and vast amounts of extra cash for polytechnics and nursery schools. She wanted 'expansion, and not contraction', she said. It never happened; if it had, her reputation in the education sector might be very different. 'In several respects,' said the *Guardian* at the time, she had been a 'more egalitarian Minister than her Labour predecessor. Her support for primary schools, polytechnics, the raising of the school-leaving age, and the new nursery programme will all provide more help to working-class children than the Labour programme actually did.'[24]

The truth was that, far from breaking with the post-war consensus, Heath's ministers still believed that the proper role of government was to administer a gently expanding welfare state, with more money being spent every year on health, education and social benefits. Behind this was the fatal assumption that, once the right dose of efficiency had been applied, Britain's economy would set off on a new burst of steady growth, the pie expanding every year so that everyone could have a bigger slice. But this was wildly optimistic, to say the least, for the economic inheritance was not as rosy as it looked. Although the outgoing Chancellor, Roy Jenkins, had left his successor a rare balance of payments surplus, his austerity had fuelled intense resentment among workers who had seen their earnings stagnate. By the autumn of 1969, there were already reports of 'anarchy' in industry, with car workers, coal miners, nurses, firemen, dustmen and local government workers all walking out in pursuit of better wages. Conscious of the looming electoral showdown, Jenkins had quietly turned a blind eye to their escalating pay claims, with some settlements soaring as high as 12 or 13 per cent. But while this was clever politics, it was extraordinarily reckless economic management. Even at the time, many observers thought that it was madness to allow workers' pay to increase so quickly at such a sensitive moment. Growth was sluggish, profits were weak and output was growing at barely 1.5 per cent a year. What was more, the cancer of inflation had already taken hold in the world economy, thanks to the Americans' disastrous overspending on the Vietnam War. As early as April 1970 the economist Michael Shanks predicted that defeat 'on the wage front' would be an object lesson in 'how dangerous it can be for governments to slacken the reins'. And whoever found himself in Downing Street after the election, predicted Lord Shawcross in *The Times*, would have to take 'the most disagreeable measures' if Britain was to escape 'runaway inflation'.[25]

In the summer of 1970, Heath's economic priorities, as he reminded his colleagues, were 'to reduce the burden of taxation and to restore the competitive vitality of British industry'. And in his first budget, unveiled at the end of October 1970, Anthony Barber did as his master demanded, slashing income tax by 6d. in the pound and corporation tax by 2.5 per cent, while cutting about £300 million in government spending, thanks to higher charges for prescriptions, false teeth, glasses and school meals, the withdrawal of free school milk for older children, the end of universal council-house rent subsidies and the imposition of admissions charges for museums and galleries. The general aim, said Barber, was to 'lessen Government interference' and to give the individual 'greater freedom in how he spends or saves his income', sentiments that delighted right-wing newspapers and outraged the Labour benches. And yet, behind the rhetoric, Barber was already seriously worried. As early as July, when he had succeeded the unfortunate Macleod, the Treasury had reported that wages and salaries were growing by 11 per cent a year. Heath urged his ministers to stand firm 'in the face of clearly excessive wage demands'. Even though it would mean strikes in the short term, he said, 'there will be long-term gains'. But a few months later, Barber reported that wage settlements in July had reached 14 per cent, even though the economy was growing at barely 2 per cent. The economy was facing 'the most severe bout of cost inflation since at least 1951', he gloomily told his colleagues; they simply must persuade the workers' representatives in the TUC to moderate their demands.[26]

Unfortunately for the government, however, the unions were in no mood to roll over. As the union leaders saw it, this was a reactionary Conservative government that had come to power promising to slash public spending and push back the frontiers of the state. Even worse, the Employment Secretary, Robert Carr, was preparing a radical Industrial Relations Bill that would drastically curtail the historic rights and free-doms of the union movement, and had already made it clear that he would not be deflected by TUC protests. And now, they thought, the government proposed to make low-paid public employees foot the bill for its battle against inflation. They watched in fury on 24 September, as Heath told ITV's Alastair Burnet that he was determined to resist 'wildly inflationary' wage demands, even if it meant a rash of strikes over the winter. And as prices inexorably rose, putting living standards in further jeopardy, so the pressure from their members mounted.[27]

Of course, Heath could have resorted to a statutory incomes policy to keep wages down; but having ruled this out only months beforehand, he was not ready for a U-turn just yet. Instead, he told Carr that the government must hold the line against big public pay increases, setting an example for the private sector. Carr duly carried this message to the

TUC, imploring them to show restraint. But it was too late. Already the strike figures for 1970 were far worse than in previous years, he told the Cabinet on 3 September, 'and there was no prospect of an early improvement'. Worryingly, strikes seemed to be getting longer, while 'militancy was also continuing to be rewarded', for example at the big GKN engineering plant in Wellington, Shropshire, where workers had just won a whopping 25 per cent increase. Both government and employers, Carr said, must 'offer strong resistance repeatedly – a single successful test case would not be enough'. But he had bad news for his colleagues: the next important public pay claim, from the local authority manual workers, was upon them, and he did not expect an easy ride.[28]

More than any other event, it was the council workers' strike of October and November 1970 that demonstrated the weakness of Heath's modernizing ambitions and set the tone for his unhappy premiership. By the middle of October, more than 60,000 workers had walked out, with another 75,000 taking part in overtime bans, one-day strikes and unofficial stoppages. It was not a strike that did great damage to Britain's economy, but it caused enormous and very visible inconvenience to millions of people, as parks and schools were closed for a lack of caretakers, as rubbish piled up in the streets, as raw sewage poured into the nation's rivers. Along the Thames and Avon, observers spotted thousands of dead fish, poisoned by the stream of pollution; in Enfield, flies swarmed out of the Deepham sewage works into the streets of London; in Tower Hamlets, troops were called out to clear the streets of decaying offal; in Leicester Square, in an uncanny preview of events at the end of the decade, uncollected bags of rubbish were piled into a foul-smelling mountain. As in the General Strike, volunteers offered to help stave off mass flooding: in Cardiff's Penarth Road pumping station, residents worked eighteen-hour days to prevent the system breaking down and sewage flooding into the streets. In London, meanwhile, a group of 'six patriots', including the Duke of St Albans's daughter Lady Caroline ffrench Blake, swept the streets around Whitehall in preparation for Remembrance Day. It was 'a demonstration against industrial anarchy', said their leader, a City economist called Patrick Evershed. 'We all believe that it was a disgrace that Mr Heath's visitors who come from all corners of the world should have to wade through debris on their way into No. 10 . . . We are all quite sure that the majority of the British public will support us in the action we have taken today.'[29]

But he was wrong. Like so many of the crises to come, the strike was a public-relations disaster for Heath. One reason the government shrank from sending troops in to run the pumping stations, for example, was their fear that it would alienate the unions and inflame public opinion (another theme repeated during many strikes in the 1970s). Even the Cabinet noted that 'there was a good deal of sympathy' with the striking workers: since park-keepers, dustmen and sewage handlers were not well paid, many people thought it was unfair to make them foot the bill for Heath's economic rigour. And in yet another preview of what was to come, the strike ended in defeat for the government, when an independent panel under Sir Jack Scamp gave in to almost all of the unions' demands and awarded the strikers an extra £2 10s. a week (a settlement of some 18 per cent) on the grounds that 'a non-inflationary settlement was never in prospect'.[30]

For Heath, it was a humiliation. Appearing on *Panorama* a few days later, he dismissed Scamp's decision as 'completely nonsensical', but refused to accept that it was time to return to an incomes policy. 'People must face up to their own responsibilities,' he said, insisting that it was wrong 'for the Government to compel the people'. Under fire, he lost his temper. 'Are you really trying to tell me the British people are not capable of facing up to their responsibilities and solving their problems in a free society?' he snapped. It was a disastrous performance, bearing out the caricature encapsulated by *Private Eye*'s fortnightly 'Heathco' parody. This cast the Prime Minister as the perennially grumpy, small-minded managing director of a beleaguered little firm, forever hectoring his staff on the correct use of the coffee machine or the right way to dispose of their plastic beakers: 'a man drowning in management-speak but entirely unable to motivate his workforce', as one account has it. It might not be as good as 'Mrs Wilson's Diary', but not even Heath's greatest admirers could deny that it had the ring of truth.[31]

Since polls showed that most people favoured some kind of pay controls, Heath's refusal to countenance a statutory incomes policy impressed neither the public nor the press. *The Times* memorably called the government's economic policy 'a mint with a hole'. Heath preferred to talk of an 'N–1' policy, in which the government would set the moral tone by encouraging settlements that were each slightly lower than the one before. But in many ways this was merely the worst of all worlds: a step away from the supposed free-market principles on which he had been elected, but without any statutory force to back it up. In any case, further humiliation was at hand. On 7 December, the power workers, who were legally barred from walking out because of the danger to public safety, began a work-to-rule and overtime ban in pursuit of a massive 25 per cent pay increase. The effect was immediate. Just before eight that morning, Labour's Tony Benn noted in his diary, the electricity suddenly blinked off, plunging his home – and millions of others, in the cold winter morning – into darkness. 'Cold, and the electricity go-slow hits harder and quicker than expected,' Douglas Hurd wrote that evening. The next day, he recorded, was 'a bad day. It is clear that all the weeks of planning in the civil service have totally failed to cope with what is happening in the electricity dispute; and all the pressures are to surrender.'[32]

More than any other dispute, it was the power strike of December 1970 that established the image of the early 1970s as an age of television blackouts and guttering candles. After just two days, power supplies were down by almost a third, and virtually every household in the country had experienced cuts. Early mornings and evenings, peak times for electricity consumption, were the worst: with cuts beginning at seven in the morning, it was common for people to be brushing their teeth or eating their breakfast when the lights suddenly went out. In London in the evenings, lines of cars snaked out towards the suburbs beneath darkened street lamps. In Liverpool, the city ring road came to a standstill as the traffic lights were extinguished; in Edinburgh, thousands of children were sent home after heating and lighting failed at eighteen schools; in Norwich, a couple returned from work to find their house in ashes because they had not realized that their electric fire, cold during the morning's power cut, had actually been switched on. In the City of London, telephone switchboards failed while banks and brokers' offices stood cold and lifeless; in Britain's car factories, workers stood drinking tea around motionless assembly lines. In Blox-wich, Staffordshire, a mother almost died of a severe haemorrhage when the power went off in the maternity ward; in Christchurch, Hampshire, a surgeon operated on an elderly woman in virtual darkness, the theatre lit only by a nurse with a hand-torch. Pubs that relied on electric beer pumps ran dry; hardware stores ran out of candles, which had rocketed in price from 4d. to 15s.; laundrettes raised their prices more than tenfold. And everywhere people sat in impotent fury as the grills cooking their breakfasts went dead and their evening's television entertainment disappeared before their eyes. Even the Queen had to take her tea by candlelight.[33]

By the fourth day of the dispute, the government was under intense pressure to give way. Many hospitals were now relying on army generators,

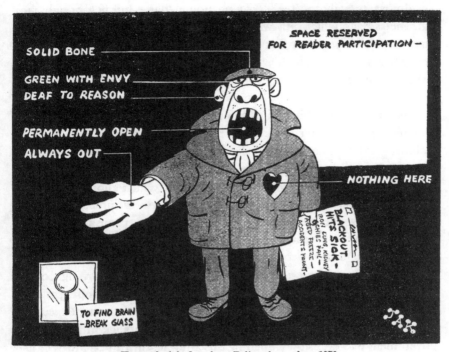

Homo-electrical-sapiens Britannicus, circa 1970.

Jak takes a dim view of the electrical workers in the *Evening Standard*, 9 December 1970. The printers were in turn so outraged by the cartoon that many walked out, interrupting production of the paper for twenty-four hours.

while there were genuine fears for outpatients with heart or kidney disease, who relied on their respirators and dialysis machines merely to survive. Outside the House of Commons, demonstrators shivering in the winter frost waved placards condemning Heath's proposed Industrial Relations Bill. Inside, Parliament was plunged into darkness, with MPs assembling for Prime Minister's Questions by the dim light of candles and paraffin lamps. 'The Commons must have looked something like it was 200 years ago,' one correspondent wrote. 'Only the quill pens and the winged collars were absent', and as the 'voices below boomed out of the gathering gloom . . . an occasional shaft of light from the windows high above the Chamber picked out landmarks such as a gleaming bald head or the white, flowing locks of Mr Michael Foot'. To many members, the occasion had an almost apocalyptic feel. 'Driving home that evening through the darkened streets, which only weeks before had been littered with rubbish,' wrote Chingford's young Tory MP Norman Tebbit, who had prudently brought his own candle, 'I wondered for how long this succession of strikes would continue.'[34]

A few days later, a group of physically handicapped patients in a Cheshire care home, stranded without heat or light, sent a telegram to 10 Downing Street. 'Don't weaken,' it read, 'we can take it.' But Heath's Cabinet had long since acknowledged that for all their fighting talk, there was simply nothing they could do to break the strike. On 12 December, the government declared a state of emergency, which allowed them to forbid the use of electricity in advertising or displays – including Christmas lights, of course – but they could hardly send in the troops to take over and run the power stations. On the same day, Reginald Maudling asked MI5's Deputy Director General, Anthony Simkins, if the intelligence service would bug a crucial union leaders' meeting the following morning. To his credit, Simkins refused point-blank, arguing that 'an eavesdropping attack against this target would take us right outside the field in which the Security Service had operated throughout my twenty-five years with it'. That the government was even contemplating this kind of scheme was a sign of its desperation, and three days later it approved a compromise, although it took hours of late-night talks between Carr, the unions and the Electricity Council before the deal was done. The unions agreed to call off their go-slow, while the government set up an official Court of Inquiry to investigate their pay claim, headed by Lord Wilberforce, a descendant of the great anti-slavery campaigner and one of the most respected judges in the country, with a reputation for pragmatism and fairness. Since the Court's terms of reference asked Wilberforce to consider 'the interests of the public and of the national economy', Heath was confident of a favourable result, while the electricians' leader Frank Chapple complained that the Court was clearly 'prejudiced before it had opened'.[35]

But when Wilberforce reported in the middle of February 1971, his findings made a mockery of their predictions. Far from keeping the settlement at or below 10 per cent, as Heath had hoped, he handed the power workers a new deal worth between 12 and 15 per cent by most calculations, and by some estimates closer to 20 per cent. The unions were naturally delighted, although they did their best not to show it; by contrast, ministers were furious, although they pretended they were satisfied. At the very least, Wilberforce had proved that strikes worked: it was no wonder that the edition of *The Times* reporting the decision had the headlines 'Hopes of Postal Strike Settlement Dashed' and 'Nurses May Seek Public Inquiry on Pay' on the next two pages. As an internal report for the Department of Employment wearily put it, the report was bound to 'influence the general attitude to wage inflation for some considerable time to come', not least since the government was already embroiled in a fresh battle, this time with the postal workers, and expected further challenges from the engineers, gas and water employees, local authority craftsmen, police and NHS craftsmen. In the event, the government prevailed against the postmen, although ministers reportedly felt sorry to have made an example of a small and moderate union. But this minor victory did not change the fact that in the strike that mattered, Heath had lost. 'Even when the government wins the battle, as it won the battle with the electricity go-slow,' said *The Times*, 'it loses the peace.' Like most newspapers, it believed that Heath was mad to have ruled out an incomes policy, not least since Wilberforce had smashed his much-vaunted pay norm into pieces. 'N−1 may be a policy,' the paper dryly concluded, but 'N+3 is a disaster.'[36]

The debacle of the Wilberforce report made it perfectly clear, if it was ever in doubt, that Heath was sailing into choppier waters than he had ever imagined on that warm June evening when he had snatched victory from the jaws of defeat. By February 1971, the government had fallen almost 8 per cent behind Labour in the opinion polls – this despite the fact that Wilson's party had descended into a bout of fratricidal bickering bitter even by its standards – while only 31 per cent said they were satisfied with Heath's record in office. His personal image, never very good anyway, had taken a battering from which it never recovered. Ensconced in Downing Street, he seemed permanently grumpy, even arrogant: when Anthony Sampson interviewed him a month after Wilberforce, he noted that although Heath seemed 'more relaxed, rather fatter', with his hair 'much longer, coming down thickly at the back', power had brought out some of his 'monarchic and eccentric tendencies'. Public relations remained a terrible problem: even in private Heath often seemed rude and dismissive, and in front of the cameras he became more stiff and pompous than ever. In *Private Eye* a few weeks later, the acerbic Auberon Waugh unmasked him as 'not human at all', but a 'wax-work'. This, Waugh thought, was 'the secret of the amazingly unattractive blue eyes, the awful, stretched waxy grin, the heaving shoulders and the appalling suntan. Even scientists admit that something has gone wrong with the pigmentation.'[37]

The early months of 1971 were not good to Heath. Not only was he losing the battle against inflation, but the situation in Northern Ireland was rapidly deteriorating, economic growth remained stagnant, and his energies were absorbed by Britain's bid to join the Common Market, which was far from universally popular. And on 4 February came news of the most humiliating kind: Rolls-Royce, one of the most famous companies in the world, 'a worldwide symbol of British technology and engineering skill', as one paper put it, had collapsed. Although it was most famous for its cars, Rolls-Royce also made diesel and petrol engines, nuclear reactors, industrial and marine gas turbines, helicopter engines and aero engines, and it was the last that had brought its downfall. In the late 1960s, egged on by Tony Benn at the Ministry of Technology, the firm had signed a fixed-price deal with the American Lockheed Corporation to make engines for the new RB-211 Tristar airbus. Unfortunately, the contract almost immediately ran into trouble; the deadline was absurdly unrealistic, the time penalties were far too harsh, and even before Heath took office Rolls-Royce had needed £20 million from Benn's Industrial Reorganization Commission. By November 1970, with its debts mounting, the firm had returned to the government and begged for a further £42 million to stave off its creditors, with an additional £18 million coming from the banks. But even while the company was waiting for the transfer of funds, the losses piled up. By February Rolls-Royce faced a staggering £110 million in production losses, far more than the cost price in the contract. Early on the morning of the 4th, the company released a simple ten-point statement, announcing that, since its losses were 'likely to exceed the net tangible assets of the company', it had no choice but to call in the receivers. As one commentator put it the following morning, a more 'shattering blow to both international prestige and industrial confidence' could hardly be imagined.[38]

The collapse of Rolls-Royce left Heath with an apparently impossible dilemma. Allowing the company to fold was unthinkable for national security reasons alone: as he grimly told the Cabinet, the 'consequential dependence of United Kingdom air defence on a foreign interest would be unacceptable'. What was more, not only the RAF and Royal Navy but 81 foreign air forces and 200 international airlines depended on 'continuing supplies and servicing of Rolls-Royce engines', and if the company simply went under the international ramifications would be enormous. The only solution, then, was for the government to step in; and yet that ran counter to everything Heath had been saying about government non-intervention and the virtues of competition. Had not his manifesto in June 1970, after all, promised 'a vigorous competition policy', rejected 'the detailed intervention of Socialism', and pledged to 'progressively reduce the involvement of the state in the nationalized industries'? Had not his industry team cut a swathe through Labour's bureaucratic state, repealing the Industrial Expansion Act and abolishing the National Prices and Incomes Board, the Consumer Council, the Shipbuilding Industry Board and Benn's beloved Industrial Reorganization Corporation? And had not his Secretary of State for Trade and Industry, the industrialist and former CBI chief John Davies, told the Commons only in November that he would avoid 'the soft, sodden morass of subsidised incompetence', and promised to stop giving money to 'lame ducks'?[39]

And yet there was rather less to Heath's economic radicalism than met the eye. Although he was often perceived – and liked to sell himself – as the champion of ruthless neo-liberalism, slashing and burning his way through piles of red tape as he rolled back the frontiers of the state, he was always much more cautious than many people realized. In opposition, he had commissioned a major report by the future minister Nicholas Ridley on how to handle Britain's gigantic nationalized industries, but while Ridley recommended taking major steps towards what was then called 'denationalization', with the ultimate goal of selling off public corporations such as coal, buses, railways, gas and telecommunications, many senior Conservatives (including, interestingly, Sir Keith Joseph) urged caution. Far from embracing Ridley's proposals, the Tory manifesto was more ambiguous than is often remembered, talking vaguely of pulling the state back from industry without offering concrete details. Even John Davies at the DTI, supposedly the standard-bearer of the new free-market approach, told the party conference that 'simply to abandon great sectors of our productive capacity at their moment of maximum weakness would be folly', and pointedly excepted the aircraft industry from his lectures about the madness of bailing out failing industries. Like Heath, Davies was devoted to economic modernization rather than ideological radicalism: the point was to improve British industry by whatever means necessary. And above all there was a basic inconsistency at the heart of Heath's policy. As the Permanent Secretary at the DTI, Sir Antony Part, later recalled, his job was both to 'disengage from industry' and to 'act like Great Britain Limited', which were mutually incompatible. Heath wanted to modernize industry and trim the power of the state, but he never seemed to realize that this might mean allowing major corporations to fall victim to market forces, condemning thousands to unemployment. When it came to the crunch, he would have to choose: stick to his guns and throw thousands out of work, or change his mind and step in?[40]

To push through the first nationalization of a privately owned industry since 1949, Heath said later, was a 'bitter shock'. But essentially he had no choice: if Rolls-Royce collapsed, not only would 80,000 people lose their jobs, but the implications for Britain's reputation would be enormous. The effects on Lockheed, which might then go under too, would 'badly sour relations with the Americans', while Willie Whitelaw told the Cabinet that the collapse 'would have the most serious implications for confidence, both in the City and internationally'. On 2 February, therefore, two days before the news was made public, the Cabinet agreed to nationalize the firm's aircraft assets and sell the rest, including the famous car division, to the highest bidder. When the news was announced to a stunned House of Commons, Labour members jeered with delight, but most Conservatives accepted that Heath had not really had a choice. Even future Thatcherites such as Ridley and Norman Tebbit agreed that Rolls-Royce was an exceptional case, while in the Cabinet Keith Joseph and Mrs Thatcher unquestioningly went along with the plan for nationalization. Only the remorselessly logical Enoch Powell condemned the government's retreat from its free-market principles, but since not a single other MP shared his view, there could be no division of the House and so he was denied the pleasure of voting against it.[41]

The next challenge, however, unfolded rather differently. Once again, its roots were in the late 1960s, when Tony Benn had helped to put together a consortium of three shipyards, known as Upper Clyde Shipbuilders, in the Glasgow docks. Since UCS consistently haemorrhaged money, it was a prime candidate for Heath's policy of disengagement. In opposition, Ridley had even put together a proposal for the 'butchery' of the Clydeside shipyards and sale of the carcass. And by the early summer of 1971, the chance seemed to have come: in desperate financial trouble, UCS needed £6 million merely to stave off insolvency. On 21 June, Davies bluntly told the Commons that he had decided it would be in 'nobody's interest' to give the firm more money. A month later, the former Labour minister and Coal Board chief Lord Robens reported that preserving UCS 'in its present form would be wholly unjustified and in the end could cause more serious and more widespread damage'. Benn's original merger plan, Robens wrote, had been 'totally mistaken', shoe-horning five different companies into one rigid structure. As a result, 'the total injection of public funds has disappeared. No improvement in facilities, no worthwhile investment has been made.' The only solution, Robens thought, was to wind up UCS, liquidate two yards and keep the other, at Govan, open for the time being.[42]

It was only with reluctance that Davies accepted the report, not because he thought it was too harsh to the shipbuilders who worked for UCS, but because keeping even one yard open seemed a little too interventionist for his liking. Even the Govan yard, he observed to his Cabinet colleagues, might not find a buyer in the private sector and would probably need an 'indefinite commitment of public support', which could not 'readily be squared with our industrial policy and would be widely resented in sectors of industry (not only shipbuilding) which are being forced to stand on their own two feet'. On the other hand, given the 'painful social consequences' of closing all three yards, Davies saw no option but to go along with the report. But when he rose on 29 July, cold and clipped as ever, to announce that some 6,000 men would lose their jobs, the result was bedlam. 'Nothing in recent years has brought more deafening scenes,' wrote one observer, as 'frontbenchers and backbenchers alike leapt to their feet, waving arms and pointing accusing fingers'. With unfortunate timing, Heath was away, leading the British team in the Admiral's Cup, and it was with merciless fury that Harold Wilson denounced his 'callous and unfeeling' treatment of the people of Glasgow. By the time Labour's Scottish spokesman Willie Ross had stepped up to the dispatch box, 'the noise was so deafening that he could only stand, without speaking'. 'This is butchery,' he cried at last, 'a cold, callous manoeuvre.' That was too much for the Tories. 'Guilty, guilty!' they chanted at Tony Benn, the architect of UCS, who sat pale and thin-lipped with anger on Labour's front bench. Only when the Speaker threatened to suspend the session did the noise die down.[43]

From the very beginning, the workers at UCS were determined not to go down without a fight. Even before Davies's announcement, they had chartered a special train to bring 400 Clydeside men and women to London, where they marched towards Downing Street, their banners streaming in the sunshine and their pipes and accordion playing 'Scotland the Brave' and 'I Belong to Glasgow'. Invited inside for a short meeting with the Prime Minister, they emerged in defiant mood. 'We were offered sympathy and only sympathy,' said the chairman of the joint shop stewards, trembling with fury. 'If he wants to get us out he will have to come and try to get us out himself. This government will be moved far more quickly than the men of the Clyde.' 'They will need to get the soldiers from the Bogside to get us out of the Clydeside,' added one of his comrades. And while a more sensitive, skilful Prime Minister might at least have persuaded them of his compassion for their plight, they clearly regarded Heath as a reactionary robot. Unemployment in the area, said the shop steward Jimmy Reid, was already running at 10 per cent: what Heath was doing was likely to double that figure, a 'prehistoric and predatory' policy. 'Mr Heath', he added, 'seemed to be a person who didn't know what a dole queue was. What is more, he didn't seem to care that much.' It was, he thought, 'the 1930s all over again, but there is one difference. We are not going to queue for the dole. We are going back to the yards and we are not leaving.'[44]

It was Jimmy Reid who became the central figure in the UCS controversy. A member of the Communist Party and Clydebank councillor as well as a UCS engineer, he was a master of publicity, inviting the media to come and watch the men defiantly continuing to work. He was the 'front man with the silver tongue', as one newspaper put it, becoming a regular on television and the elected Rector of Glasgow University, a symbol both of working-class resistance to the Heath government and of Scottish defiance in the face of English callousness. Neither political party knew what to make of him: the government were taken aback by the UCS work-in, while Harold Wilson visibly squirmed with discomfort at having to support industrial action led by a Communist shop steward. However, Wilson's natural instincts never deserted him: at one stage he even devised a truly preposterous scheme to sail a boat up the Clyde, 'visiting the doomed shipyards while Heath was yachting in the Admiral's Cup'. Tony Benn recorded that he even wanted to wear 'his outfit as an Elder Brother of Trinity House [the national lighthouse authority], which is the honorary title all Prime Ministers have'. The spectacle of Wilson sailing up the Clyde in a lighthouse-keeper's uniform would have been worth seeing. Sadly, Benn managed to squash the idea, noting (as was becoming traditional) that 'my contempt for Harold, which has been pretty high this last week, reached a peak'.[45]

Benn played a key role in the UCS work-in, not because he felt guilty over his part in the firm's demise, but because he was convinced that it would crystallize working-class opposition to the Heath government, revive the fortunes of the Labour Party and solidify his own emerging role as the tribune of the grass-roots left. The ideal solution to the shipyards' problems, he thought, was 'public ownership and workers' control', with UCS becoming a kind of standard-bearer for the new industrial politics he hoped for in the 1970s. Not only did he help to organize the shop stewards' visit to Westminster in June, he went up to Glasgow for mass rallies in Dumbarton and St George's Square, and toured the yards, shaking hands with the workers and encouraging them to stand firm. It did him no good in the Commons or the press: Davies even called him the 'evil genius of shipbuilding', a phrase gleefully adopted by most of the Conservative-supporting newspapers, while most senior Labour figures remained suspicious of his populist grandstanding. But Benn's efforts undoubtedly helped to keep the work-in on the front pages, and where he led, others on the left felt they had to follow. By August, support for the shipbuilders had reached proportions of which the government had never dreamed. John Lennon, never one to miss a bandwagon, sent a cheque of support, while on the 18th trade unions organized the biggest demonstration Scotland had seen since the war, leading some 70,000 people from Glasgow's St George's Square to Glasgow Green, with pipes and massed banners proclaiming the support of workers from Derby, Barrow, Blackpool and Wolverhampton. Benn, naturally, marched in the front row; later, he addressed the crowd, telling them that the 'shop stewards were not trying to create a little pocket of revolution in a capitalist world but were trying to engage in a serious industrial and political campaign', although the effect was rather spoiled when somebody threw a smoke bomb at him.[46]

*

On 11 August 1971, Heath returned to London weather-beaten, weary but jubilant after one of the proudest moments of his life, having captained the British team home in the 605-mile Fastnet race and secured the Admiral's Cup. For any man to bring home the most prestigious trophy in international sailing was a great achievement; for a sitting Prime Minister to have done it during his holiday was extraordinary. In the final race, Heath's beloved boat *Morning Cloud* was badly damaged, yet, he recalled, 'I cannot adequately describe in words our mounting excitement as we calculated that, despite everything, we had made it.' It was, he said later, 'one of the most exciting moments of my life'. Yet, unlucky as always, he had no time to enjoy it. As he flew back that evening, Belfast was in flames after the debacle of internment, with twenty-two people having been killed since the army began rounding up IRA suspects. Even his sporting success had become a stick with which to beat him: sailing was a rich man's habit, his critics said, and his victory was merely proof that he was more interested in his personal hobbies than in the plight of the poor and the unemployed.[47]

Little seemed to be going right for Heath in 1971. While the death toll mounted in Northern Ireland, the economy stubbornly resisted his best efforts to turn it around, and while the government struggled to hold the line against big public-sector pay deals, private employers, frightened of provoking strikes, were less obdurate. In April, Ford handed its workers a 33 per cent deal after a two-month strike, a precedent followed by the rest of the car industry. By the summer, wages were still rising at an annual rate of almost 13 per cent, far more than the government had forecast. Heath remained adamant, however, that statutory pay restraint was a recipe for disaster. It was Wilson's 'compulsory arrangements', he said in a radio interview to mark twelve months in office, that had bred 'deep resentments' among trade unionists in the first place, provoking them to 'make up the leeway' as soon as the restrictions were lifted. Wages would soon be 'increasing at a slower and slower rate', he predicted, and 'then of course the economy can expand and work will be provided by firms for people'.[48]

By this time, however, the question of providing work for people had temporarily eclipsed the nagging anxiety of inflation. The previous June, Heath had inherited a jobless total of just under 600,000 from Labour. But by January 1971, unemployment jumped to 671,000, and, instead of falling, it continued to rise, breaking through 700,000 in February and 800,000 in April, levels unthinkable just a few years before. It was no use Heath pointing out that this was simply the delayed result of Roy Jenkins's austerity during the last years of the Labour government; to his critics, it was proof that his hard-hearted policies were destroying people's lives. Instead of focusing on inflation, the press increasingly came to emphasize unemployment, demanding to know what the government was doing about it. And so the Treasury found itself in the awkward position of trying to hold down inflationary wage settlements on the one hand, while stimulating the economy to faster growth on the other. In his first full Budget at the end of March, Anthony Barber told the Commons that it would be 'irresponsible' to encourage rampant consumer demand until he had won 'a substantial reduction in the level of pay settlements'; even so, he still slashed taxes by some £550 million in an attempt to get unemployment down. As Edmund Dell, a waspish critic of so many Chancellors, remarks, it was a budget that promised to bring down both inflation and unemployment, but failed on both counts. But then the combination of the two, known as 'stagflation', was a phenomenon that nobody really understood, 'a new and ... baffling combination of evils', as Barber himself admitted.[49]

Nothing the government tried seemed to make any difference. With both exports and investment falling and Heath coming under growing criticism for the level of unemployment, the Treasury steadily edged towards greater reflation. In July, matters reached a turning point, as Barber announced an 18 per cent cut in purchase tax, the end of hire-purchase restrictions and bigger capital allowances to encourage companies to invest in new equipment, while Peter Walker unveiled a package of road, railways and housing spending worth some £100 million. This was classic Keynesian anti-recession stuff, and most commentators were broadly enthusiastic, although as *The Times* noted, the predicted 'substantial consumer boom' was bound to put pressure on the level of inflation. And yet, far from falling, the jobless total continued inexorably to rise, breaking through 900,000 in August. When the new session of Parliament opened three months later, the Queen's Speech pledged that the government's 'first care shall be to increase employment', while Heath told the nation in a party political broadcast that he was 'committed completely and absolutely to expanding the economy and bringing unemployment down'. Now very little was heard of the government's radical non-interventionist instincts: even the Post Office

Giro Bank, long slated for abolition, was saved because the government could not afford to lose 2,500 jobs on Merseyside. Enoch Powell caustically remarked that 'from this egg a whole barnyard of lame ducks will speedily be hatched'. But as Heath moved ever closer towards outright interventionism, there were few other voices of Conservative criticism. Most Tories were appalled by the rise in unemployment and wanted the government to be seen to act. Only in a few enclaves of the new free-market or monetarist thinking, such as the Institute of Economic Affairs, were there mutters of disapproval at Heath's growing apostasy. As yet, however, these were still voices crying in the wilderness.[50]

By the last weeks of 1971, it seemed that the entire country was waiting with bated breath for the moment that people had once imagined would never happen again, the moment that unemployment reached the dreaded figure of one million. The government, said one junior minister, seemed 'mesmerised' by this one, arbitrary statistic, which seemed to mean so much to politicians and the public alike. On 19 November, the latest figures put the jobless total at 970,000, provoking the Opposition to demand an immediate censure debate. A week later, more than 20,000 people joined a trade union-led march from Tower Hill to the Houses of Parliament, which ended in extraordinary scenes as demonstrators and mounted policemen fought a pitched battle on College Green. At one stage, the Speaker had to suspend the sitting after Labour politicians protested that their constituents were being attacked and arrested inside the precincts of the Palace of Westminster – an early sign of the bitterness and violence that seemed to be seeping into political life. But on all sides there was a consensus that unemployment at the current level was simply unsustainable, that it would erode the decency and civility of British life. 'It is morally, economically, socially and politically intolerable', said *The Times*, 'that unemployment should remain at its present level.'[51]

Of course, making a fetish of the figure of one million, as *The Economist* pointed out, was merely a form of statistical superstition. Unemployment had been steadily rising since the late 1960s, partly because of the severe deflation adopted after the Wilson government's devaluation fiasco in 1967, and partly because of deeper changes in the labour market, which demanded greater flexibility as old heavy industries declined. It was certainly unfair to hold Heath personally responsible when the roots of the problem lay in the late 1960s, and when he had clearly tried everything, including Keynesian spending measures, to address it. In retrospect, it is obvious that full employment as it was understood in the 1940s and 1950s was destined for the scrapheap. From the Wilson years onwards, successive governments were forced to run the economy at higher levels of unemployment simply to keep inflation in check, and even during the fat years under Tony Blair full employment never returned. Indeed, by the standards of later administrations an unemployment rate of around 4 per cent, for which Heath was mercilessly pilloried, was astonishingly good. Under Margaret Thatcher, after all, it reached three times that, and even during the boom of the Blair years unemployment remained much higher than it had been under Heath.

There is an argument that Heath should simply have bitten the bullet and explained to the nation that the days of full employment were dead. Higher unemployment, he could have told them, was not the end of the world; for most people, it would be only a temporary inconvenience, and they were now protected by far more generous benefits than had ever been available in the 1930s. What was more, it was largely beyond the government's control, and in the long run it would be a price worth paying for modernizing the economy. At any rate, this is what Margaret Thatcher told them ten years later, and it did not stop her winning three consecutive elections. For Heath's critic Edmund Dell, this proves that he lacked the necessary steel, even the political backbone, to make the tough decisions that Britain needed. But of course the early 1970s and the early 1980s were very different historical moments. Most Conservative MPs shrank from contemplating higher unemployment, convinced that it meant electoral disaster, while even newspapers like *The Times*, soon to become the chief vehicle for the new monetarism, stuck loyally to Keynesian thinking and the full-employment consensus. For men and women of Heath's generation who remembered the Depression, high unemployment remained the supreme political taboo, the great evil that the post-war settlement had been built to banish for ever. Jim Prior wrote that Heath 'utterly despised and detested the pre-war Conservative governments, who had tolerated between two and three million un-employed'. There was a case, Prior reluctantly accepted, for running the economy at a higher rate of unemployment in order to keep inflation down. But there was no way that the Prime Minister would pursue it, and most of his ministers, like Whitelaw, Carr and Prior himself, shared his views. 'The high unemployment route', he wrote, 'was counter to everything Ted believed in and had hoped to achieve for Britain.'[52]

But this did not protect him from the wrath of his opponents when the long-dreaded moment came. The New Year had begun terribly for Heath: locked in a prolonged struggle with the union leaders over his new Industrial Relations Act, he was also faced with a debilitating coal miners' strike and a bloodbath in Northern Ireland that was sliding rapidly towards outright civil war. But on Thursday, 20 January, a bad month got even worse: at that morning's Cabinet, Robert Carr reported that the latest figures, as expected, showed unemployment breaking through the one million barrier. Prime Minister's Questions that afternoon was a bear-pit: even as Heath entered the chamber, Dennis Skinner, the socialist firebrand from Bolsover, planted himself in front of him and shook his fist threateningly in his face, while Labour backbenchers chanted 'Out! Out!' Moments later, as he rose to answer his first question, another Derbyshire man, Tom Swain, walked across and slammed down the *Evening Standard* on the dispatch box, the front page carrying a stark and simple headline: '1,023,583'. For the first time in a century, Prime Minister's Questions had to be suspended. 'You ought to be ashamed of yourself!' Skinner shouted at the shaken Heath. 'You're better fitted to cross the Channel and suck President Pompidou's backside!'[53]

As it happened, Heath was indeed due to interact with the Continentals the next day, his schedule taking him to Brussels for the formal signing of the treaty marking Britain's accession to the Common Market. Like his victory in the Admiral's Cup, it should have been a moment to savour, but again it was overshadowed, partly by the fact that on his way in a woman threw ink over him (such attacks now traditional elements of Heath's prime ministerial career), but also by the prospect of defending his record against Harold Wilson in an emergency Commons debate. 'On behalf of the whole House I should like to welcome the right hon. Gentleman back from his visit to Europe,' Wilson said with merciless glee, opening the debate two days later:

> Last Friday he left these shores, the first dole queue millionaire to cross the Channel since Neville Chamberlain. I was thinking of him as he went, and I was pleased to read that he conducted a madrigal. I wish he could have been with me meeting the shop stewards of Fisher-Bendix, attempting to avert a further 750 redundancies and the total closure of that factory, following hundreds of redundancies last year ... I wish the right hon.

Gentleman could have heard the madrigal that my constituents were singing about him . . . If the right hon. Gentleman had served the cause of the right to work of the British people, a right of which he is custodian, with one-tenth of the energy which he has devoted to wooing the French President, we should not be having this debate today.

Heath and his ministers, he said bitterly, had

been proud to tear up even the mild prospectus on full employment of Sir Winston Churchill's coalition Government, and have destroyed the consensus by which post-war Governments have governed. But, above all, they are a Government who, by a combination of negligence, arrogance and wrongly directed policies, by an obsession with the balance sheet and not human beings, have produced a level of unemployment on which the whole country had thought we had turned our backs for ever.

Heath answered with his typical stiff stoicism, like some great bear fending off an attack from a polecat. He did not propose to follow Wilson, he said with grumpy dignity, 'in the personal sneers and jibes he found it necessary to make', and he agreed that unemployment was 'a human waste as well as an economic waste'. The brutal truth, he insisted, was that the government faced 'a combination of a high rate of inflation . . . with a high level of unemployment', something 'unique in British experience'. It was a line that met with some approval in the press; after the Commons had yielded the expected majority, the broadsheets' coverage of his speech was generally respectful. And yet, beneath the gruff imperturbability, there is no doubt that Heath was seriously worried. Lord Rothschild later recalled that the Prime Minister appeared 'emotionally very upset' by the unemployment figures; Jim Prior thought that he seemed 'very shaken' and that this had 'a marked effect' on his economic decision-making. Within the Cabinet, already exhausted after the battle to secure European entry and stunned by the slaughter in Northern Ireland, there seemed a mood almost of panic, even of apocalyptic fear. Already the political turmoil had seen fighting between policemen and demonstrators on College Green. And with one million out of work, with the violence in Belfast on their screens every night, and with the miners having walked out for higher pay, there seemed no knowing where it might lead.[54]

3

Ghosts of 1926

The memory of the General Strike in 1926 was still with them . . .
'I was only a boy in those days,' said Dai Evans quietly, remembering
the humiliation of the miners' defeat. 'I learnt that sometimes you
have to give in.'

'Even if it means you are being exploited?' asked Professor
Jones.

– Malcolm Hulke, *Doctor Who and the Green Death* (1975)

In the spring of 1970, the Lancashire town of St Helens seemed to have
changed little since its industrial heyday. In the town centre, dominated
by the vast, grimy Victorian town hall, chip shops and cafés jostled with
cheap shoe shops, greengrocers and the inevitable branches of Boots,
Marks & Spencer and the Co-op. From the centre stretched miles of long
Victorian streets, paved with cobbles, lit with gas-lamps, and packed
with little terraced houses of the kind familiar in every Northern town
in the country. At first glance, the streets felt almost untouched by the
affluent society. Most homes were rented, a third had only an outside
toilet, and many had no bathroom. On almost every street corner stood
a Victorian pub, with a betting shop not far away; inside, men clustered
around the heavy mahogany bars, while women were directed to a little
parlour reserved for their custom. One pub had installed a television, a
treat for the elderly men who came in to spend their days over a pint or
two; another, in a rare concession to the young, had a jukebox. St Helens
was 'a rugby league town, a man's town', wrote two lecturers from
Liverpool who visited in the spring of 1970. 'The Women's Liberation
Movement has not yet arrived: in St Helens the women do as they are
told. They play bingo while the men go drinking.'[1]

On the afternoon of Friday, 3 April, the workers at St Helens' biggest employer, Pilkington, a family firm founded in 1826 that had since become one of the world's major glass manufacturers, walked out on strike. At first the dispute was about a simple wage miscalculation, but it quickly escalated into a demand for higher pay, the strikers demanding a £10 increase in their basic weekly rate and a £5 interim deal as the price for their return to work. Over the weekend, the men's shop stewards and GMWU officials urged them to go back to work; twice, however, they voted to stay out. Within ten days, the strike had spread to seven more Pilkington factories outside St Helens, affecting more than 10,000 workers. At the end of April the GMWU struck a deal with Pilkington that gave the men a £3 weekly increase. Yet again, however, the strikers defied their leaders and chose to stay out. To widespread incredulity, a minor local grievance had turned into a national issue. When pickets prevented some men from going back to work at the beginning of May, the press had a field day: 'Siege at Tea Time!' shrieked the *Daily Express*, above a report on the 'Battle of Grove Street', where 'eight hundred screaming, punch-throwing pickets . . . flung themselves at police guarding the factory'. In fact, this was a wild exaggeration: the *Financial Times*, for example, described the fracas in terms of 'taunts' and thrown pennies. But the story captured the sense of national disbelief at a seven-week strike in an industry not known for militancy, which was only settled when Britain's most eminent trade unionist, Vic Feather, the general secretary of the TUC, stepped in to mediate at the end of May.[2]

The events in St Helens reflected in microcosm much of the wider story of trade unions and strikes in Britain in the 1970s. Far from slavishly following their shop stewards, the men consistently defied their entreaties to go back to work. For the GMWU officer responsible for the glass industry, Dave Basnett, later one of the most prominent union leaders of the late 1970s, the strike was a humiliation. There were allegations that the men were being provoked by 'subversive elements', but when representatives of extreme left-wing groups like the Socialist Labour League and International Socialists tried to contact the strike leaders, they were told to 'piss off'. Challenged about the alleged influence of Maoists on the strike, one of the men's leaders commented that if anyone could find six copies of Chairman Mao's thoughts in the whole of St Helens, 'I'll show my backside in Woolworths' window on Saturday morning. This is a good Catholic town, and good Catholic lads don't go for Communism.'[3]

Among the strikers, there was very little talk of class struggle. Most were Labour voters, though only 13 per cent actually belonged to the party; when interviewed, only three out of 187 voiced any support for more radical parties. Asked if they saw a political dimension to the strike, almost all of them said no. They showed no hostility towards their bosses; nine out of ten said they had nothing against Lord Pilkington, the company chairman. All they wanted, they said, was more money. And yet even eight out of ten admitted that the strike had taken them by surprise, and that they had walked out only reluctantly. Half of them, almost incredibly, admitted that they had walked out before knowing what the strike was actually about. Most were on strike less out of conviction than because of moral pressure from their fellows, and had no clear sense of what they hoped to achieve. And only a tiny minority found the strike exciting or liberating; most said that they found it boring, confusing and highly inconvenient. If this was what strikes were like, one said grumpily, the real impact of the dispute had been 'to make it likely that it will be another hundred years before a strike occurs at Pilkingtons again'.[4]

From the vantage point of the twenty-first century, the extraordinary prominence of the trade unions in the cultural and political life of the 1970s seems as alien as the role of the Church in medieval society. At the beginning of the decade, some 11 million people out of a workforce of 23 million belonged to a trade union, and their numbers were swelling all the time. To their admirers, their very existence defended millions of working people from being dragged back into the gruelling hardships of the Victorian age. To their critics, they were selfish and domineering, run by Communists and extremists, and single-handedly responsible for the decline of the British economy. On the right they were often loathed; on the left they were the objects of deep and often unconditional love and respect. 'You don't get me I'm part of the union,' sang the folk-rock band the Strawbs in a single that reached number two in February 1973, its lyrics often taken as a celebration of working-class trade unionism, although they were almost certainly meant sarcastically. Neil Kinnock even had it blaring out of the windows of his car as he toured his South Wales constituency a year later. What the song captured was the fact that, as the Marxist critic Raphael Samuel put it, trade unionism was 'not only a cause', it was 'something approaching a workers' faith'. Behind the mind-numbing discussions of basic rates and differentials and working-to-rule, he thought, there was 'a quasi-religious impulse at work', with the strike as a religious revival, the mass picket 'a ceremonial demonstration of strength', the hated scab who defied the picket 'a category of folk devil'. And when people on the left talked with misty eyes about the unions, they were not just thinking about bulging pay packets; to them, unionism meant 'a search for self-transcendence; the claim to collective dignity by reference to the past; the joy of a wider belonging'.[5]

In an international context, what was unusual about British trade unions was that there were so many of them. In the early 1970s, there were well over 300 different unions (although if tiny workers' associations were counted, it was more like 500), half of them belonging to the TUC. In fact, more than half of the total TUC membership actually belonged to just eleven major unions, their acronyms familiar to anybody who had ever opened a newspaper, from the TGWU, AUEW and GMWU, time-worn bastions of working-class identity, to NALGO, NUPE and COHSE, strident voices of the new white-collar public employees.* To European observers like the West German social democrat Helmut Schmidt, it beggared belief that Britain still persisted with such a fragmented, fractious union structure, in which employers often had to negotiate with several unions who were busy fighting one another, dozens of unions had fewer than a hundred members, and there were no postal ballots for official positions or secret ballots before a strike. But to talk of reforming the unions, of streamlining their procedures or making them accountable to the law of the land, was a dangerous business. Even to pick a fight with the 875 members of the Felt Hat Trimmers and Wool Formers, or the 114 Military Orchestra Musical Instrument Makers, or the 52 Basket Cane, Wicker and Fibre Furniture Makers, needed more courage and stamina than many politicians could muster, and since the late 1940s, most governments, Conservative as well as Labour, had preferred the path of least resistance. True, in 1969 Harold Wilson had

* Respectively, the Transport and General Workers' Union, the Amalgamated Union of Engineering Workers, the General and Municipal Workers' Union, the National Association of Local Government Officers, the National Union of Public Employees and the Confederation of Heath Service Employees. The other common acronym of the day, ASTMS, referred to the Association of Scientific, Technical and Managerial Staff.

made a stab at reform with Barbara Castle's White Paper *In Place of Strife*; but, while the unions had stayed united, he had lost his nerve, and the ensuing furore had almost driven him from office.[6]

At the dawn of the 1970s, very few people doubted that the unions would remain enormously successful actors on the political stage. Union membership was buoyant, surging from 44 per cent in 1968 to 56 per cent ten years later, an increase of nearly 3 million people. In particular, the unions found thousands of new recruits among women and white-collar workers. 'The pace of inflation and the sense of insecurity have galvanised not only office workers but teachers and doctors,' wrote Anthony Sampson in 1971, remarking on the 'paler and quieter men, more articulate and coherent in their talk but usually flatter in their speeches' who now rose to speak at TUC conferences on behalf of public-sector unions like NALGO and NUPE. It was said with some justice of white-collar unions that they were obsessed with their 'differentials' – the wage gaps that lifted them above their blue-collar comrades – rather than the wider health of the labour movement. But there was no doubt that they were enormously successful. NALGO, representing local government employees, saw its membership more than double between 1964 and 1979, while that of NUPE, which represented public employees, more than trebled. The most visible success story, though, was ASTMS, which swallowed up smaller unions with the appetite of a starving imperialist, scooping up doctors and technicians, administrators and managers, supervisors and foremen, at a rate of 1,000 new members a week. Its charismatic chief was the famously ebullient and well-paid Clive Jenkins, whom one reporter called 'an industrial Fluellen with the gift of tongues'. Jenkins owned a sixteenth-century country house, kept a cabin cruiser moored outside his town house on London's Regent's Canal, displayed a 'sensuous nude statuette' on his office desk, and did all he could to shatter the stereotype that all trade union bosses were grey men in glasses pouring out pompous jargon in heavy Northern accents. He was television's favourite Welshman, a regular guest on news programmes and chat shows alike, a showman and proud of it.[7]

People joined unions like NUPE and ASTMS less out of working-class solidarity (because many members were not working-class at all), but as a reaction to worrying developments such as the decline of the old industries, the rise of inflation or the government's propensity to impose wage freezes and statutory restraint. If you joined a union, the thinking ran, then at least you would have somebody to fight for you when things were tough. But it was also a vote of confidence in what the unions were best known for: strikes. When the *Economist*'s labour correspondent Stephen Milligan (later of auto-asphyxiation fame, but who then held a job that spoke volumes about the power of the unions) wrote a book about them in 1976, he noted that one obvious reason for their appeal was the fact that since the late 1960s, workers' incomes had been squeezed so tightly by high taxes, rising prices and government incomes policies. Yet he also observed that in almost every major national strike since 1965 the unions had got what they had wanted. Between 1970 and 1972, workers who walked out on strike got bigger pay rises (by 5 per cent) than those who did not. Not only had striking become a familiar, even mundane part of national life, it worked. It was no wonder, he thought, that people who had never struck before, from local government workers and civil servants to gasmen and bakers, were tempted to try it.[8]

Strikes loomed very large in the public consciousness at the turn of the 1970s. In 1968, more than 4.6 million working days had been lost in strikes; in 1969, as inflation and wage restraint began to bite, some 6.8 million days were lost. As strikes escalated during the following decade, so they not only lasted longer but involved more and more people, spreading from the docks and the mines to almost every sector of the workforce. And in some industries, the stereotype of strike-happy shop stewards was not far from the truth. The Fleet Street print unions, for example, were infamously militant and self-interested, insisting on vastly expensive over-manning (estimated by *The Economist* at an eye-watering 34 per cent), and stamping their feet at even the mildest hint of reform. Not only were their members very well paid at £69 a week, but they exercised tremendous power: if they walked out halfway through the evening, for example, there would be no paper on the breakfast table the next day. In September 1971, a pay dispute caused the loss of 9 million papers in just three nights; four years later, more disputes saw *The Times* lose hundreds of thousands of copies, while the *Mirror* disappeared from the South of England for ten days in a row. Other industries had similarly abysmal labour relations. Steel was dogged by strikes, which in 1975 delayed the blowing-in of a new blast furnace for months on end. And the car industry's strike record was justly notorious. Ford's plants at Dagenham and Halewood became national bywords for unofficial strikes, and by the late 1970s the company was increasingly reliant on its factories in West Germany, where strikes were almost unknown. British Leyland, meanwhile, was plagued by endless shop-floor disputes: in 1969, its Cowley plant reported a staggering 612 stoppages, two per day, costing an estimated 33,000 vehicles.[9]

Yet while there is no doubt that Britain's labour market was highly inefficient and inflexible, hamstrung by low productivity and deep-seated resistance to change, it is worth emphasizing two crucial points. First of all, despite all the publicity given to strikes, and despite the enormous inconvenience they caused the public, they were often more important as political events than economic. As Geoffrey Owen, the former editor of the *Financial Times*, points out in his magisterial survey of British industry since the war, strikes were a symptom, not a cause, of industrial decline. Even in the most strike-prone industries, such as cars and ship-building, they were not the only factor in what went wrong, although they obviously made it more difficult for management to turn struggling companies around. When Harold Wilson was planning *In Place of Strife* in the late 1960s, his economic adviser Andrew Graham reminded him that more working days a year were lost to illness than to strikes, which accounted for just 0.1 per cent of the 5 billion working days a year. On top of that, it is simply not true that Britain suffered more than any other country from strikes. From the United States to Scandinavia, the rise in worker unrest was a worldwide phenomenon, reflecting the pressure of inflation and the end of runaway post-war growth. People often talked about the 'British disease', making unflattering comparisons with the relatively strike-free economies of Japan and West Germany. Actually, Britain's record was not that bad. In the league table for working days lost per 1,000 workers in the 1970s, Britain finished a mere sixth, with Canada, Italy, Australia, the United States and Ireland all recording more strikes. This was much worse than its record in the 1950s and 1960s, yet not as bad as its record in the 1980s, when Britain finished third (behind Canada and Australia) in a league nobody wanted to win.[10]

For that noted political commentator Rupert Rigsby, there was an obvious explanation for the upsurge in strikes in the 1970s. 'Don't you know what's behind these strikes? All this political unrest? Russian gold!' he tells his lodgers in *Rising Damp*. This was by no means an eccentric or baseless belief. During the seamen's strike of 1966, MI5 wiretaps inside the Communist Party's run-down offices had revealed extensive cooperation between party officials and the seamen's leaders, provoking Harold Wilson to blame the strike on a 'tightly knit group of politically motivated men'. And by 1970, as scholarly studies have shown, the Communist Party was 'the major activist force' in the engineering industry in Manchester and Sheffield, the shipyards of the Clyde and the coalfields of Wales and Scotland, and had a significant role in the engineering and building trades throughout London. Communist representatives played influential roles in the leadership of the Upper Clyde Shipbuilders (most famously, through Jimmy Reid) and the National Union of Mineworkers, where the CP controlled one in four members of the national executive by late 1973. Three years later, one estimate suggested that 15 per cent of the national executives of the biggest unions were CP members, with another 15 per cent being Labour Party Marxists who often voted the same way. And Communists were particularly powerful within two factories that became synonymous with workers' unrest: the Ford plant in Dagenham, and the British Leyland plant at Longbridge, Birmingham, where Dick Etheridge and Derek Robinson (nicknamed 'Red Robbo') became the country's best-known militant shop stewards, credited with leading walk-outs that cost the company tens of millions.[11]

And yet even at Longbridge, supposedly such a bastion of Red influence, there were only about twenty Communist shop stewards out of a total of 750. By and large, the Communist Party was a very feeble institution, badly short of funds, members and inspiration. Its headquarters in Covent Garden, wrote Stephen Milligan, was 'a pathetic sight', the wallpaper peeling, the floors uncarpeted, the empty rooms lit by bare light bulbs, and only the ringing telephones signalling that the party was still alive. Rather belying the idea of growing Communist influence, its number of workplace branches fell steadily throughout the 1970s, national conferences were abysmally attended (in April 1978, for example, only fifty-two people turned up), and most local branches met infrequently if at all. And although conservative pundits often insisted that strikes must be the work of subversive agitators, MI5 reported to Edward Heath in March 1972 that 'the Communist Party does not yet control any union or exercise a decisive influence on the TUC. Its attitude to industrial disputes is tactical and it exploits rather than creates them, preferring to work through union leadership where it has a vested interest, than through the shop floor level.' This was hardly surprising: while many trade unionists were quite happy to dress up their pay claims with the rhetoric of class war and socialist transformation, they were not really interested in socialism at all. As the electricians' moderate leader Frank Chapple once remarked, 'you hear people talk about "what the workers think", but when you go along to a meeting, you'll find about six of the workers there – two Communists, two Maoists and two Labour councillors'. And although the International Socialists (later the Socialist Workers' Party) made some inroads into the unions in the mid-1970s, most unionists remained scornful or indifferent. 'It's not a trade-union newspaper,' a Yorkshire branch official said scornfully of their paper *Socialist Worker*. 'It's run by *university students*.'[12]

The truth is that many Communist shop stewards were successful in spite of, rather than because of, their politics. As one told the academic Richard Clutterbuck in 1977, most men were 'not so interested in revolutionary doctrine or world history as in better bonus or overtime rates or a decent place for a wash. Get them what they want and you'll have their loyalty.' He worked fourteen hours a day, eight at his job and six as an unpaid union official, studying the rulebook so that he could get his men a better deal, visiting families where the man had lost his job, and going round with a consolatory £10 note for men who had been hurt in an accident. His men trusted him to look after their interests, but they did not share his politics: when he stood for Parliament as a Communist, he attracted only a handful of votes. He liked to tell a story about a Trotskyist convener on a building site, whose men were furious at the lack of decent toilets, only a 'pole and a hole'. Spotting the chance to advance the crisis of capitalism, the convener called his men together and passionately addressed them on the prospects for world revolution, his talk ranging from Portugal to Cambodia, from Angola to Ethiopia. Then the Trotskyist called for a show of hands for a strike, and to his disbelief, the men voted no. As they broke up, one said sadly: 'If we have to go through all that to get a decent shit, he can keep it.'[13]

Shop stewards had a terrible press in the 1970s, represented in the newspapers and on television as exaggerated versions of Fred Kite, Peter Sellers' ludicrously stiff and self-satisfied shop steward in *I'm All Right Jack* (1959). Unlike Kite, however, most shop stewards were not interested in Communism or the Soviet Union: indeed, many were downright conservative in their attitudes. Although they were easily satirized for their plodding jargon, thick regional accents and eagerness to brandish the rulebook, most of them, said the Donovan report in the late 1960s, were 'hard-working and responsible people, who are making a sincere attempt to do a difficult job'. They were certainly not the militant bogeymen portrayed by the *Daily Express*'s highly conservative cartoonist Michael Cummings: one study found that only 17 per cent belonged to a political party, while in the GMWU only half of the shop stewards paid the political levy. A survey of white-collar shop stewards, meanwhile, found that more than half identified themselves as centre-right or right-wing, a fact that would surely have surprised many conservative commentators. They were increasingly keen to defy their union bosses, to be sure, but their chief priority was the interests of their men. Almost all of their strikes were concerned with better wages and working conditions, and instead of spending their time pontificating on the evils of capitalism, most shop stewards were far more interested in mundane things like toilet facilities, tea breaks and the prevention of accidents at work.[14]

At the time, many observers thought that the real problem with the trade unions was not so much political militancy as the impact of mass affluence. In his journalistic investigation of trade unionism, *The New Militants* (1972), Paul Ferris suggested that the driving factor in industrial action was the exaggerated material expectations of the British working classes, fuelled by advertising, films and television, a question not of escaping from poverty but of having 'butter instead of margarine, cars instead of bicycles'. Their demands had become 'higher and more insistent', remarked the *Sunday Times* in April 1972, thanks to the 'systematic selling of material opulence just outside your reach'. It was a theme beautifully captured in Margaret Drabble's novel *The Middle Ground* (1980), in which a character ponders the feelings of 'failure and rancour and despair' that have been created by the vast hoardings showing 'happy families eating Danish Bacon, glamorous women on tiger skins eating Colman's mustard, dizzy half-clad girls consuming tots of rum and an ominous new variety of Pink Martini, handsome men standing in the middle of trout streams smoking menthol cigarettes'. Even union officials agreed that their real problem was not militancy or poverty, but a revolution of rising demands. 'What people speak now is the language of expectation,' explained a TGWU official. 'You've got a right to earn, let's say, £40 a week. You don't need to feel guilty about it.'[15]

What this meant, though, was that millions of trade unionists had very different values and expectations from the old men who led them. By and large, noted Anthony Sampson, those who ran the trade unions at the dawn of the 1970s were men who had left school at 14, 'went to work in the bad years of the thirties', and took their first steps up the ladders of power during an age when mass affluence was almost unimaginable. Even as general secretaries and national icons, most led quiet and modest lives, 'an odd mixture of the homely and the high-powered, of suburban gardening and do-it-yourself, and national conferences and international seminars'. They were not rich or well paid: in 1975, most earned between £5,000 and £10,000 a year, a tenth of what their American equivalents were paid. They uncomplainingly worked long hours – eighty hours a week was not uncommon – and were proud of their unpretentious, working-class roots. Vic Feather, the exuberant head of the TUC, was the son of a French-polisher from Bradford and had been working his way up the ladder since the mid-1930s. His successor Len Murray, who took over in 1973, was the son of a Shropshire farmworker; orphaned at the age of 8, he was brought up by relatives, landed in Normandy on D-Day, worked in a Wolverhampton engineering works, went as a mature student to Oxford (where he got a First in PPE in just two years), and began climbing the ranks of the TUC in 1947. Murray presided over the trade union movement during its greatest struggles with the state, yet he was a pragmatist, not a radical, who believed in cooperation rather than conflict. Like his contemporary Billy Wright, the record-breaking England football captain who was born just a few miles away, he was the very embodiment of the wry good humour, solidity and decency of the West Midlands, yet he often seemed a man out of time, adrift at the head of his own movement.[16]

By far the two dominant personalities in the trade union movement were the heads of the two biggest unions: Jack Jones of the TGWU, and Hugh Scanlon of the AUEW. Nicknamed the 'terrible twins', they were credited (or debited) with having defeated *In Place of Strife* in 1969, and were often seen as ruthless Marxist conspirators, grasping for the levers of power. Scanlon, who turned 60 in 1971, was undoubtedly a Marxist, and presented a tough, unyielding face to the world. Brought up in Manchester, he had left school at the age of just 11 to train as an apprentice instrument-maker, became a shop steward in the engineering industry, and was a member of the Communist Party for more than two decades. Scanlon often struck observers as a very dour man, his left-wing rhetoric 'drab and repetitive'. The role of the trade unions, he once said, was 'to change society itself, not merely to get the best out of existing society', and on the right and in business circles he was virtually Public Enemy Number One. 'He wants to cause chaos. He wants to squeeze industry out of existence, to make capitalism fail,' said a Manchester personnel director in 1972. But Scanlon claimed he was a pragmatist, not a revolutionary. 'I certainly want to see socialism, but we're not going to create it by industrial chaos or by a workers' or peasants' revolt,' he told Paul Ferris. It was revealing that engineering employers, who dealt with him on a daily basis, regarded him as 'a man who keeps his promises'. And Denis Healey, no unconditional admirer of the trade unions, regarded him as one of the more likeable union bosses, largely because of his 'cynical good humour' and fondness for golf. Scanlon was also a great fan of goldfish. It was a source of great regret to him, Healey recalled, that he could never get them to breed; but then goldfish are much harder to handle than engineering bosses.[17]

If anything, Jack Jones, the head of the TGWU, was even more of a bogeyman on the right. For a man who was nicknamed the 'Emperor Jones' because of the unparalleled sway he supposedly exercised over public life, he cut a surprisingly grey figure, rather like the elderly apparatchiks who in those days reviewed parades in Red Square.* But behind the bullet head, steady gaze and thick glasses was a remarkably colourful personal history. The son of a Liverpool docker, a boyhood Sea Scout and Sunday school regular, Jones became a shipbuilding apprentice at 14, a Labour Party ward secretary at 15 and a TGWU delegate at 17. He read Marx and Engels, took Ruskin College correspondence courses, was elected a Labour councillor in Toxteth and joined the Territorial Army. In 1937, he went off to Spain to fight in the International Brigade, becoming a political commissar in the Major Attlee Company of the British Battalion. Wounded in the Battle of the Ebro, he returned home, became the TGWU's man in Coventry, left the Communist Party, and finally became his union's general secretary in 1968. By then, however, he already cut an oddly old-fashioned figure, earnest and austere, apparently the soul of proletarian incorruptibility. At the time, the *Guardian* remarked that he 'must be the last trade unionist to wear a cloth cap regularly'. A fellow union leader put it rather differently: 'Jones has a smile glinting like the sunlight on the brass plate of a coffin.'[18]

There is no doubt that Jones was a singularly thick-skinned and

*The nickname was coined by the increasingly conservative journalist Paul Johnson, after the self-made Caribbean despot in Eugene O'Neill's play *The Emperor Jones* (1920).

dedicated political operator, and, although he had left the Communist Party, his views remained far to the left of the political mainstream. The KGB colonel Oleg Gordievsky later claimed that Jones had been a Soviet agent, regularly passing Labour Party and union documents to the KGB until the Prague Spring of 1968, when he broke contact with his handlers in protest at the Soviet invasion of Czechoslovakia. Although Jones allegedly accepted KGB donations towards his holiday expenses, his motives were almost certainly ideological rather than financial. Colourless, puritanical, a great fan of Clement Attlee, he spent his holidays in a caravan in Devon, although when he took his wife on a package trip to the Algarve in 1976 his fame was such that the *Daily Mail* made it a two-column story with three pictures. He lived in a little ex-council flat in south-east London and several times turned down lucrative job offers from the private sector, even though, according to Milligan, he 'could step into the executive class any day he wanted'. And however close his links with the KGB may have been in the 1960s, they were certainly over by the autumn of 1970, when MI5 gave him a clean bill of health. 'The realities of Jones's position as General Secretary of the largest trade union in the country', the Security Service reported to the government, 'press more heavily on him that any influences the CPGB could bring to bear on him.' Indeed, by this point his extremist reputation was slightly misleading. Stephen Milligan thought that Jones was becoming 'a more thoughtful and constructive man; a man who could listen as well as lecture', while the *Financial Times* called him a 'national statesman, devoted to doing what he believes to be best for Britain's workers and their families'. Even Paul Dacre, the future voice of Middle England, told the readers of the *Express* that Jones had a 'blunt, rough-edged Scouse charisma' and was 'very far from being a monster'.[19]

One of the single biggest misconceptions about the 1970s is that Jones and Scanlon exercised unbridled power, having only to snap their fingers for their men to walk out on strike. Yet the reality was that despite their image of imperial command, their power was ebbing away as their men became more affluent, more individualistic, more focused on their own private goals. Even in 1971, Anthony Sampson thought that the age of 'unchallenged leadership' was over, that 'the members are much more questioning, the aims less certain, so that many general secretaries, while they talk like confident generals, are preoccupied with trying to prevent mutiny or desertion'. What happened at Pilkington's, where the glass workers defied their shop stewards and insisted on staying out, would become common across Britain in the following decade, as aggressive young workers on the shop floor ignored the entreaties of their elderly, cautious, often frightened and muddled leaders. And although both Conservative and Labour governments persisted in the naive belief that they could control workers' wages through a partnership with the union bosses, this was never going to work, for the simple reason that the bosses no longer had the power to impose agreements on their men. The old days of obedience and solidarity were over. 'The trouble is not that the trade unions are too strong,' one observer had presciently remarked in 1967. 'It is that they are too weak.' His name was Edward Heath.[20]

One evening in 1969, the Leader of the Opposition invited five of Britain's leading trade unionists, among them Vic Feather and Jack Jones, to dinner at his Albany flat. As luck would have it, he had first met one of them three decades before, albeit in very different circumstances. It was on the banks of the Ebro, during one of the bloodiest battles of the Spanish Civil War, that Ted Heath and Jack Jones had first shaken hands. Then still at Oxford, Heath had been part of a student delegation visiting Spain to express support for the Republican cause, and when he encountered a group of 'tough, hardened soldiers, burned by the Spanish sun to a dark tan', Jones was among them. At the time, there had been no great meeting of minds. But now, in the elegant surroundings of Heath's bachelor pad, the two men talked amiably and freely. 'There is no doubting Ted Heath's sympathy for people,' Jones later recalled, 'and we quickly established a feeling of camaraderie.' Later, the conversation turned to Heath's sailing and musical interests, and to his guests' delight Heath was persuaded to show off his new piano, and even played a couple of short pieces. 'Then Vic Feather called out, "Play 'The Red Flag' for Jack,"' Jones recalled, 'and the leader of the Tory Party cheerfully played Labour's national anthem. It put the seal on a jolly evening.'[21]

Given that Heath's premiership became notorious for industrial strife, it is remarkable how well he got on with the union bosses. In his memoirs, he wrote that the TUC chief Vic Feather was 'inherently decent' and 'a delightful man in many ways', while he found the dreaded Hugh Scanlon 'the clearest, firmest and most persuasive' of all the trade union leaders, never producing 'an argument that could be easily dismissed'. And whatever their members might think of the new Prime Minister, the general secretaries had great respect and even affection for him. Feather said later that Heath was a good man to do business with, while Scanlon praised his fairness and decency. Perhaps his greatest admirer, though, was the Communist soldier he had met on the Ebro. 'No Prime Minister, either before or since, could compare with Ted Heath in the efforts he made to establish a spirit of camaraderie with trade unions and to offer an attractive package which might satisfy large numbers of work-people,' Jack Jones later recorded. Heath, he thought, 'revealed the human face of Toryism, at least to the trade union members who met him frequently . . . Amazingly, he gained more personal respect from union leaders than they seemed to have for Harold Wilson, or even Jim Callaghan.'[22]

As a Conservative politician, Heath was naturally under pressure from his rank and file to take a hard line with the unions. Local activists' unease with the post-war consensus had been growing since at least the late 1950s, when a surge in the number of strikes, coupled with the first signs of anxiety about Britain's competitive decline, had produced a bout of soul-searching about the extent of union power. One reason that *I'm All Right Jack* had struck a chord was that it chimed so successfully with public discontent at the alleged abuses of the unions. And as strikes increased in the late 1960s, so too did middle-class hostility to trade unionism: by 1967, NOP found that 72 per cent thought unofficial strikes should be banned outright, while 82 per cent thought that industrial unrest was either planned or exploited by the Communist Party. 'The middle classes have a nightmare,' wrote Paul Ferris at the beginning of the 1970s. 'Workers with cars and jeering expressions swarm through the land, snatching new handfuls of the national cake. Governments whimper and retreat.' This was no exaggeration: during the local authority workers' strike of autumn 1970, the letters pages of *The Times* were full of complaints from middle-class homeowners distraught at the mounting piles of rubbish outside their front doors. The excellently named leader of Kensington and Chelsea council, Sir Malby Crofton, even complained that dustmen earned so much in tips that they would soon be 'in the £2,000 a year class', which suggested either that he was a very big tipper, or that he did not know many dustmen. A year later, a Norfolk haulage firm issued a blackly ironic death notice after succumbing to a seven-month strike. 'The funeral will take place on November 10 of Tina Transport which died of strangulation by the Transport & General Workers' Union,' it read. 'The immediate mourners are Miss

Christine Brown, aged 11, and Miss Beverley Brown, aged 3, whose future depended on Tina Transport. The TGWU choir will render "The fight is o'er, the battle won".'[23]

The most remarkable expression of discontent with the unions in 1971, though, came from a very unexpected source. In *Carry On at Your Convenience*, the family-run toilet makers W. C. Boggs is plagued by strikes, largely thanks to the presence of the militant, self-interested and thoroughly unpleasant shop steward Vic Spanner (played by Kenneth Cope, channelling Peter Sellers), whose Zapata moustache is an immediate sign that he is up to no good. Spanner's attitude to industrial relations is not exactly constructive: when his men complain about a planned strike, he retorts: 'If you'll pardon me, you don't have a say. This is union business.' 'But it's our union, isn't it?' another man objects. 'Exactly,' Spanner says. 'And for that reason you'll do as I bloody well tell you.' Much less subtle than *I'm All Right Jack*, this was not likely to go down well with cinema-loving trade unionists, who made up a good deal of the *Carry On* films' target audience, and they were even less likely to be pleased by scenes showing Spanner and his henchman, Bernard Bresslaw, wielding baseball bats on the picket line. As the writer Alwyn Turner points out, though, it could have been worse. Originally the film was entitled *Carry On Comrade*, and a segment with Terry Scott playing an inept union boss called Mr Allcock was cut from the finished product in a vain attempt to avoid hurting unionists' feelings. Even the cast themselves were uneasy with the film's overt message: Richard O'Callaghan, who played the young company man Lewis Boggs, lamented that it was 'all so right-wing, presenting the unions as complete asses', when he thought they were 'protecting millions of people's security in this country'. It was surely no coincidence that despite fine performances from the usual suspects, it became the first *Carry On* flop, taking five years to recoup its costs when most *Carry On* films took three days. 'There has been a ripe and earthy working-class slant to the series which has given it special appeal – and phenomenal box-office returns,' wrote the *Morning Star*'s critic Nina Hibbin, usually a great fan of the films. 'But now it has turned round and bitten the hand that has been feeding it all these years. It has betrayed its own roots.'[24]

While Heath may not have shared *Carry On at Your Convenience*'s highly jaundiced vision of the unions, he had no intention of ignoring the demands for change. Henry Ford II, chairman and chief executive of the American car giant, even told him that he was seriously thinking about pulling out of Britain because Ford was suffering so many problems with strikes. By this stage, however, much of the groundwork for the proposed reform of industrial relations had already been laid. Although Heath had refused to back *In Place of Strife* – a short-sighted decision guaranteeing that he would get no support in turn from Harold Wilson – he was well aware that it had been broadly popular with the general public. Even 60 per cent of trade unionists themselves, according to polls, agreed that unofficial strikes should be made illegal, while 77 per cent backed secret strike ballots, 65 per cent liked the idea of compulsory 'cooling-off' periods, and 58 per cent thought that agreements between unions and employers should be legally binding. In electoral terms, union reform seemed to be a winner. In opposition, Heath's team had spent years poring over different policy proposals, and he was confident that the fruit of their labour, published in 1968 as *A Fair Deal at Work*, would command popular support.[25]

Calling for a national register of trade unions, a new system of industrial courts, a code of good industrial practices, and legal enforcement of collective agreements, Heath's plan was a classic example of his thirst for modernization. He had little feel for the unions' jealously guarded traditions; instead, his goal was to make them disciplined, efficient partners in the search for higher growth. He recognized that one of their problems was that they were so fragmented, but he thought the answer was for the state to strengthen the hand of the union leaders, effectively co-opting them as allies against their rebellious shop stewards. As Heath's employment spokesman Robert Carr later explained, the problem was not 'too much trade union power, but really too little constitutional trade union power', and so the plan tried 'to bring a greater degree of stability and orderliness' into industrial relations. Carr himself was a mild, emollient man who went to great efforts to consult union leaders in the late 1960s so that the plan would be absolutely right. 'All I wanted,' he said, 'was to be an old-fashioned Minister of Labour, provided that there was a proper framework of laws around industrial relations.' And once installed as Secretary of State, Carr was confident that the government would soon reap the reward of all his hard work in opposition. His relations with union leaders were good, he had an electoral mandate from the people, and he could point to polls showing massive public support for union reform. When he briefed the Cabinet about his proposed Industrial Relations Bill in September 1970, it was hard to mistake the sense of complacency. Several union leaders, he reported, had already told him that they supported the bill, even if they dared not say so publicly. There was certainly no sense at this stage that it would become one of the most controversial pieces of legislation in modern British history.[26]

The battle over the Industrial Relations Bill opened at the beginning of October 1970, when Carr published a consultative document summarizing the provisions of his plan: compulsory secret ballots, a sixty-day cooling-off period, legally binding collective agreements, and most controversially, a National Industrial Relations Court (NIRC), with which unions would have to register, and whose decisions would have the force of High Court rulings. Registration, Carr thought, would be a smooth process. Unregistered unions would miss out on tax concessions; if they registered, however, they would be protected against being sued by firms and individuals. Meanwhile, workers' rights to join trade unions were enshrined in law; but so were their rights not to join, which struck at the cherished principle of the closed shop. Vic Feather had already warned him that the unions would not stand for it, but Carr did not listen. The wheels of legislative procedure turned swiftly: by 3 December the bill had been published, and within a fortnight it had been given its Second Reading in the Commons. As Heath told the House at the beginning of the Second Reading debate, he was convinced that its new rules would 'secure growing support from the majority of employers and trade unionists'. Polls certainly showed large public support: while 76 per cent backed the right of workers not to join a union, 73 per cent endorsed the cooling-off period, 69 per cent approved of the secret ballot, and 65 per cent supported fines for unions who broke the new rules. Even among trade union members themselves, no less than 83 per cent approved of the new National Industrial Relations Court. Faced with the force of public opinion, Heath thought, even the most intransigent union loyalists would eventually come round.[27]

The Industrial Relations Bill was Heath at his best and worst. Farsighted and ambitious, it was also absurdly complicated: Carr's consultative document took up fifty pages of close-typed text, while the published bill had 193 clauses, 8 schedules and 97 amendments. Even Carr had to have a brief to explain what it all meant. 'What it seemed to other people', he mused, 'I dread to think.' In typical Heath fashion, it took no account of the political traditions, pressures and passions of other people. Jim Prior remarked later that the bill had 'no appreciation of what made the unions tick or the real world of the shop floor', which reflected the fact that apart from Carr, none of the Cabinet 'understood industrial relations or knew industrialists, let alone any trade unionists'. A more adept politician, drawing the lesson from the failure of *In Place of Strife*, might have introduced reform gradually, building the new structures piece by piece, as Prior and Mrs Thatcher did in the 1980s. But Heath wanted it all, and he wanted it immediately. On top of that, it was madness not to make a great public show of consulting the TUC, perhaps offering a few token concessions so that the union bosses could tell their members that they had fought the good fight. For Heath and Carr to slam the bill on the table, telling the TUC to take it or leave it, was very foolish indeed. As *The Economist* had tried to tell them, the whole point of the bill was to improve industrial relations: it was a 'major public relations exercise as much as a parliamentary battle'. But then Heath was never very good at public relations.[28]

Since the TUC had already opposed Labour's attempts at reform, they were always bound to make at least a show of opposing Heath's initiative, and of course they were infuriated by his failure to consult them publicly. But it was also bad luck that the Industrial Relations Bill coincided with a period of controversy over workers' pay, with the government making a great show of its determination to face down big wage claims. Threatened by the 'N−1' pay policy, and under pressure from their members to stand up to the government, the TUC bosses found themselves prisoners of their own position: even if they had wanted to support Heath, they would have found it very difficult. When Carr presented the bill to the General Council of the TUC in October 1970, they were stunned to hear that the government would not under any circumstances compromise on its central elements, and the meeting broke up acrimoniously. And with the TUC issuing a statement that it would refuse to negotiate with the government, the Labour leadership fell into line. *In Place of Strife* was conveniently forgotten as Labour MPs did all they could to frustrate the bill's passage. In the end, it took Heath a gruelling 100 hours of parliamentary time to get it through – a record for any non-finance bill since the war – and at one point MPs had to vote continuously for almost twelve hours on sixty-three successive divisions.[29]

By 21 January 1971, when the government wearily brought down the parliamentary guillotine, the mood had soured almost beyond repair. When Willie Whitelaw announced the government's decision to bring debate to a premature end, there was an explosion of rage from the Labour benches. 'Fascist!' the Opposition yelled at him. 'Dictator!' Twenty-five times the Speaker, Selwyn Lloyd, tried to call for order, while Whitelaw stood at the dispatch box, 'roaring like the stag at bay', as *The Times* colourfully put it. Four days later, when the guillotine motion was actually debated, the atmosphere was even worse, with speeches on both sides frequently interrupted by jeers and abuse while Lloyd and his deputy, Sir Robert Grant-Ferris, struggled vainly to keep order. At the centre of the disturbances was a young Welsh MP called Neil Kinnock, who savagely denounced the government's 'class-directed legislation', and at ten o'clock led an extraordinary demonstration in which thirty Labour MPs gathered shouting in front of the Speaker's table, refusing all entreaties to sit down, some calling Lloyd a 'bloody hypocrite' and 'bloody twister'. Even after the session resumed, the abuse continued. 'It appears to me, Mr Deputy Speaker,' said Labour's Tom Swain, 'that when a man becomes a right hon. Gentleman on the Tory benches he changes biologically from a man to a pig,' at which his neighbour Arthur Lewis yelled out: 'That is an insult to pigs. Shame on you!'[30]

At last, on the night of 28 January, the House voted to guillotine the bill, trooping time after time through the lobbies, voting on clause after clause. 'We must have spent five hours actually locked in the lobby,' recorded Tony Benn, who saw some members wearily playing chess to keep awake, and others reading old copies of Hansard. 'In the final division as we went through the lobbies, we sang the "Red Flag", "Cwm Rhondda" and "We Shall Overcome",' he wrote, 'and we filed back into the Chamber and stood and sang . . . Anybody from outside would have thought we were mad but the Tories were very dispirited and we were encouraged.'[31]

For Heath, however, securing the bill's passage was not even half the battle. By the spring of 1971, the TUC had spent £120,000 to organize marches and circulate petitions opposing the bill, with its member unions putting in another £125,000. In January, the unions held a 'day of protest' at the Albert Hall, with speeches by Harold Wilson and Vic Feather, and in February they organized the biggest union demonstration in living memory, with Feather, Jones and Scanlon leading an estimated 140,000 workers from Hyde Park to Trafalgar Square, chanting 'Kill the Bill'. In

March, Scanlon's engineering workers held two day-long stoppages in protest against the bill, and on 18 March a special TUC Congress met in Croydon to discuss the next step. 'It was full of melodrama,' one journalist wrote. 'Outside the hall in pouring rain the shop stewards were chanting "Kill the Bill"; left-wing girls were handing out passionate pamphlets; Welsh miners huddled under their Victorian embroidered banners; Dundee painters, British Leyland workers, *Radio Times* warehousemen held up their scrawled protests: FEATHER DON'T BE CHICKEN. THE HUNGRY YEARS ARE COMING. YANKEE STYLES STOP WORKERS' SMILES.' Inside, the general secretaries agreed that the TUC should advise unions not to register under the terms of the bill, even though it put them in danger of being sued and losing their tax breaks. At the time, this was seen as a victory for the moderates, who had defeated Scanlon's suggestion that unions should be *instructed* not to register. But if it was a moderate victory, it was only a temporary one. For at the national congress in September the radicals carried the day, securing a majority for Scanlon's motion instructing unions to deregister and boycott the National Industrial Relations Court, or risk being kicked out of the TUC entirely.[32]

Since deregistering seemed so risky, it had never occurred to the government that the unions would try it. Carr said later that he 'certainly had a blind spot' about it, but recognized that 'it was a damnably effective tactic'. Although it meant that the unions lost the rights and immunities guaranteed by the Industrial Relations Act, it also meant that they made a mockery of the government's new framework for collective bargaining. It was a brilliantly simple way of killing the bill, especially because many employers promised to respect the unions' existing arrangements, thereby lessening the risk. By the end of November, Carr's figures showed that 28 unions had refused to register from the start, 61 had cancelled their registrations, and only 52 were still playing along, although many of them had already applied to cancel. To his colleagues, he still put on a brave face, hoping that the TUC would come round to a more 'pragmatic, realistic' stance, with white-collar unions leading the way. But the fact was that if the TUC held firm, and the unions refused to register, then there was very little the government could do. All that effort, it seemed, had been for nothing.[33]

In terms of time, morale and public opinion, the Industrial Relations Act took a terrible toll on Heath's government. He was left with the worst possible result: an Act that not only failed to set the unions' house in order, but had virtually destroyed his relationship with their leaders and had thoroughly alienated left-of-centre opinion. In the local elections of May 1971 the Conservatives suffered severe losses, and private polls found that they were seen as remote, elitist and uncaring. Worst of all, Heath had unwittingly set himself up as the unions' supreme opponent, even though he thought of himself as their friend. The theatre critic Kenneth Tynan spoke for many on the left when he wrote that he hoped 'the workers react with outright fury' to what he saw as a disgraceful attack on their historic freedoms. As unemployment mounted, so the bitterness grew, and by New Year's Day 1972, when the NIRC opened its doors for the first time, Heath's image as the sworn enemy of the British working classes could hardly have been worse. And then, four days later, came the news that the National Union of Mineworkers had rejected a last-ditch pay offer from their employers at the National Coal Board. At midnight on Saturday, 8 January, every mine in the country fell eerily silent, and one of the most decisive strikes in British history began.[34]

In the four decades since their defeat in the General Strike of 1926, Britain's miners had built a reputation for solidity, quiescence and moderation. Since that date there had not been a single national coal strike, even though mining was suffering more than most from the rise of cheap oil and the end of the old industrial economy. During the 1960s, under the chairmanship of Lord Robens, the Coal Board closed 400 pits and got rid of 420,000 miners, more than half of the workforce, yet there was remarkably little protest. Robens even managed to persuade the NUM's leadership to keep their pay demands low, so that more pits could be kept open in places like South Wales, where there was no alternative employment. At the beginning of the 1960s, coal miners had earned about 10 per cent more than manufacturing workers; at the end, they earned 3 per cent less. It was no wonder that Robens was hailed as a genius: the man who had managed to run down the coal industry without provoking a strike, bringing in mechanization, closing pits and cutting wages, yet somehow keeping the union sweet. Even in 1968, supposedly the year of revolutionary protest, there was barely a whimper when Robens closed 55 collieries and got rid of 55,000 jobs in one fell swoop. The days when governments feared the miners, it seemed, were long gone.[35]

Beneath the surface, however, resentment and frustration were mounting. Not only were miners in constant fear for their jobs, but they had seen their pay fall well below that of other working-class men, especially in the late 1960s, when they were overtaken by factory workers. In the autumn of 1969 an unofficial strike broke out in Yorkshire on the question of working hours, and in July 1970, just after Heath's election, the NUM conference voted in favour of a 33 per cent wage demand to recover their position. Just over half of the workforce voted for a strike, but the union's rules required a two-thirds majority. Instead, a wave of unofficial strikes broke out that autumn in pits across Yorkshire, Scotland and South Wales, traditionally the most militant areas, where entire communities depended on the industry for their survival. For a brief moment the government was worried: John Davies warned the Cabinet in October that if the strikes continued, they 'could cause serious damage to the country's fuel and power supplies in the coming winter'. But they soon petered out, and the government's attention moved on to other things.[36]

By this point, however, the leadership of the NUM was under enormous pressure from the left. Its rumpled Lancastrian president, Joe Gormley, was one of the labour movement's more moderate standard-bearers, interested less in sweeping political change than in gradually improving the lives of his members. But his position was never as secure as it looked, because he was surrounded by colleagues far to his left. The NUM's general secretary Lawrence Daly, who hailed from Fife, had left the Communist Party in the mid-1950s, but he remained an unashamed Marxist and kept the CP supplied with minutes of TUC General Council meetings. Gormley's vice president, meanwhile, was the Stalinist Mick McGahey, who remained in the Communist Party all his life and whose famously severe demeanour, puritanical style and extraordinarily abrasive Lanarkshire voice – the product of a life working underground and chain smoking – made him a terrifying figure in middle-class households. Like Daly, McGahey kept in close contact with the CP's industrial organizer Bert Ramelson. MI5 wiretaps revealed that McGahey regularly phoned Communist officials for advice, although his heavy accent and affection for the bottle meant that his words were often impossible to understand. Friends and admirers waxed lyrical about his fondness for poetry and warm companionship in the pub, but none of that came across on television, where all viewers could see and hear was his blazing eyes and fearsome rhetoric. 'I want the Tories to be the anvil,' he said ominously, 'and I will be a good blacksmith.'[37]

By the summer of 1971, the miners' leaders, themselves under pressure from younger elements on the left, were moving inexorably towards confrontation. In July, the NUM conference approved a Yorkshire motion calling for an average pay rise of up to £9 per week, which worked out at 47 per cent, and changed its rules so that strike ballots had to win only a 55 per cent majority. When the Coal Board's chairman Derek Ezra replied with an offer of no more than £1.80 per head, the NUM promptly declared an overtime ban and called for a strike ballot. Gormley privately advised Ezra that he would have to offer at least £3.50 to get a deal, and in other circumstances he might have obliged. The problem, however, was that the Coal Board's hands were tied by Heath's 'N−1' pay policy, which prevented them from offering more than 8 per cent. Even then, however, it was close: in December, the NUM announced that, out of 271,000 eligible miners, 145,482 had voted in favour of a strike and 101,910 against, a majority of 58 per cent. Ezra made one last offer, but the NUM executive rejected it without even putting it to the vote. When the clocks struck midnight on 8 January, the strike began.[38]

Everybody knew that the miners could not possibly win. 'Rarely have strikers advanced to the barricades with less enthusiasm or hope of success,' wrote Woodrow Wyatt in the *Mirror*. *The Times* forecast 'only marginal disruption to industry and commerce as a whole', while the *Sunday Times*'s labour correspondent Eric Jacobs wrote that, while he wanted them to win, 'I doubt they will. It is a failure of leadership to have chosen this moment, when coal stocks have rarely been higher [and] when the Government is fighting everybody's battle by resisting inflationary wage claims.' In the *Sunday Express*, Cummings drew Heath as a smirking fisherman preparing to mount a new trophy beside the postmen's leader's head; in the *Telegraph*, Garland drew Joe Gormley as an officer leading his men over the top to certain death; and the *New Statesman*'s cartoonist showed a middle-class lady in an extravagant hat telling a grinning Heath: 'So silly of the miners not to realise that we've all gone over to oil-fired central heating.' Ten days later, when Thames Television showed a documentary on the origins of the strike, they prophetically entitled it *The Miners' Last Stand*.[39]

Inside the government, there was no great alarm at the prospect of a national coal strike. Since the vote had been so close, there was every chance that the miners' unity might not last long. In any case, the winter had been mild, which meant that coal stocks were still high, even though the NUM had been operating a ten-week overtime ban. In the weeks leading up to the strike, the Coal Board had quietly distributed stocks to power stations around the country; the Central Electricity Generating Board reported that it had enough supplies to last eight weeks, and clearly the strike would be over by then. When the Cabinet met on Tuesday, 11 January, two days into the strike, there was a mood of quiet confidence. Carr told his colleagues that the NUM's efforts to rally support from other unions 'had met with a poor response', and that he expected the strike to last for 'at least a month', at which point the government might have to broker a settlement along the lines of the Coal Board's final pay offer. As for the wider impact, John Davies reported that 'the strike should have no immediate effects on the electricity or gas industries and stocks generally were good'; although there might be 'sporadic shortages', there was no reason to expect widespread power cuts. The Cabinet recognized that the miners commanded considerable public sympathy, and that 'a prolonged strike' might cause 'growing difficulties with power supplies . . . particularly if the weather were cold'. But the mood was generally upbeat, and defeat was inconceivable: 'in general discussion', the Cabinet minutes recorded, 'there was general agreement that sure handling of the dispute would be of critical importance to the continued success of the Government's policies for reducing cost inflation and the level of wage settlements'.[40]

One enormous flaw in the government's strategy, though, was that they seriously underestimated their opponents. 'Our judgement turned out to be wrong,' Carr admitted later. 'We just didn't know the miners.' Far from being divided, the miners proved to be exceptionally solid, and the NUM brought out virtually every man of its 280,000 members. What the miners had – and what the Cabinet could never understand – was an outstanding sense of tribal unity, based partly on their folk memories of struggles going back to the Victorian era, and partly on the toughness, claustrophobia and suffering of their daily grind. When one young Yorkshireman first went down the pit in the 1950s, he found it a terrifying experience, 'so full of dust you could barely see your hands, and so noisy that you had to use sign language'. Miners worked six-hour shifts with twenty minutes' 'snap time' to eat their sandwiches (although they had to scrape the black dust from their lips first). Twenty years later, a Kentish miner reported that eight out of ten men in his Snowdown pit worked completely naked because it was so hot underground, and lost so much fluid in sweat that they had to drink eight pints of water a shift, laced with salt. When *The Economist*'s Stephen Milligan visited a pit, he was horrified by what he found: the atmosphere choked with dust, the conditions 'incredibly cramped', the heat so great that 'the miners work stripped to the waist, the sweat pouring down ... confined to this darkness for eight hours a day, usually with only a plastic carton of water and a packet of sandwiches'. Accidents were common: in March 1973, seven miners were killed by flooding at Lofthouse colliery; in May, another seven died in a pit collapse at Kirkcaldy; in July, eighteen were killed in a pit-cage accident in Derbyshire. On top of all that, there was 'the Dust', pneumoconiosis caused by inhaling coal dust, an occupational hazard that blighted the lives of tens of thousands of miners, working or retired. It was, said Heath's adviser Brendan Sewill, who had visited a mine during his Cambridge student years, 'a bloody awful job'.[41]

Yet as Milligan also noted, the 'solidarity and friendliness' of the miners were legendary, and they had a deep sense of their own history. 'Sometimes it seems that 1926 was only the day before yesterday', wrote a reporter from *The Times* after visiting a South Wales pit village in February 1972. The entire community, he noted, was ready to 'fight to the finish'. And the miners commanded great respect and affection not just in the world of the trade unions, where they were seen as authentic working-class heroes, but among the public at large. Even though the newspapers thought the miners could not win, they treated them with remarkable sympathy. The *Sun*, still nominally a left-of-centre paper, offered its own 'peace plan' in typical style, headlined 'Stuff the Norm! Get the Miners Back to Work', and explaining that they were 'a special case ... because of the exceptional demands of their dirty, dangerous job', which demanded 'an over-the-odds settlement'. Even traditionally right-wing papers took a similar line. 'These men do a hard, dirty, dangerous job,' said a leader in the *Express*. 'All they ask is a decent wage. They deserve it. They should have it ... Make a start, Mr Carr – today!' And for the *Daily Mail*, which ran several features on the plight of strikers' families, the attitude of the government and Coal Board was 'not only insensitive but short-sighted', whereas the NUM had been 'restrained and responsible'. The government should set up an inquiry to meet 'the just demands of the lower-paid miners', the *Mail* said.

'Sympathy for the miners is not only a good cause. It makes sense for Britain.'[42]

With the miners cast as plucky underdogs heading for certain defeat, it was no wonder they won considerable public support. Gallup found that 55 per cent of the public supported the NUM, with only 16 per cent backing the Coal Board. Ten days into the strike, a Civil Service briefing for Derek Ezra conceded that public sympathy had 'its roots in history. We are not going to be able to change that.' Meanwhile the NUM made provisions to deal with the influx of 'members of the public . . . offering help on picket lines'. On the far left, in universities and in countercultural circles, support was particularly marked: the underground newspaper *Frendz*, one of the last survivors of the late-1960s bohemian boom, greeted the strike as a 'dress rehearsal for the uprising', and looked forward optimistically to a future of 'wildcat strikes, one-day stoppages [and] demonstrations'. What most miners would have made of support from such a publication, which was best known as a cheerleader for women's liberation, hard drugs and the Angry Brigade, can only be imagined.[43]

Yet in at least one part of the country, miners and students did form an effective alliance. By the second week of the strike, hundreds of miners from South Yorkshire had poured into East Anglia, where they had been detailed to stop the movement of coal by picketing the docks and power stations. The NUM's chief contact in the area – not exactly a hotbed of working-class socialism – was a lecturer in Norwich who happened to be a member of the Trotskyist International Socialists. He helped to arrange for the miners to be billeted with sympathetic students, and this proved a roaring success, especially at the University of Essex, whose student body had a particularly left-wing reputation. It was 'an absolutely tremendous experience', the South Yorkshire miners' leader said later. 'Our people were becoming politically educated and were becoming aware of what the class structure and the class war were', while 'we showed to the university students a degree of discipline and organisation which they had probably read about in the Marxist books, but had not seen for themselves'. As he proudly put it, 'the barriers were down'. But it does not take a cynic to suspect that for many miners, breaking down the barriers of class meant something rather different from listening to young men with beards talking earnestly about the revolution. When Lawrence Daly rang the pickets after reading some disturbing tabloid revelations, he was told: 'It's OK, Lawrence, we're doing the work – and we're getting our leg over every night.' The South Yorkshire men 'were very comfortable there', their leader admitted. 'We had difficulty in getting them home.'[44]

For the man who led the South Yorkshire miners into battle, the strike of 1972 was a turning point. Born into a poor mining family in Worsbrough Dale, Barnsley, Arthur Scargill had first gone down the pit when he was 15. The only child of doting parents, he was brought up in an intensely old-fashioned working-class atmosphere, a world of brass bands, whippets, pigeon racing and community singing, dominated by the local colliery. His father was a committed Communist and even in the mid-1980s took a staunchly pro-Soviet line, and Arthur himself joined the Young Communist League in 1955. He left the group in the early 1960s, later giving different reasons for his decision: in one version, he said that he 'objected to the moving of Stalin's body outside the mausoleum and changing the name of Stalingrad', and indeed he remained a keen admirer of the murderous Soviet dictator for the rest of his life. His biographer Paul Routledge, however, suggests simply that 'Scargill was a man in a hurry, and the Communist party got in the way'. Leaving the Young Communist League allowed him to get ahead in the local branch of the NUM, which was then fiercely anti-Communist; in any case, Scargill does not seem to have altered his principles, which remained so close to the party line as to be practically indistinguishable. As he made a name for himself within the South Yorkshire NUM as a cheeky, flamboyant, self-promoting hardliner, he made no attempt to downplay his vision of a centrally planned Marxist society with the abolition of all private property except for homes and gardens. And whenever there was pressure for a new wage demand or a strike, Scargill was always at the forefront. 'I'm completely convinced that victory is won by militancy,' he told Yorkshire Television the week before Heath's election. 'I've never known the employer who gives you anything. You get as much as you are prepared to go out and take.'[45]

Scargill was a relatively minor figure in the NUM when the strike started in January 1972, but he immediately saw the opportunity to make a name for himself. For most miners, the strike was simply about getting a better wage, but to Scargill it was 'a political battle'. 'We were in a class war,' he told the *New Left Review* three years later:

We were not playing cricket on the village green like they did in '26. We were out to defeat Heath and Heath's policies because we were fighting a government. Anyone who thinks otherwise was living in cloud-cuckoo land. We had to declare *war* on them and the only way you could declare war was to attack the vulnerable points. They were the points of *energy*; the power stations, the coke depots, the coal depots, the points of supply. And this is what we did.

Well, the miners' union was not opposed to the distribution of coal. We were only opposed to the distribution of coal because we wished to paralyse the nation's economy. It's as simple as that.

In the 'flying pickets' that he had helped to pioneer during the Yorkshire miners' unofficial strike in 1969, he had the ideal tactical weapon. Instead of staying outside their own pits, miners had been sent off around the country in cars, minibuses and coaches: 'a rapid mobile picket', in Scargill's words, 'all directed onto pre-determined targets, with five, six, seven hundred miners at a time'. In 1969, the flying pickets had worked well; and now, dispatched to docks, coke depots and power stations, they would prove an unstoppable weapon.[46]

Even though the miners had used unofficial flying pickets in 1970, the government seemed completely unprepared for their reappearance two years later. But Scargill was in his element. As the driving force in the Barnsley Area Strike Committee, he sent flying pickets to ports and power stations across the east of England, to Bedford, Ipswich and Great Yarmouth. In Yorkshire, by his own account, he ran an elaborate, almost military enterprise from a dedicated Operations Room, with a map showing the area's six ports, nineteen power stations, seventy coalmines and four steelworks, a logbook keeping track of his men from hour to hour, and four coach companies on permanent standby, with minibuses ready to ferry his men up to the gates. Other miners insisted that this was typical Scargill exaggeration, and that the pickets were a lot less organized than he claimed. But what ultimately mattered was the result, and of that there was no doubt. Slowly but surely, the pickets began to choke the life out of Britain's power network. Within two weeks, an estimated 40,000 miners were picketing 500 establishments for twenty-four hours a day, cutting off the supplies not just of coal, but of the oil and hydrogen essential to the operation of power stations, even the food for their workers' canteens. On the murky waters of the Thames, miners borrowed a power launch to picket Battersea Power Station, turning back coal and oil supplies that came by water. And where there were no pickets, sympathetic workers in other industries – who were under orders not to cross the picket line – managed to provide them. *The Times* told the story of a goods-train driver carrying oil supplies who refused to leave his yard because there were pickets on the line. His managers could see no pickets, so the driver rang the railwaymen's union and asked for help. They passed the message to the NUM, and within a short time two flying pickets had appeared on a railway bridge, unfurling a blanket with the painted slogan 'OFFICIAL NUM PICKET'. Relieved, the driver stayed exactly where he was.[47]

By the end of January, Heath was facing a more serious challenge than he could possibly have imagined. It was not just a question of the dramatic resistance of thousands of flying pickets, or even of the increasingly violent tone of some confrontations. At the Coal Board's regional headquarters in Doncaster, female clerical staff were kicked, punched and spat upon as they crossed the picket line to work; at Keadby Power Station, a lorry accidentally ran over and killed a tipsy miner. The real problem was the pickets' growing pressure on the power stations, to which the government seemed to have no answer. To be fair to Heath, both he and his Home Secretary, Reginald Maudling, were absorbed by the terrible slaughter in Northern Ireland, which reached a new low in January 1972 with Bloody Sunday and its aftermath. What that meant, however, was that even as the NUM's pickets choked off supplies to the power stations, there were still no restrictions on the use of coal and electricity. And with the Central Electricity Generating Board reporting that it was 'in a state of siege' thanks to the 'unrelenting blockade', the news suddenly got much worse for the government. As the last weekend of January approached, weather forecasters announced that a cold snap was coming. General Winter had come to the NUM's aid. On Sunday, the CEGB cut voltage across the entire national grid and shut down three power stations completely. 'There are warnings of power cuts because of these filthy mining strikes,' Kenneth Williams noted gloomily a day later. 'Oh! what a scourge and a blight is the English working man! What a dishonest, lazy bastard! Only exceeded by the Welsh and the Scots.'[48]

It was at this moment that the focus moved to an obscure suburb on the eastern side of Birmingham, a decaying industrial area of red-brick terraced streets, dilapidated pubs, dirty canals and cracked factory windows. It was here, in Saltley, that the West Midlands Gas Board maintained its coke depot, a gigantic black mountain from which dust blew into nearby homes and gardens on windy days. Usually, 400 lorries a day called at the depot, but, thanks to the strike, demand had escalated hugely. After such a mild winter, the mountain had risen to an estimated 100,000 tons of coke, and by the end of January Saltley was receiving as many as 700 lorries a day, ferrying coke everywhere from Wales and Cornwall to Lancashire and Yorkshire. There were so many trucks that Birmingham's commuter traffic began to feel the strain, and on 3 February the *Birmingham Evening Mail* ran a story on the mile-long lines of articulated lorries, headlined 'The Long, Long Queue to Load with Coke'. By five that evening, the Staffordshire NUM had organized pickets outside the depot, but they proved notably ineffective: the next day only one in 100 drivers acknowledged their entreaties to turn back, and almost 600 lorries left the depot laden with coke. On the next day, Saturday, 5 February, a further 200 Staffordshire pickets arrived at Saltley, as well as fifty policemen, and there were reports of isolated scuffles between the two groups. But still the stream of lorries continued, virtually un-hindered by the pickets. 'If the lorries wish to go in,' a police spokesman said, 'we have given instructions that the entrance must be cleared.' The Staffordshire NUM chief, however, had other ideas. 'If necessary,' he told the *Evening Mail*, 'I will bring down 300 pickets from Yorkshire to stop this exploitation at the miners' expense.'[49]

It was, of course, Arthur Scargill who answered the call. By Saturday evening, he had already agreed to send 400 Barnsley pickets in coaches to Saltley, while he drove down in his car a few hours later, arriving at three in the morning. As luck would have it, Scargill had a useful friend in the area – Frank Watters, who had recently moved from Yorkshire to Birmingham to become the Communist Party's district secretary – and they arranged for the South Yorkshire pickets to stay in the Star social club, which was part of the local Communist Party headquarters, with the promise of Salvation Army blankets and free pints at the bar. By dawn on Sunday, Scargill and several hundred men were at the Saltley gates. 'I have never seen anything like it in my life,' he said later. 'This was no coke-depot in the accepted sense. It was like an Eldorado of coke. There were a thousand lorries a day going in and you can imagine the reaction of our boys, fresh from the successes in East Anglia, fresh from the successes in Yorkshire.'[50]

That first day Scargill and his men scored a notable victory, forcing the Saltley management to close the gates before the morning was out. At least, that is how they remembered it. Later, a report for the local Gas Board's successor, British Gas, noted that the depot had not been open on Sunday at all, while Scargill and the Barnsley men had actually arrived on Monday morning, a day later than they claimed. What really happened at Saltley, in fact, is almost impossible to determine, since it is so clouded by romantic legends, claims and counterclaims. In a sense, though, the details are irrelevant. What is certain is that by the time the depot reopened on Monday, 7 February, there were perhaps 1,000 pickets – some say 2,000 – who managed, by pushing and shoving, banging and shouting, clinging onto the sides of the trucks and throwing themselves down into the road, to stop more than about fifty lorries being loaded. One account nicely captures the scene: the police in two thin lines, their arms linked, their helmets glinting in the weak winter sun; 'the miners, men of a certain age with old-fashioned haircuts, massing either side of the police corridor like a restive seventies football crowd'; and in the background a gaggle of left-wing newspaper sellers, sympathetic students, curious children and fascinated reporters. Presiding over the entire scene like a ringmaster was Scargill, who had planted himself on the roof of a grimy public toilet, loudhailer in hand, wrapped inside a thick donkey jacket with trade union badges and a less than fetching baseball cap. As if from nowhere, this junior strike delegate from Barnsley had turned himself into a latter-day medieval baron, marshalling his troops against the forces of the state. But not all the Midlands men were taken with the newcomer. 'Here's another bloody union man out to make a name for himself,' one thought – and he was not far wrong.[51]

As early as Monday evening, the *Birmingham Evening Mail* had coined the phrase 'the Battle of Saltley' to described what was going on a mile to the east of the city centre. The issue was not so much violence between the pickets and the police – in fact, despite the wild scrums that surrounded the arrival and departure of lorries, relations between the two were quite good, with cigarettes often shared in quiet moments – but violence between the miners and the lorry drivers. Most of the drivers were self-employed, owned just one lorry, and depended on regular deliveries to pay their mortgages and feed their families; crucially, very few belonged to a union. They were desperate to get through; the miners were equally desperate to stop them. 'Bottles, bricks and stones' flew through the air each time a lorry appeared; according to the *Evening Mail*, one driver was 'almost dragged from his cab' before he fought off his assailants with, rather worryingly, an iron bar. 'Bottles, stones, fruit and meat pies were thrown during the fighting,' agreed *The Times*, the pies having been provided by the TGWU. In fact, there was less violence than at many First Division football matches: in six days, 76 people were arrested (among them 61 miners, 3 drivers and, predictably, one academic) and 30 injured. But as the journalist Andy Beckett points out, with the news every evening bringing fresh pictures of jeering, screaming pickets and apparently uncontrollable violence, it was no wonder that the public came to see Saltley as a decisive engagement in the class war.[52]

On Tuesday evening, Scargill made an emotional appeal to Birmingham's engineering workers to make one last push that would close Saltley for good. 'We don't want your pound notes,' he told a local meeting of the AUEW. 'Will you go down in history as the working class in Birmingham who stood by while the miners were battered or will you become immortal? I do not ask you – I *demand* that you come out on strike.' Two days later, the TGWU and AUEW called one-day sympathy strikes, and at ten o'clock on Thursday, 10 February, Scargill had his answer. 'Over this hill came a banner,' he later recalled, 'and I've never seen in my life so many people following a banner. As far as the eye could see it was just a mass of people marching towards Saltley. There was a huge roar from the other side of the hill, they were coming the other way. They were coming from five approaches to Saltley . . . And our lads were jumping up in the air with emotion – a fantastic situation.'

In the recollections of those who were there, the last hour of the Saltley siege has become a romantic moment to set alongside any from the pages of British history. The regional secretary of the TGWU, Alan Law, remembered seeing a column of marchers 'headed by the small figure of a Scottish piper, his kilt swirling, the plaintive tune in the air over the heads of the thousands of madly cheering Birmingham workers who by now were shouting and singing, filling the air with wild delight.' His account continues in gloriously overblown style:

> Through the pickets and through the ranks of police, who parted for him like the Red Sea parted for those other marchers so many centuries ago – on he strode, followed immediately behind by his bodyguard of Scotsmen proudly smiling as they acknowledged the cheers.
> And behind them came the column of his mates, through the police cordon, into the centre of the masses, their banners held high – more and

still more of them until the whole area was full of working people standing shoulder to shoulder – surely there was no room left for more?

But the police lines parted again, and into the arena stepped the crowning glory – a single line of girls and women, their faces wreathed in smiles, taking up their places on the inner ring of pickets, waving to the cheers and claps of their menfolk, and fully conscious of the admiring glances of our friends on the picket line, whose mood seemed to have changed overnight.

What price a baton charge now?

This may sound a bit melodramatic, although Scargill, too, remembered the police being struck dumb by a 'delegation of girls' in 'bright white dresses'. In any case, Law's account certainly captures the messianic mood as 10,000 local factory workers poured into the Saltley hollow. And at a quarter to ten, with the crowd bellowing 'Close the gates! Close the gates!' the Chief Constable, Sir Derrick Capper, bowed to the inevitable. In a slightly bathetic climax, a Gas Board employee in a shabby grey overcoat materialized as if from nowhere, rather like the shopkeeper in *Mr Benn*, produced a key and locked the heavy iron gates. Law recalled that 'at that moment the sun broke through the clouds and shone on the 10,000 workers as they stood cheering and singing and on full-grown Yorkshire miners openly weeping'. And on top of his public toilet, Scargill was beside himself with joy. 'This will go down in trade union history,' he told the crowd through a borrowed police loudhailer. 'It will also go down in history as the Battle of Saltley Gate. The working people have united in a mass stand.' It was, he said later, 'the greatest day of my life'.[53]

At that very moment the Cabinet was meeting in Downing Street to discuss the progress of the strike. Jim Prior later remembered Maudling – who had promised that Saltley would not be closed – being handed a note with the bad news, which he dramatically read out to his colleagues. Indeed the minutes bear this out, recording that it was 'a victory for violence against the lawful activities of the Gas Board and the coal merchants', and 'disturbing evidence of the ease with which, by assembling large crowds, militants can flout the law with impunity'. At the very least, it was a moment rich in symbolism – both for the trade unions, for whom it represented a peak of collective solidarity and a victory over the forces of the state, and for the Conservative middle classes, who were horrified by what they perceived as the irresistible power of the mob. From February 1972 onwards, Saltley occupied a central place in right-wing mythology: not only did it fuel the growing middle-class panic of the mid-1970s, but, as Paul Routledge points out, it convinced a generation of Conservatives that they had to destroy the unions' right to secondary picketing, and created a climate that made Thatcherism possible. And for Scargill, of course, it was a turning point. It was thanks to Saltley that 'King Arthur' was born. He had begun the strike as an obscure regional union official; he ended it a tribune of the working classes, a national celebrity invited onto *Question Time*, *Any Questions* and *Parkinson* and hailed by *Harper's and Queen* as one of Britain's leaders of the future, alongside the young William Waldegrave, Patricia Hewitt and Jack Straw.[54]

Yet if Saltley was a victory, it was a purely symbolic one. Most of the coke, after all, had already gone, and Tory diehards who criticized the government for not keeping the gates open at all costs were missing the point. Symbolism apart, it made no difference to the government, the power stations or the course of the strike whether the Saltley gates were open or closed. Ironically, it would have been better for Heath to order them closed straight away, so as to deny the miners a confrontation and a propaganda victory. (In the event, of course, the decision was left to the police, not the politicians.) In any case, what really mattered was something that occupied far more of the Cabinet's time during that meeting on 10 February: the cold weather and the siege of the power stations. Just the day before, a Council of State, presided over by the Queen Mother in her daughter's absence abroad, had declared a state of emergency and imposed restrictions on shop lighting, floodlights and advertising. Desperate to end the strike, Carr told the Coal Board to raise their offer to 12 per cent, but the miners turned it down. Already the authorities had announced a programme of severe power cuts, with a third of the country losing power for four hours every day. Now, even before Maudling had been given the famous note, John Davies grimly reported that the situation was hopeless. With coal stocks immobilized, many power stations would run out of fuel by the end of the following week. Soon, the generating boards would be down to just 25 per cent of their usual supply, which would 'bring much industry to a standstill and cause large numbers of workers to be laid off' – and this at a time when unemployment was already well above a million. It now looked likely that not only would troops be patrolling the streets of Belfast, they would be guarding power stations and trying to maintain public order in a world without electricity. As Willie Whitelaw later put it, 'we looked absolutely into the abyss'.[55]

Within the corridors of power there was now a mood of abject panic. That afternoon, Carr bowed to the inevitable, announcing that the government had convened a court of inquiry on the miners' pay, with none other than Lord Wilberforce in the chair. As Heath's biographer John Campbell remarks, that the government had turned to the very man whose generosity to the power workers had disappointed them a year earlier was extremely suggestive: it was 'the clearest possible signal that they wanted only to see the strike ended as quickly as possible'. The press, conveniently forgetting their predictions of the miners' certain defeat, were in no doubt. 'We have now reached a situation which is more dangerous than that of any industrial dispute since the war,' said *The Times* the next day, judging that 'if the Court of Enquiry cannot find acceptable terms the prospect is appalling'. Many normally level-headed officials agreed: at the Treasury, Brendan Sewill heard civil servants anxiously wondering whether the government would have to 'activate the nuclear underground shelters and the centres of regional government, because there'll be no electricity and there'll be riots in the streets. The sewage will overflow and there'll be epidemics.' As Heath's aide Douglas Hurd mordantly recorded, the government was 'now wandering vainly over [the] battlefield looking for someone to surrender to – and being massacred all the time.'[56]

Desperate to fight back, Heath stirred himself to address a Conservative rally in the Philharmonic Hall, Liverpool, where he revealed that the miners had rejected an offer of between £3 and £4 a week to return to work while Wilberforce was sitting. Yet for all Heath's belligerence – which earned him severe criticism even from Conservative papers like the *Daily Mail*, which felt he had failed to show 'a grain of human understanding' – there was no mistaking the bleakness of his prognosis. 'Severe power cuts', he said, 'will mean hardship for every man, woman and child in the country. The sick and the elderly, the most defenceless members of the community, will be hardest hit . . . Millions of men and women will be put out of work as their factories close down.' In the House of Commons, meanwhile, John Davies was unveiling a literally chilling series of emergency measures. From Sunday, 13 February, he was banning the use of electricity for heating shops, offices, public halls, restaurants, and anything connected with recreation, entertainment and sport. And that was not all: the situation was so desperate that he was forced to announce 'massive restrictions in the use of electricity by industry', with most firms limited to power for just three days a week. Anyone who broke these regulations faced a three-month prison sentence or a £100 fine. On top of that, Davies warned householders that unless they cut back on their own consumption, they might find themselves in the same dark, chilly boat. 'Except where there is sickness only one room should be electrically heated,' he said grimly. 'Lights should only be used where essential.'[57]

This was terrifying stuff; yet if anything, Davies was understating the case. By now so many power stations had shut down, an internal report warned, that in three weeks Britain would be facing cuts of almost half its electricity. Over the weekend the situation deteriorated, and on Monday, 14 February, a most unhappy Valentine's Day, the government confirmed that 800,000 workers had been sent home, with plants across the country closing under the industrial three-day week. That evening, the Commons debated the government's emergency powers, in what was billed 'as likely to be one of the most super colossal parliamentary clashes of all time,' as one sketch-writer put it. And when Davies rose to speak at ten o'clock there were indeed raucous jeers from the Labour benches, but even they fell silent as he gravely outlined the situation. Even if people followed the emergency restrictions, he said gloomily, the Central Electricity Generating Board could only hold out for another two weeks. At that point, there might not even be enough power to keep essential services going; what was certain, though, was that there would be no power either for industry or for the home. Families across the country, he said, would find themselves 'without hot water and heat. As a matter of cold decision' – and at the unintentional pun, the Labour benches roared with laughter. 'Hon. Gentlemen opposite may find it exceedingly humorous,' Davies said angrily, 'but the problem of trying to deal with this issue in a serious and competent way is immense . . . This hilarity contributes nothing to one of the greatest problems we have ever had.'[58]

The next day's headlines made frighteningly bleak reading: 'Full Blackout Only Two Weeks Away, Davies Warns Commons'; 'Power Cuts Leave 800,000 Idle'; 'Even Essential Services in Danger if Situation Does Not Change.' The rest of the news was little better: the front page of *The Times*, announcing the murder of the fiftieth soldier in Northern Ireland in twelve months, carried a photo-montage of the dead men's faces, their young eyes gazing out from a page they would never see. By now, power cuts had become a fact of daily life. Not only were power stations closing, but so were factories, offices, schools. In hospitals, women were giving birth by candlelight; in the streets, there were reports of long queues as traffic lights failed. In London, Piccadilly Circus was as dark and quiet as a graveyard; on the banks of the Thames, the Palace of Westminster seemed a grey, ghostly monolith in the winter night. Across the country, pubs and restaurants were deserted; in the shops, there were shortages of matches and candles; in the newspapers, full-page advertisements warned of the 'hardships, even tragedies' if people flouted the electricity restrictions and risked three months in prison. *Blue Peter*'s presenters Peter Purves and John Noakes even advised children how to look out for their elderly relatives and neighbours, recommending that they lined their blankets with newspaper to keep warm. 'With all this newspaper,' Noakes added, 'I shouldn't go to bed with a candle, though.'[59]

Some found the power cuts exciting or nostalgic: the upper-class diarist James Lees-Milne noted that although he found reading with candles difficult, 'how beautiful the golden light they shed. How mysterious and solemn the golden light they induce.' But most were less sanguine. Writing to her friend Joyce Grenfell, the journalist Virginia Graham reported that she had only just 'turned on the tele and the cut came'. The whole business, she wrote, 'makes one wonder whether democracy is quite the answer! When we were suffering for the nation's survival during the war the task was easy, but now we seem to be silently suffering, as we watch the country brought to its knees. It's ridiculous that a quarter of a million men should be allowed to paralyse the country, with all that there coal just sitting behind gates which nobody dares open.' An NUM branch secretary on holiday in Newquay even found himself being battered with an umbrella by a furious old lady who accused him of having 'switched her electric off and fought with police'. 'You silly old twat,' he retorted, 'my electric were off too.' She promptly hit him again, and retreated only when he threatened to throw her in the harbour.[60]

On Friday, 18 February, the denouement came. The morning's papers gave a flavour of the intense pressure on Heath and his ministers: the front page of *The Times*, for example, carried a striking photograph of a nurse treating a patient at the Royal Eye Hospital by candlelight, while the lead stories reported that Ford had shut down production at its Dagenham plant, that commuter rail services had been severely cut, that thousands were marching in Belfast to protest against the sectarian murder of a bus driver, and – above all – that in a packed House of

Commons, Heath's majority on the crucial European Communities Bill had been slashed to just eight, a result marked by scenes of 'scuffling and almost fighting' between Labour backbenchers and the Liberals who had saved the government. For Heath, however, the worst was yet to come, for that morning Lord Wilberforce published his report. He did not merely lean towards the miners, as had been anticipated; he gave them almost everything they wanted. They had 'a just case for special treatment', the judge wrote, and deserved 'a general and exceptional increase', with surface workers getting up to £5 extra a week, underground workers getting £6, and coalface workers an extra £4.50. These new rates, he suggested, should be backdated to November 1971, giving the NUM an average increase of 27 per cent. As *The Times* remarked the next day, Wilberforce's report conceded 'almost all the miners' case and most of the money they demanded. It reads like a printed version of the arguments used by NUM leaders over the past six weeks.'[61]

But with their hands around the government's throat, the miners were not ready to loosen their grip. At a stormy meeting that morning at the Department of Employment on St James's Square, the NUM executive narrowly voted to reject Wilberforce's proposals and to hold out for an extra £1 a week. At eight that evening, the Cabinet met in an atmosphere of funereal gloom, the room lit only by candles, and Carr mournfully reported that the NUM had voted against the report by 14 votes to 11. (In fact, the true figure was 13–12; the miners' vice-president had lied to Carr's officials in order to present a stronger front.) Heath was trapped: as he told the Cabinet, he could hardly go well beyond Wilberforce's recommendations on the very day the report had come out; yet his government 'might find themselves unable to sustain the life of the community unless they surrendered to the miners'. Shortly after ten that night, Heath welcomed the miners' leaders to Number 10. The mood was black: Gormley remembered later that the Prime Minister was 'not "Smiling Ted" by any means. We didn't see much of his teeth that night. I wouldn't say he was humiliated, but he was very subdued.'

Heath told Gormley that there was no way he could grant the additional £1, as the miners wanted. On the other hand, he was prepared to concede ground on other issues – which was exactly what Gormley and the NUM leaders had anticipated. Now that they had the advantage, they were determined to press it home. As the night drew on, they extracted one concession after another, from free transport to the pit and free working clothes to the consolidation of miners' bonuses into shift rates that would mean a big boost to their overtime earnings. In the end, they won fifteen concessions worth an extra £100 million; at one point, their industrial relations officer was 'scratching around in his files' for long-forgotten demands passed by NUM conferences in years gone by, with Heath waving them through like an exhausted traffic policeman. When they had run out of demands, the executive voted. Even then the majority in favour of withdrawing the pickets was only 14–11, but it was enough. It was one in the morning: the strike was over, and the miners had won. Heath had not just been beaten; he had been annihilated. It was 'a grim day', he wrote later, 'for the country and for the government'.[62]

In mining communities and left-wing circles across Britain, the settlement was greeted with the biggest outpouring of joy since perhaps the end of the Second World War. 'I rejoice at the miners' victory,' the left-wing historian A. J. P. Taylor wrote to *The Times*, 'and I record that February 19 will be long remembered as a glorious day in the history of the British working class.' Battle-scarred veterans of the strike became minor local celebrities, their names applauded to the rafters. In Barnsley, Arthur Scargill came home to what the local paper called 'a hero's welcome', and 'in the streets, pubs and clubs, at further meetings in halls or pit branches, he was told by his taciturn supporters and their wives: "Well done, Arthur."'[63]

But for another proud man there were no cheers and no congratulations, only the stark reality of defeat. A few days after the end of the strike, Heath addressed the nation. Rejecting the common belief that 'the miners won a great victory' and 'the Government lost that one', he insisted that 'in the country we live in, there could not be any "we" or "they". There was only us – all of us. If the Government is defeated then the country is defeated.' There had to be 'a more sensible way to settle our differences', and he was ready to sit down with employers and trade unionists alike to work out the best way to keep prices down and yet stimulate greater growth and employment. It was, he added, 'the Government's job to see that the interests of *all* sections of the community are properly looked after'. But, he warned ominously, 'if one group is so determined to get its own way that it does not care what happens to the rest of us, then we are not living in the kind of world we thought we were, and we had better face up to it'.[64]

Public opinion strongly favoured the settlement: according to Gallup, four out of five people approved of the Wilberforce report, and sympathy for the miners, even after Saltley and the power cuts, remained high. In the press, the consensus was that Heath had been utterly humiliated; as Lord Carrington told the *Guardian*'s Peter Jenkins, there was 'true blue Tory blood all over the carpet'. For the victorious miners, however, there was nothing but praise for what *The Times* called their 'scrupulously constitutional' tactics. And yet even *The Times* admitted 'anxieties about the state of society and about growing violence', not just in Northern Ireland, but everywhere from the nation's football grounds to the floor of the House of Commons. For millions of people who had watched the miners' strike on television – when their televisions were working, that is – it had been a disturbing sign of what could happen once the bonds of civility and consensus began to fray. Even their greatest admirers had to admit that the miners had won not because of principle, but because of their sheer industrial muscle. And at a time when the limits of state power were being brutally exposed on the streets of Belfast, many people found this deeply frightening. 'The theme of anarchy and unmanage-ability', noted Tony Benn in mid-February, was creeping into the Conservative press. In the *Sunday Express*, for instance, the columnist Anne Edwards argued that the violent aftermath of Bloody Sunday and the disorder of the miners' strike were symptoms of a 'loudmouthed, lunatic hooliganism [that] is festering all over the country'. Belfast and Saltley, she wrote, had both fallen victim to 'mob violence, which excuses itself by claiming a cause', but was really 'inflicted by people with no other purpose in mind than to bash, beat up, break, scar and smash just for the kicks of doing it'.[65]

For the first time in decades, there was a palpable sense that the country stood at an ideological crossroads. Britain was 'not yet in a revolutionary situation', said the *New Statesman* portentously, but 'something resembling it' was at hand. 'I am more and more convinced that Communism must come to this country within twenty-five years,' wrote a despairing James Lees-Milne after watching the TUC leaders on television. Even in Whitehall there was gossip that the strike had been orchestrated in 'King Street', where the Communist Party had its dilapidated headquarters. And in the Prime Minister's files, a note signed by 'E' and dated 23 February warned that 'the use of violence to achieve social or political ends must increase as society becomes more complex, the vulnerable areas become more numerous, the methods of attack more sophisticated'. Next to this, somebody, probably Heath, scribbled: 'powerful: learn the lessons for . . .' But he never finished the comment – a telling sign of the sheer stress and exhaustion bearing down on this brooding, awkward, impatient man, more alone than ever as the storm broke around him.[66]

4

Fanfare for Europe

Hullo. As you probably know I've been away at a conference in Paris sorting out the final details of the merger between our company Heathco's and the large continental combine E.E.C. Ltd. . . .

I would like to state categorically once and for all: THIS NEW ARRANGEMENT DOES NOT, I REPEAT, NOT, MEAN THAT WE ARE GOING TO BE TOLD WHAT TO DO BY A LOT OF FOREIGNERS.

E. Heath, Managing Director.
Private Eye, 3 November 1972

The town of Broadstairs, nestling on the tip of the Isle of Thanet on the eastern edge of Kent, has always been a link between England and the Continent. The Romans landed on the Isle – which was then detached from the Kentish mainland – in 55 BC, and returned under Claudius a hundred years later. In the fifth century, Hengist and Horsa, by legend the first of the Anglo-Saxons, are said to have settled on the Isle of Thanet, and Viking raiding parties twice wintered in the area centuries later. By the fourteenth century, a little fishing village called Bradstow – Old English for 'broad stairs', after the steps men had cut in the soft chalk cliffs – had been established above the broad golden sands, eventually coming under the jurisdiction of the Cinque Ports. It was associated above all with fishing and shipbuilding, and was no stranger to foreign visitors: during the 1600s, Flemish refugees settled in Reading Street, while the town's stout sea walls testified to the fears of invasion from the south. In 1723, Daniel Defoe recorded that the town's population were generally fishermen, although he noted that Broadstairs was also renowned as a 'hot bed of smuggling'. Seventy years later, the town gates were urgently repaired to cope with a possible invasion from revolutionary France, and it was at Broadstairs that the imperial French eagle captured at Waterloo was brought onto English soil. And local legend has it that Broadstairs was the first English community to hear the news of Wellington's great victory – though this was a tale that the town's most famous son tactfully kept quiet about with his European friends.[1]

When Teddy Heath was growing up in Broadstairs in the 1920s, his parents used to take him for walks on the cliffs, from where on a clear day he could see the faint grey smudge of Calais and the French coast. Even as a boy, Heath was fascinated by the distant lands to the south. His father, Will, was a typical introverted Englishman, quiet, solid and serious, but his mother had travelled to Switzerland as a lady's maid before her marriage, and told stories of the voyage to her children. When Teddy was 14 he had the chance to follow in her footsteps, joining a school trip to Paris – a real treat by the standards of the day. Years later, he fondly recalled the details of the great expedition: the flight from Croydon Airport, then something that few people had ever done; the extraordinary variety of Parisian restaurants, each with its own outdoor menu to intrigue the young visitors; the 'magnificent shops' and motor showrooms, whose catalogues he kept even as an old man; the perform-ance of *Carmen* at the Opéra Comique, where he remembered seeing an attractive blonde woman in the box below struggling to keep her shoulder straps up as they 'repeatedly slipped down in a most revealing fashion'; and perhaps above all, his illicit trip to the Folies-Bergère with some friends when they were supposed to be tucked up in their boarding house – a detail he somehow forgot to mention when he eagerly told his parents all about the trip afterwards.[2]

From that moment on, Heath was hooked. As a student at Oxford in the late 1930s, he seized every opportunity for travel, spending one summer in Republican Spain and another on an extraordinary tour of Nazi Germany, where he spent many happy hours in Munich's art galleries and concert halls and also had the unusual experience of listening to Hitler at a Nuremberg rally. Afterwards, the young Heath was invited to an SS cocktail party where he was introduced to Goering ('far more bulky and genial than I had imagined'), Goebbels ('small, pale and, in that setting, rather insignificant-looking') and Himmler ('I shall never forget how drooping and sloppy [his] hand was when he offered it to me'). Two years later, in the summer of 1939, he was on a hitch-hiking tour of Berlin, Danzig, Dresden and Leipzig when news broke of the Nazi–Soviet Pact. Taking the first train out of Germany and hitching to the Channel, he arrived home in Kent only a week before Hitler invaded Poland. He did not return to his beloved Europe until June 1944, when he sailed to France as an officer in the Royal Artillery Corps, and crossed the Rhine into Germany just before VE Day. After his regiment moved into Hanover, he made it his first priority to rebuild the local opera house. 'My men must have culture,' he told his Brigade Commander. But perhaps the most memorable incident in Heath's war came months later, when he returned to the blackened ruins of Nuremberg to watch the trials of the Nazi war criminals. It was an experience that left a deep imprint on this stiff, shy but impressionable young man:

> As I left the court I knew that the shadow of those evil things had been lifted, and their perpetrators now faced justice. But at what a cost. Europe had once more torn itself apart. This must never be allowed to happen again. My generation did not have the option of living in the past; we had to work for the future. We were surrounded by destruction, homelessness, hunger and despair. Only by working together right across our continent had we any hope of creating a society which would uphold the true values of European civilisation. Reconciliation and reconstruction must be our tasks. I did not realise then that this would be my preoccupation for the next fifty years.[3]

Whatever one thinks of Heath's European commitment, there is no doubt that it was thoroughly genuine. His maiden speech as an MP in 1950 was devoted to the Schuman Plan for a European Coal and Steel Community, which became the nucleus of the modern European Union. At a time when many British politicians insisted on staying aloof from schemes of European collaboration, Heath was all for it, insisting that 'we may be taking a very great risk with our economy' by staying out. Characteristically, he had just returned from a fact-finding trip to West Germany; trips to the Continent were to be a constant feature of Heath's parliamentary career, and he often seemed more comfortable with French and German contacts than with his own party comrades. When Macmillan picked him to handle Britain's first application to join the six members of the Common Market in 1961, it soon become clear that there could be no better candidate. At the very beginning, Heath told the European negotiators that the application was 'a great decision, a turning point in our history', and his enthusiasm made a profound impression both on his own civil servants and on the representatives of the Six. And when President de Gaulle, in a stunning exhibition of diplomatic cunning, self-interest and spite, vetoed the British application in January 1963, Heath gave what was probably the speech of his life. Rejecting the view that Britain was 'not European enough', he told the assembled foreign ministers that there were 'many millions in Europe who know perfectly well how European Britain has been in the past and are grateful for it'. They should 'have no fear', he said. 'We in Britain are not going to turn our backs on the mainland of Europe or on the countries of the Community. We are a part of Europe: by geography, tradition, history, culture and civilisation. We shall continue to work with all our friends in Europe for the true unity and strength of this continent.' It was the only time in his life that this most wooden of speakers managed to move an audience to tears: when he had finished, even the female interpreters were discreetly dabbing their eyes.[4]

By the time Heath became Prime Minister, Britain had suffered the humiliation of yet another veto from de Gaulle, this time after a self-deluding and characteristically semi-ridiculous application (technically called 'the Probe') by Harold Wilson and George Brown in 1967. Revealingly, neither of the failed bids was especially popular with the public, and, even more revealingly, both were the products of desperation rather than conviction, born out of political and economic weakness. Macmillan only decided to apply to join the Common Market once his government had run into trouble and commentators were attacking him as backward and reactionary, while Wilson only applied once his ambitions to revive Britain as a white-hot technological powerhouse had been destroyed by the 1966 sterling crisis. The irony was that if Britain had joined the Common Market in the mid-1950s, as its European neighbours had hoped, then it would have done so as a military and economic superpower, still unquestionably Western Europe's pre-eminent nation. But by 1970 no serious observer could pretend that Britain still set the standards for the rest of the Continent. In productivity growth, for example, it had fallen behind not only the astonishingly industrious West Germans but the supposedly lazy French and Italians, while its GDP growth rate was just half that of the five major EEC countries (France, West Germany, Italy, Belgium and the Netherlands). On top of that, while Britain's share of world exports had collapsed from 26 per cent in 1950 to less than 11 per cent in 1970 and barely 10 per cent in 1980, West Germany's share soared from 7 per cent in 1950 to 20 per cent in 1970 and 30 per cent by 1980. From the mid-1960s onwards, in fact, Britain cut a very miserable and unimpressive figure beside the buoyant French and West Germans. It was true that the French had their problems with student unrest and the Germans with domestic terrorism; but then Britain had plenty on its plate in Northern Ireland. And not only was unemployment much higher than in France and West Germany, but Britain's inflation record was truly abysmal. The Germans might be unhappy with an inflation rate of 6 per cent in 1975; but they had only to look across the Channel, where it had reached almost 25 per cent, to remind themselves that they must be doing something right.[5]

When Heath won the election in 1970, it was common knowledge that he planned to apply for Common Market membership as soon as possible. This was not merely a personal project, though; it was a vision shared by almost all senior Conservatives. The party's detailed report recommending European entry, for example, had actually been prepared under Heath's predecessor, the strongly pro-American Sir Alec Douglas-Home. But as with other emotive issues of the late 1960s such as immigration and the abolition of capital punishment, there was a strong whiff of elitism about pro-Europeanism. Not only were most Tory associations dead set against entering the Market, but most Tory voters were very sceptical, too. Throughout the 1960s, in fact, public opinion had been a mixture of indifference, confusion and outright hostility, with support rallying only whenever the British economy seemed particularly dire. In April 1970, just weeks before the election, Gallup found that just 19 per cent of voters supported British entry, with more than 50 per cent rejecting even the idea of holding talks. On the other hand, most business leaders strongly backed the idea of entering a bigger European market, and the CBI was particularly enthusiastic: a year later, a survey of 1,000 firms found that 95 per cent backed joining the Common Market. The civil service was broadly enthusiastic, too, with the notable exception of the Treasury. And although Heath's drive to win British membership is often seen as one man's lonely crusade, the truth is that his successes were built on foundations laid by others. He actually inherited much of the team that organized the bid from Harold Wilson; all the files were prepared, all the planning was in place, and a lot of work was already out of the way. Indeed, one of the little secrets of British politics in the early 1970s was that Wilson had been planning a new bid once he won re-election. The Labour government had even fixed a date for negotiations to begin, which makes Wilson's decision to turn against Europe immediately after his defeat look even more cynical and unprincipled.[6]

What distinguished Heath from his contemporaries, therefore, was not the commitment itself but its unusually personal nature, rooted not just in his travels on the Continent but also in his deep love for its musical heritage, his contacts with European politicians and his experiences during the Second World War. Harold Wilson might have applied to join the Common Market in 1967, but he said himself that he had 'never been emotionally a Europe man', while his policy adviser Bernard Donoughue observed that Wilson was 'basically a north of England, non-conformist puritan . . . continental Europeans, especially from France and southern Europe, were to him alien. He disliked their rich food, genuinely preferring meat and two veg with HP sauce.' This even extended to holidays, which Wilson famously spent on the Scilly Isles, as well as to cheese. After one Downing Street lunch, Donoughue recorded that Wilson had been delighted to have English cheese, because he much preferred it to French.[7]

But then Wilson was also a fan of the Commonwealth, in which Heath took no interest whatsoever. And Wilson was strongly pro-American to the extent of modelling himself on first John F. Kennedy and then Lyndon Johnson, whereas Heath was unusual among modern British prime ministers in his total indifference to all things American. The irony was that although Johnson treated Wilson as an inconvenient but obsequious nuisance, the next President, Richard Nixon, was hugely excited by Heath's victory and hoped that they would become great friends. Like Heath, Nixon was a conservative modernizer from a humble provincial background, a self-made man distinguished by his lofty vision, brooding intellect, grumpy demeanour and permanent social unease. In some ways they should have been natural soulmates – they could have bonded, for instance, over their shared interest in classical music, their mutual disregard for women, or their fondness for wildly overcomplicated incomes policies. To Nixon's bewilderment, however, Heath rebuffed his attempts to strike up a special relationship. Henry Kissinger, Nixon's supremely cynical Secretary of State, wrote later that they were shocked by Heath's 'unsentimentality' and 'reserve', which left Nixon feeling like a 'jilted lover'. But Heath had no time for misty-eyed visions of Anglo-American partnership. All the special relationship achieved, he said later, was 'to estrange us from our European colleagues ... Now there are some people who always nestle on the shoulder of an American president. That's no future for Britain.'[8]

In his profound affection for European culture and complete lack of interest in anything American, Heath cut an unusual figure among contemporary British politicians. And yet although there had been plenty of anguished commentary about the supposed 'Americanization' of British life in the 1950s and 1960s, from supermarkets and advertising to fast food and television, what was much more striking was the extent to which Britain was becoming 'European'. The pop act that recorded most number one hit singles in the 1970s, for example, was not Rod Stewart, Elton John, the Bay City Rollers, the Sex Pistols or any other emblematic British singer or group of the day; it was a Swedish group, Abba, who sang in heavily accented and occasionally slightly strange English. Admittedly they made their great breakthrough in the unmistakably English surroundings of the Brighton Dome, built in 1805 for the Prince Regent and connected to the famous Pavilion, but the occasion was distinctly European: the nineteenth Eurovision Song Contest, held in April 1974. In many ways the contest was a typical product of the 1950s, conceived as a well-meaning effort to bring old enemies together, although more often than not it merely exposed the depths of Continental depravity – for example in 1968, when Cliff Richard was disgracefully cheated of victory by Franco's vote-rigging. By the early 1970s, however, it was a serious business, commanding international viewing figures unequalled by anything other than major sporting events. The BBC took it so seriously that in 1971, when the contest was held in Dublin, they deliberately chose a Northern Irish singer, Clodagh Rogers, to minimize Anglo-Irish tensions (although she still got death threats from the IRA). Indeed, terrorism was a constant concern: when the contest was held in Stockholm in 1975, the authorities took massive precautions against a rumoured attack by the Baader–Meinhof Group, and at the eighteenth edition, held in Luxembourg and the first to feature an Israeli entry, the audience were memorably advised not to stand up while applauding in case they were shot by the security forces. Mercifully, the Brighton event was free of any such horrors, although it did feature a half-time performance by the Wombles.[9]

Although Abba's success obviously depended on their talent for writing irresistibly catchy songs, they were not the only example of European infiltration into the British charts. When the abominable 'Chirpy Chirpy Cheep Cheep' topped the charts for five weeks in the summer of 1971, for example, the most common explanation was that people were trying to recapture the spirit of their holidays in Spain, where it had been everywhere that summer. In fact, it had been recorded for the Italian market by Middle of the Road, a Scottish pop group who specialized in Anglo-Latin crossovers, and even they thought it was awful. Their drummer later remarked that they needed two bottles of bourbon before they could start work, for 'we were as disgusted with the thought of recording it as most people were at the thought of buying it'. But three years later, the curse of the Armada struck again, this time in the form of the Swedish singer Sylvie Vrethammar, whose hit 'Y Viva España' – 'This year I'm off to sunny Spain ...' – captured the excitement, the hedonism and the sheer awfulness of package tourism in its early years.[10]

As a Broadstairs boy, Heath was well placed to appreciate the seismic changes that had overtaken British holiday habits. Like so many seaside resorts, the little Kentish town had long relied on a flood of big-city holidaymakers in the summer months; Charles Dickens, for example, was a great fan, visiting almost every year from 1837 to 1859. By the early 1970s, however, resorts like Broadstairs were losing their lustre, outshone by the new craze for touring caravans, the newfound popularity of more distant stretches of rural England such as Devon, Cornwall and the Lakes, and above all, the sun-bleached concrete monoliths of Torremolinos and Benidorm. Heath himself chose to take pride in the changing patterns of tourism: in the official programme for the 'Fanfare for Europe' celebrations in January 1973, he expressed his delight that 'many more of us in Britain, in particular young people, travel to other European countries than a decade ago', with holidaymakers becoming 'steadily more "European" in terms of our knowledge and contacts'. But it was resorts like Broadstairs that paid the price in boarded-up shop-fronts, abandoned amusement arcades and crumbling hotels. Already Northern resorts like Skegness and Cleethorpes, with their wet and windy reputations, were struggling for custom. On the Wirral, the resort of New Brighton fell into total disrepair, with its ballroom ravaged by fire in 1969, ferries across the Mersey discontinued in 1971, and the promenade pier torn down six years later. Even the fictional seaside town of Fircombe in *Carry On Girls* (1973) is a miserable place of slate-grey skies, driving rain and empty hotels: in the film's opening shots, we see a family sheltering from the rain in the shelter of a derelict pier, while a sign behind them reads 'Come to Fabulous Fircombe', with graffiti adding 'What the hell for?'[11]

The sentiment would have appealed to the acerbic Tory politician Alan Clark, who was not impressed by the venue for their party conference in October 1973. 'Isn't Blackpool appalling, loathsome?' he wrote in his diary. 'Impossible to get even a piece of bread and cheese, or a decent cup of tea; dirt, squalor, shanty-town broken pavements with pools of water lying in them – on the Promenade – vulgar common "primitives" drifting about in groups or standing, loitering, prominently.' It was no wonder that as soon as the conference was over, hundreds of Blackpool hoteliers decamped en masse to Spain, heading for the very resorts that were destroying their livelihoods. 'It was like being in Blackpool except we had this wonderful sunshine,' one later recalled. 'It was November and the main topic of conversation was, "Amazing sun, isn't it? We couldn't do this in England."'[12]

The father of package tourism is often identified as the former Reuters journalist Vladimir Raitz, who flew thirty-two students and teachers in an old American Dakota to Corsica in 1950, with the intrepid pioneers staying in a makeshift camp of army surplus tents. By the end of the 1960s, his company, Horizon, was one of Britain's biggest package operators, with tours to Majorca, Minorca and Ibiza, the Costa Brava, Costa Blanca and Costa del Sol, the Algarve, Bulgaria and Crete. At this stage, though, package holidays abroad accounted for barely 8 per cent of the total holidays taken by British families, partly because travellers were only allowed to take £50 a year out of the country. In January 1970, however, the rules were amended to allow individuals to take £25 each per trip, and from then on the boom seemed unstoppable. By 1971, British tourists were taking more than 4 million holidays abroad; by 1973, some 9 million; by 1981, more than 13 million. The two-week trip to Spain with Horizon, Cosmos or Thomson became a great status symbol of the mid-1970s: children who might once have been delighted by a few days in Bognor now pestered their parents to take them to Benidorm, desperate to keep up with their more affluent classmates.

For people who had grown up with the limited horizons of working-class life in the 1950s and 1960s, that first trip abroad was often an unforgettable experience, all the way from the endless, harried queues at the airport to the atmosphere on the plane itself, thick with anticipation and cigarette smoke, and then the shock of the heat, the light and the unfinished hotel. 'Stepping off the plane at Ibiza airport was incredible,' a clerk from Burnley recalled of her first trip abroad. 'The doors opened, the heat flooded in and the smell of musk and pine mixed with cigar smoke . . . Unbelievable. Coming from a grey northern mill town, you can imagine when we saw all the lovely white painted houses with geraniums growing from the balconies, we felt we were in another world.' And some holidaymakers reported that the experience made them look on their native land in an entirely new light. In June 1970, a reader who had recently visited the Spanish coast wrote to the *Mirror* noting that 'there were no aggro boys, no vandalism, all the telephone boxes were clean and all the phones worked. It was hardly necessary to lock up cars and little children could go anywhere unmolested.' Four days later,

"What worries me, Doris, is that if my union's strike in our motor-factory goes on much longer, our new car won't be ready to take us to the Costa Brava during the next strike"

Holidays on the Spanish coast were becoming the norm as early as 9 August 1970, when Michael Cummings drew this *Daily Express* cartoon mocking the selfishness of the unions.

another reader wrote in. 'I appreciate that he did not see any aggro boys,' he commented wryly, 'but did he notice the armed police, the censored press, the jails crowded with people who merely expressed their dislike of the Franco regime?'[13]

Not all British holidaymakers enjoyed the Continental experience. Arthur Scargill, who usually took his holidays in Cornwall, eventually plucked up the courage to take his family to the socialist paradise of Bulgaria, but the overcharging and petty corruption infuriated him so much that, on his return, he announced: 'If that's Communism, they can keep it.' A more common complaint was that with package companies overwhelmed by the demand, their planes were often scheduled to make two or three return journeys from Britain to Spain a day, with no room for manoeuvre when things went wrong (as they invariably did). In the early 1970s, delays of half a day or more were extremely common: the managing director of Gaytours later admitted that 'if a flight was six hours late, that was good'. And with few organizations to fight for holidaymakers' rights, service was often downright abysmal: one woman who flew for the first time from Birmingham to Majorca in the early 1970s later recalled that water leaked onto her shoulder throughout the flight, the pull-down table 'came off in my hands' and when the steward tried to wheel a duty-free trolley through the cabin, one of the wheels fell off and rolled down the aisle. 'Of course we never complained,' she mused. 'Most people never dreamt of complaining in those days.'

But times were changing. In 1969, the BBC launched its weekly *Holiday* series, which was often devoted to scandals and scams, and in 1974 ITV followed suit with *Wish You Were Here*. Non-existent hotels, beaches that looked nothing like the picture in the brochure, surly locals and atrocious plumbing were all common complaints, but the dark side of the package experience was rarely better captured than in the film *Carry On Abroad* (1972), in which the familiar team visit the 'paradise island' of Elsbels, courtesy of the optimistically named Wundatours. In traditional fashion, their hotel is not quite finished; the drawers have no bottoms, the electrical fittings explode when turned on, and the taps produce sand, not water. They have no need of alarm clocks, either; every morning they are woken by a dawn chorus of pneumatic drills and cement mixers, which for all too many British visitors was an even more unforgettable part of the Mediterranean soundtrack than the songs of Middle of the Road and Sylvie Vrethammar.[14]

In *Carry On Abroad*, the British visitors themselves are hardly models of good behaviour. After a drunken night out in the local town, the entire tour party ends up in the cells, winning their release only after one of the women seduces a policeman. Unfortunately, this was less far-fetched than it sounded; drunk with the heat, the sense of freedom and the local liquor, many holidaymakers did drop their inhibitions in a way that would have been unthinkable at Broadstairs. A common stereotype of British tourists was that women were particularly liable to lose their self-restraint on holiday, opening their arms to the first smooth-talking Don Juan they bumped into. 'Once they bridge that strip of English Channel,' says Terry Collier in *Whatever Happened to the Likely Lads?*, 'they drop everything: reserve, manners, morals and knickers' – and this, of course, was before the heyday of Faliraki and Magaluf. But there was also a hefty dose of class prejudice in all this. Social class still played a large role in determining where people went on holiday: according to the British Home Tourism Survey in 1978, manual workers were far more likely to visit seaside resorts, while professional families were more likely to go on 'country holidays where mountains and moorlands, lakes and streams are the attraction'. And as early as the mid-1970s, mass working-class tourism had become the subject of savage social commentary. In *The Golden Hordes* (1975), Louis Turner and John Ash complained that package holidays were reducing the Mediterranean to a vast 'pleasure periphery', with all sense of cultural distinctiveness submerged beneath a mountain of cheap souvenirs and a vast flood of baked beans, sun-tan lotion and pints of Skol. Tourists were the 'new barbarians of our age of leisure', they wrote, treating their hosts as little better than performing monkeys in a zoo enclosure, and expecting them to put up with behaviour they would never have contemplated at home. But perhaps nobody put it better than *Monty Python*'s Eric Idle in 1972, with his violent rant about the hordes of tourists 'carted around in buses surrounded by sweaty mindless oafs from Kettering and Coventry in their cloth caps and their cardigans and their transistor radios and their *Sunday Mirrors*, complaining about the tea.' 'Yes, yes,' agrees Michael Palin's travel agent, hoping to shut him up. But it is no good: from his nightmarish vision of the 'party from Rhyl' who cannot stop singing 'Torremolinos, Torremolinos' to his horrified memory of the 'drunken greengrocer from Luton' with last Tuesday's *Daily Express* and firm views on Enoch Powell, Idle is only just warming up. And who could blame him?[15]

The most common bone of contention, though, was the food. As Idle's disgruntled tourist notes, the first item on many supposedly 'international' hotel menus often bore a disturbing resemblance to warmed-over Campbell's Cream of Mushroom soup. In fairness, many tourists were glad of anything that reminded them of home, recoiling in horror from the supposedly greasy, garlic-infested local fare. Accounts of the early days of package holidays teem with stories of holidaymakers gagging at the sight of pasta, noodles or grilled fish, manfully trying to eat spaghetti with a knife and fork, or even marching into the kitchens and ordering the local cooks to prepare them a traditional British meal, which no doubt won them plenty of friends in the Mediterranean catering trade. When Hunter Davies accompanied Tottenham's footballers on a trip to Nantes in November 1971, he wryly observed their horror as they were served steaks with little daubs of garlic butter. 'They all said they hated garlic,' he noted, and 'they tore at it furiously, swearing, and wiped all marks of it from their steak'.[16]

Within just a few years, however, even working-class tastes were changing. By 1975, Newcastle United's Malcolm MacDonald was telling *Shoot* that he liked 'all types of food . . . Indian, Italian, Greek or plain old English'. By now there were already thousands of Indian takeaways from Scotland to Cornwall, thanks to the flood of Commonwealth migrants in the 1950s and early 1960s, while in 1976 the number of Chinese takeaways officially overtook that of fish and chip shops, with kebab shops not far behind. Then there were the theatrical Italian trattorias with their 'low-slung lighting, strings of empty Chianti bottles, bread-sticks in tumblers, and conically folded napkins of unearthly whiteness and rigidity', as one writer put it in 1974, or the Greek and Cypriot tavernas that sprang up during the political turmoil of the early 1970s which drove thousands of refugees to London. Increasingly, too, foreign foods were finding their way into the ordinary British household, from beef goulash and lamb moussaka to coq au vin and chilli con carne. 'Why should you wait for a dinner party to enjoy them?' asked adverts for Brie and Camembert in 1978. Even the laziest cooks had the opportunity to experiment, thanks to Vesta's mouthwatering 'Package Tour' ready meals. From Italy came Beef Risotto ('the real taste of the Continent'); from India came Curry and Rice with Chicken ('Pineapple, apples and sultanas, coriander and cumin make this delicious curry'); and from China, with added political correctness, came Chow Mein with Crispy Noodles ('You like, yes?').[17]

The other obvious European innovation was wine, hitherto a treat reserved for the rich and famous, or perhaps for special occasions, but now an essential ingredient of even a modest suburban dinner party. Tottenham's players might hate garlic, but their manager Bill Nicholson liked his wine; Davies noted that his taste for Sauternes was 'the only sliver of middle-class life which appears to have rubbed off on him'. When Nicholson had been growing up in the 1920s, one of nine children in a working-class Yorkshire family, a taste for wine would have been condemned as sissified French pretentiousness. As late as 1950, only 5 per cent of the population drank wine once a week or more, 36 per cent drank it on special occasions only, and 59 per cent said they never touched it at all. But tastes were changing. In 1960, the British drank 3.6 pints of wine per head per year; by 1971 they drank 7 pints, by 1973 9 pints, by 1975 11 pints and by 1980 almost 20 pints. One obvious reason was that it was cheaper than ever, with the duty having been slashed when Britain joined the EEC; another was that people picked up the taste on holiday; a third was that wines were advertised more successfully, being associated with glamour, luxury and ambition, and aimed particularly at young women. As *The Times*'s wine critic Pamela Vandyke Pryce pointed out in 1973, there was still a long way to go, given the keenness for chilling wines to 'iced lolly texture', filling glasses to the absolute brim or knocking back vast amounts of Blue Nun, Black Tower and Mateus Rosé. 'You'll like this, sir,' a wine waiter tells a diner in one memorable *Private Eye* cartoon. 'It'll make you very drunk.' Still, although later generations poured scorn on the wine-drinkers of the 1970s – Alan Partridge, for example, is a big fan of Blue Nun – the point is not that British tastes were inherently terrible but that they were simply untutored, since the great majority had only started drinking wine within the last twenty years. But then as Basil Fawlty so rightly observes, it is 'always a pleasure to find someone who appreciates the *boudoir* of the grape. I'm afraid most of the people we get in here don't know a Bordeaux from a claret.'[18]

The government formally opened talks with the members of the EEC in Brussels at the end of October 1970. Originally, the head of the team had been Anthony Barber, but when he was promoted to Chancellor, his place was taken by the much more colourful Geoffrey Rippon, who had a quick mind, a healthy impatience with details, a fondness for large cigars and – unusually for the time – a telephone installed in his car, much to the amazement of his officials. As on previous occasions, the talks were mind-numbingly boring to all but the most dedicated Euro-enthusiast, with endless haggling over New Zealand cheese and butter, Caribbean sugar, the Community tariff, and economic issues such as sterling's role as a world currency. Tedious as they might seem, however, these were hardly unimportant issues: the Common Fisheries Policy, for example, proved a bitter bone of contention for years afterwards, with British trawlermen complaining that they had been done out of a living by the government's surrender to European interests.

At the time, the Labour Party protested furiously that Heath had caved in to his Continental chums, and in later years Heath's name was mud among Conservative Euro-sceptics, who blamed him for Britain's excessive contribution to the EEC budget (later partly recovered by Mrs Thatcher) and the abomination of the Common Agricultural Policy, a gigantic subsidy scheme for inefficient, obstreperous French farmers. But the brutal truth is that the British were hardly in a position to dictate their own terms. If they had entered the Common Market in the 1950s, as the Europeans had urged, then they would have had a much bigger say in its rules and conventions, so the Common Agricultural Policy might never have got off the ground. But by 1970 it was too late; as the chief civil servant in the negotiating team, Sir Con O'Neill, later noted, the British were faced with a staggering 13,000 typewritten pages of European enactments, all reflecting compromises between the existing members, and they were hardly likely to make friends by demanding that all these issues be reopened. The only solution, O'Neill said, was to 'swallow the lot, and swallow it now', which inevitably meant bad bargains on dairy products, fishing rights and the EEC budget. That was the price Britain paid for having stayed aloof for so long; the choice was not between bad terms and good terms, but between bad terms and nothing.[19]

Whatever the outcome of the negotiations, it would all be for nothing if the French again vetoed Britain's application. From the very beginning, Heath knew that he had to succeed where Macmillan and Wilson had failed, persuading the French that Britain was genuinely committed to the cause of European unity, and was not merely a stalking horse for American influence. 'It was to the French that we should pay attention,'

Douglas Hurd wrote later, summarizing his master's views. 'We must gain friends in France and outmanoeuvre our enemies.' This was easier said than done, of course. Fortunately, General de Gaulle, Britain's chief antagonist in the past, was off the scene, having died suddenly in November 1970. His successor, Georges Pompidou, was a shrewd banker with rural origins and pragmatic instincts, not a nationalistic showman like de Gaulle. Even so, Pompidou was not necessarily sympathetic to Britain's application; indeed, he harboured a deep suspicion of Harold Wilson, dating from an unfortunate incident in 1967 when Wilson had turned up late and dishevelled for an official dinner because he had been at a Commons debate on Vietnam – a moment, Pompidou thought, that spoke volumes about Wilson's subservience to American interests. But as luck would have it, Heath was already a good friend of Pompidou's private secretary Michel Jobert, whom he had first met, bizarrely, on a beach in Spain in 1960. Rather implausibly, Heath had gone to Spain to try to lose weight, and was lying on the beach one day when Jobert came across and murmured: 'If you don't eat any more, you'll never be able to deal with de Gaulle.' The diet was forgotten; the two men called for sherry and prawns, and a close friendship was born. A few years later, when Heath gave a series of lectures on European integration, he made sure to send them to Jobert. 'Pompidou knows that you are serious,' the Frenchman reported back a few weeks later.[20]

In May 1971, Heath and Pompidou were due to meet for the first time in Paris, and Heath prepared as though he were a schoolboy facing an exam that would decide his entire future. 'For hours on end the Prime Minister sat under a tree, dunking biscuits in tea,' Douglas Hurd remembered. 'Experts were produced individually and in groups . . . They each had their session under the tree, while ducks from the park waddled amorously across the lawn, and over the wall on the Horse Guards workmen banged together the stands for the Queen's Birthday Parade.' It was clear, however, that mood music was more important than mastery of detail: what mattered was to persuade Pompidou that the British were ready to become good Europeans. Interviewed on *Panorama* a few days before the summit, Pompidou explained that the 'crux of the matter is that there is a European conception or idea', and 'the question to be ascertained is whether the United Kingdom's conception is indeed European'. He even mischievously told a French newspaper that Britain must agree that French was the main language of the EEC, because

English was the language of the United States. But Pompidou had not taken into account Heath's capacity for linguistic vandalism, for when Broadstairs' favourite son recorded a message to be shown on French television, the results were truly excruciating. The next day, when Heath arrived at Orly airport and said a few words in French for the cameras, the welcoming party had to stifle snorts of derision. Heath might consider himself a good European, but never had the language of Voltaire and Flaubert been so cruelly abused.[21]

Fortunately, Pompidou was in a forgiving mood, and when the two men met at last on 20 May, the talks were a triumph. Leaving their officials behind, Heath and Pompidou decided to thrash out the issues on their own, accompanied only by their interpreters. They 'clicked', Con O'Neill recalled later. 'They liked each other and they trusted each other.' Outside, their advisers waited nervously, anxious that their masters were merely exchanging amiable pleasantries without getting down to brass tacks. But they need not have worried. At the lavish banquet at the Elysée Palace that night, wrote one reporter, the room 'glowed with the warmth and satisfaction of an estrangement ended and a friendship regained'. Pompidou's remarks at the dinner were notably generous – 'Through two men who are talking to each other, two peoples are trying to find each other again' – and the next morning's talks continued in similar vein. Indeed, they went so well that, instead of calling a press conference immediately after lunch, Pompidou suggested they keep talking. It meant that Heath would have to miss an important race in his beloved *Morning Cloud*, but in the interests of Britain's European future, he thought it was worth it.

At last, at nine that evening, the two men emerged for a press conference in the splendid gilded Salon des Fêtes, the very room in which de Gaulle had announced his devastating veto in 1963. By now the waiting press-men were convinced that something had gone badly wrong, and even Heath's senior advisers were pale with nerves since – in typical style – their boss had decided to tease them by saying nothing and looking as miserable as possible. Their surprise was therefore all the greater when Pompidou broke the good news. 'Many people believed that Great Britain was not and did not wish to become European, and that Britain wanted to enter the Community only so as to destroy it or to divert it from its objectives,' he said. 'Many people also thought that France was ready to use every pretext to place in the end a fresh veto on Britain's entry. Well, ladies and gentlemen, you see before you tonight two men who are convinced of the contrary.' Even Heath could not suppress a broad smile at that. 'It was marvellous to see the looks of astonishment on the faces of so many of those present,' he later wrote. 'We had secured success and also triumphed over the media. For me personally, it was a wildly exciting moment. Just forty years after my first visit to Paris, I had been able to play a part in bringing about the unity of Europe.'[22]

With Pompidou's blessing, the British team now found the waters a lot smoother. The French negotiators adjusted their positions overnight, deals were reached on everything from New Zealand butter to the sterling balances abroad, and at the end of June Geoffrey Rippon returned in triumph from Luxembourg, 'wearing a red tie and with a scarlet hand-kerchief sprouting jauntily from his jacket pocket', reported *The Times*, as though he had picked up a dash of Continental flamboyance. Even Heath's men privately admitted that the terms were not perfect, but to have got them at all was a great achievement, and there seemed every chance that Britain could press for changes in the years to come. Mean-while, Heath wasted little time in parading his accomplishment before the British people. On 7 July, the government issued a White Paper setting out the terms, accompanied by a glossy 16-page brochure on the case for British membership. 'Either we choose to enter the Community and join in building a strong Europe on the foundations which the Six have laid,' said the White Paper, 'or we choose to stand aside from this great enterprise and seek to maintain our interests from the narrow – and narrowing – base we have known in recent years.' And on television that night, Heath was in typically sweeping but banal form. 'For twenty-five years we've been looking for something to get us going again,' he told the nation. 'Now here it is. We must recognize it for what it is. We have the chance of new greatness. Now we must take it.'[23]

What was conspicuously lacking from Heath's case for joining the EEC was any admission that it might affect Britain's national sovereignty and self-government. In his broadcast to the nation, he talked in terms of renewing Britain's prestige, explaining that joining the EEC would be 'a chance to lead, not to follow', allowing Britain to 'fulfil the role we have played so often in the past'. As his biographer remarks, one of the paradoxes of Heath's European vision was that it was rooted in 'sturdy English patriotism', with the Prime Minister convinced that Europe was the ideal platform on which to display Britain's inherent greatness. But it made no concession to the argument that, by joining the EEC, Britain would be giving away its national sovereignty. In his fine history of Britain in Europe, Hugo Young suggests that sovereignty did not seem a key priority in the early 1970s, with economic issues apparently much more important. But not only did maverick Euro-sceptics like Enoch Powell, Michael Foot and Tony Benn make great play of Heath's alleged surrender of sovereignty and the European threat to the sanctity of Parliament, but the thirty-nine Tories who ultimately voted against the bid often cited sovereignty as their central concern. Rather than meet their arguments head on, Heath preferred to sweep them under the carpet. His White Paper claimed that there was no question of 'any erosion of essential national sovereignty' but instead proposed 'a sharing and an enlargement of individual national sovereignty in the general interest', which was so vague as to be practically meaningless. Meanwhile, Heath's ministers deliberately avoided admitting that European Community laws would take precedence over British law, even though they knew perfectly well that this was the case.

This does not mean, however, that the British people were duped by a sinister federalist conspiracy. Rather, as one historian writes, they were 'told what they wanted to hear', becoming partners in a 'compact between a disingenuous governing class and a people too preoccupied with the economic problems of the day to pick a fight over a constitutional issue which even the most politically astute knew would not begin to affect their lives for many years to come'. From Heath's point of view, this was not deception so much as careful political strategy – something all too rare during his time in office. 'If Heath had laid it on the line, what he thought it would lead to,' Denis Healey said later, 'he wouldn't have got it through. He thought it was more important to get it through, even if it was ignorant and misunderstanding acquiescence rather than support, than to let it go. And I suspect he was right about that.'[24]

Since Harold Wilson had been looking forward to taking Britain into Europe himself, the spectacle of Heath and Pompidou exchanging smiles like love-struck teenagers must have been deeply infuriating. As grammar school and Oxford boys from modest backgrounds, as dynamic modernizers fascinated by the machinery of government, the two rivals had a lot in common. For years Wilson had held the upper hand; during the late 1960s he had dismissed Heath's clumsy attacks in the Commons with almost embarrassing ease. All that had changed, however, in a few hours in June 1970. Once the cheeky, cheerful prodigy of British politics, the former Boy Scout had taken defeat very badly indeed. It was a 'terrible trauma' for him, one aide said, while others remarked that Wilson seemed exhausted, demoralized, even burned out, a careworn and untidy figure who relied on handouts from his very shady business friends just to keep his office going. It was revealing that when the BBC's David Dimbleby asked about his finances for the controversial documentary *Yesterday's Men* in 1971, Wilson kicked up an enormous fuss with the BBC governors. In the old days, when he was younger, fitter and quicker-witted, he would simply have come up with a smart reply. And even in the Commons, where he had once carried all before him, he seemed tired and apathetic, his speeches perfunctory when they had once been dazzling. As Anthony Sampson reported in 1971, he seemed shrunken, diminished, 'mesmerised by his memory', forever harking back to the past when once his eyes had been firmly fixed on the future.[25]

In some ways this made Wilson the ideal leader for a miserable, backward-looking party. The Labour Party was a deeply unhappy ship in the early 1970s, defeat having cast it into yet another debilitating bout of feuding and factionalism. Its problems ran deep: after the humiliating devaluation of the pound, Wilson's approval rating had sunk to unprecedented depths, while the party had been crushed in one local election after another, losing control of cities like Sheffield and Sunderland, as well as all but four of London's thirty-two boroughs. Beyond that, however, lay a deeper problem. As the party's industrial heartlands were transformed by economic change and social mobility, so its core vote entered a steady decline. Even in the late 1950s, political experts had wondered whether Labour could ever hold its own in an increasingly affluent society, but Wilson's invocation of science and modernization had temporarily papered over the cracks. Now, in defeat, there was a palpable sense of horizons narrowing as Labour turned inwards, relying more and more on the council tenants of the North, Scotland and Wales, on public-sector workers and on the trade unions. Paradoxically, its parliamentary representatives were increasingly well-educated and middle-class, their politics driven by conscience rather than class. In 1966, the Labour benches contained more university graduates than the Tory ones for the first time, and by October 1974 no fewer than 182 Labour MPs had university degrees.[26]

Revealingly, they included 22 journalists, 25 university lecturers, 32 barristers and 38 schoolteachers, but only 19 miners – a far cry from the first Labour representatives at the dawn of the century. And many of the newcomers burned with righteous anger, impatient to see injustice banished by a genuine social revolution. For Wilson they had only contempt; increasingly, they looked for inspiration to the messianic figure of Tony Benn. Once the former Viscount Stansgate had been Wilson's semi-comic technological protégé, safely confined to redesigning stamps and opening the Post Office Tower. But with Labour in the wilderness, Benn took the opportunity to reinvent himself as a latter-day Puritan demagogue, the heir to the Levellers and champion of participatory democracy, workers' control and massive nationalization. Many of his colleagues openly scoffed at his ostentatious gestures of proletarian solidarity, such as when he formally asked the BBC to stop calling him Anthony Wedgwood Benn, or when he deleted all references to his expensive education from *Who's Who*. But mocking Benn was now a risky business: nobody had more support among the high-minded young activists who increasingly dominated Labour's constituency parties.[27]

Even without the issue of Europe, Labour would have slid into bickering and factionalism after 1970. Wilson's government had been disfigured by almost unbelievably self-serving disloyalty from his senior ministers, who seemed to spend more time plotting against their leader than actually doing their jobs, while Wilson made matters worse by trying to play his 'crown princes' off against one another. And once he had lost his image as a winner, he also lost his ability to restrain their mutual dislike. By 1971 the party seemed to be subsiding into indiscipline, with senior figures trying to outdo one another by moving ever further to the left. Looking around that year's Labour Party conference, one journalist wrote that he could almost see in the rows of faces 'the layers of political geology' as the rock face crumbled, from the 'pacifists with their bright eyes and violent convictions' to the 'small bands of Marxists', from the 'cranky fringe parties handing out angry pamphlets in the foyer' to the 'Oxford intellectuals' who still believed they ought to be running the show. It was no wonder that, even then, political commentators wondered whether the party could survive without a major split. In January 1974 Wilson's former Commonwealth Secretary George Thomson, now one of Britain's two European Commissioners, told a friend that even if Labour won the next election 'the internal strains would be so great as more or less to paralyse it'. If Labour lost, he mused presciently, 'he thought it would split, giving rise to a new Social Democratic Party'. He was a few years too early; but he was right all the same.[28]

It was around Europe that the fault lines developed. Labour had always had its fair share of European enthusiasts, most of them members of the liberal coterie that had gathered around Hugh Gaitskell in the late 1950s and early 1960s (even though Gaitskell himself was passionately anti-European). To them, the cause of Europe had an almost religious intensity: it was the cause, they thought, of tolerance, of progressivism, of liberalism, of cosmopolitanism, and their high priest was a man who embodied all of these characteristics, or at least tried to, the former Chancellor Roy Jenkins. But they were never more than a minority, and their generally moderate politics (regarded as right-wing by Labour standards) automatically made them targets of suspicion. 'The pro-Market fanatics', said the firebrand Barbara Castle, were 'sanctimonious middle-class hypocrites', and plenty of her colleagues agreed with her. There was a long tradition of Little England insularity inside the Labour Party, an introverted desire to build socialism in one country, a Methodist suspicion for the corrupt Catholic ways of the wine-drenched Continent, which might appeal to Tories but could never compete with an honest pint of workers' ale (or in Tony Benn's case, a gallon of tea).

By the early 1970s, this had evolved into the firm belief that the Common Market was a millionaires' conspiracy, designed to crush British socialism for ever. This was, after all, an age in which there was no dirtier word in the socialist lexicon than 'multinational', with companies being excoriated not just because they were pillars of capitalism but because they were owned by foreigners. The EEC was therefore the perfect target – not least because it was so close to the despised Heath's heart. It was a 'rich nations' club', Michael Foot told the voters of Ebbw Vale, opposed to 'the interests of British democracy [and] the health of our economy'. It would destroy 'the real power of the people to control their destiny', agreed Neil Kinnock – this, of course, some years before he became a European Commissioner himself. 'Beating capitalism in one country is enough of a task. Beating it in several countries – without even having a solid domestic base – goes too far even for me.'[29]

It was in the unmistakably English surroundings of Blackpool, at the Labour conference in October 1970, that Wilson first realized he had a serious problem on his hands. In theory at least, he could ignore the fact that the conference had come dangerously close to endorsing outright opposition to EEC entry. But he could not ignore what happened in January 1971, when more than a hundred of his own MPs signed an early day motion opposing EEC entry 'on terms so far envisaged', or in May, when Jim Callaghan gave a blistering speech warning that British membership of the Common Market would mean a 'complete rupture of our identity' and a retreat into 'continental claustrophobia'. In a memorably chauvinist passage, Callaghan poured justified contempt on Pompidou's suggestion that French should be the sole language of Europe. That 'the language of Chaucer, Shakespeare and Milton must in future be regarded as an American import', Callaghan said mockingly, was totally unacceptable. 'If we are to prove our Europeanism by accepting that French is the dominant language of the Community, then the answer is quite clear and I will say it in French to prevent any misunderstanding: *Non, merci beaucoup*.'[30]

This was good knockabout stuff, but for Wilson it was deeply disturbing. Although he and Callaghan got on fairly well, they had been undeclared rivals since the early 1960s, and the popular former Home Secretary was seen as embodying the solid centre of the party, the darling of the trade unions, the 'keeper of the cloth cap'. By his very presence he seemed to define the centre ground; where he went, scores of Labour MPs followed. And since Wilson could never shake the suspicion that Callaghan was plotting a coup against him, he decided to step in before his rival laid claim to the anti-European mantle. 'He is totally obsessed by the leadership question now,' noted Tony Benn after they met to discuss Europe in June. 'The risk that Jim Callaghan might stand against him is something that worries him very much.'

Never mind that Wilson himself had once been all for EEC membership; as he had shown before, nobody in British politics was a better or more unscrupulous adept of the dark arts of party one-upmanship. So, after months of hedging and waiting and vague ambiguities, he chose the occasion of the party's Special Conference on the Common Market, held in Westminster on 17 July, to nail his colours to the mast. With typical Wilson cleverness, he did not come out against the principle of Europe, only the practice. The problem, he said, was the terms: 'I reject the assertion that the terms this Conservative Government have obtained are the terms the Labour Government asked for, would have asked for, would have been bound to accept.' Nobody believed him, but that was almost beside the point. 'It's all over bar the shouting now,' wrote Benn, 'and he feels he has warded off Jim Callaghan's assault on the leadership, which he almost certainly has.'[31]

But that was far from the end of the matter. Labour's pro-European wing – the 'Marketeers', as they were known – were horrified by Wilson's apparent treachery, especially since it confirmed what many of them had suspected for years: that he was a duplicitous, untrustworthy political fixer, unfit to wear the mantle of their beloved Hugh Gaitskell. Above all, Wilson's most dangerous rival, Roy Jenkins, was outraged at his perfidy. Jenkins himself was not exactly the soul of self-denying constancy: even while serving as Wilson's Chancellor in the late 1960s, he had maintained a network of personal supporters in the Commons, and on more than one occasion came close to launching a leadership putsch. In June, he had even tried to strike a deal with Wilson, promising that if the leader stayed true to the European cause, then 'there could be no question of the Labour Europeans joining in any intrigue with Callaghan or anyone else to embarrass him, still less to endeavour to replace him'. But this, of course, was little less than blackmail: if Wilson had accepted, he would not only have alienated much of the left and centre of his own party, he would have made himself a prisoner of the Jenkins camp, his leadership dependent on his European enthusiasm. Fortunately for him, his principles were endlessly flexible, so he was able to wriggle out of it. But Jenkins's principles were not. He already cut a slightly semi-detached figure in the Labour Party of the early 1970s, a sleek and self-consciously sophisticated lover of croquet, tennis, fine wines and aristocratic women. 'With his big smooth head he looks like an aristocratic egghead,' one profile remarked in 1971, calling him 'the most improbable leader of a workers' party'. Even then, observers commented that he seemed 'more like a Liberal than a Labour leader', more at home with the memory of Asquith, whose biography he had written, than with the modern reality of Arthur Scargill. And as Jenkins saw it, Europe left no room for compromise. It was 'a battle between outward-looking tolerance and generosity of spirit on the one hand', wrote his friend David Marquand, 'and mean-minded Pecksniffian narrowness on the other'.[32]

Jenkins issued his declaration of war just two days after Wilson had come out against the terms of the EEC bid. At a raucous meeting of the Parliamentary Labour Party, he insisted that 'socialism in one country' (or 'pull up the drawbridge and revolutionise the fortress', as he witheringly put it) was 'not a policy, just a slogan'. The atmosphere sizzled with revivalist passion; Jenkins later wrote that the speech attracted more 'violent applause' than any other of his career, with many Labour MPs hammering their desks in approval and one Scotsman even banging his shoes on the table, as if in homage to Khrushchev. On the left, however, the reaction was horror and disgust. In the Commons smoking room afterwards, left-wing Euro-sceptics huddled in angry conclaves, and as Jenkins passed, Barbara Castle, no stranger to hysterical over-reaction, said bitterly: 'Roy, I used to respect you a great deal, but I will never do so again as long as I live.' As for Wilson, he characteristically saw the issue purely in terms of his own leadership, not in terms of Britain's long-term future in Europe. The next morning, Tony Benn found him 'extremely agitated', issuing wild threats against Jenkins and talking of walking away from the party leadership, but underneath all the bluster 'desperately insecure and unhappy'. All in all, it was a pretty pathetic spectacle of introversion and feuding, played out in the full gaze of the media and the public. And with Jenkins adamant that Britain's European future must come before party unity, there seemed little prospect of an end to hostilities. 'I saw it in the context of the first Reform Bill, the repeal of the Corn Laws, Gladstone's Home Rule Bills, the Lloyd George Budget and the Parliament Bill, the Munich Agreement and the May 1940 votes,' Jenkins wrote later.[33]

What finally pushed Jenkins overboard was a wheeze that Benn himself had cooked up at the end of 1970, which was for the next Labour government to call a national referendum on the issue of Europe. At first, Wilson rejected the idea outright; at the time, only Callaghan realized that it offered the ideal way to paper over Labour's European divisions, remarking sagely: 'Tony may be launching a little rubber life-raft which we will all be glad of in a year's time.' But by the beginning of 1972 Wilson had come round. Although a referendum would be unprecedented, it was the perfect way of appeasing the sceptics without completely conceding the issue. Jenkins, however, loathed the idea of referendums, not least because this most self-consciously elitist of politicians saw them as 'the likely enemy of progressive causes from the abolition of capital punishment to race relations legislation'. When the Shadow Cabinet voted to back the scheme in March 1972, Jenkins demanded the right to speak against the decision, and when this was denied, he promptly resigned as deputy leader. 'It was the only way he could see to lance a swelling boil of misery and guilt,' his friend David Marquand wrote later, and Jenkins's letter seethed with righteous anger, denouncing Wilson's 'relentless and short-sighted search for tactical advantage'. In the process, however, he comprehensively demolished his last chance of becoming Labour leader. Like the last deputy leader to resign, George Brown, he made no secret of his bitter contempt for Wilson's endless compromises, but his bombshell was no more effective than Brown's. Although Jenkins still commanded the ardent support of a small group of right-wing admirers, his reputation within the broader Labour Party, where loyalty and solidarity were still seen as the supreme virtues, was in ruins. A Harris poll in October found that 79 per cent of Labour supporters preferred Wilson, with a pitiful 5 per cent picking Jenkins. A few days later the party conference formally approved the referendum scheme, and the twin issues of Europe and the leadership had been settled at last.[34]

Roy Hattersley wrote later that the day Jenkins resigned was the moment 'the old Labour coalition began to collapse'. In the light of what happened later, it did indeed look like a dress rehearsal for the launch of the SDP, with two other members of the Shadow Cabinet, George Thomson and Harold Lever, resigning in sympathy and Bill Rodgers, David Owen, Dickson Mabon and Dick Taverne all leaving their junior shadow positions. Even in the short term, it did tremendous damage to Wilson's reputation. As the *Telegraph*'s Colin Welch wryly remarked, the gulf between the public images of Jenkins and Wilson was enormous: on the one hand 'an almost saintly figure, heroic, shining, guided only by honour and high principles, even to the sacrifice of his own career'; on the other, 'a dark serpentine crawling trimmer, shifty and shuffling, devious, untrustworthy, constant only in the pursuit of self-preservation and narrow party advantage'. Wilson himself found this deeply infuriating: during a Shadow Cabinet meeting, he once snapped: 'I've been wading in shit for three months to allow others to indulge their conscience.' By now, however, there was not much he could do about it; trapped into a position of wriggling ambiguity, he had become for many observers the incarnation of everything that was wrong with British politics in the 1970s: its narrowness, its short-termism, its petty positioning, its navel-gazing introversion. On the Labour right, he was regarded with something like repugnance; even on the left, he was seen as merely the best of a bad bunch. He was 'the principal apostle of cynicism, the unwitting evangelist of disillusion', declared an extraordinary leader in the *New Statesman* in June 1972. 'We say it with reluctance but we believe it to be true. Mr Wilson has now sunk to a position where his very presence in Labour's Leadership pollutes the atmosphere of politics.'[35]

This was strong stuff, though not entirely baseless. It might well have been better for all concerned if Wilson had retired after 1970, bequeathing the leadership to the tougher, more reassuring Callaghan; certainly his historical reputation would be much higher if he had. And yet there was something to be said for his undeniably slippery tactics during the European debate. At a time when Labour might easily have torn itself apart, Wilson at least managed to hold the party together. Even Denis Healey, who generally held his leader in very low esteem, thought that he showed 'great courage in refusing absolutely to reject British entry in principle'. Whereas Callaghan would probably have demanded a stance of outright opposition, and Jenkins would have split the party by declaring wholehearted support, Wilson's implausible complaints about 'the terms' actually kept the principle of European membership alive. What this meant is that when Labour returned to office, it was committed to holding a referendum rather than automatically taking Britain out of Europe. Wilson may have looked like a weasel, but in the long term, his approach worked: Labour stayed together, and Britain stayed in Europe. It was sheer 'duplicity', writes the pro-European Hugo Young, but it was 'nonetheless one of Wilson's finer hours'. Of course, Britain's European destiny was above all Edward Heath's achievement. But his great rival perhaps deserves a share of the credit – or the blame.[36]

While Labour's senior figures were busy tearing into one another with the brutal relish of First Division footballers on a muddy Saturday afternoon, the Prime Minister had already turned his thoughts to the battle for public opinion. In May 1970, he had made the vague but ringing promise that Britain would enter the EEC only with the 'full-hearted consent' of its Parliament and people. But with just one in five voters backing European membership at the time of the election, winning public consent would clearly take some doing. Even after negotiations had begun, Gallup found that one in three people thought their standard of living would decline if Britain joined the EEC, while fully 73 per cent thought that their food bills would rise 'a lot'. Even in April 1971, just before Heath's historic summit with Georges Pompidou, nearly 70 per cent of the public said they opposed British membership, most citing rising prices as their biggest concern. But although the economic dimension was clearly the most important, many people did have reasons that were more cultural, almost spiritual, for resisting European entry. Asked in July whether they would lose their British identity if the country went into the Common Market, 27 per cent thought 'a lot' and 62 per cent 'some'. If Heath wanted to win them over, his adviser Michael Wolff told him, his appeal must not only address the prices issue, but should be 'based on high ideals and national destiny and should be particularly aimed at youth'.[37]

Heath's answer was the biggest state publicity campaign since the war, with a Cabinet committee coordinating a vast range of nationwide talks and events, including almost 300 public speeches by government ministers. Not even holidaymakers were safe: on beaches across the country, families basking in the summer sun were accosted by girls in tight T-shirts with the logo 'SAY YES TO EUROPE!', who were handing out copies of a free newspaper called the *British European*. Inside, graphs showed Europe's faster growth rate and the great welter of economic benefits that would come Britain's way, while national icons such as Kenneth More and Bobby Moore assured readers that they were all for European cooperation. But the message was not all food bills and productivity charts: 'EUROPE IS FUN!' screamed the cover, next to a photograph of a Page Three lovely in a skimpy Union Jack bikini. 'More Work But More Play Too!' Needless to say, this kind of stuff drew widespread derision: in the Commons, one Labour MP mockingly charged that Heath's ministers were 'as frenetic in their enthusiasm to convert public opinion as the Chinese Christian who decided to baptise his troops with a hosepipe'. But they were undeterred: even the government's White Paper on the terms for entry was recruited into the campaign, with no fewer than 5 million copies distributed in Post Offices as a 16-page booklet with a fetching green and black cover. It was a telling sign of public indifference, though, that the reaction was 'muted enthusiasm and often perceptible lack of interest'. In Trafalgar Square's Post Office, which had the longest counter in Britain, the booklets were piled almost to the ceiling, but they were 'barely touched' by customers. 'Most people are rather bored by it all,' explained a middle-aged housewife. 'They are sure we are going in anyway.'[38]

In the press, the mood was overwhelmingly pro-European. Both *The Times* and the *Guardian* were extremely keen from the very beginning, as were the *Sunday Times*, the *Observer* and *The Economist*, while the *Telegraph*, reflecting its loyalty to Heath, moved off the fence and into a position of unquestioning support, telling its readers that when MPs finally came to decide the question, 'they will be passing a judgement on a civilisation, a culture, an economic union, a nascent defence capability, above all an idea of Europe that cannot be rejected without grievous results for Europe's future and our own'. The *Mail* had been wavering since the early 1960s, but as soon as Wilson and the trade unions declared their opposition, it announced it was strongly in favour. So was the *Sun*, which boasted that it had been in favour of EEC membership for its entire lifetime, while the bestselling *Mirror* ran a stream of fiercely pro-European pieces. 'Are a people who for centuries were the makers of history – and who can again help to make history – to become mere lookers-on from an off-shore island of dwindling significance?' demanded a ferocious editorial in July 1971. Even its lighter pieces often had a pro-Market slant: there was even a 'Guide to the Euro-Dollies', reporting on how they rated as kissers. Only the *Express* stood 'alone – with the people', as it put it, warning that the talks had been 'a victory won by French diplomacy over British interests'. It was therefore delighted when Prince Philip, making one of his trademark public interventions, waded into the debate to attack the Common Agricultural Policy. 'The people admire his good sense,' said the *Express*, 'and wish it were more widely shared by our rulers.' But its competitors were less impressed. The Prince was a 'chump', said the *Mirror*, while the *Sun* thought it was high time 'our sailor Prime Minister told the sailor Prince which way the wind blows'.[39]

In cultural circles, too, the mood was strongly pro-European. When the magazine *Encounter* organized a symposium of writers and intellectuals in the summer of 1971, forty-six respondents were in favour and only seventeen against. Still, the sceptics were joined by such impressive names as Anthony Burgess, who claimed that 'England is to be absorbed, her own distinctive character sordined, and the end of a great Empire to be completed in the bastardisation of a great empire-building nation', while Kenneth Tynan told *The Times* that the EEC was 'the most blatant historical vulgarity since the Thousand Year Reich'. It was a 'capitalist bloc', Tynan wrote in his diary, sounding 'the deathknell of socialism in

Western Europe', although the fact that these thoughts followed a long anecdote about Britt Ekland's knickers rather deflated the impression of progressive commitment. But not all theatrical diarists of the day were sceptics, for Kenneth Williams sent Heath a letter in May 1971 'saying I admire him very much; do hope he gets us into Europe'. And even *Doctor Who* came out in favour of the Common Market. A week after Heath had signed the Treaty of Accession in January 1972, the Doctor and his companion Jo arrived on the planet Peladon, which had just applied to join the Galactic Federation, much to the displeasure of its High Priest and presumably the Peladonian equivalents of James Callaghan, Kenneth Tynan and the *Daily Express*. The High Priest insists that the Federation will 'exploit us for our minerals, enslave us with their machines, corrupt us with their technology', but he is eventually unmasked as a double-dealing blackguard. Meanwhile Jon Pertwee's Doctor, like some infinitely more dashing Ted Heath, convinces Peladon's King that only Federation membership can bring the modernization his people need. But the Doctor has to come to terms with his own prejudices, too; for among the members of the Federation are the once-terrifying Ice Warriors, now reformed. At first these towering Martian reptiles seem certain to prove the villains of the piece – but once they have saved the Doctor's life, it becomes clear that they are simply *Doctor Who*'s answer to Willy Brandt and Helmut Schmidt.[40]

Not surprisingly, public opinion began to shift under this barrage of commentary. What is clear from the polls is that most people did not really know what to think about the EEC, and did not care much either way. Public support ebbed and flowed with bewildering speed: just a year after 70 per cent of the public had proclaimed themselves against, polls in July 1971 showed the pro and anti camps dead level – but then a few months later the pro camp had collapsed again and the opponents were 12 per cent ahead. Conservative supporters naturally rallied to Heath, and local constituencies reported overwhelming support by the end of 1971, but there was no sense of a 'Great Debate'. The historian A. J. P. Taylor grandly claimed that it was 'the most decisive moment in British history since the Norman Conquest or the loss of America', but most people were content to follow the advice of their favourite politicians or columnists rather than dig out the White Paper and decide for themselves. Perhaps the best reflection of public opinion was the experience of the Conservative official who was sent to Liverpool on a mission to gauge local attitudes to Europe. On arrival, he stopped a woman in the street and asked what she thought of the Common Market. 'Where are they building it, love?' she asked.[41]

Once the terms had been agreed, Heath's central priority was to get the appropriate legislation through the House of Commons. This was trickier than it looked, since there were bound to be Tory rebels, and he might need to rely on support from the Labour right. Of all his parliamentary critics, by far the most persistent, elegant and passionate was his implacable adversary Enoch Powell, once a keen supporter of the Common Market, but now the fiercest of sceptics. As early as February 1970, Powell had warned that entry into the EEC would mean absorption 'economically, legally, commercially and politically' into a European super-state. And as Heath's negotiations neared their goal, Powell's warnings became ever more apocalyptic. If Britain signed the Treaty of Rome, he told the Commons in January 1971, it would 'lead to an irreversible alienation of our separate sovereignty'. He denied that Britain even had a basic European identity: her place had always been with her back to Europe 'and her face towards the oceans and the continents of the world'. The battle in the Commons, he said, was a 'life and death struggle for its independence and supreme authority', a struggle 'as surely about the future of Britain's nationhood as were the combats which raged in the skies over southern England in the autumn of 1940. The gladiators are few; their weapons are but words; and yet their fight is everyman's.'[42]

If Powell had merely been a lone maverick, then Heath would have had nothing to worry about. The problem, though, was that at least thirty Conservative MPs, most on the right of the party, shared his views and were expected to vote against the government when it came to the crunch. By the middle of October 1971 the moment of truth was at hand, with the House being asked to give its approval of the government's decision to join the EEC, and the atmosphere crackled with tension, every day bringing fresh reports of 'nose-counting, arm-twisting, weak knees and stiff upper lips'. If Heath had had his way, the government would have ploughed unswervingly onwards, demanding the loyalty of its supporters, and might well have crashed to defeat. But he was lucky to have in Francis Pym an outstandingly clear-sighted Chief Whip, who managed to persuade him – after weeks of trying – that it would be better to allow a free vote on the grounds that he wanted a true reflection of the will of the House, rather than a vote on purely partisan lines. That way, Pym argued, they might lose a few more Tory votes, but they would be able to pick up far more Labour rebels, who would be much happier to defy their party leadership if they were not technically voting with the government. As Heath himself admitted, it was only through 'Pym's wise instinct' that he eventually secured a majority in perhaps the single most important Commons vote of the late twentieth century.[43]

Although the debate opened on 21 October, it was not until a week later, on Thursday 28th, that it reached its nail-biting climax. The atmosphere that night was thick with tension and excitement, the peers' and diplomats' galleries crowded with spectators, even the entrances to the Palace of Westminster jammed with demonstrators, well-wishers and curious passers-by who just wanted to be on hand for a genuinely historic occasion. 'See the Ambassadors' Gallery over there?' muttered an old attendant, showing a nice sense of irony. 'Haven't seen it so full since we used to matter in the world.' Among the observers was Jean Monnet, father of the European project, who had long dreamed of seeing Britain join hands with its neighbours, and now sensed that the moment was at hand. Even many parliamentary correspondents, cynical by nature and by trade, thought that this was Parliament at its best, showing off the varied rhetorical styles of no fewer than 176 MPs, all the way from Dennis Skinner to Enoch Powell. The final night alone offered a fine array of parliamentary talents, from the flamboyant Michael Foot to the languid Reginald Maudling, from the debonair Jeremy Thorpe to the avuncular Jim Callaghan. Even Jeffrey Archer got a word in, although it was only to complain about the queues outside. And while Harold Wilson, who opened the night's debate for the Opposition, was on unusually feeble form – 'soporific' and 'well below the level of events', according to the watching Douglas Hurd – the Prime Minister made a brave stab at matching the momentousness of the occasion. 'I do not think that any Prime Minister has stood at this Box in time of peace and asked the House to take a positive decision of such importance as I am asking it to take tonight,' Heath began, before turning to the great changes that were overtaking the world in the early 1970s – the rise of multi-polar diplomacy, the decline of the Cold War, the emergence of China and the onset of economic globalization. He ended, however, on an unusually personal note:

Throughout my political career, if I may add one personal remark, it is well known that I have had the vision of a Britain in a united Europe; a Britain which would be united economically to Europe and which would be able to influence decisions affecting our own future, and which would enjoy a better standard of life and a fuller life . . .

When we came to the end of the negotiations in 1963, after the veto had been imposed, the negotiator on behalf of India said: 'When you left India some people wept. And when you leave Europe tonight some will weep. And there is no other people in the world of whom these things could be said.' . . . But tonight when this House endorses this Motion many millions of people right across the world will rejoice that we have taken our rightful place in a truly united Europe.[44]

When Heath had sat down, the House voted. The only questions were how many Tories would rebel against their Prime Minister, and how many Labour members would follow Roy Jenkins into the government lobby. Some of Jenkins's friends were seriously worried for his safety: at lunch, Roy Hattersley had excitably suggested organizing a bodyguard to get him out of the Commons and into a getaway car, which even Jenkins thought was ridiculous. Even so, there was a gaggle of Labour MPs waiting for him outside the government lobby, glaring ominously when Jenkins walked past. And when the tellers finally announced the verdict to a packed House – the Ayes 356, the Noes 244 – there was an extraordinary explosion of feeling, a surge of delight and anger of a kind rarely seen in the oak-panelled solemnity of the Commons chamber. 'Fascist bastard!' some Labour loyalists screamed at the serene figure of Jenkins, while others physically pushed and punched his fellow rebels. One Labour member, Reg Freeson, yelled 'Rat-fucker! Rat-fucker!' in Jenkins's face (although the latter arguably had the last laugh, noting with relish in his memoirs that the hard left eventually kicked Freeson out of his Brent seat in favour of Ken Livingstone). 'It was awful', Tony Benn admitted in his diary. But passions were running high: even the usually austere Enoch Powell was not immune. 'It won't do! It won't do!' he shouted at his own front bench.[45]

News of the vote travelled fast. All evening, Harold Macmillan had been waiting on the cliffs beside Dover Castle with a great bonfire prepared by the European Movement, and as the news broke at 10.30, he set the beacon alight to the cheers of 500 onlookers. Far away in the inky night, an answering flame burst into life, a beacon of goodwill on the Pas de Calais. At Folkestone, the town's beauty queen lit seven rockets to symbolize Britain's new partnership with the original Six, and there was enthusiastic applause as the French lit an answering beacon in Boulogne. In West Germany, where broadcasters brought the news live from London, the word YES flashed repeatedly on the screen, and moments later the Chancellor, Willy Brandt, faced the press to announce 'a great day for Europe'. In Hamburg, where Queen Juliana of the Netherlands was attending a gala banquet, more than 300 guests burst into applause when she announced the news. 'This is what I have been waiting for during the last twenty-five years,' Jean Monnet told French television. 'Now it's the turn of the youth of Europe.'[46]

For one man above all it was a moment of supreme joy, the sweetest of his premiership, perhaps of his political career. Edward Heath was never a great man for public displays of emotion; after a drink or two with supporters in the Commons bar, he went on to a party in Admiralty Arch for Jean Monnet, but then quietly slipped away. He thought back to 'the battlefields of France, Belgium and Holland, to the rallies of Nuremberg and to Wendell Willkie's voice, crackling over a radio set at my command post in Normandy in 1944, speaking of "One World".' And when he reached the sanctuary of Number 10, this most reserved, most repressed of men went up to his private sitting room, sat at his clavichord and poured his emotions into Bach's First Prelude and Fugue for the Well-Tempered Clavier. After ten years of struggle, he had realized his dream. But only when the 'still, small voice of the clavichord' rang around the silent room, 'at once so serene, so ordered and so profound', did he find peace and fulfilment at last.[47]

On 22 January 1972, Heath arrived in Brussels for the formal signing of the Treaty of Accession. Many of Britain's most senior politicians, including Macmillan and the Liberal leader Jeremy Thorpe, were on hand to lend moral support; pointedly, Harold Wilson preferred to go to a football match. It should have been another joyous moment, and Heath later recorded that as he sat at the long table in the Palais d'Egmont, the world's press assembled before him, he felt an intense thrill. But as so often in Heath's career, dark clouds all but blotted out the sun. Back home, the news that unemployment had just topped one million had put his government under tremendous pressure, while the miners' strike was just weeks away. And that morning, as he was climbing the great marble steps to the Assembly Hall, a young German woman, infuriated by plans to redevelop Covent Garden, pushed her way through the line of spectators and hurled a bottle of black ink over his head and shoulders. Heath himself admitted that he felt 'shattered'; it took an hour of frantic scrubbing by his aides before he was even vaguely presentable, and newspapers reported that the whole business left him visibly upset. No modern Prime Minister ever had worse luck.[48]

Although Heath had signed the treaty amid all the pomp and ceremony Brussels had to offer, Britain was not quite there yet. For the next few months, the government's legislative energies were absorbed by a gruelling drive to bring British law into line with the Common Market's regulations, which meant getting a European Communities enabling bill through the Commons without it being shot down either by the determined Tory rebels or by Wilson's Labour Party. This was not the stuff of glamorous public politics, of great oratory or tabloid front pages; it called for exhausting, niggling, time-consuming parliamentary management, sapping the government's strength and attention at a time when the miners' strike, the collapse of the Industrial Relations Act and Heath's industrial and economic U-turns were dominating the headlines. Since Jenkins and the Labour rebels, having nailed their colours to the mast of European unity, had now retreated reluctantly into the party fold, the arithmetic was terribly tight, and Heath himself spent hours trying to persuade Tory dissenters not to bring down the government. After 300 hours of debate, however, the government managed to bring down the parliamentary guillotine, an unusual measure that provoked more wrath on the Labour benches but brought the gruelling process to a merciful end. It was no wonder that Heath's Chief Whip, Francis Pym, danced a jig on the Commons floor when the battle was won.[49]

Britain formally joined the European Economic Community on New Year's Day 1973, the beginning of a new chapter in the nation's history.* Already, British representatives had played their part at a summit in October 1972 to discuss the goal of economic and monetary union in 1980, while the nation's first two European Commissioners, Sir Christopher Soames and George Thomson, were making their final preparations to join the new Commission. It was not quite the glorious

---

*Denmark and Ireland also joined on the same day.

occasion that some had hoped, however; with the Labour Party refusing to take up its seats in the European Parliament, there were only 21 British representatives, instead of the allotted 36. The unions, too, refused to enter into the party spirit, announcing that they would boycott the Community's Economic and Social Committee. All the same, few British observers could entirely suppress a twinge of emotion as, that crisp January morning, the Union Jack was hoisted outside the Community's Brussels headquarters. The fact that it was upside down was entirely beside the point.[50]

In the press, the big day was generally hailed as a watershed, the beginning of a bright new era of international friendship, economic growth and renewed diplomatic purpose. 'Any lingering idea that the British are a stuffy lot who believe that God created the English Channel to preserve them from foreigners and their funny ways gets ditched today,' said the *Mirror*. Lord Goodman, the chairman of the Arts Council, wrote in *The Times* that Britain had embarked on a 'splendid adventure' that would 'enable us to graduate from a nation of shopkeepers, trading only from our own back door, into a nation of industrialists, financiers and scientific and efficient agriculturalists'. Even the *Express* played along, if a bit grudgingly. Its front page boasted a picture of the first British baby born in the new era, Debbie Busby, 'the Euro-baby who could not care less', while the accompanying story assured readers that her 19-year-old mother Sylvia thought of her child as British, not European. In a front-page editorial, the *Express* observed that British entry still 'DOES NOT carry the approval of the majority of the British people', but since the decision had been taken, 'it would be fatal to hang back'. And there was a warning for Britain's new partners. 'Let there be no doubt: If it becomes clear that there is no place for Britain in the developing European Community, Parliament has a way out. So watch out Europe – Here we come!'

Among the great mass of the population, however, Britain's European destiny provoked barely a flicker of interest. Membership was 'accepted by most people with resignation, if not enthusiasm', admitted Lord Goodman, noting that 'the issues are too complicated for mass enthusiasm', and that although people would happily dance in the streets at the end of a war, or mourn the death of a beloved monarch, 'to expect them to dress themselves up in woad or plait a maypole because we have successfully negotiated a customs treaty is to underrate their sense of proportion'. If anything, however, he was underplaying public scepticism. *The Times*'s poll found that just 38 per cent of people were happy at the thought of European entry, with 39 per cent unhappy and 23 per cent undecided. And in the *Mirror* – which hailed Britain's first day in the Common Market as 'A Day in History', and claimed that children leaving school in the 1980s 'will have to be Anglo-European to survive' – a more detailed survey shattered any illusions that Britain had become European overnight. 'Would you like to see these "Common Market customs"?' the paper asked:

	Yes	No
Regular wine with meals	23%	21%
More pavement cafés	11%	34%
More shops open on Sunday	5%	40%
Coffee and roll for breakfast, not bacon and eggs	13%	58%
Pubs open all day	18%	44%

And in the *Express*, the columnist Jean Rook – one of the most popular journalists of her generation – spoke for the millions who shuddered at the thought of pavement cafés, Sunday shopping and coffee and rolls for breakfast. 'Since Boadicea,' she reminded her readers, 'we British have slammed our seas in the faces of invading frogs and wops, who start at Calais. Today, we're slipping our bolts. And, of all that we have to offer Europe, what finer than contact with our short-tongued, stiff-necked, straight-backed, brave, bloody-minded and absolutely beautiful selves? To know the British (it takes about 15 years to get on nodding terms) will be Europe's privilege.'[51]

For Edward Heath, there was no question of allowing the great moment to pass without celebration. He had already appointed an official committee to plan a nationwide festival, chaired by Lord Goodman and including such eminences as the V&A's director Roy Strong, the new head of the National Theatre, Peter Hall, and the BBC's new director of programmes, David Attenborough. 'Fanfare for Europe', the event was called, and Heath hoped that it might enter history as a great national celebration to rival the Great Exhibition and the Festival of Britain. But with a budget of just £350,000, the Fanfare was always facing an uphill struggle, and the fact that four out of ten people were still opposed to EEC membership made it hard to arouse much public enthusiasm. Heath should be 'ashamed of himself', Dennis Skinner bitterly told the Commons. 'Can he tell us how the British people can celebrate a national disaster in the middle of a wages freeze?' They would 'certainly be prepared to celebrate the opportunities of improving their real living standards', Heath retorted stiffly – stubbornly ignoring polls which showed that almost three-quarters of the population, whatever their views on the EEC, believed the Fanfare should not even be taking place at all.[52]

It was entirely characteristic of Heath's single-mindedness, his self-centred introversion and his complete misreading of public opinion that he arranged for the Fanfare's opening night on 3 January, a gala at Covent Garden, to be devoted to classical music, precisely the kind of thing least likely to win over the sceptical masses. When the Queen, Prince Philip and the Prime Minister arrived at the Royal Opera House, splendidly attired and looking forward to an evening of high culture, they were greeted by 300 anti-European protesters chanting 'Sieg Heil', which was hardly the ideal start. In his memoirs, Heath records an evening of incomparable delight in a hall bedecked with pink roses: readings from Judi Dench and Sir Laurence Olivier, recitals by Elisabeth Schwarzkopf, Geraint Evans and Kiri te Kanawa, and performances of Britten's *Spring Symphony* and Beethoven's Ninth, conducted by Carl Davis. 'Many great performances have graced that world-renowned stage,' Heath wrote, 'but few can have been more moving or more appropriate. Performers and audience then mingled afterwards for a splendid dinner at Lancaster House . . . My heart was full of joy at the recognition that Her Majesty the Queen had given to our country's great achievement.' He did not mention the protesters; nor did he mention the look of horrified distaste, quickly suppressed but there all the same, that crossed the Queen's face when Carl Davis conducted his 'modern' adaptation of the National Anthem, a classic instance of Heathite reform gone wrong.[53]

Much of the rest of the Fanfare was pretty desperate stuff. In London the V&A mounted an exhibition of 'Treasures from the European Community', while the Whitechapel Art Gallery put on an exhibition of European sweet-wrappers. In Cardiff, the Caricature Theatre mounted a stage show 'for all the family' in French and English; in Scotland, gas and electricity showrooms organized demonstrations of Continental cooking. In York Minster, there was a concert by something called the 'Great Universal Stores Footwear Band'; in Lincoln's Inn, there was a tin-whistle concert, charitably described by one observer as 'an evening of nameless Irish wails'; in Hull, actors and poets at the local Arts Centre put on a show around the impossibly glamorous theme 'Hull is the Gateway to Europe'. Then there was the bizarre international friendly held at Wembley on 3 January, in which a team of players from the six original EEC members took on a united British-Danish-Irish team from the new member states. To be fair, the organizers attracted some stellar names – Pat Jennings, Bobby Charlton, Johnny Giles and Peter Lorimer for the 'Three', Dino Zoff, Franz Beckenbauer, Ruud Krol and Johan Neeskens for the 'Six' – but with only 36,000 bothering to turn up, the crumbling old stadium felt cold and empty. To add insult to injury, reported the *Guardian*, 'the loudest cheer of the night greeted the news on the information board that Norwich City had reached the final of the League Cup'. All in all, the general experience was summed up by what happened in the little town of Ivybridge, Devon, where the pro-European mayor managed to organize a parade led by a teenager dressed as Britannia, and invited the townsfolk to line the streets and wave European flags. But as the odd-job man who put out flags along the route remarked, most people 'didn't know what they were doing, they didn't know what was going on. It was a big con-job. It wasn't a celebration of going in; it was literally a good excuse for a booze-up on someone else's expense.'[54]

Heath refused to hear a bad word about the Fanfare for Europe, and for the rest of his life he rarely failed to wrap himself in the blue and gold banner of the European Community, or to describe Britain's entry in January 1973 as his proudest hour. For critics hostile to the European project, of course, it was his lowest betrayal, the moment when the political elite ignored public opinion and inveigled Britain into a Franco-German cartel in defiance of history and tradition. Arguments about the value of Britain's membership inevitably come down to personal preju-dice, but it is worth pointing out that January 1973 hardly turned out to be the beginning of a new golden age, and the promised economic miracle never materialized. On the other hand, it was hardly a moment of apocalyptic disaster either. In any case, what many people forget is that if Heath had fallen under a bus in 1969, Britain would still have entered eventually. Both the Conservatives and Labour had already made one application each, Wilson was already planning a second bid, and the weight of business and Fleet Street opinion was almost impossible to ignore. But this does not detract from the fact that, by his own lights, Heath pulled off a major accomplishment. He was lucky to come to power at exactly the right time, when de Gaulle had given way to Pompidou, but it took enormous determination, diplomatic effort and parliamentary skill to manoeuvre Britain past the rocks and into the high seas. His biographer rightly calls it 'the one unquestionable success of his premiership', and, for the rest of his life, foreign politicians treated him as a respected elder statesman, a man of vision and drive who had decisively changed the course of history.[55]

What he did not do, however, was to change the basic attitudes of the British people. For all the popularity of the Eurovision Song Contest and *It's a Knockout*, the town-twinning and the au pair girls, the Spanish holidays, Scandinavian duvets, French wines, Italian restaurants and West German cars, there remained a deep cultural gulf between the British and their Continental neighbours – in their own minds if nowhere else. Even though the public voted to remain in the EEC when Wilson finally put the question to a referendum in 1975, there was never any sense of enthusiasm, of mission, even of common culture. For one thing, member-ship coincided with a wild surge in the domestic money supply and world commodity prices, so people associated the EEC (a bit unfairly) with inflation; for another, the economic picture for the next few years was so dire that it destroyed the case that Brussels was the great saviour. Two out of three people in 1974 thought that Britain should have 'developed links with the Commonwealth rather than joined the Common Market', and for the rest of the decade – the year of the referendum being a notable exception – barely one in three described EEC membership as a 'good thing', while as many as 40 per cent thought that it was a 'bad thing'.

Within a few years, meanwhile, Brussels had become a dirty word, a symbol of banality and bureaucracy rather than idealism and friendship: when John Osborne sneered in the *Observer* that Jerusalem would never be built 'in the typists' pools and conference rooms of Brussels', he was aiming at the easiest of targets. And as W. H. Auden had once perceptively noted, attitudes to Europe still had a strong class dimension. The 'High-Brows', he said, could not conceive of life without Europe's 'literature, music and art'. But to the 'Low-Brows', 'abroad is inhabited by immoral strangers', and 'an Englishman who goes there often, still worse, decides to live there, is probably up to no good'. Even in the age of the package holiday, these stereotypes still held firm: although millions of Britons now roasted on the beaches of Spain, they insisted on surrounding themselves with reminders of home, from fish and chips and warm beer to the *Daily Mirror* and kiss-me-quick hats, and shuddered at the thought of interacting with the locals.[56]

Old prejudices died hard. When a group of West Germans arrived on holiday in England in October 1975, they were stunned to find their hotelier taking down their food order as 'two eggs mayonnaise, a prawn Goebbels, a Hermann Goering and four Colditz salads'. And when they asked him to stop mentioning the war, he retorted, 'You started it . . . You invaded Poland', and finally snapped, 'Who won the bloody war, anyway?' Of course Basil Fawlty set out with decent intentions; at the beginning of *Fawlty Towers'* most famous episode, he admonishes the suspicious Major: 'Forgive and forget, Major. God knows how, the bastards.' And even when suffering from concussion, he does his best: 'All in the Market together, old differences forgotten, and no need at all to mention the war.'[57]

But then how could he possibly forget it, given its ubiquity in British cultural life in the 1970s? Even in the year of Britain's accession to the EEC, millions of people were being treated to the gigantic (if excellent) documentary series *The World at War* every week on ITV. On the BBC, meanwhile, series like *Dad's Army*, *Colditz* and *Secret Army* attracted more than 10 million viewers a week and spanned almost the entire decade, re-creating a lost golden age when Britain mattered in the world and had prevailed against overwhelming odds in a clear-cut struggle of good against evil. In *Till Death Us Do Part*, Alf Garnett never shuts up about the 'bloody Huns'; in *Whatever Happened to the Likely Lads?*, Terry Collier loves to moan about his German ex-wife; in *Rising Damp*, Rigsby is never happier than when recounting how he got his 'war wound' in the North African desert. And with boys' comics like *Victor, Tiger* and *Commando* wallowing in war nostalgia and anti-German feeling, it was no wonder that in 1974 only 13 per cent of the population said they liked Germans, with the majority describing them as 'violent, lacking in tolerance, and unfriendly' – and hostility being strongest among the young.[58]

But the incident that revealed most about British attitudes to Europe concerned another project close to Heath's heart: the long-discussed dream of building a tunnel under the Channel to link the French coast with his native Kent. In March 1973 the government announced plans to build the Channel Tunnel, issuing a White Paper which observed that 'Britain is no long economically or socially an island'. A few weeks later, Heath and Pompidou finalized the deal, and in December the Channel Tunnel Bill passed its Second Reading by 18 votes. But when Harold Wilson returned to Downing Street, he could hardly wait to kick the idea into touch. 'An island is an island,' Barbara Castle wrote in her diary after the Cabinet had agreed to drop the scheme, 'and should not be violated. Certainly I am convinced that the building of a tunnel would do something profound to the national attitude – and not certainly for the better.' In July 1977, Bernard Donoughue made the mistake of mentioning the tunnel scheme as a possible answer to unemployment in the construction industry. 'This would be the worst thing that could ever happen to Britain,' Peter Shore said angrily, jumping to his feet and 'waving his arms . . . How old was I? Did I not remember 1940? We would be invaded by Germans coming through the tunnel.' Donoughue thought he was 'quite mad'. But Shore's was not a minority view: despite all Heath's efforts, despite all the foreign holidays and Continental ready meals, Britain in the mid-1970s remained a deeply inward-looking society, suspicious of foreigners and hostile to the outside world. In the final analysis, most people would probably have agreed with the words of Alan Clark, who idly remarked to Dennis Skinner in the Commons tea-room queue one day: 'I'd rather live in a socialist Britain than one ruled by a lot of fucking foreigners.'[59]

5

The Green Death

*Our ancestors made machines and the machines destroyed the
earth, causing earthquakes and volcanoes that killed men by the
hundreds of thousands. That is why the Spirits decreed that the
making of machines was an abomination.*
    – John Christopher, *The Prince in Waiting* (1970)

*Imagine when the holocaust comes and these places are all deserted
and there are thistles growing on the motorway . . . and there's
grass growing over the jukebox . . . and honeysuckle coming out
of the espresso, yeah . . . and tadpoles swimming in the ladies.*
    – Steven Poliakoff, *Strawberry Fields* (1977)

For Howard and Barbara Kirk, the academic couple at the centre of
Malcolm Bradbury's novel *The History Man* (1975), life should be
perfect. They live in a renovated Georgian terraced house in the south-
coast university town of Watermouth. Their walls are lined with books
and African masks; their shelves overflow with bottles of wine. Their
kitchen is a temple to the organic fashions of the day, full of French
casseroles and earthenware dishes; 'the long table is scrubbed pine, the
shelves on the walls are pine, there are pine cabinets, and pine and rush
chairs, and rush matting on the floors'. As a fashionable sociology lecturer
and media don, Howard is the darling of the town's left-wing party
circuit, while Barbara is 'a *cordon bleu* cook, an expert in children's
literature, a tireless promoter of new causes'. They even look 'the way
new people do look': Howard with his Zapata moustache, white sweat-
shirts, 'hairy loose waistcoats' and 'pyjama-style blue jeans'; Barbara
with her 'frizzled yellow hair', green eyeshadow and long kaftan dresses

that show off the fact she is not wearing a bra. They are busy, popular, fashionable people, at the cutting edge of cultural life. And yet they are always looking back to the past, to the undelivered promise of the 1960s, to an unfulfilled 'hazy dream' of 'expanded minds, equal dealings, erotic satisfactions, beyond the frame of reality, beyond the limits of the senses'. 'Do you remember,' Barbara asks her husband, 'when things were all wide open and free, and we were all doing something and the revolution was next week? And we were under thirty and we could trust us?' 'It's still like that,' Howard protests. 'Is it really like that?' she asks. 'Don't you think people have got tired?'[1]

Laments for the lost promise of the 1960s were a common theme of bohemian life during the age of stagflation. By the time Malcolm Bradbury wrote his brilliant satirical novel, the emblematic boutiques of Swinging London had conceded defeat in the face of surging rents and recession, while the underground press, once associated with so many idealistic dreams, had largely collapsed amid plummeting circulation and bitter factional infighting. Radicals liked to claim that the counterculture had been broken by the 'establishment', citing the Oz obscenity trial in the summer of 1971, when the underground paper's three editors were briefly imprisoned and had their hair forcibly cropped after being prosecuted for showing Rupert Bear in various pornographic poses. A year later, when a group of anarchists were found guilty of the Angry Brigade bombings, which had targeted banks, embassies, shops and the house of the Home Secretary, Robert Carr, it did seem that the state had crushed the spirit of rebellion. But the truth was that even without those landmark trials, the counterculture was doomed, as its look and style were appropriated by mainstream enterprises and its rebellious energy drained away in the economic crisis of the early 1970s. As early as January 1971, John Lennon gloomily told an interviewer:

> The people who are in control and in power and the class system and the whole bullshit bourgeois scene is exactly the same except that there is a lot of middle-class kids with long hair walking around London in trendy clothes and Kenneth Tynan's making a fortune out of the word 'fuck'. The same bastards are in control, the same people are runnin' everything, it's exactly the same. They hyped the kids and the generation.
>
> We've grown up a little, all of us, and there has been a change and we are a bit freer and all that, but it's the same game, nothing's really

changed . . . The dream is over. It's just the same only I'm thirty and a lot of people have got long hair, that's all.[2]

Lennon was a bitter man, but his sentiments were not unusual. 'The feeling of community that was about to emerge three years ago has shattered and split,' wrote the radical activists Edward Barker and Mick Farren in 1972. 'Flower power's failure', they concluded, proved that society was 'not even prepared to tolerate the existence of any minority who attempted to live according to other principles, no matter how peaceful or self-contained their culture might be'. A tiny minority, like the Angry Brigade, reacted by falling for the supposed glamour and efficacy of violence, like their far more effective and dangerous international comrades in the Baader–Meinhof Group and the Red Brigades. But most turned inwards, whether wry and wistful or sour and disillusioned. And while some historians argue that the early 1970s were 'the real Sixties', it did not seem like that at the time. What had once called itself the 'underground community' broke up; as one writer puts it, 'squatters became home-owners; local activists became adventure playground leaders; utopians joined the Labour Party'. Certainly by 1972, with the underground press in ruins, the counterculture was effectively dead. When police broke up the illegal Free Festival in Windsor Great Park in August 1974, arresting 220 people amid scenes akin to a pitched battle, many saw it as the requiem mass for an era of freedom and experimentation. 'The Isle of Wight, Glastonbury, these were the great manifestations of the alternative culture of love, dope, sounds, macrobiotic food, tripping, instinctive anarchism, youth, the new lifestyle,' wrote the jazz musician George Melly in an obituary for the 1960s in the *Observer* a few days later. 'The last bastion of all that was that free festival in Windsor last week and . . . the law moved in with truncheons and shut the whole thing down . . . My spirit mourned for Windsor, the pathetic and perhaps the last manifestation of peace and love.'[3]

Perhaps the best barometer of the changing mood was the theatre. Where once radical playwrights, inspired by the likes of Harold Pinter, Joe Orton and Kenneth Tynan, had looked forward to a brave new world, they now looked back in anger. As the critic Michael Billington puts it, in the early 1970s 'there was a sense of hopes dashed, of things winding down, of individual lives confronting intractable problems', so that the abiding themes of the new generation were 'disappointment, disillusion and a pervasive sense of despair'. In Trevor Griffiths' play *The Party*, which opened at the National Theatre just after the announcement of the three-day week in December 1973, a group of revolutionary socialists plan the way forward during the Paris disturbances of May 1968; yet all the time, we know that there will be no revolution, that the future does not lie with the radical left, that their dreams will turn to ashes. Howard Brenton's play *Weapons of Happiness* (1976) makes a similar point: when a group of well-meaning radicals stage a sit-in at a London crisps factory, their naive utopianism comes over as reckless and self-indulgent rather than brave or admirable. And in his friend David Hare's play *Teeth 'n' Smiles* (1975), suggestively set in the last year of the 1960s, a radical rock band see their dreams literally go up in smoke after a farcical gig at a university ball, their idealism deflated by sharp reality. 'The fringe has failed,' Brenton observed in 1974. 'Its failure was that of the whole dream of an "alternative culture" . . . The truth is that there's only one society – that you can't escape the world you live in. Reality is remorseless. No one can leave.'[4]

And yet across the national landscape – from the communes of mid-Wales to the antique shops of Camden Lock, from the squats of Notting Hill to the Victorian enclaves of university towns across the country – the 1960s had left a deep impression. Like Howard and Barbara Kirk, most of the young men and women who had seen themselves as bohemians or freethinkers in the late 1960s ended up older, wiser, mildly disillusioned but still fiercely idealistic residents of what might be called the counter-culture belt, in the leafy streets of gentrifying urban villages, in run-down Georgian squares, in renovated Victorian townhouses and Edwardian garden flats. In 1974, the journalist Mary Ingham, who as a girl had expected to be married with children by her mid-twenties, found herself, aged 27, still sharing a shabby flat with a group of university friends in a dilapidated Regency crescent overlooking a park. One of her flatmates had gone back to university, two worked in publishing, another was a polytechnic lecturer and the fifth worked for a homeless charity. They lived in amiable squalor 'among books and pieces of flowered pottery'; they argued late at night about 'entry to the Common Market, Marxist politics, astrology'; they mingled with 'fringe theatre actors and media people at noisy parties overflowing with wine, garlic bread and vegetarian delights'; they went to encounter-sessions with feminists and social workers in their 'platform-sole boots, long peasant dresses and baggy trousers'.[5]

At that very moment, Jonathan Raban was observing the lives of his neighbours in the scruffy yet increasingly upmarket neighbourhoods of north and west London, a world of Japanese lampshades, white paint and stripped-pine stereo systems. 'Here children play with chunky all-wood Abbatt toys,' he noted; 'here girl-wives grill anaemic escalopes of veal; everyone takes the *Guardian*.' They worked in 'journalism, publishing, TV'; they 'cooked out of raggy Elizabeth David Penguins', smoked pot, listened to Pink Floyd and earnestly discussed R. D. Laing and Michel Foucault. Visiting Ceres, a macrobiotic restaurant on Porto-bello Road, he imagined the life of one of 'the girls who drift about the store, filling wire baskets with soya beans, miso and wakame seaweed': her seriousness, her narcissism, her sense of 'inner virtue' and her 'latent violence'. In her room, he thought, she might drink honey and grape juice and eat brown rice. On her shelves, he imagined the rows of paperbacks: *Slaughterhouse 5*, *Steppenwolf*, *The Macrobiotic Way*, *The I-Ching*, the poems of Rod McKuen and Leonard Cohen, and 'Louis MacNeice's coffee table book on astrology (an awkward Christmas present from her father)'. And if she read a newspaper, of course it would be the *Guardian*, which later caught the tone of semi-bohemian middle-class life so well in Posy Simmonds's cartoon of Wendy Weber, the well-meaning feminist former nurse, now married to a bearded polytechnic lecturer called George. They wear 'soft, frayed, patched, ethnic, woolly comfortable old clothes'; they eat lentil curries and vegetarian quiches; they drink expensive wines from Marks & Spencer. As a sociologist told *Punch* in 1977, theirs was the world of muesli and au pairs, discussion groups and nut salad, 'wholemeal bread, encounter therapy, finger paint-ing, dabbling in the occult, nudity'.[6]

And while they no longer demonstrated about Vietnam, as they had as students in the late 1960s, there were plenty of brave causes left. In the middle-class dinner party described in Margaret Drabble's novel *The Middle Ground* (1980), a group of lecturers and journalists talk over the cheese of 'the simple life, of communes in Wales, of modern technology and solar heating, of Wordsworth and the romantics, of nature and Rousseau'. They were the kind of people who subscribed to *The Ecologist* and joined Friends of the Earth, who read *The Lord of the Rings* and *Watership Down*, who called public meetings to stop the extension of the M3 or the development of Covent Garden. A decade before, writing about the Festival of Britain, Michael Frayn had captured the world of

In the sunshine of June 1970, Edward Heath and his women MPs, with Margaret Thatcher second from right, greet their new dawn. Reality, however, soon hit home: by October, a council workers' strike meant that piles of rubbish were festering on the streets of London.

The moral fibre of Britain's youngsters provoked considerable anxiety during the early 1970s. Above, boys play on the streets of west London before the 1970 FA Cup Final. Below, a photographer catches secondary school boys smoking, May 1972.

For the elderly, Edward Heath's new Britain could seem a frighteningly alien place. Above, an old woman waits to be evicted from her dilapidated flat, 1973. Below, shoppers return to the brave new world of north London's Highbury Quadrant.

Despite their reputation, the union bosses were less powerful than they seemed. Above, the TGWU's Jack Jones strikes a suitably imperial pose, flanked by the AEU's Hugh Scanlon and the Vehicle Builders' Alf Roberts. Below, postal workers heckle their leaders after the collapse of a strike, March 1971.

Young and old, rich and poor: in February 1972, there was no escape from the power cuts. Fashion buyer Sally Hayton has breakfast with her father in their Fulham flat, while in Hillcrest Avenue, Edgware, Sheryl Hart does her homework by candlelight.

Margaret Thatcher looks delighted on her first day as Secretary of State for Education, June 1970. To some critics she was the 'Milk Snatcher'. But to the children of Harwood Primary School, shown protesting in 1973, she was something much worse: a 'Loo Snatcher'.

the 'radical middle classes – the do-gooders; the readers of the *News Chronicle,* the *Guardian,* and the *Observer;* the signers of petitions; the backbone of the BBC ... who look out from the lush pastures which are their natural station in life with eyes full of sorrow for less fortunate creatures, guiltily conscious of their advantages, though not usually ceasing to eat the grass'. He called them the Herbivores. And never had the name seemed more fitting than in the early 1970s, the years when green was good and small was beautiful.[7]

In 1971, the *Yorkshire Post* gave its annual award for non-fiction to a title that must have struck fear into the souls of all who read it. Written by the science journalist Gordon Rattray Taylor, *The Doomsday Book* begins ominously with a long quotation from the Book of Revelation. On the very next page, Taylor warns his readers that mankind is facing an 'eventual population crash', an 'apocalypse' that will probably wipe out a third of humanity. Thanks to 'crowding, pollution and a disturbed balance of nature', the planet itself is at risk. The land has been over-farmed, the seas have been over-fished, the air is full of chemicals, and 'Spaceship Earth', with its fragile crust of land and thin band of atmosphere, is on the brink of collapse. The temperature is steadily rising; the icecaps are melting, the seas are rising, and as man releases more carbon dioxide into the atmosphere, so the planet is getting hotter and hotter. Even more worrying than global warming, however, is the threat of global cooling: scientists are already warning that the Earth stands on the brink of an ice age, and the distinguished British scientist James Lovelock has predicted a drop of 4 °F by 1975 and 'the start of a new ice age well before 1980'. But the time has long since passed for arguments about numbers. The priority, Taylor argues, is 'to stabilize world population growth'. Britain should adopt the 'realistic target' of halving its population in fifty years, aiming for 30 million people in 2030. 'Man', he concludes, 'has reached a turning point in his history.'[8]

With its apocalyptic tone, scattershot approach and wild warnings of a coming ice age, Taylor's book was a quintessential product of the early 1970s. But although environmentalism is often thought to have been born in the age of oil shocks, coal strikes and communes, the truth is that Britain's green movement has a long history. The first society to protect 'Commons, Open Spaces and Footpaths' was founded as far back as 1865, while the National Trust, the Royal Society for the Protection of Birds, the Fauna Preservation Society, the Metropolitan and Public Gardens Association and the Camping Club were all founded between 1880 and 1910, during the heyday of late Victorian and Edwardian conservationism. And although the twentieth century is often seen as the century of the city and the car, groups like the Ramblers' Association, the Council for the Preservation of Rural England and the Pure Rivers Society were set up in the 1930s, the Attlee government set up the Nature Conservancy, the first agency dedicated to protecting wildlife, in 1949, and more than 200 local societies dedicated to the environment had been established by the late 1950s.

But it was in the decade that followed, as the high-minded middle classes turned their attention to the spread of factory farming, the growth of suburbia and the blight of pollution, that conservationism began to acquire a genuinely significant following. Membership of the Ramblers' Association (obviously a form of leisure, though a green-tinged one) doubled between 1962 and 1972; meanwhile, coverage of environmental issues in *The Times* increased by 280 per cent between 1965 and 1973. Of course, these were not yet issues that concerned the great majority of the population. Ramblers, conservationists and early eco-activists tended to be middle-class couples working in the professions, the arts and (as per the stereotype) teaching. All the same, as early as the mid-1960s there was a palpable sense of momentum and enthusiasm.[9]

As a reaction against modernity, industrialization and big business, and as a celebration of the pastoral, the organic and the small-scale, the environmental movement naturally appealed to the youngsters who made up the counterculture of the late 1960s. But the counterculture did not 'give birth' to environmentalism, as is often thought. Not only did the green movement come first, but it appealed to plenty of people who were not hippies at all. There had always been a strong strain of pastoral romanticism in English culture (and the American historian Martin Weiner, in a book beloved by Thatcherites but derided by many scholars, even argued that the High Tory suspicion of capitalism lay at the root of Britain's economic problems). What is certainly true is that by the mid-1960s plenty of people were becoming worried about the social costs of economic growth. In his book *The World We Have Lost* (1965), for example, the historian Peter Laslett evoked an age before 'progress' and industry, a vanished English landscape in which 'the whole of life went forward in the family, in a circle of loved, familiar faces, known and fondled objects, all to human size'. Two years later the LSE economist E. J. Mishan published *The Costs of Economic Growth*, warning that the pursuit of progress led only to 'the waste land of Subtopia', a world with less and less room for individualism, religion and the family. 'Growthmania', Mishan warned, was 'more likely on balance to reduce rather than increase social welfare'; in the meantime, the 'rich local life centred on township, parish and village' had been cruelly destroyed. And at the same time, the economist Barbara Ward published her groundbreaking *Spaceship Earth*, in which she asked readers to imagine themselves as the crew on a precarious space voyage, depending 'for life itself' on their fragile earth, which was being 'contaminated and destroyed' by man's reckless arrogance. She drew her central image from the pictures astronauts had sent back of the beautiful blue-green Earth hanging in space; it was to prove a lasting and highly influential metaphor.[10]

It was one of Ward's friends, however, who published the best-known green manifesto of the 1970s. Born in Bonn just before the First World War, Fritz Schumacher had emigrated to England in the late 1930s and worked for a time as a statistician at Oxford before becoming chief economic adviser to the National Coal Board and a part-time adviser to the Labour Party. He was a strange, contradictory man, with a brilliant mind, an impatient manner and a sharp tongue, as well as a vague sense of spiritual yearning that became increasingly intense as his career seemed to stall. For much of the 1950s, as his ideas for the future of Britain's coal industry were ignored by the Coal Board, he felt frustrated and aimless, and he began to pour his energies into a succession of eccentric hobbies, from astrology and yoga to Eastern religions and organic foods, which were nowhere near as fashionable then as they would be ten years later. In particular, Schumacher found comfort in gardening, which he approached with his usual fierce energy. In 1950 he bought a house with four acres of land in rural Surrey, and he began to cultivate the land, not with the chemical-intensive techniques popular at the time, but with organic methods, which most people had long since abandoned. For support he turned to a small fringe group called the Soil Association, and in 1970, the year he retired from the Coal Board, Schumacher became its president.[11]

It was not Schumacher but his editor, Anthony Blond, who came up with the title for his book, which was originally called 'The Homecomers'. Struck by the power of the fashionable catchphrase 'Black is Beautiful',

Blond suggested *Small is Beautiful* – a phrase that not only captured Schumacher's ideas very nicely, but seized the imagination of the emerging environmental movement. For although Schumacher's book was really just a compilation of lectures and articles, through it ran a constant thread of anti-modernist radicalism, urging a retreat from the industrial and the large-scale, and a realization that 'man is small, and therefore small is beautiful'. He had flirted with Buddhism since the late 1950s, when he had been sent as an adviser to the Burmese government, and argued for what he called 'Buddhist' economics, celebrating 'the joy of work and the bliss of leisure'. Britain's decline, he thought, was rooted in spirituality as well as economics. The nation had sold its soul for the promise of ever-expanding abundance; it needed to rediscover the pleasures of small-scale farming, of tending the soil, of looking after animals, of thrift, balance and self-sufficiency. There was nothing inherently wrong with technology, or even with industry itself; but if the breakneck rush towards massive industrialization continued much longer, the world was heading for catastrophe. Yet Schumacher was neither a pessimist nor a doom-monger. By taking action in their own small way, he argued, millions of ordinary people could change the world; by switching to organic farming, for example, or by keeping their own animals, or merely by leading quieter, more modest lives. 'Everywhere people ask: "What can I actually *do?*"' he concluded. 'The answer is as simple as it is disconcerting: we can, each of us, work to put our own inner house in order.'[12]

It was not surprising that Schumacher's vision struck such a chord with readers in the early 1970s. 'England is the country, and the country is England,' Stanley Baldwin had famously said half a century before, evoking what he thought to be timeless images of Englishness: 'the tinkle of hammer on anvil in the country smithy, the corncrake on a dewy morning, the sound of the scythe against the whetstone, and the sight of a plough team coming over the brow of a hill', something that would 'be seen in England long after the Empire has perished'. But he was wrong about that. For when visitors to the countryside looked out across the rolling acres of English farmland, they now saw a landscape utterly transformed.

Farmers were far more productive than ever before (the average cow produced 200 gallons more milk than she had in the 1950s, while the typical hen laid twice as many eggs) and during the 1970s they became expert at lobbying for grants and tax breaks, as well as picking up an estimated £1.5 billion in subsidies from Brussels in just seven years. Once mocked as backward and reactionary, they grew fat on the proceeds of the Common Agricultural Policy, which encouraged production regardless of cost or quality, and they used their large profits to invest in fleets of combine harvesters, tractors and Land Rovers. But they seemed to have lost something of their souls in the process. Small farmers were steadily being driven out by ambitious businessmen like Jack Eastwood, the broiler-chicken millionaire who owned 12,000 acres in Northampton-shire, or Bernard Matthews, the Norfolk turkey tycoon, famous for his 'Bootiful!' catchphrase. In 1971, one writer recorded that there were now barely 350,000 farm workers left in Britain. Soon the typical farm would 'consist of a farmer, his wife and a lot of machinery'. Farmers were no longer husbandmen; they were factory managers, often working for a pension fund that had bought the farm and leased it back to its original owner. And even at this stage, they had become dependent on the market for convenience foods, producing vast quantities of peas and beans for Birds Eye, Findus and Marks & Spencer. 'Processions of pea-picking machines like mechanical dragons roar into the quiet farms of East Anglia,' wrote Anthony Sampson, 'racing from one field to the next, working all night under arc-lights to devour their quota.' Farmers already had to produce 'always the same width of pea, the same fat-content of pork-meat, the same size of apple all over the country'. As one bitterly remarked: 'You can farm against the weather, but you can't farm against Birds Eye.'[13]

Efficiency came at a heavy cost, not just to the traditional relationship between the people and the countryside, but to the landscape itself. It was not merely the vast fields of sugar beet and oilseed rape; as the historian Robert Colls writes, it was the 'bulldozed hedgerows, the cut-down woods, the conifer plantations, the nitrates, pesticides and dubious feedstuffs, the battery cages and broiler sheds, the slurry tanks, the giant machinery, and the sheer emptiness born of planning policies designed to prevent smallholders from repopulating and reworking the land'. Encouraged by subsidies and supermarkets to turn the land into a gigantic industrial operation, farmers tore down anything that stood in the way of profit, from hedgerows and woodlands to meadows and wetlands. With Whitehall handing out grants for this very purpose – a classic example of modernization gone mad – farmers were ripping out more than 10,000 miles of hedges a year, indifferent to the cost in beauty and wildlife. And as woods and hedgerows disappeared, so the countryside lost much of its variety: the birds and butterflies, the roaming animals and wild flowers that had been there for centuries, sacrificed to the insatiable demands for cheap food and instant profit. By 1980, when Marion Shoard, a former official at the Council for the Preservation of Rural England, published her broadside *The Theft of the Countryside*, Britain had already lost a staggering 24 million trees, 150,000 miles of hedgerow and a third of its woodlands, meadows, streams and marshes. Norfolk had lost 45 per cent of its hedges, Devon 20 per cent of its woodlands, Suffolk 75 per cent of its heathland, Bedfordshire 70 per cent of its wetlands. The landscape was 'under sentence of death', she wrote. And the executioner was not 'the industrialist or the property speculator', as city-dwellers often assumed, but 'the figure traditionally viewed as the custodian of the rural scene – the farmer'.[14]

But while the 1970s were tough years for rural England, its landscape violated, its villages increasingly deserted as post offices were closed and bus services cancelled, they were not much better for towns and cities. When many people got up and looked out of their bedroom windows, they saw not the brick and stone contours of settlements that had developed organically over the centuries, but wildernesses of concrete and tarmac, utopian post-war visions that had gone horribly wrong. Take the nation's second city, Birmingham, once a beacon of enlightened Victorian town planning, but rebuilt in the early 1960s as a monument to modern brutalism, its city centre dominated by a vast inner ring road and the huge slab of the Bull Ring, earning it a national reputation for choked flyovers, soulless towers and rain-sodden concrete. At the time, the travel writer Geoffrey Moorhouse praised it as 'the most go-ahead city in Europe', yet as early as 1972 *The Times* was lamenting that while the old city centre had had 'a quality and warmth of its own', the new was like a 'large and chaotic building site' with all traces of history and distinctiveness suffocated by a 'wave of concrete'. It was no wonder that four years later the BBC used its flyovers and underpasses as the backdrop to Philip Martin's gritty series *Gangsters* (1976–8), which broke new ground in its depiction of the seedy corruption, organized crime and casual racism beneath the surface of the modern British city. As one local woman put it when she wrote to the local paper about the redevelopment of Paradise Circus: 'Where could another Paradise be found that is so completely and utterly soulless?'[15]

While Birmingham was justly notorious for its concrete bleakness, other towns and cities fared little better. In Margaret Drabble's state-of-the-nation novel *The Ice Age* (1977), a woman arrives in the Yorkshire town of Northam to find that 'the developers' have done their worst: as she steps out of the station, she sees 'an enormous roundabout, the beginning of a flyover, a road leading to a multi-storey car park, and an underpass', but no signs of human life. She struggles through the underpass with her bags 'in the stink of carbon monoxide, shuffling through litter, walled in by high elephantine walls, deafened and sickened', only to emerge on a traffic island, cut off from the distant shops by four lanes of roaring traffic. 'This was an environmental offence as bad as a slag heap,' she thinks, feeling a surge of hatred towards the people responsible. Among them, as it happens, is her own husband, a successful property developer. In a nicely caustic passage, Drabble shows him contemplating an architect's model of a new concrete building, conscious that 'the grass would be covered in dog shit, that the trees would be vandalized and killed' – but not caring, because 'that would not be his fault, or the fault of his property company. It would be the fault of the people.'[16]

Of course this was a caricature. At the time, most planners saw themselves as pioneering social engineers, using the proceeds of growth to banish the cramped and insanitary slum conditions that had blighted working-class lives for generations. As disciples of Le Corbusier's dictum that 'to save itself, every great city must rebuild its centre', they did not see themselves as reckless vandals. In their own minds they were progressive egalitarians, tearing down what another of Drabble's characters calls the 'mucky little alleyways', and putting up bold, clean blocks, wide avenues and generous car parks. And yet Drabble's caustic portrait was a highly seductive one, for by the mid-1970s developers and planners were almost universally loathed. 'The answer to the terraced, two-up, two-down house is a grey skyscraper with its head lost in the clouds; to the crowded street, a stretch of unbroken grass big enough to fight a war on; to the corner grocer's, a yawning shopping plaza,' wrote Jonathan Raban in 1974. 'Behind all these strategies lies a savage contempt for the city and an arrogant desire to refashion human society into almost any shape other than the one we have at present.' Even the chief planner of the Greater London Council, David Eversley, conceded:

'The Planner' has become a monster, a threat to society, one of the most guilty of the earth-rapers. Suddenly he has become a breaker of communities, a divider of families, a promoter of neuroses (first noticed as 'New Town Blues'), a feller of trees and bringer of doom by noise, visual intrusion and pollution, a destroyer of our natural heritage, a callous technocrat razing to the ground a large proportion of Britain's historic buildings. He is regarded as a dictator, a technocratic law unto himself, outside the processes of democratic control.

Indeed, if anyone doubted that planners were the root of all evil, they needed only to listen to Douglas Adams's radio series *The Hitchhiker's Guide to the Galaxy* (1978), in which Arthur Dent's intergalactic adventures begin when the Earth is demolished to make way for 'a hyperspatial express route'. As the Guide itself puts it, the alien race responsible, the Vogons, are 'one of the most unpleasant races in the galaxy. Not evil, but bad-tempered, bureaucratic, officious and callous.' Typical planners, in other words.[17]

If there was one building that symbolized the damage done to British cities in the heyday of modernist planning, it was the high-rise tower block. Conceived as a cheap way to get people out of their run-down tenements and into clean, safe council accommodation with all the latest amenities, tower blocks were heavily promoted by both Conservative and Labour governments in the 1950s and 1960s. Crucially, they were quick and easy to build, which meant immediate results for politicians and planners alike; equally importantly, they were seen as a progressive alternative to the sprawling suburban estates that were steadily devouring the countryside. So when Harold Wilson promised voters that Labour would build half a million new homes a year by 1970, tower blocks naturally filled the gap. Between 1964 and 1968, local authorities built, on average, almost 40,000 high-rise flats a year, with the biggest concentrations coming in Greater London, Glasgow, the West Midlands and the North-west. In London alone, there were more than 68,000 high-rise flats by the time the boom ended. In Birmingham there were 24,000, in Liverpool 19,000, in Leeds 12,000, and in Glasgow, where city authorities prided themselves on building bigger and taller than anyone else, high-rise flats constituted a staggering three-quarters of all new housing built in the 1960s. By the time the planners lost faith in high-rise solutions – thanks partly to the gas explosion at Ronan Point in 1968, but also to the fact that funds were running out as the economy tightened – more than 1.5 million people, generally in some of Britain's poorest urban areas, found themselves looking out of a grimy window ten, twelve or twenty storeys in the air.[18]

By the turn of the decade, the newspapers were already full of stories about the nightmarish experience of high-rise living. To working-class families used to living cheek by jowl with their neighbours on crowded terraced streets, or to couples who had long dreamed of their own little house and garden, the brutal concrete reality of estates like Glasgow's Red Road, Sheffield's Park Hill or Hunslet Grange in Leeds came as a deep disappointment. A survey for the Department of the Environment in 1973 found that high-rise residents suffered from more health problems because they were less likely to go for walks or exercise, while other studies found that the elderly and children were more likely to get respiratory infections from being trapped inside all day. The infirm and disabled lived in terror of the lifts breaking down, as they often did; parents lamented that their children had nowhere to play; residents of all ages complained bitterly at the lack of a garden, the absence of shops and the culture of teenage bullying, drug abuse and gang violence. Vandalism was a constant problem: shut up inside all day, many teenagers almost literally had nothing better to do, and as early as the mid-1960s almost one in three high-rise residents complained that graffiti, litter and damage were everyday problems. At the Avebury estate in Southwark, vandalism was so bad that just four years after the blocks were finished, they had to be repaired at a cost of £2 million, a sixth of what they had cost to build.

On top of all that, many system-built flats were shoddily and cheaply put together. Their concrete walls were soon stained with rainwater and damp, growing lichen and fungus and sometimes developing deep structural cracks. Built with undue haste and a cavalier lack of care, they proved enormously expensive to maintain: on one Portsmouth estate where water had leaked behind the concrete cladding panels, it cost the local authority a cool £1.5 million to repair just two towers. And in a survey of sixty local authorities at the end of the 1970s, the architecture writer Sutherland Lyall found that almost all had been forced to spend vast amounts of money repairing cracked cladding, leaking roofs and damp walls that were barely a decade old, coming to a total of at least £200 million. But while architects insisted that they were hard done by, blaming the local authorities for not spending more to maintain the blocks and the tenants themselves for treating them so badly, it was of course the residents who suffered most. As many as four out of ten told researchers they felt lonely and cut off; in London and Sheffield, half of the residents interviewed said they would move immediately if they had the chance.[19]

By the early 1970s, the tower block had become a powerful metaphor for the shattered ideals of the post-war consensus, associated in the public mind with graffiti, drug addiction, unemployment and crime – as well as with the arrogance of middle-class planners, infected with the spirit of social engineering, who had tried to force design solutions on working-class families without bothering to find out what they actually wanted. And when writers and reporters visited high-rise estates in the early 1970s, they did so with a sense of sadness and horror. Arriving in the Millbrook estate in Southampton, 'a vast, cheap storage unit for nearly 20,000 people', Jonathan Raban found a dismal scene of glowering concrete blocks, deserted service roads and poorly maintained grassland 'patrolled by gangs of sub-teenage youths and the occasional indecent-exposure freak'. Inside, most of the people he interviewed complained of theft and vandalism; even their milk bottles and milk-money regularly disappeared, and many admitted that they would not risk hanging their clothes in the communal drying areas. Of course Millbrook was still a long way from the world imagined by J. G. Ballard in his dystopian novel *High Rise* (1975): a futuristic forty-storey housing complex containing a swimming pool, a supermarket, even a school, in which the residents turn on one another, forming aggressive clans, fighting brutally for territory and food, withdrawing into a degenerate society of murderous, cannibalistic hunter-gatherers. Even so, in an age of growing anxiety about public violence and family breakdown, Ballard's vision was still too close for comfort.[20]

For although Britain's high-rise utopia had not yet degenerated into cannibalism, it had nonetheless become a potent symbol of social break-down. In the autumn of 1976, the journalist Christopher Booker visited Sir Denys Lasdun's groundbreaking sixteen-storey Keeling House in Bethnal Green, completed two decades before. Architectural handbooks often hailed it as a masterpiece, their pictures showing 'its concrete gleaming white in the sun'. But Booker found it hard to imagine that he was looking at the same building: a 'tatty and forlorn' council block, 'its concrete cracked and discolouring, the metal reinforcement rusting through the surface, every available inch covered with graffiti'. Inside, only one lift was working; 'piles of old cigarette packets and broken bottles' lay in the corners; and throughout there was an overwhelming 'stench of urine'. If this was the best that architectural modernism could do for London, then it was no wonder that just five years later the GLC began a programme of demolishing its least popular tower blocks, some of them barely ten years old. The high-rise utopia, as the distinguished geographer Alice Coleman wrote a few years later, 'was conceived in compassion but has been born and bred in authoritarianism, profligacy and frustration. It aimed to liberate people from the slums but has come to represent an even worse form of bondage.' It was meant to be 'a form of national salvation'. Instead, it had become 'an all-pervading failure'.[21]

In August 1972, the diarist James Lees-Milne spent a pleasant weekend visiting a variety of upper-class friends, artists and fellow historians in the Dorset countryside, one of the least spoiled landscapes in southern England. 'All the people we met this weekend', he noted when he got back, 'were highly intelligent aesthetes, all deeply apprehensive about the dire threat to the landscape, in fact to the whole earth.' Yet these people, who to him represented 'the highest standards of civilisation', were 'powerless to stop the devastating flood of spoilation', which he blamed on 'the vast mindless, faceless majority with no principles but personal greed'. Six months later he made another trip, this time to Shropshire, where he was horrified to find the countryside 'dotted with modern bungalows'. He was particularly depressed by the sight of Bridgnorth, looking out from 'its delightful acropolis' over 'an ocean of factories and horrors'. As always, though, his aesthetic judgements were seasoned with a heavy dose of snobbish contempt. 'The conglomeration of wires, pylons, ill-placed factories and execrable villas is so horrifying that I utterly despair of the landscape,' he recorded.

> I know that people say there has always been change which is resented by the old. But never, never has there been such devastating change as in my lifetime, change always for the worse aesthetically, never for the better. The public *en bloc* are blind to hideous surroundings. I prefer to stay at home in my ivory tower and never go on expeditions rather than be affronted at every familiar turn with a substitute architectural monstrosity.[22]

Lees-Milne was quite wrong about 'the public'. Just a few weeks later, taking the new Poet Laureate, Sir John Betjeman, on a trip to inspect the architectural 'horrors' inflicted on the city of Bath ('one's vision of hell'), he was taken aback by the warmth of their reception. When they went for lunch, the waitresses immediately recognized Betjeman; so did the staff in the bookshop they visited next, the attendants in the Pump Room and the cashier in the Midland Bank, who immediately rushed to get the manager. 'Just as well I had not told the Bath Preservation committee that he was coming,' Lees-Milne recorded sourly, 'for he would have been mobbed.' No doubt this owed a great deal to Betjeman's accessible, witty verse, to his cuddly teddy-bear television persona, and to the natural charm and humility with which he treated his admiring fans. But it also owed something to his reputation as Britain's leading champion of conservation: the man who had fought vainly to save Euston Arch and had kept St Pancras alive, the man who had savagely punctured arrogant redevelopment in his poem 'The Planster's Vision', the man who gave his time and energy in the early 1970s to save Southend Pier, Liverpool Street station and Holy Trinity Church, Sloane Street. It was partly thanks to his reputation as the man who had stood up to the bulldozers that Betjeman got an unprecedented 6,000 letters of congratulation when he was made Laureate. And whatever Lees-Milne thought about the public's attitude to modern architecture, the fact that Betjeman got some fifty letters a day on 'threatened buildings, redundant churches, old market places, Victorian town halls, etc.' tells a rather different story.[23]

In previous decades, conservation had been regarded as a faintly cranky pursuit, the province of artists, eccentrics and intellectuals, three groups to whom most right-thinking people gave a very wide berth indeed. But as the demographic make-up of inner cities and rural villages changed, so the articulate, affluent newcomers began to raise their voices. Many were children of the mid-1960s, brimming with self-righteous passion. Unlike their predecessors, they were not content merely to form discussion groups; they wanted to make a difference. There were early signs of this new spirit in the 1960s, when middle-class pressure groups blocked two deranged schemes to build a relief road across Christ Church Meadow in Oxford and a tunnel underneath the centre of Bath; the location of these protests gives a clue to the kind of people attracted to conservationism. Not surprisingly, it picked up plenty of recruits in the gentrifying enclaves of London at the turn of the decade: in Gospel Oak, for example, where residents fought to save their nineteenth-century artisan houses from demolition, or in De Beauvoir Town in Hackney and Railton Road in Brixton, where residents preserved their Victorian streets from the bulldozer. Near the British Museum, long-held plans to demolish the area between Great Russell Street and Bloomsbury Way were finally abandoned in 1975 after years of bitter debate. So was an even more demented scheme to level and redevelop Covent Garden (the market having closed in 1974, although its last days are wonderfully captured in Alfred Hitchcock's film *Frenzy,* made two years earlier), which collapsed only after a vociferous protest campaign spearheaded by the *Evening Standard*'s Simon Jenkins. And most famously of all, a seventeen-year battle raged over the fate of Tolmers Square, just west of Euston, a cluster of run-down Georgian buildings that had been lined up for redevelopment as a gigantic and highly lucrative office complex. Squatters, Asian immigrants, trade unionists and even students from nearby University College London joined the crusade against the developers; in the end, though, both sides lost, with Camden Council turning it into a particularly soulless council-flat complex.[24]

In the meantime, not one but two schemes to build a new London airport had come to a sticky end. In January 1971, the Roskill Commission announced that a site had been selected in the Bedfordshire village of Cublington, well placed for access to motorways, the Midlands and the north of the capital. To get this far had taken four years of hearings and well over £1 million, but the scheme lasted only six weeks. Not only would the airport destroy a thirteenth-century church, a Georgian rectory and acres of perfect farmland, but it also threatened the country house of the Conservative political hostess Pamela Hartwell. She pulled some strings, various Tory MPs were persuaded to come out against the report, and within two months it was dead. So the government adopted a new site: Maplin Sands, a stretch of mudflats off Foulness Island in the Thames estuary. In characteristic Heath style, the plans were suitably ambitious: two runways by 1980, with two more built in the next decade; an eight-lane motorway into the heart of the City of London; a 'brand new jet city' of 300,000 people with the airport at its centre; even a high-speed railway to whisk passengers at 125 miles an hour through the Essex marshlands. The council backed it; so did the trade unions. But the locals were not so sure: one group, the 'Defenders of Essex', distributed posters warning of 'Jackboots over Essex'. As projected costs surged, Maplin began to look increasingly far-fetched, and in January 1974 the government reluctantly admitted that the plan was back under review. When Labour returned to office two months later, the new Environment Secretary, Anthony Crosland, who had mocked the scheme as 'Heathograd', wasted little time in scrapping it.[25]

But it was not just in the capital that conservationists won significant victories. In Berwick-upon-Tweed, an alliance of the local historical society and the Chamber of Trade overturned a scheme in 1970 to knock down part of the town's Elizabethan walls, calling themselves 'the authentic voice of the people'. Two years later, near Dumbarton, the fifty-five households of the little village of Dullatur – a high proportion of them professionals, clerical workers and university lecturers – defeated a plan to destroy their 'bucolic isolation' with a giant housing estate. In *Coronation Street*'s Weatherby, residents even organized an Action Group in February 1974 to stop the planned redevelopment of their beloved street. And across the land, conservationists whispered the name of their new folk hero, John Tyme, a lecturer in environmental studies at Sheffield Polytechnic. Almost no hearing or new motorway scheme went ahead without Tyme's rumbustious presence, striking fear into the heart of planners everywhere. In December 1974, he disrupted a hearing on an extension to the M16 in rural Essex. A year later he appeared as the star witness in a melodramatic hearing on plans for a four-lane road through the Aire Valley, which was eventually suspended after scenes of 'shouting and scuffling', a first for a planning inquiry. And in February 1976, after the hearing had been restarted, he was on hand to watch dozens of protesters fight their way through lines of stewards and occupy Shipley Town Hall, which was surely the most exciting thing to have happened in that corner of Yorkshire for decades.[26]

Perhaps the most colourful scenes, though, came at Winchester during the baking summer of 1976, where Major General Raymond Edge, the planning inspector, convened hearings on a planned M3 extension that would slash through the city's beloved water meadows. 'From the start,' reported *The Times*, 'it was clear that most of the 800 or so people crowded into the sweltering Guildhall had no intention of allowing the inquiry to proceed. Throughout the morning and afternoon they kept up a constant barrage of boos, handclaps, cheers and stamping of feet.' At one point, in a rare moment of solidarity between sailor and soldier, the town's excellently named MP, Rear Admiral Morgan Morgan-Giles, tried to intervene from the balcony, but he was shouted down. Meanwhile, Major General Edge's voice was constantly drowned out by chanting and singing, and when he tried to order television cameras out of the hall, fighting broke out between police and cameramen. The high point of the drama, however, came when the hearing resumed two weeks later. On this occasion, when Major General Edge refused to let John Tyme read a statement objecting to the inquiry on procedural grounds, all hell broke loose, with the crowd roaring, chanting and clapping, while the beleaguered Major General spent the next half-hour 'pointing at individuals, asking them to be silent, and, when they refused, ordering the stewards to eject them'. Order was restored only when Tyme got to read his statement after all, but, as *The Times* reported, pandemonium broke out again that afternoon when 'Mr Tyme burst back into the room. His shouted message was drowned out in cheers and applause, and police reinforcements were called.' In an extraordinary climax, the crowd started singing 'Jerusalem' and 'Land of Hope and Glory' while Major General Edge implored them to leave. At last, the police had to clear the building, dragging some of the audience with them. Among them, the press noted delightedly, was John Thorn, the headmaster of Winchester College. 'I will be back!' he shouted at Major General Edge, like some public school Terminator. Not even the chaotic planning inquiry in Tom Sharpe's novel *Blott on the Landscape* (1975), the hilarious and very timely story of Lady Maud Lynchwood's battle against the fictional M101, could compete with that.*[27]

What lay behind many of these protests was not just a love of the countryside or a fascination with Victorian architecture, but a revulsion from technological modernity and a renewed love affair with an idealized national past. At one level, conservationism was an exercise in nostalgic escapism, a way of banishing the depressing headlines about strikes, terrorism and inflation, and returning to a supposedly more settled, orderly age, when Britain still ruled the waves, the lower orders knew their place and tower blocks did not yet blight the horizon. But since so many gentrifiers read the *Guardian* and voted Labour, it was less a form of reactionary conservatism than simply yet another consumer fad. For much of the 1960s, at least until the hippy craze that set in from about

---

* In the long run, though, the conservationists lost the war, for in the 1990s the M3 was extended through Twyford Down.

1967, cultural fashion had been bound up with visions of the future, with optimistic projections of the coming Utopia, with the glamour of the Space Age. But with the shock of the Vietnam War, the collapse of Harold Wilson's modernization programme and the new vogue for resurrecting the Victorians and Edwardians, the future fell out of fashion. And by the early 1970s, with man's horizons shrinking and even the space race running out of steam, modernism itself seemed out of date. White heat was passé; rustic romanticism was the latest thing.[28]

The cult of the past found expression in a huge variety of ways. Local and family history societies, industrial archaeology groups, oral history associations and amateur history 'workshops' thrived; so too did museums, despite the entrance charges levied by the Heath government in 1970. Often seen as a product of the Thatcher years, the heritage industry was alive and well long beforehand: these were boom years for the manufacturers of china figurines, the sellers of artfully distressed-pine furniture, and the National Trust shops offering historically themed trinkets and toiletries to weekend visitors. These were good years, in fact, for the National Trust, full stop. Having been put onto more business-oriented, commercial lines at the end of the 1960s, it experienced astonishing growth in the next decade, with its membership rolls expanding from a healthy 158,000 in 1965 to 539,000 in 1975 and more than a million in 1981; as David Cannadine puts it, this was unquestionably 'the most successful recruitment drive ever undertaken in Britain in peacetime'. Country houses had never been so popular: when the government refused to accept the palatial Mentmore Towers in lieu of inheritance taxes, with the result that it was sold at auction in 1977 to the deeply disreputable Maharishi Mahesh Yogi, the public outcry was loud and long. Where country houses had once been associated with shiftless aristocrats lounging around on the backs of the poor, they were now popularly linked with a lost golden age of social order, deference and decorum, a far cry from the hooliganism and pornography of the present. Intellectuals often winced at the stunning commercial success of books like Mark Girouard's *Life in the English Country House* (1978), and above all Edith Holden's *The Country Diary of an Edwardian Lady* (1977), perhaps the most unlikely bestseller of the decade. But as Roy Strong perceptively remarked after staging the enormously successful 'Destruction of the Country House' show at the V&A in 1974, 'in times of danger' Britain's 'environmental heritage . . . represents some form of security, a point of reference, a refuge perhaps, something visible and tangible which, within a topsy and turvy world, seems stable and unchanged'.[29]

Both high and low culture seemed saturated with nostalgia in the early 1970s. In poetry, Geoffrey Hill's magnificent *Mercian Hymns* (1971) looked back to the eighth-century kingdom of Mercia under the Anglo-Saxon Offa; in pop music, nominally 'progressive' bands like Yes, Genesis and Led Zeppelin evoked an imagined past of Arthurian knights, Pre-Raphaelite maidens and perilous quests, subjects that would have seemed downright bizarre back in the days when 'Telstar' was number one. On the high street, shoppers queued to buy gentle autobiographical tales by the rural Yorkshire vet James Herriot (later televised as *All Creatures Great and Small*), no fewer than eight of which featured in the bestseller lists in 1976, or to place orders for Portmeirion's bestselling 'Botanic Garden' range of Victorian-themed pottery, which was so popular that shops ran out of stock. In the cinema, audiences revelled in the nostalgic escapism of *The Railway Children* (1970), based on E. Nesbit's popular children's tale, the film that endeared Jenny Agutter to thousands of furtive middle-aged men. There were tales of patriotic derring-do like *The Eagle Has Landed* (1976) and *The Thirty-Nine Steps* (1978, which bears almost no relation to Buchan's original but became famous for the splendid scene of Robert Powell hanging from Big Ben), and Agatha Christie adaptations such as *Murder on the Orient Express* (1974) and *Death on the Nile* (1978), which were conceived, the EMI studio boss admitted, as an antidote to 'all the gloom and doom in the country'. And then there was Peter Hall's *Akenfield* (1974), an adaptation of Ronald Blythe's bestselling oral history of a Suffolk village. Made with only a skeleton script and a cast of 150 amateurs, *Akenfield* was an astonishingly beautiful and evocative depiction of rural life from courtship and marriage to education and work, based around a young man's dilemma about whether to leave behind the familiar rhythms of the countryside after the First World War for a new life in Australia. Unsparingly honest and austere, this was more than uninformed nostalgia. Yet the public loved it: almost 15 million tuned in when *Akenfield* was shown on ITV in January 1975. The next day, even Hall's taxi driver told him how much he had enjoyed it.[30]

On television, evocations of the past were enormously popular, from *The Six Wives of Henry VIII* and *The Long March of Everyman* to

Colditz and *I, Claudius*, from *Pennies from Heaven* and *The Duchess of Duke Street* to *Dad's Army* and *Last of the Summer Wine*, reflecting not merely the BBC's unparalleled skill at making costume dramas but also the public appetite for depictions of a quieter, happier age. When the BBC launched *The Pallisers*, a stunningly elaborate 26-part version of Anthony Trollope's novels adapted by the rakish novelist Simon Raven, the on-screen world of Victorian elegance and courtroom drama made for a stark contrast with the political headlines of the day – for this was January 1974, with the papers full of the three-day week and the death throes of the Heath government, when some commentators were gloomily pondering a future of authoritarianism or revolution. But as the *Radio Times* explained, *The Pallisers* was set in a very different world, when 'the political affairs of the nation were frequently conducted in the luxurious, and sometimes frivolous drawing-rooms of London Society'. Past and present collided, however, when strikes at the BBC meant that the last two episodes were not finished in time; in the end they were shown five months later, rather undermining the impact of the series.

In general, though, viewers seemed reluctant to draw contemporary lessons from series set in the past. After the ninth episode of the hugely popular *The Onedin Line*, a family drama serial based around a Victorian shipping line watched by tens of millions in the early 1970s, researchers asked viewers if they thought James Onedin's 'commercial struggles' had 'any relevance to the industrial problems of today'. Most saw no link at all: 'I enjoy the drama and don't look for hidden meanings' was a typical response. A similar kind of escapism lay behind the success of perhaps the most successful of all the costume dramas of the 1970s, LWT's *Upstairs, Downstairs* (1971–5), a lovingly detailed portrait of Lord Bellamy's household in Edwardian London, a vision of Britain as a stable hierarchy in which the lowliest servant had her place, just as the richest aristocrat had his. Yet even in *Upstairs, Downstairs*, reality has the cruel habit of breaking in: the series ends with the General Strike and the Wall Street Crash, two moments anticipating the industrial conflict and economic crisis that would have been so familiar, and so worrying, to contemporary viewers.[31]

Even the clothes people wore often reflected the retreat from modernity into an idealized version of history. When Brentford Nylons, once advertised with unrelenting frequency on ITV by Alan Freeman ('All right? Stay bright!'), went bust in February 1976, it seemed to set the seal on a period in which the synthetic future of the 1960s had been rejected in favour of a much more organic, folksy, flowing look. In fashion and cosmetics alike, the space-age look was dead, replaced by a druggy pastiche of Pre-Raphaelite beauty which in turn gave way to a succession of retro styles from art deco elegance to Joan Crawford film noir, at once nostalgic, escapist, elegant and camp. For Biba, the emblematic London boutique of the early 1970s, it always seemed to be the day before yesterday, a world of elaborate art nouveau patterns, of muted, swirling mulberries, browns, plums and purples, of impossible glamour and unspeakable decadence. When Biba took over the art deco Derry & Toms department store in Kensington High Street, the result was a vast fun palace of nostalgic escapism, 'a free ticket to a 1930s Disneyland dropped suddenly in the centre of London', as one newspaper diarist put it when the store opened in September 1973. 'It's like seeing old Hollywood movies on a Sunday afternoon,' said one shopper, a student from UCL. 'I can just imagine Ginger Rogers and Fred Astaire dancing over the marble floors.'

Ominously, though, she had come out without her chequebook, adding: 'It's best seen and not bought.' That was precisely what most people thought about the new Big Biba, and explains why it lasted less than two years. By contrast, perhaps the most influential designer of the decade always kept a close eye on the pounds, shillings and pence, and became a rare symbol of British commercial nous. 'Her clothes possess precisely the qualities demanded by a certain sort of customer who might once have been considered a bit strange and arty crafty but is now a recognized mainstream in fashion,' one fashion writer observed in 1972. '[Laura] Ashley clothes fit in with hypo-allergenic cosmetics, milk face washes, ethnic dress, conservation and home grown food, and there is no reason why they should go out of style any faster than the ideas they seem to complement so well.'[32]

For some people, looking backwards was not enough. Like the hippies of the late 1960s, they wanted to escape inwards and outwards, to slip the bonds of rationality and modernity, to leave behind all reminders of a flawed, compromised, polluted world. In academic enclaves and urban villages, semi-hippyish writers such as Carlos Castaneda, Erich von Däniken and Robert M. Pirsig, with their accounts of prehistoric shamanism, ancient extraterrestrials and the relevance of Zen Buddhism in a technology-obsessed world, all enjoyed brief and highly undeserved bursts of success. By the mid-1970s, no fashionable household was without a copy of at least one of them, often ostentatiously displayed alongside the pot plants, semi-erotic prints and obligatory recording of *Tubular Bells*. Even more popular, though, especially in the long run, were the works of a writer who had grown up in a world very different from that of macrobiotic restaurants and progressive rock, yet became an inspiration for millions of romantic dreamers not just in Britain but across the world.

As a distinguished Oxford philologist during the middle decades of the century J. R. R. Tolkien had cut a deliberately tweedy, nostalgic figure. Yet when he died in 1973 his fame had spread well beyond the literary-academic circles in which he was most at home. He had begun work on his Middle-earth stories while recuperating from wounds suffered during the Battle of the Somme: even then, his influences, from William Morris and Richard Wagner to the neo-medievalism and mythological revival of the Victorians, were themselves backward-looking. Yet as early as 1968 – just over ten years after he had published the last part of *The Lord of the Rings* – his worldwide sales had hit 3 million. By 1979, the *Evening News* estimated that only the Bible had sold more copies worldwide than *The Lord of the Rings*, and a year later his total sales exceeded 8 million. And contrary to myth, his readers were not all Californian hippies lost in a fog of marijuana smoke. In January 1972, the *Sunday Times* reported that the paperback edition of *The Lord of the Rings* was selling a steady 100,000 copies a year in Britain alone. Not even death could diminish his appeal: in 1977, when Allen & Unwin published *The Silmarillion*, a compilation of Middle-earth legends written for Tolkien's own amusement, the initial print run of 600,000 copies was a record for a British hardback. But the publisher's vision was rapidly validated: as they had anticipated, *The Silmarillion* went straight to the top of the bestseller list.[33]

Tolkien's books would never have been so successful if they had appealed only to the strange coalition of sweaty male teenagers, pale-faced girls and lank-haired prog-rock songwriters with which they became associated. As Tolkien's *Times* obituary noted in 1973, his little hobbits 'embodied what he loved best in the English character and saw most endangered by the growth of "subtopia", bureaucracy, journalism and industrialization'. As a quiet pastoral people, at home with the land

and their pipes, the hobbits made perfect heroes for a generation who distrusted authority and self-aggrandizement, while his portrait of evil – Saruman with his 'mind of metal and wheels', the Orcs with their love of 'wheels and engines and explosions', the blackened land of Mordor, with its industrial slag-heaps, its air filled with ash and smoke, its Dark Tower dominating the horizon – is a blistering indictment of modernity, industrialization and the contemporary urban nightmare. For Tolkien, as for the environmentalists of the early 1970s, there were few greater crimes than the rape of the landscape. When the corrupted wizard Saruman turns from good to evil, he symbolically cuts down the trees around his fortress to make way for machines. Similarly, when the hobbits return home, they are horrified to find the Shire turned into a modern wasteland, with even their beloved old mill pulled down and replaced by a brick monstrosity, used not for grinding grain but for some un-specified industrial purpose. It was little wonder that green campaigners loved the book: when Greenpeace sailed into the French nuclear testing zone in 1972, one of their activists noted in his diary that he had been reading Tolkien, and 'could not avoid thinking of parallels between our own little fellowship and the long journey of the Hobbits into the volcano-haunted land of Mordor'. *The Lord of the Rings* 'is at once an attack on the modem world and a credo, a manifesto', wrote the former literary *enfant terrible* Colin Wilson in 1974. 'It stands for a system of values: that is why teenagers write "Gandalf lives" on the walls of London tubes.'[34]

The only book that rivalled *The Lord of the Rings* as both a bestseller and a 'manifesto' was another work of fantasy written for personal entertainment. Its author, Richard Adams, was an Oxford-educated civil servant in (appropriately) the Department of the Environment, who originally made up his story of talking rabbits to amuse his two daughters during a long car journey to see Judi Dench in *Twelfth Night* at the RSC. Eventually, he decided to write it down and sent it to thirteen different publishers, all of whom rejected it. Only the one-man publishing house of Rex Collings agreed to take it, and even Collings had his doubts. 'I've just taken on a novel about rabbits, one of them with extra-sensory perception,' he wrote to a friend. 'Do you think I'm mad?' But when *Watership Down* appeared in the shops in November 1972, its success was phenomenal. Early reviews were ecstatic: the *New Statesman*'s critic wrote that he found himself 'checking whether things are going to work out all right on the next page before daring to finish the preceding one', while *The Economist* declared that if there was 'no place for "Watership Down" in children's bookshops, then children's literature is dead'. To Adams's surprise, his book picked up not only the Carnegie Medal but the *Guardian* Children's Fiction Prize, while Penguin immediately snapped up the rights and brought out a Puffin paperback for children and then a Penguin edition for adults. By 1974, when the *Sunday Times* bestseller list first appeared, *Watership Down* was Britain's fastest selling book; by the end of the decade, this epic story of rabbits searching for a new warren, originally written for children, had sold more than 3 million copies – most of them to adults.[35]

Like *The Lord of the Rings*, *Watership Down* resonated with readers in the early 1970s precisely because its themes – the individual against the collective, the small against the great, the organic against the machine, the natural world of fields and woods against the man-made one of roads and bulldozers – seemed so timely. What sets the narrative in motion is the destruction of the rabbits' home to make way for 'high class modern buildings', as a sign puts it, and everything man-made – cars, roads, traps, gassing devices – seems alien and threatening. As Christopher Booker put it, the book offered 'escape from the unspeakable, inhuman world we are creating for ourselves with technology', and a 'dream of getting back to a simpler, natural world'. As in *The Lord of the Rings*, however, the novel's eco-politics came with more than a hint of old-fashioned conservatism, showing how the emerging green sensibility blurred the lines between left and right. The critic Alexander Walker called it 'a cosy idealisation of England's past . . . where everyone had their place in the warren and kept to it, women were thought to be satisfactorily defined by their role as home-makers, and the Welfare State had not yet turned hardy individual initiative into marrowbone jelly. In short, a High Tory myth.' But of course there was more to the book than political symbolism, not least an exciting story that entertained readers of all allegiances. In the midst of juggling briefs on the planned Sex Discrimination Bill, the new government's plans for massive industrial intervention and a bitter battle about pay-beds in the NHS, Labour's Barbara Castle retreated to bed one Saturday in July 1974 with a copy of Adams's bestseller. 'It was bliss to give in and to be able to read something other than an official document,' she recorded. 'I found great comfort in *Watership Down*.'[36]

Most writers of the mid-1970s, however, portrayed nature in a much darker light, emphasizing its propensity to fight back against human exploitation, even to destroy mankind itself. In 1976 alone, two competing pulp thrillers, Richard Doyle's *Deluge* and Walter Harris's *The Fifth Horseman*, showed Britain being engulfed by monstrous floods. In the latter, in good science-fiction style, the terror has been unleashed by man's own arrogance, with North Sea oil drilling (then a topical subject) having destroyed the seabed and brought a tidal wave crashing over Britain's shores. As one character sagely puts it: 'Nature abhors a vacuum ... We're taking out oil and gas, and putting nothing back.' But the book that really set the standard for nature biting back was James Herbert's gory blockbuster *The Rats* (1974), whose terrifyingly graphic vision of feral black rats swarming across London, leaving a trail of mutilated corpses in their wake, drew ferocious criticism from shocked reviewers. As the writer Alwyn Turner points out, while the murderous rats obviously tapped readers' 'folk memories of Pied Pipers and plagues', they were also inspired by contemporary headlines. There had been fears of rats running amok during the council workers' strike of October 1970, when bags of rubbish lay uncollected in the streets. Five years later, after an unofficial strike in Glasgow left more than 50,000 tons of 'rotting garbage' in the city's streets, some in piles twenty feet high, the army had to be called in to deal with the infestation of vermin. Perhaps it was no coincidence, then, that giant rats featured as deadly adversaries not only in *The Rats*, but in television adventure series such as *Doomwatch* ('Tomorrow, the Rat', 1970), *The New Avengers* ('Gnaws', 1976) and *Doctor Who* ('The Talons of Weng-Chiang', 1976). In Turner's words, nothing better symbolized 'the inability of science to deliver a brave new world' than the rearing figure of a giant rat – even if it was played by a glove puppet.[37]

Television played a central part in framing the new environmental concerns of the day, especially through the semi-fantastic adventure series that were so popular with children and adults alike. *Doomwatch* was a particularly prescient example: first broadcast in February 1970, it was partly conceived by Dr Kit Pedler, the head of electron microscopy at the University of London's Institute of Ophthalmology. As the unofficial scientific adviser to *Doctor Who*, Pedler had co-created the Cybermen four years before as a way of articulating his concerns about the effects science and technology would have on man's essential humanity, but now he wanted to take a more realistic approach. As his long-term collaborator Gerry Davis told the *Radio Times,* they wanted to create a series that would investigate 'what was happening in the world', questioning the narrative of 'scientific progress' that had dominated the headlines in the 1950s and 1960s.

Doomwatch follows the activities of the Department for the Observation and Measurement of Scientific Work, a government unit set up to appease the green lobby, but which acquires more teeth than its sponsors expected. Its director, Dr Spencer Quist (John Paul), worked with the Americans on the atomic bomb during the war, but has become a haunted and brooding man after his wife died of radiation poisoning. Meanwhile his deputy, Dr John Ridge (Simon Oates) is a *Jason King*-esque playboy with extravagant shirts, a Lotus Élan and a penchant for slapping his female colleagues on the behind. Each week, more than 12 million people tuned in to watch them confront the latest man-made menace, from a plastic-eating virus in the first episode to chemical waste, computer brainwashing, factory pollution and nuclear weapons. Thirsty for profit and indifferent to the ecological costs, big business never emerges in a good light; neither do the government nor the civil service, both of which try to obstruct Doomwatch at every turn. A thick but enjoyable streak of paranoia ran through the programme, epitomized by the moment in the third series when Ridge, driven to a breakdown by the government's refusal to tackle pollution, steals some phials of anthrax and threatens to hold the world to ransom, presenting viewers with a rare chance to see an eco-terrorist in a cravat. Needless to say, the press loved the show: while the *Mirror*'s television critic initially claimed that *Doomwatch* was 'unbelievable', the global pollution scandals of the early 1970s gave it a sense of context, and before long Davis was telling the *Daily Mail* that it was 'a staggering coincidence that many of the programmes we put out turn into reality a few days later. Of course we do our research in scientific journals but that does not explain everything.' The *Mirror* even set up its own 'Doomwatch' unit to investigate environmental issues. 'Call in Doomwatch!' the paper urged its readers. 'They are ready for action!'[38]

Since *Doomwatch* shared not only many of its writers but its cast and production team with *Doctor Who*, it was perhaps not surprising that the older series also became an unashamed champion of the new environmentalism. The very first *Doctor Who* story of the 1970s, 'Spearhead from Space', introduces us to an alien enemy that infiltrates the plastics industry, bringing shop-window dummies to life with murderous effect, and soon Jon Pertwee's Doctor finds himself working with a United Nations team to fight off weekly threats from mad scientists and alien invaders. But while this era of the programme's history owed much to precursors like *Quatermass,* it also reflected the cultural concerns of the early 1970s. Barely a week went by without the Doctor infiltrating some top-secret research establishment, often in defiance of the government and the military, and discovering a terrible elemental threat to the world's existence, unleashed by mankind's heedless meddling. As the critic James Chapman astutely remarks, it is telling that the Doctor's foes in these years tended to be green-skinned organic monsters – Silurians, Sea Devils, Axons, Ogrons, Draconians – rather than the silver metallic robots that had proliferated during the years of 'white heat'. In 'Doctor Who and the Silurians' (1970) and 'The Sea Devils' (1972) the threat even comes from the planet itself, as it is revealed that the Earth once belonged to two highly intelligent reptile species, who retreated into hibernation hundreds of millions of years ago and have been awakened by – surprise, surprise – a nuclear power research centre. Indeed, given that the series was initially conceived as a way of educating children about science, it is striking how badly scientists come out of *Doctor Who* in the 1970s. If they are not drilling to tap the power reserves hidden beneath the Earth's crust, releasing a toxic slime that turns people into hairy lunatics ('Inferno', 1970), then they are leading ill-fated geological expeditions in the far future and infecting themselves with anti-matter ('Planet of Evil', 1975). Disaster always ensues, but they never, ever learn. 'Listen to that!' the Doctor yells at the mad scientist in 'Inferno'. 'It's the sound of the planet screaming out its rage!'[39]

As in *Doomwatch,* the succession of ecological disasters inevitably takes its toll on the morale of the Doctor's friends. In 'Invasion of the Dinosaurs' (1974), the Time Lord finds modern London deserted after an infestation of very poorly realized dinosaurs, who have been brought through time by a group of radical environmentalists. It transpires that this is all part of Operation Golden Age, a plan to return the Earth to 'an earlier, purer age' before it was soiled by technology and pollution, and the conspirators include not only a group of renegade scientists, but an ecologically minded government minister and the Doctor's friend Captain Mike Yates, who has become obsessed with the dangers of industrial development. Despite the havoc, the Doctor has some sympathy for their motives, but insists that the best answer is to 'take the world you've got and try to make something of it'. And when his more literal-minded ally Brigadier Lethbridge-Stewart suggests that the conspiracy leader must have been mad, the Doctor retorts: 'Yes, well of course he was mad. But at least he realized the dangers that this planet of yours is in, Brigadier. The danger of it becoming one vast garbage dump inhabited only by rats . . . It's not the oil and the filth and the poisonous chemicals that are the real cause of pollution, Brigadier. It's simply greed.'

But by far the most radical *Doctor Who* story of the era, as well as the best remembered, was 'The Green Death', broadcast during the summer of 1973. This time, the Doctor and his assistant Jo investigate some strange goings-on at a disused coal mine in South Wales, where a miner has been found dead. ('It's exactly your cup of tea,' the Brigadier points out. 'The fellow's bright green, apparently, and dead.') The cause, it turns out, is toxic waste from a local chemical factory, which has not only given birth to a poisonous green slime that kills all who touch it, but is also breeding terrifying giant maggots. No doubt many viewers had already guessed that the factory was up to no good when its managing director appeared at the beginning of the story promising a group of unemployed miners 'wealth in our time', but they surely could not have guessed the chilling reality behind the façade. For, as the Doctor discovers, Global Chemicals, the multinational corporation that owns the factory (motto: 'Efficiency, productivity and profit'), is actually run by a megalo-maniac super-computer, the BOSS, indifferent to ecological damage and human life. To defeat it, he has to forge an unlikely alliance with a group of environmentalists based in the local Wholeweal commune. Their leader, Professor Cliff Jones, is a Nobel Prize-winning biologist; the Doctor has been looking forward to meeting him, but is taken aback when Professor Jones turns out to be a long-haired, denim-clad hippy, now working on a fungus substitute for meat. In a clear victory for the forces of environmentalism, however, it is precisely this fungus that kills the toxic slime. Meanwhile, the Doctor's ditzy companion Jo has fallen head over heels for Professor Jones's ecological message, insisting: 'It's time to call a halt, it's time that the world awoke to the alarm bell of pollution instead of sliding down the slippery slopes of, of whatever it is.' At the end of the story she announces her intention to marry him, rubbing salt in the wound by telling the Doctor that 'he reminds me of a sort of younger you'. Capitalism, chemicals and computers have been defeated, the hippies have won the day, and the Doctor drives off disconsolately into the night, alone with only the memory of a hearty fungus meal to console him.[40]

Most ecological fantasies of the 1970s were rather less heart-warming. With the headlines full of pollution and the bookshelves groaning with predictions of disaster, unutterable catastrophe tended to be the order of the day, especially in stories for children. In John Christopher's trilogy *The Prince in Waiting*, *Beyond the Burning Lands* and *The Sword of the Spirits* (1970–72), we find ourselves in a future England that has reverted to medieval customs and superstition, a bloody, paranoid world of walled cities in which dabbling with machines is a crime punishable by death. The landscape is littered with relics of modernity – one character ties his horse to a piece of wood on which are painted the words 'RADIO TV DEAL', 'something that meant nothing' – but it is also full of the casualties of science, such as 'polymufs', people disfigured by genetic mutations, who are treated like menial slaves. People in this neo-medieval future live in small wooden houses, conscious that their 'ancestors had built in stone and metal, their houses hundreds of feet high, and had died under the rubble of their tumbled pride'. But it transpires that the priestly Seers, who preach anathema towards machines, are secretly preserving the wisdom of the ancients, and have a bunker full of machines beneath Stonehenge. In the climax to the first book, they explain to the youthful hero that 'the earth itself rebelled' against the scientific arrogance of their ancestors: it 'shook and heaved and everywhere men's cities tumbled and men died in their ruins'.

> The worst of it did not last long, days rather than weeks, but it was enough to destroy the world of cities and machines. Those who survived roamed the shattered countryside and fought each other for what food there was.
>
> Gradually they came together again . . . They returned to their old places, at least to the villages and the small cities. Not to the large ones which were left as rubble. They did as they had done in the past – grew crops, raised cattle, traded and practised crafts and fought. But they would have no truck with machines, identifying them with their forefathers' ancient pride and the reckoning which had followed. Anyone found dabbling with machines was killed, for fear of bringing down fresh destruction.[41]

Hatred of machines was a popular theme of apocalyptic fiction in the 1970s. The BBC series *The Changes* (1975), adapted from Peter Dickinson's novel *The Devil's Children*, imagines a future in which mankind is filled with an overwhelming revulsion against modernity, smashing machines and banning even the mention of technological terms as society reverts to a brutal, pre-industrial order. In its chilling opening scenes, all kinds of machines – televisions, radios, toasters, cookers and cars – suddenly give out a strange, unsettling noise, filling people with an unstoppable urge to smash and destroy them. This time, however, there is a rather more upbeat conclusion. The programme's young protagonist, a secondary school girl called Nicky, decides to find out what lies behind this Luddite madness, and traces its origins to a quarry deep in the mountains, where miners have disturbed a rock identified as 'the oldest on Earth', a living entity that has been disturbed by man's industrial activity (just like the Silurians in *Doctor Who*, although here the stone seems to be an incarnation of the legendary Merlin). Only when she has begged the stone for forgiveness – and received by telepathy some home truths about man's greed and pollution – is the terrible process reversed, the world apparently having been restored to 'balance' between nature and machine – although what that means is anybody's guess.[42]

In April 1975, only a month after the conclusion of *The Changes*, the BBC showed the first episode of what would become the last word in eco-catastrophe dramas. Thanks to its terrifying global-pandemic opening, its earnest back-to-the-land message, its endless shots of Volvos trundling down country lanes, and its cast of balding men in parkas and feisty women in dungarees, *Survivors* captured the spirit of the mid-1970s better than almost any other cultural product of the day. It follows the adventures of three plucky survivors – Greg, an engineer, Abby, a middle-class housewife, and Jenny, a young secretary – in the aftermath of a devastating pandemic that has wiped out the vast majority of the world's population. In the opening titles, we track the progress of the deadly virus from a Chinese laboratory, where a scientist has become accidentally infected (do they never learn?), across the Western world. And in 'The Fourth Horseman', the show's first and arguably best episode, we watch as society crumbles in the face of what appears at first to be merely flu. When we first meet Abby (Carolyn Seymour), she is playing tennis in her Home Counties back garden against a serving machine. When she leaves the court, the machine continues to pump out balls, but we know it will stop eventually – as will all other machines on the planet, although for very different reasons. And as Abby cooks her husband's dinner, listening to the news of the illness striking London, she muses prophetically on the fragility of civilization. 'I never thought what happens to a city if it all breaks down, all at the same time,' she says. 'There's no power, no lighting or cooking. And food, even if you get it into the city, you can't distribute it. Then there's water, sewage, ugh! Things like that.'

Soon afterwards, Abby falls ill; when she awakes, not only is her husband (Peter Bowles, in pre-bounder days) dead, but so is everyone else in the village. Together with a handful of like-minded survivors, she faces the overwhelming challenge of eking out a decent life in a world without electricity or running water, without government or police, without televisions or telephones, supermarkets or hospitals. In this Hobbesian world, the very concepts of affluence and technology have lost their meaning. And while the little group of survivors establishes a rudimentary commune in a country house, they are not fleeing the modern world from choice, like the hippies of the early 1970s, but because they have no alternative. The cities have been reduced to cesspits: when Jenny flees London, she is leaving a city collapsing into anarchy, the streets jammed with traffic, the hospitals choked with corpses. Later, when the survivors visit a supermarket in search of provisions, they find it crawling with rats; from the ceiling hangs a corpse, a sign around its neck reading 'LOOTER'. When they make it back to London in the second series, they find a city haunted by vermin and disease: although a little commune survives at the Oval and still has heat and light, it has to maintain an electric fence to keep the rats out, and is ruled by a fascistic despot. The future lies not in the city but in the countryside; as the series progresses, the survivors become increasingly self-sufficient, giving the lie to Abby's despairing claim that they are 'less practical than Iron Age man'. Indeed, by its third season *Survivors* often seemed like a how-to guide for viewers expecting an imminent apocalypse, patiently following its characters as they teach themselves gardening and medicine, grow wheat and make soap, and even set up a rudimentary government, with its own approved currency. There is even a happy ending, as they rediscover the means to generate power: a sign that the narrative of human progress, for good or ill, can begin again.[43]

*

In interviews to promote the first series of *Survivors*, the show's creator Terry Nation claimed that the idea had come to him long before the oil shock of 1973. But in an age when petrol pumps seemed in danger of running dry and the next power cut was always just around the corner, his series struck a powerful chord. In particular, its fascination with self-sufficiency took up one of the most fashionable and popular themes of the day. Previewing the show in April 1975, the *Radio Times* advised its readers that 'in a survival situation, the only things we would have to rely on would be our hands and our muscle power'. Helpfully, the magazine recommended a couple of good reads on how to provide for a family in the event of disaster: '*Food for Free* [by Richard Mabey] is literally that: plants you can pick up in the hedgerows. And John Seymour's book on *Self-Sufficiency* actually tells you how to kill a pig – and how many of us would know how to do that? Dismiss the technical approach and think primitive!'

Thinking primitive was all the rage in the mid-1970s: the *Radio Times* piece, for example, was illustrated with a montage of other exciting titles, from *The Vegetable Garden Displayed* and *The Rearing of Chickens* to *The Small Commercial Poultry Flock* and *Soil Conditions and Plant Growth*. When Terry Nation showed his interviewer a carved wooden ornament and asked: 'Who cut the tree down? Who made the steel to create the saw to cut it down? Who dug the coal to feed the furnace to make the steel? Who dug the iron ore out of the ground?', he was merely echoing the ideas of one of the gurus of the self-sufficiency movement, John Seymour, who liked to ask audiences to work out the processes behind even the most basic household items. And when Nation's survivors were shown painstakingly learning crafts from scratch and building up a body of knowledge to pass on to the next generation, they were following all the principles of Seymour's manifesto, *Self-Sufficiency*. No doubt they would have benefited from a trip to the Centre for Alternative Technology, which had been founded in a disused slate quarry outside Machynlleth two years previously, opened its doors to the public in 1975 and soon became Europe's most successful eco-centre. And if only they had had a subscription to the magazine *Practical Self-Sufficiency*, founded in the same year, then they might have picked up all sorts of useful tips. 'The country faces grave economic difficulties and the likelihood of severe shortages,' an editorial in the first issue began ominously.

Rapid inflation, unemployment, soaring food prices, chemically adulterated foods and the increasing dehumanising of our Society have all contributed to a growing awareness of the need to be more self-reliant – to grow more of our own food – to make less demands on a welfare state which can no longer cope with the needs of its citizens . . . The need is for direct experience of the whole and natural life, irrespective of the situation in which we find ourselves – whether it be in the centre of a city or in a commune in Wales. This is of paramount importance, not only for us, but for our children – for knowledge and experience gained in childhood are never lost.[44]

The founders of *Practical Self-Sufficiency* were a husband-and-wife team, David and Katie Thear, who had started running an organic small-holding in rural Essex after David was made redundant. But it was another husband-and-wife team, Tom and Barbara Good, who were to become the poster children of self-sufficiency, thanks to the great success of the BBC sitcom *The Good Life*, which began life just two weeks before *Survivors*. In less skilful hands the show might have become painfully worthy, but thanks to the accomplished writing of John Esmonde and Bob Larbey, and perhaps even more to the performances of Richard Briers and Felicity Kendal, it became one of the fondest-remembered comedies of the decade. One of the keys to its appeal was that unlike the characters in *Survivors*, the Goods never take themselves too seriously and are actually not very good at self-sufficiency. Although they set out with the best of intentions, Tom throwing up his job as a Surbiton draughtsman designing the plastic toys in cereal packets, their failures are more notable than their triumphs: their goat is always escaping, there are all sorts of mishaps with their pigs and chickens, and their beloved peapod burgundy is practically undrinkable. Their relationship with their next-door neighbours Jerry and Margo, the souls of suburban respectability, affords plenty of opportunities to poke fun at middle-class conventions, but it must have been a rare viewer who did not, from time to time, have a sneaking sympathy for poor, beleaguered Margo. There could, after all, be something unbearably self-righteous about even the most well-intentioned defender of the planet. The feminist paper *Spare Rib* reported the case of 'an ecologically orientated' mother who 'chews up her baby's food for him rather than use the blender that she has been given. She believes that turning on the blender contributes unnecessarily to the pollution produced by electric power plants.' Not even Tom and

Barbara were that bad, although the series did have one or two detractors. 'Saw Richard Briers in a comedy series,' recorded Kenneth Williams after watching the second episode. 'It was terrible. Not a laugh line in it.'[45]

Although self-sufficiency was never more than a minority interest, composting, recycling and tending allotments did enjoy growing and sustained popularity. Even the *Daily Mail* Ideal Home Exhibition eagerly jumped aboard the bandwagon, with displays showing the homeowners of 1975 how they could make wall lights from empty tin cans, rugs from old cardigans, a lamp from cigarette packets, a chair from drainpipes and a table from corrugated iron sheeting, which was surely carrying recycling to post-apocalyptic extremes. For some people, however, growing one's own vegetables and saving on electricity were not enough: as Gordon Rattray Taylor had shown in *The Doomsday Book*, the situation was so desperate that only collective action could stave off disaster. One such group were the members of the Conservation Society, which had been founded in 1966 (by James Lees-Milne, among others) after a series of letters to the *Observer* about the dangers of massive population growth. During the next few years, the society devoted itself not only to population policy, family planning and abortion reform, but to water conservation, national parks projects, the problems of disappearing hedgerows, the urgent need for recycling and the campaigns against Concorde and the Maplin scheme. With fewer than 5,000 members in 1970, it was hardly a mass movement, but two years later it scored a notable triumph by exposing cyanide dumping in Warwickshire, a coup that paved the way for the Deposit of Poisonous Waste Act. By the beginning of 1973 its membership reached more than 8,700, but then it began to decline – not because of any defects on the society's part, but because another group had captured the limelight.[46]

In February 1971, the environment reporter of *The Times* alerted his readers to a new publication, *The Environmental Handbook*, which had been produced by a small group of young activists in a little office space in Covent Garden. It was 'a good 40p's worth for all do-it-yourself environmentalists', he thought, quoting its message to readers: 'Be as subversive, clever, radical, yet constructive as you possibly can.' Its authors certainly lived up to their own injunction. On 10 May, sixty young members of Friends of the Earth (inspired by a similarly named association across the Atlantic) marched from Pall Mall to Schweppes House in Connaught Place, demanding that the company change its policy of having non-returnable bottles. When they arrived at the firm's headquarters they listened to a poetry reading, as was then obligatory at protest marches. But it was what they did next that caught the attention of the press, as they ceremonially dumped some 1,500 glass bottles on the doorstep, with the warning that more would follow unless Schweppes gave in. It was a brilliant public relations coup (aided by the fact that, amazingly, not one of the bottles broke): the next day, *The Times* reported, 'supporters of FOE's campaign kept the telephone ringing in the group's tiny office'.[47]

From a small band of radical students (the British branch's founder, Graham Searle, had been vice president of the NUS just a year beforehand), Friends of the Earth mushroomed into one of the largest and most influential green groups in the country. Within barely a year, *The Times* was calling it 'the most effective pressure group probably since the days of Shelter under Mr Des Wilson'. In 1971, Friends of the Earth had eight local branches; by 1976 there were 140, and by 1980 there were 250, with 17,000 people having registered as supporters. It succeeded because it was daring, irreverent, clever and often funny; crucially, it was also highly decentralized, allowing local activists to set their own tone. It was a new kind of organization, assertive and dynamic rather than nostalgically conservationist, aiming not just to preserve what was left of nature, but to roll back the tide of industry and pollution. It produced pamphlets on everything from roads and pollution to uranium mining and the whaling industry; it stopped Rio Tinto-Zinc mining for copper in Snowdonia, and lobbied the government for a ban on imported products made from endangered species. Funnily enough, though, the one thing it did not do was to persuade Schweppes to change its policy on returnable bottles.[48]

A common criticism of groups like Friends of the Earth was that they were merely opportunities for spoiled middle-class do-gooders to get together and indulge their bleeding hearts, and that they offered nothing to working-class households who supposedly had neither the time nor the money to worry about footling issues like the future of the planet. Trade union leaders, for instance, tended to be highly suspicious. 'My members have achieved decent living standards and they want further improvements,' boasted the electricians' leader Frank Chapple. 'They can identify with the advance of new technology and its benefits, not with the muesli-eaters, ecology freaks, loony leftists and other nutters who make up the anti-nuclear brigade.' But perhaps the fiercest critic was Labour's shadow environment spokesman, Anthony Crosland, whose obsession with economic growth meant that he was virtually blind to the campaigners' argument. In a sense, Crosland was still dining out on his reputation as the rising star of the 1950s; as he grew older and wearier with the disappointments of office, his thinking became coarser, more rigid, closed to new ideas. Conservationism, he told his wife, was 'morally wrong when we still have so many pressing needs that can only be met if we have economic growth'. The environmentalists suffered, he thought, from a 'middle-class and upper-class bias' (which was a bit rich coming from the Highgate public school boy who had set out to smash the grammar schools), and they were 'kindly and dedicated people, but were usually affluent and wanted to kick the ladder down behind them' (ditto). Invited on television to debate the point with representatives of environmental groups, Crosland ostentatiously dropped off to sleep during a short film about the dangers of development; afterwards, he claimed that he had merely been 'resting his weary eyes'. Perhaps it was not surprising that, as one of his fellow MPs told him, he was 'more hated by environmentalists than any man I know'.[49]

In some respects, though, Crosland's analysis was not far short of the mark. Environmentalism appealed above all to the well-meaning, well-educated middle-class professionals who throughout Britain's modern history had written letters to the press, signed petitions and attended public meetings. A survey of people who read the new magazine *The Ecologist* in 1971, for example, revealed that 59 per cent belonged to the professional middle classes, with a very high proportion of teachers and scientists, and a further 33 per cent were students and sixth-formers. Indeed, in many respects the ecology movement was the natural successor to CND, which had fallen from fashion after the nuclear test-ban treaty of 1963 and the rise of détente. Not only was there a strong social and cultural affinity between CND and environmentalism – what might be called the *Guardian*–folk music–chunky knitwear tendency – but there is some evidence that many people moved instinctively from one movement to the other, following the tides of political fashion. They were the heirs to the dissenters and Nonconformists of old, the kind of people who had once inveighed against bishops, slavery, armaments and empire – which automatically invited the suspicion of well-heeled politicians like Crosland who fancied themselves as tribunes of the working classes. When one of Crosland's old Oxford pupils went to a Friends of the Earth meeting in December 1977, for example, he was impressed by their enthusiasm but disturbed by their bourgeois leanings. 'They were an overwhelmingly middle-class group,' recorded the former Viscount Stansgate, now plain 'Tony' Benn. 'They appeal to some radicals and dissenters, but I felt they could be drawn into the mainstream of establishment opinion without actually making any difference to the way in which society was run.' He advised them to 'turn your mind to the power structure' – which, given that Benn was then Secretary of State for Energy, was precisely what they had been trying to do all evening.[50]

One of the remarkable things about environmentalism – confusing to some, refreshing to others – was the way in which it blurred the traditional ideological division between left and right. While both the Tories and Labour made growth and modernization their central objectives, environmental groups' challenge to modernity made it hard to locate them within the conventional spectrum.* A good example was the magazine *The Ecologist*, which was launched in July 1970 by Edward Goldsmith, known as Teddy. Born into a wealthy banking family and the elder brother of the ruthless financier James Goldsmith, Teddy was a rich man, free to travel the world indulging his passion for anthropology and his fascination with what he called 'tribal peoples'. He became convinced not only that tribal societies were being wiped out by economic progress, but that the human race itself was at risk, with man's basic nature as a hunter-gatherer having been eroded by centuries of decadence. By the end of the 1960s, Goldsmith had decided that it was time to fight back, and so he invested £20,000 of his own money, as well as £4,500 of his brother's, in the new magazine. More funds came from rich friends like the eccentric casino owner John Aspinall, who ran Mayfair's Clermont Club, kept a tigress and two brown bears in his private zoo, and spent his spare time fantasizing about a right-wing military coup. And the first issue of *The Ecologist* was apocalyptic to say the least, with a cover story warning of world famine, urgent appeals for population control and a public sterilization drive, and a suitably melodramatic editorial by Goldsmith himself. It was 'only a question of time', he wrote, before

---

* Stephen Poliakoff's play *Strawberry Fields* (1977), for example, features a far-right group called the English People's Party, violently opposed to immigration and pollution, and obsessed with the rape of the countryside and blight of the motor car; one character calls it a 'sort of conservation wing of the National Front'.

the planet's resources were exhausted, and then 'that already tottering technological superstructure – the "technosphere" – that is relentlessly swallowing up our biosphere, will collapse like a house of cards, and the swarming human masses, brought into being to sustain it, will in turn find themselves deprived of even this imperfect means of sustenance'.[51]

The Ecologist was a big fish in the pond of the early green movement: as the historian Meredith Veldman remarks, it was a 'slick, well-produced and expensive publication', and 'brought an air of professionalism to a movement often beset by amateurism'. Many of its themes – the dangers of nuclear power, the threat of motorway expansion, the folly of supersonic aircraft, the blind brutality of industrial farming – reflected what other green groups were saying in the 1970s, and the magazine was rarely less than provocative. On the other hand, Goldsmith's obsession with the 'hunter-gatherer' ideal and his insistence that tribal societies were 'the normal units of social organization', which in almost every issue were obediently echoed by his assistant Robert Allen, struck more than a few readers as downright odd. In its respect for nature, its fascination with community, its rejection of materialism and its obsession with a lost pre-industrial golden age, *The Ecologist* was not so different from other green groups, or indeed from *The Lord of the Rings* and *Watership Down*. But when Goldsmith demanded an immediate end to immigration, or ferociously condemned welfare programmes that interfered with the 'natural controls' of infant mortality, or denounced women's liberation, he seemed less like a nostalgic idealist and more like a cranky archreactionary.

In some ways, indeed, his magazine blurred the lines between two very different kinds of groups in the early 1970s: the middle-class conservationists and environmentalists fretting about the state of the world, and the discontented Mayfair playboys muttering about toppling the government and turning the clock back. And on occasion, its obsession with hunter-gatherer medievalism produced positively bizarre results, such as when, in July 1975, Robert Allen produced a wild encomium to the Khmer Rouge, who had just had forced Cambodia's entire population to march into the countryside in a bloody attempt to build peasant Communism from the ground up. 'They seem to be doing their best to ensure that urban parasitism cannot reoccur,' Allen wrote, commending them on their decision to close the factories, smash up the banks and destroy the towns' water supplies. 'They deserve our best

---

wishes, our sympathy and our attention. We might learn something.'[52]

For a brief period, however, *The Ecologist* genuinely set the tone of environmental debate in Britain. Its undoubted high point came in January 1972, when the magazine published a special issue billed as a 'Blueprint for Survival', which sold out immediately, was then published as a book by the small imprint of Tom Stacey, and was finally picked up by Penguin. As usual, its guiding lights were Goldsmith and Allen, and the message, laid out in detailed bullet-point form, was as doom-laden and melodramatic as ever. Much of the world would run out of food 'within the next 30 years,' it warned; the reserves of all but a few metals would be gone 'within 50 years', and 'the breakdown of society and the irreversible disruption of the life-support systems on this planet' would come 'within the lifetimes of our children'. Not unpredictably, Goldsmith advised his readers that only a 'stable society', abandoning pretensions to material progress, but embracing man's hunter-gatherer instincts, could save the world. Industrial development must cease; population must be tightly controlled; and people must live in self-sufficient units of no more than 500 people each, with the political system conducted on a largely local basis. And in some ways the Blueprint's vision sounded distinctly authoritarian. 'There is no doubt that the long transitional stage that we and our children must go through will impose a heavy burden on our moral courage and will require great restraint,' it warned, adding that 'legislation and the operations of police forces and the courts will be necessary to reinforce this restraint'.[53]

If nothing else, the Blueprint was a brilliant public relations coup. Before it was published, Robert Allen asked thirty-six eminent scientists and conservationists for their approval, including Peter Scott, Sir Julian Huxley, Professor C. H. Waddington, Professor W. A. Robson and Sir Frank Fraser Darling, a member of the Royal Committee on Environmental Pollution whose Reith Lectures had done much to arouse public anxiety about environmental damage. Allen then printed their names on the inside front cover, giving careless readers the impression that they had written the Blueprint themselves. He also managed to get Sir Frank Fraser Darling to chair a press conference on the day the magazine came out, ensuring yet more publicity: indeed, the next day saw reports in almost every national newspaper, including on the front pages of both *The Times* and the *New York Times*. Even in his wildest dreams, Goldsmith could hardly have hoped for better coverage. In the *Guardian*, Anthony Tucker compared the Blueprint's impact to that of the Communist Manifesto; in *The Times,* a long leader concluded that its thesis was 'too plausible to be dismissed'; in the *Sunday Times,* Lewis Chester wrote that it was 'nightmarishly convincing'; and even the *Daily Mail* thought that its 'prophecy of a world blindly careening towards self-destruction remains profoundly disturbing', and that 'the prophets of doom deserve to be heard with as much respect as those who continue to worship the Gross National Product'. If that were not enough, a week or so later 187 scientists, including nine Fellows of the Royal Society and twenty university professors, signed a letter to *The Times* explaining that though they were unable to sign the Blueprint because of its errors of fact or emphasis, they welcomed it as a 'major contribution to current debate' and a reminder that only population control, conservation and recycling could save the planet. 'Now letters are written daily to *The Times,*' recorded James Lees-Milne, a great admirer of the Blueprint, 'and everyone who thinks at all realises that the future of the earth is literally at stake.'[54]

Although the Blueprint was, perhaps fortunately, never put into effect, there is no doubt that it caused a considerable stir. In the Commons, the junior environment minister Eldon Griffiths called it a 'quite remarkable document', and Goldsmith even got to present his ideas to the Environment Secretary, Peter Walker, at an informal meeting in February 1972, although nothing really came of it. All the same, environmentalism seemed to be on the march. In January both the *Lancet* and the *British Medical Journal* published letters signed by dozens of doctors demanding immediate action to halt global over-population, while on the very same day that *The Ecologist* published the Blueprint for Survival, the American ecological doom-monger Paul Ehrlich addressed a capacity crowd at Westminster's Central Hall, telling them that Britain held 'the key to the entire problem', and that 'educated people look a great deal to England to lead the way'. In radical environmentalist circles, it was hard to miss the feeling of millenarian excitement, of 'high euphoria', as one of Goldsmith's colleagues later remembered. In the very near future, it seemed, all politics would be green.[55]

It was in Coventry, of all places, that this new mood bore concrete results. Towards the end of 1972, a group of friends started meeting in a local pub to discuss their shared interest in environmental issues, and in the New Year four of them – Tony and Lesley Whittaker, who were both solicitors, an estate agent called Michael Benfield and his assistant Freda Saunders – decided that it was time to do their bit. (Revealingly, Tony Whittaker was a former Conservative activist, and had already tried to interest the mainstream parties in environmental issues, but with no joy.) On 31 January, the *Coventry Evening Telegraph* carried an advertisement inviting support for a new political party, PEOPLE, with the goal of winning power by 1990. By later standards, their message was both uncompromising and thoroughly bleak, calling for an end to economic growth, strict measures to limit population and the radical levelling of social distinctions through a National Incomes scheme. It also bore the heavy imprint of Teddy Goldsmith, who merged his own abortive Movement for Survival with the new group, and whose austere views influenced their first manifesto. Their goal was to field 600 parliamentary candidates at the next general election; in the event, partly because it came more quickly than they were expecting, they actually fielded just five and won a mere 4,576 votes. It did not help that their first colour scheme, coral and turquoise, came out as red and blue on their cheaply printed flyers; or that the press, assuming that they were yet another left-wing sect, consistently called them the People's Party. When a second election was called for October 1974 they did even worse than before, winning a feeble 1,996 votes. At this stage they might easily have collapsed. The Whittakers decamped to the West Country to start a new life of self-sufficiency, but in their absence the party changed its name to the Ecology Party and in 1979 managed to field 55 candidates. To almost universal surprise it picked up almost 18,000 votes, not bad going for a party with just 500 members. The Green Party – as it was eventually called – was on its way.[56]

In many ways the green movement of the 1970s was a failure. It never dislodged economic growth from the forefront of the political agenda; indeed, as the economy lurched close to the abyss in 1974 and 1975, environmental issues faded from the headlines, not reappearing until a decade or so later. To some extent, environmentalism was a middle-class fad, as its critics had claimed, and its strident, apocalyptic tone, so redolent of protest movements in the early 1970s, meant that it never attracted a mass following. The young man who placed a personal ad in *The Ecologist* in March 1974, hoping for a partner to 'share the remaining years of industrial civilisation' and experience the 'end catastrophe', may well have found a girlfriend eventually, but it is hard to believe that he was a very jaunty date. Even Jonathon Porritt, the Old Etonian baronet who chaired the Ecology Party in the late 1970s and became one of Britain's best-known environmental campaigners, conceded that 'there was too much doom and gloom in the early seventies, and there's a limit to how much people will take'. They may have laughed along with Richard Briers and Felicity Kendal, but most were too attached to their comforts to contemplate a life of self-sufficiency, and while they may have enjoyed watching *Survivors* on Wednesday nights, they had no desire to re-enact it themselves.[57]

And yet there is another side to the story. The green movement may have disappeared from the headlines, but environmental concerns continued to seep into the mainstream, with consumer groups and publications like *Which?* taking up issues like pollution and over-packaging. In cities and town centres, there was no return to the unchecked philistinism of the 1950s and 1960s. Although development continued, it was more sensitive to the historic landscape, and attempts to knock down much-loved Victorian or Edwardian buildings typically provoked angry public debates. Industrial agri-business still ruled the countryside, but in 1978 Labour introduced a conservation bill that was inherited by Michael Heseltine and eventually passed as the Wildlife and Countryside Act of 1981. The Ecology Party slowly picked up recruits, Friends of the Earth went from strength to strength, and more established groups like the RSPCA, the RSPB, the National Trust and the Council for the Preservation of Rural England attracted millions of supporters and acquired a more assertive, even mildly radical edge. And in a piece entitled 'How people have been made to care about their surroundings', *The Times* noted that by the summer of 1975 there was already a vast array of unsung little groups and societies: 'organizations for the preservation of ancient monuments, birds, canals, friendless churches, green belts, rights of way, steam engines and village ponds; for the promotion of archaeology, tree planting, light railways, public transport and road safety; and opposed to airports, motorways, Concorde and much else'. They might not win every battle; they might even lose more than they won; but the revealing and heartening thing was that they were fighting at all.[58]

And there were other legacies, too. Thanks to Elisabeth Beresford's wonderful characters, a generation of children were converted to the joys of recycling by the Wombles of Wimbledon Common, who first appeared on television, making good use of the things that they found, in February 1973. Meanwhile, it was thanks to the conservationist, backward-looking spirit of the early 1970s that traditional country crafts – basket-weaving, pottery-making, iron-working – were saved from extinction, and that the antique shop became such a familiar and much-loved fixture in the alleys and back streets of little towns across the country. It was thanks to the well-meaning muesli-eaters of the 1970s that macrobiotic restaurants and wholefood shops became common sights in big cities, gradually evolving into the vegetarian restaurants and organic cafés that later generations took for granted; and it was partly thanks to the sandal-wearing members of the Campaign for Real Bread that the sliced white loaf did not destroy traditional baking for ever. And it was thanks to the Campaign for Real Ale – founded in 1971 by a stereotypical group of bearded do-gooders, one of whom, Roger Protz, was expelled from first the Socialist Labour League and then the International Socialists for being too left wing – that keg beers like Watney's Red Barrel and tasteless lagers like Skol and Hofmeister did not kill off the traditional ales of England, and that British drinkers could hold their heads high in the beer halls of the world. These groups were much mocked at the time, and indeed there was often something faintly ridiculous about them. But it is only a slight exaggeration to say that whenever a modern Briton eats brown toast for breakfast or has a pint of proper beer after work, he ought to mutter a quiet thank-you to those real-life Wombles of the early 1970s.[59]

6

A Bloody Awful Country

For God's sake bring me a large Scotch. What a bloody awful country!

– Reginald Maudling, 1 July 1970

You may not totally eliminate the IRA, but the army has the power and certainly the intention of reducing the level of violence to something which is acceptable.

– Reginald Maudling, 15 December 1971

It was late on Friday afternoon, when the working day is winding down and thoughts are turning to the blessed relief of the weekend, that a police car, two army Land Rovers and four armoured personnel carriers of the Royal Scots Guards turned off the heavily Catholic Falls Road, Belfast and into the narrow, brick-terraced warren of streets below it. Their destination was 24 Balkan Street, where the Official IRA had hidden a small cache of weapons just days before, and, as the Scots Guards sealed off the street, their major and a group of Royal Ulster Constabulary men searched the house. But by the time they emerged, carrying fifteen pistols, a machine gun, a rifle and some ammunition, it was to a scene rapidly descending into chaos. At either end of the street, crowds of angry residents had surrounded the Scots Guards, pushing and shouting. And as the soldiers regained the safety of their personnel carriers, the crowd was on them, banging on the doors and trying to rock them from side to side. In the confusion, one of the drivers tried to reverse past the crowd, but he had barely got his one-tonne Humber into gear when he heard a sickening crunch. Without meaning to, he had reversed his vehicle into one of the local men, crushing him against the spikes of the iron railings at the edge of the street. From the crowd there came a great howl of rage, then the clatter of stones, raining down on the armoured personnel carriers. The soldiers radioed for help, and minutes later more Royal Scots roared into the Falls. It was not even 5.30; most people were still at work. But already the evening's bloodshed had started.

By six o'clock, the narrow brick streets of the Lower Falls – streets that would have seemed immediately familiar to the residents of countless British industrial towns – were the backdrop for what might have been a medieval pitched battle or a vision of the Inferno. As more and more troops were sucked into the warren, each detachment supposedly going in to rescue the last, thick clouds of CS gas drifted down the alleyways and along the back streets, under doorways and windows, into bedrooms and kitchens, choking and suffocating men, women and children alike. As terrified residents cowered behind their doors, they heard the ominous percussion of nail and petrol bombs, and then the louder bangs of grenades and gelignite. High in the skies above Belfast, where the army's commander was watching events from his helicopter, it must have seemed like a scene from Bosch or Breughel, hundreds of angry figures scurrying furiously through the little streets, the landscape dotted with bursts of flame and clouds of smoke. At seven, Brigadier Hudson gave orders for the troops to regroup outside the Falls. Already residents had started erecting makeshift barricades, setting light to tyres, mattresses and old bits of furniture, while the word on the street was that the Official IRA were on their way with guns.

But Hudson had no intention of giving up. By eight o'clock he had 3,000 men stationed just outside the Falls, among them units of the Black Watch and Life Guards whose ship had docked in Belfast only that afternoon. Twenty minutes later, he sent them in and sent them in hard, with instructions to clear the barricades, disperse the rioters and secure the area. Now there were no half-measures, and when the first shots rang out from the IRA men in the shadows, the soldiers fired back; one officer's log recorded that some 1,500 rounds of ammunition were fired that night. Yet again there was no escape from the CS gas; indeed, this time canisters smashed through roof tiles into attics, filling the houses with smoke. On the doorsteps stood little bowls of vinegar, left by housewives for their men to protect them from the gas; in the dark back alleys, IRA snipers ran for cover. Such was the chaos, the clouds of gas, the confused hell of bullets and shouting and screaming, that it was a miracle only four more people were killed and forty-five injured. Even so, these were terrible scenes to be unfolding on a Friday night in one of the United Kingdom's great old ports. By ten o'clock, in fact, the situation seemed so far out of control that the army's commanding officer in Northern Ireland, General Sir Ian Freeland, decided it was time for drastic measures. Above the noise of battle, a new sound broke through: a clipped, upper-class English voice, booming from loudspeakers in a helicopter high in the sky, declaring that the Falls were under curfew, and ordering all civilians to get off the streets immediately or risk being shot.

The two-day curfew imposed on the Falls Road from the evening of Friday, 3 July 1970 was one of the pivotal moments in Northern Ireland's descent into sectarian bloodshed. As the army moved in to search the Falls, there were reports of more gun battles across Belfast, while three bombs went off in the city centre, the biggest at the offices of the city's Unionist *Belfast News Letter*. Clouds of CS gas still hung in the air as the armoured personnel carriers moved through the shattered streets, littered with debris, ash and broken glass. Toddlers watched with handkerchiefs pressed over their mouths as the Black Watch moved from house to house, kicking in locked doors, ripping up floorboards, tossing family photographs and religious trinkets contemptuously to the floor. For many, this was their chance to get their revenge on the IRA bastards who had been shooting at them; some, however, felt qualms of unease as they smashed their way through one house after another, like an invading army on foreign soil. Inside, parents hugged their children close as they heard the tramp of the soldiers' boots; in some houses, trapped IRA men sat clutching mugs of tea, their guns hidden, their taut faces trying to contain their fear. No house escaped, and by the time the curfew was lifted, the army had arrested more than 300 people and collected some 100 firearms, 100 homemade bombs, 250 pounds of explosives and 21,000 rounds of ammunition. But their haul came at a heavy price; too heavy, many thought.

'Some of the houses I had seen were totally wrecked,' said the Provisional Sinn Fein activist Marie Moore, who led a group of women to bring bread, milk, tea and sugar to the imprisoned residents on Sunday morning. 'Holy statues were smashed on the floor. Family portraits and pictures were smashed. Furniture was ripped and overturned. Windows were broken and doors off the hinges. Some of the people who'd been beaten were still lying there, bloody and bruised.' Perhaps she exaggerated a little. But when a senior British officer looked into allegations of looting and pillaging, he estimated that about sixty of them were true. And when residents saw two hard-line Unionist politicians touring the area in an army Land Rover, like colonial officials surveying the repression of the natives, even the most moderate struggled to contain a surge of fury. For the men and women of the newly formed Provisional IRA, who had spent the last few months seething at their fellow Catholics' apparent passivity in the face of British occupation, it was a moment to savour. Women who had once given soldiers cups of tea now slammed their doors or spat in their faces; children who had once watched the armoured personnel carriers passing with fascinated awe now threw stones and chanted abuse. 'Thousands of people who had never been republicans now gave their active support to the IRA,' one of the Provisionals' rising stars, a young man called Gerry Adams, wrote later. As men and women poured furiously out of their homes in the moments after the curfew had been lifted, a helicopter cruised overhead, a British officer repeating through a loudspeaker: 'We are your friends. We are here to help you.' But nobody was listening.[1]

When Edward Heath became Prime Minister, the agony of Northern Ireland was already several years old. The so-called Six County state, which had been detached from the rest of Ireland in the Partition of 1922 and ruled since then by the Ulster Unionist Party, had a strange and uneasy relationship with the rest of Britain. It was part of the United Kingdom, but although its Protestant majority often described themselves as British, it was not technically part of Great Britain. Meanwhile, although the Republic of Ireland still maintained that the Six Counties were part of Ireland, most southern politicians had lost all interest in the province and consistently ignored its minority Catholic representatives. Since the late 1960s, however, Northern Ireland had found itself making international headlines thanks to a deadly cocktail of industrial decline, sectarian tensions and the violent repression of civil rights marches. Since 1963 its patrician Prime Minister, Captain Terence O'Neill, had falteringly tried to guide the province towards modernization and reform, partly by trying to attract international investment and partly by trying to reach out to the Catholic minority, who suffered from voting, housing and job discrimination. But as so often happens, his tentative reforms proved the worst of all worlds. At a time when the Belfast shipyards were struggling to stay alive, O'Neill's programme alienated working-class Protestants who were already frightened for their jobs, pushing them into the arms of anti-Catholic demagogues like the evangelical minister Ian Paisley. And by 1966, a group of working-class loyalists from Belfast's staunchly Protestant Shankill Road had already founded the vigilante Ulster Volunteer Force (UVF) and committed the first murder of the Troubles, drunkenly killing a Catholic barman in cold blood.

But on the other side, too, O'Neill's reforms failed to satisfy the demands for change. From August 1968 onwards, Catholic nationalists mounted a series of high-profile civil rights marches, demanding an end to gerrymandered voting, the elimination of job and housing discrimination, and the abolition of the unionist state's security force, the B Specials. In the background, however, hovered the spectre of Irish unity, which was utterly unacceptable to their Protestant neighbours. Meanwhile, television pictures of the marchers being beaten by Protestant policemen were flashed around the world, horrifying most British observers. In Northern Ireland, however, the chief effect of the marches was to crank up the tension. Protracted rioting saw the first barricades go up in nationalist parts of Belfast and Londonderry (or Derry; the confusion over its name reflects the sectarian passions at the heart of Northern Irish life), and in August 1969 the violence reached a terrifying climax when pitched street battles in Derry's Bogside ignited three days of bloodshed across Northern Ireland, with 8 people killed, 750 injured, and 1,500 Catholic and 315 Protestant families expelled from their homes. With the overwhelmingly Protestant Royal Ulster Constabulary so clearly hated by the Catholic minority, the government in Westminster was left with no choice but to send in British troops to maintain order. Initially the troops were seen as the protectors of the Catholics, who greeted them with smiles, cheers and fish and chips. But the man who ordered them in, Labour's Home Secretary James Callaghan, was never so naive as to think that the honeymoon would last. Sending in the army 'was the last thing we wanted to do', he said later. 'We held off until the last possible moment, until we were being begged by the Catholics of Northern Ireland to send them in. What an irony of history.'[2]

Like most of his ministers, Heath knew next to nothing about Northern Ireland and had little interest in its affairs. But he had only been in office for three days when his Cabinet Secretary, Sir Burke Trend, handed him a memo that made deeply disturbing reading. Events since the spring of 1970 had made a mockery of predictions that the troops could be withdrawn in a matter of months; indeed, far from dying down, the fires of sectarian hatred seemed to be reaching a new intensity. At the end of March, rioting on Belfast's Ballymurphy estate had seen British troops in action for the first time against Catholic youngsters, prompting General Freeland to warn that in future petrol bombers risked being shot dead. As Trend saw it, these events were merely a taste of what was to come. For the situation to improve, he wrote bluntly, it would take a 'miracle'. More likely was that it would 'remain much as it is – stabilized by the presence of British troops and trembling on the edge of disaster but never quite tipping over', which would mean an 'intolerable' burden, 'in terms both of men and money'. But there was a still worse possibility. 'It could get worse and finally tip over the edge,' Trend wrote; 'the Northern Ireland Government proving incapable of holding the position, civil war breaking out within the Province and Dublin being compelled to intervene. This would present us with a political and constitutional crisis of the first order.'[3]

The sheer intractability of the problem facing Heath in Northern Ireland was nicely summed up by his very first dilemma: should he impose a ban on the Protestant marching season, which had provoked so much violence the year before? As one historian remarks, 'it was a case of being damned if he did and damned if he didn't', for a decision either way would inevitably inflame one of Northern Ireland's communities. In the end, he left the decision to his Home Secretary, Reginald Maudling, who elected to let the marches go ahead under strict supervision from reinforced security forces. It was the first of many disastrous decisions, for what looked to Maudling like a sensible compromise was seen in Belfast and Derry as a nakedly partisan surrender to unionist interests. At the end of June the marching season got under way amid scenes of almost apocalyptic violence, and when Protestant mobs threatened to overrun the Catholic Short Strand enclave in East Belfast, the Provisional IRA made their first appearance on the streets, blasting away in a fierce gun battle around St Matthew's Church. Six people were killed that weekend and 200 injured; ten soldiers ended up in hospital, homes and businesses suffered half a million pounds' worth of damage, and hundreds of Catholic workers were expelled from the shipyards. For the Provisional IRA, which had been founded only months earlier, it was a terrific public relations coup and the moment that they staked their claim to be the heroic defenders of the embattled Catholic minority. For the government, though, it was a catastrophe. Surveying the wreckage afterwards, the British government's official representative in Belfast remarked to a friend: 'That was the greatest single miscalculation I have ever seen made in the course of my whole life.' It was made under extreme pressure, when there was no right answer; even so, it was the first mistake of many.[4]

It is a myth that the tragedy of Northern Ireland in the late 1960s and early 1970s was simply inevitable. Although people were deeply shaped by their political and religious traditions, often looking to the conflicts of the past for inspiration and guidance, they were not prisoners of history. Picking up the gun was a matter of choice, not destiny; for every disaffected, unemployed young man who found solidarity and excitement in a paramilitary brotherhood, there were hundreds who did not. But the conflict also owed much to the decisions of individual political leaders: not just people who consciously sought to inflame the conflict, like the anti-Catholic preacher Ian Paisley and the Provisional Sinn Fein president Ruairí Ó Brádaigh (born Peter Brady), but moderate politicians who made things worse by indifference, inaction or incompetence.

Of the second group, Reginald Maudling was perhaps the supreme example. For all his superficial cleverness and charm, Heath's Home Secretary cut a sadly diminished figure in the early 1970s, his mind coarsened by drink, his attention distracted by his corrupt business interests. Even his name seemed suggestive: a blend of 'muddle', 'maudlin' and 'dawdling'. As one contemporary profile put it, he was a 'great rambling, untidy hulk of a man with epicurean girth, a ready grin, and sardonic humour', staggering into action 'like an overweight prizefighter who would rather sink back into the corner and take the bell'. Maudling knew little about Northern Ireland and cared even less; on his first visit to the province, just four days after the Short Strand gun battle, he made a terrible impression. To the nationalist MP Paddy Devlin, he was 'plainly out of his depth and bored rigid', while even General Freeland thought that he seemed 'completely ignorant'. And as his plane back to London climbed into the sky the next day, Maudling let out a great sigh of relief. 'For God's sake bring me a large Scotch,' he exclaimed. 'What a bloody awful country.'[5]

If Maudling offered only a caricature of leadership, then the Prime Minister of Northern Ireland, Major James Chichester-Clark, was little better. A former Irish Guards officer and County Londonderry farmer, Chichester-Clark was a typical product of the unionist landed gentry: slow, decent and sensible, and totally out of his depth. To be fair, he was in a hideously difficult position, trapped between the British government, the Catholic minority and his own unionist electorate. Such was the tension and paranoia that with every concession, from voting reforms to the abolition of housing discrimination, he pushed more Protestant voters into the arms of Ian Paisley. And with every new report of violence, every bomb attack, every shooting, he faced more demands for a tough military crackdown. But while Chichester-Clark patently lacked the skill to juggle all these competing pressures, the truth was that even the most gifted politician would have struggled. Not only was Stormont a deeply compromised regime in the eyes of the nationalist minority, but once British troops arrived in Belfast the Northern Irish government was little more than a caricature, a client state at the mercy of its master. As early as May 1969 – even before the army was sent in – Callaghan had warned his Labour colleagues that scrapping Stormont completely 'might be forced on us', although the Cabinet minutes noted that 'the difficulties of direct rule, which would probably have to be imposed against the wishes of the majority of the population, would be very great'. By the summer of 1970 the Home Office had drawn up detailed contingency plans for direct British rule, and on 9 July, after the debacle of the Falls Road curfew, Burke Trend raised the issue with Heath and Maudling. If the situation deteriorated much further, Trend said, 'we must be prepared . . . to suspend the Parliament at Stormont . . . and to place the executive government of Ulster in the hands of a nominee of our own'.[6]

While Heath hesitated, the initiative on the shabby, careworn streets of Belfast was quietly passing to a group of men who had very different priorities for Northern Ireland. After its last military campaign was crushed in the 1950s, the tiny Irish Republican Army – which was banned on both sides of the border – had turned instead to Marxism, hoping to build a working-class coalition and bring Irish unity by peaceful means. Despite the bloody events of 1969, the IRA's leaders refused to indulge in what they saw as sectarian violence; instead, they hoped to coax the movement towards political participation both north and south of the border. For many older IRA men, however – often highly conservative Catholics who nursed a visceral hatred of the British and the unionist state – this was anathema, while a group of young militants, seasoned in the street battles of Belfast and Derry, insisted that the IRA take up arms to defend its people. Graffiti across Belfast that summer – 'IRA = I Ran Away' – hammered home the message: if the IRA wanted to maintain their image as the standard-bearers of the republican cause, they needed to return to the gun. At the end of August 1969, a small group of Belfast hardliners got together to plan a new direction, and a month later they launched a coup within the city's IRA. On 18 December, twenty-six delegates secretly elected a new Provisional IRA Executive and Army Council, and ten days later they issued a public statement reaffirming their commitment to defend 'our people' against 'the forces of British Imperialism' and to build a united thirty-two-county Irish state, by force if necessary. Finally, on 11 January 1970, the IRA's political wing Sinn Fein underwent its own split into rival Official and Provisional wings. The Provos – the group who brought the IRA back to the forefront of international attention and struck terror into the hearts of thousands of families not merely in Northern Ireland but in mainland Britain too – were born.[7]

Although apologists for the IRA later claimed that the Provisionals were above all a defensive organization, formed to protect Catholic communities from Protestant attack, this is not really true. There were clear continuities between the Provos and the old IRA of the 1950s, and almost all of the Provos' original leaders, such as 'Seán MacStíofáin', 'Ruairí Ó Brádaigh', David O'Connell, Billy McKee, Joe Cahill and Seamus Twomey, had been active in the IRA for decades; indeed, most had served time in British or Irish prisons. Even younger recruits often came from republican families of long standing: so Gerry Adams, then a West Belfast boy in his early twenties, came from a family in which both his father and uncle had been IRA men, while his mother's family also had impeccable IRA connections. As the historian Richard English points out, it is a myth that Adams became involved because of his anger at the repression of the civil rights marches. In fact, he seems to have joined the Belfast IRA in 1965, when he was 16, well before the civil rights movement had got under way.

From the very outset, in other words, the Provisionals saw themselves as the heirs to a long tradition of republican violence (or 'physical force', as they euphemistically called it). They saw the Six County state as utterly unredeemable; in the words of Adams's collaborator Martin McGuinness, it was 'a unionist state for a unionist people'. Whatever they might claim later, they were not interested in reforming it, only in tearing it down in the name of Irish unity. Peaceful reform was for the effete Marxists of the Official IRA; indeed, one of the major reasons the Provos had walked out was that they believed in violence. Only the gun, they thought, would bring down Stormont and bring home to the British the costs of keeping Northern Ireland within the United Kingdom. On top of that, it would give their Catholic people a chance to strike back, to regain some pride after the attacks and humiliations of 1969 and 1970. The Irish people, said the *Republican News* in September 1970, 'must realise that British imperialists do not respect, fear or pay much attention to people who beg, grovel or crawl for favours or concessions ... If we do not respect ourselves, we need not expect our British overlords to respect us. If we act like slaves and lickspittles, we deserve to be treated as such.'[8]

During the mid-1970s, some on the extreme left of British politics hailed the Provisionals as non-sectarian Marxists standing up for the rights of the working classes. This was nonsense. There was always a strong element of sectarianism in Provo thinking, and their reputation for hitting back at the Orangemen was part of their appeal. Although they took their own Irish Catholic identity extremely seriously, most refused to believe that Protestant unionists were anything other than self-deluding Irishmen. When the journalist Kevin Myers asked Seamus Twomey if there was a risk of provoking a Protestant backlash, Twomey exploded: 'THERE IS NO BACKLASH BECAUSE DEEP DOWN THE PROTESTANT PEOPLE WANT A UNITED IRELAND, only they don't know it yet,' which suggested an interesting relationship with reality. Their left-wing identity, too, was only skin-deep: many senior figures were extremely pious and conservative Catholics, opposed to abortion and contraception. 'Seán MacStíofáin', the Provos' first chief of staff, even refused to bring contraceptives over the border to be used as acid fuses for bombs.

But then MacStíofáin was a very peculiar character by any standards. His real name was John Stephenson; far from being some oppressed child of West Belfast, he had been born and bred in Bethnal Green. His father was English; his mother, although of Protestant Irish descent, was Bethnal Green through and through. His Irish Catholic identity, like his 'Hollywood Darby O'Gill brogue', as Myers put it, was entirely self-created; even many of his own comrades found it hard to take him seriously. He certainly made a very unlikely hero for British left-wingers who fancied themselves as progressive freethinkers. 'Seán's problem is that he spends all his time going around trying to prove to everybody that he's as Irish as they are,' the Official IRA's Marxist chief Cathal Goulding once remarked, 'and in the IRA he had to show that he was more violent than the rest.'[9]

At first, the British army saw no great threat from the Provisional IRA. Behind the barricades, officers even held informal talks with Provo representatives to get a sense of the mood on the streets. As late as January 1971, indeed, there were still secret links between military intelligence and the Provisional command. All the time, however, the Provos were preparing for the great offensive. Their growth was slow and they remained relatively obscure, but by the middle of 1970 they could count on about 1,000 active supporters across Ireland, from armed street fighters to the people who ran their safe houses. Their biggest problem seemed likely to be getting their hands on some guns, but their luck was in. In 1969, the Irish government in Dublin had agreed to make money available for the Catholic victims of Protestant attacks, and much of this money found its way into the hands of the Provos, who used it to buy arms. What was more, elements within the Irish government – notably Charles Haughey and Neil Blaney, but possibly even the Taoiseach, Jack Lynch, himself – arranged for Irish Army intelligence to buy and ship guns to the Provisionals in the spring of 1970, an extraordinarily reckless and dangerous decision, given what was to follow.

Finally, any group claiming the mantle of the IRA could expect considerable moral and financial support from across the Atlantic, where Irish families still toasted the Easter Rising and damned the British Empire. In particular, it was American money that paid for the massive shipments of Armalite rifles to the Provos in the early 1970s, with most of the cash coming from the Provo front organization NORAID. Smugglers even used the cruise liner QE2 as cover, bringing over half a dozen Armalites with every voyage, sometimes tucked down the legs of their trousers. By the late summer of 1970, therefore, the Provos had enough weapons to start a small war. 'There were Belgian FN semi-automatic rifles, assault rifles, self-loading rifles and M1 carbines,' one IRA man later recalled. 'People didn't question where they came from. Just the fact that the weaponry was there made people feel a lot more at ease.'[10]

By this stage, the Provos had already made their first impression on the people of Belfast. Having killed five Protestants in the gun battles of late June, they had established what one historian calls their 'ghetto credibility' over the more restrained Official IRA, and their aid to Falls Road families during the disastrous army curfew only added to their lustre as defenders of the Catholics. It is worth repeating the fundamental point that even *before* these landmark events, the Provos were bent on a campaign of armed unrest. For all their claims that they acted only in self-defence, they were violent revolutionaries before they were protectors of their communities. Still, there is no doubt that the Falls Road curfew gave them an enormous boost, both in morale and in recruitment. Crucially, it shattered the relationship between Northern Irish Catholics and their British protectors, so that whereas the IRA's standing orders in September 1969 dictated that British soldiers were 'not to be shot', after the Falls curfew 'all Brits' were 'acceptable targets'. More broadly, it destroyed any remaining illusions that politics in Northern Ireland could be resuscitated on the basis of mutual trust. For nationalists, the attack on the Short Strand and the so-called 'rape of the Falls' confirmed that the British army was merely the tool of the repressive unionist state; for unionists, however, these events were a terrifying reminder of the threat of the IRA and its Catholic supporters. On both sides, moderate voices were almost drowned out by the hubbub of fear and anger. As a moderate nationalist councillor later remarked, 'overnight the population turned from neutral or even sympathetic support for the military to outright hatred of everything related to the security forces. I witnessed voters and workers turn against us to join the Provisionals. Even some of our most dedicated workers and supporters turned against us.'[11]

Behind the grey drabness of the urban landscape, the dilapidated Victorian brick façades, the 'mean houses, tiny streets, endless rain', old enmities were rising to the boil. And in the narrow terraced streets and bleak, grey estates – the 'tiny, lightless kennels' reeking of 'coal smoke, sour milk and the rancid liquids of reproduction', as Kevin Myers put it – the air tingled with anticipation as before a storm. Every week brought a fresh wave of IRA bombs aimed at Protestant shops and businesses across the capital, with the year's hundredth explosion, an unhappy and ominous landmark, coming on 15 September. A report for the Ministry of Defence warned of 'inflamed sectarian passions . . . deliberately exploited by the IRA and other extremists', but Heath and

Maudling still believed that Stormont must be given every chance to restore order before they resorted to the drastic option of direct rule.[12]

Yet although the marching season passed off without more major incidents, the mood was bitter, nervous, tense. And if anyone doubted the fierce passions that lay beneath the surface, they needed only listen to the increasingly common stories of punishments meted out to girls who had fraternized with British soldiers – many of them teenagers who had merely gone along to the discos set up as part of the army's hearts and minds campaign. One soldier never forgot coming across a young girl's body tied to a lamp post late one night. She had been held down so that her head could be shaved; then hot tar had been poured over her, and she had been covered with feathers. 'The tar actually ran down her neck and the front of her breast,' the soldier remembered, 'and her hands were badly affected where she'd clawed at her face to get it off. And the feathers were just stuck to the tar. We had to cut her away from the lamppost and take her to hospital. She was very badly burned . . . I felt utter revulsion for the type of person that had the mentality to do it – just because a human being had decided to go and dance for a couple of hours at an army barracks.'[13]

It was not until the early hours of Saturday, 6 February 1971, during street fighting near Belfast's Ardoyne area, that the potential costs of the conflict were brought home to the British public. Trouble had been brewing in the area for days, and when fighting broke out late on Friday night, the army sent in a unit of the Royal Artillery. The men had just finished a six-week tour along the Irish border and had returned to Belfast for a break; they were still lugging their kit off the troopship when the orders came through to restore order in the Ardoyne. Trained to deal with rioting crowds, they had no concept of what awaited them. 'The crowd was in front of us, throwing bricks, bottles, petrol bombs, everything that was going,' one soldier remembered. 'Then all of a sudden the crowd parted and this chap just popped out with a machine gun and just opened up.' The chap in question was Billy Reid, a Provisional IRA volunteer, and one of his bullets hit Gunner Robert Curtis in the chest, killing him instantly. The first British soldier to be killed in Northern Ireland, Curtis was just 20 years old, a Newcastle boy who had been married for thirteen months. His wife, also 20, was three months pregnant. In the army and among the general public alike, there was widespread horror and incomprehension. Curtis's father told the press that he had no idea 'what my son died for'. His wife's mother, meanwhile, said that her daughter thought the troops should be brought home immediately, and 'the mobs left to fight it out among themselves'.[14]

The troops did not come home, of course. The government was committed to restoring law and order to the troubled province, even if that meant stepping deeper into the quagmire. When Heath's Cabinet met three days later, Maudling told his colleagues that the 'renewed disorder in Northern Ireland was being deliberately fomented by the militant wing of the Irish Republican Army', while the Defence Secretary, Lord Carrington, added that 'the disorder was no longer an inter-communal matter', since 'a situation approaching armed conflict was developing'. Even at this early stage, the Cabinet were worried that 'public opinion in Great Britain was beginning actively to resent the situation'; reports suggested that 'many people would favour abandoning the Province to its fate, a course which the Government could not contemplate' – not least because of the international outcry that would greet British withdrawal and the sectarian anarchy that would almost certainly ensue. 'The general public', the Cabinet agreed, 'should be helped to realise that the disorder was no longer the result of communal strife or rebellion against political injustice but was the outcome of deliberate terrorism by the IRA.'[15]

This was not just political spin: although Heath gets a bad press for his policy in Northern Ireland, and made more than his fair share of dreadful mistakes, he set out with the best of intentions. In his detailed study of Heath's policy in his first twelve months, the historian Jeremy Smith concludes that 'on the issue of reform, on future north–south connections, on political change within Northern Ireland and even the constitutional link with the United Kingdom, the British government was positive, open-minded and mildly radical'. Of course, this does not sit well with simplistic views of the conflict in which the British are cast as clichéd stage villains. But the fact remains that in the crucial months of late 1970 and early 1971 it was the Provisionals who set off bombs, intimidated local residents, murdered soldiers and deliberately escalated the conflict. Of course, they were not stage villains either. But while Heath had everything to lose from violence, they thought they had everything to gain.[16]

If anybody thought that Gunner Curtis's death would bring an end to the violence, the events of the next few days destroyed their illusions.

The following Tuesday, five BBC engineers were killed by an IRA land-mine near a transmitter in County Tyrone; the mine had been meant for a passing army patrol. A week later, a second British soldier, 22-year-old John Laurie, was shot by the IRA, and on 26 February Provo snipers shot and killed two RUC men patrolling in the Ardoyne. For many observers, however, it was what happened on the evening of Wednesday, 10 March that marked Northern Ireland's descent into anarchy. That night, three young Royal Highland Fusiliers – Dougald McCaughey, 23, and the brothers John and Joseph McCaig, just 17 and 18 respectively – were enjoying a quiet pint in Mooney's Bar in the centre of Belfast. They were off duty and wearing civilian clothes; in those days, there were no restrictions on soldiers visiting pubs and clubs on their evenings off. When a friendly stranger, introducing himself as a former soldier, offered to buy them some drinks and asked if they would like to come to a party, they readily agreed. It was only hours later, when a group of schoolchildren on a remote country road came across three corpses with bullet holes in the backs of their heads, that it became clear that the stranger was a member of the Provisional IRA, an Ardoyne man who had been kicked out of the SAS for mental instability after killing a civilian in Cyprus.

The murder of the three young Highlanders left many observers numb with disgust; it was telling that, even though they had been killed by an IRA unit, the Provisionals' leadership refused to accept responsibility. 'After all the horrors of recent weeks and months, Ulster people have almost lost the capacity for feeling shock,' observed a local newspaper editorial. 'But the ruthless murder of three defenceless young soldiers has cut to the quick. These were cold-blooded executions for purely political purposes.' Protestant and Catholic leaders united to condemn the killers; from Dublin, Jack Lynch branded them the 'enemies of all Irish people', and said that the atrocity brought 'Belfast closer to the abyss'. And yet on the streets, where it counted, the murder of the three men only stoked the passions higher. Kevin Myers noted that their deaths 'caused much quiet satisfaction amongst republicans', since as Scots they were 'pre-sumed to be Protestant and Glasgow Rangers supporters'. The consensus now was that 'British soldiers simply had what was coming to them'. Some talked openly of civil war: even Myers's Catholic taxi driver told him with shining eyes that 'the war's coming and it's going to be serious', that 'the Provies have fresh gear coming from America' and that 'there'll be people dying in this town who've never fucking died before'. And in the army, there was now a mood of white-hot fury, a grim determination to strike back against the thugs who had slaughtered three unarmed men. Harry McCallion, a working-class Scottish Catholic in the elite Parachute Regiment, remembered that he and his comrades heard the news in silence. 'I looked at the faces of the older soldiers around me,' he recalled. 'I read on them the same thing: "Just wait until we get across" . . . For me and everybody at the table, that was the major turning point.'[17]

For unionists, the murder of the three Scottish soldiers provided definitive proof that the IRA were nothing more than barbarians, poised to destroy the very basis of the state they loved. Few had much faith in the British government or even in the army, which they blamed for not cracking down properly on the republican subversives in their midst. Many working-class Protestants, already frightened for their jobs and livelihoods, decided that they would have to take up arms to defend themselves, like their ancestors before them. By the spring of 1970, local communities across Belfast were already organizing vigilante 'defence associations' to protect themselves against their old enemies in the IRA. Like their counterparts in the nationalist community, these early loyalist groups put the blame on their adversaries, insisting that they wanted only to defend their families; as so often in sectarian conflicts the world over, violence and hatred were rooted in fear that the other side would strike first. Martin Snodden, a 16-year-old boy who joined the UVF in 1970, killed two people in a bomb attack and became an activist for reconciliation after being released from prison, recalled that on his estate – a unionist enclave in a predominantly nationalist area – there were 'daily attacks on Protestant families', including stonings, shootings and 'riot situations'. Snodden's grandfather had been a B Special and his father a member of the Ulster Defence Regiment: for an impressionable teenager, picking up a gun was a way of defending his family, asserting himself as a man, and associating himself with the history of his people. He felt 'a combination of fear and love', he said; 'fear for what could happen and what was happening in the area at the time but also a wider sense of love for my whole tradition and the country that I had grown up in'.[18]

In homage to the three Scottish soldiers, young loyalists across Belfast set up what they called 'Tartan' groups, teenage gangs who roamed the streets of their estates harassing Catholic families whom they blamed for supporting the IRA. In their flared jeans, bovver boots and tartan scarves, the Tartans looked like nothing so much as Glaswegian football hooligans; indeed, when the Shankill Young Tartans marched back from watching their team, Linfield, they would often pause to throw missiles at the Catholics in Unity Flats. Unlike ordinary hooligans, however, they had the chance to graduate from throwing stones to throwing bombs. Whereas most English youths were content merely to parade the colours of their team, the future loyalist Eddie Kinnear used to travel to school every day with a rucksack bearing the initials SYT (Shankill Young Tartan), YCV (Young Citizens Volunteer) and UVF (Ulster Volunteer Force). That said, however, it is worth remembering that most people never joined a paramilitary organization. When the loyalist vigilante groups banded together to create the Ulster Defence Association (UDA), complete with a military hierarchy just like the IRA's, it attracted tens of thousands of volunteers. Yet when the UDA's recruiting sergeant visited one Belfast estate already guarded by baseball-bat-wielding vigilantes, the response was something less than overwhelming enthusiasm.

'He walked in in full combat uniform,' recalled the watching Sammy Duddy, 'put a Union Jack on the table, a Bible on top of it and a Sterling sub-machine gun in the middle of the lot. He says, "Right, we're all here to join." I was nearly killed in the queue to get out. There was a mad rush for the door.' Of the fifty vigilante teenagers, he estimated, only fourteen joined the UDA. Duddy was one of them, becoming the group's press officer. Unusually for a paramilitary, he maintained a double life as a drag artist by the name of Samantha, performing in loyalist clubs in fishnet tights, a black wig, heavy mascara and scarlet lipstick. In his heyday, he was known as 'the Dolly Parton of Belfast'.[19]

For the Stormont government, the murder of the three Scotsmen was a catastrophe, a symbol of its total failure to impose the rule of law on a sectarian conflict rapidly lurching out of control. 'The telephone exchange of one Belfast newspaper was swamped with callers,' reported *The Times,* 'many of whom were demanding not only the immediate intensification of security measures but the resignation of the Chichester-Clark Government.' At the very least, Chichester-Clark needed to make a dramatic gesture, and Unionist hardliners hoped that he would urge the army to introduce internment under the Special Powers Act. Internment – the detention of IRA suspects without trial – had been used on both sides of the Irish border with great success as recently as the 1950s, and there were persistent rumours that the government was going to reintroduce it. Indeed, in December 1970 Maudling and the Defence Secretary, Lord Carrington, had considered plans to hold IRA suspects on the troopship HMS *Maidstone,* and the following February a secret army report identified a possible site at the disused Long Kesh airbase, near Lisburn. Clearly this would be a controversial and risky step, yet in the immediate aftermath of the three Scots' deaths, there seemed a decent chance that even some Catholics would accept it as a way to stop such atrocities happening again. Gerry Fitt, the founder of the SDLP and spokesman for moderate nationalism, privately urged the British to introduce 'the immediate internment of all Provisional IRA men known to the police in order to rid Belfast of intimidation'.

Even south of the border, where the Dublin authorities were increasingly disturbed by IRA recruitment and gun-running, harsh measures might not be entirely unwelcome. In December 1970, Ireland's Minister of Justice, Desmond O'Malley, had publicly threatened to introduce internment to crush the republicans' 'secret armed conspiracy', and six months later the Irish government set up 'special criminal courts' without juries to handle IRA terrorist trials. And even though Chichester-Clark had publicly ruled out bringing back internment, arguing that it would create more problems than it solved, the pressure seemed irresistible. Two days after the murders of the three soldiers, thousands of angry unionists descended on Stormont, waving Union Jacks and carrying placards demanding immediate internment, the rearming of the RUC and a major army offensive into 'no-go' areas. It was time, said the Unionist hardliner Harry West, for the murderers to be 'rooted out'.[20]

On 16 March, Chichester-Clark flew to London. To the surprise of his hosts, though, he did not ask for internment, because both the army and the RUC had warned him that it would provoke serious street protests and that given the poor state of intelligence on the IRA, it would be impossible to pick up all the right people. (This was a view echoed in London: when Heath's Cabinet first discussed internment in February, they agreed that it must remain a last resort because it was bound 'to exacerbate communal tensions afresh'.) Instead, Chichester-Clark wanted a broad security crackdown, with at least 3,000 more British troops sent in to occupy the nationalist 'no-go' areas, to impose curfews and cordons, and to forestall what he melodramatically warned might be a 'general uprising' against the IRA. This idea was a non-starter: army chiefs were adamantly opposed to the thought of their men becoming sitting ducks on nationalist estates, while Heath had no desire to throw thousands more men into a British Vietnam. So when Chichester-Clark flew back to Belfast, it was with a British offer of just 1,300 extra men, nowhere near enough to satisfy his increasingly vituperative critics on the right of the Unionist Party. For this decent man, painfully out of his depth, it was the final straw. Two days later, he decided to ring Maudling and announce his resignation.[21]

Chichester-Clark's departure unfolded in blackly comic circumstances. Maudling, it turned out, was giving a lecture at Merchant Taylors' school, and when his Special Branch bodyguards approached him with news of the Stormont Prime Minister's call, they found him having lunch with the headmaster – a lunch 'made up entirely of whisky', one said. Although Maudling then headed back to London, his car mysteriously 'broke down' in Watford, preventing him from taking the call – a breakdown probably arranged by his officials, given that by now he was steaming with booze. Instead, Chichester-Clark was put through to Heath himself, a very different prospect from the lazy, amiable Maudling. 'What is the reason?' Heath snapped when Chichester-Clark mumbled about resigning. 'In what way are you disappointed? . . . Well, I don't know what your justification for thinking that is . . . You're responsible for your own intelligence, and you've agreed that it's extremely weak . . . Well, I don't understand what you mean by saying that.'

Every time Chichester-Clark tried to justify himself, largely by blaming the British, Heath stamped all over him. The transcript reads like an account of a bulldozer crushing a rabbit:

HEATH: Can you give me any examples where the IRA could have been apprehended and we failed to take action?

CHICHESTER-CLARK: No, I can't, no.

HEATH: Well, then, Prime Minister, you can't give me a single example. How can you say that we are just sitting there and doing nothing? On the one occasion that you raised with me at Chequers, we immediately took action.

CHICHESTER-CLARK: Well, indeed, I appreciate that. I am not really trying to dispute that. I am not really trying to dispute that . . .

Poor Chichester-Clark was not so much out-argued as overwhelmed. To a man of Heath's obstinate rigidity, the notion that Chichester-Clark would walk away was simply unfathomable. 'What exactly is your personal position?' he demanded angrily. 'Have you told the Cabinet that you intend to resign? . . . So in fact the decision is taken? . . . I see.' And when Chichester-Clark muttered that he intended to blame the British army, Heath exploded. 'Well, all I can say is that I consider that absolutely unjustifiable,' he snapped. 'I shall make it quite plain from here that it is absolutely unjustifiable. In fact it bears very little relation to the truth. I think it is doing immense harm to Northern Ireland and I think it makes the position of any successor of yours absolutely impossible. Absolutely impossible.' That was the end of that; it would have taken a man with a much stiffer backbone than Chichester-Clark's to stand up to Heath in this form. 'Well, I will certainly look at what I propose to say again,' he said weakly. 'The last thing I want to do is to do anything that is in any way unhelpful.' But Heath was in no mood to be magnanimous. 'I don't think there is anything further to discuss,' he said bluntly. 'Goodbye.'[22]

Chichester-Clark's successor was a very different proposition. As the heir to the world's biggest shirt-making company, Brian Faulkner saw himself as the spokesman for Northern Ireland's business interests, rather than the old landed gentry. Unlike most of his Unionist colleagues, he had not served in the Second World War and, perhaps to compensate, cultivated a brusque, no-nonsense style. As Stormont's Minister for Home Affairs in the late 1950s he had taken the credit for crushing the IRA's last major campaign, and he was reputed to be the best administrator that Unionist politics had ever produced. Cunning, energetic and fiercely ambitious, he saw himself as the only possible saviour of Northern Ireland, not least because his tough line had a strong appeal to the Protestant working classes. Indeed, even before Chichester-Clark's resignation, Heath had told his Cabinet that Faulkner might be the only man who could stop the rise of 'the extreme right wing' in Unionist politics. If Faulkner failed, then Britain would have to take over. But Faulkner had no intention of failing, and in his first words after his election by the Ulster Unionists he struck a predictable theme. His priority, he said, was 'law and order . . . What we need on this front are not new principles but practical results on the ground in the elimination not only of terrorism and sabotage but of riots and disorder.'[23]

Far from the situation improving in Faulkner's first few months, however, it got steadily worse. With an average of two bombs going off a day, the people of Belfast were becoming used to the distant thump of another explosion, the plumes of smoke, the smell of cordite, the sight of bleeding, crying casualties. On Sunday, 11 July, the Provos twisted the knife with a fresh bombing offensive along the route of the Orange marches planned for the Twelfth, as well as an attack on the *Daily Mirror*'s new Belfast printing plant. By now Faulkner's words were looking like yet more empty promises. So far, 1971 had seen 300 explosions, 320 shooting incidents and more than 600 people rushed to hospital, while 10 soldiers and 5 policemen had lost their lives. And as Faulkner mulled over the latest terrible headlines, there seemed only one way forward. As he saw it, he had already offered concessions to the nationalists by promising the SDLP that their representatives could chair two new committees reviewing government policy and legislation; now it was time to balance the equation. Internment was risky, but it had worked for him in the late 1950s, and it would shore up his shaky Protestant base. On 2 August, *The Times* reported that Faulkner's most vociferous critic, the former Home Affairs minister William Craig, was already calling for new leadership and the foundation of an armed Protestant reservist force on the lines of the old B Specials. Three days later, Faulkner flew to London and formally asked Britain to introduce internment.[24]

Heath and his ministers were well aware of the arguments against internment. In March, the British representative in Belfast had reported that Army Intelligence estimated that they would catch only 20 per cent of the Provisionals' membership ('and then mostly small fry'), while the RUC had advised that 'there would be a lot of younger people whom the police did not know and who would not be picked up'. The new commanding officer in Belfast, General Sir Harry Tuzo, observed in July that the arguments against it were 'very strong' and that it would be 'primarily a political decision', not a military one. And at the end of the month, the Taoiseach, Jack Lynch, had warned that there was no way he could introduce internment south of the border without splitting his own party. Heath 'should reflect very seriously' before taking such a 'grave step', he told the British ambassador in Dublin, warning that 'it would produce an explosion that it would be impossible to contain . . . With the extreme unionists apparently on the rampage, all the [Catholic] moderates would identify themselves with the internees.' Even when the ambassador raised the prospect of direct British rule, Lynch 'reverted

again and again to the immediate problem of the unwisdom of internment, saying that surely we had enough troops, police and intelligence
resources to manage without it'.[25]

It could hardly be said, then, that Heath was unaware of the dangers.
The problem, though, was that he was now totally committed to Faulkner.
If he turned him down and Faulkner resigned, then the only alternative
might be direct rule, which nobody in Westminster wanted. And there were
possible compensations: not only might internment break the back of the
Provisional IRA, but as Maudling pointed out, it might be the only way
to forestall a 'Protestant backlash' against the Catholic minority. At six
on the evening of 5 August, therefore, Heath told Faulkner he could
have what he wanted. He noted, however, that internment 'could not be
said . . . to be justified by any military necessity', but was 'a political act,
which would be thought to be directed against one faction and must
accordingly be matched by some political action, in the form of a ban on
marches, which would represent its counterpart in relation to the other
faction'. Faulkner tried to wriggle out of a ban on Orange marches,
but Heath stood firm. Internment 'should be seen to be impartial in its
application', he added, 'and it would presumably be desirable for this
purpose that those interned should include a certain number of Protestants'.
This was good advice. Unfortunately, Faulkner did not heed it.[26]

When Richard McAuley went to bed on the night of Sunday, 8 August
1971, he found it difficult to get to sleep. Like thousands of other Belfast
teenagers, he was waiting nervously for his A-level results to come in the
post the next morning, and he did not drift off until almost three. But
when he finally awoke at half-past seven and came downstairs, there was
no sign of the post – or the postman. 'There was a barricade at the top
of the street,' he remembered.

> It was incredible. In our street! Barricades! I didn't understand it. Stories
> were going around that people were being lifted out of their homes and the
> word was that internment was in. And there I was asking people, 'What's
> happened to the postman?' They were all saying, 'His van's probably at the
> top of the street.' And my A-level results were with him. Then I thought to
> myself, 'Internment? . . . They can't do it. They wouldn't be so daft.'

But they had; the postman never came that day. So Richard and a couple
of friends hurdled the barricades and walked the short distance to school,

where they found their results. Richard's were good; he went to St Joseph's College to train as a teacher, fulfilling a lifetime's ambition. But he never graduated; instead, he dropped out a few years later, and joined the Provisional IRA.[27]

'Operation Demetrius', as it was called, was a shambles, a debacle, a disaster for the cause of peace in Northern Ireland. Acting on intelligence provided by the RUC, British troops sealed off streets across the province and snatched a total of 342 men in a series of dawn raids, whisking them off to various makeshift camps, most famously at the Long Kesh airbase. Some of their captives were indeed IRA activists, and they did manage to extract some decent intelligence. But whatever slight benefits they gained were overwhelmingly outweighed by the mistakes, the terrible public relations and the ferocity of the reaction. The RUC's files on the IRA were horrendously out of date; the split between the Officials and the Provisionals, as well as the emergence of the militant new generation, meant that they were not even close to identifying the key players. Their intelligence, one British officer said, 'was very, very poor'. He himself had the unenviable task of storming into a house at four in the morning to pick up an 'elderly gentleman who was well into his eighties who was rather proud to be arrested'. 'I'm delighted to think that I'm still a trouble to the British Government,' his captive said wryly, 'but I have to tell you I've not been active since the Easter Rising.' Needless to say, he was soon released; indeed, no fewer than a hundred people were released after just two days, which says it all about the quality of the RUC's information.[28]

But internment was no laughing matter. Kevin Duffy, a 21-year-old joiner from the little country village of Moy, was watching television with his mother when soldiers surrounded the house and threatened to kick the door in unless he gave himself up. He had never joined the Provisionals, the Officials or any republican group; he had never been connected with the civil rights groups; his only qualifications for arrest were that he had learned Gaelic and was a member of the Gaelic Athletic Association. And he was, of course, a Catholic. Despite what Heath had said in London, and despite Maudling's encouragement to 'lift a few Protestants', every single one of the 342 people arrested that morning was a Catholic.[29]

Faulkner always insisted that the policy had been a success. The army was excising 'a deep-seated tumour', he said, which was 'not a pleasant business. Sometimes innocent people will suffer.' But as news of the raids spread across Belfast, anger turned into outright fury, and fury into violence. In Catholic areas, women banged hundreds of dustbin lids to warn of approaching army vehicles while teenagers dragged together cars, mattresses, old furniture, even builders' skips and rubble to construct makeshift barricades. Milk vans were seized and their bottles converted into petrol bombs; paving stones were torn up and smashed into missile-sized fragments. As smoke rose over the bleeding city, the first reports of deaths reached the local press: in two days, seventeen people were shot dead, ten of them Catholic rioters shot by the British army, while enraged mobs forced 7,000 people out of their homes. Buses came to a standstill, and thousands of people stayed away from work: a wise decision, given that almost every hour brought news of fighting breaking out somewhere else in the city. In the Ardoyne, at least 200 houses were ablaze by Monday evening, as Protestant families fled their homes after attacks by nationalist mobs. Many set fire to their own houses to ensure that Catholic families would not take them over, and as the crowds of fleeing refugees straggled down the roads, some defiantly flying the Union Jack, IRA snipers and British soldiers exchanged gunfire in the streets. 'All shops were closed, and the destruction of so many lorries and tankers meant that the city was running out of food and fuel,' wrote Kevin Myers, who watched the devastating scenes in the Ardoyne with fascinated horror. 'A perpetual pall of smoke hung in the city's skies, its acrid vapours accosting everyone who stepped out of doors . . . Belfast was paralysed.'[30]

Reginald Maudling spent the day relaxing by his swimming pool in suburban Hertfordshire, rousing himself from time to time to ring Whitehall and ask how things were going. In interviews over the next few days, he blandly repeated Stormont's propaganda that internment was a terrific success, telling the *Guardian* what his biographer calls the 'outright lie' that he had merely been following army advice. And when the BBC's Robin Day asked why the army had not arrested any loyalists, Maudling came out with the absurd line that 'if any Protestant organisa-tions were behaving like the IRA we should treat them in precisely the same way' – which completely missed the point that not only had the loyalist UVF committed the first murders of the Troubles, but the UDA was even then building up its strength on Protestant estates. Within the army, however, there was much less complacency. As one officer put it, internment had been a 'complete disaster'. Among other things, it destroyed the last vestiges of a moderate political consensus in Northern

Ireland, with the SDLP walking out of public bodies and organizing a rent and rates strike until the internees were freed. And by turning so many Catholics against the British, internment completed what the Falls curfew had begun, utterly undermining the hearts and minds campaign the army had been conducting for two years. One account of the Troubles calls it 'a misjudgement of historic proportions'; Maudling's biographer even calls it 'one of the great blunders of recent British political history'. The tragic irony was that neither Heath nor the army had wanted to introduce it in the first place. But by listening to Faulkner, Heath had committed one of the worst errors of his career. The big winners, of course, were the Provisionals, who not only survived with their weapons virtually untouched, but could now count on huge support on the nationalist estates. 'That's when it became clear to me', said one Belfast woman who joined the Provos, 'that the Brits were here to suppress the Catholic minority, and for no other reason.'[31]

"In our next riot, boys, we must do better. We've only been able to provoke one British soldier to give Paddy a tiny cut on his drinking finger."

Initially, most papers scoffed at claims that the army and the RUC had tortured internees in Northern Ireland. Here, Cummings addresses the issue with his usual sensitivity in the *Daily Express*, 27 October 1971.

What made internment even more of a disaster, however, was the treatment of the prisoners. Incarceration in the bleak solitude of Long Kesh, which with its low Nissen huts and barbed wire fences looked like a Nazi concentration camp, was bad enough, but as early as mid-August Irish newspapers began running reports that suspects were being tortured by the army and the RUC. One Belfast man, for example, told the *Tyrone Democrat* that he had been made to run over broken glass; others reported suffering violent beatings, being forced to stand spreadeagled with hoods over their heads, or being subjected to white noise and bright lights. But while the government insisted that this was merely IRA propaganda – and indeed republicans gleefully repeated allegations of brutality as loudly as possible – the terrible reality was that the stories were true. In April 1971, the army and the RUC had held a secret meeting in Belfast to plan the interrogation of suspects if internment were intro-duced. During colonial operations in Palestine, Malaya, Kenya, Cyprus and Aden, intelligence officers had already perfected what they called the 'Five Techniques', which involved making suspects stand spreadeagled against the wall for hours on end, putting hoods over their heads, subjecting them to white noise, giving them only water to drink and a little bread to eat, and keeping them awake for days on end. There was nothing new about these techniques, and they owed nothing to anti-Irish racism, as some republicans claimed. They were merely part of the army's colonial repertoire, and it never occurred to its officers that, quite apart from any moral considerations, they might not be suitable within the United Kingdom itself. For one thing, they had explicit government approval. As Lord Carrington later told his colleagues on GEN 47, the special Cabinet committee set up to handle Northern Ireland, both he and Maudling had approved the 'proposed methods of interrogation' the day after internment was announced. As the minutes blandly con-cluded, 'the lives of British soldiers and of innocent civilians depended on intelligence. We were dealing with an enemy who had no scruples, and we should not be unduly squeamish over methods of interrogation in these circumstances.'[32]

The memories of men interrogated according to the Five Techniques make chilling reading. The Belfast republican Liam Shannon, for example, claimed that he had been beaten constantly before being hooded, spread-eagled and exposed to white noise for a solid seven days, and then interrogated with a bright light shining in his face, 'like something you see in KGB films'. Other men were treated to more rudimentary methods: Tommy Gorman recalled being 'battered, just battered, for three days. There was no subtlety to it. It was just, you were hauled out of bed at two o'clock in the morning and brought in and questioned, battered against the wall.' That two men as intelligent as Maudling and Carrington thought that such techniques were acceptable in Northern Ireland is a reminder that British officials often saw the conflict through a colonial prism. If the techniques had been appropriate for Aden, they thought, there was no reason why they would not work in Belfast. Even so, it beggars belief that they genuinely thought the techniques could be kept quiet. As early as August 1971, the pressure was such that Heath set up an inquiry under Sir Edmund Compton to investigate the allegations. But before it could report back, a major investigation by the *Sunday Times*'s Insight team on 17 October uncovered eleven potential cases of torture. And while Compton's report concluded that there had been no 'physical brutality as we understand the term', a second inquiry by the Privy Council a few months later produced rather different results. Two of the three-man panel backed the government, but the third, Lord Gardiner, was blistering in his condemnation of techniques 'which were secret, illegal, not morally justifiable and alien to the traditions of what I believe still to be the greatest democracy in the world'.

After that there could be no going back. On the same day the report came out, Heath announced that the Five Techniques would never be used again. The damage, however, was done. 'If I, as a Catholic, were living in Ulster today,' Graham Greene wrote to *The Times,* 'I confess I would have one savage and irrational ambition – to see Mr Maudling pressed against a wall for hours on end, with a hood over his head, hearing nothing but the noise of a wind machine, deprived of sleep when the noise temporarily ceases by the bland voice of a politician telling him that his brain will suffer no irreparable damage.'[33]

Internment was a public relations catastrophe. Viewed from Dublin or New York, it gave the impression that the arrogant imperialists were once again stamping with brutal callousness on a defenceless people. And even in mainland Britain it provoked fierce criticism. Ever since troops had been sent to protect the Catholics in 1969, a minority on the far left had insisted on seeing them as the equivalent of the American troops fighting in Vietnam, reducing the conflict to a simplistic morality tale of imperialists and insurgents. And although the Provisional IRA were one of the least countercultural organizations imaginable, they became the unlikeliest of folk heroes in the squats and festivals, the polytechnic classrooms and hippy communes that made up the far-left landscape in the Heath years. As early as the summer of 1971, marchers in London waved placards reading 'GAY LIBERATION FRONT SUPPORTS BATTLE FOR FREEDOM IN IRELAND'. It probably says it all that John Lennon, always keen to advertise his bleeding heart, went along to one march waving a countercultural newspaper with the headline: 'For the IRA – Against British Imperialism'.

Two years later, a coalition of 'trade unionists, housewives, students and ex-soldiers', as they rather disingenuously called themselves, gathered at Fulham Town Hall to set up the Troops Out Movement, modelled on the American movement against the Vietnam War. Although this organization professed to be entirely non-partisan, much of its money and muscle came from Tariq Ali's International Marxist Group. Its literature frequently defended IRA atrocities while devoting vast swathes of newsprint to the alleged crimes of the British army. The province's unionist majority, meanwhile, were either dismissed as imperialist puppets or ignored altogether. And while the Troops Out Movement never came close to securing mass support, its arguments did filter slowly into the mainstream. 'Give Ireland back to the Irish,' sang Paul McCartney and Wings in 1972, in a single that was banned for political reasons by the BBC, although they might have done better to suppress it for crimes against musical taste. Certainly nobody could accuse McCartney of excessive sophistication: 'Great Britain you are tremendous / And nobody knows it like me / But really what are you doing / In the land across the sea?'[34]

Still, Lennon and McCartney were hardly unusual in knowing so little about the conflict in the land across the sea. Instead of explaining the roots of the troubles, the tabloids often preferred to feed their readers' worst fears, such as when the *Mirror* told its readers that the IRA had 'hired assassins from behind the Iron Curtain to gun down British troops', or when the same newspaper claimed that the IRA had recruited 'British Trotskyists and Marxists' to organize 'a blitz of shopping centres, railway stations and other government offices'. And behind the ignorance lay centuries of dislike, suspicion and outright prejudice. In Glasgow, Protestant Rangers fans cheered the news of army offensives in Northern

Ireland, while Celtic fans sang bloodthirsty Fenian songs. Even on BBC programmes, overt anti-Irish sentiments were not uncommon. In *Till Death Us Do Part,* Alf Garnett is forever thundering against 'the Micks', while few Irish viewers could have been entirely delighted by Sybil Fawlty's verdict on the builder O'Reilly in September 1975: 'Not brilliant? He belongs in a zoo! . . . He's shoddy, he doesn't care, he's a liar, he's incompetent, he's lazy, he's nothing but a half-witted thick Irish joke!' And once the Provisionals launched their mainland bombing campaign in 1973–4, there were brief spasms of fierce anti-Irish harassment, with reports of Irish pubs and clubs being attacked in major cities. 'Even mates that I've worked with for years, Eddie from Wales, I've seen him blank me,' said one Irishman living in London. 'Mates in the pub, they come out with comments like "Bloody Irish murderers, they should all be shot."'[35]

Yet what is most striking about British attitudes to Northern Ireland is the sheer indifference. Although more than a million Irish men and women lived in Britain in 1971, making up more than 2 per cent of the population, the conflict in the Six Counties never became a major electoral issue; indeed, between the two major parties there was an undeclared but virtually unbroken consensus. Beyond Westminster, most people simply could not care less. In September 1969, just after British troops had been sent to Belfast and Derry, an NOP survey found that people ranked Northern Ireland rock bottom in a list of ten problems confronting the government. Even at the height of the violence, it lagged well behind public anxiety about the economy. In fact, as the conflict got worse during 1972, so Northern Ireland actually *receded* as an issue. By April 1973, less than 10 per cent of the population described the conflict as Britain's biggest problem – a proportion that steadily fell in the next few years. As an American reporter astutely remarked, the 'televised spectacle of suffering in Ulster has become monotonously familiar', with the images of weeping mothers and bombed-out homes now 'stale with repetition, an O'Casey drama with no last act'.[36]

It is ironic, therefore, that foreign observers, especially in Ireland or the United States, often imagined that the average Briton dreamed of Belfast's pebble-dashed council estates with misty eyes and a thumping heart. In fact, as early as February 1971 the government was worried that the public was 'beginning actively to resent the situation', and that 'many people would favour abandoning the Province to its fate'. Although

polls had originally shown strong support for Britain's military intervention, they soon swung around: by 1974, just 32 per cent favoured
keeping the troops in Ulster, while 59 per cent thought the government
should bring them home – although few people felt strongly enough to
do anything about it. Far from taking sides, most people regarded
unionists and nationalists alike with baffled horror. By 1973, 44 per cent
agreed that the people of Northern Ireland were intolerant, while only
20 per cent thought them hard-working and just 14 per cent described
them as friendly. 'I hate Bernadette Devlin as much as I hate the Revd.
Ian Paisley, if anything worse,' recorded the diarist James Lees-Milne, a
good barometer of conservative opinion, in January 1971. And even
atrocities on the mainland provoked not a great wave of sympathy for
unionism, but a surge of contempt for *all* Northern Ireland's combatants,
whether loyalist or republican. 'I loathe and detest the miserable bastards
. . . savage murderous thugs,' wrote Lord Arran in the *Evening Standard*
in October 1974. 'May the Irish, all of them, rot in hell.'[37]

But the truth was that many of them were there already. In the
aftermath of internment, Northern Ireland sank into the bloodiest period
in its history, an orgy of bombings and shootings in which even the most
terrible atrocities were almost overlooked amid the carnage. By now, any
remaining trust between the rival communities had completely broken
down. As in so many sectarian conflicts, each side looked on the other
with horror and fear, arming itself in case its enemy struck first. By
September, soldiers, paramilitaries and civilians were dying almost every
day in shooting incidents and bomb attacks, and at the end of the month
the conflict reached a new low when the Provisional IRA detonated a
100-pound bomb in the Four Step Inn on the Shankill Road. It was half-
past-ten at night; the lounge was full of local residents watching television,
and when the bar's roof collapsed, twenty-seven were badly injured and
two were killed. One of the dead men, Alexander Andrews, was so badly
disfigured by shattering glass that his son could only identify him by his
shoes. It was a naked sectarian attack, brutal and cold-blooded, and it
unleashed a cycle of violence that seemed likely to consume the city itself.

On 4 December, the UVF took their revenge by planting a 50-pound
bomb in McGurk's Bar in the city centre, a sleepy, Catholic-owned pub
with no republican connections, in which old men liked to chat about
the horses over a pint. Patrick McGurk himself, who was serving behind
the bar when the bomb went off, miraculously survived the explosion;

when he came to, he was told that his wife and daughter were among the fifteen people killed. It was a ghastly, terrible scene, the stuff of some sick nightmare, but the blood feud was not over yet. Exactly one week later, the IRA bombed the Balmoral Furnishing Company on the Shankill Road. It was a busy, bustling pre-Christmas Saturday, and the street was packed with shoppers. Two men were killed; so were two infants, aged just 1 and 2. 'Women were crying. Men were trying to dig out the rubble,' one man said later. 'One person was crying beside you and the next person was shouting "Bastards" and things like that. I didn't actually see the babies' bodies as they had them wrapped in sheets, but the blood was just coming right through them. They were just like lumps of meat, you know, small lumps of meat.' The next day, he walked along to a local UDA meeting and announced that he wanted to volunteer. He was prepared to do 'whatever it took to defend the people of my area', he said. And so it went on. This was the United Kingdom in December 1971.[38]

7

Love Thy Neighbour

The stink of the blacks made him sick. He hated spades – wished they'd wash more often or get the hell back where they came from. This was his London – not somewhere for London Transport's African troops to live.

            – Richard Allen, *Skinhead* (1970)

AGGRO BRITAIN: '*Mindless Violence' of the Bully Boys Worries Top Policeman*

            – *Daily Mirror*, 14 June 1973

By the beginning of the 1970s, the British Empire had been consigned to history. As one colonial possession after another had declared independence during the 1950s and 1960s, so the swathes of imperial pink that had once covered maps in classrooms across the country had vanished. When Edward Heath flew to Singapore for the first Commonwealth Conference in January 1971, it was as the chief executive of a rusting industrial conglomerate, once a market leader but left now with just a handful of tiny, scattered subsidiaries: Hong Kong, the Seychelles, St Vincent, the Falkland Islands. Heath could not even console himself that Britain had left a noble legacy, for the record of the newly independent countries, from the permanent tension between India and Pakistan to the civil war in Nigeria, from the ethnic bloodletting in Cyprus to the reactionary defiance of Rhodesia, made for shameful reading. Only two years before, Kenya had become a one-party state, while Uganda's President Milton Obote, once a hero of the struggle for independence, now ruled as a virtual dictator, imprisoning and torturing anyone who dared criticize him. And what was even worse from a British point of view was that the new post-colonial leaders seemed to have no respect for their old imperial masters, no sense of obligation or community. For when Heath arrived in Singapore, it was to an atmosphere of bitterness and recrimination, with African leaders queuing up to denounce his policy of selling arms to South Africa in return for the use of the Simonstown naval base. And when he faced his severest critics – Zambia's Kenneth Kaunda, Tanzania's Julius Nyerere and Uganda's Obote – he found it hard to keep his patience. 'I wonder how many of you', he finally snapped, 'will be allowed to return to your own countries after this conference?'[1]

At the time it sounded like a typical example of Heath's absurd rudeness. In fact, it turned out to be a remarkably accurate prediction, for a week later Milton Obote was on his way home from Singapore when the news broke that he had been toppled by a military coup. After Obote's flagrant corruption, his intolerance of dissent and his threats to British commercial interests in Uganda, his replacement seemed like a breath of fresh air. All political prisoners, announced Major General Idi Amin, would soon be released, while he hoped to hold 'free and fair' civilian elections as soon as possible. And since General Amin had a reputation of being pro-British, noted *The Times,* his rise to power was greeted 'with ill-concealed relief in Whitehall'. As a young man he had not only been the Ugandan light heavyweight boxing champion, he had been a warrant officer in the King's African Rifles, holding the highest rank possible for a black African, and in 1961 had been one of the first two Ugandans given a Queen's Commission. He had even learned to play rugby, being selected as a reserve forward for the East Africa XV to face the touring British Lions in 1955. The story goes that his Scottish officers used to hit him on the head with a hammer to inspire him before big games: perhaps that explains why he rarely seemed the sharpest of intellects. 'Idi Amin is a splendid type and a good player,' one officer reported, 'but virtually bone from the neck up, and needs things explained in words of one letter.' By January 1971, however, that was precisely what Uganda needed – or so most British observers thought. Amin was 'not a man of intellect or political finesse', admitted the *Guardian,* 'but [one] with great ability at man-to-man straight talking with ordinary soldiers'. He would be 'a welcome contrast to other African leaders and a staunch friend to Britain', announced the *Telegraph.* 'Good luck to General Amin.'[2]

It did not take long for the *Telegraph* to realize its mistake. Within months of the coup, it was clear that Amin had no intention of surrendering power to a civilian administration, and clear too that beneath the blustering, jovial exterior was a thoroughly aggressive, cunning and unscrupulous political operator. To *Punch*'s columnist Alan Coren, who regularly parodied Amin's clumsy ignorance, his grandiose pretensions and his thick African accent, he seemed merely a 'buffoon'. But the Ugandans imprisoned and murdered under his increasingly paranoid regime were not laughing. And neither were the 60,000 Asians – most of them originally from Gujarat in India – who had come to Uganda during the days of the British Empire, working as clerical staff, bankers and tailors.

Racial tensions had been growing since Ugandan independence, exacerbated by the fact that the Asians were generally well educated, affluent and socially exclusive, keeping themselves apart from their black African neighbours. 'We were the visible middle class,' recalled the columnist Yasmin Alibhai-Brown. 'We didn't much care for independence when it came in 1962, and we did what was necessary – bribes, public demonstrations of support for this minister or that – anything that could keep us living enchanted lives in a natural paradise.' Between the two communities was a thick wall of racial tension: when she played Juliet in a school production alongside a black African Romeo, her own father refused to speak to her for three years. And even before Amin took power, the temperature was rising. Among the Asians, rumours spread that Africans were raping their daughters; among the black Ugandans, there were stories that the 'greedy' Asians were hogging all the best jobs, were sending money overseas, were 'cheating, conspiring and plotting' to undermine the state. They were the easiest of targets; too easy for Idi Amin to resist. 'I want the economy to be in the hands of Ugandan citizens, especially black Ugandans,' he told a military assembly on 4 August 1972. Since the Asians were 'sabotaging the economy of the country', all those with British passports should pack their bags. They had ninety days to leave.[3]

For Heath and his ministers, Amin's bombshell left them facing a terrible dilemma. On the one hand, they recognized that Britain had a moral obligation to accept the Asians, not merely because they faced persecution and expulsion, but because an estimated 57,000 of them held British passports. As the Foreign Secretary, Sir Alec Douglas-Home, reminded his colleagues four days after Amin's announcement, 'we could not disclaim responsibility for British passport holders even if we so wished'; in any case, the impact on Britain's reputation overseas would be catastrophic. But public opinion within Britain was a very different matter. Like most of his ministers, Heath had always been determinedly moderate on questions of race and immigration; indeed, his dogged refusal to play the race card and his decision to sack Enoch Powell for rocking the boat on immigration had upset many grass-roots Tories in the last years of the 1960s. But his position in the election campaign of 1970 had been clear. Public opinion overwhelmingly demanded an end to mass immigration, so an end must be made. In October 1971, therefore, the government had passed a landmark Immigration Act bringing up the drawbridge. From now on, only so-called Commonwealth 'patrials' with a parent or grandparent born in the United Kingdom (which meant they were likely to be white) had the right to settle in Britain; all other Commonwealth citizens had to apply for work permits, just like everybody else. Some observers detected a hint of racism in the distinction between 'patrials' and the rest; indeed, Reginald Maudling told his colleagues that since assimilation was 'all but impossible' for Asians, immigration ought to be limited to people from a 'cultural background fairly akin to our own'. But Heath's ministers were, by and large, a liberal-minded lot, and certainly far more tolerant than the majority of the population. They closed the door to mass immigration not because they were racist reactionaries, but because public opinion – as manifested in one poll after another – demanded it. The Act worked and the furore died down – until Idi Amin reignited it.[4]

At first, even as terrified Ugandan Asians were desperately calling friends and relatives in Britain to beg for help, the government tried to play for time. On 12 August, Heath sent his urbane European troubleshooter, Geoffrey Rippon, to Kampala to persuade Amin to change his mind or, at the very least, to extend his deadline. Unfortunately the former rugby forward made it clear that he would not yield an inch of ground. 'I have already made up my mind. Finished!' Amin melodramatically told the press corps. 'This is British imperialism. I am not going to listen to imperialist advice that we should continue to have foreigners controlling the economy.' What was more, once Rippon had gone home, the Ugandan president increased the stakes by withdrawing his promised exemption for selected Asian professionals. 'They could not serve the country with a good spirit after the departure of other Asians,' he explained. And with Amin standing firm, the British government had no real choice. 'We will accept our responsibilities,' Rippon announced. 'If people are expelled and they are United Kingdom passport holders, then however unreasonable that expulsion may be, and however inhumane and unjust the conditions in which it is brought about, we have to accept the responsibility . . . I don't think anyone in a situation like this can stand aside and say, "Oh, it's no concern of ours."' Other senior Conservatives took a similar view. It was a question of 'honour and decency', said Reginald Maudling, now exiled to the back benches. 'If homes elsewhere in the world cannot be found for them,' agreed Sir Alec Douglas-Home, 'we must take these unlucky people in.'[5]

Since the Labour leadership agreed that Heath had no choice but to accept the refugees, the Ugandan crisis never became a partisan issue. Almost all senior politicians, in fact, agreed with *The Times* that even though Britain had recently accepted immigrants 'at a faster rate than most similar communities would find tolerable . . . the ultimate responsibility for British citizens lies with Britain'. But it was an academic anthropologist, Nicholas David, who put it best in a letter to the paper the next day. The Ugandan Asians, he pointed out, were 'our colonial legacy', and it was the Conservative government of Harold Macmillan that had given them their British passports. To discriminate between different colours of passport holders would be to follow the examples of Nazi Germany and South Africa. 'These islands are indeed over-populated, reason enough to discourage all immigration,' he concluded, 'but unless we are to forsake what we say we stand for, we cannot refuse entry to fellow subjects of the Queen who have no other country of their own.'

And yet Dr David, like the editor of *The Times* and like Heath himself, was in the minority. In the tabloids there was talk of a 'deluge' of immigrants, a 'flood' of newcomers that would put Britain on 'panic stations'. In cities with already large Asian populations, which were bound to attract considerable numbers of refugees, there were howls of protest from local councillors. 'We are virtually full up,' insisted the Labour leader of Leicester City Council, encouraging residents to send letters of complaint to the government. By early September, the council had even taken out an advertisement in the *Uganda Argus* imploring Asians not to come to Leicester, while Bolton Council collected thousands of signatures to a petition demanding that they stay out of Bolton, too.

And day after day, letters pages burned with the fury of correspondents worried that their country was about to be overrun, their homes, jobs and opportunities threatened by tens of thousands of foreigners who, through a fluke of history, happened to have British passports. 'I have every sympathy with these unfortunate Asians, some of whom I have counted as friends for many years,' wrote the former Conservative MP Sir John Fletcher-Cooke (whose friends must have been hastily revising their social diaries). 'But both they and the British Government failed to realize that peoples of one culture or background will never willingly share power, political or economic, with those of another culture.' And for another *Times* reader, Katherine Fussell, who called herself 'an ordinary British subject and housewife', the question was one of 'hard everyday facts':

> The Clydeside shipyard workers have fought extremely hard for their daily bread, the dockers are in a struggle for theirs, the transport workers are wondering what will happen to some of their jobs, at the Norwich shoe factory women staged a stop-in to save theirs. Not all these fights are successful in these times of much unemployment.
>
> Mines have been shut down, and we hear of men in all walks of life offered redundancies in place of their work. White and black citizens of this country cannot buy or rent a house easily. Many young folk cannot get married because of the housing problem or if they do they live with in-laws and many marriages fail. Young school leavers, white and black, are on the streets with nothing to think about or do, they draw the dole! The future is bleak indeed.
>
> This situation should not be aggravated by a large influx from any country. These people if allowed in must be housed, fed and found work. Schools must be found to take the children. If they are given national assistance they will strain the economy already at breaking point . . . Let the Government make it clear to these people from any country wanting to come to us, that the immigration quota remains and they must wait their turn when they will be more than welcome.[6]

For some people, however, the Ugandan Asian crisis was a godsend. For the right-wing Monday Club, which had been set up to oppose decolonization in the 1960s, it was an opportunity to attract new supporters and stoke up opposition to Heath within the Conservative Party. As early as 7 August it had issued a statement insisting that the 'so-called British Asians are no more and no less British than any Indian in the bazaars of Bombay'. They had 'no connexion with Britain either by blood or residence', explained the Buckinghamshire South MP Ronald Bell, and should 'go back to their own country', meaning India (a country that had already ruled out accepting large numbers). And although there was no chance that the Tory leadership would take a blind bit of notice of the Monday Club's pronouncements, its members could console themselves that Britain's best-known politician agreed with them. 'All the talk of "British passports" is spoof,' Enoch Powell told a Conservative lunch in Wolverhampton on 14 August. The passports, he explained with his characteristically fierce logic, gave no 'entitlement to enter this country' and implied 'no connexion with the United Kingdom itself', and while the government might feel morally obliged to accept an 'infinitesimal' share of the refugees, it had no obligation to take them all.[7]

As the crisis wore on, so Powell's rhetoric became more strident. 'In order to govern a people and to lead them, you must enter into their feelings and their fears, and they must know you enter into them,' he told a Round Table audience a few weeks later. And yet 'at this moment hundreds of thousands of our fellow citizens here in Britain are living in perpetual dread: they dread for themselves, or they fear for the future, or they dread for both'. He singled out the elderly, 'who live in actual physical fear', as well as those who feared for their children, 'who feel as if they are trapped or tied to a stake in the face of an advancing tide'. But 'beyond all these, and including all these', Powell said, 'are those who watch an alteration, profound and irrevocable, which they feel powerless to arrest or to protect against, engulfing the places, the towns, the cities which they knew and which they thought were theirs'. And if Heath's government would not address their fears, then 'another must'.[8]

By 1972, Powell was comfortably the most popular politician in the country, voted 'Man of the Year' in a BBC poll two years running. Once the youngest professor in the British Empire and the youngest brigadier in the British Army, the MP for Wolverhampton South West now cut a brooding, isolated figure, a prophet to his admirers, a pariah to his enemies. In full flow in the House of Commons he often seemed icily logical, pressing his argument to its conclusion without regard for the sensibilities of his audience. In fact, he was a man of smouldering passions, from Housman and Nietzsche to High Anglicanism and hunting. As a newspaper profile had put it when he ran against Heath and Maudling for the Tory leadership back in 1965, he had 'the taut, pale face of a missionary, and the zealous energy of a man who is not afraid of the stake'. Ever since his extraordinarily divisive 'Rivers of Blood' speech (a phrase he never actually used) in 1968, he had been in the political wilderness, and had not even spoken to Heath since his dismissal from the Shadow Cabinet. Yet while his doom-laden predictions ensured him the hatred of students and the liberal left, they had also made him enormously popular with the general public; indeed, three out of four people told pollsters they agreed with him. His appeal crossed regional and party boundaries: he was regarded as a courageous, independent man, the tribune of the voiceless masses. And the more that student demonstrators tried to drown him out, the more his support seemed to grow. During the general election campaign of 1970, Tony Benn had histrionically claimed that 'the flag hoisted at Wolverhampton is beginning to look like the one that fluttered over Dachau and Belsen'. Two weeks later Powell almost doubled his majority, and afterwards some analysts suggested that he had attracted as many as 2 million working-class voters to the Conservative Party. He had tapped into a widespread feeling, wrote the *Guardian*'s Peter Jenkins, that 'the politicians are conspiring against the people, that the country is led by men who had no idea about what interests or frightens the ordinary people in the backstreets of Wolverhampton'.[9]

Then as now, Powell's views and career were widely misunderstood. Often caricatured as a fire-breathing reactionary, he actually held remarkably liberal views on many social issues. Not only did he vote for the legalization of homosexuality and the abolition of hanging, but his most celebrated parliamentary speech was a withering attack on British atrocities in the Hola detention camp in Kenya, which even Labour observers thought was one of the most moving Commons speeches they had ever heard. And although he loathed the project of European union and regarded the United States with deep distaste, it is hard to see a man who taught himself French, German, Spanish, Portuguese, Hebrew, Italian, Russian and Urdu as a xenophobic Little Englander. Set against all that, however, is the fact that in April 1968 Powell gave a speech that thousands of immigrants found deeply unsettling, even terrifying; a speech that repeated some of the racist urban myths of the day in terms that were bound to prove inflammatory; a speech that horrified even some of his oldest and closest friends. And whatever the nuances of Powell's own

With his trademark moustache and blazing eyes, Enoch Powell was a gift to the cartoonists, and in this image for the *Daily Express* (10 April 1972) Cummings links him with immigration, the EEC and Northern Ireland. It is easy to be shocked by the racial caricatures, but it has to be said that Bernadette Devlin makes a fine mermaid.

position, which was often much more complicated than his critics allowed, there is little doubt that genuine racists drew comfort from his stand. From Wolverhampton, which had virtually no history of racial antagonism before the speech, there came reports of white youths attacking immigrants and chanting 'Powell, Powell'. And according to the National Front's organizer in Huddersfield, his speeches 'gave our membership and morale a tremendous boost. Before Powell spoke, we were getting only cranks and perverts. After his speeches we started to attract, in a secret sort of way, the right-wing members of the Tory organizations.'[10]

The irony, though, is that even as Powell's speech effectively destroyed his political career, it made his name as a national icon. As far as the general public were concerned, all the complexities of Powell's career, from his liberal attitudes to homosexuality and hanging to his radical free-market economic ideas, were reduced to just one issue: race. To those frightened by immigration or alienated from the political system, he became an overnight hero. 'He's the finest man in the country,' one elderly Blackburn woman told Jeremy Seabrook, prompting a chorus of approval: 'He should be Prime Minister.' 'He started too late with all this black business. He should have started sooner.' 'He speaks the mind of all the white – well, three quarters of the white people in this country.' 'I think Enoch is a marvellous man, and I hope that some day he's Prime Minister.' 'He's whiter than white is Enoch. Whiter than white.' In popular culture, meanwhile, support for Powell was used everywhere from episodes of *Coronation Street* to spin-off novels from *The Sweeney* to identify resentful, racist or reactionary working-class characters. 'Enoch's Dreaming of a White Christmas', sings Albert Steptoe in one *Steptoe and Son* Christmas special, while Alf Garnett is never slow to invoke the sage of Wolverhampton. 'It's a pity old Enoch ain't in charge,' he mutters in an episode of *Till Death Us Do Part* from January 1974, while behind him, to the hilarity of the audience, a black electrician arrives to fix his broken television. 'He'd sort them out. He'd put the coons down the pits, he would.'[11]

As opinion rallied against the Ugandan Asians, it was Powell's name that protesters invoked to justify their opposition. When 400 Smithfield meat porters, joined by groups of dockers and porters from Covent Garden, marched on Westminster on 24 August, they carried placards reading 'ENOCH WAS RIGHT'. Two weeks later they organized a second march, this time to the headquarters of the TGWU, again carrying banners proclaiming their determination to keep 'BRITAIN FOR THE BRITISH'. But while the Smithfield porters had seized national attention four years before, marching on the House of Commons in an unsuccessful attempt to have Powell restored to the Shadow Cabinet, there was an unexpected twist this time. Just days after the second march, Granada's *World in Action* team recruited one of the more vehement anti-immigration porters, Wally Murrell, to travel to Uganda and interview people on all sides of the crisis. Murrell was in Kampala for only three days before Amin kicked him out, yet on his return he confessed that he had changed his mind. 'I must admit that when I saw what one Asian family had to give up to leave the country it influenced me,' he said. 'What impressed me while I was there was the violence that was only just beneath the surface. I was convinced that there would be a bloodbath if they stayed.' Many of his fellow porters were horrified by his apostasy: when he appeared on *World in Action* to retract his opposition, he was bombarded with obscene phone calls. 'He does not speak for us,' one porter angrily told the press. But others were more supportive. 'All morning blokes came up to me individually,' Wally said after his first day back at Smithfield, 'and said they respected what I had done and admired me for speaking out.'[12]

Wally Murrell was not, of course, the only person whose compassion for the Ugandan Asians trumped his concern that Britain was becoming overcrowded. In Leicester, leaders of the Asian community raised £10,000 to provide for the expected influx of refugees, took over 200 houses due for demolition and even prepared to set up temporary classrooms for the refugees' children, staffed by teachers who had previously run schools in Uganda. 'We must not put all the burden on the British Government or people,' explained H. S. Ratoo, chairman of the British Asian Welfare Committee. 'We must take the responsibility and make preparations to help the people.' But it was not only Asians who went out of their way to welcome the exiles. By the middle of September, the government's Ugandan Resettlement Board was reporting that 2,000 people had written to offer rooms in their own homes, and by the end of the month a further 3,000 had followed suit. In the Isle of Wight, stereotypically a conservative part of the country with virtually no black or Asian residents, a Ventnor hotelier offered to put 90 Asians up at his hotel, while Fred Sage offered to house 500 refugees at his Bay View Holiday Park in Gurnard. Another proprietor, Bertram Wrate, even offered to put up 100 refugees in his nudist camp at Blackgang. And all the time, despite the torrent of criticism in the tabloid press, clothes, blankets and supplies poured in. 'We know many of you didn't really want to leave your homes and jobs in Uganda,' *The Economist* assured the refugees.

> You know we didn't really want you to come here, because we have problems with homes and jobs here. But most of us believe that this is a country that can use your skills and energies . . . You will find that we, like other countries, have our bullies and misfits. We are particularly sorry about those of our politicians who are trying to use your troubles for their own ends. And we're glad your British passport means something again.[13]

In an ideal world, Heath and his ministers would have liked the Ugandan Asians to disappear somewhere else: to India, perhaps, or to Canada, which agreed to take several thousand. There was clearly no chance that Idi Amin would change his mind: he was 'fundamentally irrational and unreliable', Robert Carr, the Home Secretary, wrote in early August. As an emollient and strikingly liberal man, popular on both sides of the House, Carr had not been an obvious Tory candidate to run the Home Office; indeed, in a period of high public anxiety about law and order, it might have been better for Heath if he had chosen a more authoritarian figure. But from the refugees' point of view, Carr was the perfect Home Secretary, persuading his Cabinet colleagues to approve £750 per family towards their travel expenses as well as subsidies for local authorities faced with mass arrivals. He was no fool: whenever the Cabinet discussed the issue, the threat of a popular anti-Asian backlash was never far from their minds, and Carr conceded that they should not give the refugees so many benefits that they lost all public sympathy. By and large, however, his handling of the crisis was a rare model of compassion and competence, although it was also made a lot easier by the fact that fewer Asians arrived than had been predicted.[14]

By the middle of September, it was clear that only about 25,000 refugees were coming to Britain, with others going to Canada, Australia or elsewhere in Africa. The Resettlement Board was working well, Carr reported on 21 September; local authorities were dealing smoothly with the inflow; and above all 'the public now seemed disposed to accept the [Asians] as genuine refugees'. At the party conference a few weeks later, Carr even recorded a notable rhetorical triumph, swatting aside Enoch Powell's attempt to humiliate the leadership over immigration and securing a two-to-one mandate for the government's approach. If they had abandoned the Ugandan Asians, Heath reminded a Tory audience at the end of November, 'they would be rotting in concentration camps prepared by President Amin, and they would be there simply because of the colour of their skin and the fact that they held British passports. That would have been the sight presented to us on our television screens night after night this Christmas. I cannot believe that anyone in this country would have regarded such an outcome as acceptable.'[15]

All in all, the Ugandan crisis brought the best out of Edward Heath. A few years earlier, Harold Wilson had rushed through an emergency bill to stop the mass influx of Kenyan Asian refugees. But even though Heath's government was under even greater pressure over immigration, he never wavered in his view that Britain had a moral obligation to its passport holders in their hour of need. For once his mulish obstinacy shone through as courageous commitment: the more that right-wing critics slammed his refusal to follow public opinion, the more he seemed determined to honour Britain's moral and legal obligations. Not surprisingly, representatives of Britain's Asian community were full of admiration. Heath's policy, said Praful Patel of the All-Party Committee on United Kingdom Citizenship, was 'in the highest traditions of justice and fair play so often shown by the British people. The decision to accept responsibility for these people is a tremendous credit for the Government. It vindicates our trust in them.' And there were moving words from a group of Indian students who wrote to *The Times* at the beginning of September:

> Some of us have been in your country and as young Indians we have come to love and respect Britain. We have experienced the welcome and hospitality in your homes. We have been struck by the concern your people have for other nations ... We have been inspired by the British Government's readiness to accept the Uganda Asians with British passports at a time when the country faces unemployment, crisis in industry and in Northern Ireland.
>
> Your Government has shown true statesmanship in honouring past promises and in fighting for humane treatment to be given to these men, women and children. This adherence to moral responsibility by British leaders is encouraging when expediency and national interest decide policies the world over.

For a group of foreigners – especially from a former imperial possession – to write of their admiration for British politics in the early 1970s was rare indeed. On this occasion, though, Heath deserved it.[16]

At the beginning of the 1970s, perhaps a million Caribbean, Indian and Pakistani immigrants and their children lived in Britain.* Although there were pockets of black and brown life right across the nation, immigrant communities tended to be concentrated in heavily urbanized areas, especially where there had once been plenty of low-paid jobs and cheap housing. More than half of the immigrant population lived in London and the South-east, and a further 16 per cent lived in Birmingham, Wolverhampton and the industrial towns of the West Midlands, with smaller clusters in Lancashire, West Yorkshire and the East Midlands.

* A definitive figure is virtually impossible, and the official census figure of 650,000 in 1971 is surely too low. The Institute of Race Relations came up with the figure 1 million in the late 1960s.

The biggest group were the Indians, who accounted for about 30 per cent of the total, and who had already made a deep impression on British cultural life through their restaurants, of which there were perhaps 2,000 in 1970, serving cheap, anglicized curries to young couples and late-night revellers. Then came the West Indians, who accounted for 25 per cent and were overwhelmingly concentrated in London and Birmingham. In 1971, the official census recorded a Caribbean population of 170,000 in the capital alone, which was surely an underestimate. The third biggest group, at 13 per cent of the total, consisted of Pakistani families, often from poor rural village backgrounds. Many settled further north in the textile towns of Yorkshire and Lancashire, which in the 1950s and 1960s had a thirsty demand for cheap unskilled labour: in Bradford, there were about 50,000 Pakistani residents by the early 1980s.[17]

These were not, of course, the only immigrant communities in Edward Heath's Britain. By the late 1960s, there were already around 75,000 Greek and Turkish Cypriots in London alone, having fled the political unrest in their native land. After the Turkish invasion in 1974, about 10,000 more followed, most of them Turks settling in the north-east of the capital, where they opened innumerable restaurants, bars and community centres. And then there were the Hong Kong Chinese, easily Britain's quietest and least assimilated major immigrant group – so quiet, in fact, that even racist campaigners sometimes forgot they were there. The 1971 census put the Chinese population at 96,000, almost all of them working in the catering trade. By this point, Chinese restaurants were even more popular and numerous than Indian ones. In many areas, their willingness to work long hours meant that they virtually supplanted (and often physically took over) the old fish-and-chip shops, and by the early 1970s virtually every sizeable town had developed a taste for chow mein and sweet and sour sauce. Yet even though the Chinese population almost doubled during the 1970s, there was no repeat of the racist panics of the Edwardian era, and no talk of the yellow peril. For one thing, they were widely dispersed across the country; for another, they worked such long hours and were so discreet that they were rarely even noticed. Ironically, although critics often complained that immigrants did not even try to fit in, the ones who provoked least hostility were those who made least effort to do so.[18]

Ever since mass immigration from the Commonwealth began in the early 1950s, successive governments had been anxious to make sure that the newcomers found productive work and a chance to make their way up the ladder. Initially there seemed good reason for optimism: a study in 1970 found that many immigrants had readily adapted to new challenges, with 18 per cent of both Indians and West Africans finding professional or technical work and another 19 per cent getting clerical jobs. But by the mid-1970s it was worryingly obvious that progress had stalled. One problem was that thousands of immigrants had chosen to live in industrial towns with falling populations and cheap housing – precisely those places, in other words, that suffered most in the economic troubles of the 1970s. And since the mills and factories that would once have given newcomers a foothold on the ladder were closing down, they often found themselves condemned to low-paid manual jobs in dreary, dilapidated, depressed towns that the rest of Britain had forgotten. By 1975, government figures showed that unemployment among immigrants was twice the national average, while young black school-leavers were four times less likely than their white counterparts to find jobs. Education was not always the answer: a year later, more figures suggested that one in four West Indian and Asian university graduates now worked in manual trades, compared with only a tiny proportion of white graduates. And by the beginning of the 1980s, it was clear that the decline of Britain's manufacturing industries had taken a heavy toll on the ambitions of its immigrant population. In 1984, eight out of ten Caribbean men and seven out of ten Asian men were still working as manual labourers – compared with only five out of ten whites. And instead of moving up the property ladder, immigrants found themselves trapped at the bottom: in London, for example, some of the most run-down, violent and intimidating housing estates virtually became immigrant reservations, such as the Holly Street Estate, Hackney, or Broadwater Farm, Haringey. Here too racial discrimination clearly played its part, but to an extent the newcomers were simply the helpless victims of economic history.[19]

Outside London the situation was little better. Nottingham, for example, had attracted a sizeable immigrant population in the 1950s and 1960s thanks to its history as a major textile town. By 1971, Commonwealth immigrants accounted for about 6 per cent of its total population, and a council official estimated that there were 10,000 West Indians, 4,000 Indians and 3,000 Pakistanis. Instead of being dispersed across the city, they were packed into a few seedy, neglected inner-city neighbourhoods such as St Ann's, Lenton and Radford. But this was not merely a matter of choice. Despite the race relations legislation of the late 1960s, housing discrimination was still a fact of life: in February 1971 Nottingham's Fair Housing Group, which had close links to the council, local estate agents and building societies, reported that 'discrimination still continues to appear in various forms when an immigrant intends to purchase a house in one of the suburban areas of the city'. It was 'so subtle', the report claimed, 'that even the Race Relations Act has become powerless to prevent it'.

In interviews, immigrants consistently complained that white residents refused to sell to them, that neighbours put pressure on sellers to pull out, that building societies were reluctant to give them mortgages or would ask for an impossibly high deposit. In Nottingham, seven out of ten said that they had suffered housing discrimination, while almost eight out of ten complained of employment discrimination too. Time and again, they said, they were turned down without an interview, or told that the job had been filled as soon as the interviewer discovered they were black. One man rejected for a salesman's job, for example, was told that 'customers might not like a coloured man calling on them', even though the interviewers admitted that he was perfectly 'fit for the job'. So it was hardly surprising that no fewer than nine out of ten West Indians told researchers that they had been deeply disappointed by the realities of British prejudice. 'We thought England was the home of justice – so we got quite a shock,' one said. 'The least little trouble they'll turn round suddenly and say why don't you go back where you come from,' another lamented. 'I was not expecting at all any prejudice or discrimination,' admitted a third. 'As a matter of fact I did not know I was a coloured man until the English tell me. Somebody referred to me as a coloured person on the bus once and that was the first time I knew who I was.'[20]

That many people were prejudiced is not in doubt. In the same survey, six out of ten white Nottingham residents agreed that 'English' people should have priority in council housing. 'It's our bloody country so we should get first chance,' one said. 'Because the English fought to keep out the invaders and all both governments have done since is to open the doors to them all,' said another. 'We've fought two wars to keep our country English so we should have priority,' insisted a third. And an even greater proportion (67 per cent) agreed that the 'English' ought to have priority in employment, too, even though this was technically illegal under the Race Relations Act of 1968. 'It's our country. I know some blacks are born here but I still think the Englishmen should have priority,' one said. 'It's England isn't it? I'm Alf Garnett. He said that when God made this earth he allotted a little bit to everybody. I've got no intention of going to India,' said another. 'I'm not prejudiced,' said a third. 'It's just an Englishman's right.'[21]

Although Nottingham was badly affected by the economic downturn of the 1970s, other towns were even harder hit, and there prejudice took on a sharper, more aggressive edge. In Blackburn, Jeremy Seabrook found 'an elaborate system of legends, myths and gossip' surrounding the town's 5,000 Pakistani immigrants, who made up just 5 per cent of the total population. One man told him that 'this chap, white chap' had heard noises in his loft one night, and upon ascending had found 'a great long row of mattresses in the roof, all the length of the street, and on every one is a Pakistan [sic]'. Another man reported hearing that a Pakistani had managed to get £40 from the social services to pay for his car repairs (although even he admitted: 'I shouldn't think the Social Security'd be as generous as that'). In fact, Seabrook had heard it all before: these were common urban myths of the day, repeated in towns across the country and always involving some mysterious friend of a friend. But they were none the less virulent for being false. Visiting a Victorian terraced house in a run-down area, Seabrook met a crowd of middle-aged and elderly white women who were almost falling over each other to tell him that the Pakistanis were benefit cheats. As Seabrook saw it, the women were clearly frightened of being stranded in immigrant-dominated areas, their homes losing their value, their moral attitudes becoming obsolete in a disturbing new social and cultural landscape. The Pakistanis spat on the street, they complained; they blew their nose between their thumbs and fingers, instead of using a handkerchief; their wives did not even bother to scrub their front steps, as proper Blackburn women did. 'We're being driven out, no doubt about it,' one said passionately. 'We're going back to the Stone Age,' said another woman, 'where they can just do as they like on the pavement ... It's like a jungle living here. People are very bitter. And if they can't live like we live I think it's time they went back.'[22]

As Seabrook pointed out, these kinds of resentments – which often seemed more bitter and outspoken in the 1970s than in the decades beforehand – were only partly the result of racial prejudice. He noticed that many of the Blackburn women seemed uncomfortable with their own sentiments: afterwards 'there was a certain uneasiness in the room, a sense of shame, the shame of people who have unburdened themselves to a stranger'. They knew that racial prejudice was wrong, which is why they often insisted that they were not prejudiced themselves ('but . . .'). 'This business about colour is all wrong,' one told him. 'I had some Italians live next door to me, and nicer people you couldn't wish to meet . . . They make me sick when they say it's on grounds of colour. It's not the colour at all.' Of course this was not really true: 'the colour' – understood broadly as the immigrants' attitudes, habits and values, as well as their appearance – was clearly a factor. But there was more to it than atavistic hatred, Seabrook thought: there was a sense of loss, of helplessness, of nostalgia for an idealized industrial working-class world with strict moral and social boundaries, a world that seemed to be slipping away. The women's anger was 'an expression of their pain and powerlessness confronted by the decay and dereliction, not only of the familiar environment, but of their own lives too'.[23]

In many ways, racial prejudice was becoming increasingly unacceptable in Edward Heath's Britain. In the political arena, overt racism was largely unknown, and most politicians trod extremely carefully. For almost all ambitious politicians, fear of being attacked by the press as a 'racialist' was much greater than the appeal of pandering to working-class sentiments. It was revealing, for example, that even when tabloid newspapers were attacking immigration, they took care to present themselves as tolerant and open-minded, insisting that their opposition was based on economic or environmental factors rather than questions of skin colour. Even though more than eight out of ten people agreed with Enoch Powell in the spring of 1968 that immigration had gone too far, seven out of ten told a Race Relations Board survey that they regarded themselves as tolerant and would happily drink with a black man at the pub. And for the *Daily Mirror*, still seen as the voice of the ordinary working man, even this was not enough. 'The immigrant population – especially the second generation immigrants – don't want simply to be tolerated,' an editorial thundered. 'They are NOT economic units. They are human beings. They are citizens of this country here to build a new life for themselves and their families. It is as fellow citizens and fellow human beings that they are entitled to be accepted.'[24]

Fine words indeed; yet by the early 1970s, it was clear that racial prejudice was more deeply entrenched than it had seemed. This was, after all, a world in which the highly educated James Lees-Milne, a lover of the arts and driving spirit in the National Trust, saw nothing wrong in recording his horror that 'half the inhabitants [of London] are coloured'. They were 'aliens with alien beliefs', he wrote in 1977, 'and no understanding of our ways and past greatness. England to them is merely a convenience, a habitation, rather hostile, where wages are high and the State provides.' This was tame stuff, though, compared with the views of Philip Larkin, arguably Britain's finest poet, who complained to his mother in 1970 that 'one child in eight born now is of immigrant parents', and in fifty years' time 'it'll be like living in bloody India'. Of course people often write controversial or politically incorrect things in their diaries or to their families and close friends. Perhaps Larkin was only joking. But it still says much that such a thoughtful and sensitive poet (albeit one with extremely conservative man-of-the-people opinions) was happy to send his friend Anthony Thwaite a Jubilee poem bemoaning 'the rising tide of niggers', or to tell Robert Conquest that one of his poetic tips on 'How to Win the Next Election' was to 'kick out the niggers'. And it also says much that in one of the first Inspector Morse novels, *Last Seen Wearing* (1977), Colin Dexter's intellectual detective, arguing with a Maltese bouncer in a strip-club, readily calls him a 'dirty little squit' and a 'miserable wog' – and that his sidekick, Sergeant Lewis, then a Welshman, clearly thinks nothing of it.[25]

As so often, it was humour that best revealed the limits of racial tolerance. Racist banter in the workplace, for example, was very common. 'I went for a job up the road,' one black 18-year-old told the *Sunday Times* in 1973, 'and the man he says, "You don't mind if we call you a black bastard or a wog or a nigger or anything because it's entirely a joke."' When the applicant answered that in that case he could 'keep his job', the man insisted that he was 'not colour prejudiced', the standard formula of the day. But it is easy to see why the employer might have thought that such 'jokes' were acceptable. Popular culture in the early 1970s was saturated with humour and attitudes that later generations would regard as shockingly racist. Jokes about black men and 'Pakis' ('I saved a Paki from drowning the other day. I took me foot off his head') were the common currency of pubs and working men's clubs. In Trevor Griffiths' play *Comedians* (1975), which follows the fortunes of a group of aspiring Manchester stand-up comics, almost all of them fall back on racist mockery to impress their first audience, from jokes about black physical endowment ('a big black bugger rushes in [to the toilet]. Aaaah, he says. Just made it! I took a look, I said, There's no chance of making one in white for me is there?') to a particularly offensive joke about a Pakistani on a rape charge ('They bring the girl in and the Pakistani shouts, She is the one, Officer. No doubt about it'). Yet this is one of the few jokes that make an impression on the visiting talent scout, for whom racist material is clearly nothing untoward. 'It was a different act, the wife, blacks, Irish, women, you spread it around,' he says admiringly to another comedian.[26]

What Griffiths' play captured – and what made it controversial and deeply uncomfortable viewing when it was adapted for television four years later – was the raw, resentful tribalism of much working-class comedy in the 1970s. Even television stand-up often had a racist edge: almost no edition of ITV's hugely popular show *The Comedians,* which gave a regular platform to Northern working-class comics such as Bernard Manning, Stan Boardman and Lennie Bennett, was complete without a handful of racist jokes. What was remarkable, though, was that the tellers included black comedians themselves. The South Yorkshire comedian Charlie Williams, the son of a Barbadian soldier who had settled in Barnsley, played for Doncaster Rovers in the 1950s before turning to the club circuit and was a great favourite with television audiences. As a black man with a cheerful demeanour and strong Yorkshire accent, he cut a confusingly ambiguous figure, defying easy stereotypes. Yet although Williams was a role model for a younger generation of black performers, and may well have been the most popular black Englishman in the early 1970s, his material was controversial even at the time. Among all the jokes about the minutiae of Northern working-class life – the 'boxes of broken biscuits, terraced houses, outside lavatories, the coalface, scrumping apples', as his obituary put it – he regularly fell back on jokes about his own colour. 'If you don't shut up,' he would tell hecklers, 'I'll come and move next door to you.' And while Williams sometimes poked fun at racial stereotypes – 'When Enoch Powell said: "Go home, black man", I said: "I've got a hell of a long wait for a bus to Barnsley"' – his act could hardly be described as particularly subversive.

More often than not, in fact, Williams simply reinforced the racist clichés of the day, delighting audiences with his remarks that he had been 'left in the oven too long' or was sweating so much that he was 'leaking chocolate'. 'During the power cuts,' he once joked, 'I had no trouble at all because all I had to do was roll my eyes.' He even joked about being a cannibal, telling a story about a man he invited to dinner: 'Halfway through the meal he says: "I don't like your mother-in-law." So I said: "Leave her on the side of the plate and just eat the chips and peas."' This kind of material guaranteed Williams an enthusiastic reception: when he topped the bill at Scarborough in 1973, he broke box-office records. But was he merely pandering to white prejudice, or was he blazing a trail for other black comedians? He certainly inspired Lenny Henry, by far the most successful black comedian of the next generation, who admired his energy and courage in taking to the stage. Not all black observers, however, were impressed by Williams's eagerness to do routines about 'darkies', 'Pakis' and 'coons'. 'He thinks he can hide behind his Yorkshire grin,' one correspondent wrote to the *Guardian,* condemning Williams for not 'speaking for his brothers'. But that was highly unrealistic: a professional comedian who performed Black Power routines would not have lasted long on ITV.[27]

Lenny Henry's own career was not without its ambiguities. One of seven children born to Jamaican parents in Dudley, he made an immediate impact on the club circuit as a teenager and won ITV's *New Faces* competition in 1976 when he was just 17. Almost immediately, however, he joined the touring version of the *Black and White Minstrel Show,* which attracted sell-out audiences almost every year in the major cities and seaside resorts. Looking back later, he admitted that there were two voices in his head: one told him that there was a 'fundamental problem' with appearing alongside grinning minstrels in blackface; the other told him to 'take the money and have a great time'. In fact, it is obvious why an ambitious teenage comedian would join the Minstrels. By the mid-1970s, they had a place in the *Guinness Book of Records* as the world's most popular stage show, and when Henry joined he found himself performing for twenty-two consecutive weeks at the Blackpool Opera House before 3,000 people a night. For an aspiring performer, this was an unbeatable education in cabaret and pantomime, and it made it easier for him to block out the protesters who sometimes heckled from the stalls, or the publicity photographs that showed him alongside blacked-up performers pretending to take off his make-up. Like most of the other performers, he told himself that the costumes were merely a distraction, that the essence of the show was the sets and the songs, and he accepted the conventional wisdom that it was 'not a racial show'. Ultimately, though, he was no fool, and the protests of his friends finally changed his mind. In 1979, 'going mad' with frustration, he walked out. 'The mistake wasn't in doing the show and getting stage time and getting experience and learning to time a joke,' he said later. It was in not realizing that, as a 'second generation West Indian guy', he had no place in a show based on racial caricatures.[28]

Defenders of the *Black and White Minstrel Show* often insisted that it was merely innocent, harmless fun, without any racial dimension, and that its critics were humourless killjoys. In fact the television show, which began in 1958, was dogged for much of its run by quiet murmurs of discontent within the BBC and angry protests from race relations groups. In some ways it beggars belief that neither the producers nor the performers could detect any hint of racism in routines that showed grinning men in blackface serenading pretty white women. 'It depicts my race as singing, dancing, laughing, idiotic people,' Clive West, a young Trinidadian who organized a petition calling for its cancellation, told *The Times* in 1967. But although West collected 200 signatures blaming the programme for causing 'misunderstanding between the races', the Minstrels refused to budge: as their producer George Inns put it, 'how anyone can read racialism into this show is beyond me'. And in their defence, the Minstrels could point to their enormous popularity with the British public. They regularly attracted audiences of more than 12 million, drawn to the old-fashioned and highly accomplished song-and-dance routines: as late as 1976, when the show had already lost some of its lustre, the Minstrels' Christmas special was still among the top five programmes of the season. Millions of people clearly thought the routines were perfectly acceptable, and there is no evidence that the producers were deliberately prejudiced. 'Not one of us ever gave a thought to racism,' the performer Les Want later told a BBC documentary. 'We didn't connect it with black people, because the original shows were white people blacked up. It never felt offensive.' Yet by the mid-1970s – much to Want's disappointment – the show had lost its supporters in the BBC. In an era when black performers like Lenny Henry and Floella Benjamin were becoming mainstays of the television schedules, not even the most conservative television executives could defend a show trading in blackface caricatures. In July 1978 it was cancelled, never to return.[29]

It is probably unfair to single out the *Black and White Minstrel Show* for special condemnation. In general, television and film culture during the 1970s was remarkably indifferent to racial sensitivities, and attempts to include black characters were often ludicrously clumsy. Superficially, Roger Moore's debut as James Bond, *Live and Let Die* (1973), might look like a rare attempt to embrace black culture and promote black performers: most of the cast are black, and the producers drew inspiration from the 'blaxploitation' genre then popular with American audiences. In fact, the film makes even Ian Fleming's novel look like a model of racial liberalism. While Moore has never been more effortlessly urbane, the film's black characters, almost without exception, are villainous hoodlums, and the post-colonial black politician at its centre turns out, surprise, surprise, to be a part-time gangster and drug smuggler. 'A white woman has been tied to a post and a black man dressed in animal skins is laughing crazily and wielding a massive poisonous snake,' writes one Bond aficionado, reliving the experience of watching the climax as a 10-year-old in Tunbridge Wells. 'Around them hundreds of voodoo worshippers are screaming and convulsing.' Even when Bond appears to rescue Jane Seymour, the black revellers are 'too busy rolling their eyes and waving old cutlasses to offer proper resistance'. And not even his pioneering sexual encounter with a black woman – who of course turns out to be a traitor and dies almost immediately – can quite dispel the impression of unthinking, endemic racism, which makes the film 'such a shameful experience on each viewing' – albeit a bizarrely enjoyable one.[30]

By this point, black faces were becoming increasingly common on British television. *Crossroads* introduced its first black character – Melanie Harper, played by Cleo Sylvestre – in January 1970, cleverly teasing the audience by presenting her as Meg Richardson's daughter (although she turns out to be adopted). Four years later it became the first television soap to feature a black household – the James family, born in Jamaica – and in the summer of 1977 it presented viewers with the first interracial romance, between the Cockney mechanic Dennis Harper and the Asian receptionist Meena Chaudri. But while the producers of *Crossroads* handled race with rare sensitivity, others were rather less adept. Spike Milligan was a particular offender: his crude portrayal of the half-Irish half-Pakistani Kevin O'Grady ('Paki-Paddy') in *Curry and Chips* (1969) was so bad that ITV cancelled the show after just six episodes. When Milligan blacked up again with John Bird for *The Melting Pot* (1975), playing a Pakistani father and son who live in a London rooming house alongside a black Yorkshireman and a Chinese Cockney, the BBC pulled the plug after a single episode, afraid of a public backlash. And even the infinitely superior *Rising Damp* (1974–8), in which much of the comedy derives from the tension between the racist Rigsby and his black lodger Philip, is not altogether comfortable viewing today. Don Warrington's Philip is clearly the most sympathetic character: suave, dignified and intelligent, as befits the 'son of a chief'. Yet it is Rigsby who has all the best lines, for instance when he worries whether Philip's behaviour will change 'when he hears the drums', or when he suggests that Philip's being a chief merely means that 'his mud hut is bigger than all the other mud huts', or when he opines that 'when they first had petrol stations out there, they spent three years worshipping the pumps'. As with Alf Garnett, the laughter track leaves no illusions about the audience's sympathies. When Rigsby opens his mouth to deliver a fresh put-down, the viewers are laughing with him, not at him.[31]

But it was another sitcom, Thames Television's *Love Thy Neighbour* (1972–6), which best illustrated the limits of racial tolerance in the early 1970s. Although later regarded as a terrible embarrassment, it was extremely popular in its day: indeed, from 1973 to 1975 it reigned as Britain's favourite sitcom. The basic situation is very simple: a West Indian couple, Bill and Barbie Reynolds, move in next door to the white working-class Eddie and Joan Booth. The two women get on well; the two men take an immediate dislike to one another and are soon hurling insults such as 'Choc-ice!' and 'Snowflake!' over the garden fence, to the evident delight of the studio audience. Almost incredibly, when the show started there was much talk of it as a highly charged version of *Till Death Us Do Part,* using satire to tackle the problem of racism in modern society. Thames's head of Light Entertainment predicted that it would 'take some of the heat out of race relations', while the *TV Times* made the extravagant claim that it was 'about racial prejudice – with a difference. It should make us laugh a lot . . . and think a lot, too.' That *Love Thy Neighbour* made many people think a lot, however, is very hard to believe.

As numerous academics have pointed out, the premise of the show seemed almost deliberately designed to *stop* audiences thinking seriously about the roots of racial tension. So the white racist, Eddie (Jack Smethurst), is shown as backward in almost every way: a Labour voter, a trade union member, a Manchester United supporter, a *Daily Mirror* reader, he is a relic of a dying working-class world who insists that 'equal rights does not entitle nig-nogs to move in next door'. By contrast, the black couple are models of self-improvement and upward mobility: rather implausibly, Bill (Rudolph Walker) is a devoted admirer of Edward Heath. In other respects, though, he is just another caricatured black man, 'a happy go lucky Jamaican with strong Conservative views', as publicity for the inevitable spin-off film put it, with a comically childish high-pitched laugh. Meanwhile his wife, Barbie (Nina Baden-Semper), seems to be a sensible modern woman with a swanky stereo. Deep down, though, she is just another voluptuous black siren in a bikini and hot pants, who spends much of her time being ogled by white men. And throughout the series runs a thread of aggressive racial hostility that to modern eyes seems deeply distasteful. In one episode, 'Operation Aggro', Eddie organizes a petition to 'Keep Maple Terrace White' and throws dog muck over the fence, narrowly missing his black neighbour. In others, he denounces Bill to his face as a 'coon', a 'bloody nig-nog', 'Sambo' and 'King Kong', while for good measure he dismisses other immigrant groups as 'Fu Manchu', 'Gunga Din' and 'Ali Baba'. Yet Bill himself is hardly a model of tolerance. Quick to dismiss Eddie as a 'honky', a 'snowflake' and a 'racialist poof', he admits to his wife that he would not want black neighbours himself because of their impact on house prices. Amazingly, though, Rudolph Walker claimed to be 'excited' by the scripts. 'Here are white men writing for blacks,' he said proudly, 'and there isn't a hint of the Uncle Tom.'[32]

Since *Love Thy Neighbour* attracted large audiences for eight series over four years, millions of people presumably found it hilarious. What now seems extraordinary, though, is that many critics complained that it was too tame and inoffensive. It was 'quite bland', said the *Telegraph*'s reviewer after the first two episodes, while the *Observer* thought it 'all very nice and soft-centred and predictable'. In *The Times*, Barry Norman even commended the programme as 'a step in the right direction', but thought that 'Eddie's mild little jokes about spades and sambos and nignogs have no shock value and indeed are so gentle and so comfortable that the words themselves acquire a sort of respectability. Anyone, listening to Eddie, who has ever thought of black men as spades or nignogs might well feel reassured that this is precisely how we ought to think of them.' As time went on and the programme lost any pretence of having a satirical edge, however, the criticism became sharper. Black viewers unsurprisingly found the programme – and especially its implied moral equivalence between the racist and his victim – deeply disturbing: in July 1975, a spokeswoman for the Race Relations Board told *New Society* that she had not 'met a black person who isn't offended to hell by it'. And as the critic Chris Dunkley pointed out in September 1972, it was 'a little frightening that the loudest laugh from Monday's audience, and even a little shower of applause, was elicited by a joke about a Negro's house-warming party: the "White Honky" threatened that his house would get really warm when somebody burned it down. There seems precious little hope of cathartic benefit in cracking jokes like that.' But as so often in the 1970s, many people simply could not understand why others were complaining. 'Who can really take offence', asked James Murray of the *Daily Express,* 'if kids in school playgrounds nowadays copy the epithets of Eddie and Bill and call each other "Choc ice" and 'Snowflake"? It's got to be an improvement on "nigger".'[33]

In the early hours of Tuesday, 7 April 1970, a 50-year-old kitchen porter called Tosir Ali was returning home from his work at a Wimpy Bar in central London when he ran into two white youngsters armed with knives. He bled to death at the door of his building on St Leonard's Street, Bow, just moments from the safety of his flat. At first the police ruled out racist motives. But it soon became clear that the murder was part of a pattern of brutal attacks on Asian residents in East London, and especially on the East Pakistani* community packed into the narrow streets around Brick Lane. In one incident, two Asian workers at the London Chest Hospital were badly beaten by a gang of white youths; in another, the imam of the East London Mosque was taken to hospital after being beaten with an iron bar and kicked in the face; in a third, Pakistani mourners at the funeral parlour beside the mosque were taunted and bombarded with bottles. In what many champions of racial integration saw as a worrying development, the local Pakistani Workers' Union announced it was organizing vigilante patrols to protect local families. But *The Times* sympathized with their feelings. 'The Pakistani community in London are now badly frightened and very resentful,' its lead editorial explained on 14 April. 'They are coming to regret their reputation for gentleness. If nothing further is done to protect them, the time will come when they will fight back.' It was time, the editorial concluded, for a

---

* East Pakistan became Bangladesh in 1971.

crackdown on violence and 'a few exemplary punishments in the courts. That was what put a stop to further violence after the Notting Hill race riots in 1958 and it may be necessary to demonstrate again with all the force of the law that young thugs will not be permitted to establish the pattern of race relations in Britain.'[34]

The next few weeks were a grim time for race relations. In Brick Lane, tension escalated into a full-scale race riot at the end of April; in Luton, gangs of white youths roamed the streets looking for Pakistani victims; in Wolverhampton, the Indian Workers' Association advised its members to stay at home after dark after a string of attacks by white youngsters. And in each case, the newspapers levelled the blame at a new and uniquely disturbing figure. At one level, as the latest teenage folk devil to haunt the nightmares of Middle England, the incarnation of primeval violence and working-class rebellion, the skinhead was the descendant of the Teddy Boy and the Mod. But whereas both Teddy Boys and Mods were stereotypes of upward mobility, being working-class youngsters with unprecedented freedom, self-confidence and cash in their pockets, skinheads were defiantly backward-looking. With their cropped hair and steel-capped boots, they had originated in East London as a working-class riposte to the 'nancy-boy' hippies who dominated press coverage of youth culture. Skinheads were self-consciously hard; they were un-apologetically working class; and above all, they were white. They hated hippies, but they hated immigrants even more. 'We're being exploited, the working class,' one East End skinhead explained. 'It's hard for us to fight for our job and our house, but with them here as well, trying to get our houses, it's another opposition ... I'll tell you another thing, when you stand next to these people that have just come over here, they fucking stink.'[35]

Although the summer of 1970 marked the high point of the skinhead panic, they did not go away. Indeed, thanks to a stream of astonishingly popular thrillers by the pulp novelist James Moffatt (writing as Richard Allen), skinhead culture spread well beyond the capital, appealing to disaffected working-class teenagers seduced by its heady mixture of violence, resentment and tribal identity. Racism was always a major element of its appeal, cementing the loyalties of men who felt adrift in a world of deep economic anxiety and social change. 'It was like the black hole of Calcutta down my factory,' lamented one East London hooligan who joined West Ham's notorious Inter-City Firm. 'You'd get them all standin' in a mob, all talkin' that chapatti language an' all that, an' you never know whether they're talkin' about you.' He looked forward to the weekend rampages against immigrants, when he and his fellow supporters would 'steam round an' kick fuck out of the Pakis' – a chance, as he saw it, to proclaim their white working-class masculinity, to stand up to the effeminate middle classes and job-stealing immigrants who were trying to keep them down. As skinhead culture merged almost seamlessly into the growing culture of football hooliganism, so the post-match 'Paki-bashing' became just another weekend ritual alongside the pie and the pints. And even after skinheads had faded from the headlines, their attacks continued to blight the lives of immigrant families. In London alone, Gurdip Singh Chaggar was killed in Southall in 1976, Altab Ali, Kennith Singh and Ishaque Ali were murdered in Whitechapel, Newham and Hackney respectively in 1978, and Akhtar Ali Baigh was killed in Newham a year later. In the East End, reported a local trade union group, there were 110 racist attacks just in the autumn of 1977, 'an almost continuous and unrelenting battery of Asian people and their property'.[36]

What made the racist violence of the 1970s even more unsettling was that many immigrants felt utterly abandoned by the authorities. 'The Pakistanis of East London', one observer remarked in April 1970, 'have unquestionably lost confidence in the police', and who could blame them? Despite the fact that London now had an immigrant population in the hundreds of thousands, the Metropolitan Police was staggeringly white, with only 'ten coloured policemen', to use the terminology of the day. Although the new Met commissioner Robert Mark devoted considerable effort to attracting more black and Asian recruits, by 1976 there were just 70 black police officers in a force more than 22,000 strong. Many encountered persistent mockery and hostility from their fellow recruits, which was hardly surprising given the prevailing prejudice within the ranks. But London was hardly exceptional. Most police officers, reported the Select Committee on Race Relations and Immigration in 1971, believed blacks were more likely than whites to be criminals, even though the statistics actually showed that levels of crime among blacks were no higher. In Nottingham, a city with almost 20,000 immigrant residents but *not a single* black or Asian policeman, efforts to organize race relations seminars were undermined when, at the end of one session, a group of veteran officers started chanting 'Enoch, Enoch, we want

Enoch!' And when the sociologist Maureen Cain investigated police attitudes in 1973, she reported that most officers thought 'niggers' or 'nigs' were 'pimps and layabouts, living off what we pay in taxes'. 'Have you been to a wog house?' one officer asked her. 'They stink, they really do smell terrible.'[37]

For many immigrant families, police hostility was an unpleasant but sadly inevitable part of life in Heath's Britain. In Nottingham, 31 per cent of West Indians and 36 per cent of Pakistanis thought that the police gave them 'less favourable treatment'. Many complained that the police turned a blind eye to racist attacks: one man, who called the police after a neighbour's son smashed his windows, recalled that they were initially very sympathetic, but changed their tune when they discovered that the boy was white. Even more distressingly, one in five Nottingham immigrants claimed that the police regularly beat up blacks and Asians – an allegation dismissed at the time, but one that matches accounts from other cities. For black youngsters growing up in London, Mike and Trevor Phillips wrote, the police were 'a natural hazard, like poisonous snakes or attack dogs off the leash'. A survey in 1972 found that almost all of the capital's West Indians thought the police discriminated against them, and one in five claimed to have had direct experience of police racism. One man later remembered that 'as black kids, you couldn't go anywhere without a copper creasing your collar . . . and if they didn't like your face, if your face didn't fit, or you was a bit too lippy, as most black kids are, you'd get a little kicking'. Similarly, Herman Ouseley, later chairman of the Commission for Racial Equality, recalled that in Brixton he 'didn't even wait for a bus', since 'just being black and being on a street was very frightening because you were seen as acting suspiciously'.[38]

Even at this early stage there were warnings that police harassment was stoking the flames of racial tension. In 1970 black protesters besieged the police station in Caledonian Road, Islington, while a year later repeated police raids on the Mangrove restaurant in Ladbroke Grove culminated in the embarrassment of the Mangrove Nine trial, where a white jury acquitted seven out of nine black activists accused of affray. Black protest often focused on the excessive zeal, to put it mildly, of the aggressive Special Patrol Group, a kind of force within the force, which was repeatedly sent into South London to target young black muggers. In 1975 the SPG stopped 14,000 people and arrested some 400, almost all of them young black men, in Lewisham alone. The tabloid press often hailed the SPG as the cutting edge of the modern force; to many Caribbean families, however, it was the epitome of white racism and police harassment. But black patience was not inexhaustible. As early as 1972 there were reports that local groups were forming self-defence associations, and representatives of the West Indian Standing Conference warned a parliamentary committee that unless the police ended their 'systematic brutalization of black people', there would be 'blood on the streets of this country'. This was no exaggeration: two years later, scuffles at a fireworks display at Brockwell Park, Brixton, escalated into a pitched battle between white policemen and black youths, with allegations of brutality on both sides. Miraculously, nobody was seriously hurt, but it was a sign of things to come.[39]

While the harassment of ethnic minorities undoubtedly reflected the prejudice shared by many police officers, it also owed something to the intense pressure on them to crack down on public disorder. Police officers were told to keep an eye out for 'coloured young men' on the London Underground, for example, not just because their superiors had highly reactionary ideas about black criminality, but because almost every week the press were demanding a more aggressive approach to policing. The Heath years were a period of deep anxiety about law and order, not only because one corner of the United Kingdom seemed on the brink of civil war, but because so much of modern life seemed infected by the virus of public violence. What the *Mirror* called 'AGGRO BRITAIN' was more than fantasy: it seemed a genuine reflection of a world in which there was an armed bank robbery in London every six days, police estimated that 3,000 professional robbers were loose on the streets of the capital, and almost no major football match passed off without drunkenness, damage and disorder. The statistics in London alone made sobering reading. In 1968 the Metropolitan Police had reported 299,000 indictable crimes, but by 1971 the total had surged to 340,000, rising to 414,000 in 1974 and 567,000 in 1978. (It is worth noting, though, that these figures are still small compared with the peak in the early 1990s, when there were 945,000 offences a year.)[40]

Behind these figures lay an unsettling sense that the times were out of joint, that something had gone wrong, that the forces of violence and disorder were gaining the upper hand. 'It was a year which began and ended in violence . . . the year of the international terrorist,' *The Times* concluded gloomily at the end of 1972, looking back at the massacres in Londonderry and Munich, the American bombing of North Vietnam and a rash of terrorist atrocities in Italy, Israel, Japan and the United States, not to mention the domestic controversies of the miners' strike, the collapse of Heath's industrial relations plan and the furore over the Ugandan Asians. Amid this international lawlessness and domestic disarray, it was no wonder so many people thought the barbarians were at the gates, or that so many – the overwhelming majority, in fact – supported the return of the death penalty. 'Violence has reached such a pitch', recorded James Lees-Milne, in words that would undoubtedly have drawn approving nods from millions of his countrymen, 'that only violence can restrain it. The thugs of this world cannot be checked by light sentences and comfortable cells, but by being executed, got rid of by the quickest, least offensive means, a prick in the arm and a gentle slipping away to God knows where.'[41]

Of all the symptoms of public disorder, one of the most frightening was the rise of mugging. The word first appeared in the British press in August 1972, when an elderly widower, Arthur Hills, was stabbed to death outside Waterloo station as he was going home from the theatre. It was, said the *Mirror* a few days later, 'a frightening new strain of crime', imported from the United States, where such atrocities were apparently endemic. Of course it was not really new at all: as a leading QC pointed out in *The Times* a few days later, mugging was almost exactly the same as the 'garrotting' that had obsessed Victorian headline writers a century before. But the word carried disturbing connotations. Since the late 1960s, British papers had reported with horror the surge in violent crime across the Atlantic, where American cities seemed to be sliding into a brutal cycle of decay, delinquency and disorder. Mugging was an American phenomenon, associated with the black gangs who supposedly controlled the mean streets of cities like New York, Chicago and Detroit, and British newspapers shuddered at the thought that it was coming east. 'Britain seems to be edging too close for comfort to the American pattern of urban violence,' lamented the *Birmingham Evening Mail* in March 1973 after a controversial mugging case in the city's Handsworth neighbour-hood. 'I have seen what happens in America where muggings are rife,' agreed Jill Knight, Edgbaston's Conservative MP. 'It is absolutely horrifying to know that in all the big American cities, there are areas where people dare not go after dark. I am extremely anxious that such a situation should never come to Britain.'[42]

Mugging was more than robbery with violence. As the tabloids saw it, mugging was alien, threatening, even subversive; it hinted at the dangers that lay beneath the surface of modern city life; above all, it was immediately associated with young black men. White criminals were rarely identified as muggers; black ones almost always were. And at a time when the economy was sliding into chaos, the government appeared powerless in the face of the unions and traditional expectations seemed to be undermined by feminism, permissiveness and social mobility, the press coverage of mugging – often described as a 'disease' or a 'virus' – quickly began to assume the proportions of a full-blown moral panic. By the late autumn of 1972, mugging was the word on everybody's lips. Long articles explored 'the making of a mugger' or asked 'why they go out mugging', while editorials called for more police patrols, tougher prison sentences and what the *Sunday Mirror* melodramatically called an all-out 'war' on muggers. A typically blunt *Sun* editorial entitled 'Taming the Muggers' gives a sense of the tone:

> *What are the British people most concerned about now?* Wages? Prices? Immigration? Pornography? People are talking about all of these things. But the *Sun* believes there is another issue which has everyone deeply worried and angry: VIOLENCE IN OUR STREETS . . . Nothing could be more utterly against our way of life, based on a common sense regard for law and order . . . If punitive jail sentences help to stop the violence – and nothing else has done – then they will not only prove to be the only way. They will, regrettably, be the RIGHT way. *And the judges will have the backing of the public.*

Indeed, with polls indicating that 70 per cent of people wanted the government to show greater urgency in the war on mugging and 90 per cent wanted tougher punishments for muggers, it was no suprise that judges, politicians and policemen alike were quick to take the hint. Local councils organized 'anti-mugging patrols' armed with walkie-talkies and guard dogs; the Metropolitan Police stationed extra men outside Underground stations; and the new Chief Inspector of Constabulary described mugging as his 'highest priority' and promised that his men would 'stamp [it] out'. And by early November even Prince Philip had waded in, telling an audience at the Royal College of General Practitioners that 'mugging and child-bashing were symptoms of unhealthy communities and a cure had to be found for the "disease"'.[43]

As a group of cultural theorists at the University of Birmingham pointed out in a hugely influential study six years later, the furore over mugging was driven as much by sensationalist headlines and racial prejudice as by a genuine increase in crime. It was no coincidence that the death of Arthur Hills, supposedly Britain's first mugging, came just a week after Idi Amin had announced the expulsion of the Ugandan Asians and at a time when the papers were full of angry letters about the predicted 'flood' of penniless immigrants. If poor Mr Hills had died a few months earlier, his murder might well have been ignored. Coming when it did, it became a symbol of wider anxieties about crime and immigration. But as the Birmingham theorists saw it, the 'moral panic' about mugging had even deeper roots, stretching back to the aftermath of the Moors murders in 1965, when the newspapers had first taken aim at the so-called 'permissive society'. This panic was under way, they argued, even 'before there [were] any actual "muggings" to react to', reflecting white middle-class unease at a time of social and economic change. Far from being a reaction to a terrifying epidemic on Britain's streets, they thought, the mugging furore had actually been 'constructed' by an unholy alliance of journalists, judges, politicians and policemen as a 'mechanism for the construction of an authoritarian backlash, a conservative backlash: what we call the slow build-up towards a "soft" law-and-order society'.[44]

In many ways this kind of analysis now feels almost as dated as platform shoes, the Ford Granada and the music of Emerson, Lake and Palmer. There is no doubt that the mugging panic owed a great deal to wildly sensationalist press headlines, nor that it was fuelled by deeper popular anxieties about immigration, the decline of the inner cities and the plight of the economy. But the decisive factor was surely something the Birmingham theorists persistently downplayed: the genuine reality of rising crime. It is true that crime had been steadily rising for most of the century, and that the biggest increase actually came in the late 1950s. But it is not hard to see why so many people felt genuinely unsafe in the early 1970s. By far the most likely victims of crime, after all, lived in working-class neighbourhoods that had recently suffered enormous upheavals as planners tore down the Victorian slums and erected gigantic new tower blocks in their stead. Old friends and relatives had moved out, unfamiliar new groups were moving in, and the much-loved bulwarks of the neighbourhood – the corner shop, the pub, the cinema, even the church, the landmarks that had once represented community and stability

– were disappearing. On television, respectable values seemed to be in retreat; in the shops, everyday prices had reached astronomical levels; in the headlines, all was doom and despair. And in this context – the context of derelict terraces and struggling factories, of concrete council flats sodden with rain and covered with graffiti, of empty churches and broken-down football grounds – it is no wonder that people became so frightened.

The crime figures themselves, meanwhile, leave no room for doubt. At the time the mugging panic began, the crime rate had increased by 5 per cent annually for the past seven years, while Home Office statistics showed violent crime increasing by a whopping 62 per cent between 1967 and 1971. And of course it did not stop there: as people moved away from the embrace of the traditional working-class neighbourhood, as the bonds of family and community frayed, as unskilled and manufacturing jobs dried up, as the old moral sanctions came into disrepute, so the appeal of crime became steadily greater. By 1974, every single category of crime was showing a significant annual increase: theft, for example, jumped by a staggering 71 per cent in London and 42 per cent overall. No doubt some of the apparent increase was down to changes in measurement, but not all of it. And while fashionable academics liked to dismiss popular fears of crime as middle-class 'hysteria' fanned by the sensationalist press, the fact remains that while there were 1.6 million serious crimes in England and Wales in 1970, there were almost 2.8 million ten years later. The victims were rarely affluent sociologists or well-paid journalists; they were the poor, the elderly, the downtrodden, the forgotten. Not even Britain's best-loved street was safe: when *Coronation Street*'s Ernie Bishop was shot and killed by armed robbers in January 1978, the tabloids reacted as though the last bastion of innocence had been contaminated. 'It mustn't happen,' insisted John Betjeman in the *Mirror*. But it did. And as thousands of the soap's regular viewers would readily have testified, something like it was happening somewhere in Britain almost every day of the week.[45]

In many ways it was to Edward Heath's credit that he never exploited the anxiety about rising crime for his own political ends. Unlike the majority of his own activists, he remained steadfastly opposed to the death penalty, not least because he had once commanded a firing squad during the war and never forgot what an awful experience it had been.

Given how much attention the press paid to crime during his premiership, it is remarkable that he said virtually nothing about it at all. If anything, his first Home Secretary, Maudling, was even more liberal, even refusing to engage party members in debate about capital punishment because he found their views so distasteful. When Maudling's financial corruption forced him out in the summer of 1972 – a time at which the press furore about crime was reaching boiling point – it is highly revealing that Heath replaced him with the even milder-mannered Robert Carr, whose liberal opinions cut little ice with ordinary Tory activists. The truth is that, as one historian remarks, Heath insisted on acting 'as a national statesman and not merely as the leader of a political party', which would make a nice epitaph for his entire career but also highlights his greatest weakness. For although Heath's handling of immigration and race relations brought high marks from historians, it won him few friends among the Conservative rank and file. To many ordinary Tory members, as to Enoch Powell, it seemed part of a disturbing pattern. And as Heath seemed to move further to the centre, so others rushed to fill the space on the right.[46]

When the National Front was founded in 1967, there seemed little chance that it would ever attract more than a handful of supporters. The post-war decades had not been kind to the far right: tarred by association with the Nazis, the various fringe groups descended from the inter-war British Union of Fascists spent as much time fighting one another as they did winning support on the streets. Even Sir Oswald Mosley, the only figure on the far right with any national reputation, failed miserably to appeal to a mass electorate. Standing on an anti-immigration platform in Kensington North in 1959, he won just 2,621 votes, and when he stood in Shoreditch and Finsbury in 1966 he fared even worse, polling a pathetic 1,126 votes. Other leading figures on the far right were even less successful. Andrew Fountaine, a Norfolk landowner's son who fought for Franco in the Spanish Civil War and made a stir at Conservative party conferences in the late 1940s by condemning Labour as a party of 'semi-alien mongrels and hermaphrodite communists', pinned his hopes on the youth of the nation. 'The man who can gain the allegiance of the Teddy Boys', he grandly remarked, 'can make himself ruler of England.' But although Fountaine set up an 'Aryan camp' for boys on his Norfolk estate, Britain's teenagers proved rather more interested in shopping and pop music than racism and street violence. Somehow it said it all that

Fountaine could not even win the support of his own mother, who used to heckle him during his public meetings.

In 1967, Fountaine led his minuscule British National Party into a merger with two other far-right groups, the League of Empire Loyalists and the Racial Preservation Society, to create the embryonic National Front. Six months later a fourth group, the Greater Britain Movement, joined the fledgling organization, and its leader, John Tyndall, would become the National Front's key figure during the 1970s. Tyndall was by any standards a deeply unappealing figure, a dedicated neo-Nazi who was briefly imprisoned in 1966 for illegal ownership of a gun and who made no secret of his extremist views. Among other things, he blamed the Holocaust on a 'food shortage', hoped to see 'the whole democratic regime come crashing down', promised to eliminate the 'cancerous microbe' of Jews in Britain, denounced mixed marriages and promised to expel the 'droves of dark-skinned sub-racials'. Unfortunately for Tyndall, however – though not for anybody else – his appeal was strictly limited. His Greater Britain Movement had just 138 members, which meant that it was smaller than many local working men's clubs, and even the embryonic National Front had no more than 1,500 active members, most of whom came from Fountaine's old BNP. To put this into context, if all the active members of the National Front in 1970 had lined up one Saturday afternoon at Walsall's Fellows Park, they would be outnumbered more than three to one by people who had come to watch their local football team.[47]

In many ways the general election of 1970 confirmed the impression that the National Front was a pitiful fringe outfit, posing no threat to the established parties and no real danger to law and order. It managed to put up only ten candidates, all in areas of high immigration and working-class resentment where the NF was supposed to be strong. And with Enoch Powell attracting anti-immigration voters to the much more respectable bosom of the Conservative Party, the NF's results were appalling: just 1.9 per cent in Cardiff, 2.3 per cent in Leicester, 4.7 per cent in Wolverhampton, 5.5 per cent in Deptford and 5.6 per cent in Islington. To most observers, therefore, it seemed that the NF had effectively missed the anti-immigration boat. And yet other election figures told a rather different story. In the local elections of 1969 the NF had made striking inroads into former Labour strongholds, attracting 12.5 per cent in Huddersfield, 10 per cent in Cardiff and 11.5 per cent in

Wandsworth and West Ham. In the local elections of 1970, too, the NF did better than expected, winning 11 per cent in Huddersfield and coming second to the Tories in one Wolverhampton ward.

These voters, thousands of them, were people who had been almost forgotten amid all the media excitement about the pace of change in the Swinging Sixties, people who felt betrayed by the major parties and were horrified at the rising crime figures, the transformation of the working-class urban landscape and the influx of so many newcomers with strange habits and coloured skin. They were people like Barry Watts, a teenager from an Irish family who moved from a dilapidated back-street terraced house to one of north London's roughest council estates in 1970, and later became a keen advocate for the National Front. 'You see them natives on TV, dancing around in the jungle,' Barry said scornfully. 'I says, we've got 'em living next door to us. We don't like that. Their music, the food, the smell, they're different. Their whole attitude to life is different to ours. You got to put a gas mask on to get past their door.'

As Barry Watts's words suggested, race was at the very core of the National Front's appeal. Yet this was not the whole story. Although plenty of people were prejudiced in the early 1970s, most did not vote for the National Front, while not all National Front supporters thought in terms of nothing but race. 'We're for the old folks, we're for them,' Barry earnestly insisted. 'We think they should get a better deal. And the kiddies, somewhere for them to play. Better schools.' In other circumstances, a boy from his background might have become a Labour activist. But he did not think much of Harold Wilson's Labour Party. 'They are out to help the rich, they are all for the people with the money,' he said. This was a common theme among the National Front's sympathizers, reflecting the fact that not only were Labour MPs increasingly well educated and middle-class, but big-city constituency parties were being taken over by people who read the *Guardian* rather than the *Daily Mirror*. At a time when their jobs were disappearing, their incomes had stagnated and their values were being dismissed as anachronistic, the urban white working classes felt abandoned by the 'wine and cheese set with their posh accents and big words', said a gruff local councillor who represented Barry's north London estate. He denied being a 'racialist' himself, praising the midweek football league ('the only thing that works in this borough') for integrating 'dozens of black kids, and Greeks, and Turks'. But he had no time for his council colleagues or the community workers, all 'long hair and plimsolls', who 'come here and think they can tell you how to live'. 'These people fall over backwards to do anything for black people,' he said contemptuously. 'They give money to squatters, Bangladeshis, the lot.'[48]

For many of the National Front's supporters, therefore, their aggressive feelings about race and immigration were tightly, almost indistinguishably bound up with all sorts of other resentments, from their suspicion of middle-class do-gooders to their fury at the destruction of their old neighbourhoods. Indeed, a survey of National Front supporters in Harlesden at the end of the 1970s found that its appeal was grounded less in abstract ideas of racial superiority than in rather more mundane, bread-and-butter concerns – jobs, housing, crime, obscenity – that had little to do with immigration itself. But for many of these people, racism made an ideal prism through which to view the world, partly because it tapped into the latent prejudice with which many people had grown up. As the journalist Martin Walker explained in 1974, 'unemployment was explained as black workers taking British jobs; bad housing as blacks jumping the council house queue; clogged health and social services were the fault of diseased immigrants taking the place of deserving Britons; bad schools were the cause of illiterate black kids, and crime was their fault too'. It was, Walker thought, a 'potent and poisonous combination', not least because 'the bad schools, the bad housing and the unemployment' were most visible in precisely those 'run-down, inner-city areas with poor housing in which immigrants have tended to congregate'.

So it was that the National Front began to gather support in those areas that had been partially cleared in the slum clearances of the 1950s and 1960s, landscapes where traditional working-class communities had been uprooted and rehoused in grey, grim tower blocks. It appealed to teenagers who saw no future after school and to manual workers frightened for their jobs; to shopkeepers resentful of their Asian competitors and to small self-employed businessmen worried about inflation; to Second World War veterans who felt cheated and abandoned and to teenage football fans addicted to the camaraderie of the terraces. To all of their grievances it offered a deceptively simple answer: what had happened to working-class Britain since the war was the fault of the newcomers and the stuck-up Oxford-educated politicians who molly-coddled them. 'Why do I fight for the National Front?' one man asked rhetorically:

Why, because I don't want parts of my country to become no-go areas, where I feel I can't walk without the risk of being knifed or mugged. I don't want to be with black people. I don't want a multi-racial country. Why should I? I've got nothing in common with them . . . why should I be forced to live with them? I want to be able to go into a pub, I want to be able to go to work without seeing a black face. The National Front is saying the sort of things I want to hear . . . I want to be just with our own. I don't want to live in a system that falls over itself to favour blacks. If there's anything going in this country, I want it for myself. We've suffered enough in the past, and now it's our turn. We've had one flabby government after another saying, 'We've got to learn to live together.' Well, why? They don't have to live with them, killing goats, wailing at dusk and fasting and being a nuisance.[49]

In some ways it is remarkable that the far right did not make deeper inroads into decaying working-class areas in the late 1960s and early 1970s. If it had been better organized, more disciplined and more united, or had benefited from the leadership of an articulate and credible politician, it might have made a handsome profit from the slow decline of Labour support and the dying agonies of the Heath government. Fortunately, the leaders of the various far-right factions were a very bizarre and unsavoury bunch, whose rhetorical extremism repelled far more people than it attracted and who seemed never happier than when engaged in bafflingly obscure internal feuds. Tiny fringe groups like Self-Help and the British League of Rights, which might perhaps have picked up disaffected Conservative voters, undermined their own appeal by banging on about Zionist conspiracies, the influence of 'Big Finance' and the dangers of racial 'mongrelization'. Meanwhile the League of St George, which at least had the sense to pick a good name, espoused a particularly virulent form of National Socialism as well as the pagan cult of 'Odinism', a weird mishmash of Norse and Celtic mythology. In a society that venerated the memories of national solidarity and sacrifice against the Nazis – indeed, one in which the Second World War was rarely off the television screens for more than an hour or two – this kind of stuff was fatally counterproductive. But then the far right's leaders were hardly the best and the brightest. Colin Jordan, the founder of the anti-Semitic British Movement, did have a second-class history degree from Sidney Sussex College, Cambridge. But the former Coventry maths teacher's ambitions to become Britain's answer to Adolf Hitler were cruelly frustrated when, in May 1975, he was convicted of stealing 'a box of chocolates and three pairs of red women's knickers' from a branch of Tescos in Leamington Spa. As even the most faithful Nazi would have to admit, this was hardly the behaviour of a future *Führer*.[50]

The biggest thing in the far right's favour in the early 1970s, in fact, was an event over which it had no control: the coming of the Ugandan Asians. Within hours of the government's announcement that it would honour the refugees' British passports, John Tyndall had organized a demonstration by a hundred National Front activists outside Downing Street, which he followed up by personally delivering a petition to Number 10. Meanwhile it was the National Front that organized the supposedly non-partisan march of the Smithfield meat porters. On 22 August the National Front's Ron Taylor, armed with leaflets and a loudspeaker, had toured Smithfield calling for action, although he was careful to play down his party affiliation. The Ugandans 'could be black, blue, green or red for all we cared', he disingenuously told the press, 'but most of our blokes have sons or daughters waiting for council houses . . . If there was room for them you would not catch me saying anything about them.' But when the porters marched on Westminster two days later the organizers' claims that there was 'no racialism involved' rang very hollow. Many carried placards with National Front insignia, and as they marched they sang 'We don't want the Asians', 'We don't want to integrate', and a version of 'Rule, Britannia' containing the line 'Britons never, never, never will be spades'. Outside Rhodesia House and South Africa House they stopped and cheered, and whenever they saw black passers-by, they booed and made monkey noises. Indeed, some organizers made no secret of their fascist associations. Dan Harmston told reporters that he was proud to be a supporter of Sir Oswald Mosley, 'one of England's great patriots'. 'Afro-Asians are the greatest racialists in the world,' he added. 'They have no intention of integrating with each other, let alone with us.'[51]

Against the background of economic uncertainty and industrial turmoil, the Ugandan Asian furore was a gift to the National Front. At Heathrow, demonstrators brandished placards warning that there were too many people in Britain already; in Manchester, pickets handed out more than 2,000 National Front leaflets; in Hounslow, demonstrators occupied the Town Hall during a council meeting and read out a statement of protest; in Ealing, Leicester and Blackburn, organizers called open-air public meetings attracting busloads of supporters from across the country. By October the party newspaper *Spearhead* was bragging that 250 new members had joined in a matter of weeks, while Head Office was fielding 100 enquiries a day. Even allowing for exaggeration, these were bountiful days for the far right: as the journalist Martin Walker wrote, Idi Amin 'was the best recruiting officer the NF ever had'. By the end of the year, he thought, the National Front had 800 new recruits, and, more importantly, its rhetoric seemed to be striking home. Leaflets on the Ugandan Asian issue were designed to tap into a host of loosely related anxieties, from unemployment and housing to strikes and Europe, as the party competed to attract disgruntled Labour and Tory voters alike. 'If the British people have to worry about fighting for a job in the face of a tide of cheap immigrant labour, and are occupied in trying to get decent housing in competition with teeming millions of immigrants,' one read, 'then they will not have time to think about how the International Big Business Establishment is robbing them with such gigantic swindles as the Common Market.'

At a time when neither of the major parties inspired much confidence, this approach paid handsome dividends. In the local elections of June 1973 the National Front recorded its best performance yet, picking up more than 15 per cent of the vote in Leicester (including more than 20 per cent in three out of ten wards), 24 per cent in Blackburn and 25 per cent in Staines. In Bristol, where its record had been abysmal, the National Front's four local candidates picked up between 8 and 18 per cent of the vote; in Dartford its three candidates attracted just under 14 per cent; in Nottingham a new branch fought in two wards and won 22 and 14 per cent. Even more striking, however, was the party's performance in May's West Bromwich by-election. In many ways this was perfect National Front territory, a seedy, dilapidated industrial town with a large population of Pakistani foundry workers, close not only to Powell's Wolverhampton heartland but also to the Black Country constituency of Smethwick, notorious for sending the Conservative Peter Griffiths ('If you want a nigger neighbour, vote Labour') to Westminster nine years before. Never before had the National Front thrown itself so vigorously into a Westminster election: supporters drove up from London every weekend, parading with Union Jacks and pretty girls, while the candidate Martin Webster, a fat man who dubbed himself 'Big Mart', promised to 'send back the coloured immigrants'. And even though many observers tipped the National Front to pick up hundreds of disaffected Conservative votes, the result nevertheless came as a shock. As expected, Labour's Betty Boothroyd won the seat with 15,907 votes, while the Tories came second with 7,582 votes. Few had anticipated, however, that the National Front would win 4,879 votes (16 per cent of the total): the best result in its history by a huge margin.[52]

'The National Front's challenge to Mr Heath' was the title of *The Times*'s post-mortem two days later, which thought that the two major parties needed to be 'more open' about 'the facts about the immigrant community [and] the social tensions to which it undeniably gives rise'. This was sensible advice, yet neither party seemed willing to grasp the nettle. In some ways, this hinted at the growing gulf between middle-class politicians and the people they represented: in an age when new Labour MPs were more likely to be lecturers than miners, many white working-class voters felt that their voices were being squeezed out of the political arena. But it was also a testament to the underlying moderation of British politics in the early 1970s that despite all the strident rhetoric of the day, no ambitious office-seeker wanted to risk being dubbed the next Enoch Powell.[53]

In some ways, the National Front at the beginning of 1974 was still a very unimpressive force. As Martin Webster himself had predicted after West Bromwich, the party struggled to match expectations in the next general election, winning a national average of just 3.3 per cent in February 1974. In West Bromwich, its share fell to 7 per cent; in Leicester, it won fewer than 8,000 votes; in Wolverhampton, where the party had campaigned hard to pick up Powell supporters, it won just 5, 4 and 3 per cent of the vote in the city's three parliamentary seats. And yet few observers thought there were grounds for complacency. In just seven years, the party had established 30 branches and 54 groups around the country, as well as an estimated 20,000 paid-up members. Its activists were highly visible on the streets of major cities, distributing thousands of leaflets that did not confine themselves to race and immigration but tackled issues such as crime, inflation, Northern Ireland, the EEC and industrial unrest. In a telling sign of its broadening ambitions, it was now targeting university students ('Don't be bullied by the crackpots and gangsters of the extreme left') and schoolchildren ('Are you tired of younger students being bullied or subjected to the alien cult of mugging?'). It was true that 3.3 per cent was hardly an impressive sign of national support; yet as observers pointed out at the time, the Nazi Party won only 2.6 per cent of the vote in Germany in 1928 but was running the country just five years later. We know now that the National Front never broke through to become a serious political force. But nobody could have known that then.[54]

Perhaps it would be wrong, though, to end on such a bleak note. For the biggest immigration story of the decade, the arrival of the Ugandan Asians, had a happier ending than could have been predicted. When the first refugees trooped off their planes at Heathrow and Stansted, the men's faces drawn with anxiety, the women's saris limp and sodden with rain, their prospects seemed depressingly bleak. Most had only what they could stuff into their battered suitcases, and even then many had been robbed at gunpoint in Entebbe airport. 'Every piece of baggage was thrown open on the ground and most of the valuables we had, including rings and watches, were taken away,' a former haulage contractor told reporters after the exhausting nine-hour flight to Heathrow. Others told stories of relatives being harassed, injured and even killed: one student told journalists at Stansted that his uncle had been shot and thrown into a municipal skip, while another man, still trembling with outrage, claimed that Amin's soldiers had stripped his wife of her jewellery and threatened to cut their throats. And in the corner of an airport waiting room, a reporter spotted the 'tired, puzzled-looking' figure of Khanji Dhanji Karsan, a 35-year-old Kampala builder in a second-hand army greatcoat and a green balaclava. Exhausted, nervous and awkward, Mr Karsan spoke only two or three words of English. He had arrived with 'no friends, no money, no relatives and only the haziest ideas about the country in which he found himself'. All that he had was a grubby black notebook, pushed into his hand by an anonymous well-wisher at Entebbe airport. Inside were three phone numbers, one in Welwyn Garden City, one in Kensal Green and the third for 'Hitrow Airport'. The last the reporter saw of him, he was boarding a coach for the government transit camp at Stradishall, Suffolk, the notebook clutched firmly in his hand.[55]

But despite the trauma of their arrival, the refugees settled far more comfortably into British life than anybody had expected. By July 1973, all but 2,000 had found permanent homes, and many resettlement camps had already closed down. Most moved to areas where there were established Indian communities, such as north-west London, Birmingham and above all Leicester, where their restaurants, jewellers and sari shops lit up the Belgrave Road and became a driving force in the city's evolution from a decaying manufacturing town into the centrepiece of the new multiracial Britain. Brimming with brains, ambition and commercial enthusiasm, they became the outstanding success story of post-war immigration. To be sure, they still faced prejudice and discrimination, their children often teased at school, their achievements ignored or belittled. Yet that only added to the achievement of people like the Trivedi family, who arrived at Stansted in September 1972 with a few suitcases, two pet African parrots, and less than £30 in Ugandan currency. A few months earlier, Mr Trivedi had been a shoe salesman earning £1,500 a year; now he had virtually nothing. Yet just two weeks after his arrival, he had moved his family into a rented terraced house in Willesden, north London, paid for by his new job as a London Underground guard, his wife's job as a machine operator in a small components factory, and his eldest daughter's job as a typist in the West End. Some people might have wallowed in self-pity, but Mr Trivedi was grateful merely to be alive and to have the chance of a new start. 'I am halfway on my feet,' he said proudly, 'and that is what really counts.' And if his new white neighbours had only shown the same initiative, guts and self-reliance, then Britain in the 1970s might have been an altogether happier place.[56]

8

The Limits to Growth

The issue is not about the fairly narrow gap between the parties on wage inflation, nor even about the threat of a further bout of most damaging inflation, but about the fundamentals of our constitution and our way of life. For who is now governing the country? The elected government at Westminster or the trade unions?

– Letter to *The Times* from John Stokes MP, 20 April 1972

In March 1972, a group of management theorists at the Massachusetts Institute of Technology published a report on the 'predicament of mankind'. They had been working for two years on a computer model of the entire global economic system, funded by the giant Fiat and Volkswagen car empires and sponsored by a group of international industrialists, scientists and management consultants who called themselves the Club of Rome. Feeding their computers with data on population growth, food supplies, capital investment, industrial output, resource depletion and pollution, the MIT researchers believed they had produced the first genuinely scientific prediction of where the world was heading, and it made deeply depressing reading. Even in the most optimistic scenario, they predicted, mankind's food and resources would run out in 2100. The world was like 'a pond on which a water lily is growing'. Every day the lily was doubling in size; if it grew unchecked, it would take just thirty days to choke off all other forms of life. But at the moment it seemed small, 'and so you decide not to worry about cutting it back until it covers half the pond. On what day will that be? On the twenty-ninth day, of course. You have one day to save your pond.' If they were right, the post-war dream of an infinitely expanding affluent society was over: hence the title of their report, *The Limits to Growth*.[1]

Even at the time, experts queued up to pour scorn on *The Limits to Growth*'s apocalyptic predictions. The report was 'such a brazen, impudent piece of nonsense', thought Professor Wilfred Beckerman of the University of London, that 'nobody could possibly take it seriously'. And yet as he later told *The Times*, he was horrified to discover that it was actually 'taken very seriously in high places and amongst a wide public, including some officials in Whitehall'. This was no exaggeration: the new president of the European Commission, the West German politician Sicco Mansholt, issued an open letter calling for governments to act on the report's conservationist recommendations, while there were even rumours that its authors had been invited to Downing Street to meet Edward Heath. And with the report's paperback edition costing just £1, it was hardly surprising that its gloomy conclusions were soon filtering through to a mass audience. (By the end of the decade, indeed, an estimated 4 million copies had been sold in thirty languages.) From a British point of view, after all, its timing could hardly have been better. For when the report was formally released on 1 March 1972, the miners' strike had been over for barely ten days. At a time when electricity supplies were only just returning to normal, *The Limits to Growth* struck a powerful chord. And at a time when candle manufacturers were struggling to keep up with demand, the MIT team's predictions of strikes, shortages, blackouts and queues seemed the stuff not of fantasy but of everyday reality.[2]

By any standards, the first two months of 1972 had been a terrible time for the government. Heath's biographer calls them 'the most dreadful short period of concentrated stress ever endured by a British Government in peacetime'. And although the end of February brought a short breathing space for the embattled Prime Minister, he cut a distinctly gloomy, weary figure, exhausted by the struggle to secure European entry, preoccupied by the slaughter in Northern Ireland, bruised by the furore over unemployment and bloodied by the humiliation of the miners' strike. The self-confident victor of 1970 had long since disappeared; now Heath seemed more remote than ever, secluded inside the Downing Street bunker with a handful of aides, apparently happiest when poring over policy details or conducting marathon negotiations with Vic Feather and Jack Jones. The journalist James Margach, who had known him for twenty years, thought that power made him 'authoritarian and intolerant'. It certainly made him a lot fatter: he now cut a very heavy figure whenever he appeared for his glacial, self-consciously presidential press conferences in the grandiose surroundings of Lancaster House. More and more he surrounded himself with Whitehall mandarins such as Sir William Armstrong, the head of the Home Civil Service, whom union bosses nicknamed the 'Deputy Prime Minister'. No Prime Minister and civil servant had ever had a closer relationship, and by the end of 1972 Sir William was virtually the number two man in the government. He had 'great personal charm and charisma,' one aide later told Hugo Young, as well as 'a desire to be known, an appetite for the front line.' But many ministers worried that Armstrong, who seemed increasingly pessimistic about the future of the country, had rather too much influence. 'Messianic was a good word,' remarked Jim Prior. 'He drove us along; some people thought here was this great public figure, this ice-cold civil servant, this dispassionate observer – if *he* looks at it this way, we *must* be right . . .'³

A week after the MIT experts issued their depressing predictions, *The Times* published a long editorial entitled 'A Turning Point for Mr Heath'. Its message was clear: on issues from inflation and unemployment to Northern Ireland and Europe, Heath must show that he led 'a learning Government . . . accepting the lessons of their own experience'. He must personally learn from 'the mistakes that were made in handling the miners' strike', and must 'take no notice of critics who despise concili-ation'. '"George, be a King"', the paper insisted, 'is bad advice to a Prime Minister – after all it cost Britain America.' To many people, the thought of Heath changing his mind was about as likely as the Beatles getting back together. But this was to misread the man. For all his personal stubbornness, Heath was ultimately a pragmatist. And as the quintes-sential product of the post-war consensus, he shuddered at the thought of an age of limits. Like his old boss Harold Macmillan, he believed that rapid economic growth was the key to national prosperity and political survival. So did Sir William Armstrong, and at a Chequers seminar in November 1971, Heath listened with approval as Armstrong suggested that 'we should think big, and try to build up our industry onto a Japanese scale. This would mean more public spending. We should ask companies what they needed in the way of financial and other help, and give it to them.' This completely contradicted what Heath had promised in his manifesto. But to the surprise of some onlookers, he nodded enthusiastically. 'Fine,' he said, 'and of course we must give it only to the good ones, not the bad ones.'[4]

They began, however, with one of the bad ones. On 24 February, barely a week after the end of the miners' strike, John Davies told his Cabinet colleagues that he had decided – in total contravention of his previous undertakings – to put up £35 million to save the doomed shipbuilding yards on the Upper Clyde. He frankly admitted that there was little chance of UCS becoming commercially viable, but explained that the end of shipbuilding on the Clyde might have disastrous consequences in terms of mass unemployment and public disorder. The local Chief Constable, David McNee, had even suggested that he would need 15,000 extra policemen to maintain order if the yards went under, and, given what was happening in Belfast, as well as what had happened during the miners' strike, the government were not prepared to take that risk. Since the yards were not likely to become viable even in five years, the Cabinet minutes recorded, 'the case for Government intervention was principally a social one'. In private, Davies even admitted that 'if the general level of unemployment was lower and economic activity was reviving more rapidly, he would not have felt it necessary to recommend financial support for the three yards on the scale now envisaged'.[5]

Given what Davies had said eighteen months before about leaving lame ducks to their fate, this was clearly a U-turn of enormous proportions. There were roars of delight from the Labour benches when he announced the news four days later, and many people saw the decision as a victory for Jimmy Reid and his fellow shipbuilders, whose work-in had been vindicated. On the right, however, the decision looked like a sign of panic in the face of unemployment, a disturbing surrender to the threat of public violence. Listening to her colleague, Margaret Thatcher felt a sense of 'tangible unease', while *The Economist* lamented that if the government had to throw £35 million at any industry, 'one of the worst possible economic choices is shipbuilding, whose future probably lies in low wage countries and certainly does not lie so many miles up the Clyde'. As the magazine later put it, the government seemed to have 'lost its nerve'.[6]

In his memoirs, Heath admitted that the U-turn over UCS had been a mistake. It gave the impression that the government was 'baling out companies as a panic reaction to the prospect of seeing the employment figures rise to about 1 million', he wrote. 'In hindsight . . . we were wrong.' Not untypically, he put all the blame on Davies, cattily observing that 'John had been unlucky rather than incompetent' and that 'the demands of the job were proving too much for him'. But although Davies was demoted later that year, Heath's account leaves much to be desired. He had approved the UCS bailout not as a one-off, but because it tallied with his new approach, which was to make a dynamic bid for economic growth in order to get unemployment down, win back the friendship of the trade unions, and give Britain the best possible chance of making a splash in Europe when it joined the Common Market in January 1973. In part, as Edmund Dell suggests, this was a strategy born of sheer panic: facing the massive resistance of the trade unions, Heath had blinked, preferring to put people back to work rather than pay the price for free-market principles in mass unemployment. But it also tallied with all his personal instincts. When Harold Macmillan had been in a tight spot in the early 1960s, he had backed a 'dash for growth', hoping that a consumer boom would somehow help the economy break through the fetters of inflation and the balance of payments. And now that Heath was in trouble, he fell back on his patron's example. As Douglas Hurd later wrote, it was not that he 'lost his nerve' because he was 'frightened of the political consequences of unemployment'. It was more that a policy of radical expansion 'appealed to his underlying belief' in 'sustained growth' as the answer to all Britain's problems. The laissez-faire overtones of the 'quiet revolution' had been all very well, but they had not yielded the results that Heathco's chief executive expected. With the country plunging into the vastly enlarged markets of Europe in January, he wanted a quick fix, and he was prepared to do whatever it took to get it.[7]

On 21 March 1972, Anthony Barber rose to Conservative cheers to unveil his second Budget. It was, he said, 'the first Budget since Parliament took the historic decision that we should join the European Economic Communities', providing 'an unparalleled opportunity' to sell British goods and services abroad. But it was also a Budget conceived against a background of high unemployment, 'which has persisted despite the unprecedented action to counter it which has been taken over the past year'. Though present policies would eventually bring a recovery, they would not do so quickly enough 'to meet the challenge of Europe', and so the time had come for radical action to 'help British industry to modernise, to re-equip and to reorganise to meet the challenge of greater international competition'.

What Barber wanted above all was a faster rate of growth, and he unveiled the extraordinarily ambitious target of 10 per cent growth within just two years, to be achieved through a massive boost to demand. Not only did he slash £1 billion off income tax, he also cut purchase tax by £140 million, increased social security and pensions by some £21 million a week, and announced a vast range of incentives for industry, from generous tax allowances for new plant and machinery to regional investment grants in struggling areas (which had been explicitly repudiated in the Conservatives' manifesto). To call it a giveaway Budget was an understatement. For ordinary taxpayers and businessmen alike, it was as though Father Christmas had brought several years' worth of presents in one go. With public sector borrowing up to almost £3.5 billion, there was of course an enormous risk of inflation. But Barber told the House that there was no danger that his stimulus proposals would send prices up; on the contrary, he explained, the boost to business profits and productivity would actually help to keep inflation down – not least because the unions, inevitably impressed by the government's commitment to full employment and economic growth, would refrain from demanding big pay increases. It was the most ambitious Budget in living memory: no wonder that as the Chancellor sat down, his voice hoarse, his backbenchers gave him a standing ovation.[8]

In later years, when Barber's Budget had become a byword for reckless profligacy, the rationale behind it would often be overlooked. The basic philosophy was very similar to the dash for growth under Macmillan in 1963, the premise being that if the government could only urge the economy on to a faster rate of growth, the resulting gains in output and productivity would put an end to the debilitating cycle of 'stop-go'. Back in the early 1960s, the Wilson government had been forced to apply the brakes after barely a year, the reason being that the boom had stimulated huge demand for imports, which consequently pushed Britain's balance of payments deep into the red and heaped pressure on an already beleaguered pound. But in 1972, the thinking ran, the situation was very different. Thanks to Roy Jenkins's austerity, Britain had built up a healthy balance-of-payments surplus, and on top of that, Barber was determined not to allow an 'unrealistically' high pound to 'distort' the domestic economy. With the economy free to expand, he hoped, the gains in productivity would be so great that they would more than make up for any surge in prices, thereby keeping inflation down. And to be fair, plenty of people agreed with him. Many Tory MPs were delighted by such an expansionist Budget, while the most common complaint among Labour MPs, for whom no Budget could be too generous, was that he had not gone far enough. The economist Sir Roy Harrod, once the protégé of John Maynard Keynes, predicted that the boom would have no adverse effects on inflation, while *The Times*'s only complaint was that Barber had been too timid.[9]

One of the Budget's few perspicacious critics was one of Barber's predecessors as Chancellor, Roy Jenkins, who predicted from the Labour side of the House that in due course it would lead to 'swingeing and unacceptable public expenditure cuts' and 'substantial tax increases' – as indeed, in the long term, it did. Remarkably, however, one of the biggest sceptics was Barber himself. He always had profound doubts about the recklessness of the stimulus, as did many of his advisers, who knew that the balance of payments was already deteriorating and that there was a real risk of sending inflation into overdrive. 'A lot of people within the Treasury were worried,' recalled his special adviser Brendan Sewill, while a senior civil servant later claimed that, although 'the Chancellor went along with it', the Budget had been conceived not in Number 11 but in Number 10, by 'the Prime Minister and one or two of the spending ministers' who thought that it was a formula for political recovery. Unfortunately, it was a formula only for disaster, a classic example of politicians over-stimulating the economy because they lacked the backbone to resist public criticism or the patience to wait for their previous measures to take effect. Thanks to Barber's stimulus measures the previous year, unemployment would have come down anyway, but by throwing even more money at the economy Heath was stoking the flames of inflation. At any time it would have been a naive, irresponsible gamble. But with the world economy in a state of deep uncertainty and international currencies in deepening disorder, this was the worst possible time for such an expensive mistake. It was the product not only of good and noble intentions, but of panic and arrogance, and it was a classic example of a disease to which British politics was peculiarly prone in the 1970s: the economics of wishful thinking, based on rosily optimistic predictions that were never, ever vindicated.[10]

The dash for growth unleashed by Barber's Budget took place against the background of two seismic economic events. First, there was the collapse of the Bretton Woods system, which had kept monetary order through fixed exchange rates since the end of the Second World War, laying the foundations for the great post-war boom. Thanks largely to the decline of the dollar, Bretton Woods had finally disintegrated in August 1971, and was replaced by a temporary realignment under the Smithsonian Agreement at the end of that year. Meanwhile, the six countries of the EEC, together with Britain as an aspiring member, formed what was nicknamed the 'Snake', a primitive version of the Exchange Rate Mechanism in which members agreed to keep their exchange rates from fluctuating more than 2.25 per cent against one another. But this proved no more successful than its sequel. The pound would probably not have lasted long in the Snake anyway, but, thanks to Barber's dash for growth, sterling was bound to come under enormous pressure. As the Budget took effect and British consumers began to spend heavily on imports, the pressure became unsustainable. At last, on 23 June, the Chancellor made the historic announcement that the pound was to float freely, its value determined by the markets rather than by a fixed exchange rate. Strictly speaking, this should have been an embarrassment for the government, a rebuke to their European ambitions and a hint of the dangers of unchecked growth. Indeed, the fact that the pound fell steadily from $2.60 to $2.38 in just twelve months hardly suggested great international confidence in the British economy. Yet since a floating pound removed the fetters on domestic expansion, the reaction at home was one of delight. *The Times* hailed Heath's 'insight', 'courage' and 'confidence' in allowing the pound to float, while many Tory backbenchers were overjoyed at the thought of the economy surging ahead without being checked by petty considerations about exchange rates. That a floating pound made the risks of inflation all the greater seems not to have occurred to them.[11]

The second development – and one that made the Barber boom seem even more reckless – was the Bank of England's radical reform of the financial system in the autumn of 1971. During the 1960s, Britain's major clearing banks had operated under strict lending regulations which meant that they lost business to the so-called 'secondary' or 'fringe' banks, smaller, upstart institutions which did not have to play by the same rules and therefore muscled in on the market for credit. In an attempt to spur competition, create a level playing field and perhaps kill off the secondary banks, the Bank unveiled a new system in September 1971, known as Competition and Credit Control, which lifted the ceilings on bank lending. As *The Times* put it, the Bank had changed 'the traffic lights from red to green' in a bid to push the banks towards 'greater competition and efficiency': precisely the kind of measure that Heath loved. It was obvious that in the short term there would be a sharp rise in credit, and hence in the money supply. What nobody seemed to realize, though, was that, since this coincided with a property boom, the drastic explosion of global commodity prices and Barber's giveaway Budget, the surge in the money supply would be impossible to control.[12]

The explosion in credit after September 1971 was extraordinarily reckless by any standards. In 1970, new bank lending to the private sector had come to £1.3 billion; in 1971, £1.8 billion. But as banks rushed to take advantage of their new freedom, it soared in 1972 to a staggering £6.4 billion, reaching £6.8 billion a year later. Meanwhile, the broad money supply, then measured as M3 (meaning notes, coins, money in deposit accounts and private bank deposits in foreign currencies), was wildly out of control, growing by 28 per cent in 1972 and then by exactly the same rate a year later. These figures were bad enough; what was worse was that all of this new credit was not going into industrial expansion and investment, as Heath and Barber had hoped, but something much less productive. For since bank rate in 1971 was just 5 per cent, even though the retail price index had hit 10 per cent, this meant that real interest rates were effectively negative. Assuming that the situation remained roughly the same, anyone who borrowed money at a decent rate would be able to make a killing provided they invested in something that held its value – and the obvious thing was property.[13]

Property prices had been booming since the late 1960s, thanks above all to the office-building spree that had transformed the skylines of London, Birmingham and Manchester. But when the Bank of England lifted its credit restrictions the boom began to turn into a bubble. With the major clearing banks now competing in the credit market, the smaller secondary banks found themselves squeezed out. So they turned to property lending instead, assuming that in an age of inflation it represented the ideal safe bet. The effect was extraordinary. In the first two years of the bubble, with secondary banks almost throwing money at property developers, entrepreneurs and even ordinary families, house prices went up by an astounding 70 per cent, the biggest margin in living memory.

By 1973, office space in central London cost five times as much as it did in New York, while for the first time, property prices became the stuff of popular fascination. With inflation outstripping mortgage rates, it made sense to buy; indeed, if they got the right deal, some people found themselves paying literally nothing for their housing costs. In particular, young couples who would once have been happy to rent now threw themselves headlong into the capital's property market, rushing to buy houses and flats in run-down areas such as Islington, Camden Town, Brixton and Notting Hill. It was the Barber boom that established all the clichés of the capital's fashionable middle-class young: the white stucco house-fronts and the stripped-pine interiors, the antique door handles and the painstakingly sourced fireplaces, the overflowing pot plants and the earthenware jars, the *Guardian* on the coffee table and Led Zeppelin on the record player. In his book *Soft City* (1974), Jonathan Raban described what happened to one small square on the Islington–Holloway border: the profusion of estate agents' boards, the overnight swarm of builders and interior decorators, the transformation of brick and stucco fronts, the unexpected crowds at lunch hour in the pubs, the arrival of 'Nigel and Pamela, Jeremy and Nicola' in their Renaults and Citroëns. The local landlords duly took note, 'shaking their heads gloomily at the absences of bathrooms and the damp patches and the jags of falling plaster' and suggesting that their tenants might be better off in a new council flat somewhere else – so that they could sell the property and cash in on the great gentrification game.[14]

Needless to say, this was not quite what Heath had envisaged when he set the economy on its dash for growth. The point of Barber's Budget had been to 'provide the climate in which industry can have the confidence to re-equip and expand', not to give 25-year-old couples the chance to become property tycoons. As Heath saw it, he had given the City everything it wanted, slashing corporate taxes, lifting state controls and pulling the government out of industry – and yet the only result had been high unemployment and continued industrial stagnation. In private, he lectured industrialists and bankers on their unpatriotic refusal to invest in new staff and equipment; in public, he exhorted them to do better, telling the Young Conservatives that there was 'not much virtue in a private enterprise system if its practitioners are always trying to find clouds in the sky as an excuse for staying indoors'. But with entry to the Common Market looming in January 1973, he simply could not understand why businesses were not frantically gearing up for the new competition. Well, he thought: if British business was too timid, slothful and unimaginative to invest in the future, then he must force it to do so. Of course this meant dropping all his rhetoric about pulling the government out of industry, but, as he later put it, this was merely a 'sensible, pragmatic and practical response to a disappointing state of affairs' – the classic language of the Heathco technocrat. The aim, he told the *Evening Standard,* was to 'regenerate our entire industrial capacity' so that Britain would be 'in a very advantageous position when we are in the European Economic Community'. The goals of efficiency, modernization and competition were still exactly the same. All that had changed was the means. 'Once the industrial climate in Britain had changed, and our companies had acquired some positive momentum,' he wrote later, 'then the government could gradually withdraw.'[15]

In the meantime, what was needed was drastic action. During the early months of 1972 Heath had commissioned a three-man civil service team, headed by Sir William Armstrong, to draft the appropriate legislation, and on Budget Day, Anthony Barber unveiled the proposed Industry Act to a stunned Commons. It gave the government more sweeping powers over industry than most Conservatives had ever imagined, not only creating an Office of Fair Trading and Consumer Protection committee, but restoring the old system of regional grants to areas of high unemployment and creating a special agency, the Industrial Development Executive, to hand out hundreds of millions of pounds to hand-picked companies. Ripping up the principles of 1970, the Industry Act seemed to turn the clock back to the Wilson years, when Tony Benn and MinTech had been in the business of picking winners, encouraging mergers and creating vast industrial conglomerates like British Leyland and Upper Clyde Shipbuilders. But when John Davies explained the details to the House the day after the Budget, he was in bullish form. In the 'rapidly changing world industrial and commercial environment', he said, 'the government cannot stand aside ... We have decided to take powers to help industry to modernise, adapt and rationalise to meet these new and changing circumstances.'[16]

In the Commons, nobody could quite believe their ears. 'Davies made a great "U-turn" speech on the Budget in which he totally withdrew everything he had ever said about lame ducks,' wrote Tony Benn, 'and the House just roared with laughter.' In fact, Benn was delighted by the new measures, not just because they restored the principles of his beloved Ministry of Technology, but because they made an excellent blueprint for massive state intervention along much more radical lines. The Industry Act was 'spadework for socialism', Benn gleefully told the Commons, with the 'largest subsidies by the taxpayers to the regions that we have ever known; to industry generally, and to shipbuilding in particular, with total expenditure far exceeding anything that has been brought forward by previous Governments', and he promised to use its powers 'when we inherit power again, more radically than the right hon. Gentleman himself will use them'. Not surprisingly, there were reports of serious dissatisfaction on the Tory benches, especially among the two or three dozen backbenchers who saw themselves as champions of the free market. The chairman of the 1922 Committee, Sir Harry Legge-Bourke, even told the government that it was 'a Socialist Bill by ethic and philosophy', although he went along with it because the depressed areas were in dire need of help. And yet the future champions of Thatcherism – men like Nicholas Ridley, John Biffen and even Enoch Powell – were conspicuous by their quiescence. At a time when the government appeared beleaguered, they had no wish to make its life even harder, even if they were horrified by its apparent lurch to the left. In the end, the Industry Act sailed through with remarkably little opposition.[17]

As *The Economist* put it, Heath now had 'a blank cheque to give money to industries in trouble', and in his Cabinet he had the perfect man to spend it. As a former City buccaneer with bags of youthful enthusiasm, Peter Walker was itching to get his hands on British industry, and in the autumn of 1972 Heath gave him his head, naming him as the new chief of the Department of Trade and Industry. Unlike his backbench critics, Walker saw nothing wrong with the state taking a commanding role in industry; indeed, he told the party conference a year later that 'the object of the "new capitalism" is that harnessing of economic growth to the creation of a civilised society'. By this point, the new regime had been in place for twelve months, spending £55 million on regional development grants and almost £77 million on aid to industry, creating more than 50,000 new jobs in the process. And that was not all. Under Walker's aegis, the government handed out £1 billion to the coal industry, reorganized the gas industry under one national body, British Gas, and set up British Nuclear Fuels Ltd. and a Nuclear Power Board. There was £16 million for the machine tools industry; there was £26 million for

ICL, the computer conglomerate set up by Tony Benn; there was even £5 million for Meriden, the doomed motorcycle firm in the West Midlands, later notorious as one of Benn's ill-fated workers' cooperatives. Walker certainly could not be faulted for lack of effort: his junior minister, the flamboyant and similarly expansionist Michael Heseltine, even organized a series of breakfasts with captains of industry, the rationale being that 'if you excited them' first thing in the morning, 'they would go straight back and do something about it'.[18]

Heath and Walker always denied that the Industry Act amounted to a massive programme of socialism, as their Thatcherite critics later claimed. In a lecture in October 1972, Walker's junior minister Christopher Chataway, a former Olympic runner who had been a pacemaker for Roger Bannister's four-minute mile, told his fellow Conservatives that although the government would not 'prop up' bad managements and failing firms, it was 'bad economics as well as bad social policy' to allow major British companies to collapse because of subsidized international competition or 'severe market dislocation'. For Chataway, Walker and Heseltine, the Industry Act was merely a home-grown equivalent of what, say, de Gaulle had done in France or the Liberal Democrats had done in Japan, using the power of the state to regenerate and modernize British industry so that it could compete freely on the world stage. There is an argument that their experiment might have worked if it had been tried for longer, or if it had been tried in less turbulent economic conditions, and Heath always insisted that it was a lot better than Mrs Thatcher's policy of leaving industry to fend for itself, often resulting in massive job losses. (Actually, the difference between them was often exaggerated: in her first term, Mrs Thatcher followed Heath's example by ploughing vast sums of money into nationalized concerns like British Steel and British Leyland before selling them off.)

But whether the Industry Act was really the answer to the British economy's problems is very doubtful. For one thing, it was far too complicated and bureaucratic, a typical complaint during the Heathco years, trying to solve every conceivable problem – regional disparities, deep-seated unemployment, consumer protection, competition with the members of the EEC – all at once, usually by throwing money at them. There is no doubt that British industry badly needed modernization, but, as John Campbell remarks, 'throwing Government money at favoured projects and bribing firms to set up where they would not otherwise have done was not the way to do it'. Throughout the post-war years, British governments had had a lamentable record of picking industrial winners, and Heath's was no exception. It was telling, as Campbell points out, that a House of Commons report into regional policy in 1974 described it as 'empiricism gone mad, a game of hit and miss, played with more enthusiasm than success'. And it was even more telling that by 1974, both Heath and Walker had become intensely impatient and frustrated with what they saw as the caution and conservatism of British employers and managers. What they never seem to have realized was that no matter how much public money they spent, economic miracles simply could not be conjured into being overnight.[19]

There was one other obvious problem with Heath's new policy of massive industrial expansion. Unless he was very careful, rapid economic growth was bound to trigger a new wave of inflationary pay claims, and any illusions that the government could simply face down the unions had been blown away by the miners' strike. In any case, not only had an exhausted government lost much of its thirst for confrontation, but the pressure of public opinion and Fleet Street commentary for a more consensual approach proved irresistible. Since yet more strikes would obviously undermine Heath's drive for growth and modernization, he was keen to strike a conciliatory note. 'We still have to find sensible means by which sensible men can reach sensible agreements before there is any question of industrial action,' he told an audience of Scottish Conservatives in May 1972, and a few weeks later he told the Press Association that he was 'working to find ways of checking more effectively pay claims which go far beyond the rise in prices'.

In private, meanwhile, he was already reaching out to the union bosses. Throughout the early months of 1972, Sir William Armstrong and a group of 'Four Wise Men' – the TUC general secretary Vic Feather, the CBI's Campbell Adamson, the Treasury chief Sir Douglas Allen and Sir Frank Figgures, head of the National Economic Development Council – had been meeting secretly to discuss a more consensual way of running economic and industrial affairs. Meanwhile, just a couple of weeks after the end of the miners' strike, Heath invited the General Council of the TUC, including Jack Jones and Hugh Scanlon, for drinks at Downing Street, kicking off with cups of tea and moving on to whisky before the night was out. He had always got on well with the union bosses, and with the strike tactfully forgotten, they were soon back in the old jovial routine. According to the TUC's notes, the Prime Minister was clearly in peace-making mood. He wanted to work out 'common objectives' to meet 'the changing needs of an industrial society', he said, assuring them that his priorities were to encourage 'steady expansion of the economy, a decrease in unemployment . . . and a steady rise in living standards'. Perhaps it would be too much to say that he had rekindled the romance, but the TUC bosses were certainly impressed enough to agree to another date. Heath was 'a very decent man, there's no question about that', Jack Jones said. 'He was prepared to be patient and listen to our point of view and our arguments and, within his limits as a Conservative Prime Minister, I think he did try to respond.'[20]

Unfortunately for Heath, thousands of ordinary trade unionists did not share their bosses' opinion. Although the Industrial Relations Act had been badly undermined by the unions' refusal to register, it remained on the statute book, a glaring signal (as they saw it) of the government's reactionary war on the working classes. Months of pay restraint, strikes and the tumultuous climax to the miners' dispute gave existing political and social differences a sharper edge: it was telling that, according to Gallup, three out of five people in the spring of 1972 believed that there was a class struggle in Britain, the highest proportion for decades. In the rhetoric of parliamentary debates, as well as on shop floors, on picket lines and in university classrooms, the language of class warfare came increasingly naturally to the tongue, partly because of the popularity of pseudo-Marxist ideas in the late 1960s and early 1970s, but also because a stuttering economy lent a new bitterness to old divisions. Even a family tuning in for an evening's escapism were confronted with the class struggle, whether it be *Till Death Us Do Part*'s endless backbiting between right-wing Alf Garnett and his layabout Liverpudlian son-in-law, the defiant working-class hedonism of Stan Butler and Jack Harvey in *On the Buses*, or the earnest proletarian sentiments of *Play for Today* instalments such as Jim Allen's *The Rank and File* (based on the Pilkington glass strike), Jeremy Sandford's *Edna the Inebriate Woman* (alcoholism and homelessness), Tom Clarke's *Stockers Copper* (a Cornish clay mine strike in 1913) and Dominic Behan's *Carson Country* (working-class life in Protestant Belfast in 1920) – all of which appeared between May 1971 and October 1972.

And whereas politicians in the early 1960s had often sought to dampen class differences – for example, Harold Wilson's attempt to woo middle-class voters with his promises of 'white heat' – the generation taking their seats in the 1970s impatiently rejected the compromises of the past. The young Neil Kinnock, who entered the Commons in 1970 and quickly became famous for his blazing condemnations of the 'class-ridden Government' and its 'disgusting and doctrinaire' policies, stood out only for his red hair and gift of the gab, not because his rhetoric was especially unusual. His fellow left-winger Eric Heffer even wrote a book called *The Class Struggle in Parliament* (1973), advising the working classes that there was a difference between 'ordinary laws', which they should obey, and 'class laws', which they should not. For Kinnock and Heffer, Heath's stiff appeals for national unity and clumsy references to One Nation were merely window dressing, disguising the fact that he was a stubborn, callous reactionary who cared nothing for the common man. Even his hobbies of classical music and sailing were seen as emblems of class tyranny, elitist habits well beyond the reach of the ordinary worker. Heath was 'unfair', 'uncharitable', 'faceless and heartless', said the *New Left Review*. 'His hatred of the poor, the unlucky, the undeserving, is absolutely genuine,' wrote Paul Johnson (then on the left) in a particularly overblown piece in the *New Statesman* in February 1972. 'When he dilates on these categories of the nation, he cannot keep the contempt from his voice. To him failure is not merely a sign of incompetence but of immorality, to be punished in the next world but especially in this.'[21]

If Heath thought that the end of the miners' strike would banish the dark clouds of winter and bring a return to consensus, he was greatly mistaken. Within a matter of weeks a new and equally bitter confrontation had captured public attention. For years, discontent had been simmering in the docks over the introduction of new working practices, notably 'containerization', which threatened the jobs of the notoriously militant, tough and clannish dockers. In an attempt to avoid clashes with the unions, cargo-handling firms were increasingly trying to avoid employing them, but in March 1972 an unofficial shop stewards' committee in Liverpool began blacking lorries whose drivers refused to sign a pledge to abide by union rules. One family-run haulage business, Heaton's, promptly took the matter to the new National Industrial Relations Court, claiming that the dockers were trying to force their drivers to break their contracts. It seemed a clear-cut case: the NIRC handed down a £5,000 fine, and then a further £50,000 fine in April. Under the terms of the Industrial Relations Act, the dockers themselves were spared the burden of paying up; instead, it was their union, the TGWU, who had to foot the bill. This put the union leadership in a dilemma, since technically they did not recognize the court, and had refused to be represented at its hearings. But the TGWU boss Jack Jones, supported by the TUC, successfully argued that it would be better to pay the fine rather than risk having their assets seized for contempt of court; and so on 2 May, two days before the deadline, the union paid up.[22]

Complicated as it already was, however, the case did not end there. By this point, the dock strike had spread. Even though Jones appealed to the dockers to stop, a national shop stewards' committee now urged workers in ports across the country, from Hull to Tilbury, to join the blacking action. The NIRC promptly ordered Jones to discipline his members within three weeks or face further penalties, but he refused, arguing that it was union policy to defend 'the right of shop stewards to exercise their responsibilities', even when that meant defying his instructions. And if this gave the impression that the unions were out of control, then other events seemed to confirm it, for by now the government was facing yet another, completely unrelated strike. On 13 April, the three rail unions rejected an 11 per cent pay offer from British Rail and declared a work-to-rule, which inevitably meant severe disruptions and cancellations, especially on commuter lines around London. Disastrously, Heath decided to make this a point of confrontation, perhaps out of desperation to show his mettle after defeat by the miners, and that very evening Anthony Barber pledged that the government would not be 'blackmailed by sectional groups seeking their own interest'. One Tory backbencher even told *The Times* excitedly that 'if the railwaymen bring the nation to a standstill the Government will challenge Labour to a general election' – a preview of things to come, although nobody knew it at the time.

In the meantime, this seemed an excellent opportunity to show off the powers of the Industrial Relations Act, and Heath's new Employment Secretary, Harold Macmillan's rather ineffectual son Maurice, applied to the NIRC for a compulsory cooling-off period. This was granted; the railwaymen duly cooled off, and two weeks later returned to the fray more determined than ever, resuming their work-to-rule and imposing an overtime ban. By Saturday, 13 May, an unlucky day for travellers, the railways were facing massive shutdowns and the government had decided to fire its second barrel, as John Campbell puts it, by ordering a compulsory ballot as laid down in the new Act. Obeying the law, the railwaymen went away and voted, returning a 5–1 margin in favour of further action. Now the government really did look ridiculous. After all that effort, the Industrial Relations Act had made no different whatsoever, much to the fury of commuters. At last, the unions accepted a 13 per cent pay deal, less than they had wanted, but making a mockery of Heath's initial insistence that he would never give in. *The Times* spoke for many in its withering verdict that it was 'not political strength but political obstinacy to fight to a finish for a principle in a policy that is not going to work'. Heath must write off the dispute as 'the last twitch of an expiring policy', the paper solemnly said, and look for 'more effective ways of countering wage inflation'.[23]

But it was the dockers who finally reduced the Industrial Relations Act from failure to farce. On 13 June, the morning after Heath had surrendered to the railwaymen, the Court of Appeal, chaired by Lord Denning, ruled that the NIRC had been wrong to impose fines on the TGWU. Jack Jones could have his money back; instead, the individual shop stewards would have to settle the fines. This was a catastrophe for the government: not only did it completely undercut the Industrial Relations Act, which was supposed to make unions responsible for the behaviour of their members, but it opened the way for shop stewards to defy the court and get themselves sent to prison, turning themselves into martyrs to the cause of the trade unions. Robert Carr was so depressed he felt he 'might as well jump off Westminster Bridge', while Heath was aghast that, as he put it, 'even though [the dockers] had been using their strength to bully and blackmail the nation, they could now pose as the underdogs'.[24]

As it happened, three London dockers were already before the NIRC, accused of leading an illegal picket of the Chobham Farm container depot on Hackney Marshes. One was the chairman of the National Port Shop Stewards' Committee; another, the secretary, was a member of the Communist Party. All three could hardly contain their excitement at the thought of being sent to prison and turned into working-class heroes: when the news that the NIRC had charged them with contempt of court reached the picket lines, one shop steward remembered, the mood was 'like a holiday, a bank holiday. They were sitting on the roofs, on the balconies.

All the traffic was stopped. I've never seen anything like it in my life.' Almost overnight, a relatively minor case had turned into a major national crisis. By Friday, 16 June, the NIRC had signed arrest warrants for the three men, tens of thousands of dockers had walked out and Britain's ports were at a standstill. On the front page of *The Times,* the faces of the three men, weather-beaten, bushy-whiskered and defiant, glared out from beneath a headline reporting that the dockers had called on the miners and railwaymen to join them on the picket lines. Inside, the High Court official delegated to arrest the three men admitted to feeling 'a little bit scared' at the prospect. Standing just over five feet tall, James Dorling, the 'Tipstaff', said nervously: 'I hope there won't be any trouble and that they'll come out of the picket line quietly. I'll get them in the car and be away to Pentonville.' But others were less sanguine. 'The Government does not seem to realise', noted the former *Mirror* boss Cecil King, 'that, as has been shown in the case of the miners and the railwaymen, this is all a trial of strength and the unions are stronger than the Government.'[25]

What happened next, however, defied all predictions. On Friday morning, just minutes before the three self-declared martyrs were about to be arrested, the Dickensian figure of the Official Solicitor, whom few people had even known existed, applied for the prison orders to be quashed on the basis that there had not been enough evidence to convict them. Legally speaking, this was very sharp practice indeed, and most people assumed that the government had simply come up with an arcane ruse to escape from a tight spot. But the truth was that one of the prime movers was none other than Jack Jones, who had no desire to turn his rebellious shop stewards into left-wing heroes, or to make Edward Heath's life even worse than it already was, and had instructed the TGWU's lawyers to get the dockers out. Meanwhile, Lord Denning was under similar pressure to find a solution. 'We were influenced perhaps by the state of the country, by the realisation that there would be a general strike, which would paralyse the whole nation,' he admitted later. Hilariously, the dockers were furious at missing out on a spell behind bars, and their reactions were irresistibly reminiscent of, say, Leeds United's footballers after yet another Cup Final defeat. 'It's a bloody liberty. They had no right to do it,' said Vic Turner. 'It's a bloody disgrace,' agreed Alan Williams, at 29 the youngest of the three. 'If they had let us be arrested by the weekend there would have been a general strike. I am absolutely choked.'[26]

Two of the men, however, eventually got what they wanted. Defying both the NIRC and their own union, the dockers continued to mount their pickets, and at last, on 21 July, the court ordered the arrest of five shop stewards for picketing the Midland Cold Storage depot in East London. Four were taken that day to Pentonville prison; almost unbelievably, the only one to avoid capture, Vic Turner, turned up outside the prison the next day to protest against the arrest of his friends, and was promptly taken inside himself. By this time, industrial relations across the country were sliding into chaos. Already the capital's lorry drivers, mounting an action *against* the dockers, had brought all roads out of the Port of London to a total standstill, but the arrest of the 'Pentonville Five' brought matters to a climax. By the next day, not only had every major docks in Britain fallen silent as the workforce walked out, but thousands of electricians, bus drivers, printers and even meat porters joined the strike, claiming that the government had launched an unparalleled assault on the nation's working people. 'Exports worth millions of dollars a day to the country's fragile economy piled up on idle piers,' reported the American magazine *Time,* 'while thousands of tons of Guernsey tomatoes, grapes from Cyprus and Australian apples rotted in the ships' holds or were destroyed.' Fleet Street was brought to its knees; for five days there were no national newspapers. In the Commons, Labour MPs chanted 'Heil Hitler' and gave mocking Nazi salutes as Heath desperately insisted that the Industrial Relations Act was still working, while Tony Benn rather absurdly claimed that the Pentonville Five would go down in history beside the Tolpuddle Martyrs. On 24 July, Heath refused Vic Feather's entreaties to suspend the hated act. The next day, Hugh Scanlon persuaded the TUC to vote for a one-day general strike, the first since 1926.[27]

Given the circumstances, it seemed odd that Heath was not more worried. *The Economist* remarked that the government appeared 're-markably relaxed and it was plain that Mr Heath had decided that this was not going to be his general strike week'. The reason became clear in the late morning of Wednesday, 26 July, when the Law Lords unexpectedly delivered their ruling in the original case of the lorry drivers at Heaton's. Since their decision had not been expected for weeks, many people suspected that they had come under political pressure, but it seems more likely that they speeded up the timetable themselves, conscious of the threat to public order if they delayed. In the event, their decision could hardly have been better timed, for they threw out Lord Denning's decision in the Appeal Court and declared that the TGWU was liable for prosecution after all, rather than its shop stewards. The NIRC immediately ordered the Pentonville Five set free, and that evening they were out, carried on the shoulders of a cheering crowd like conquering heroes. As numerous experts pointed out, this was a very strange decision: given that the men had been imprisoned for contempt of court, not for blacking, the Law Lords' decision should really have made no difference. Since the men showed no contrition, and continued to voice their scorn for the court, the case could hardly have been said to have strengthened respect for the law; indeed, since it so obviously smacked of political convenience, it destroyed any last shreds of respectability that still clung to the NIRC. But the government hardly cared: the Pentonville Five were out, the TGWU quietly paid the fines, and the sympathy strikes petered out.[28]

With the Pentonville case resolved, the dock strike dragged on for another two weeks, the government having to declare yet another state of emergency at one stage to guarantee food supplies. In the end, the dockers grudgingly agreed to the terms of a report drawn up by Jack Jones and Lord Aldington, chairman of the Port of London Authority, which provided for ports to charge extra for containers not packed by dockers, and effectively guaranteed them a job for life, hardly a very good way of modernizing Britain's creaking and painfully old-fashioned ports. What was most revealing, however, was the way in which the strike ended. After delegates voted at Transport House on 16 August to approve the terms, they were jostled and punched by dozens of dockers waiting angrily outside. Some two dozen men, meanwhile, forced their way into the building and angrily confronted Jack Jones while he was trying to hold a press conference. He had sold them out, they insisted; and as he tried to explain, some threw water, ripped-up union cards and even a metal ash-can at him. Outside, more dockers confronted television reporters trying to get their side of the story, smashing their cameras and kicking one man to the ground. 'Smash the fucking lot up,' one said bluntly, 'that's what we want to do.'[29]

If the turbulent events of the summer hinted at the widening gulf between the union bosses and the men they led, they also marked the final disintegration of Edward Heath's plans for industrial relations. Not only did polls show that one out of two people now saw the Industrial Relations Act as a threat to order in the workplace, but employers themselves had lost confidence in it, many refusing to invoke it or even adding clauses to collective agreements specifying that they were not legally enforceable. Above all, the dockers' and railwaymen's strikes had made an utter mockery of the National Industrial Relations Court, which in the public mind had been reduced to a meaningless arm of the government. Even Heath himself quietly dropped mentions of the legislation from his speeches, and although it remained on the statute book, it ceased to be a meaningful presence. Whether it could ever have worked, given the unions' determination to break it, is very doubtful; certainly its massive, unwieldy bureaucracy did it no favours. In the long run, it was probably a necessary prelude to the reforms carried out in the early 1980s, with the Thatcher government learning from Heath's mistakes and introducing legislation more slowly and carefully, building a new structure brick by brick. In the short run, however, its failure seemed to confirm a growing sense that authority was breaking down, from soldiers being murdered in the back-streets of Belfast and the Law Lords bending over backwards to neutralize the threat of a general strike, to the police turning a blind eye to a new wave of pornography and muggers supposedly running riot on Britain's streets. In Whitehall, there was a pervasive sense that the state had lost control of public order; in the polls, the government lagged thirteen percentage points behind even Harold Wilson's ageing, disorganized and faction-ridden Labour Party. And it was little wonder that two out of three people told the Harris organization that summer that the unions were more powerful than the government, or that the same number thought that Britain was doomed to permanent industrial unrest.[30]

Yet while some Tories were already muttering that Heath ought to ask the electorate for a new mandate to crush the unions, the Prime Minister himself remained surprisingly upbeat, presenting an unusually relaxed image on *Panorama* at the end of July and appearing 'extremely confident' when he welcomed a group of industrialists for whisky at Downing Street ten days later. The truth was that, with Barber unleashing a dash for growth and the Industry Act giving the government unprecedented power to bail out struggling businesses, Heath was confident that the coming economic boom would utterly transform his prospects. In particular, he was increasingly hopeful that despite the terrible headlines about strikes and class warfare, his charm offensive with the union leaders was about to pay off. In a series of secret meetings over the summer of 1972, he had tried to persuade Vic Feather that the future lay in a 'tripartite' partnership between the government, the employers and the unions. As always, he believed that simply by sitting down and talking, reasonable men would be able to come up with rational, consensual solutions, with no need for confrontation, and in July he told the TUC General Council that 'the government, the CBI and the TUC had a common interest' and should work together to build a 'sensible consensus'. This was a very different Heath from the callous reactionary of left-wing propaganda, but he was being absolutely sincere; indeed, some of his Conservative colleagues began to worry that he was rather too keen on the union leaders. 'He became infatuated with them. Insisted on meeting after meeting,' Douglas Hurd later told the journalist Hugo Young. 'Was the only member of the Cabinet who actually enjoyed the meetings. Of course the union men loved them too; this was their way of life.'[31]

From the middle of July onwards, Heath arranged a series of ten tripartite meetings with the CBI and the TUC, taking up a total of fifty-two hours and demanding vast amounts of effort and paperwork from his Employment and Treasury ministers. The business representatives did not impress him very much: they were 'under-prepared and in-experienced', he grumbled later, noting that his ministers sometimes had to help them with their own arguments. On the other hand, he had nothing but admiration for the TUC men: 'widely experienced, immensely knowledgeable ... and skilled in persuasively putting their side of an argument'. This came through to everyone who saw him in action: the CBI chief Campbell Adamson later complained that Heath clearly 'loved the trade unionists more than he loved the industrialists', and seemed 'much more able to agree with them than with his own kind, as it were'. Coming from a Conservative Prime Minister, however, this was a risky approach. However much Heath liked to hark back to the 1930s and 1940s, seeing himself as the incarnation of One Nation patriotism, many party activists were itching for a fight with the unions and distinctly uneasy with the thought of a partnership with them. More seriously, Heath never seems to have realized that the union leaders were deeply political animals, subject to pressure from below and marked by social loyalties and ideological convictions he never really understood. Even if they wanted to work with him, it was very doubtful whether they could persuade their members to go along with it. But then Heath would not be the last Prime Minister to make the mistake of overestimating the union bosses' power, the discipline and solidarity of their members, and their chances of delivering the orderly settlement he craved.[32]

On 26 September, Heath welcomed the TUC and CBI to Chequers and unveiled the most ambitious corporatist programme in peacetime history. Under the agreement, the government would be committed to achieve a 5 per cent growth rate for the next two years; the CBI would agree to a 5 per cent price limit on goods in the shops; and the TUC would pledge to accept pay rises of no more than £2 a week, the pill sweetened with the promise of aid to pensioners, 'threshold' payments to protect consumers from higher prices when Britain entered the EEC, and help for the low paid. If they accepted his plan, he grandly told them, the result would be a 'new era of cooperation', carefully worked out to match 'what the country can afford'. Even the most militant union leaders were impressed by Heath's commitment. 'We Would Be Mad Not To Do It', declared a long leader in *The Times* the next day, explaining that Heath's plan was vital 'to the future of the British economy and conceivably even to the survival of democracy in Britain'. The alternative, the newspaper declared grimly, holding out the example of the military regime in Brazil, was 'to go on with inflation until the conditions become so intolerable that authoritarian rule becomes almost unavoidable and certainly popular'. This was dramatic stuff. But the TUC said no. Although Vic Feather allowed that Heath's plan offered 'a good deal of fair play to a good many people', the unions wanted more: the repeal of the Industrial Relations Act, for example, as well as stricter price controls and more concessions on rents and VAT. The next evening, Heath went on television to address the nation, imploring the TUC to see sense in some of his most consensual, conciliatory rhetoric yet. 'Think nationally,' he begged them; 'think of the nation as a whole. Think of these proposals as members of a society that can only defeat rising prices if it acts together as one nation.'[33]

Even at this stage, Heath remained convinced that the TUC would come round. The possibility that the union leaders would shrink from becoming his 'social partners', and might prove much more introverted, conservative and self-interested than he hoped, seems not to have occurred to him. When the talks resumed on 16 October, after the party conference season, he was stunned to discover that Scanlon and Jones had dug in their heels, and were insisting that the CBI must agree that price rises would be controlled by law, while wage rises remained entirely voluntary. Since this was so one-sided as to be politically impossible, it is hard to resist the suspicion that the union leaders simply wanted a pretext for the talks to fail so that they would be spared the challenge of becoming the government's formal partners. On 25 October, Heath reported to the Cabinet that the TUC had so far not budged an inch. He was willing to concede ground on housing, rents and even the Industrial Relations Act, he told his colleagues, but 'Parliament and public opinion' would never allow him to give in to their demand for statutory control of prices only. On the 26th, he welcomed the negotiators to Downing Street for a gruelling seventeen-hour marathon, running from 9 a.m. to almost four o'clock the next morning, with only two hours' break; on 30 October, they had another seven-hour session; on 1 November, they argued for another eight hours. Heath was exhausted, his eyes red-rimmed with frustration and fatigue, but still he hoped for a breakthrough. 'At Number Ten again till midnight while the endless tripartite talks go on – or rather don't go on, as it is almost all separate little huddles in every room and passage – including mine,' wrote Douglas Hurd during a break on 1 November. 'EH hanging on still, against almost every calculation, to his hope of an agreement. Just a small chance he can wear them down.'[34]

At 10.30 on the morning of 2 November, after very little sleep, Heath briefed his Cabinet on the progress of the talks. Although he had not yet abandoned hope, the fact that he was already thinking about the battle for public opinion if they collapsed – with the TUC presented as the culprits – was a sign of how things were going. By this stage, he had also decided on the only option if they did fail: 'an emergency "freeze" of prices and incomes for a limited period', followed by legislation 'to put on a more permanent statutory basis the type of arrangement on which the Government had hoped to find voluntary agreement with the TUC'. Late that afternoon the warring parties met again over a cold buffet supper, but it was no good. At ten o'clock the talks broke up, a sombre Feather telling the waiting reporters that the government had 'missed a golden opportunity to secure the cooperation of the trade union movement'. But this was disingenuous; the government could hardly have done much more to appease the unions' demands, short of giving them a deal so one-sided that it would have provoked mirth in the press, horror among employers and a rebellion on the Tory benches. The supreme irony was that Feather himself, as well as most moderate trade union leaders, had actually been happy to accept Heath's offer. It was Jones and Scanlon, the two most militant leaders but also those most under pressure from radicals in their own unions, and therefore with most to lose, who had dug in their heels. In any case, the chance was gone. The next morning, Heath summoned his Cabinet to approve the next step. It was 'a matter of great regret' that the talks had failed, the minutes noted, but 'there was unanimous agreement that nobody could have done more than the Prime Minister'.[35]

Three days later, Heath rose in the House of Commons to announce the biggest U-turn of his premiership. With the tripartite talks having collapsed, he said, the government had no choice but to institute statutory measures in pursuit of the goals he had outlined six weeks before. There would be an immediate freeze on all wages, prices, rents and dividends, lasting ninety days and then renewable for another sixty days, with fines of up to £400 for companies who ignored it. This was just Stage One of a long-term policy; in the New Year the government would announce the plans for Stage Two. Given everything that Heath had said, stretching back to the late 1960s, about the folly of a statutory incomes policy, this was an extraordinary retreat, 'the biggest reversal of positions' since he had come to office, as Harold Wilson, who knew a thing or two about reversing his position, gleefully pointed out. From the Labour benches, Heath's old Oxford friend Roy Jenkins elegantly wondered whether he had 'now abandoned his constantly reiterated view that a statutory policy could only make inflation worse in the long run, or does he now regard the short-term situation that he has produced as so disastrous that he cannot afford any longer to think about the long run?' Even Heath was seen to wince at that; his pay policy was not the same as Labour's policy in the 1960s, he said stiffly, because whereas they had been shrinking the economy, he wanted to expand it. It was a dreadfully feeble reply; no wonder Labour MPs delightedly yelled 'Resign!'

But it was from Heath's own side that the most damning criticism came. 'Does my right hon. Friend not know', Enoch Powell asked with silken contempt, 'that it is fatal for any Government or party or person to seek to govern in direct opposition to the principles on which they were entrusted with the right to govern? In introducing a compulsory control of wages and prices, in contravention of the deepest commitments of this party, has my right hon. Friend taken leave of his senses?' Even coming from an old rival and dedicated adversary, this was strong stuff: as Powell resumed his seat there were 'intakes of breath and whistles of amazement'. 'Seldom in recent years can a Prime Minister have been so bitterly denounced by one of his own backbenchers,' wrote one parliamentary correspondent. In reply, Heath barely bothered to disguise his fury. 'This Government was returned to power to take action in the national interest when required to do so,' he said stiffly, and then sat down. The debate moved on; the Tories dutifully cheered. But Powell's question hung in the air, and its author sat motionlessly in place, his eyes fixed on his enemy, wrapped in a 'sinister, glowering silence'.[36]

Powell's dramatic intervention was rooted not merely in personal hatred but in ideological conviction. The Wolverhampton MP had never forgiven Heath for sacking him from the Shadow Cabinet after the 'Rivers of Blood' speech in 1968, but as one of the Conservative Party's few unashamed free-market ideologues he was also genuinely appalled by his rival's economic policies. As early as April 1971 he had torn into Anthony Barber with the relish of a predator, warning that by inflating the money supply to tackle unemployment the government was only making matters far worse in the long run. Even if pay controls were voluntary, he said later, they were 'totalitarian' and 'Fascist'. Powell agreed that inflation was the supreme danger: indeed, in October 1973 he called it 'a social evil, an injustice between man and man, and a moral evil – a dishonesty – between Government and people, between class and class'. But Heath's bureaucratic attempts to contain it struck him as not merely counterproductive but downright immoral. 'No rules can be laid down in advance, or administered by any body of men or Government, so as to decide, prescribe and order, without the most evident and unacceptable injustices, how all prices and wages are to start to move in relation to one another,' he told the Commons in the summer of 1973. Nobody had a convincing answer; even Tony Benn noted that it was 'a brilliant academic analysis'. 'People listen to him fascinated by his intellect and clarity,' Benn wrote, 'and he mesmerises Labour MPs like rabbits caught in a headlamp.'[37]

Although Powell's heresy over immigration put him beyond the pale for many politicians, he was not quite a voice crying in the wilderness. By allowing himself to be associated with a radical agenda that he did not really believe in, especially after the Selsdon Man furore, Heath had aroused expectations among right-wing backbenchers that had now been thoroughly disappointed. Even before the election, the clever Tory maverick John Biffen had told Hugo Young that Heath was merely a 'super management consultant', a 'technocrat in politics' with 'no resources of affection or respect to fall back on'. And as early as the summer of 1971, when the government opened the coffers to fight unemployment, economic liberals such as Biffen and Jock Bruce-Gardyne made no secret of their displeasure. As Biffen later put it, 'Ted donned the rather tatty fabrics of socialism and they didn't look any more decorative on him than they had on Harold Wilson.' When Anthony Barber unveiled his notorious boom a year later, the backbench liberals, as well as the growing coterie of monetarist converts associated with the Institute of Economic Affairs, were horrified. In July 1972, the economist Alan Walters, then a part-time adviser to the Central Policy Review Staff, sent Heath a paper warning of 15 per cent inflation in two years' time (an underestimate, as it turned out), only to be ignored and eventually relieved of his job. That November, Walters helped to put together a public 'Memorial to the Prime Minister', signed by eight prominent monetarists, warning that 'profligate' public spending was out of control, and begging Heath to slow the growth of the money supply. Of course the government took no notice. But on the Tory benches, something was stirring.[38]

For a generation of Thatcherite Conservatives, influenced by the likes of Powell and Biffen as well as by the free-market Institute of Economic Affairs and the converted Sir Keith Joseph, Heath's U-turn over incomes policy was the greatest of his many betrayals. As early as September 1973, a group of disaffected right-wingers set up the Selsdon Group, convinced that the free-market values of 1970 had been sacrificed by a crypto-socialist government obsessed with the 'Middle Ground' and indifferent to genuine 'Conservative principles'. This was Thatcherism in embryo, dripping with contempt for Heath's endless U-turns, his betrayal of the Selsdon promises, his appeasement of the unions, and his craven return to inflationary public spending. And in one sense they had an almost unanswerable case. As events were to show, incomes policies were not a very good way of fighting inflation. They might keep a tight lid on inflation in the short term, but, as Wilson had already found in the late 1960s, they could not last for ever. As soon as the lid was lifted, the frustrated expectations of millions of workers boiled over, and the invariable result was more inflation than ever. In the Commons, Heath explained that Stage One was only a temporary expedient, buying time for him to reach a voluntary deal with the unions. If that failed, he would simply move into the next stage of a long-term policy, with the lifting of the lid endlessly postponed. The irony, though, was that he had missed a deeper point. By the end of 1972, pay deals were only one factor in the rising inflation, which was driven by soaring world commodity prices and by the wild monetary incontinence of the credit boom. Not even the toughest incomes policy in the world could do much about them.[39]

In a broader sense, though, Heath's critics were wrong. Their image of Heath in 1970, after all, was based on Harold Wilson's 'Selsdon Man' caricature, which made him appear much more radical than he really was. Unlike Powell or Biffen, he was never really a free-marketeer; instead, he thought of himself as a technocratic modernizer, using whatever tools were necessary to turn Britain around. Although he had borrowed free-market language in 1970, this was what his biographer calls 'the opportunism of Opposition'. In fact, ideology left him cold; to the perennially impatient and empirical Heath, all that mattered was results. As his friend Robert Carr later explained, the U-turns were merely 'tactical', while the 'strategy' – to turn Britain into a dynamic, competitive, high-growth economy – 'remained very strong and coherent'. And in this respect, far from being a botched and bowdlerized version of Thatcherism, his approach was not so different from that of his old mentor Harold Macmillan, another modernizer scarred by memories of the Hungry Thirties. Indeed, with its talk of planning, its wage freezes and its mad dash for growth, the Macmillan government looks uncannily like a dry run for Heath's stint in Downing Street.[40]

The crucial point, though, is that, like Macmillan before him, Heath was governing at a time when the old Keynesian consensus, however battered and bruised, was still deeply embedded in the body politic. As the horrified reaction to the figure of one million unemployed in January 1972 shows, the press and the general public were still tightly attached to full employment. And if Heath *had* followed Powell's advice and taken a strict free-market approach, matters would surely have worked out very differently from how they did later under Mrs Thatcher. When he took office in 1970, after all, there had been no miners' strike, no oil crisis, no inflation at more than 25 per cent, no IMF crisis and no Winter of Discontent. Although there was a deep thirst for modernization, there was little appetite for the radical surgery of the early 1980s. Indeed, given how violently people reacted to what Heath actually did in his first couple of years, he might well have provoked a general strike if he had adopted even more Thatcherite policies. And unlike Mrs Thatcher, he would have got little support from the press, the Civil Service or even much of his own party. Not only were many Tory MPs desperate for him to take action against unemployment, but even newspapers like *The Times*, which later backed Mrs Thatcher all the way, were still firmly attached to full employment, statutory incomes policies and big-spending Keynesian expansion. Perhaps most revealingly, the principal architects of Thatcherism – Sir Keith Joseph, Sir Geoffrey Howe and the future Prime Minister herself – did not spend the early 1970s begging Heath to take a harder line. Instead they spent them inside his Cabinet, nodding and smiling at his alleged U-turns, and, in the cases of Joseph and Thatcher, enthusiastically throwing around enormous sums of public money. At that stage, the idea that they were the sworn enemies of the post-war consensus would have seemed absurd.[41]

This explains why, at the time, Heath's supposed U-turn attracted surprisingly little criticism outside the hard-core Selsdon Group. By the summer of 1972, with wages rising at almost 17 per cent a year, not only was the Treasury pressing for statutory restraint but newspapers across the spectrum, from *The Times* and *The Economist* to the *Guardian* and the *New Statesman*, were begging the government to change tack. 'A statutory incomes policy', said *The Times* in a leader entitled 'How To Fight Inflation' on 16 June, 'ought to be a normal part of national economic policy' – a remark which, coming from the paper most asso-ciated with the rise of monetarism, revealed how deeply social democratic assumptions were embedded in the political establishment. Indeed, Heath's old rival for the Tory leadership, Reginald Maudling, never lost an opportunity to remind colleagues that he backed a sweeping statutory policy. 'The old classical economics are no longer relevant to a wholly new political situation,' Maudling told his colleagues in the spring of 1972, calling for 'a far greater degree of systematic control over incomes and prices than we have ever contemplated before'. That a mainstream Conservative was calling for such overt corporatism was a sign of the uncertainty of the day. And even *The Economist*, usually a reliable indicator of free-market thinking, warned in October that inflation posed such a threat to British life that keeping wages and prices down would be worth 'the billion pounds or so a year of emollient economic sillinesses' involved in Heath's partnership with the unions.[42]

And yet although the press applauded the U-turns, there was no disguising the growing sense of unease. With his stiff, impatient manner, Heath had never been especially popular with the Tory grass roots, and he personally had no feel for the party in the country. Confronted by the extravagantly hatted housewives, blue-rinsed ladies, retired colonels and nasal-voiced small businessmen who stuffed envelopes and organized jumble sales on the party's behalf, he often looked as though he had trodden in something. But not only were activists less than impressed with their leader's charm, they were deeply worried by what was happening to their country. It was in the Heath years, after all, that many of the phenomena we lazily associate with the late 1960s – long hair, obscenity, soft drugs, way-out fashions, even superficial things like flared trousers, tie-dyed shirts, long sideburns and affected hippy slang – became popular outside a few corners of London, slowly seeping into the mainstream of British youth culture, to the horror of many middle-aged parents. When they studied their copies of the *Telegraph*, the *Express* or the *Mail* at the breakfast table, they were shocked by the litany of strikes and demonstrations, the tide of pornography and football hooliganism, the student sit-ins, the feminist protests and the Ugandan Asians. When they looked at Britain, they saw a breakdown of politeness and public order, a collapse of discipline and self-restraint, a mounting sense of vandalism, greed and self-interest, embodied by individuals from Arthur Scargill to George Best. And on top of all that, middle-class voters complained of being 'ground between the cost of living on the one hand and a more or less fixed income on the other', as an internal Tory report put it in January 1972. 'Honest middle-class people, good citizens, people with principles and standards' had been abandoned 'in a vacuum', wrote a local official a year later. There was 'a general fear about the state of our society', the party's Advisory Committee on Policy reported in March 1973, and a 'feeling that we are not in control'.[43]

Heath's failure to appease middle-class anxieties was one of his greatest tactical blunders. As so often, he saw himself as a national spokesman, not a party leader: as Norman Tebbit later put it, the government appeared so eager to please the union bosses that it 'seemed always to dump its friends in an effort to buy its enemies'. By contrast, Heath's handling of his own MPs was so inept that it might have been an object lesson in how to prepare one's own downfall. Almost every Prime Minister has to put up with backbench grumbling at one time or other, and by the end of 1972 many Tory MPs were distinctly restless, registering their discontent by electing Heath's old enemy Edward du Cann as chairman of the 1922 Committee. But the problem was not merely disquiet at the Industry Act and the new pay policy. What really infuriated many backbenchers was Heath's dismissive treatment of his own rank and file. He may not have seen them 'as cattle to be driven through the gates of the lobby', as the *Spectator*'s Patrick Cosgrave claimed in December 1972, but he certainly treated them with reckless rudeness, consistently refusing to hear their complaints, to take unwelcome advice, or even to acknowledge that they were there at all. One Tory backbencher later confided to Simon Heffer that Heath had once told him that there were 'three sorts of people in this party: shits, bloody shits and fucking shits'. He certainly treated most of them as though they belonged in the final category. Rebellion was not yet inevitable. But with every snub and slight, every greeting ignored and every grumpy remark, Heath was creating the conditions for an uprising.[44]

9

Metro-Land

Well, what's wrong with being the same as everyone else? What's wrong with trying to make a little bit of modest progress?
– Bob Ferris, in *Whatever Happened to the Likely Lads?* (1973)

As London's commuters trudged home on the dark winter's evening of Monday, 26 February 1973, the headlines made for miserable reading. With the unions in revolt against Stage Two of Heath's pay policy, more than half a million people, from Civil Service clerical staff and non-medical hospital staff to train drivers, firemen and Ford car workers were planning to walk out in the next three days. Both the railway network and the London Underground were expected to shut down, and experts were already warning of chaos on the roads. So gloomy were the predictions of traffic jams on the main routes into Britain's major cities that thousands of people were expected to stay at home. So it seemed supremely ironic that the highlight of that night's television was a BBC2 film celebrating London's first and fastest Underground line, the Metropolitan, the original artery of the capital's commuter network.[1]

Edward Mirzoeff's film *Metro-Land,* which follows the poet Sir John Betjeman along the Metropolitan Line's north-western branch from the heart of the capital into rural Buckinghamshire, was not so much a tribute to the capital's public transport network as a lyrical celebration of what had followed in its wake: the sprawling suburbs of Greater London, from Neasden and Harrow to Pinner and Amersham, a mosaic of grand houses and modernist stations, country hedgerows and suburban golf courses, mock-Tudor villas and art deco cinemas. During the early decades of the century, Metro-land had been a marketing slogan, designed to promote both the line and the housing estates that sprang up around its stations. It was a symbol of the middle classes and of Middle England, of suburban gentility and material ambition; it was a marriage of urban and rural, neither town nor country, tantalizingly close to London but (at least according to the brochures) surrounded by quiet, empty fields. Millions dreamed of owning their own Metro-land home, their own bow-windowed, fake-timbered house in Harrow or Ruislip. Intellectuals saw it as the supreme symbol of narrowness, materialism and sheer bad taste, the symbol of mass affluence and suburban banality. Yet even suburbia's most virulent critics temporarily put their hatred aside after Betjeman's tribute to Rickmansworth and Chorleywood, so taken were they with his blend of melancholy and celebration. In the *Observer*, Clive James called it an 'instant classic', and predicted that it would be repeated 'until the millennium'. But the review Betjeman liked best came in affectionate verse from his friend Simon Jenkins in the *Evening Standard*: 'For an hour he held enraptured / Pinner, Moor Park, Chorley Wood. / "Well I'm blowed," they said. "He likes us. / Knew one day that someone should."'[2]

What was so striking about *Metro-Land*, as Betjeman pottered amiably from a half-timbered mansion at Harrow Weald to the golf course at Moor Park, was his deep affection for London's suburban fringes, which emerged as far more interesting and quirky than most viewers had suspected. For the Poet Laureate to be waxing lyrical about the joys of Neasden (the 'home of the gnome and the average citizen', as he put it) seemed quite extraordinary, for everyone knew that the suburbs were terrible places, dull and soulless at best, claustrophobic and confining at worst. In *Private Eye*, for which Betjeman had once written, Neasden was the symbol of everything base, boring and banal, the very worst of Middle England, the place where romance and imagination came to die. Indeed, hatred of the suburbs had an impressive pedigree: in the early years of the century, intellectuals from George Bernard Shaw and G. K. Chesterton to E. Nesbit and E. M. Forster had queued up to denounce their 'dullness and small-mindedness'. To the high-minded and well bred, the fact that Metro-land represented a dream come true for millions of ordinary families, not just in London but across the nation, was beside the point. Intellectuals loathed its mock-Elizabethan façades, its quiet leafy streets, its crowds of clerks on the station platforms at dawn and dusk. For the writer Cyril Connolly, the suburbs were 'incubators of apathy and delirium', while Graham Greene shuddered at their 'sinless, empty, graceless chromium world', Suburbia is 'just a prison with the cells all in a row,' says the narrator in George Orwell's novel *Coming Up for Air* (1939), imagining thousands of clerks, just like himself, 'with the boss twisting his tail and his wife riding him like the nightmare and the kids sucking his blood like leeches'.[3]

Although the 1950s and 1960s had been decades of tremendous growth for housing estates and New Towns, Metro-land's image remained as bad as ever. Architects and planners were quick to condemn what they saw as the suburbs' ugly, monotonous conservatism, while in the novels, plays and films of the period, to be suburban is to be cheap, crass, joyless and materialistic. Urban legend had it that the suburbs were unfriendly, loveless places, without warmth or community, where husbands mechanically washed their cars every weekend and wives pined for excitement behind their net curtains. Even pop and rock music, which had millions of followers in the suburbs, presented the same mocking picture. The Kinks' album *Muswell Hillbillies* (1971), which affectionately evokes the Davies brothers' youth in the suburbs of North London, was a rare exception: more conventional was the attitude of the punk bands of the late 1970s, which took a uniformly hostile view of suburbia and its inhabitants. The very first lines of the Members' song 'Sound of the Suburbs' (1978), for instance, caustically describe the atmosphere of a 'same old boring Sunday morning': Dad outside washing his car, Mum in the kitchen cooking Sunday dinner, Johnny upstairs annoying the neighbours with his electric guitar. That the same year saw the release of Siouxsie & the Banshees' 'Suburban Relapse', narrated by a housewife who snaps and lashes out while washing the dishes, reinforces the impression that punk bands had their knives out for Metro-land. The suburbs were 'middle-class' and 'puritanical', full of people 'always going on about Hitler,' remarked the singer Siouxsie Sioux – actually Susan Ballion from Bromley.[4]

The most sustained and popular indictment of suburbia, however, came in the television sitcoms so popular in the mid-1970s. In a sense, the fact that so many sitcoms were set in greater Metro-land, from *Bless this House* and *Happy Ever After* to *Butterflies* and *George and Mildred*, was a testament to its newfound place at the centre of Britain's physical and imaginative landscape. And yet their portrait of a monotonous world of lonely, frustrated housewives and henpecked husbands might have been scripted by the upper-class intellectuals of the inter-war years.

When Terry Collier first visits his friend Bob Ferris's new estate in *Whatever Happened to the Likely Lads?*, his indictment is pure Cyril Connolly. 'There's just something depressing about these estates,' Terry says gloomily. 'It's the thought of you all: all getting up at the same time, all eating the same sort of low-calorie breakfast, all coming home at half-past-six and watching the same programme at the same time and having it off the same two nights of the week.' The only way residents can 'tell the difference' between the individual houses, he concludes caustically, 'is by the colour of your curtains.'[5]

But while Bob angrily defends his new suburban existence, pointing out that his new home represents a 'little bit of modest progress', not all sitcom characters were so content with their lot. The struggle of the individual against his suburban shackles is one of the central themes of mid-1970s comedies, encapsulated most famously in the series *The Good Life* (1975–8) and *The Fall and Rise of Reginald Perrin* (1976–9). In the former, the Goods begin the series as a classic suburban couple: Tom a draughtsman designing toys for cereal packets, and Barbara a perky middle-class Surbiton housewife. But the real incarnations of Metro-land are their neighbours, Jerry and Margo Leadbetter (played by Paul Eddington and Penelope Keith): the former urbane, ambitious but a little henpecked; the latter one of the great fictional characters of the era, a humourless, snobbish social climber, a pillar of the Pony Club, the Music Society and the local Conservative Party. Hers is a world of manicured respectability, with everything in its place and no room for surprises – which is precisely why the Goods' decision to become sustainable farmers horrifies her so much. And no doubt Margo would have been equally appalled by the antics of Reginald Perrin (Leonard Rossiter) in David Nobbs's series – an ostensibly respectable middle-class executive, driven to the brink of a nervous breakdown by insecurity and impotence, by simmering rage at late-running trains, by the sheer monotony of life in Metro-land.[6]

As a bored middle-aged sales executive for a company making trifles and ice cream, Reggie Perrin was well placed to appreciate the changing world of middle-class work. When men like Reggie entered the workplace in the mid-1950s, most middle-class workers expected to follow a straight and stable career path, often spending their entire lives within the same organization, rewarded not just with progressively rising salaries, pension plans and investments, but with a sense of professionalism, status and respect. Men who worked for established institutions such as banks and insurance companies often talked of having a job for life. 'If I worked hard, I had a really worthwhile career ahead of me,' reflected one man, who left school in the early 1960s and joined Lloyds Bank. 'In return for that, the bank expected loyalty from me and my colleagues, but it repaid that loyalty by the job continuity and the salary and career opportunities which were offered to us.' Another man, who joined the Prudential, echoed his sentiments. 'The Pru were good employers,' he said later. 'We always felt they liked their pound of flesh, with perhaps a drop of blood as well, but they looked after us if we were in trouble.'[7]

Although the disappearance of these cosy assumptions is often associated with Thatcherism, the signs had been there for years. For a new generation of ambitious white-collar workers, often boys from working-class homes who owed their success to a grammar-school education, the old values of deference, hierarchy and organizational loyalty held little appeal. Writing in the *Radio Times* in 1968, one social analyst described a typical example: a working-class boy who had passed his eleven-plus, left school to join an office equipment firm, became a travelling salesman and bought a suburban home with all the trimmings, including a pink plastic pelican on the manicured front lawn. Married at 27, he had joined the local Conservative Party and sent his children to private nursery schools, and he had no intention of resting on his laurels. Thrusting, ambitious, he was precisely the kind of man Edward Heath admired and that Reggie Perrin hated, and he was a common archetype in the popular culture of the 1970s. In John Betjeman's poem 'Executive', published in 1974, he is the 'young executive' with clean cuffs, a Slimline briefcase, a company Cortina and a scarlet Aston Martin, as well as a 'speed-boat which has never touched the water', named *Mandy Jane* 'after a bird I used to know'. In Alan Ayckbourn's play *Absurd Person Singular* (1972), he is the socially inept, much-derided contractor Sidney Hopcroft, who claws his way up the ladder by turning himself into a local property tycoon, and ends the play a triumphant proto-Thatcherite figure, literally forcing his architect and banker friends to dance to his tune in a game of musical forfeits. And in Martin Amis's novel *Success* (1978), he is the aggressively proletarian Terry Service, who goes to evening classes, works in an open-plan office in a 'big efficient building' fittingly called Masters House, and rapidly overtakes his arty half-brother Gregory. 'The yobs are winning,' Gregory says in despair – a sentiment often repeated during the following decade.[8]

For those like Terry Service, willing to work long hours and clamber over their colleagues to get up the ladder, the rewards were great. Many observers lamented the new culture of middle-class materialism: writing in *Encounter* in October 1974, the market-research pioneer Mark Abrams warned that 'the value system of most people in Britain today is solidly grounded in materialism', and that many were satisfied only by 'the act of spending by itself . . . almost irrespective of what is bought'. But neither the woes of the stock market nor the cancer of inflation could check the new 'money culture', as some called it. By the end of the decade even the mass-market *Daily Mail* had a Wednesday 'Money Mail' page offering advice on financial affairs, while the Ideal Home Exhibition at Olympia opened a special Money Mail section in 1979, including stands run by the Stock Exchange and the School Fees Insurance Agency.[9]

But with greater rewards came greater pressures. In *Whatever Happened to the Likely Lads?*, the ambitious Bob admits that for all the trappings of success – the secretary, the company car, the candlelit dinners and foreign holidays – he is virtually sick with worry about 'the sheer volume of things you have to do: study, go to work, service the car, claim rebates on the rates, worry about whether I can take Thelma to Morocco' – a far cry from his lazy friend Terry's daily grind of betting shops and billiard halls. But Bob was far from alone: in workplaces across the country, expectations and anxieties were greater than ever. Open-plan offices replaced the old warrens of hierarchical little rooms, so that everyone could see what their colleagues were up to. Perhaps not coincidentally, even before the advent of Thatcherism and the Big Bang, City workers were giving up their long lunch breaks in favour of spending more time at their desks. Executive dining rooms began to die out, City restaurants reported falling lunchtime demand, and in 1979 Robin Birley opened the Square Mile's first sandwich bar in Fenchurch Street. Even the beloved tea trolleys of old were disappearing, replaced by vending machines that were no good at making tea but made a better fist of providing Nescafé instant coffee – the ideal drink for a highly pressured, hard-working environment in which white-collar executives faced the real prospect of being sacked if profits fell, if they failed to meet their targets, or, even more frighteningly, if a computer could do their job more cheaply and more quickly.[10]

It was hardly surprising, then, that researchers in the mid-1970s found that managers and executives were spending more and more time at weekends worrying about their work. 'When I'm in the bath or mowing the lawn, I'm often trying to figure out some problem or other,' confessed a sales manager from Sutton. 'If you saw me very happily sitting in the garden with a drink at my side I might be thinking over a problem,' agreed a manager from Caterham. 'If you came along beside me you might be talking to me for ten minutes and I wouldn't hear you, I'd be so concentrated.' Perhaps it was no surprise, either, that so many marriages broke up. 'I said that I never take work home,' said a service manager from St Albans. 'That's true – not paper work. But unfortunately it remains in my head. There are the usual domestic problems as a result.' And with wives and mothers increasingly joining the workplace, the report's conclusion was bleakly prophetic. 'Strains will be inescapable,' wrote Michael Young and Peter Willmott, warning that if the trends continued, 'there will inevitably be more divorces'.[11]

Even though more middle-class managers brought their work home at evenings and weekends, the suburban home remained an idealized refuge from the pressures of the office. Mass home ownership was a relatively recent phenomenon: in 1950, just over one in four families had owned their own home, but by 1970 half of them did so. And although intellectuals derided the mock-Tudor or mock-Georgian houses of the suburbs, with their clipped privet hedges and regimented flower beds, their garden gnomes, sundials and rockeries, the vast majority of British families held them in high esteem. Almost nine out of ten people told researchers in 1968 that a suburban house represented 'the ideal home'. And since so many people, even relatively young couples, could remember the cramped terraced streets and crowded tenements of old, it is hardly surprising that owning their own home meant a tremendous amount to them. It was not just a question of wealth and status: it meant success, comfort, liberation. In the first episode of *Whatever Happened to the Likely Lads?*, Bob Ferris's suburban home on the new Hillfields estate in Killingworth is not quite finished, but he and his fiancée Thelma are already entertaining themselves by looking at slides of the estate being built. 'Oh Bob! The damp course!' says Thelma with feeling. 'My house!' muses Bob. 'You know, I can't get used to saying that.' '*Our* house,' she gently corrects him. 'I know, pet. It's our house,' he concedes, trying the words out for size: 'Chez nous.'[12]

For fictional couples like Bob and Thelma or the Leadbetters in *The*

Good Life, as well as for millions of real-life couples, the home assumed tremendous importance because it was the centre of the nuclear family. Researchers agreed that the extended family had almost entirely died out: as early as the 1940s, surveys had revealed a ubiquitous dream of marriage, two children and a quiet suburban life, unencumbered by parents-in-law and other relatives. With husbands and wives spending far more time together – playing with their children, shopping, pursuing hobbies, going on holiday – the home was not merely a place where people ate and slept, but where they relaxed, entertained and expressed their values and desires. And just as possession of the right appliances had been a crucial badge of status during the 1950s and 1960s, when millions of people had rushed to buy televisions, fridges and washing machines, so the right furniture and decorations assumed tremendous importance in the 1970s.[13]

In the early days of Metro-land, suburban semi-detached houses had preserved a kind of rustic-modern blend, as though the look and values of the English countryside had been trapped and tamed within a distinctly non-rural roadside setting. And despite the fact that most families were more remote from agriculture than ever, this nostalgic ethos still dominated suburban life in the 1970s. Both new estates and individual houses often had faux-rustic names ('The Larches', 'Rose Hill', and so on), while most families liked to decorate their homes with ornaments and knick-knacks that looked back to an idealized past: reproductions of Constable paintings and Dutch landscapes, Swiss mountain views and gypsy-girl portraits, old-fashioned clocks and barometers, plaster plaques and china models of thatched country cottages, intricate little clipper ships and galleons, china statuettes and painted plates, and of course the flight of ceramic ducks winging their way across the wall. As time went on, these were joined by mementoes of holidays in Spain or France. But the overall effect was both nostalgic and socially ambitious, like the rows of leather-bound encyclopedias that would be proudly displayed in the sitting room, or the stripped-pine furniture that became so popular in the mid-1970s.

The tragedy, of course, was that while all these things were meant to lift the household into a higher social class, they became unmistakable and faintly comic markers of suburban aspirations to gentility. In Piers Paul Read's novel *A Married Man* (1979), the protagonist, a left-wing barrister, is deeply embarrassed by his mother's collection of china statuettes because her 'bad tastes betrayed not only her origins but also her pretensions, for she believed that her collection, although not quite equal to the treasures of Castle Howard, was a step in that direction'. Yet he is also 'ashamed of his own embarrassment', because he knows it is unfair to expect her to have the good taste of the upper middle classes. 'It was the social connotations which he minded most,' he admits, 'as if she had spoken with a regional accent or had smelt of sweat because she never took a bath. His objections to her china ornaments were snobbish objections and he knew it.'[14]

But the obsession with nostalgia was not confined to ornaments. The very design of the home, its wallpapers, curtains and carpets, was often deliberately 'period', to use a popular term of the day, as though the right furnishings would sprinkle timeless elegance on a nondescript suburban house that might have existed for only months. Mock-Georgian tables and chairs were supposedly 'hand-carved' by craftsmen in the 'traditional' way, while a typical advert in the *Sunday Times* in 1977 offered the 'Ambassador' silver-plated 'Georgian' tea and coffee set, designed to be 'displayed proudly in the home' (rather than, say, actually used). Stripped-pine and wood furniture was enormously popular: the travel writer Jonathan Raban recorded in 1974 that London shops 'like Habitat, Casa Pupo, and David Bagott Design sell home-made-looking tables and chairs in bulky stripped pine which are actually mass produced and mass-marketed'. In gentrifying areas like Kensington and Islington he had seen supposedly '"craftsmen's" shops selling roughly identical lines in clear-varnished wood', while friends boasted stereos in 'grainy deal cabinets' and even a 'stripped-pine fridge'.

On their walls, ambitious couples stuck highly decorated, heavily textured Laura Ashley wallpaper; on their floors, they placed fur rugs and extravagantly patterned carpets; in their bathrooms, they laid synthetic tiles imitating mosaics or marble. The effect was meant to be lush, luxurious, elegant. In fact, since many Laura Ashley or William Morris patterns had been intended for much bigger rooms, the real effect was often dark and claustrophobic, a wild collision of lurid patterns, which is why the 1970s became a byword for bad taste. But like the barrister's mother in Piers Paul Read's novel, most people had grown up in much more straitened circumstances, had never learned the difference between 'good' and 'bad' taste, and simply wanted to emulate their social superiors. To a newly affluent couple, the juxtaposition of a mock-fur rug, a gleaming stereo in a stripped-pine cabinet, a row of Toby jugs,

Morris-style curtains and faux-velvet wallpaper meant elegance and class. Only later, long after the decade had become synonymous with the colour brown, did they look back and shudder.[15]

The popularity of home decorating was just one illustration of the increasingly domesticated, family-centred world of leisure in the Heath years. Where husbands had once gone out to the pub with their friends, they now stayed at home, perhaps pottering about the garden, mowing the lawn, weeding and planting bulbs. Gardening had long been held up as a symbol of the British character, but never had it been more popular: by 1970, four-fifths of all homes had a garden, and an estimated 29 million people regularly lavished time on their little plot of earth, tending their flower beds, building their patios and piling up their rockeries. And although gardening was widely seen as a symbol of British conservatism, individualism and domesticity, it also reflected the technological innovations and mass affluence of the day. *Gardener's World*, shown on BBC2 from 1968, was one of the channel's most popular shows, while garden centres were besieged at weekends by couples hunting for plastic tools, chemical weedkillers and Flymo's pioneering electric hover-mowers. So popular was gardening, in fact, that it played an increasingly central role in the long-running Ideal Home Exhibition. In 1974, for the first time, gardens dominated the Grand Hall, with an enormous and rather baroque interpretation of the Hanging Gardens of Babylon mounted overhead. It was revealing that some of the exhibition's longest queues formed outside the Garden Advice Centre, set in a mock English cottage garden – and revealing too that its panel of experts included television stars such as Percy Thrower and Geoff Hamilton.[16]

If the popularity of gardening, which was second only to watching television as the most popular leisure activity in the country, testified to the modesty and conservatism of everyday life in Metro-land, then so did other favourite hobbies and habits, from country drives, car-cleaning and stamp-collecting to the pony clubs and music societies beloved of *The Good Life*'s Margo. Instead of radically recasting tastes and attitudes, in fact, the affluence of recent years often worked to reinforce them. So while Britain had long been renowned as a nation of animal-lovers and bird-fanciers, it was not until the 1970s that many middle-class families acquired a dog (which was expensive to maintain), or that membership of the RSPB rose above 100,000. Even young men supposedly at the vanguard of glamour and affluence, such as the working-class footballers interviewed by Hunter Davies during his season with Tottenham Hotspur, led markedly conservative lives, settling down in mock-Georgian homes in Enfield and Epping and spending their weekends playing golf and tennis. Britain was still George Orwell's nation of stamp-collectors and pigeon-fanciers, wrote Anthony Sampson in his *New Anatomy of Britain* in 1971, a nation of 'lawn-mowers, pets, caravans and, inevitably, do-it-yourself . . . the greatest nation in Europe for handymen and potterers-about'. What emerged, he thought, was 'a broad picture . . . of the British living a withdrawn and inarticulate life, rather like Harold Pinter's people, mowing lawns and painting walls, pampering pets, listening to music, knitting and watching television'.[17]

One obvious addition to the list of hobbies, however, was shopping. It was not long since most housewives had visited their local high street several times a day, with food kept covered in the larder rather than chilled in the fridge. Even in 1971, according to one survey, the average housewife went shopping for groceries three times a week. But at least one of those trips was now a 'major' trip, usually to a supermarket. By the beginning of the decade there were about 3,000 little supermarkets in Britain, and bigger versions were on their way. In September 1972, Carrefour opened the first out-of-town, 60,000-square-foot 'hyper-market' in Caerphilly, and a second opened in Telford a year later. Despite the warnings of environmental campaigners and consumer advocates, they proved enormously popular; so popular, indeed, that Carrefour took the unusual step of asking customers to stay away because the traffic jams were so bad. And where Carrefour led, others were quick to follow. By 1974, Asda had opened 27 'superstores' of more than 25,000 square feet, while the Co-op had opened 23, Fine Fare 21, Tesco 20 and Morrisons 11. Although some protesters objected that they were bound to damage local traders, a much wider complaint was that there were not enough superstores, and press reports often suggested that, in this respect as in many others, Britain was lagging well behind its neighbours. A spokesman for Debenhams even predicted that the 'trendy, out-of-town superstore with its cut-price shopping and easy parking will become a British institution'. *The Times*, however, thought this was a little unlikely. Town centres would continue to thrive, it observed, because most people would surely baulk at having 'to travel three or four miles for shopping'.[18]

What *The Times* had overlooked was the phenomenon of shopping not as a necessity but as a pleasure, a leisure activity in itself. Although some housewives complained that they missed the local gossip of the high street, others said that they actively relished the vast choice of the hypermarket. As one explained in 1974, she loved supermarket shopping 'if I've got the time and lots of money, and I know I can choose all these lovely foods'. And of course many housewives no longer went shopping alone. Even in the late 1960s, more than one in three husbands regularly accompanied their wives on shopping trips, and by 1982 one in four husbands often did the grocery themselves, armed with a shopping list and stern instructions 'what to buy where'. Children also played their part: it was estimated in 1970 that they exercised some influence over 15 per cent of family purchases, especially cakes, biscuits, confectionery and cereals, which were often packaged with toys or offers appealing to youthful consumers. Shopping, in other words, had become yet another kind of family entertainment, and canny entrepreneurs were quick to cash in. By 1976, the nation's first major shopping centre had opened at Brent Cross, north London, and within three years it had been followed by similarly vast malls such as the Mander Centre in Wolverhampton and the Arndale Centre in Manchester, temples to the new gods of affluence, consumerism and material ambition.[19]

In many respects, what people bought at these new shopping centres was simply 'more of the same', as the historian Arthur Marwick puts it. By the late 1970s, almost all households had at least one television, 88 per cent had a fridge, 71 per cent a washing machine and 52 per cent a car. Only half, though, had a telephone, and just 3 per cent a dishwasher, which was a treat reserved for the richest or most forward-thinking. There was much talk of calculators and home computers, but not until 1980 did Spectrum release the pioneering ZX-80, which sold an unprecedented 50,000 units and paved the way for Britain to lead the world in computer ownership during the Thatcher years. Video recorders, too, were keenly anticipated, but few families owned one: by the end of 1978, just 136,000 had been sold, although in the long run home videos obviously represented the beginning of a seismic shift in broadcasting and entertainment. And there were other signs of change in what people bought in 1978: the £1 billion spent on DIY products, for example, or the surging sales of wine, soft drinks, perfumes and deodorants, or even the staggering 44 million pairs of jeans.[20]

In terms of white goods, though, the big success story of the 1970s was the deep freezer. In 1970 only about 4 per cent of British homes had one; by 1972, 8 per cent; by 1978, 41 per cent, a tenfold increase in just eight years. Frozen food was already associated with laziness, obesity and morbid addiction to the television: during the 1950s, Elizabeth David had bitterly attacked restaurateurs and housewives alike for using frozen peas, and in 1972 the critic Barry Norman mocked 'the average pleb, dozing in his carpet slippers in front of his set with his pre-frozen dinner congealing on his lap'. None of this, however, seemed to deter the average pleb. By the mid-1970s, even small grocery stores had brought in freezer chests to hold Birds Eye fish fingers, McCain's oven chips and Walls ice cream, with frozen Vesta curries, coq au vin and chicken à la king for the adventurous. Meanwhile, dedicated 'freezer centres' had made their first appearance on the high street, the most successful, Iceland, having been opened in Oswestry in 1970 by a group of bored Woolworths employees. Woolworths promptly fired the founders from their day jobs, but, like most things from Shropshire, the venture proved a roaring success. By 1975, there were fifteen Iceland stores across the northern Midlands and North Wales, and three years later Iceland opened its first superstore in Manchester. Meanwhile, by the beginning of the 1980s Birds Eye were making almost £13 million a year from their frozen Oven Crispy Cod, £12 million from their Steakhouse Grills and £5 million from Viennetta ice cream. They had rather missed the boat, however, on that other great frozen success story, the pizza, which accounted for a staggering £60 million a year in total sales by 1983. As one marketing man explained, the pizza looked set to become 'the beans on toast of the eighties'.[21]

Frozen food, which probably transformed the British diet more than any other innovation of the post-war years, succeeded simply because it was so convenient. With middle-class Britons working longer and more irregular hours, and with even married women flooding into the workplace, frozen food naturally appealed to harassed parents and exhausted mothers. There was even a minor genre of frozen-food cookbooks, advising women how to prepare shepherd's pies, casseroles and goulash in bulk before parcelling them into containers for freezing, how to quick-blanch peas and carrots before freezing them too, and even how to freeze cottage cheese, pâtés and, bizarrely, sardine sandwiches. Convenience was all; even cooks who disdained frozen food often found themselves tempted by dishes like Marks & Spencer's Chicken Kiev, launched in 1976 to become the unrivalled bestseller of the 'ready meal' world. Then there was Cadbury's Smash, a packet of granules aimed at people too busy (in other words, too lazy) to make their own mashed potatoes, and famously advertised on television by a group of robotic Martians. Even the Great British Breakfast was not immune from the lust for convenience: by 1976, a study for Kellogg's found that only 20 per cent of the working public began the day with bacon and eggs, compared with 40 per cent who ate cereal and 25 per cent who had nothing but a cup of tea or coffee. And as people became used to speed at home, so they demanded speed when they ate out: it was in 1974 that the sinister arches of McDonald's were first raised over the streets of London.[22]

The paradox is that while many people ate terribly during the 1970s – an evening meal of a boil-in-bag chicken curry followed by Angel Delight, say, or tinned chilli con carne and Neapolitan ice cream – the possibilities for eating well were greater than ever. Popular accounts of the decade often present it as a time when chillies, aubergines and courgettes were unheard of: when Sam Tyler, the detective from the future in the BBC's twenty-first-century series *Life on Mars*, ponders buying olive oil and coriander, Gene Hunt warns him that in Trafford Park 'you've got more chance of finding an ostrich with a plum up its arse'. But Britain in 1973 was not just a wasteland of spaghetti hoops and cheese-and-pineapple skewers. Visiting inner-city Nottingham a few years earlier, researchers had been struck by the Central European delicatessen selling Polish delicacies, the Indian shops stocking 'sweet potatoes and yams', the Chinese chop suey restaurants and the 'crowded Italian corner-shop . . . with its baskets of aubergines and green peppers outside, and inside a passing glimpse of pasta in every shape and size'. Still, while most people were keen to try new things, their tastes remained strikingly conservative. When Piers Paul Read's barrister protagonist takes his mistress out for lunch, they have 'avocado pear with prawns' followed by fillet steak; when Kingsley Amis's Oxford don Jake Richardson makes himself a slap-up dinner, he has 'avocado pear with prawns' again followed by trout with almonds and Brussels sprouts; and when a policeman in Margaret Drabble's novel *The Ice Age* (1977) describes the best meal of his life, it consists of pâté, prawn cocktail, steak and chips, and Black Forest gateau. And when Gallup asked people in 1973 to choose their 'perfect meal if expense were no object and you could have absolutely anything you wanted', the ideal menu turned out to be sherry, tomato soup, prawn cocktail, steak and chips, sherry trifle and cheese and biscuits, a line-up almost identical to the one people had chosen twenty-five years previously.[23]

One thing that had changed, though, was that more and more middle-class couples liked to entertain friends and colleagues to dinner in their own homes, partly as a way of showing off their perfect lawns, three-piece suites and collections of china figurines, but also as a chance for the (almost always female) cook to demonstrate her mastery of the new culinary trends. Previously a habit reserved for the rich, the dinner party was the supreme suburban ritual of the 1970s and the ultimate test of a wife's organizational skills, which is why women's magazines spent so much time advising on everything from the best pre-dinner drinks – Campari and soda, say, or Bacardi and coke – to the ideal books to leave on the coffee table. As for the food, many cooks turned for inspiration to the highly elaborate recipes of writers like the Anglo-American television chef Robert Carrier, presenting a waist-expanding selection of pastry crescents, heavy cream sauces, stuffed vegetables, lobster soufflés, sweet and sour meatballs or veal goulash, served with a chilled bottle or two of Mateus Rosé. Contrary to popular belief, however, there is no evidence of people swapping partners on these occasions; in any case, the average housewife would have been far too worried about the state of her sherry trifle to contemplate a quick tumble with Terry from Accounts.[24]

By far the biggest influence on the suburban cook was a pretty young woman who first appeared on television in September 1973, presenting simple ten-minute recipes in a converted BBC weather studio and coming across, in the words of the *Telegraph*'s reviewer, as 'a friendly, unaffected young housewife at home in the kitchen'. The daughter of a Bexleyheath ironmonger, Delia Smith had left school in the late 1950s without a single qualification, and spent the 1960s working as a hairdresser, shop assistant, washer-up and waitress. After becoming interested in cooking at her workplace, a little Paddington restaurant, she began taking notes on popular dishes, and even visited the British Museum's Reading Room to bone up on recipes from the past. In 1969, she landed a job writing recipes for the *Daily Mirror*'s new lifestyle magazine, and three years later she moved to the *Evening Standard*, where she stayed for twelve years. By this point her first book, *How to Cheat at Cooking* (1971), had already done well, and she was on her way to becoming a publishing phenomenon. *The Evening Standard Cookbook*, *Frugal Food* and *Cakes, Bakes and Steaks* soon followed, but her biggest success was *Delia Smith's Complete Cookery Course*, published in three annual volumes from 1978 onwards to accompany her BBC series. Often lampooned, not least for her deep Catholic faith and vociferous support for Norwich City, she could not, however, be dismissed. No other British cook, not Elizabeth David, not Fanny Cradock, not Marguerite Patten, had more influence over what ordinary people had for dinner.[25]

The key to Delia's success was that her recipes, unlike those of other cooks, were designed for real people too busy to worry about elaborate sauces and time-consuming marinades. Her very first cookbook, the aptly titled *How to Cheat at Cooking*, encouraged readers to use packet sauces and Smash, and not to be afraid of 'tarting up . . . tinned, packet, frozen or dehydrated goods'. Frozen Findus ratatouille or Birds Eye baby onions in cream sauce, Delia advised, could be 'poured over chops or steak to give them an edge'. And she even suggested that busy hostesses serve 'Baked Fish Fingers', a concoction of tinned tomatoes, mushrooms and grated cheese poured over fish fingers, which would be unlikely to fool even the least observant guest, even if, as Delia recommended, there were 'plenty of top-drawer cook-books placed on full view'. Later, of course, she played down the cheating element, and by the mid-1970s Findus ratatouille had disappeared from her repertoire. But her recipes always catered for nervous, insecure and busy cooks – in other words, the great majority of the population. She was a 'down to earth sort of cook', reported *The Times* before her first television appearance, adding that she called herself 'the poor woman's Elizabeth David', was not ashamed of never having studied at cookery school, and practised at home in 'a pair of old jeans that I can get dirty'. As Joan Bakewell remarked seven years later, Delia was in the vanguard of the changes brought by 'the fast-food revolution, freezers and working wives', but 'not so far ahead as to be freaky'. Her recipes were simple and reliable, always a little behind the latest trend, reassuring viewers that 'nowadays' olive oil was quite acceptable instead of salad cream, or introducing them to such novelties as 'cream, bacon and onion tart' (actually quiche Lorraine) or crusty brown bread as an accompaniment to main courses. Her sets were semi-rustic and suburban, her style democratic without being patronizing. 'We live in homes like Delia Smith's, among people like Delia Smith,' Bakewell wrote, '. . . or so she persuades us.'[26]

While Delia Smith presented an image of the perfect suburban house-wife, polite, pretty and endlessly competent, there were other, rather more caustic visions of the domestic hostess. No suburban social event of the 1970s has been more celebrated than Abigail's party, even though in Mike Leigh's *Play for Today* we never meet the teenage Abigail or hear anything but rumours of her notorious gathering. Instead we are confronted by the ghastly Beverly Moss (Alison Steadman), whose suburban drinks party, complete with faux-brown leather sofas, beige wallpaper, bowls of nibbles, plenty of Bacardi and coke and Demis Roussos on the record player, turns domestic entertaining into excruciating black comedy. Beverly is of course a monster: a middle-class social climber, a sexual vulture, a snob obsessed with liking, having and saying the right things. She is the prisoner not only of her insecurities but also of her ambitions: we are meant to laugh at her suburban pretensions ('Is it real silver?' 'Silver plate, yes'), just as we are meant to laugh at Laurence, her overworked estate-agent husband, with his leather-bound volumes of Shakespeare ('Not something you can actually read, of course'), his L. S. Lowry prints and his efforts to impress guests with Beethoven's Ninth. This is a vision not merely of social climbers desperately trying to impress their neighbours, or even of families falling apart in an age of cultural change, but of all the vices of Metro-land, combined and exaggerated: its materialistic one-upmanship, its sexual voraciousness, its lack of community and feeling, its aggressive individualism. As Bernard Levin wrote at the time, it is 'a study of the mores, attitude, conduct and speech of Affluent-Yobbonia', of people without roots, 'torn loose from history, faith, spirit, even language, because they are torn loose from themselves.'[27]

Mike Leigh was not, of course, the only dramatist of the day to unearth what he saw as the insecurity, loneliness and sheer misery behind the façade of contented middle-class affluence. Although Alan Ayckbourn's plays invariably made audiences howl with laughter, the bard of Scarborough was a master at picking apart the seams of marriages and families, uncovering the gruesome hypocrisy beneath the ritualistic Sunday lunches and housewarming parties of suburban life. There is surely no better scene of the decade, for example, than the famous Sunday evening dinner in *Table Manners,* part of his trilogy *The Norman Conquests*, in which the anxieties and unhappiness of Ayckbourn's characters – the fussy, pedantic Reg, the angrily buttoned-up Sarah, the dowdy, frustrated Annie, the bumbling, awkward Tom, the dryly waspish

Ruth and the outrageously needy, predatory Norman – are mercilessly but hilariously laid bare. 'Come on now, don't cry,' Norman tells Annie at the end of a disastrous family weekend. 'I'll make you happy. Don't worry. I'll make you happy.' But happiness seems impossibly distant. For all their obvious affluence, their Home Counties lifestyle and their protestations of contentment, all six characters end the trilogy as they began: deeply lonely, frustrated, resentful people, victims of their own expectations, and of each other.[28]

And yet, for all their comic brilliance, *The Norman Conquests* and *Abigail's Party* were misleading guides to suburban life. For although writers liked to imagine that suburbanites were selfish, unhappy, lonely people, forever teetering on the brink of some terrible Reggie Perrin-style breakdown, the fact is that most people found life in Metro-land warm, sociable and thoroughly enjoyable. As early as 1960, researchers had comprehensively debunked the caricature of joyless, atomized social climbers (a cliché first coined by sneering upper-class intellectuals at the turn of the century), reporting that suburban couples were 'friendly, neighbourly and helpful to each other' and enjoyed a rich life of clubs and societies. In the much-mocked New Towns, too, friendliness and contentment tended to be the rule, not the exception. To the working-class couples with small children who moved to the New Towns, they represented privacy, security and comfort: one Hemel Hempstead woman, for instance, burst into tears on her first day there because she was so happy. 'We had a garden for the children to run in,' she recalled, 'we had a house, a home of our own and we could shut the front door and we didn't have to worry about anybody.' And even the most derided new settlements had their fans. When researchers visited the forbidding concrete blocks of Cumbernauld in 1968, they found that eight out of ten people (most of whom had come from the Glasgow slums) were pleased with their new homes, while nine out of ten liked their neighbours. Cumbernauld was 'a happy town', reported *The Times*. 'The people are friendly, more of them have cars and telephones than Glaswegians do, there is no teenage problem and there are more than 100 clubs and societies in the community . . . So much for "new town blues".'[29]

Despite all the travails of the economy in the next few years, the bloodshed in Northern Ireland, the battles between governments and unions, the headlines about crime and decadence, the talk of crisis and national breakdown, there is no reason to believe that this picture changed. Of course many families were deeply affected by the major events of the day, from soaring food prices and petrol shortages to public spending cuts and job losses. For those lucky enough to be in steady, well-paid jobs, however, life was good, especially as they watched their mortgages disappear thanks to inflation. Provided that they could ignore the newspaper stories about British decline, there was much to enjoy: a brand-new company car, next year's foreign holiday, a trip to the new shopping centre or even a lazy afternoon tending the garden and watching *The Big Match*. Even the terrorism expert Richard Clutterbuck, writing in a book entitled *Britain in Agony: The Rise of Political Violence* (1978), reflected that in late 1974, one of the lowest moments in the country's modern history, a Labour activist had reminded him that 'despite the almost permanent atmosphere of economic crisis, Britain was at that moment more prosperous in real terms than at any point in our history and that the majority of us, especially at working level, had the highest standard of living we had ever had'. Despite all the problems, indeed, most people still enjoyed affluence, mobility and opportunities of which their parents could never have dreamed. Perhaps it was not surprising, then, that in 1977 a major survey found that a staggering 82 per cent of people were satisfied with life in Britain, compared with only 68 per cent in France and 59 per cent in Italy. For many people, in short, life was good.[30]

For one social group in particular, the political and economic shocks of the seventies hardly registered even as distant rumbling on the horizon. Unless their parents were unusually political, most children were barely affected by the major news stories of the day, which is perhaps one reason they later remembered the 1970s so fondly. As one schoolboy of 1973 later put it, while the news programmes were 'crammed with bombings, mass strikes, unemployment and financial ruin', he 'happily sat . . . swinging my legs, enjoying the candles' intimate light, reading comics [and] picking my nose'. And although a 12-year-old Essex girl recorded on New Year's Day 1974 that 'as the power & energy crisis is still on, it looks as if we'll soon be using candles and riding bikes everywhere', her other diary entries during the national crisis were taken up with camping expeditions, trips to sweet shops and Chinese takeaways, the purchases of records and bubble bath, and the compilation of David Cassidy scrapbooks. Only the weekly editions of *Top of the Pops* ('Dear Me, It's been a good day today. *Top of the Pops* was on at 7.55pm. Suzi Quatro was on and Bay City Rollers, Barry White, Alvin Stardust, Gilbert O'Sullivan, Hollies, David Bowie, Queen. I can't think of any others') marked the passing of the seasons – as well as the inevitable but never less than sensational transfer of her affections from one spotty youth to the next.[31]

Children in the 1970s were obviously fortunate to be growing up in an age of free state education and national health care, but they were also lucky to be growing up at a time when, thanks to the boom in living standards since the 1950s, affluence had gently trickled down the generations. Very few had to put up with the outside toilets, cold running water and shared tin baths that their parents had known, and many took for granted the space hoppers and chopper bikes that later became clichéd emblems of the decade. Even working-class children could expect to get pocket money from their parents: a survey of sixth-formers at a very mixed north London comprehensive in 1974 found that most got about £2 a week, while many took part-time jobs at the weekends, earning between £2 and £6 for a day's work. The working-class Essex girl we met earlier was too young to have a job, but her older sister earned £3 every Saturday at Littlewoods in Romford, while the 12-year-old diarist regularly bought new clothes, records and make-up. And although class inequalities meant that children from very rich and very poor backgrounds had very different life chances, British children in the 1970s arguably had more of a common culture than any generation before them. Rich or poor, all but a tiny minority had a stake in the world of Action Man, *Star Wars* and Scalextric, yo-yos, roller-skates and Sindy dolls, Uno, Mastermind and the Magna Doodle.[32]

What dominated children's cultural lives above all, however, was the small screen. While *Blue Peter*, *Jackanory* and the excruciating *Why Don't You?* aimed to educate and uplift, most children preferred the colourful adventures of *Mr Benn*, *Ivor the Engine*, *The Wombles* and the gloriously melancholy *Bagpuss*. For slightly older children, meanwhile, *Doctor Who* was at its peak in the 1970s, pitting Jon Pertwee and then Tom Baker against an imaginative if rather unconvincing range of foes from Daleks and Cybermen to man-eating plants, giant slugs and a giant rat – the latter one of the worst-realized monsters not merely in the show's history, but in the history of human entertainment. Moral campaigners fretted that the Time Lord's adventures were too frightening for children: his encounter with plastic policemen in 'Terror of the Autons' (1971) was discussed in the House of Lords, while the Church of England's consultant psychiatrist blamed Pertwee's swansong 'Planet of the Spiders' (1974) for 'an epidemic of spider phobia among young children'. An internal BBC report even claimed that *Doctor Who* was the single most violent programme on television, although, as *The Times* pointed out, comparing *Doctor Who*'s violence with real violence was 'like comparing Monopoly with the property market in London: both are fantasies, but one is meant to be taken seriously'.

In any case, children clearly liked to be frightened, and viewing figures regularly topped 10 million. It is telling that after one particularly violent adventure, 'The Seeds of Doom' (1976), children wrote in to express their appreciation. 'I think it was one of the scariest ones of all, I liked the bit when the plants were taking over, and I also liked the monster,' was a typical comment, while another young correspondent commended the producers on their ingenious ways of killing people (strangled by tendril, crushed in compost machine, and so on). Sadly and foolishly, however, the BBC eventually yielded to parental criticism: in 1977 the programme's horror content was toned down and the production team, which soon included Douglas Adams of *The Hitchhiker's Guide to the Galaxy* fame, struck a more comic note. But by that stage the moral campaigners had a new target, for the fuss about *Doctor Who* was as nothing compared with that surrounding *Grange Hill*, which began in 1978 and horrified many parents with its boisterously realistic portrait of comprehensive school life.[33]

One reason that children's television aroused such alarm was that even the producers themselves thought youngsters watched far too much of it. A typical weekday afternoon schedule in February 1978, on the day *Grange Hill*'s first episode appeared, began at 1.45 with *Mr Men*, with the pleasures of *Play School*, *Jackanory*, *Screen Test* and *Grange Hill* to come before *Paddington* rounded things off at 5.35. Even Shaun Sutton, the BBC's head of drama, worried that parents were allowing their children 'to watch too much and so denying them much of the rich diversity which should be enlarging their developing years', when there were 'books to be read, arts and crafts to be learnt, and games to be played'. And yet there is no evidence that television destroyed children's appetite for reading. The Puffin Book Club, founded in 1967, had 50,000 diminutive members by the early 1970s, each receiving a copy of the quarterly *Puffin Post* (or *The Egg* for very young readers), and membership eventually peaked at a staggering 200,000 in the early 1980s. By this point, Puffin were selling well over 3 million children's paperbacks a year, while more than 3,000 new books flooded annually into the marketplace. Many of these broke new ground in children's fiction: writing in 1980, the critic Elaine Moss predicted that a twenty-first-century historian would be interested in novels that were 'beginning to reflect the multicultural nation . . . [and] contemporary situations that cut across class and colour', such as Jan Needle's story of an immigrant Pakistani family in Bradford, *My Mate Shofiq* (1978). There were deliberately anti-sexist books, such as Gene Kemp's celebrated *The Turbulent Term of Tyke Tiler* (1977), in which naughty, athletic Tyke turns out, in a surprise twist, to be a girl; there were also 'social realist' stories revising the cherished myths of the Second World War, such as Nina Bawden's *Carrie's War* (1973) or Robert Westall's *The Machine Gunners* (1975). And there was even a revisionist account of the most cherished childhood fantasy of all, thanks to Raymond Briggs's grumpy, working-class *Father Christmas* (1973) – who still has an outside toilet.[34]

Revealingly, however, most children seem to have had similar tastes to their parents; while they liked novelty and appreciated realism, they were reluctant to dispense with old favourites, much to the despair of progressive teachers. A survey in 1972 found that Enid Blyton was still 'easily the most popular' writer among children from 6 to 11, followed by C. S. Lewis and Beatrix Potter. And while Captain W. E. Johns, the creator of Biggles, was clearly in decline, Arthur Ransome, E. Nesbit and A. A. Milne were still far more popular than most of their modern competitors; in fact, only Michael Bond, the creator of Paddington Bear, came close. At the time, critics insisted that the survey must be biased towards middle-class children, and could not possibly represent the tastes of the nation. But when the Schools Council carried out a wider poll in 1977, it turned out that the three most widely read children's books in Britain were C. S. Lewis's *The Lion, the Witch and the Wardrobe* and Enid Blyton's *The Secret Seven* and *Five on a Treasure Island* – published in 1950, 1949 and 1942 respectively, and unashamedly old-fashioned even when they were written. Old values died hard – as the success of J. K. Rowling, who spent the 1970s as a Gloucestershire schoolgirl writing fantasy stories to entertain her younger sister, would later confirm.[35]

In the 1970s, as in other decades, teenagers were the focus of considerable social anxiety, blamed for everything from street crime and promiscuous sexuality to the decline of patriotism and the plight of the economy. Young people, wrote J. B. Priestley in his survey of *The English* (1973), were 'inept, shiftless, slovenly, messy', because 'unlike their fathers and grandfathers, they have not been disciplined by grim circumstances'. This last bit was true, but there was no evidence that they were any more shiftless or slovenly than previous generations; only that attitudes and discipline had softened, which meant that they wore their hair longer and more scruffily, or refused to give their elders the automatic respect they demanded. There was certainly little evidence of a yawning cultural generation gap: when Jeremy Seabrook visited Blackburn, he found that local teenagers were just as suspicious of immigrants and keen on hanging as their parents. Like teenagers everywhere, they worried that they were missing out on some wildly debauched metropolitan party to which everyone else had been invited: life in Blackburn, they complained, was 'bloody boring'. They were 'sensual, acquisitive and fundamentally quiescent', Seabrook thought, and, despite their flared jeans and long hair, they differed from their parents only in their 'commitment to enjoyment and consumption', for which he puritanically blamed the affluent society.[36]

Actually, Seabrook's verdict was not much fairer than Priestley's. It is hard to accept that young people were greedier and more selfish, given that this was a decade in which more teenagers than ever gave their time to charity, in which membership of the Cubs, Brownies, Scouts and Guides reached record levels, in which the number of Community Service volunteers increased by six times, and in which tens of thousands worked for their voluntary Duke of Edinburgh awards. And despite the stereotype that sees young people in the 1970s evolve from hairy hippies into spittle-flecked punks, a glance at photographs from the decade confirms that most were neither. They might make half-hearted gestures towards rebellion – growing their hair, perhaps, or buying an ill-advised pair of leather trousers – but most stayed on the straight and narrow. As a survey of 16-year-old girls found in 1975, the vast majority dreamed of getting married and having children, just like their parents before them, with only a minority worrying about getting good jobs, and none of them mentioning rebelling or dropping out. And it is worth bearing in mind that of all age groups, the biggest swing to Mrs Thatcher in 1979 came among voters aged between 18 and 24 – in other words, precisely those people who a few years earlier had been chewing their pens in O-level physics classes, dreaming of Marc Bolan or Olivia Newton-John, and trying to ignore the headlines that condemned them as feckless wastrels.[37]

What dominated teenagers' cultural lives, just as in the 1950s and 1960s, was pop music. Some things had changed: most independent labels had died out, and almost all major British artists had signed with the big multinational conglomerates: EMI, Decca, Polydor, RCA and CBS. Many independent record shops, too, were struggling: by 1977, 34 per cent of all singles and 30 per cent of albums were bought in Boots, Woolworths and WH Smith, which had moved in to dominate the music market. Television, meanwhile, wielded enormous influence over teenage tastes. Every Thursday, some 15 million people tuned in to watch *Top of the Pops*, which meant that invitations to appear were highly prized. When groups could not make it (or more rarely, refused to come), they were replaced with nubile dance troupes like Pan's People, conceived as a treat for the dads. But most weekly line-ups were both impressively star-studded and bizarrely eclectic. On 18 April 1974, for example, the Essex teenager recorded her delight at seeing 'the Wombles, Glitter Band, Mott the Hoople, Sunny, Limmie & Family Cooking, Jimmy Osmond, Terry Jacks, Abba, Bay City Rollers, Wizzard'. A week later, to her horror, she missed it, having been forced to help her parents tow their caravan to Chelmsford. But she made sure to catch the next edition, in which Abba, the Wombles and the Bay City Rollers returned and were joined by Peters and Lee, Status Quo and the crooner Vince Hill, whose lustre had faded since his heyday in the early 1960s – an indication of how quickly teenage tastes had changed. 'I feel sorry for him,' she confided, 'coz he appeared and he's not really appreciated.'[38]

The other obvious difference from the teenage culture of the 1960s was the extraordinary tribalism of musical tastes. Of course this had always been there in embryo, in the division between Mods and Rockers for instance, or between hippies and skinheads. But as the critic Ian MacDonald points out, pop music in the 1960s was a 'half-invented art form'. Artists as different as, say, Cilla Black and the Rolling Stones were still seen as part of the same world, while the Beatles and the Kinks experimented wildly with different instruments, lyrical styles and even musical genres, so that their admirers 'never knew from bar to bar what was coming next'. Between about 1967 and 1969, however, a gulf opened up between pop on the one hand, and rock on the other, reflecting not just the difference between singles and albums, but between younger and older listeners, the latter now demanding more self-consciously serious and stimulating material. To people who loathed all popular music, the difference between Slade and the Bay City Rollers, or between Nick Drake and Leo Sayer, must have seemed footling and arbitrary; but to teenagers in the early 1970s, it loomed very large indeed. Pop music was catchy and commercial, designed for the radio and the singles charts; rock songs were meant to be authentic and artistic, and often lasted for what seemed hours. Rock was worthy but difficult; pop was cheerful but trite. Rock appealed to adults, pop to teenagers. 'Rock was not only a thousand watts louder,' writes Philip Norman; 'it was also a thousand times more serious.'[39]

With artists under such pressure to conform to established, market-friendly stereotypes – the fresh-faced young balladeer, the dreamy-eyed singer-songwriter, the badly behaved long-haired rockers – it is not surprising that magazines like *Melody Maker* and the *New Musical Express* lamented the death of creativity. In February 1972 the *NME*'s assistant editor Nick Logan dismissed what he called 'mini-phenomena' like the Faces, Slade, and T.Rex, and complained that he had spent 'three or four years waiting in a post-Beatles limbo for a new *real* phenomenon to present itself'. Even David Bowie, perhaps the only chart star of the early 1970s who preserved the old spirit of permanent reinvention, came in for criticism: to the *NME*'s Roy Carr, for example, he was a triumph of 'hype and hoax', a 'singing boutique who appeals only to freaks'. Revealingly, both Logan and Carr had started writing for the magazine in the late 1960s, and while they may have been only ten years older than their readers, ten years is an enormously long time to a teenager. But then generational battles are as much a part of teenage culture as surliness, spots and self-loathing. When T.Rex released 'Children of the Revolution' in September 1972, the *NME*'s reviewer Danny Holloway dismissed its 'nursery-school lyrics' before mournfully predicting that 'the soldiers of Teenage Wasteland will send this one straight to Number One'. (In fact, it peaked at number two, breaking T.Rex's sequence of four consecutive chart-topping singles.) And the magazine's letters pages often smouldered with teenage fury at the snobbery of its 25-year-old critics. 'I'm sick and tired of letters from people who say yesterday's music has a higher standard than today,' wrote an angry B. Randall of

London SE9. They must be 'deaf or daft or both to think that the oldies can be compared with today's music. Can't they see the music scene has changed? Or are they all locked away in dark rooms, listening to wind-up gramophones?'[40]

What really defined pop and rock music in the early 1970s, though, was its sheer fragmentation. No group dominated the charts, the media or the imagination of the young in the same way that the Beatles and Rolling Stones had done a few years before. At the end of 1971, it seemed possible that Marc Bolan's group T.Rex, whose theatrical style epitomized the new craze for 'glam rock', might establish themselves as an enduring force. Their singles 'Get It On', 'Ride a White Swan' and 'Hot Love' accounted for almost 4 per cent of all British record sales that year, both Paul McCartney and John Lennon anointed them as their successors, and 'Whispering' Bob Harris, host of the BBC's *The Old Grey Whistle Test*, announced that they had 'got to be the next Beatles, if they're not already'. By early 1972, with the band's album *The Slider* boasting 100,000 advance orders, the press was talking excitedly of 'T.Rexstasy' and Bolan's self-satisfied features seemed likely to become a defining image of the decade. However, he then lost his way, partly because of his own narcissism and fondness for the bottle, but also because it was extremely difficult to combine artistic ambitions with making chart-topping records for 14-year-old girls.[41]

By 1975 Bolan had almost vanished from sight; now the great phenomenon was the Bay City Rollers, a clean-cut, tartan-clad group from Edinburgh, whose single 'Bye Bye Baby' held the number one spot for six weeks and sold almost a million copies. Like T.Rex, the Rollers' public appearances inspired scenes of hysteria reminiscent of the Beatles at their peak. 'Their audience is aged between 10 and 15, and their enthusiasm can realistically be compared with Hitler's Nuremberg rallies,' reported *Melody Maker* after one concert in Edinburgh. 'Girls were being trodden underfoot in the melee and the front row of seats became dislodged from the floor and smashed as more and more surged into the crowd. There were at least a dozen cases of fainting, and twice girls pretended to be overcome in order to be lifted up stagewards.'[42]

But while the band's domineering manager Tam Paton (later convicted of gross indecency with teenage boys) boasted that they would be 'as big as the Beatles', nobody took him seriously. The market was now far too sophisticated and the audience far too fragmented – by age, class and region, as well as by taste and temperament – for any group to repeat the Liverpool quartet's extraordinary commercial and critical success. Between, for example, Slade and Genesis, two emblematic bands of the early 1970s, there yawned a vast cultural chasm. Both enjoyed dressing up: Slade's Noddy Holder usually sported a top hat decorated with silver discs, while Genesis's Peter Gabriel wore costumes so ludicrous – fluorescent bat-wings, a flower-petal mask, a diamond helmet – that he would have made a first-class monster on *Doctor Who*. Beyond that, however, they had almost nothing in common. Holder was the son of a Wolverhampton window-cleaner, whose skinhead band had become the epitome of cheerful, unpretentious glam rock. Gabriel, on the other hand, was a former Charterhouse boy who claimed inspiration from J. R. R. Tolkien and Arthur C. Clarke and said that his twenty-three-minute epic 'Supper's Ready' (1972) described 'the ultimate cosmic battle for Armageddon between good and evil in which man is destroyed, but the deaths of countless thousands atone for mankind, reborn no longer as Homo Sapiens'. Never less than ambitious, Gabriel once remarked that his band's 'role as musicians . . . may well be providing bourgeois escapism'. What Noddy Holder would have thought of this can only be guessed at: he was content, he said, to be a 'Black Country yobbo'.[43]

By this stage, pop music had already lost the exaggerated subversive, utopian associations of Swinging London and the Summer of Love. If anything, it had reverted to something very similar to the picture before the Beatles' breakthrough in 1963: a bewildering kaleidoscope of singers and bands, competing for attention in a highly crowded but socially fractured market, with the singles charts often dominated by one-hit wonders and novelty records like Middle of the Road's 'Chirpy Chirpy Cheep Cheep' (1971), or the Royal Scots Dragoon Guards' version of 'Amazing Grace', the biggest-selling single of 1972. And although bands like the prototypical heavy metal outfit Led Zeppelin – who refused to release singles, let alone appear on *Top of the Pops* – continued to make headlines for outlandishly bad behaviour, pop music in the age of Pink Floyd and Elton John seemed to have lost much of its ability to shock. By the end of 1973, the days when John Lennon and Mick Jagger had been media folk devils, hailed as champions of a new generation and voices of protest against the established moral order, seemed long gone. Looking back on a year that had produced Mike Oldfield's *Tubular Bells*, Emerson, Lake and Palmer's *Brain Salad Surgery*, Yes's *Tales from Topographic Oceans*, Pink Floyd's *Dark Side of the Moon*, Genesis's *Selling England by the Pound* and, hilariously, Rick Wakeman's *The Six Wives of Henry VIII*, not even the most defiantly countercultural critic could deny that rock had become distinctly respectable. And when *The Times* was hailing *Tales from Topographic Oceans* as 'the ultimate bridging of the gap between the music of the academy and the tunes of the discotheque', and predicting that its 'third movement' would be 'studied 25 years hence as a significant turning point in modern music', then the Mods and Rockers really did seem like ancient history.[44]

In January 1974, when the glam-rockers the Sweet released their new single 'Teenage Rampage', its co-writer Nicky Chinn told *Melody Maker* that he was 'trying to convey the changing behaviour of kids, who now more than ever before are going rampant'. Teenagers, he said, were 'having a bigger effect on life than ever' and 'to ask whatever happened to the teenage dream is a load of cock'. The band's guitarist Andy Scott, however, was rather less bullish. 'We've only released the song for the sake of having a hit,' he said bluntly, adding that he didn't even like it himself. And when *Melody Maker* asked young music fans for their reaction to 'Teenage Rampage', it turned out that very few agreed with the 28-year-old Chinn. Many hated the teenage label. 'I think of myself as a person, not as part of an anonymous horde,' said Christine Harrison, 15, from Manchester. People like Chinn 'put teenagers in a bad light', said 16-year-old Ada McMahon from Edinburgh, adding that 'parents are too easily influenced.' Pop records were a 'gross exploitation of teenagers' views and feelings', agreed Tim Potts from Newcastle, while Oldham's Kevin Lee thought that adults who 'use the word [teenage] for song titles should be treated with contempt'. It should be 'a criminal offence,' he added, 'to cash in on the idiot hordes of 13 to 16-year olds who are brainwashed into thinking they're the same just because their age group is mentioned'.

But the last word belongs to 15-year-old Steven Knight of Crouch Hill, London. The very mention of the word 'teenager', he said scornfully, merely made him think of surfboards and 1950s rock and roll. 'I visualise a useless, worthless struggle of kids arguing with their parents as to how late they can stay out,' he went on, 'a struggle which they would soon grow out of and be ashamed of when reminded.' Given that so many of the teenagers of 1974 would vote for Mrs Thatcher five years later, perhaps he was not far wrong.[45]

For a small minority of children and teenagers, life was very different from middle-class fantasies of suburban bliss. In 1970, when the Child Poverty Action Group claimed that 3 million children were growing up in poverty, many people objected that it had included families able to afford washing machines and televisions. But while no definition of poverty won universal agreement, other studies published that same year showed that many children were clearly blighted by their poor upbring-ing. An LSE study showed that one in five large families in London was living below the government's official poverty level, some children even having to make do with coats instead of blankets in winter. A conference organized by the housing group Shelter produced the claim that 7 to 10 million Britons were 'camped on, or down beyond, the boglands of poverty', being shut out from the delights of the affluent society, deprived of luxuries and leisure, and forced to make do with welfare handouts, poor diets and damp, dilapidated council accommodation. And in January 1971, the chairman of the Child Poverty Action Group, the future Labour maverick Frank Field, issued a revised estimate that one million children grew up in families beneath an income level of £16 a week, which was the poverty line agreed by the government's Supplementary Benefits Commission. More likely to be smacked by their exhausted parents, to suffer from illnesses, to have bad diets and bad teeth, they were also less likely to have help with their school work, to go on holidays and outings, and even to be read to at night. And for the unluckiest children, falling through the welfare net, disadvantage could turn into abuse. In 1973 the nation was horrified by the case of Maria Colwell, a 7-year-old girl battered to death by her stepfather after social services ignored more than thirty complaints from her Brighton council-house neighbours – and not the last tragedy of its kind.[46]

In the autumn of 1972, two young researchers arrived on the Mon-mouth council estate in Islington, north London, to begin a project on working-class youth culture. What they found could hardly have been more remote from the leafy suburbs of Betjeman's *Metro-Land*: a low-rise GLC housing complex trapped between two busy main roads, first occupied in 1960 but never properly finished, a 'twilight zone with high rates of delinquency, mental breakdown and suicide'. Just a short bus ride from the West End, the estate's 1,200 maisonettes offered a 'familiar contrast between the private trappings of affluence – colour TVs, kitchen units, and fitted carpets – and public squalor – halls and stairways strewn with garbage and covered with graffiti, lifts that don't work and telephone boxes smashed up'. Many children were drawn into criminality before they had even reached double figures; led by a manic 13-year-old, one gang had occupied a disused local pub, using it to store their booty from robberies and raids, but reserving one room for 'shitting and pissing'. Between the Monmouth youngsters and their neighbours on the Denby council estate, which was dominated by widowed pensioners and black immigrant families, there was a long history of tension. In particular, Irish and black teenagers hated each other; the Irish often complained that the 'jungle bunnies' would 'turn you over' for money if they caught a white boy on his own. And when a group of well-meaning social workers and squatters tried to turn the pub into a youth centre, with a disco as the centrepiece, their dreams were quickly shattered. The disco soon succumbed to endemic racial violence, and when a kaftan-wearing hippy tried to organize hand-holding 'encounter sessions' to dissipate the tension, the teenagers beat him up so badly he ended up in hospital. It would have been funny if it were not so sad: by the time the researchers left in 1974, all they could foresee for the children of the estate was violence, racism and unemployment.[47]

Like so many of the council estates planned and built in the 1940s and 1950s, the Monmouth estate had originally been a symbol of modernity and opportunity, the embodiment of the reforming spirit that was going to turn Britain into the New Jerusalem. The transformation in the estates' image, however, was astonishingly quick: by the early 1970s, writes one historian, they had already become symbols of 'dependence on state benefits, of a morass of indebtedness to the council and the moneylender, of isolation from neighbour and kin and society at large'. Once they had been praised for their bold appearance and modern amenities; now they were 'feared for their violence, their vandalism, their inhuman scale and their dog-eat-dog collective life'. Visiting Blackburn in the summer of 1969, Jeremy Seabrook found 'empty sweeping vistas of disfigured concrete, neglected grass verges and uncontrolled privet hedges ... crumbling kerbstones, blocked drainpipes that stain the walls with a rust-coloured overflow ... extinguished street lights, overflowing dented dustbins'. They were as 'impermanent as refugee camps', he thought, inviting 'violence and negation'. The mood of their inhabitants was a 'sullen and passive indifference': in the ill-stocked, threadbare shops, he watched women queuing with 'dirty aprons and draggled dresses' poking out from beneath their coats, their children dressed in outsize Fair Isle sweaters and cracked plastic jackets, 'the uniform of jumble sales and charity'.[48]

This picture, of course, was far from universal. Even in the early 1980s, when the estates seemed to have reached rock bottom, there were pockets of success, from grass-roots youth associations, day-care centres, summer festivals and food cooperatives to surveys showing that some estates were genuinely happy, welcoming places. On one Hammersmith estate in the late 1970s, for example, kinship and community had not disappeared; indeed, 77 per cent of tenants had relatives living nearby and 62 per cent felt they could rely on their neighbours in the event of an emergency. Yet other London estates were deeply miserable and troubled places, the inevitable problems of poverty, welfare dependency and lack of opportunities exacerbated by their grim concrete architecture. And as working-class white families moved out to suburbs and New Towns, so the poverty of the estates acquired a racial dimension. By the mid-1970s, black and Asian families were beginning to dominate crumbling pre-war estates like White City, Kingsmead, Kennington Park and Kingslake. Even on the new system-built concrete Holly Street estate in Dalston, more than 75 per cent of new arrivals were black by 1977. Only six years old, Holly Street had once been a symbol of the technological optimism of the late 1960s, its four twenty-storey towers housing more than 1,000 families. Yet by the end of the decade it was a byword for water leaks, vermin infestation, vandalism, muggings and racial violence. In a single week in 1980, there were twenty-one separate break-ins. The corridors were a 'thieves' highway', one visitor wrote, while at the corners of the blocks were 'dark passages, blind alleys, gloomy staircases'. By now the fear of mugging was so great that if people went out at night they 'stick to the lit areas and walk hurriedly'. Many compared it with the worst estates of New York or Chicago; it was certainly a long way from the New Jerusalem.[49]

The plight of Holly Street makes an appropriate metaphor for what happened to much of inner-city London in the 1970s. With the capital's decline as a working port – thanks not only to changing trade and export patterns, but also to the extraordinary intransigence of London's dockers, whose introverted, clannish politics were notorious even among other trade unions, and made modernization impossible – its manufacturing base collapsed. In everything from the car and engineering industries to furniture-making, vehicle parts and even sweet-making, factories closed and jobs were wiped off the map. Between 1966 and 1974 alone, the capital's manufacturing workforce fell from 1.29 million to 940,000, and it fell even further and faster during the late 1970s and 1980s. As an industrial city, London was ceasing to exist. And as middle-class and skilled working-class workers moved out to the New Towns and suburbs of Hertfordshire, Essex, Surrey and Kent, so the city's character radically changed. By 1981, the population of inner London had fallen by a staggering 26 per cent in just twenty years; at 2.35 million, it was barely half the figure in 1901. The turnover was astonishing: two-thirds of the people living in Islington in 1961 had moved out by 1971, and more followed in the next ten years. Formerly respectable working-class districts were increasingly dominated by immigrants, tower blocks and unskilled poor workers, as well as a smattering of young middle-class bohemians in the vanguard of the gentrification craze. And in areas like Islington, the contours of the city's future were already being sketched in draft: on the one hand, the affluent young, well-educated and well-paid, with an insatiable appetite for commerce and entertainment; on the other, the people of the towers, often shut out from jobs and opportunities, and condemned to lives of crime and dependency.[50]

As early as the mid-1970s, therefore, there was already a sense of two Londons emerging, side-by-side: the city of the gentrifiers, and the city of the council estates. But what struck most visitors at the time was the capital's sheer seediness: the dirty, run-down, dilapidated streets, the sense of mistrust and disappointment that hung in the air like a fog. The terrible Moorgate tube disaster of February 1975, when a Northern Line commuter train smashed into a bricked-up tunnel, killing forty-three passengers, was a freak accident blamed on driver error; but the very fact that it was never properly explained somehow seemed a symbol of the deteriorating quality of life in the capital. 'You feel in this city that despair is washing the walls and is eating into hearts of people,' recorded Kenneth Williams in 1971, 'and so the music gets noisier, the dancing more frenetic & fragmented, the conversations more wry and ruefully cynical . . . and the confrontations more & more stalemate'. Six years later, a Thames Television survey found that 'more than half the people living in London would like to move out because they do not like the neighbourhood'. The heart of the West End, the journalist Clive Irving told American readers, had become 'a semiderelict slum', blighted by 'tacky porno shops, skin movies, pinball arcades, and toxic hamburger joints', while 'behind neon façades the buildings are flaking and unkempt'. Even the 30-year-old writer Jonathan Raban, a newcomer to the capital, was struck by the physical decay of his Notting Hill neighbourhood. With its transient population of West Indian youngsters, unkempt hippies and struggling young mothers, it might be picturesque in the sun, he wrote, but 'on dull days one notices the litter, the scabby paint, the stretches of torn wire netting, and the faint smell of joss-sticks competing with the sickly sweet odour of rising damp and rotting plaster'.[51]

London's fictional image reflected a similar sense of decay and decline. 'Rat City', the Art Attacks called it in their punk-rock single of 1979; 'It's so shitty.' Perhaps they were inspired by one of the most successful contemporary visions of London, James Herbert's bestseller *The Rats* (1974), the book that effectively reinvented the British horror genre. Here, London is a city eaten away from within by giant, feral rats, which hunt down people in packs, becoming so bold that they take over a tube station, a school, a cinema. And the book's teacher hero knows who to blame: 'the councils that took the working class from their slums and put them in tall, remote concrete towers,' the 'same councils' that tolerated 'the filth that could produce vermin such as the black rats'. This was an extreme example, admittedly, but few other depictions of the city would have gone down well with its tourist board. As early as July 1971, when John Schlesinger's film *Sunday, Bloody Sunday* reached the cinemas, it was clear that the carefree fantasies of Swinging London, supposedly 'the most exciting city in the world', had long since evaporated. Here, London is a sad, haunted city of drug addicts, harassed homosexuals and looming economic collapse, setting the tone for the decade to come. 'Up-ended dustbins and capsized vegetable barrows are being sick all over the pavement; rubbish bags slump like tramps against shop windows; rabid pigeons, too fat to fly, squawk among the filth,' the narrator observes in Martin Amis's novel *Success*, published seven years later. Turning into Queensway, past the 'great continents of Middle-Eastern immigrant workers' and the 'shock-haired nig-nog' selling orange juice from a fridge, he looks in vain for a sign saying 'English Spoken Here'. And when the heroine revisits her old respectable working-class neighbourhood in Margaret Drabble's novel *The Middle Ground* (1980), she finds it 'derelict, abandoned', its unfinished tower blocks 'raw, ugly, gigantic in scale', a 'wilderness of flyovers and underpasses and unfinished supports', a 'no man's land' in the aftermath of war.[52]

What happened to London in the 1970s was by no means unusual. As skilled working-class and lower-middle-class families moved out of Birmingham inner-city districts like Sparkbrook and Small Heath, the brick terraced streets attracted a new population of students, squatters and immigrants. In Whalley Range, Manchester, where middle-class families were disappearing to the Cheshire suburbs, their old Victorian villas were converted into single-occupancy flats, often becoming shabby student bedsits. And then there was Liverpool, which the planner Lionel Brett, Viscount Esher, called 'the *locus classicus* of the collapse of the inner city: the loss of the go-ahead young; the consequent shrinking of the tax base, yet no diminution of the number of under-privileged needing multiple support, of young children, of the impoverished old; the loss of jobs within reach of the centre; and above all the failed, frightening environment'. Only the success of the city's leading football team, twice European champions in the 1970s, represented a point of pride. But when, just weeks after Liverpool's second European Cup victory, the city's industrial development officer reported that it had suffered 'an unprecedented level of plant closures and redundancies', it was a reminder of what really mattered.

Later, the Thatcher governments would take much of the blame for Liverpool's woes. But, as in so many other areas, the rot had set in well before then. There was already a sense, a reporter wrote in June 1978, that 'Britain had decided simply to write Liverpool off'. Crippled by strikes, the docks were in deep decline, while the new Kirkby housing estates were a 'planning catastrophe on a very large scale', with mugging, vandalism and arson endemic, and their inhabitants mocked as 'drunken, semi-literate idlers who beat their wives' and 'marauding mobs of mini-muggers'. And across the city, the rule for calculating unemployment was simple: take the national figure, and double it. To get the figure for Kirkby, double the figure for Liverpool; to get the figure for Toxteth, the inner-city district where most black immigrants lived, treble it. The unemployment rate among young black men, *The Times* reported sadly, was 'getting on for 50 percent, four times the city average, and eight times the national'.[53]

What was really strangling Liverpool was not union militancy or government indifference, but the inexorable logic of economic history, the same thing that afflicted once-prosperous Northern mill towns like Bradford, Oldham and Nelson, or West Midlands engineering towns like Dudley and Wolverhampton. In Bradford, for example, some 50,000 people had been working in textiles in 1964, a third of the town's workforce; by 1974, however, the equivalent figure was almost down to 25,000, and it continued to fall afterwards. Bradford's Manningham district, where the serial killer Peter Sutcliffe used to drink in the early 1970s, had once been a handsome middle-class Victorian neighbourhood; by Sutcliffe's time, however, it was fast becoming one of the worst inner-city slums in the North of England, a wilderness of sex shops, betting shops, seedy drinking clubs and decrepit workers' cafés. Customers who followed the 'Toilet' signs in the Lahore restaurant would 'find themselves stumbling across a piece of waste ground where half a dozen cats were fighting each other over a hen's head', while at the corner, prostitutes solicited in the darkness. 'Chapels and mills are suddenly exposed by demolition, marooned in a tangle of convolvulus and mallow like the carcasses of huge extinct saurians,' wrote Jeremy Seabrook of Blackburn, though he could have been talking about any one of dozens of Northern industrial towns. The well-to-do had long since moved out to what he dismissively called their 'joyless Arcadia of inflated Wendy-houses'; meanwhile, 'the centre of the town is left increasingly to the poor, the old and the immigrants'.[54]

'Left-over people', the former Animals keyboardist Alan Price called them in his album *Between Today and Yesterday* (1974), a collection of songs built around the experience of growing up in working-class Jarrow. The institutions that had once given texture and meaning to industrial working-class life – the factory, the chapel, the council estate, even the pub and the football club – seemed to be in deep, unstoppable decline. The very landscape was changing: terraced streets ripped down and replaced with monolithic concrete blocks; mill chimneys and colliery engine houses crashing down in clouds of dust; pubs and chapels converted into carpet showrooms or flats for ambitious gentrifiers. When Terry Collier, back from five years in West Germany, tours his old haunts in *Whatever Happened to the Likely Lads?*, he is horrified by the transformation of the Newcastle he loved. Standing on top of a new multi-storey car park, he reels in shock when his friend Bob tells him that this was the site of the old Go-Go rock club. 'The Go-Go?' he exclaims. '*Gone?*' The Roxy, too, where he used to sink the pints and ogle the girls, has disappeared, demolished to make way for a new civic centre. Only Eric's fish-and-chip shop remains, a forlorn relic of the old world, alone in a wasteland of building sites and tower blocks. 'None of our memories is intact,' Terry says sadly.[55]

Even working-class political culture, which had given life to the Labour Party and still found expression in strikes, marches and local meetings, seemed 'narrower, more introverted and more brittle', as local branches fell under the sway of middle-class teachers, lecturers and social workers – who in turn adopted what the Labour MP and political historian David Marquand called 'an explosive mixture of pseudo-proletarianism, insular populism and mostly shallow neo-marxism', like some grotesque parody of genuine working-class values. Behind the misleading arithmetic of the electoral system, Labour's vote was steadily shrinking: from 48 per cent in 1966, it fell to 43 per cent in 1970, 37 per cent in both February 1974 and 1979, and a mere 28 per cent in 1983, when its anti-modernization, even reactionary rhetoric was shrillest. Marquand thought it was trapped in the past, 'a product of the age of steam, hobbling arthritically into the age of the computer', appealing above all to 'the casualties of change rather than to the pacemakers, to declining areas rather than to advancing ones'. When the BBC made a documentary on Harold Wilson and his senior colleagues in 1971 and called it *Yesterday's Men,* they provoked the biggest row between the Corporation and the Labour Party that anybody could remember. In the long run, however, the title was more fitting than any of them realized.[56]

But it would be a misleading portrait of Britain that focused entirely on decline, decay and disappointment. Change brought prosperity as well as poverty: in East Anglia, for example, the growth of agri-business, the opening of the M11 motorway and the development of a new economy based on technology and computers brought unparalleled growth to old market towns such as Norwich and Ipswich. In Cambridge, the nation's first science park opened in 1970 and proved a sensational success, hosting 25 technology firms by 1980 and more than 1,000 by the end of the century. Further east was an even more compelling success story: Felixstowe, already on its way to becoming the nation's busiest container port, its workforce drawn from former agricultural labourers, its rapid growth a deterrent to the labour disputes that crippled London and Liverpool. And even the capital had its boom areas, most notably Croydon, the epicentre of the new vogue for suburban office blocks. By 1970, it was already the tenth biggest town in the country, with a big new shopping centre, a multi-storey car park and more than fifty office buildings taller than nine storeys. 'Mini-Manhattan', observers called it, and its rise seemed relentless; by the end of the decade, East Croydon station was reckoned the busiest outside central London.[57]

It was another, even more derided outpost of Greater Metro-land, however, that most clearly pointed the way to the future. In March 1970, developers unveiled the plans for the last of the New Towns, a 'city of the future' in rural north Buckinghamshire, based on an American-style road grid, 'landscaped parks', a 'health campus' and a spanking new shopping mall to mark the town centre. 'Los Angeles, Bucks', wags called it, but its ethos was pure Metro-land, its advertisements showing off the projected landscape of lakes, fields and bridleways, an expanse of manicured green dotted with new homes. The planners had big ambitions: 70,000 people by 1981 and more than 250,000 by the 1990s, with 'Mr and Mrs 1990' at the forefront of their thinking. Even in 1972 they were anticipating a brave new world of fibre-optics and computers: homes were fitted with cable to allow Mrs 1990 'to stay at home, dial her shopkeeper on her audio-visual telephone, and choose the Sunday lunch as the camera scans the shelves'. Talk of a monorail, that emblematic transport dream of the 1960s, had already been abandoned; instead, this was to be a town centred on the car, although the developers had plans for a 'dial-a-bus' scheme, in which a passenger would dial his destination into the nearest bus stop, and a 'central computer' would send 'the nearest bus' to pick him up. There were plans for golf courses, water-skiing, a 'water bus' zipping to London along the Grand Union Canal, even 'an orchestra floating on a lake with the audience listening from the banks'.[58]

Like all New Towns, Milton Keynes was the subject of criticism and mockery from the very beginning. Newspapers eagerly reported the developers' problems in securing enough labour and materials to build tens of thousands of homes, while inflation and government cuts meant that the budget was endlessly revised. When the first families began to arrive in the mid-1970s, there were the usual unrepresentative reports of disappointment and loneliness, as well as genuine complaints about poor sound insulation and draughty windows. And when the *Daily Telegraph*'s Christopher Booker went to inspect the site in July 1974, he made no effort to disguise his horror and contempt. Unlike the 'leafy, affluent' suburbs of Los Angeles, he found 'hundreds of grim little misshapen boxes, in brick or corrugated metal, turned out by machine'. Milton Keynes, he thought, was the 'ultimate monument' to 'the utterly depersonalized nightmare which haunted Aldous Huxley in *Brave New World* just forty short years ago'. It was with something approaching glee that he predicted that 'in the present economic climate . . . the chances must be high that over the next decade Milton Keynes will simply become a pathetic national joke, falling ever further behind its ambitious schedule, and finally grinding to a stop in a sea of mud and rusting contractors' equipment, unsold houses and half-finished factories'. And 'in the name of the poor people who will actually have to live there', he said, 'such a horrible mistake must never be made again'.[59]

But he was wrong. Milton Keynes was neither a horrible mistake nor a pathetic joke; it was, in fact, a great success. By May 1973, Tesco, British Oxygen, Legal & General and the Abbey National had already committed themselves to opening offices or warehouses in the new town, and by the end of the 1970s more new jobs had been created in Milton Keynes than in any other city in Britain, with the exception of the North Sea oil boomtown of Aberdeen. And although housing completions had fallen behind demand, that was simply because industry and jobs were coming to Milton Keynes much faster than anybody had expected. By the end of 1973, the developers had finished more than 5,000 homes, and by 1976 the town's population already stood at 76,000 people. The majority of these people, defying the stereotypes of suburban fragmentation and New Town blues, were very happy with their lot. As the town's chief architect later proudly put it, they had 'voted with their feet'. And in 1975, even before the shopping centre and other amenities had been opened, a survey found that between 83 and 95 per cent of the residents were pleased with life, while only four families out of 290 questioned said that they wanted to go back to their old homes.[60]

Milton Keynes thrived because it matched the ordinary ambitions of hundreds of thousands of British families: a steady middle-class job, a neat suburban home, a little garden and a safe environment to bring up children. The editor of the *Architectural Association Quarterly* was probably going a bit far when he said in 1975 that it represented 'the nearest thing we shall get to Utopia'. But in its mundane, understated way, Milton Keynes was the apotheosis of Metro-land, the ultimate blend of social mobility, material ambition and conservative cultural values. It was 'not much of a place to look at', another visiting journalist reported in 1976, but there was 'much to admire' in the gentle, low-level design of the housing estates and 'the absence of graffiti and vandalism'.

It lacked grandeur or romance; it was 'low-profiled, commodious, efficient, unpretentious'. But that was exactly what people wanted – people like Henry and Lilian Foulds, a retired couple who had left their two-bedroom maisonette in Hackney for a neat bungalow in Milton Keynes. Instead of staring at a skyline of tower blocks and chimneys from a 'four-walled prison', they now spent their days in the garden, 'growing nasturtiums, roses, peas and beans'. They took walks down to the canal; they caught the bus to Wolverton for a 'hot plate of chips' or to Bletchley for a 'nice cup of tea'. They were surrounded by children, but unlike in London, they had no fears of harassment or vandalism. And with informal support from a 'good neighbour' paid by the Development Corporation, Henry and Lilian had made plenty of friends in the area, including a neighbour who grew strawberries and cheerfully swapped his surplus produce for their lettuce and beans. Some might mock, but after a lifetime working in the capital, this to them seemed a taste of paradise, their own private version of Betjeman's *Metro-Land*. It was 'like a holiday', they told an interviewer in 1980. And what about London? 'We don't long to go back, not even for a visit.'[61]

10

Who Needs Men?

The writer in residence spoke. 'Look, are you trying to tell us . . .
Is – what? – is Mr Richardson trying to tell us he believes that?
About women being equal to men? Does he believe it?' He looked
around the room as if pleading for enlightenment. 'I mean, you
know, like really *believe it?'*
                – Kingsley Amis, *Jake's Thing* (1978)

But they're like chaps, these days, like fellas, like blokes.
                – Martin Amis, *Success* (1978)

In December 1973, with the headlines full of industrial unrest, economic
meltdown and international terrorism, the youthful viewers of *Doctor
Who* were introduced to the time traveller's latest female companion.
For ten years the Doctor's companions had tended to be pretty young
girls who spent most of their time screaming, falling over and asking
the Time Lord to explain the plot. Now, however, Jon Pertwee's Doctor
seemed to have met his match. In the opening episode of 'The Time
Warrior', he arrives at a secret research establishment to investigate the
disappearance of Britain's most eminent scientists, only to find that
a plucky young investigative journalist, Sarah Jane Smith (Elisabeth
Sladen), has got there first. From the moment she walks in, her hair cut
fashionably short, her trim figure enclosed in a brown flared trouser-suit,
it is clear that Sarah Jane is a distinctly modern woman. And when the
Doctor gently suggests that she make him a cup of coffee – as her
bubbly predecessor, Jo Grant, had done countless times – her anger is
immediate: 'If you think I'm going to spend my time making cups of
coffee for you . . .!'

Undeterred, the Doctor continues to talk down to her, but Sarah is having none of it. 'Kindly don't be so patronising,' she snaps a few moments later, and then: 'Stop treating me like a child.' Even when, having stowed away aboard the TARDIS, she finds herself imprisoned in the Middle Ages, her feminist passion burns as brightly as ever. 'She spits fire,' one of her medieval captors says ruefully. And although Sarah Jane and the Doctor soon become fast friends, she remains a champion of what she calls 'women's lib'. 'Harry, call me "old girl" again,' she warns a fellow companion, a bluff naval surgeon, 'and I'll spit in your eye.' In fact, not even the shock of travelling to distant worlds in the far future can dent Sarah Jane's feminist ardour. Trapped in the middle of a miners' strike on the planet Peladon, she is distressed to discover that the locals have decidedly unreconstructed attitudes to women in politics. 'It would be different if I was a man,' sighs Queen Thalira. 'But I'm only a girl.' 'Now just a minute!' Sarah exclaims. 'There's nothing "only" about being a girl!'[1]

When *Doctor Who* began, the notion of a young female companion standing up to the Doctor, demanding to be taken seriously and insisting that a woman was just as good as a man, would have been almost inconceivable. Back in 1963, the Doctor's first female companions had fulfilled highly traditional or stereotypical roles: the shy teenage granddaughter, the earnest school history teacher, the kooky dolly bird, and so on. But by the beginning of the 1970s, women's lives and expectations had changed a great deal in a very short amount of time. To be sure, there were still glaring inequalities: far fewer women than men attended universities or went into the world of work, women were generally paid far less than men, and women in senior managerial or executive positions were almost unknown. As late as the mid-1960s, *The Times* noted that middle-class families still often sent their daughters to 'lightweight schools' that trained them in cookery, needlework and domestic management instead of maths, physics and chemistry. And it was revealing that when Heath announced his Cabinet in June 1970, it contained just one woman, Margaret Thatcher, who as Education Secretary was handling that part of the public sector traditionally associated with serious-minded middle-class women like herself. It was telling that when her local newspaper asked whether she would like to be the first woman Prime Minister, her reply was emphatic: 'No, there will never be a woman Prime Minister in my lifetime – the male population is too prejudiced.'

And that prejudice often expressed itself in unexpected but doubtless highly frustrating ways. If Mrs Thatcher, snatching a few moments' break from a hard night's work at the Department of Education, had gone unaccompanied into a nearby pub, she would have attracted glares of suspicion, if not outright hostility. And she would have been well advised to banish all thoughts of a late-night hamburger. For until the end of 1971, women were banned from entering Wimpy bars after midnight without male companions, on the grounds that the only women on their own at that hour must be prostitutes.[2]

If a young woman from the twenty-first century, following in the footsteps of Sarah Jane Smith, were catapulted back in time to the early 1970s, she would no doubt be shocked at the petty prejudices, restrictions and inequalities that still governed the lives of most British women. And yet at the time, the overwhelming impression was one of enormous change and opportunity, driven by the rise of labour-saving technology, the availability of contraception and consequent fall in the birth rate, and the expansion of white-collar work. A girl who came of age in the late 1960s could expect educational and economic opportunities that would have been denied to her mother and grandmother. More likely to stay longer in school, she could marry when and if she wanted, have children when she wanted, and pursue her own career even after marriage. As Brian Jackson recorded in 1968, even the average housewife found her load lightened by 'such humble things as the proliferation of effective cleaning materials, more easily prepared food, the practical information in women's magazines'. The change in the 'personal quality of women's lives', he wrote,

> has surely been immense. Contraception removes fears about love-making, eats into that thick nest of taboos built protectively around working-class sex. Your children don't die. Neither do you. The plastics revolution removes almost intolerably hard physical work from the home. And the demands of home are easier to bear, knowing that there is the chance of working years – with the social life, the skills and the income they will bring.[3]

For young women in the early 1970s, the unexpected reality of these new opportunities could be both invigorating and bewildering. The journalist Mary Ingham, who was born in 1947, had grown up imagining 'being married at 22, quite old really, and settling down to raise a family at 25'. But 'at university 22 suddenly didn't seem so old', so she mentally revised her plans. Then '25 came and went without the wedding and 27 without the children', and as she approached 30 in the mid-1970s, she found herself still sharing a flat with ex-student friends in a dilapidated Georgian terrace in London. Life had turned out completely differently from the visions she had nurtured as a teenager. 'So much of what I was groomed and rehearsed for just didn't apply by the time I grew up,' she wrote, 'because so many new opportunities had opened up for women: free, reliable contraception, abortion, easier divorce, job opportunities.' She felt both excited and adrift, lost in a world whose landscape was still unformed, whose contours were not yet clear. And like many women, she turned to her contemporaries for solidarity and support. 'How better to enter a new territory but together?' wrote the feminist playwright April de Angelis. 'How could the strange landscape be mapped singly when no apprenticeship had been served?'[4]

For most of the 1950s and 1960s, feminism was widely supposed to have disappeared. On the left, it was often seen as divisive, distracting and self-indulgent: at the Labour Women's Conference in 1969, one delegate even condemned pressure for equal opportunities and equal pay, insisting that if women 'could not sacrifice five years for their children before the children went to school they did not know what they were missing'. When Barbara Castle, then easily the best known female politician in the country, was asked to address the TUC on the fiftieth anniversary of women's suffrage, she found it 'agony'. 'It's time we stopped thinking in these women *v.* men terms,' she wrote afterwards. 'As long as we are so sexually conscious about our work we will never really get ourselves "assimilated", any more than the immigrants will.' These attitudes were by no means confined to older women. Even articulate, outspoken young women like Shirley Williams – the daughter of the pioneering women's rights campaigner Vera Brittain – rejected the feminist label, which was thought to belong to the lost age of the suffragists. It was, she said, 'a matter of generations'. And the young Sheila Rowbotham, who went to grammar school and Oxford in the early 1960s and later became one of Britain's best-known feminist writers, thought that feminists were 'shadowy figures in long old-fashioned clothes who were somehow connected with headmistresses who said you shouldn't wear high heels and make-up. It was all very prim and stiff and mainly concerned with keeping you away from boys.'[5]

All this changed in a very short space of time, roughly between 1968 and 1970. One key influence was the bohemian underground of the late 1960s, which was fertile soil for ideas of liberation and self-realization, and which included prominent future feminists such as Rosie Boycott, Germaine Greer and Rowbotham herself. In fact, although the well-educated young men and women who made up the counterculture thought of themselves as radicals and revolutionaries, their sexual politics were unattractive, to say the least. The gospel of free love was supposed to be a way of challenging bourgeois ideology; it was also, of course, a way for young men to blackmail women into sleeping with them. 'Chicks', as the underground journalist Richard Neville called them, were told that they were conservative or boring if they refused male attention. 'It was paradise for men in their late twenties: all these willing girls,' one woman later recalled. 'But the trouble with the willing girls was that a lot of the time they were willing not because they particularly fancied the people concerned but because they felt they ought to.' Another woman reflected that although she thought she was 'breaking all the taboos', 'we had our own taboos and one of them was we couldn't talk about our problems or admit to being unhappy'. She was 'unfulfilled', she said sadly. She rarely 'had an orgasm, because the men were so selfish'; but she lacked 'the confidence to say, "No, that's not right, I don't want to do that."'[6]

Since so many intelligent, articulate young women felt that their underground colleagues were using them simply 'for fucks and domesticity', as another put it, their rebellion was only a matter of time. In 1969, Rowbotham persuaded her colleagues on the radical newspaper *Black Dwarf* to devote an issue to 'the Year of the Militant Woman', including articles on equal pay, birth control, childcare and sex. In her lead article, Rowbotham gave voice to her resentment at women's low pay and restricted opportunities as well as 'something else besides, a much less tangible something – a smouldering bewildered consciousness with no shape – a muttered dissatisfaction which suddenly shoots to the surface and EXPLODES'. Women wanted, she said, to 'drive buses, play football, use beer mugs, not glasses', and not to be 'wrapped up in cellophane or sent off to make the tea or shuffled into the social committee'. These were 'only little things', she granted, but 'revolutions are made of little things'.

While Rowbotham's piece struck a chord with hundreds of like-minded young women, it was nevertheless revealing that in the personal ads, the male designer had inserted: 'DWARF DESIGNER SEEKS GIRL:

Afghan coats . . . earnest expressions . . . preposterous hairstyles . . . a casserole recipe: these squatters, photographed in 1974, might have come directly from Central Casting. But mainstream pop culture could look just as ridiculous: below, chart-topping Slade show off the glam-rock look, late 1973.

The black faces on Britain's streets, like this woman at Brixton market, testified to the pace of social and cultural change in the early 1970s. Even the Channel was no longer the ultimate barrier: on 28 October 1971, to the short-lived delight of the tabloids, Parliament approved Heath's historic decision to join the EEC.

Even Germaine Greer, photographed here in 1971, might have found Peter Wyngarde's Jason King something of a challenge, although it is hard to say whether she would have been annoyed most by his sexist views, his enormous tie or his outrageous moustache.

Below, David Bowie crosses the gender line as Ziggy Stardust, May 1973.

'No sex please, we're British!' Above, a group of 'pregnant men' campaign for better birth control provision, February 1972. Below, Lord Longford launches the paperback edition of his report on pornography, six months later.

Head girl type to make tea, organize paper, me. Free food, smoke, space. Suit American negress.' Rowbotham was not amused: this was, she wrote later, 'the seedy side of the underground: arrogant and prejudiced', and it explained 'the anger which was shortly to cohere' among many of her female peers. One letter to the radical paper *Idiot International* in October 1970 speaks volumes. 'Will you please tell me', the correspondent asked, 'how you reconcile publishing information on Women's Liberation and adverts which read "Dave seeks aware chick" and "the most delicious new cunt on the screen"? You are making me weary and sick with your stupidity.'[7]

While Rowbotham and her fellow radicals drew encouragement from the new wave of feminists across the Atlantic, they also looked for inspiration to a group of rather less exotic women closer to home. In Hull, Lil Bilocca led a group of fishermen's wives campaigning to improve the safety of trawlers after two were lost in bad weather in January 1968. As first they were mocked: the secretary of the Hull Trawler Officers Guild remarked that 'the idea of forming a women's committee to fight battles for the men is to my mind completely ludicrous'. But the scorn only spurred the women on, provoking them to set up Hull's Equal Rights Group, one of the first such women's groups in the country. Other women, flexing their muscles for the first time, met similar derision. Later that summer, a group of sewing machinists brought the giant Ford plant in Dagenham to a standstill when they walked out demanding equal pay and the status of skilled workers. The 'Petticoat Strike', as the press mockingly called it, fizzled out after three weeks, although the women did win a pay rise. In the long term, though, it was more significant than many much longer strikes, because it pushed the principle of equal pay into the headlines and became an inspiration for women workers and trade unionists across the country.[8]

At the TUC conference later that year, a succession of women rose to denounce the 'industrial apartheid' that reduced them to being 'the slaves of slaves'. And by the late spring of 1969, when Rowbotham and other bohemian young women joined a thousand trade unionists on a pioneering Equal Pay march to Trafalgar Square, there was suddenly a sense of excitement at the possibility of change. Rain poured down on the demonstrators, but their spirits were high. Rowbotham scribbled down slogans from the forest of placards: 'BARBARA GETS HERS WHY NOT US', 'WE WANT A CHANCE TO PROVE WE CAN DO THE WORK OF ANY

MAN', and from a group of Stoke pottery workers, 'EQUAL PAY NOW. WE MAKE MUGS, BUT WE ARE NOT MUGS'. It was their first demonstration, the Stoke women told her, and they were a 'bit nervous': 'You hear such funny things about what goes on at them.' But despite the nerves and the weather, Rowbotham sensed a mood of tremendous excitement and adventure. 'Everyone I talked to felt this was only the beginning,' she wrote in *Black Dwarf*. 'The movement for EQUAL PAY NOW is going to get bigger, noisier and more determined. And it's not just about equal pay. You can't challenge the economic subordination of women without immediately highlighting the total secondary social position. Something is stirring. Something which has been silent for a long time.'[9]

Although equal pay had never been one of Labour's priorities, pressure from the trade unions – which were increasingly conscious of their growing female membership – almost immediately paid off. With so many women flooding into the workplace, only diehard reactionaries rejected the principles of equal pay and equal opportunities. In an influential leader in May 1968, *The Times* called employers' failure to make allowances for mothers and married women 'gross discrimination' and 'a great waste of potentially useful skills'. What was worse, only one in ten women earned more than £16 a week, with half earning less than 5s. an hour, a pittance by male standards. Change must come 'with all deliberate speed', the paper said, and so it did. In January 1970, Barbara Castle introduced an Equal Pay Bill to compel employers to pay men and women equally within five years. Revealingly, she presented it as 'a measure for efficiency as well as equality': like most women of her generation, she was uncomfortable with the moralistic politics of militant feminism. Some employers objected that it would put them out of business, while Enoch Powell characteristically condemned it as reckless meddling with the free market. But with polls showing that both men and women overwhelmingly supported the principle of equal pay, most senior Conservatives were keener to proclaim their pro-women credentials than to stand in the bill's way. Addressing the National Council of Women in May 1970, Edward Heath promised that his government would help working women to advance 'with perfect freedom and every chance of promotion'. Equal pay legislation, 'while vital, is only the beginning', he said, for 'a revolution in the hearts and minds of men will be needed if equal job evaluation is to be translated into real equality'.[10]

As a man notorious for his brusque and dismissive attitude to women, Heath made a very implausible feminist revolutionary. It is certainly hard to imagine him as one of the protesters at the Miss World contest at the Albert Hall in November 1970, when concealed agitators hurled smoke bombs, flour and general abuse at the bewildered presenter, Bob Hope. Perhaps more than any other event, it was this moment that catapulted radical feminism into the public consciousness, although Miss World herself was less than impressed. 'I do not think that women should ever achieve equal rights,' she said, 'I do not want to. I still like a gentleman to hold back a chair for me.' As the academic Laura Mulvey, one of the protest's organizers, later mused, it was not an event that 'attracted people to the movement', but it did get it 'much more widely known'. Even the heir to the throne felt compelled to offer an explanation for the protesters' shocking behaviour, revealing his own deeply considered thoughts on the vexed question of modern gender relations. 'Basically,' said Prince Charles, 'I think it is because they want to be men.'[11]

For many feminists, though, a more significant event was the first National Women's Conference, held at Ruskin College, Oxford in February 1970. The organizers, who included Sheila Rowbotham and other socialist activists, expected 100 people to turn up; in fact, they got 500, so many that they had to move their sessions to the Oxford Union building nearby. They discussed papers on the family, work, crime and women's history; they called for equal pay, free abortion and contraception, and all-day childcare to allow mothers to work. Most of the delegates, according to reports, were 'young women, many of them students with long flowing hair, trousers and maxi-coats', although 'here and there were middle-aged mothers and housewives from council estates'. In between sessions on woman's resistance in history and the inspirational example of the French Revolution, 'clusters of young women in the ragged fur coats and with the long, straight hair of the 1960s generation could be seen talking intensely about everything under the sun'. Rowbotham had 'never seen women in that mood before, hearing people speak who'd never spoken before, seeing people inspired to do things they wouldn't have done in the past'. To take part in seminars and workshops with so many women was 'terrifically exciting', agreed another delegate, Michelene Wandor. 'You thought, "This is the first time anybody's noticed this and, by God . . . it's going to be different tomorrow."'[12]

Although there had been women's groups before the Ruskin conference, it marked a genuine turning point, inspiring hundreds of women to set up their own organizations. According to one estimate, scores had been established across the country within months of the conference. In London, with its population of affluent, articulate, politically motivated young women, there were four feminist groups in the autumn of 1969 (in Tufnell Park, Belsize Lane, Ladbroke Road and Peckham Rye), seven groups by the turn of 1969 (including Sheila Rowbotham's group in Hackney), fourteen by the middle of 1970, and no fewer than fifty-six by the end of 1971, from local organizations to specialist subject and study groups. In the beginning, Rowbotham recorded, the Hackney group had met in one another's front rooms; by 1971, however, there were so many members that 'we no longer even knew one another's names', so they had to split into two 'consciousness-raising' groups. Most belonged to the umbrella London Women's Liberation Workshop, which had premises in Covent Garden and combined the functions of a bookshop, a social centre and a clearing house for information, and published a newsletter and the radical paper *Shrew,* which the different local groups took it in turns to produce. When the Hackney group had a go in October 1970, they focused on the issues of playgroups and nurseries, as well as running stories about the plight of housebound mothers and an interview with a local West Indian woman about 'nurseries, abortions, racism and relationships with men'. Two years later, when they had a second go, the subjects included 'black women's position in the labour market ... teachers, secretaries, trade unions, equal pay, housework, motherhood, relationships with children'. It was not exactly a hilarious read; on the other hand, it was often a lot better written and more pragmatic than the underground papers of the late 1960s.[13]

Although feminists were later stereotyped as dungaree-clad harridans with their heads in the clouds, their demands in the early 1970s were extremely practical. At the first International Women's Day rally in March 1971, more than 1,000 women marched from Hyde Park Corner to Trafalgar Square in a blizzard (they had an unenviable knack for picking days of appallingly bad weather) in support of the four goals agreed at Ruskin: equal pay, equal education and career opportunities, twenty-four-hour nurseries, and free contraception and abortion on demand. Even this, however, was a bit much for the newspapers. The *Evening Standard*'s man on the spot reported that the crowd had mostly been 'girls from colleges, sad bed-sitters in North London or the smarter, liberated areas like Hampstead', many of whom had left their bras behind and therefore boasted 'defiantly if awesomely pendulous' breasts. In the *Telegraph,* meanwhile, one female columnist wrote that although some of her sisters' 'nags' had a point, the problem was their 'tone of voice'. The 'overriding impression that Women's Lib with all its Socialist-orientated frenzy suggests', she wrote, 'is of a deep sexual unhappiness among its members'. ('Don't bother to write an article,' a friend had advised her; 'just print their photographs.') In any case, the 'battle of the sexes' had gone on too long already: 'Can't we drop it? Morbidly interesting though it may be I shall not attend the flop of the year. I shall stay at home and with my children watch "Dr Who". It's far more exciting – to this thrill-seeking female anyway.'[14]

Yet despite the carping, there was a genuine sense of utopian excitement about the early years of what the press called the 'women's lib' movement. 'Demonstrations became fun,' the writer Zelda Curtis later recalled. 'Women musicians sent us dancing along the route; women choirs sang songs by women for women; women's theatre groups dressed up as brides and house drudges to confront the onlookers; new, bright and cheerful banners flew, green and purple everywhere; and "choice" became the core word of our campaigns.' And as was often the case with campaigns rooted in the counterculture, there were some splendidly pretentious and laughable moments. In 1971, for example, the Women's Street Theatre Group put on their *Flashing Nipple Street Theatre Show,* consisting of women with flashing lights attached to their clothing at the groin and breast areas. Later, they mounted an agitprop piece in the women's toilets at Miss Selfridge on Oxford Street, while *Sugar and Spice,* which they put on in Trafalgar Square on International Women's Day, 1971, included a display of 'a huge deodorant, a large sanitary towel, and gigantic red, white and blue penis'.[15]

Of course it was easy to laugh at the real-life Sarah Janes in their flared jeans and dungarees, with their earnest lectures on patriarchal oppression and the need to rename history '*herstory*', or their peculiar mania for taking intimate photographs of their genitals and blowing them up as wall posters. Yet not all feminist efforts were so extravagant or so easily derided. They set up playgroups, nurseries and playgrounds, they fought for equal pay on the shop floor, and they built a coalition of tiny local groups and major national organizations such as the National Council for Civil Liberties, the National Joint Council of Working Women's

Organizations and Women in Media. It is true that their members were overwhelmingly young, well educated and middle-class, and much of their rhetoric reads now as turgid, self-indulgent, pseudo-Marxist waffle. But their efforts undoubtedly had a wide impact on the lives of many thousands of others, from the children in the playgrounds they set up to the nervous women who visited their centres for advice on escaping their abusive husbands. Above all, no social movement of the 1970s posed a bigger challenge to the complacent assumptions of British society, from the bedroom to the workplace, from laws and customs to pay and politics – a testament to the underappreciated vigour of national life during a supposedly dreary period.[16]

It was female activists, for example, who capitalized on the growing unease about domestic violence, which until the late 1960s had rarely even been discussed. One criminological survey suggested that almost two-thirds of the women murdered between 1967 and 1971 were killed by their husband or lover; another, analysing more than 3,000 cases of violence in Scotland in 1974, found that one in four involved husbands hitting wives. 'An astonishing number of wives', said the *Sun*, 'accept violence as part of the normal relationship between a man and a woman.' From 1971, however, there was somewhere for victims to go, thanks to the activist Erin Pizzey, who set up the Chiswick Women's Aid refuge in Goldhawk Road, the first such centre in the country. Even she was taken aback by its success: by May 1973, the centre was receiving 100 telephone calls a day, and by the end of the decade there were 99 women's aid groups and 200 refuges across the country, many funded by charities or the government. It was thanks in part to Pizzey's tireless activism, especially her groundbreaking book *Scream Quietly or the Neighbours Will Hear* (1974), that the Labour MP Jo Richardson introduced what became the Domestic Violence Act of 1976, which allowed women to get court injunctions to restrain their violent husbands. And yet, revealingly, Pizzey did not consider herself a typical feminist: indeed, she had opened the Chiswick centre only after walking out on a local women's group where, she later recalled, she 'heard shrill women preaching hatred of the family'. During the 1980s, she became a hate figure for radical feminists after accusing them of hijacking her crusade against domestic violence and using it as a front for their campaign against men and the family. But her legacy is incontestable. As the Labour MP Jack Ashley told the Commons in 1975, 'it was she who first identified the problem, who first recognised the seriousness of the situation and who first did something practical by establishing the Chiswick aid centre. As a result of that magnificent pioneering work, the whole nation has now come to appreciate the significance of the problem.'[17]

But domestic violence was not the only dirty little secret exposed during the early 1970s. There were 'thousands of households across the country where rape will be committed tonight, carefully camouflaged by the sacraments of marriage', Jill Tweedie told *Guardian* readers in January 1972. Indeed, rape was much in the news during the 1970s, partly because feminists insisted that it was far more common than hitherto believed, but also because of shocking high-profile cases like that of Peter Cook, the 'Cambridge Rapist', who conducted a campaign of terror against local women for nine months before he was given a life sentence in 1975. Not all rapists, however, received similar treatment. In June of the same year, a judge allowed one rapist to appeal because 'the girl was not without sexual experience and the intimidation had been mild', while a week earlier another man escaped with only a suspended sentence after raping a woman at knifepoint.

And in a third horrifying case in June 1977, the Court of Appeal handed a suspended sentence to a Guardsman, Tom Holdsworth, who had attacked a teenage barmaid after she refused him sex, ripping out her earrings, fracturing her ribs and causing injuries to her genitals that a doctor likened to those suffered in extremely complicated childbirth. 'It does not seem to me that the appellant is a criminal in the sense in which that word is used frequently in these courts,' said Mr Justice Wien. 'Clearly he is a man who, on the night in question, allowed his enthusiasm for sex to overcome his normal behaviour.' Almost unbelievably, the three justices decided to set Holdsworth free on the grounds that the sentence would ruin his promising army career; as for the victim, meanwhile, they noted that she would have suffered less if only she had agreed to have sex with the man. By any standards, this was an astonishingly callous verdict, and in a long editorial, *The Times* argued that it proved the point of those who argued that rape victims were consistently mistreated by the justice system. Such was the furore, in fact, that the next day the paper broke with its usual practice and published the entire text of the judgement. 'We apologize for printing passages of such a sickening nature,' a disclaimer read, 'but feel that this transcript is necessary to enable readers to form their judgement.' Indeed it was: few people reading the full account of what the poor girl had suffered could have had anything but contempt for the judges, as well as for the criminal himself.[18]

While it would be many years before the police and the courts treated rape victims with the sensitivity they deserved, the subject had at least ceased to be taboo by the late 1970s. London's first Rape Crisis Centre was opened in 1976, a year later women in Edinburgh held the first Take Back the Night march, and by the end of the decade Britain had sixteen rape crisis centres, paid for by charitable trusts. But it was television's oldest soap opera that arguably did most to publicize the shock and suffering visited every year upon countless women. On 19 October 1977, almost 13 million people watched open-mouthed as *Coronation Street*'s Deirdre Langton (Anne Kirkbride), was attacked and sexually assaulted underneath a viaduct. In the following episode, she was shown breaking down in tears and confessing to a friend, but refusing to go to the police out of shame, and later episodes traced the aftermath of the assault, with a traumatized Deirdre refusing to go out or to sleep with her husband.

Where the programme broke new ground was that it refused to move on from the story, showing how Deirdre remained in shock long after others had almost forgotten the incident. In the episode on 7 November, for example, she finally goes into work, but breaks down when a man comes into the office where she has been left alone. On 16 November, when her husband takes her for a night out and the babysitter compliments her on looking 'dead sexy', she again breaks down, and the next episode ends with her standing on a motorway bridge, staring down, apparently about to throw herself off. As it turns out, a lorry driver eventually talks her down, and after confessing to her husband she agrees to see a psychiatrist. By *Coronation Street*'s standards, this was strong stuff. But given how many people watched it, and the place the series occupied in the popular imagination, it probably did as much to persuade people about the terrible effects of sexual assault as any number of feminist tracts.[19]

Since so many early feminists were highly articulate, literate young women, their movement left an unsurprisingly deep imprint on the world of arts and letters. Although there were a vast quantity of feminist papers and newsletters, many of them short-lived, easily the best known was *Spare Rib,* which was founded by a collective of young women in the

380

summer of 1972, The driving forces, Rosie Boycott and Marsha Rowe, were just 20 and 26 respectively, with very little journalistic experience. Between them, however, they managed to scrape together the necessary funds: Rowe went to consciousness-raising groups and feminist meetings, while Boycott, by her own account, went to 'a large number of parties and talked the whole idea up to anyone who would listen in the hope that they'd forget [my] age and inexperience and come over with the cash'. And somehow, by early 1972, they had done it. They borrowed typewriters from friends, picked up desks, chairs and filing cabinets from the offices of the defunct underground paper *INK*, and raised thousands of pounds at a succession of parties. Working by candlelight during the power cuts of early 1972, they sent out questionnaires to discover what women wanted from a feminist monthly; and finally, in June, they were ready to go.

The whole point of *Spare Rib* was that it was not like other feminist papers. Compared with its competitors, Boycott said later, 'it was a very straight-looking magazine: it was clearly designed, it was clearly printed, it looked nice'. Rowe agreed: they wanted above all 'to be accessible', to be 'professional' and to be 'in WH Smith'. At first, she said, they emphasized 'very traditional women's role things' like make-up and cookery, simply because they were desperate to attract a wide female readership. This brought them fierce criticism from older and more radical feminists; even their launch party was invaded by gay activists dressed as clowns, who told them that they were 'selling out' and that *Spare Rib* was 'straight and bourgeois'. But that was nonsense: *Spare Rib* was clearly not just another glossy women's magazine, and even in the design and layout, the debts to the underground press were obvious. The cover might show two attractive women and promise 'Georgie Best on Sex', but inside there were pointed feminist cartoons, an article on the campaign to get better wages for night cleaners, a story on the suffrage movement, and a recipe for a banana and raw cabbage salad that would have received short shrift from *Woman's Own*. As one writer puts it, 'article by article . . . it laid bare the intricate workings of gender inequality in Britain', from the drudgery of housework to a woman's fear of going into a pub on her own. Predictably enough, the founders soon fell out among themselves, and Boycott eventually parted company with the others. But sales were better than they could possibly have imagined: 20,000 for the first issue alone. Revealingly, though, most copies were sold in London and university towns; it was not easy to find in the newsagents of Wakefield, Wigan or Wolverhampton.[20]

Boycott and Rowe's ambitions were not limited to magazines. In June 1973 they attended the first board meeting of a new publishing imprint, Virago, which presented itself as 'the first mass-market publisher for 52% of the population – women'. This was the brainchild of Carmen Callil, an Australian in her mid-thirties, who had been working for the now-deceased *INK* and had decided that she would 'change the world by publishing books which celebrated women and women's lives, and thus spread the message of women's liberation to the whole population', while also banishing 'the idea that it had anything to do with burning bras or hating men'. Inside every book was printed the message 'Virago is a feminist publishing company', together with a quotation from Sheila Rowbotham: 'It is only when women start to organise in large numbers that we become a political force, and begin to move towards the possibility of a truly democratic society in which every human being can be brave, responsible, thinking and diligent in the struggle to live at once freely and unselfishly.' But Callil's new venture was more than a political statement; it was to prove an extremely successful imprint, publishing major writers like Kate Millett, Adrienne Rich, Eva Figes, Angela Carter, Juliet Mitchell, Lynne Segal and Elaine Showalter, and rediscovering forgotten classics of women's writing such as Antonia White's *Frost in May* and Vera Brittain's *Testament of Youth*, which was adapted as a BBC television serial in 1979.[21]

Virago's success reflected the broader accomplishments of women writers during the post-war years. Even before the revival of feminism, women's writing was enjoying a golden age: novelists such as Doris Lessing, Iris Murdoch and Margaret Drabble had been writing superbly and sensitively about women's experiences for years, anticipating many of the concerns that feminists would make their own in the 1970s. The plight of women banished to a life of domesticity, as the critic D. J. Taylor points out, is a constant theme in A. S. Byatt's novels: in *The Game* (1968), an Oxford don's wife, once a promising academic, now a frustrated housewife, admires the heroine's books because they explore the 'real boredom' of 'intelligent women, who are suddenly plunged into being at home all day'.[22]

Then there was Angela Carter, whose heady blend of feminism, science fiction and magic realism delighted, baffled and repelled readers in equal measure. In *Love* (1971), a relatively conventional novel by her standards, the innocent, trusting female protagonist, callously betrayed by her uncaring husband, ends up gassing herself. In the surreal and violently explicit *The Infernal Desire Machines of Doctor Hoffman* (1972), meanwhile, the female characters freely use their sexual allure and desires as weapons to proclaim their own independence. But it was Carter's next book, *The Passion of New Eve* (1977), which became perhaps *the* emblematic feminist novel of the decade, albeit a disturbingly peculiar one. The plot defies easy summary: to put it very simply, Evelyn, a male English professor in a dystopian New York, impregnates a young black nightclub dancer, forces her to have an abortion, and then spends the rest of the novel being punished for his aggressive masculinity. Captured by a cult of Amazonian desert women, he is brought before a mother-goddess, who tells him: 'You've abused women, Evelyn, with this delicate instrument that should have been used for nothing but pleasure. You've made a weapon of it!' Evelyn is promptly transformed through surgery into Eve, a woman: when he protests, one of his captors remarks: 'Is it such a bad thing to be like me?' Eve spends much of the rest of the novel being raped; at the end, after being symbolically reborn in the womb of time, she is offered her old male genitals, which have been frozen in ice. But she 'bursts out laughing' and refuses them; instead, she sails out to sea, in search of her new Eden.[23]

By far the best-known feminist writer of the 1970s, however, was neither British nor a novelist. Born in the middle-class suburbs of Melbourne in 1939, a privately educated convent-school girl who studied Elizabethan drama at Cambridge and became a leading light in the underground of the late 1960s, Germaine Greer was a tirelessly flamboyant figure even by the standards of her fellow bohemians, her undoubted energy supported by a fierce thirst for publicity and desire to shock. The historian Lisa Jardine recalled meeting her at Cambridge in the late 1960s, the setting a formal dinner in the women's college of Newnham. What happened next was a classic example of the Greer effect:

> The principal called us to order for the speeches. As a hush descended, one person continued to speak, too engrossed in her conversation to notice, her strong Australian accent reverberating around the room.
>
> At the graduates' table, Germaine was explaining that there could be no liberation for women, no matter how highly educated, as long as we were

required to cram our breasts into bras constructed like mini-Vesuviuses, two stitched white cantilevered cones which bore no resemblance to the female anatomy. The willingly suffered discomfort of the Sixties bra, she opined vigorously, was a hideous symbol of male oppression.

I'd like to be able to recall that we hallooed and thumped the tables, or that we erupted into a spontaneous roar of approval, a guffaw of sisterly laughter. We should have done, but we didn't. We were too astonished at the very idea that a woman could speak so loudly and out of turn, and that words such as 'bra' and 'breasts' (or maybe she said 'tits') could be uttered amid the pseudo-masculine solemnity of a college dinner.

But Greer's activities went well beyond shocking bluestockings at formal dinners. She wrote a gardening column for *Private Eye,* contributed articles for the controversial underground paper *Oz,* and edited the Dutch paper *Suck,* for which she famously posed 'stripped to the buff, looking at the lens through my thighs', as she later put it. 'Face, pubes and anus framed by vast buttocks, nothing decorative about it. Nothing sexy about it either. Confrontation was the name of the game.'[24]

What transformed Greer from a bohemian Amazon with a weird taste in exhibitionism into the world's most celebrated icon of women's liberation was her book *The Female Eunuch,* which was published in October 1970. A deliberately provocative attempt to bridge the gap between academic writing and crowd-pleasing polemic, the book argued that not only do men hate women, they teach them to hate themselves through the institution of the suburban, consumerist nuclear family, which denies their sexuality and turns them into 'female eunuchs'. Women had become 'separated from their libido, from their faculty of desire, from their sexuality', Greer explained. 'Like beasts, for example, who are castrated in farming in order to serve their master's ulterior motives – to be fattened or made docile – women have been cut off from their capacity for action.' They needed to cast off the shackles of the family, throw themselves into sexual action, and embrace their own distinctive physicality. 'A woman should not continue to apologise and disguise herself,' she wrote witheringly, 'while accepting her male's pot-belly, wattles, bad breath, farting, stubble, baldness and other ugliness without complaint.' Only a woman who had tasted her own menstrual blood, she added, could consider herself genuinely liberated.[25]

Greer admitted later that *The Female Eunuch* was far from perfect, its scattershot argument clearly derived from the fashionable ideas of the late 1960s, from the iniquity of consumerism to the supposedly irresistible power of sex to bring social change. And what is often forgotten is that the reviews were mixed to say the least. In the *Listener,* Greer's fellow Australian exile Clive James called it a 'brilliant attack on marriage and on the psychological preparation for it, and on the nuclear family which is a result of it', although even he noted that a lot of the argument could be traced back to the Edwardians. But other critics disliked her strident, hectoring tone: 'as often with hastily-written polemic,' noted *New Society,* 'there is a good deal of nonsense.' There was rather too much 'nagging', agreed Penelope Mortimer in the *Observer,* commenting that Greer's advice to women on how to handle their lovers came close to being a 'contemporary manual on How to Get Your Man'. Still, there could be no argument with the sales figures. Published in October, it had been translated into eleven languages by the following summer and had almost sold out its second print run. By 1971, Paladin's paperback edition, which boasted a striking cover image of the naked female torso as a metallic swimming costume, hanging from a rail, was being reprinted every month to meet the demand. The *Sunday Mirror* even bought the serial rights and in March 1971 ran three weeks of extracts, billed as 'a series to challenge the woman who thinks she's feminine – and the man who likes her that way'.[26]

Whether everybody who bought *The Female Eunuch* actually read it is beside the point. It was one of those books that came to symbolize a particular historical moment, a book that everybody of a certain class and age thought they simply had to own. It made Greer a media star, writing columns for the *Sunday Times* and co-presenting a Granada comedy show with, of all people, Kenny Everett. Many of her fellow feminists, however, were outraged. Before *The Female Eunuch,* Greer's reputation had been that of a sexually voracious rebel rather than an earnest women's liberationist. She had not even turned up to the Ruskin conference and showed little interest in joining consciousness-raising sessions or building playgrounds and childcare centres. For the serious-minded Sheila Rowbotham, she was a 'scare crow radical', more interested in entertaining the media than in putting in the hard graft that would bring social change. Like other feminists, Rowbotham preferred more earnest tracts such as Eva Figes' *Patriarchal Attitudes* (1970), or Juliet Mitchell's *Women in Society* (1971), a frankly turgid blend of Marxism and radical feminism.

But to the general public, Germaine Greer was feminism incarnate, freely discussing everything from her sexual experiences to the self-indulgence of hippies, often in shockingly coarse and caustic language. Her 'wit and style and intelligence and beauty and guts made her impossible to ignore', the admiring Rosie Boycott said later. 'There were loads of people writing equally serious works who you could just dismiss because they looked depressing and they were hangdog.'[27]

Whether Greer's book made more converts than the unsung activists who never made the headlines is impossible to say. Between them, though, they made a deep impression on British society in the early 1970s, not least because, with so many more women going to university and flooding into the workplace, they found such a receptive audience. It is revealing that although the newspapers continued to mock 'women's lib', they all made strenuous efforts to attract female readers, which often involved concessions to the feminist agenda. The *Guardian*'s women's page famously became a bastion of feminist ideas – although at one stage it was temporarily dropped under pressure from activists who argued that women should not be patronized with their own page. Yet what was even more revealing was the *Daily Mail*'s campaign to present itself as a modern woman's paper, complete with the slogan 'Every Woman Needs Her *Daily Mail*'.

Even the *Sun*, despite the evidence of Page Three, billed itself as a woman's paper. Larry Lamb, its first editor, rather dubiously claimed that it was the first paper 'to recognise the obvious truth that every other reader is a woman'. It was 'in tune with the new mood of *feminine* feminism', he said, 'as opposed to militant feminism', and he prided himself on addressing women, not just about 'clothes, slimming, knitting and babies', but about 'matters emotional and matters political . . . men and money, sex and sin, sport and crime'. The *Sun* even had a dedicated department of female journalists nicknamed the 'Pacesetters' who were given their own section, called 'the pages for women that men can't resist' – although in practice their stories tended to be even more skewed towards sex than the rest of the paper.[28]

And then, of course, there was *Cosmopolitan*. Launched in 1972 as an offshoot of the American original, this was a woman's magazine with a difference, aimed not at the housewives who had traditionally made up the women's market, but at upwardly mobile, ambitious young professionals. Its ideal reader was 'lively, sensual, fun, adventurous . . .

honest with herself', or so the adverts claimed. Its first editor, Joyce
Hopkirk, made no secret of the fact that sex and men were central to
her strategy: as one early reader put it, the first issue read as 'a guide
to getting, keeping (and if necessary getting rid of) your man'. 'How To
Turn a Man On When He's Having Problems in Bed', read the headline
on the first cover, although other items ('Michael Parkinson Talks About
His Vasectomy') were rather less enticing. The ideal reader, Hopkirk
explained, was aged between 18 and 34, 'although she will be addressed
as if she's 25', and the magazine would address her as a woman, not just
'as a wife and mother'. She would be 'very articulate, intelligent but not
intellectual . . . smart and ambitious', with 'brains as well as a body'. It
was clearly a formula that worked: within twenty-four hours the first
issue had sold out. For the rest of the decade, Cosmopolitan reigned
supreme as the magazine for go-getters. Oddly, though, it was Penthouse's
publisher Bob Guccione who put his finger on the key to its appeal. 'They
want to see the kind of woman who is being idealized for men,' he
remarked of Cosmopolitan's readers in 1972. 'They want to see what
the ideal values are.'29

Film and television producers also tried hard to appeal to female
audiences, although the end products were not always to feminists' liking.
Few television series of the mid-1970s were complete without their share
of tough, self-reliant women: Carolyn Seymour's Abby Grant in the first
series of Survivors (1975), for example, a middle-class housewife who
finds extraordinary reserves of strength in the midst of a global plague;
or Siân Phillips's Livia in I, Claudius (1976), who unrepentantly poisons
her way through the first generations of the Roman imperial family; or
Jacqueline Pearce's magnificently camp Supreme Commander Servalan
in the science fiction series Blake's 7 (1978–81), an irresistible combination
of ruthlessness and sex appeal who haunted the daydreams of more than
a few anorak-wearing adolescents. Then there was Felicity Kendal's
Barbara Good in The Good Life (1975–8), whose jeans and dungarees
immediately proclaimed her status as a liberated woman, while even
Penelope Keith's sitcom characters Margo Leadbetter and Audrey fforbes-
Hamilton (in To the Manor Born, 1979–81) were formidable presences.
Indeed, across the board there was a clear effort to show female characters
as more independent and assertive. So when Sarah Jane Smith was written
out of Doctor Who in 1976, she was replaced not with a more conventional
sidekick, but with Leela, a savage huntress in skins, supposedly named

after the Palestinian hijacker Leila Khaled. As a feminist icon, however, Leela was limited by the fact that she appealed so obviously to male viewers. 'She is a bit of a Woman's Movement sort,' wrote the television critic Stanley Reynolds; 'a militant is Leela and she kills with a knife with the ease of a Royal Marine Commando.' But deep down, he suspected, 'the leggy Leela is there for the dads and more earthy 14-year-olds, rather like those appalling rhythmic girls who practise dancing each week on *Top of the Pops*'.[30]

Since there were so few British films in the 1970s, it is hard to make out a similar pattern. By far the most successful film actress of the early 1970s, Glenda Jackson, was the perfect symbol of liberated womanhood, her politics 'a sort of diffused feminism, militant up to a point, but not calculated to frighten the bankers in their counting-houses', as the critic Alexander Walker put it. In films such as *Women in Love* (1969), *Sunday, Bloody Sunday* (1971) and *A Touch of Class* (1973), she played articulate, assertive, often deeply pragmatic women, more forceful than the screen characters played in the 1960s by, say, Julie Christie, winning Oscars for the first and third. Jackson's ostentatious disdain for stardom – she often talked of her desire to retire and plunge into 'social work' – was perfect for the mood of the early 1970s. But so were her dismissive quotes about men: 'One heck of a lot of outlay for a very small return from most of them.' She would have made an entertaining companion for Roger Moore's splendidly unreconstructed James Bond; instead, the producers of Britain's best-known film series continued to cast pneumatic sirens such as Jane Seymour and Britt Ekland. But even Bond eventually faced the challenge of women's liberation. In *The Spy Who Loved Me* (1977), he seems to meet his match: a gorgeous KGB agent, Major Anya Amasova (played by Barbara Bach, later unaccountably married to Ringo Starr), who is just as daring, witty and accomplished as he is. Of course Bond ultimately gets the upper hand (not least by 'keeping the British end up' in the final scene), but Anya strikes plenty of blows for her sex along the way. Bach herself, however, was not a Bond fan: the character, she said, was 'a chauvinist pig'.[31]

Even the most obviously chauvinist film series of all did its best to engage with the spirit of Sheila Rowbotham and Germaine Greer, although it is hard to imagine either of them enjoying it. In *Carry On Girls* (1973), we find ourselves in the seaside town of Fircombe, whose weak-willed Mayor (Kenneth Connor) gives way to demands for an old-fashioned beauty pageant – which will, of course, be organized by Sid James, here in the guise of the distinctly sexist Councillor Sidney Fiddler. However, Sid has not bargained for the fiercely militant 'women's libbers' on the town council, led by June Whitfield's redoubtable Augusta Prodworthy and supported by her sidekick Rosemary, who wears a shirt-and-tie, cardigan and trousers, just in case there is any doubt about her being a lesbian. Predictably enough, the film has great fun with the women's libbers: a policeman calls Rosemary 'this gentleman', a bra-burning ritual rapidly degenerates into a farcical inferno, and Mrs Prodworthy, who opposes the building of a men-only toilet, is given the extraordinary line: 'We will squat upon this erection to man's so-called superiority!' Less predictably, however, the feminists win the day, sabotaging the beauty contest with oil, itching powder and sneezing powder, in an exaggerated replay of the events at the Miss World contest three years earlier. Ten years earlier, the film might have ended with them frustrated; instead, the pageant falls apart. Not even Sid James, it seems, can hold the line against the women's libbers.[32]

Since Sally Jordan never went to the cinema, she is unlikely to have appreciated *Carry on Girls*. She liked watching films, but her husband never took her out and she was reluctant to go on her own. In any case, there was always too much to do. Every morning, as dawn broke over their London council estate, her husband brought her tea in bed; but from that moment, there was no rest. In little more than an hour, she said, 'I come down, lay the table for breakfast, get dressed, and then I charge around doing what I can: the children make their own beds. I make my bed, I carpet sweep: if I'm hoovering, I leave that till I come home, I dust, draw curtains, drink tea, smoke a million fags with nerves, and then I make sure the children are all dressed and ready for school.' Then it was time to go out to work. Sally was a shrink-wrapper ('I know it sounds ridiculous,' she said, 'but that's what I actually am. I would rather describe myself as a shrink-wrapper than as a housewife. I pack tins in cellophane, and the cellophane shrinks'), and she worked every day from nine till one. Then she came home, prepared her dinner, and started the washing and ironing, washing some clothes by hand and shoving others into the machine, and later hanging them out on a line or taking them down to the launderette. At half past three, it was time to pick up her daughter; there was the children's tea to prepare, and her husband's dinner, and 'after that I wash up, put the dishes away, sweep the floor, wash the floor', she explained. Then she put the children to bed, and at last, 'I come down, make a cup of coffee, and then I sit down!'[33]

Nothing was more likely to make a radical feminist shudder than contemplating the lot of the average housewife. The very word struck them as deeply offensive, and they regarded stay-at-home wives and mothers as a slave underclass, so deeply oppressed that they did not even realize the extent of their own plight. 'Abolish the housewife role, abolish the family,' was the recommendation of Ann Oakley, a feminist writer whose interviews provided the basis for her pioneering study *Housewife* (1974). Like many of her contemporaries, she was appalled by what seemed the blatant unfairness of the division of labour within the home. Even though almost half of all married women, like Sally Jordan, were working either part-time or full-time by the early 1970s, they still did the lion's share of work at home. In 1970, one extensive survey of family life in the Home Counties (the most affluent, middle-class area of the country, where attitudes were likely to be most progressive) found that women with part-time jobs still did 35 hours of housework a week, while women working full-time did 23 hours. Men, meanwhile, did just 9 hours, very little of it involving dull, repetitive tasks such as cleaning and ironing. The advent of feminism had little immediate effect: in the mid-1970s, another survey reckoned that men did 'less than 10 per cent of routine domestic work'. And although there was much talk of young men sharing the burden, a study in 1984 found that nine out of ten married women still did the washing and ironing on their own; seven out of ten did all the household cleaning; and five out of ten still did all the shopping.[34]

Not surprisingly, many housewives suffered from terrible loneliness. In Ann Oakley's survey of forty housewives, almost all said they often found their work boring or unsatisfying, and many admitted that they felt abandoned during the day. 'I could be murdered here and no one would know. When the milkman comes, it's an event,' said the wife of a lorry driver, while a shop manager's wife said that she often got 'this feeling that unless you go out and talk to someone, you'll go stark raving mad'. Sally Jordan's was an exceptionally bad case of a housewife abandoned at home by her husband and expected to work all hours of the day. 'Even before you go to bed you've got something to do –

emptying ashtrays, wash a few cups; you're still working,' she said sadly. Her husband, a dustman, barely lifted a finger to help her; he refused to change their children's nappies, to push a pram or even to set foot inside a supermarket, presumably because these were not things a 'real man' did. He disapproved of Sally going out without his permission – 'It's all right for a man, but it's not all right for a woman', he told her – yet he went to the pub every single night, weekdays and weekends. 'I'm a very lonely person,' Sally admitted. 'I suppose I'm frightened of my husband to a certain extent. I've always been led to believe that a man is the boss of the home, and I feel I can't get that idea out of my mind. My marriage is like boss and employee; I take orders from my husband.'[35]

In this context, Oakley's verdict that Sally was 'deeply oppressed' seems absolutely right; revealingly, however, her male doctor diagnosed her as 'neurotic'. She was certainly no feminist: she told Oakley that a man had the right to run his family as he wanted, and that a woman's place was in the home. 'Right from birth you're like a robot, you're programmed,' she said; 'it's as if you're born, you get the toys – the prams and everything – and then later on you get the real things.' Yet she was unable to break the cycle. Even though she would have liked to buy her daughter 'trains and motor cars', she had in fact got her a miniature cot, a doll, a little pram, even 'a little washing machine' and an ironing board. Asked what she thought of women's liberation, her reply was highly revealing. 'I don't fancy burning my brassieres,' she immediately shot back. 'I say equality is all right to a certain extent. A woman can never be as equal as a man: although they're not inferior, they'll never be quite as equal . . . If it's equality so far as women MPs are concerned, why not women dustmen? And I don't think women could do it. So I therefore say men are the stronger sex in some things, but not in all things.'[36]

Sally's values were by no means unusual. Asked if she envied her husband, another of Oakley's housewives, an outgoing redhead called Patricia Andrews, admitted that she often told him: 'I wish I was the bloke.' But when she was asked if she would like to go out to work while her husband stayed at home, her answer was firm: 'I don't think men can look after the children and do the housework and everything like we do. It's not the same. I'd think the man was a bit funny, wouldn't you? Lazy sod.' Like Sally, she worked hard: washing and cleaning every morning, then shopping and cooking, and more housework at weekends. 'I never sit down in the morning,' she said; 'I never even have breakfast.

I don't sit down until half-past four when I watch *Crossroads*.' But her story was different from Sally's, illustrating the point (often ignored by radical feminists) that no two housewives' lives were exactly alike, and that some actively enjoyed their work. One obvious difference was that Patricia's husband, a delivery man, was relatively keen to help: he happily fed the children, changed their nappies, went shopping for supplies, made the evening meal every night and washed up every Sunday and sometimes in the week.

Perhaps this explained why Patricia clearly felt much less oppressed, and even admitted that sometimes she 'really liked doing housework' and that it gave her a sense of pride. Oakley saw this as false consciousness. A less patronizing verdict, though, might be that Patricia knew what she liked better than her visitor did. As the journalist Mary Ingham pointed out a few years later, Oakley was so determined to present housewives as an oppressed underclass that she dismissed the testimony of women who said they felt happy and fulfilled. 'I don't find it a terrible chore, and I enjoy cooking,' one housewife told her. 'I know it's old-fashioned, but I see it as a labour of love. Andrew is out there slogging away for us and I'm doing my bit on the home front.' 'I'm going nowhere, but fortunately my life is rather full,' said another. 'I like not having to keep to a timetable, and I do have a lot of control in the house. It's my territory . . . I don't feel I've missed out on anything by putting my husband and children first.'[37]

The fact is that, despite the condescending stereotype that all housewives must be lonely and frustrated, many insisted that they cherished their freedom and independence, and certainly preferred it to the alternative, which was often a low-paid menial job. And it is not true that housework gave women no opportunity to win status and respect. As one historian writes, it was 'of major economic, social and cultural importance', for the skills of the housewife helped to determine the social standing of her family, and 'provided the means by which the family presented itself to the world'. And yet as families came under increasing pressure to maximize their earnings and thus to share in the opportunities of the affluent society, so the number of housewives steadily fell. It is a myth that the 1960s changed everything: even in 1951, one in five married women was working, and by 1961 it was more like one in three. Economics was not the only factor: as women were better educated, so they were likely to have loftier career goals, and as contraception freed them from the routine of childbearing, so they tailored their family lives to suit their ambitions. But one crucial and much underrated development was the economic transition from labour-intensive heavy industry, which obviously suited men, to white-collar clerical and service work, which women could do just as well. In other words, not only were there more women who wanted to work, there were more jobs for them to do. By 1971, almost 47 per cent of married women were working, and by 1981, 54 per cent. Most were only part-time; even so, it marked a radical change from the days when women had attracted frowns of disapproval if they stayed in work after marriage.[38]

The influx of women into the workplace inevitably brought subtle changes in the dynamics of the office. 'Would you let your daughter work in an open-plan office?' asked an *Observer* feature in 1968, noting that male employees were so afflicted with 'visual distraction' that one 'had to turn his desk sideways to avoid seeing the miniskirts'. Two out of three secretaries, reported the *Mirror*, wanted 'modesty boards' to 'stop the boss peering at their legs', although by the mid-1970s, when longer skirts and trousers had ousted the mini-skirt, the issue was less pressing. But there were other changes, too. Cartwrights, the biggest mill in Huddersfield, employed 2,000 people at the beginning of the 1970s, a growing proportion of them 'mill girls'. One visitor noticed that the men, whose workplace conversation often consisted of sexual banter, were clearly 'embarrassed' mentioning sexual matters in front of the women, as though they were 'trespassing against traditional ideals of womanly purity and, at a deeper level, the securities of family life'. If a woman joined in with their sexual banter, he noted, 'she immediately lost their respect': one man who happily joked with his female neighbour one moment ('Have you got a match?' 'Yes, your face and my arse') contemptuously dismissed her as 'a common thing' the next. In interviews, the men almost universally voiced the belief that 'the different worlds of work and home should remain separate', not so much because they thought that women were inferior, but because their presence made them feel uncomfortable. It challenged their 'basic categories of thought about women', who were meant to be maternal, domesticated creatures, protected from swearing and sexual banter. 'I wouldn't like my girlfriend to have to work here,' one said: 'not from t'work point of view, but from what they have to put up with and t'language they have to hear.'[39]

In June 1970, the *Daily Mirror* held a competition to celebrate the new importance of working women, asking female readers to write in about their experiences in the workplace. The winner was Ivy Williams, a welder from Hemel Hempstead, who carried off the reward: 'the difference between her pay and a man's rate for the same job for three years'. As gimmicks go, it was a brilliant way of illustrating the fact that in 1970 a woman was generally paid less than two-thirds per hour of what a man earned for the same work. Yet it was a measure of how much things had changed that both parties agreed this was no longer accept-able. The Heath government was already preparing a Sex Discrimination Bill when it fell from office; a year later, Labour passed a heavily revised and expanded Sex Discrimination Act outlawing discrimination in em-ployment, education, training, housing and the provision of goods and services. And these landmark laws were enforced by a new Equal Opportunities Commission, which was empowered to launch invest-igations and to take action against wrongdoers.

On the radical right, some complained that the EOC was a damnable interference with the free market and the rights of employers; on the radical left, however, there were complaints that it did not go nearly far enough. In its first two weeks, the commission was inundated with more than 2,500 enquiries about sexual discrimination. But Britain had no real tradition of civil rights legislation, proving discrimination turned out to be a difficult and lengthy business, and the grim economic climate of the day was hardly the ideal time for an assault on embedded inequalities. By the late 1970s, the *Guardian* was already dismissing the EOC as a 'wet lady-like body too concerned with holding its skirts down against the rude winds to have a go at entrenched masculine strongholds'. And despite the high hopes, working women still lagged a long way behind their male counterparts. By the end of the decade, most still worked either part-time or in jobs where there were almost no men anyway. In 1980 the Women and Employment survey found that 63 per cent of women worked in areas that were virtually women-only (like nursing), where their low pay could not legally be challenged. As the *Sunday Times* had presciently put it ten years earlier, 'the woman's dilemma is not so much equal pay as gross and systematic lack of opportunity'.[40]

Since the EOC was so toothless, many women looked elsewhere for help. Historically, the trade unions had been seen as bastions of male chauvinism, but times had changed. Visiting Blackpool for the annual conference of the Textile Factory Workers' Association in April 1972, Tony Benn was 'very struck by a woman trade unionist who demanded maternity leave for women textile workers', who automatically lost their jobs if they had children and had to start from the bottom if they returned to work. 'She put it so toughly and the men looked so shifty,' Benn recorded, 'that all of a sudden it focused my mind on what the things are that change society.' In fact, by 1975 one in four trade union members was a woman, and by 1980 almost one in three. They were particularly prominent in white-collar public sector unions: during the 1970s, the female membership of NALGO went up by 141 per cent, of NUPE by 236 per cent, of COHSE by 309 per cent and of ASTMS by a staggering 721 per cent.

Indeed, although the strikes of the 1970s were later remembered for burly men in donkey jackets warming their hands around braziers, the picket lines often had a distinctly feminine feel. Wives' support groups played key roles in the miners' strikes of 1972 and 1974 – for example, forcing local grocery stores and fish-and-chip shops to lower their prices, or buying food collectively for their families – while both the Grunwick strike of 1976–8 and the massive public sector strikes of early 1979 were largely driven by low-paid women. It was often female trade unionists, moreover, who led the way in campaigning for nurseries and abortion rights, and against rape and domestic abuse. In 1978, the TUC organized a march of 100,000 members against interference in the abortion laws. And a year later, it published a ten-point 'Equality for Women' charter, which called not merely for equality but for positive action to promote opportunities for women.[41]

But it was not only in the unions that women were making an un-precedented impact. Not only did the 1970s see Britain's first female party leader and Prime Minister, it also saw a gradual trickle of women into the professions, so that by 1977 they made up 60 per cent of schoolteachers, almost 14 per cent of GPs and 8 per cent of barristers (although by later standards those last figures now look astonishingly low). Newspapers excitedly reported on the first female jockeys, Lloyds underwriters and RSPCA inspectors. Cambridge University appointed Dame Rosemary Murray as its first female vice-chancellor, while the BMA made Dame Josephine Barnes its first female president. In a piece on the effects of the Equal Pay and Sex Discrimination Acts in February 1976, *Time* magazine noted that Sotheby's had made 24-year-old Libby

Howe the first female auctioneer in its 232-year history, while 'Linette Simms, 43, black and the mother of six, is now tootling along as the first woman among 350 male London school-bus drivers after previously being turned down because of her sex'. There was even a 'women's revolt' inside MI5, where in November 1972 female employees circulated a petition demanding better promotion prospects, and by the end of the decade female officers (among them the future spy chief Stella Rimington) were at last allowed to run their own agents. And even that bastion of the old order, the Stock Exchange, once one of the capital's stuffiest and most conservative gentlemen's clubs, gave in to pressure for change, electing its first women members in March 1973. Bizarrely, one of the reasons given for barring them had been the lack of adequate toilets. But with the opening of the new Stock Exchange Tower on Threadneedle Street, which had excellent facilities, the game was up for the diehards.[42]

When we look back at the flood of women into the workplace and the rise of feminism, what we often forget is that they had enormous implications not just for women but for men, too. The days when a husband could confidently expect automatic deference and respect from his wife were over; in some households, the woman even earned more than the man. Men had been exposed as 'vulnerable, dependent, emotional human beings', terrified of being judged on their sexual performance, announced *Cosmopolitan*. Perhaps this was an exaggeration, but in an age when the old hunter-gatherer stereotype seemed to have run its course, the very nature of masculinity was apparently up for grabs. In 1977, the acerbic journalist Christopher Booker wrote that Britain had entered the 'Age of Mother', with 'masculine' qualities such as 'prudence, firmness and conservatism' replaced by 'feminine' qualities such as 'intuition, dash, youthful glamour' and 'narcissism, self-love, weakness, irrationality and permissiveness'. Under Edward Heath's 'petulant parody of masculinity', Booker claimed, 'firmness, rationality, authority and other "male" qualities were at a very low ebb in English life'. As for Harold Wilson, his were apparently the characteristics of 'a man with a very strong "feminine" side – the pursuit of the outward appearance, guile, winning ways, intuition, conciliation and outward show, punctuated by outbursts of petulance'. And the symptoms of the wider 'collapse of the "masculine"' could be seen in 'almost every walk of national life – from the reign of a kind of effeminate, unstructured permissiveness in morals, education and the arts . . . to the craze which swept politics and industry for every kind of "corporatism", for building up ever larger, more amorphous groups into which everyone could huddle for protection'.[43]

It was in the home that the transformation of male identity was most apparent. For decades, men and women, especially in working-class towns, had led virtually segregated lives. Men spent their daylight hours with their workmates and their evenings and weekends at the pub or watching sport; women stayed at home and built up entirely separate circles of friends, based around 'feminine' activities such as knitting, bingo and watching television. But as affluence eroded the old bastions of segregation, this was clearly on the way out. Young couples now expected to spend far more time together, and research in 1970 found that a typical married man in his thirties or forties spent just five hours a week with his friends, compared with fifty-three hours with his family. Men now devoted almost all their weekends to their immediate families, whether gardening, doing DIY around the house, taking the car for a spin, or going on some outing or shopping trip. More men, too, were happy to take on a share of domestic tasks, even those that were traditionally seen as 'feminine'. The 1970 survey found that 70 per cent of professional and managerial men helped with cleaning, cooking and childcare, 16 per cent just did the washing up, and only 14 per cent did nothing, while fully 80 per cent of clerical men lent a hand with cleaning, cooking and the children. Working-class men, though, were much more reluctant to help: one in four refused to do anything, often claiming that their mates would think them 'effeminate' if they did.[44]

But partly because of these class connotations, it was increasingly unfashionable for men to do nothing around the home. Even the kitchen was no longer a mystery, thanks to Len Deighton's pioneering graphic cookbooks, in which rugged real men master the culinary arts to produce Continental casseroles worthy of Harry Palmer. As so often, sportsmen led the way, and football magazines often showed stars of the day lending a hand with the housework: Tottenham's Steve Perryman armed with a carpet-sweeper in a bizarre montage of domestic tasks, say, or the Scottish full back Tommy Gemmell ('an enthusiastic cook') stirring a pot and struggling to muster a smile while wearing an apron patterned with baby elephants. In his interviews with the Tottenham squad in 1972, Hunter Davies found that some players were almost prehistoric in their attitudes.

Pat Jennings, for example, said proudly that he had 'never washed a dish' because 'in Ireland, men don't do any housework', while the future Premier League manager Joe Kinnear, then a cocky 25-year-old, said that he would 'just want my wife to be a woman, you know, bring up the kids. I'd be the boss.' But several readily owned up to helping at home: Mike England dried the dishes and put his children to bed; Martin Peters washed up, put his baby to bed and changed the nappies; Terry Naylor helped with the baby and said he wanted 'to give my wife all the help I can. She works hard in the house.' Perhaps unsurprisingly, it was the most mature member of the squad who helped the most. 'I think I should do my share. Juny has a hard day in the house so it's only fair I should help,' Alan Mullery explained, adding that he always did the washing up when *Coronation Street* was on, so that his wife could watch it. He had changed his daughter's nappies when she was a baby, and still took charge of bath-time when he was at home. 'I love it,' he said. 'I wouldn't miss it for anything.'[45]

With their enormous collars, garish shirts, patterned ties and painstakingly curled, shaggy hair, the Tottenham players were excellent advertisements for male fashion in the early 1970s. Long hair, beards, floral designs and extravagant colours had once been seen as reliable signs of decadence, deviance and general degeneracy: now, thanks to cheaper dyeing and production techniques as well as the aesthetic legacy of the counterculture and the influence of overtly nostalgic designers such as Ossie Clark, they had found their way onto the provincial high street. Television and film heroes of the early 1970s, from Peter Wyngarde's Jason King to Roger Moore's James Bond, often dressed in gigantic flares, powder-blue suits and lurid cravats that Richard Hannay or Bulldog Drummond would have found very disturbing indeed. When Moore appeared in the ITC series *The Persuaders!* (1971–2), he was credited with designing his own clothes: given the preponderance of orange silk shirts and polka-dot ties, however, his taste looks decidedly questionable.

To be fair, though, it was only a few years since men's clothes had been almost entirely grey, so it was not surprising that so many men wanted to experiment with wildly radical colours and styles – which is one reason why the look of the early 1970s now seems so horrifically tasteless. Television commercials showed handsome young men in clothes in which their fathers would never have been seen dead, from crotchbulgingly tight Terylene flares to garish floral shirts. Meanwhile, aftershave commercials invited men to follow their wives in dousing themselves with pungent aromas, from Old Spice ('the mark of a *man*', according to its advertisements) to Brut (endorsed by the reassuring masculine boxer Henry Cooper). Even underwear was undergoing something of a revolution. 'Bring a little colour to your cheeks,' read the caption on full-page magazine adverts for Lyle & Scott briefs in 1971. 'You may be forced to wear pin-stripes on the outside. But you've surely got more room to manoeuvre on the inside.' The even skimpier Undercover-Masters briefs, meanwhile, were billed as 'masterful, masculine styling', although it is hard to imagine that, say, Christopher Booker would been happy wearing 'Sugar Pink' or 'Flame Red' pants.[46]

If there was one individual who came to symbolize the apparent changes in masculinity in the early 1970s, that man was the rake and adventurer Jason King, as portrayed by Peter Wyngarde in the ITC shows *Department* and *Jason King*, which ran from 1969 to 1972. The word 'camp' hardly does justice to a character described by *Jason King*'s publicists as 'flamboyant, extrovert, a lover of the good things in life': his wardrobe includes silk lavender dressing gowns, suede jackets, snake-skin shoes, a vast array of cravats and a selection of kaftans and kimonos, while he wears his hair in a vast bouffant and sports an outrageous Zapata moustache. Once, hair like this would have been little short of a criminal offence, but in the early 1970s longer hair was all the rage, a fashion that had slowly filtered down the social pyramid from upper-middle-class hippies to ordinary working men. By 1972, many working-class football fans wore their hair so long that they 'could have passed for hippies, except for their big heavy boots'. And even politicians wore their hair longer. Once installed in Downing Street, Edward Heath grew some impressively bushy sideburns, while front-bench Labour politicians such as Harold Wilson, Roy Jenkins and Anthony Crosland (though not, notably, the conservative Jim Callaghan) took to the campaign trail in 1974 with distinctly shaggy, uncombed hair very different from their neat, clipped styles ten years earlier – a transformation that aptly symbolized what had happened in the meantime to their modernizing ambitions.[47]

For some men, however, long hair remained a source of deep anxiety. Tottenham's manager Bill Nicholson, who had been born in Yorkshire in 1919, wore his own hair in a military crew cut and genuinely loathed long hair. When the club's youngsters won the Youth Cup in 1971,

Nicholson rejected their first team photo, which would be sent to their proud parents, because their hair was too long. The boys were sent off to have it cut, and then the picture was taken again. This kind of antipathy was not unusual. In the opening episode of *Rising Damp* (1974), Rigsby regards the student Alan's long hair with utter contempt and suspicion: when Alan points out that Jesus had long hair, Rigsby retorts: 'He didn't have a hair-dryer, though, did he? Didn't give himself blow-waves!' Reports that his new lodger has short hair fill Rigsby with delight, although he is rather less ecstatic when he turns out to be black. In the first episode of *Whatever Happened to the Likely Lads?*, too, hair is a bone of contention: returning from the army, Terry is shocked by his friend Bob's elaborate bouffant, which Bob does not even allow him to touch, and which symbolizes his status as a domesticated, tamed fiancé. And in *Fawlty Towers*, Basil Fawlty is outraged when his guest Mr Johnson (the swaggering, shaggy-haired Nicky Henson) proves a great hit with the ladies. Sybil, however, is rather taken with their hirsute guest. 'You seem to think that we girls should be aroused by people like Gladstone and Earl Haig and Baden-Powell, don't you?' she goads her grumbling husband. 'Well, at least they had a certain dignity,' Basil retorts. 'It's hard to imagine Earl Haig wandering around with his shirt open at the waist, covered with identity bracelets.' Mr Johnson, he thinks, looks like an 'orang-utan' – although as Sybil points out 'monkeys have *fun*; they know how to *enjoy* themselves. That's what makes them sexy, I suppose.'[48]

Since Basil found Mr Johnson outlandish and offensive, he would not have enjoyed being in the audience at the Rainbow Theatre on Seven Sisters Road on 19 August 1972, when Mick Jagger, Rod Stewart, Elton John, representatives of the music press and almost 3,000 fans gathered to witness an even more outrageous vision of masculinity. The sound of Beethoven's Ninth Symphony, played offstage by the organist from Procul Harum, echoed around the dilapidated former cinema as vast clouds of dry ice poured onto the stage, followed in short order by three awkward-looking men in silver jumpsuits, and then the main attraction: a slim young man wearing silver boxing boots, a greenish jacket open to the waist to reveal his bare torso, and a shock of violently dyed blood-red hair above his pale, spectral face, the cheekbones tinged with rouge. This was Ziggy Stardust; or rather, it was David Bowie, whose theatrical creation was the talk of the rock world in the summer of 1972. The onlookers were enthralled. 'Judy Garland hasn't left us!' wrote the critic from *Plays and Players*. 'David Bowie, his delicate face made up to look like hers, has the guts, the glitter, the charm of Garland and yes, even the legs.' Nobody seemed to mind the overtly homosexual overtones – Mick Jagger even got out of his seat and danced – except one man. 'That's it!' Elton John was overheard telling a friend. 'He's gone too far. He's through!'[49]

Bowie is often seen as one of the defining cultural personalities of the early 1970s, not merely because of his shifting sexuality and androgynous image, but because his emphasis on image, theatricality and pastiche, as well as the narcissism of his stage persona, seemed characteristic of the era. Born in suburban Bromley, the son of a charity promotions officer and a cinema usherette, he had broken into pop music first as a Mod and then as a folk singer in the mid-1960s. But he was always fascinated by ideas, masks and marketing slogans, reflecting not only his brief stint in an advertising agency after leaving school, but also the sheer theatricality of British pop music in the age of the Beatles. Although he enjoyed modest success after his first hit single, 'Space Oddity', it was not until the invention of Ziggy Stardust, three years later, that he really broke through to national fame. By now, glam rock was all the rage, a genre perfectly suited to (and partly influenced by) Bowie's obsessive interest in dressing up. With its sense of the theatrical, its simultaneous looking ahead to the future and ransacking the past, and its emphasis on the invented persona of the star as a work of art, glam was bound to appeal to a former advertising man who had studied mime and *commedia dell'arte*. But there was also another element to its culture of dressing up: a strain of androgyny inherited from forerunners such as Mick Jagger, who had famously worn a dress in the Hyde Park concert in 1969, and Ray Davies of the Kinks, whose song 'Lola' (1970), the story of a boy falling for a transvestite, anticipated much of what was to come.[50]

From a relatively early stage, Bowie's publicity traded on his androgynous looks and ambiguous sexuality. In April 1971, he raised eyebrows by posing in what he called a 'man's dress' on the cover of his album *The Man Who Sold the World*, and in January 1972 he told *Melody Maker* that he was gay, with the caveats that he had little 'time for Gay Liberation', despised 'all these tribal qualifications', and supposed he was 'what people call bisexual'. Even so, the interviewer, Michael Watts, clearly had his doubts: after Bowie's words 'I'm gay, and always have been', Watts noted that there was 'a sly jollity about the way he says it, a sly smile at the corner of his mouth'. And although Bowie played on his bisexual image throughout his Ziggy Stardust and Aladdin Sane phases – for instance, appearing on the *Russell Harty Plus* show in January 1973 in a bizarre green quilted tuxedo and yellow trousers, heavily made up and with his eyebrows replaced with thin red pencil lines – it was never clear how serious he was. Two years earlier, after all, he had told an American reporter that his performances were 'theatrical experiences', and that rock music needed to be 'tarted up, made into a prostitute, a parody of itself'. And in May 1973 he confided to *Melody Maker*'s Ray Coleman that 'this decadence thing is just a bloody joke. I'm very normal.' Two decades later, he even admitted that 'the irony of it was that I was not gay. I was physical about it, but frankly it wasn't enjoyable . . . It wasn't something I was comfortable with at all.'[51]

Bowie was not the only example of glam rock's ostentatiously androgynous style. Marc Bolan, for instance, told *Melody Maker* that he considered himself 'bisexual in appearance', and wore high-heeled shoes and glitter around his eyes to accentuate 'the feminine aspect'. But the gender-bending vogue had its limits. Arriving for an interview with long ash-blond hair and mascara around his eyes, Bowie's guitarist Mick Ronson explained that 'having a gay image' was merely 'the "in" thing, just like a few years ago when it was trendy to walk around the streets in a long grey coat'. 'I'm gay', he said cautiously, 'in as much as I wear girl's shoes and have bangles on my wrists' – which was to say, not at all. Meanwhile Slade's Dave Hill, who wore costumes so outlandish that even other glam rockers blanched, claimed: 'I couldn't be camp if I tried, because my background is working-class.' And music fans who followed Bowie's lead and came out of the closet often encountered far more hostility than he did. In most places, wearing glitter and mascara was a sure way to ask for a beating: a boy from north London's Monmouth estate who arrived to meet his friends one evening 'looking like David Bowie, complete with make-up and streaked hair', was greeted with so many wolf whistles, jeers and 'fairy' jokes that he beat a hasty retreat. And when *Melody Maker*'s reviewer met two gay Bowie fans waiting to hear him in Dunstable Civic Hall, even he could not resist a few quips about their moist eyes and trembling hands, or about how the two boys had since 'become very good friends'.[52]

Male homosexuality had been decriminalized in 1967 thanks to years of pressure from groups like the Homosexual Law Reform Society, supported by such eminent figures as Clement Attlee, A. J. Ayer, Isaiah Berlin and J. B. Priestley, as well as numerous Anglican bishops and Nonconformist ministers. Of course a homosexual subculture had existed long before that, centred on particular London pubs and clubs, but the disappearance of legal sanctions meant a dramatic change in the lives of gay men and women – although obviously prejudice did not disappear overnight. By the end of the 1960s the word 'gay', which had had sexual connotations for centuries, was being increasingly used as a synonym for 'homosexual', and in October 1970 two students at the LSE, impressed by the progress of the American gay rights movement, set up the Gay Liberation Front. The GLF had three core principles – the validity of the homosexual orientation ('Gay is Good'); the importance of being frank and open ('Coming Out'); and the importance of working with 'brothers and sisters' to bring change – and within weeks it had almost 200 members. At its first demonstration, held on 27 November, some 150 people assembled to protest against the arrest of a young man for gross indecency on Highbury Fields, and the movement rapidly acquired a national reputation. In February 1971, the GLF even joined the mass march against Heath's Industrial Relations Bill, although the content of its leaflets – 'nearly one million trade unionists are homosexual' – and the slogans on its placards – 'POOF TO THE BILL' – meant that its members were told to march at the back, where they would attract less attention. In the next day's *Evening Standard*, a cartoon showed a group of sturdy middle-aged union leaders studying the press cuttings. 'Well, I make it eighty to one hundred and fifty thousand,' one says worriedly, 'depending on whether you include the "Gay Liberation Front", or not!'[53]

Predictably enough, many people refused to take the GLF seriously. *Private Eye* ran a long feature on 'Poove Power', complete with a merciless but admittedly very funny statement from the group's president, Trevor X. It was time for 'ACTION NOW, SWEETIES!' Trevor insisted, to win 'equal rights with women', 'free use of the Pill', a 'squeaky voice in Parliament' and the establishment of nationwide 'Poove Guidance Councils'. If these demands were ignored, he warned, Poove Power would take drastic action, from a 'Gay Moratorium' ('all of us will just put on some nice clothes and go and walk about'), to a 'Pretty Candlelight Demo' and a 'Mass Mince-In in Hyde Park'. 'We pooves,' he concluded, 'are on the march . . . We shall overcome, sweeties!'[54]

Despite the scorn of the *Eye*, the GLF initially went from strength to strength. By the spring of 1971 it had so many members that meetings had to be held in the vast Middle Earth club in Covent Garden. But then its decline was swift. As in so many of the radical protest movements of the late 1960s, its members soon fell out among themselves, and within a year it had effectively collapsed, although it left in its wake all sorts of gay groups and communes, especially in London, Meanwhile the paper *Gay News*, which was first published in the summer of 1972 to mark the first Gay Pride march from Trafalgar Square to Hyde Park, was selling more than 20,000 copies a fortnight within four years. Crucially, the GLF also bequeathed an unprecedented spirit of assertiveness among young gay men, manifested in support groups, helplines, professional and trade union associations, theatre groups and so on. And thanks partly to this new mood, but also simply to the fact that homosexuality was no longer a crime, gay men and women were far more visible on the streets of London. In Earl's Court, for instance, Jonathan Raban watched men gathering every evening in 'the varied uniforms of the gay ghetto: in their leathers, in peacock gear of wool and velvet, or, transformed for the night in drag, titupping on high heels in Jayne Mansfield shirtwaists, their faces looking like spoiled gouache paintings with rouged lips and powdered cheeks'.[55]

Homosexuality certainly enjoyed unprecedented visibility in the 1970s, from the explicit sexuality in Angus Wilson's novel *As If By Magic* (1973), which shocked some readers and earned him hate mail, to John Inman's mincing Mr Humphreys in the sitcom *Are You Being Served?*, and from John Hurt's pioneering performance as Quentin Crisp, 'one of the stately homos of England', in the BBC play *The Naked Civil Servant* (1975) to Tom Robinson's catchy singalong 'Glad to Be Gay', written for the Gay Pride march a year later. Even recent history acquired a pinker tone, thanks to books like Nigel Nicolson's *Portrait of a Marriage* (1973), which exposed the bisexuality of his parents Harold Nicolson and Vita Sackville-West. In some ways, therefore, it did seem that Britain had turned a corner. 'What a satisfactory life his must seem now,' the *New Statesman*'s reviewer wrote after watching the portrayal of Quentin Crisp:

> And to think too how many ex-colonial governors, retired generals, and remaindered judges and statesmen and commissioners of police must have sat biting their knuckles in fury as *The Naked Civil Servant* unreeled. Once

in palmier days they might have anticipated that one day a grateful nation would be bestowing on them the kind of affectionate, graceful tributes that they now saw being lavished on this frightful pansy. Changed, utterly changed. For them now the long years of neglect and debilitation in Surrey or Wilts, the slow descent into the unlauded grave. And for Quentin Crisp at last a place in the sun. A lovely transformation.[56]

But this was surely going too far. Many gay men and women still felt compelled to conceal their homosexuality, such as the ice skater and Olympic gold medallist John Curry, who had a long-running affair with the actor Alan Bates (who also had an affair with Peter Wyngarde), or Larry Grayson, presenter of *Shut That Door* and *The Generation Game*. Above all, of course, the Liberal leader Jeremy Thorpe went to enormous lengths to hide his homosexual past, including allegedly plotting to murder his erstwhile lover Norman Scott. As the *Sunday Telegraph* put it after Thorpe had gone on trial in 1979, his story was a 'cautionary tale on the dangers of going out in the world with a time-bomb strapped to your chest'.[57]

But what it also suggested was that public suspicion of homosexuality – at least as Thorpe perceived it – died hard. Perhaps people were less ready now to agree with sentiments like those voiced by Charlotte in Stephen Poliakoff's play *Strawberry Fields* (1977), who thinks that 'they're worse than rats, those sort of people'. But an NOP poll of almost 2,000 people in 1975 found that only four out of ten approved of gay couples living together openly, while half thought that they should 'never' be allowed to become teachers or doctors. Two years later, Gallup found that most people felt that while it was all right for gay men to work in 'sales, staff or the armed forces', they should be banned from becoming 'teachers, doctors or prison officers', and that fewer than three out of five thought that homosexuality should be legal. Indeed, outright hostility to homosexuality remained a powerful element in British social life, especially outside London. When the novelist Angus Wilson came out in the mid-1970s, he was bombarded with hate mail ('Why don't you take a long rope, find a tall tree and hang yourself by the neck until you are dead – YOU DEPRAVED FAGOT [*sic*]'), not least because he was a key figure in the protests against British Home Stores in 1976, which had forced a trainee manager to resign after he was shown kissing his boyfriend in an ITV documentary. Prosecutions of gay men for indecency actually went up, not down, in the early 1970s, although convictions no longer had such a devastating impact on people's lives. And gay men still ran the risk of being attacked by 'queer-bashers', like the gang of teenagers who killed Michael de Gruchy, a solicitor's clerk, on Wimbledon Common in 1970, or the building workers who killed Peter Benyon, a 32-year-old librarian, in 1978.[58]

Of course traditional versions of masculinity – strong and silent, gruff and gritty – endured, too. The skinhead craze, for example, first emerged on the estates of East London between 1968 and 1970, at precisely the moment when the hippy look was invading the high street, the Gay Liberation Front was organizing its first campaigns, and sensitive viewers were averting their eyes from Jason King's kaftans. 'Stylized hardness', as one account puts it, was central to the skinhead ethos: in their 'violent masculinity, their community loyalty and collective solidarity, their violent opposition to outsiders and any males who looked "odd"', they ostentatiously looked back to a decaying version of working-class manhood. Skinheads have often been discussed in the context of racism or football hooliganism, but at a time when middle-class radicals and feminists were much in the news, they made no secret of their hatred of 'dirty' hippies, 'pampered' students and, above all, 'queers'. It takes no great imagination to see that the symbols of skinhead identity – the cropped hair, the steel-capped workmen's boots, the straight-leg Sta-Prest trousers and button-down shirts – were adopted as diametrical opposites of the 'effeminate' fashions of middle-class bohemians. And while students were earnestly proclaiming their solidarity with feminists and homo-sexuals, skinheads prided themselves on their moral conservatism, their attachment to tradition, their affiliation with their working-class territory. 'If you live up on the Leys,' remarked one football hooligan from an Oxford council estate, 'then you have to fight or else people piss you about and think you're a bit soft or something.'[59]

And while it was easy to dismiss this young man, and others like him, as mindless thugs, the truth is that there were probably far more skin-heads in the early 1970s than there were gay liberationists. By 1972, one book even argued that they constituted 'by far the biggest single group among this country's teenagers', even though their aggressive working-class identity repelled middle-class critics. Asked what they were all about, one skinhead gave a wonderfully revealing reply. 'What are we for? Nothing really,' he said. 'We're just a bunch of blokes.'[60]

*

For many men, young as well as old, the transformation in traditional gender roles in the early 1970s was at once ridiculous, bewildering and threatening. The sexist joke in Trevor Griffiths' play *Comedians* (1976) – 'I'm in a pub down town and this liberated woman person collars me, she says, You're a brutal, loud-mouthed, sadistic, irrational, sexist, male chauvinist pig. I said, I suppose a quick screw is out of the question?' – was one of many circulating in the mid-1970s, reflecting anxieties about the pace of change. Of course such jokes were nothing new, but they seemed to acquire a more bitter edge in the 1970s, as though reflecting the insecurity and hostility of the determinedly old-fashioned male. And as women moved into new arenas, so they had to put up with a great deal of ribaldry and ridicule, which sometimes deterred all but the most thick-skinned. Women who went onto the Stock Exchange floor, for instance, had to be careful what they wore: wearing all-red, for example, invited the nickname 'Pillar Box', while trouser suits were definitely beyond the pale. 'I was the Night Nurse,' one newcomer, still in her teens when she went onto the floor in 1975, later recalled; 'there was Sweaty Betty, Super Bum, the Grimsby Trawler, the Road Runner, Stop Me And Pick One. They were very cruel. Stop Me And Pick One was because she had acne.' Even the highest echelons of government were not safe. When Barbara Castle wore a trouser suit to a strategy meeting at Chequers in August 1975, her Cabinet colleagues reacted with childish excitement. 'She is just the size of my first girlfriend,' Denis Healey said, as a group of male ministers gathered to admire Castle's outfit. 'I can tuck her under my armpit!' – and he proceeded to do so. It is hard to imagine many of Edward Heath's ministers treating Margaret Thatcher in quite the same way.[61]

In many ways, old attitudes died hard. Advertisements traded on old stereotypes in ways that feminists found unacceptable: a famous photograph taken in 1979 showed a Fiat billboard with the slogan 'If It Were a Lady, It Would Get Its Bottom Pinched', below which someone had spray-painted 'If This Lady Were a Car She'd Run You Down'. Even the *Yorkshire Miner*, the *Pravda* of Arthur Scargill's empire, ran Page Three pin-ups, provoking the journalist Anna Coote to challenge him to a public debate in the spring of 1979. Hilariously, the paper's editor Maurice Jones, who was also on the platform, chose the occasion to launch a bitter tirade against the outrage of dungarees, which he clearly regarded as a sign of dangerous lesbianism. Given that the audience mainly consisted of feminists, this was a bold gambit, although, in a nice refutation of the stereotype, none of them was actually wearing the offending garment. But the *Yorkshire Miner* was hardly alone in its defiantly anachronistic stance. The *Guardian* women's page, running a story about the first woman principal probation officer in 1973, treated her husband as a hero because he was content to eat 'casseroles from the freezer which she prepares when time permits'. 'Women's Lib could do worse than pin a medal on him!' the piece concluded, surely rather missing the point that women's lib was meant to be about more than men settling for frozen dinners.[62]

Publications for the next generation were no better. When *Shoot* introduced its teenage readers to the 1970 'Goal Girl Finalists' – ten 'dolly birds' in their underwear who had entered a contest to find 'the best-looking fans in football' – it was not exactly striking a blow for women's liberation. And as the academic Angela McRobbie pointed out in a famous essay, the emblematic girls' magazine of the 1970s, *Jackie*, was hardly a feminist bible. In almost every *Jackie* story, the teenage heroine is defined almost entirely by her good looks and her quest to find a boyfriend; the only other things that matter are pop music, make-up and fashion. It was, however, a highly successful formula. By 1976, *Jackie* was selling more than 600,000 copies a week, and was easily Britain's bestselling teenage magazine. Its popularity was yet another sign that, despite the supposed revolution of the 1960s, many people, young as well as old, still had strikingly conservative tastes. 'I was addicted to *Jackie*,' one woman said later. 'The stories were all the same, and either had a happy ending when the boy and girl got together for ever, or a sad ending, in which case the last two drawings were the boy walking off into the sunset and the girl sitting with tears in her eyes saying, "Red was a loner." I'd feel sad all through Maths.'[63]

It does not take a radical feminist to work out that one reason Page Three proved so successful in the 1970s, apart from its obvious aesthetic attractions, was that it represented a way of putting women back in their box, showing them as unthreatening sex objects rather than as assertive, independent subjects. This was a theme not just of the tabloids, but of popular culture in general: for every cheap thriller or television show that featured a strong female character, there was another that revelled in old-fashioned male chauvinism. The notoriously lecherous exploits of Benny Hill's television persona – forever panting with a mixture of

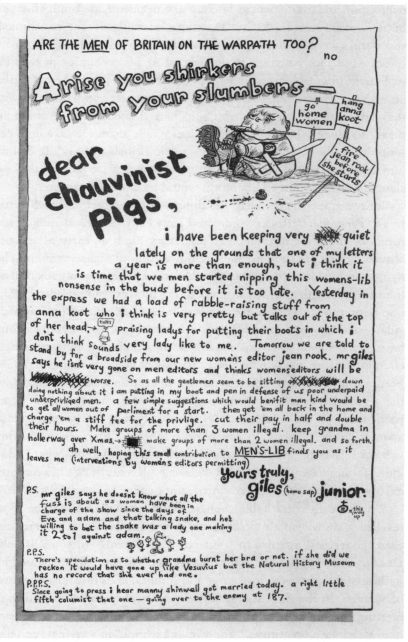

Enraged by the feminist opinions of Anna Coote and the impending arrival of
Jean Rook, Giles calls for 'Men's Lib' in the *Daily Express*, 2 May 1972. The style
is pure Molesworth; the sentiments are pure Kingsley Amis.

exhaustion and excitement as he chases some pneumatic beauty in a tiny bikini – were merely the most obvious example. In the enormously successful 1971 film version of *On the Buses*, the story follows the efforts of Stan and Jack to frustrate the despicable Blakey's attempt to bring in female bus drivers, who will clearly ruin the roguish, masculine atmosphere of the depot. We are meant to sympathize with the men when they attack the newcomers with spiders and laxatives, just as we are meant to laugh when they torment Jack's ugly sister Olive, whom one writer calls 'the most abject female figure in British comedy'. To call the film unreconstructed would be an understatement; a more brutal on-slaught against women's liberation would be hard to imagine.[64]

But other, less aggressively reactionary shows were not much better. In *The Persuaders!*, Roger Moore and Tony Curtis are gentlemen adven-turers of the most outrageously predatory kind: as early as the title sequence, they are shown admiring the bottom of a passing bikini-clad nymph, 'more like a pair of middle-aged, medallion-wearing sex tourists than the debonair playboy crime-fighters they are supposed to be', as one critic put it. Women are either mindless sex objects or diabolical villainesses; there is no middle ground. No doubt the heroic couple would have got on well with Jason King, who, despite his extraordinarily effeminate attire, might have been a parody of male chauvinism. 'You've been yapping all day about women's liberation and the equality of the sexes,' Jason tells his female companion, a photographer, in one particularly painful exchange. 'What contribution has your sex made, apart from the obvious, to, say, photosynthesis?' 'Just give me a drink, will you?' she says wearily. 'Navigation?' he asks pointedly. 'I bet I know more about navigation than you do,' she replies hotly. 'Well,' says Jason nastily, 'then you can find your own stumpy way to the drinks table.'[65]

What is really remarkable, though, is how often the films of the 1970s revelled in showing male violence towards women, often without making even the feeblest attempt to condemn it. In Dennis Potter's BBC play *Double Dare* (1976), the central character, a writer, almost overflows with sexual frustration, insecurity and simultaneous lust for and hatred of women. In the final scene, fantasy and reality collide as, during a meeting with an actress in a London hotel, he thinks he can overhear a man attacking a prostitute: '"You stinking whore," he's saying. I can hear it. He hates her. Hates her! She's biting and kicking and – that's it! I *knew* it would happen! I knew! Hands round her throat! Squeezing the life out of her, the sex out of her, the *pretence* out of her.' By this stage, he has reached a paroxysm of aggression and excitement. Only as the ecstasy dies down does he realize that he was only imagining it – and that in a terrible twist he has vented his feelings on the actress he was with, who now lies strangled and lifeless on the bed.[66]

Of course Potter's highly personal, tormented vision was hardly representative of British popular culture in the 1970s. Even so, it is worth noting that the strangling of sexually active, intensely desirable women is a key element of another black comedy of the day, Alfred Hitchcock's film *Frenzy* (1972), in which the jovial 'necktie murderer' Bob Rusk (Barry Foster) pursues attractive conquests with all the zest of the *Persuaders!* heroes, the only difference being that he gets his kicks out of choking them to death. In the Michael Caine thriller *Get Carter* (1971), meanwhile, the female characters, almost universally weak, untrustworthy and licentious, all meet decidedly sticky ends. Carter's niece is sucked into the underworld of porn films, his mistress has her face slashed to ribbons, and his voluptuous landlady, whom he has already seduced, is attacked by gangsters. Meanwhile, Carter beats up and tortures the prostitute Glenda, eventually locking her in the boot of his car (where she is drowned), and kills another prostitute, Margaret, a key link in the conspiracy, by stripping her naked and forcibly injecting her with heroin – a particularly brutal scene in a film overflowing with masculine aggression towards women.

And yet by the standards of the early 1970s the misogyny of *Get Carter* was not especially shocking. Ken Russell's dementedly extravagant *The Devils* (1971) wallows in female sexuality, hatred and irrationality: indeed, for scenes of naked nuns in a religious frenzy, nuns sexually assaulting a statue of Christ, and nuns pleasuring themselves with charred human bones, there is nothing to touch it. That the same year also saw the release of Sam Peckinpah's film *Straw Dogs* (Cornish yokels lay siege to American boffin and sexy wife), in which a notorious rape scene shows Susan George apparently enjoying being anally violated, suggests that this was no accident. Horror films of the day, too, showed women as dangerously unstable, sexually obsessive creatures, verging on the demoniacal, like the monstrous red-coated dwarf in *Don't Look Now* (1973), and a few years later Hollywood would make a speciality of punishing sexually promiscuous young girls in memorably gory ways. Even James Bond got in on the act. Few people could have been surprised when Sean Connery slapped Jill St John in *Diamonds are Forever* (1971), yet even the most embittered chauvinist must have winced when Roger Moore, of all people, hit Maud Adams in the face not once but twice in *The Man with the Golden Gun* (1974).[67]

Perhaps mercifully, British culture had no real equivalent of Norman Mailer, the aggressively macho American novelist who transformed himself into virtually a full-time critic of women's liberation as his literary powers waned. The nearest it came was probably the eternally disputatious Kingsley Amis, formerly a very keen lover of women (or 'cocksman', to use his own terminology), whose novels became increasingly acerbic in the late 1970s as his sexual potency declined and his second marriage began to crumble. Feminist critics frequently accused him of being a misogynist, and although his books were a good deal more complicated than that, his protagonists often have some very robust things to say. In *Jake's Thing* (1978), the central character, the middle-aged Oxford don Jake Richardson (an updated version of Amis's most famous hero, Jim Dixon), cannot contain his horror at the thought of admitting women to his college. 'It's the men who are going to be the losers,' he says angrily, for there will be

> women everywhere, chattering, gossiping, telling you what they did today and what their daughter did yesterday and what their friend did last week and what somebody they heard about did last month and horrified if a chap brings up a *topic* or an *argument*. They don't mean what they say, they don't use language for discourse but for extending their personality, they take all disagreement as opposition, yes they do, even the brightest of them, and that's the end of the search for truth which is what the whole thing's supposed to be about.

In the last lines of the book, Jake returns to the theme. After months of seeing therapists about his fading libido, he is finally told that the problem is purely hormonal and can be corrected easily enough. He does a 'quick-run through of women in his mind', taking in

> their concern with the surface of things, with objects and appearances, with their surroundings and how they looked and sounded in them, with seeming to be better and to be right while getting everything wrong, their automatic assumption of the role of injured party in any clash of wills, their certainty that a view is the more credible and useful for the fact that they hold it, their use of misunderstanding and misrepresentation as weapons of debate,

and so on, right up to

> their pre-emption of the major share of feeling, their exaggerated estimate
> of their own plausibility, their never listening and lots of other things like
> that, all according to him.

(That last phrase is wonderfully ambiguous.) His decision, then, is clear:
'No thanks,' he says.[68]

Amis bitterly resented biographical interpretations of his novels. Still,
there is no doubt that he was animated by a fierce loathing of therapy
culture and women's liberation, both of which he associated with his
wife Jane, who went to women's groups and consciousness-raising
sessions ('GROUPS and WORKSHOPS and crappy new friends', as he
once put it). In *Stanley and the Women* (1984) the message is even more
pointed: the book's female characters are almost entirely loathsome, and
the satire of feminism and therapy culture is unremittingly bitter. 'I
thought you'd given women a pretty good going-over in JT [*Jake's
Thing*],' wrote an amused Philip Larkin. 'Still got some more to say, eh?'
This was 'not another JT by any means,' Amis wrote back. 'None of the
sentimental mollycoddling that women get in that.' Not surprisingly,
therefore, many critics hated the book, although the academic Marilyn
Butler, writing in the *London Review of Books*, managed to interpret it
as a subtle demolition of anti-feminism, which Amis thought was 'balls'.
Indeed, several major American publishers turned it down for fear of
sparking feminist outrage, which did nothing for Amis's attitude toward
feminism, or indeed Americans. But by this point his public attitude to
women (always more complicated than the misogynist stereotype) had
hardened into another of his deliberately provocative acts. Even his
beloved Mrs Thatcher was not above criticism. 'She doesn't like being
disagreed with,' he told Larkin in 1982. 'FUCKING WOMAN SEE.'[69]

While other literary novelists tended to steer clear of such contentious
territory, the writers of cheap thrillers had no such inhibitions. In Pamela
Kettle's hilariously bad *The Day of the Women* (1969), a feminist political
party, IMPULSE, wins the 1975 general election and inaugurates a
reign of terror. 'A female Prime Minister . . . human stud farms run by
women . . . mass rallies at Buckingham Palace to celebrate the day of the
dominating woman': all were signs of 'high-heeled fascism, a dictatorship
of unbridled power lust', according to the paperback blurb. The master
of this kind of thing, though, was the pulp science-fiction writer Edmund

Cooper, whose views on women's liberation were full-bodied, to say the least. In an interview with *Science Fiction Monthly* in 1975, he commented that men were right to be suspicious of high-flying career women, because 'most women are going to get themselves impregnated and piss off shortly after they've mastered the job and got themselves a decent salary'. He was in favour of 'equal competition', though, because then 'they'll see that they can't make it. We have had free education in this country for a great many years, but where are the good female mathematicians? Where are the good female scientists? Where are the female Beethovens? They've gone back home to wash the dishes and produce children.'[70]

These views shone through in his books: in *Five to Twelve* (1968), for example, twenty-first-century Britain is run entirely by women, with men reduced to 'chattels', not only few in number but physically dwarfed by their Amazonian mistresses. This terrible situation, we discover, is all down to the Pill, which liberated women from their own biology and made them 'both in the literal and in the metaphorical sense, impregnable'. One man, a 'troubador' with the bizarre name of Dion Quern, tries to resist, but, like Orwell's Winston Smith, he meets a tragic conclusion. In *Who Needs Men?* (1972), meanwhile, twenty-fifth-century Britain is again dominated by women, lesbian orgies are all the rage and Nelson's Column has been renamed Germaine's Needle. The plot follows the adventures of Rura Alexandra, 'Madam Exterminator', who is leading the effort to wipe out the last men hiding in the Scottish Highlands. But even she is vulnerable to the most dangerous weapon of all – love – as she falls for her opponent, Diarmid MacDiarmid, 'the last remaining rebel chieftain'.[71]

While feminists bitterly resented the caricature that they were all man-hating, fire-breathing dragons, it is nevertheless true that some presented to the world a very strident face indeed. The London Women's Liberation Workshop, for instance, was gripped by a furious row in 1974 about something called the 'CLIT Statement', a series of American articles advocating total separation from men and condemning heterosexual women as 'collaborators'. By this stage, men had been banned from the Workshop offices, while the movement was already splintering into rival 'socialist' and 'radical' factions, the latter apparently having the upper hand. In November 1974, one member complained about hostility to mothers and their little boys, while the rival socialist publication

Red Rag claimed that 'women with boy children have been turned away from the Kingsgate women's centre' and that 'women in the office have refused to speak to men over the phone', even when the men were ringing to voice their support. By the mid-1970s, in fact, it barely made sense to talk of a united 'women's movement' when many groups spent as much time fighting each other as they did campaigning for change. 'Political lesbianism' was the latest slogan, again borrowed from across the Atlantic, as radicals argued that feminists had a duty to express themselves sexually only with other women. This did not go down well, however, with more moderate activists, and when the next national Women's Liberation conference was held in Birmingham in 1978, the mood was so bitter that nobody ever wanted to call another one. Even in terms of public relations, the event was a disaster: with radicals arguing for a complete rebellion against the laws and institutions that entrenched male dominance, the movement seemed to be living up to all the stereotypes of its critics.[72]

This partly explains why, although most women by the end of the decade proclaimed themselves in favour of equal pay and equal opportunities, so many were reluctant to identify themselves as feminists. For women who had chosen (or been compelled) to become housewives, feminism could easily feel like a slap in the face, apparently mocking their husbands and children, and suggesting that they had wasted their lives as glorified domestic servants. Too often radical feminists – most of whom, of course, were highly educated, middle-class young women – sneered at the views and values of women like the housewife Patricia Andrews, who agreed with feminism 'in moderation' but said that 'these women they usually have on television just put me off completely and utterly; they think men are dirt'. They did not 'want men at all', she added, not inaccurately. 'They're not really interested in being equal with men; they're just interested in completely domineering [*sic*] men and being absolutely self-sufficient.'[73]

Anecdotal evidence suggests that most women probably felt the same way; it was common to hear women complaining that feminists were middle-class snobs, a 'very exclusive club for about twenty women, who all talked to each other', as one put it. This was unfair, but it had a grain of truth, and the impression proved difficult to shift. Interviewing her old classmates as they turned 30 in the late 1970s, Mary Ingham found that although they all believed in equality, they often regarded feminism as 'extremist nonsense'. And these attitudes transcended generational boundaries. At a London comprehensive in 1974, not one of the teenage pupils in a girls-only sex education class said that she approved of women's liberation. No doubt the mockery of the media had played its part. Still, in many ways this was surely feminism's greatest failure.[74]

In 1978, the Hayward Gallery exhibited a gigantic sculpture, *Brick Knot*, by the artist Wendy Taylor. The press photograph, showing the artist making the final touches inside a 40-foot-long twist of brick, seemed a superb metaphor for what had happened to the cause of women's liberation, caught in the coils of its own self-regard. But perhaps it was not surprising that feminism seemed to have run out of steam. Being an activist was hard work: as Sheila Rowbotham recalled, all the solidarity and good humour in the world 'could not prevent a culture of complaint and protest from wearing thin as time passed and the world went on just the same – or pretty much the same'. Utopian hopes curdled into bitterness, consciousness-raising descended into self-indulgence, confidence turned into anger. Most women still had low-paid jobs in the 'feminine ghetto' of the service industries and public sector, and after years of slow progress, their earnings began to fall behind men's again in the late 1970s, when they were hit hard by the government's public-sector pay restraint. In the same year that Taylor exhibited *Brick Knot*, figures showed that only 1 per cent of bank managers, 2 per cent of accountants and 5 per cent of architects were women. The cause of women's liberation seemed to be 'running out of breath', wrote Mary Ingham. Even in north London, the epicentre of the movement in the early 1970s, the magic had gone. In the autumn of 1978, Sheila Rowbotham's Hackney group 'dwindled to a halt', while the women's centre they had helped to set up in Islington closed down. Their golden age, it seemed, was over.[75]

And yet the picture was much more complicated than a simple one of failure and defeat. When Carla Lane's BBC2 sitcom *Butterflies* first appeared in November 1978, some critics saw it as an old-fashioned celebration of the traditional nuclear family, with Wendy Craig's bossy housewife Ria sparring with her taciturn dentist husband (Geoffrey Palmer), like some upmarket *Terry and June*. In fact, it perfectly captured the mood of the moment, delicately poised between feminism and conservatism. Ria is far from an old-fashioned housewife; bored, frustrated, she yearns for something more, for some excitement to leaven her suburban routine. She is no feminist, but she believes in equality and she dreams of having an affair with her friend Leonard. Yet at the same time she cannot bring herself to break with the settled routines of family life. She still does the cooking – albeit atrociously – and looks after her two grown-up sons, feckless wasters who take her for granted even more than her husband does. Critics who dismissed the series as backward-looking, in other words, were missing the point: *Butterflies* might not capture the experiences of activists at the front lines of the women's movement, but it did reflect the lives of millions of women who were drawn to some elements of feminism, inhabited a cultural landscape that bore its imprint, and yet were reluctant to break entirely with the values they had learned as children. There were many more Rias than there were radicals, which is one reason the series proved so successful.[76]

By this stage, public attention was increasingly focusing on the woman who would soon dominate British life. Feminists almost universally loathed Margaret Thatcher, not merely because they disliked her social and economic policies, but because they despised what she symbolized: her accent, her manner, her hats, her husband and two children, her provincial, suburban attitudes. The feminist writer Beatrix Campbell even argued that Mrs Thatcher's rise to power ended an emerging bipartisan consensus on women's rights, representing a shift to the hard-right politics of the family and a new language of moral populism. It is certainly clear that Mrs Thatcher was no friend to feminism: asked about it at her very first press conference as Conservative leader, she replied simply: 'What has it ever done for me?' Her social services spokesman, Patrick Jenkin, was one of the few politicians who spoke out aggressively against women's liberation. In 1977, he notoriously declared that 'quite frankly I don't think mothers have the same right to work as fathers do. If the good Lord had intended us to have equal rights to go out to work he wouldn't have created men and women.'[77]

Interviewed by the *Hornsey Journal* in April 1978, Mrs Thatcher made her own position very clear. 'You are a feminist –' the questioner began, before she cut him off: 'No, I'm not a feminist.' 'Well, you are a feminist, but not a militant feminist,' he pressed on. 'How do you think you have helped women, and where do you think militant feminists have gone wrong?' 'I think they've become too strident,' she said earnestly. They had done great damage to the cause of women by making us out to be something we are not. Each person is different. Each has their own talents and abilities, and these are the things you want to draw and bring out. You don't say: 'I must get on because I'm a woman . . .' You should say that you should get on because you have the combination of talents which are right for the job. The moment you exaggerate the question, you defeat your case.[78]

And yet there was another side to the story. Mrs Thatcher's own career, after all, was a glaring refutation of Patrick Jenkin's argument: despite being the mother of two young children, she had gone out to work without a second's thought. In 1952, she had written a piece entitled 'Wake Up, Women' for the *Sunday Graphic* urging women to 'play a leading part' in business, politics and national life. 'The idea that the family suffers', she insisted, 'is, I believe, quite mistaken. To carry on with a career stimulates the mind, provides a refreshing contact with the world outside – and so means that a wife can be a much better companion at home.' She even called for a woman Chancellor or Foreign Secretary, which at the time, as her biographer remarks, was a 'startlingly radical thought'. And in an article for the Young Conservatives' publication *Onward* two years later she was even more explicit. 'Some men I know are far too ready with the phrase "woman's place is in the home,"' she wrote, 'forgetting that their own daughters will almost certainly have to earn their living outside the home, at any rate for a time.' If a woman had talent and ambition, she concluded, 'it is essential both for her own satisfaction and for the happiness of her family that she should use all her talents to the full'.[79]

Mrs Thatcher's career was, in many ways, the story of a dedicated career woman triumphing over sexist prejudice. Throughout the 1950s she worried that her sex counted against her within the Conservative Party, and even after being adopted as the Tory candidate for Finchley she confided to a friend that 'anti-woman prejudice' still lingered 'among certain Association members'. Once she was in Parliament, her femininity counted as an asset, up to a point: it meant that she stood out from all the middle-aged men in grey suits, it gave her an extra weapon with which to charm Tory grandees, and it probably helped her to advance up the ladder of office. But it also worked against her: because she was a woman, colleagues took her less seriously and dismissed her ideas, and because she was a woman, the press focused unerringly on her outfits, her hats and her efforts to juggle work and family. Even after she became party leader, the fact that she was a woman still counted against her in some quarters, and made it easier for critics to dismiss her as an aberration.[80]

In some ways, therefore, her story was much more representative of the lives of other, unsung British women than we often remember. And while she was no feminist herself, her victory in 1979 – something unthinkable only a few years before – made a supremely fitting end to a decade that had seen women win unprecedented gains and publicity, even if they had not travelled as far as the feminists would have liked. As one woman put it in July 1978, on the fiftieth anniversary of the Equal Suffrage Act: 'Women are tired of being patronised and condescended to. We are bored by being considered as a curious and endangered species. We are certainly not "more deadly than the male" – indeed as history emphasises, we are noticeably less deadly. If our homes and our families remain central to us and our concerns, they are no longer our horizon.' It could easily have been Sarah Jane Smith talking. In fact, it was Mrs Thatcher.[81]

The Ravages of Permissiveness

BASIL: *All this psychiatry, it's a load of tommy-rot. You know what*
they're all obsessed with, don't you? . . . You know what they
say it's all about, don't you? Hmm? Sex. Everything's connected
with sex. Coh! What a load of cobblers!
   – Fawlty Towers, 'The Psychiatrist', 26 February 1979

ROBIN DAY: *Why should a man of your charm and personality have*
to go to whores for sex?
ANTONY LAMBTON: *I think that people sometimes like variety. I*
think it's as simple as that and I think that impulse is understood
by almost everybody. Don't you?
   – Panorama, 25 May 1973

On Friday, 16 April 1971, a retired Shropshire schoolmistress went to
the cinema. Mrs Mary Whitehouse was one of a hand-picked audience
invited to the West End premiere of Dr Martin Cole's film *Growing Up*,
a thirty-minute sex education film – 'in colour', as the papers excitedly
noted – that broke new ground not just in the frankness of its advice,
but in the explicitness of its imagery. As the eclectic audience of schoolteachers, educationalists, moral campaigners and wide-eyed teenagers
watched with a mixture of fascination, horror and indifference, they saw
full-frontal nude shots of teenage boys and girls, long sequences showing
a teenage boy and a young woman masturbating, and to cap it all, a
fifteen-second shot of a couple actually having sex. And even though
Mrs Whitehouse had spent the previous eight years campaigning across
the land against the ravages of obscenity and permissiveness, she had
never seen anything like it. As she emerged pale and blinking into the

spring sunlight of Soho, she made her feelings quite clear. 'Educationally speaking, it is a rotten film,' she said angrily, 'which makes children no more than animals.' It was 'balderdash', agreed her friend Lord Longford, who was already beginning to carve out a reputation as a moral campaigner in his own right. But not all of the audience shared their horrified reaction. 'It was good,' remarked Janet Caunt, a 16-year-old from Baldock in Hertfordshire. 'I think this is the sort of film that is needed. I did not find it at all embarrassing. It was done very tastefully.'[1]

The man at the centre of the *Growing Up* storm, Dr Martin Cole, was not, perhaps, a very good advert for sexual permissiveness. As Mrs Whitehouse immediately pointed out, he was neither a doctor of medicine nor a trained teacher; in fact, he was a 39-year-old biologist who, while working at Birmingham's Aston University, had become involved with the nationwide campaigns for legal abortion and free contraception, setting up Birmingham branches of the Abortion Law Reform Association and Pregnancy Advisory Service, and then his own 'Institute for Sex Education and Research'. Cole himself admitted that he had an 'obsessional' interest in sexual freedom, which he traced back to a 'crisis over guilt over masturbation' that he had suffered when he was 17. And whereas earlier campaigners for sex education had urged a self-consciously sensible, even conservative approach, he made no secret of his highly libertarian views. 'I think teenagers should be promiscuous,' he told the *Guardian*. 'I think being promiscuous can, in many cases, be a vitally important part of growing up.' At least he practised what he preached: unfortunately for the image of his film, he had already been married and divorced twice when the scandal broke. Even more unfortunately, he had only just married again, this time to an attractive former student, sixteen years his junior. And when his critics discovered that his wife worked in his clinic as a 'surrogate therapist', sleeping with paying customers who said they had sexual problems, his image as a 'decadent middle-aged roué' and glorified brothel-keeper was confirmed. 'Sex King Cole', some papers called him, or just plain 'Dr Sex'.[2]

Given the extraordinarily explicit content of his film, Cole must have realized that *Growing Up* would provoke a storm. Immediately after having seen it, Mrs Whitehouse wrote to the Archbishop of Canterbury, Dr Michael Ramsey, who duly issued a measured but nonetheless hostile verdict, explaining that Cole's enthusiasm for sex outside marriage made it 'unsuitable for use in schools'. In Birmingham, meanwhile, the local education authority demanded that Cole put on a special screening, and once they had seen it, they banned it. There were rather more drastic consequences for one of the amateur actors involved in the film, for the masturbating woman turned out to be a 23-year-old Birmingham teacher called Jennifer Muscutt, who was promptly suspended from duty. Meanwhile the controversy was threatening to spill over into the national political arena: on 21 April, the Education Secretary, Margaret Thatcher, told the Commons that although she had not seen the film, she had sent one of her 'professional advisers' and understood that it 'shows the sex act and some sequences on masturbation'. Although she had no direct power to ban it, she said earnestly, she was 'very perturbed' at the thought of it being shown in schools, and urged local authorities to treat it 'with extreme caution'. But her advice was probably unnecessary: by the end of the year, there was no record of it having been shown to schoolchildren anywhere. Desperate to drum up publicity, Cole agreed to a screening at, of all places, a Birmingham strip-club, but then changed his mind when reminded that if he took money in return for letting people watch it, he could be charged as a pornographer. Finally, the affair reached a kind of bathetic climax when he showed the film to students at Oxford University. According to the student newspaper, though, the general reaction was awe at the unusual athleticism of the couple having sex ('one could sense every male beginning to doubt himself') – not, perhaps, the reaction Cole had anticipated.[3]

The odd thing about the *Growing Up* controversy was not so much the furore about a film that virtually no one had ever seen, but the fact that people were arguing about sex education at all. Until the late 1960s, sex education had rarely been a subject of public debate, and most politicians took the line that as 'an effective tool in the fight against venereal disease', its introduction was a welcome development. Most experts agreed that children were woefully uninformed about sex, with neither parents nor teachers inclined to enlighten them. Two out of three teenage boys, the researcher Michael Schofield reported in the mid-1960s, had been told nothing by their parents, and much of what passed for their knowledge was 'inaccurate and obscene'. And even after the *Growing Up* scandal, there was still a strong sense in political circles that sex education should be defended as a good thing. When Mary Whitehouse asked her to give parents the legal right to remove their children from sex education lessons, Mrs Thatcher refused point-blank, although she added that she hoped that schools would respect the views of parents who had strong objections. And in a Commons debate in May 1971 Mrs Thatcher even stood up for sex education against her own backbenchers. They should not let *Growing Up* make them 'get the whole subject out of perspective,' she said, for 'some very excellent work on sex education is being done in the schools in a way of which the parents approve and which is tasteful and satisfactory to all concerned'.[4]

And yet already the reaction against liberalized sex education was gathering pace, thanks not only to the noisy protests of conservative commentators and Christian pressure groups, but also to a broader sense of disquiet that the 'traditional' British family was under threat. In the nine months after the *Growing Up* controversy, the press reported the establishment of Lord Longford's unofficial commission to investigate pornography; the foundation of a group called the Responsible Society, aimed at reversing the tide of sexual permissiveness; the launch of an anti-permissive religious revival movement in the Nationwide Festival of Light; and blazing controversies over sex and violence in four major films, *The Devils*, *Family Life*, *Straw Dogs* and *A Clockwork Orange*. Against this background, sex education seemed to many people a symbol of a gathering storm of moral corruption, splintering families and sexual chaos, promoted by an unholy coalition of addled-headed liberals and profit-crazed pornographers. Even Rupert Murdoch's *Sun*, the newspaper that best exemplified the new fascination with sex and self-gratification, thought that 'people are getting sick of a society which has made emotional and physical demands on people whose minds and bodies are too unformed to cope'. And in an atmosphere of 'sexual jealousy, unemployment and social conflict', agreed the women's style magazine *Nova*, this was the 'authentic voice of the British backlash'.[5]

In the public memory, the 1960s are now indelibly stamped as the decade of the sexual revolution, a watershed in social history marked by a new mood of liberalism and tolerance, the retreat of the state from private life and a move towards greater sexual freedom and self-indulgence. Historians often write of a 'permissive moment' between roughly 1958 and 1970, when decades of public pressure bore fruit in the relaxation of laws governing everything from gambling, suicide and obscenity to divorce, abortion and homosexuality – a 'historic shift', as one scholar puts it, that meant individual morality was no longer governed by law, and that a gay man, for example, could pursue physical happiness without being hounded by the state. At the same time, at least according to the conventional wisdom, technological innovations like the Pill were radically changing everyday sexual behaviour both within and outside marriage. 'It is no longer possible,' the novelist Margaret Drabble told readers of the *Guardian* in 1967, 'to deny that we face the certainty of a sexual revolution.' Thanks to the 'new contraceptive techniques', Drabble explained, 'a woman need no longer dread pain, or years of motherhood, or even, on the crudest level, discovery, as the result of her sexual activities. Nor, on a higher level, need she fear the guilt of bringing into the world a child for which she may not be able to provide. She is free now, as never before.'[6]

In fact, the lazy stereotype of the permissive, self-indulgent 1960s is enormously misleading. The landmark reforms of the era, such as the abolition of capital punishment and the legalization of homosexuality, were passed in defiance of public opinion and remained deeply contro-versial: when the magazine *New Society* conducted an extensive poll on public attitudes in 1969, 'easier laws for homosexuality, divorce, abortion, etc.' was ranked as comfortably the most *unpopular* change of the decade. Of course things were gradually changing, largely as a result of greater prosperity and education: sex before marriage, for example, was much less of a taboo than it had once been, and by the end of the 1960s only one in four men was a virgin on his wedding day (although, intriguingly, two out of three brides *were* still virgins). By and large, however, the great majority of the British population – who rarely feature, of course, in rose-tinted retrospectives of the Swing-ing Sixties – remained remarkably conservative both in attitudes and in behaviour. Even most teenagers, supposedly in the vanguard of permissiveness and self-gratification, made very unconvincing sexual revolutionaries. Research by the pioneering sociologist Michael Schofield found that most teenage boys in the mid-1960s not only expected their bride to be a virgin, but agreed that a boy should marry a girl if he got her pregnant. Schofield's teenagers had great respect for marriage, disliked homosexuality and generally led lives of remarkable chastity: more than two out of three boys and three out of four girls were still virgins. And even at the end of the decade, other surveys reported similar findings; in *Sex and Marriage in England Today* (1971), Geoffrey Gorer wrote that although attitudes were becoming more tolerant, only one in ten people was even vaguely promiscuous, and overall 'England still appears to be a very chaste society'.[7]

Of course this flies in the face of the tiresome and sadly invincible myth that sexual intercourse began in 1963, with the advent of the Pill as the decisive factor. In fact, while the Pill first went on trial in the glamorous settings of Birmingham and Slough in 1960, most women could not get hold of it until ten years later. Only a handful of pioneering Brook Advisory Centres – mocked at the time as 'teenage sex clinics' – handed out the Pill to young single women, while the much bigger Family Planning Association network catered for married couples only. By the end of the decade, therefore, Geoffrey Gorer found that only 4 per cent of single women were taking the Pill, while fewer than one in five young married couples used it – typically, affluent young professionals, because at that time the Pill was the only drug for which doctors were allowed to charge a fee. In other words, although the advent of the Pill is often seen as both a symbol and an instigator of sexual liberalization, the early story of the Pill is a much better reflection of the sheer conservatism of moral attitudes. It was only in 1968, after all, that the Family Planning Association grudgingly allowed some of its branches to give contraception to unmarried women. And for all the excitement in the press about the wonder contraceptive drug, many people remained suspicious of the Pill. Many men disliked giving up their control over contraception, and working-class couples were much less likely to use it than middle-class ones. When the *Evening Standard* commissioned a poll in 1971 asking whether it should be available to single women, 32 per cent still said no, with opposition highest among women over 65. Most younger women who had tried it were great fans; even so, one in three women under 44 and even one in five women under 24 opposed giving it to unmarried women – a useful reminder that not everybody was swept up in the enthusiasm for change.[8]

The crucial breakthrough in the availability of the Pill came in 1970, when, under pressure from the government, the Family Planning Association instructed all its clinics to make it available to single women. This was without doubt a landmark moment: although the pioneering Brook clinics had led the way in legitimizing the provision of the Pill to young women, there were so few of them that they could not possibly reach the majority of the population. From 1970, however, hundreds of FPA clinics were required to make provision for single women, and five years later, the FPA having been absorbed into the National Health Service, contraception was made free for all women, married or single. At the time, some Tory backbenchers and tabloid critics made a great fuss about 'sex on the rates'. Yet within just a few years it was clear that as a relatively simple and highly effective form of contraception, the Pill was enormously popular. As early as 1973, surveys showed that 65 per cent of young women had taken it, and this rose to 74 per cent two years later. And even though a health scare – based on reports in the *Lancet* in 1977 that the Pill increased the risk of thrombosis in older women – temporarily damaged its popularity, there is no denying its overall impact: by the end of the 1980s, almost nine out of ten young women had taken it. For the first time women had a reliable contraceptive about which there was no need to feel squeamish or embarrassed – 'It's absolutely safe and no fiddling about – so natural,' 'It's just like not using any-thing and you can really relax and enjoy it,' women told an interviewer in 1970 – and for the first time they had complete control over their own fertility. The Pill meant that 'sex was not a big risk any more and neither were men', one young woman recalled. Even after she stopped taking it, she still basked in the confidence it had brought. 'I was allowed to have what I liked,' she said, 'and did not have to be frightened of sex because it could trap me into things. I didn't have to be punished.'[9]

One of the many myths about the Pill was that because it gave women control over their own fertility, it represented an extraordinary and revolutionary breakthrough, opening the door to a new age of heedless promiscuity. We tend to forget, though, that men and women had been using reasonably reliable methods of birth control for years, such as the condom or the cap. Even after 1970, many women stuck to more familiar devices, and it is not true that it immediately inaugurated an era of wild abandon. In 1972, a survey of 3,000 women for the *Sunday Times* concluded that 'the more promiscuous you are, the *less* likely you are to be on the Pill'. Yet there is no doubt that the popularization of the Pill did mark a crucial turning point, not just in behaviour, but in the way people talked and thought about sex. As the medical researcher Ann Cartwright pointed out in 1970, 'an oral contraceptive could be discussed more easily and with less embarrassment than methods related to the vagina, penis or sexual intercourse', prompting people to talk much more openly about the entire subject. And in a broader sense the Pill came to symbolize a whole series of related innovations, from the new divorce and abortion laws to the spread of family planning clinics and the general acceptability of various forms of birth control. We commonly think of all this as a 'sexual revolution', although the crude division into pre-revolutionary monasticism and post-revolutionary hedonism obscures the fact that some people had been buying condoms, sex manuals and the services of prostitutes for decades anyway. As the historian Hera Cook points out, the events of the late 1960s and early 1970s were merely the latest stage in a long history of change – a 'long sexual revolution', indeed – stretching back to the nineteenth century. And yet the Family Planning Association's decision on the Pill in 1970 makes as good a dividing line as any. With that decision, generations of women were handed unprecedented control over their own fertility, breaking the historic bond between sex and childbirth. From that point onwards, there was no going back.[10]

Ironically, the crucial point about the sexual revolution is that it made sex not more but *less* important. Before the early 1970s, having sex had 'immense emotional, economic and symbolic weight' attached to it, as Cook puts it, because to sleep with another person was 'tantamount to choosing them as a life partner'. Even in the kitchen-sink plays and novels of the early 1960s, for example, having sex is a literally life-changing moment and something to be taken intensely seriously. The plot of Stan Barstow's novel *A Kind of Loving* (1960) shows the consequences of getting it wrong: when Vic, the protagonist, gets an office typist pregnant, he is condemned to spend the rest of his life with her, even though he clearly does not love her. But by the mid-1970s this had clearly changed. The bohemian academics Howard and Barbara in Malcolm Bradbury's *The History Man* (1975) or the Robin Askwith character in the film *Confessions of a Window Cleaner* (1974) may have sex with anybody they fancy, but they take it much less seriously: the ubiquity of contraception and availability of abortion have taken the danger out of it. And of course this helps to explain why, from the mid-1970s onwards, sex became the perfect vehicle for advertisers and marketing men. Supposedly liberated from its 'social ceremony and emotional baggage', no longer seen in terms of a life-changing commitment, it was increasingly presented as the ultimate consumer luxury. As Jeremy Seabrook noted after observing teenage girls discussing their love affairs in Blackburn, 'their concern with their sexuality, their looks, their sensuality, is readily turned to profit', from cosmetics that promised to make girls more alluring to magazines offering tips on getting and pleasing a man. And all of this hammered home the simple message that sex was no longer serious; it was fun.[11]

With the link between sex and childbearing broken, the new orthodoxy emphasized sex as pure pleasure, not just a means of self-indulgence but a form of self-expression. 'An active and rewarding sex life, at a mature level, is indispensable if one is to achieve his full potential as a member of the human race,' wrote the Californian sex therapist David Reuben in his manual *Everything You Always Wanted to Know About Sex (But Were Afraid to Ask)*, published in 1969. Of course sex manuals were nothing new: between 1941 and 1964, Eustace Chesser's *Love Without Fear* had sold an estimated 3 million copies, despite being available only through mail order and in backstreet shops. But in its emphasis on pleasure rather than procreation, on gratification rather than reproduction, Reuben's manual typified the new mood. Even the wording of the title – 'sex' rather than 'love' – reflected the deeper change, a point made even more emphatically by another bestseller three years later. Published in 1972 by the London-based obstetrician, anarchist and poet Alex Comfort, *The Joy of Sex* was an urbane, explicit sex manual modelled on a cookery book: hence the subtitle, 'A Gourmet Guide', and the section titles 'Starters', 'Main Courses' and so on. Groundbreaking in the frankness of its recommendations, the book also boasted some now splendidly dated illustrations that gave the male participant a shabby beard and the woman a luxuriant growth of underarm hair. But the illustrations were not the only things that soon proved anachronistic. Prostitutes, Comfort explains at one point, are usually motivated by 'an active dislike of males', while 'the expression of erotic astonishment on the face of a well-gagged woman when she finds she can only mew is irresistible to most men's rape instincts'. These sections, needless to say, did not survive in later editions. But they did no harm to the original version's prospects: not only did it sell hundreds of thousands of copies in Britain, it spent a stunning seventy weeks in the American bestseller list between 1972 and 1974, and never went out of print.[12]

It is impossible to know how many people actually followed Comfort's recommendations, or indeed how many read the book for titillation rather than instruction. But there is little doubt that in the course of one generation, sexual behaviour and attitudes had undergone a tremendous change. Now that having sex was no longer a necessarily life-changing decision, manuals, newspapers and medical experts alike began to treat it not as a private expression of intimacy between husband and wife, but as the ultimate form of recreation. Just as contemporary travel guides opened readers' eyes to the pleasures of Mediterranean holidays, just as cookery books recommended exotic new dinner-party recipes, so magazines like *Cosmopolitan* advised readers to set their standards ever higher, urging them to maximize the quantity and quality of their orgasms, the bewildering variety of their partners and positions, the intensity and frequency of their sexual experiences. Even the female body was no longer sacrosanct; to anybody who read *Cosmopolitan*, it seemed less like a temple and more like a playground. 'To awaken your body and make it perform well, you must train like an athlete for the act of love,' advised another manual, *The Sensuous Woman*, in 1970. In this context, the idea of remaining chaste until your wedding day seemed not merely unproductive but downright bizarre. The days when nice girls said no seemed to be long gone: by 1978 a divorced teacher in her thirties could write to *Cosmopolitan* complaining that 'nowadays you go out with a man and it's simply assumed that you are an emancipated woman who will fall into bed'.[13]

Of course not all women fell into bed on their first date: in a survey published in 1976, the researcher Michael Schofield reported that only 60 out of 376 young adults he interviewed were genuinely promiscuous (although even this figure marked a dramatic shift from ten years earlier). Still, given the context, the disgruntled teacher's suitors were not being excessively optimistic. In the first half of the 1950s, most girls had lost their virginity between the ages of 19 and 23; by the first half of the 1970s, most lost their virginity between 17 and 20. Perhaps more importantly, the vast majority of young women by the mid-1970s lost their virginity before they were married. As late as 1963, two-thirds of the population had believed that sex before marriage was immoral (even though many people fell short of their own high moral standards). By 1973, however, just one in ten people did so, and as attitudes changed, so did behaviour. More than 86 per cent of women who reached adulthood in the first half of the 1970s had sex before marriage, and by the end of the decade premarital chastity had almost died out. By the late 1980s, in fact, fewer than 1 per cent of women were virgins on their wedding day – an extraordinary transformation given that the equivalent figure in the late 1960s was more like two out of three. At the same time, the taboo on unmarried couples living together was clearly evaporating, not just among the young, but among their elders too. When the journalist Mary Ingham interviewed a group of 30-year-old women at the end of the 1970s, many recalled that their parents had actively encouraged them to live together before marriage. One young couple, Shirley and John, were always 'worried' how much their parents knew about their relationship, yet, as Shirley recalled, in 1971 her mother 'suggested it would be cheaper if we lived together and I thought heavens, it's my mother saying that!'[14]

From one perspective, of course, the sexual revolution of the 1970s represented a genuine moment of liberation, allowing generations of young men and women to experience physical pleasures, apparently free from guilt or consequences, that had been denied their predecessors. And yet even at the time perceptive observers recognized that despite the naive optimism of the manuals and magazines, sexual self-indulgence did not come without a cost. One obvious consequence, for instance, was the stunning rise in illegitimacy. In 1964, just 7 per cent of children had been born out of wedlock; by 1971, the equivalent proportion was up to 8.4 per cent, by 1981 almost 13 per cent, and by the 1990s it was well on its way towards 40 per cent. It is true that single parents and illegitimate children were no longer ostracized as they once had been: in 1967 special tax allowances were extended to unmarried mothers, in 1975 illegitimate children were granted inheritance rights, in 1976 family allowances were extended to the first child in a one-parent family, and in 1979 the Law Commission recommended that courts no longer distinguish between legitimate and illegitimate children – all of which infuriated conservatives, for whom the state itself was undermining the traditional family. Even so, single mothers still found life hard and society highly censorious, which perhaps explains why abortion clinics saw so much trade.[15]

When abortion had been legalized in 1967, most people had seen it as a long-overdue measure to regulate an appallingly dangerous back-street business. Most historians agree that there were perhaps 100,000 illegal abortions a year during the 1950s and early 1960s, many of them horrifyingly rushed and bloody affairs in dingy flats and dirty bathrooms. As the vast majority of the public saw it – as well as the Anglican churchmen who were in the vanguard of the movement for change – legalizing abortion was a humane and sensible measure to safeguard the lives of thousands of frightened women; by the mid-1960s, polls showed that at least seven out of ten people supported it. What nobody had expected, however, was that the abortion figures would then go through the roof; indeed, most experts predicted that after a brief flurry, abortion would decline as better contraception and sex education made it unnecessary. In fact, the opposite happened. In 1968, there were 23,641 abortions; a year later there were 58,819; a year after that there were 83,851; and by 1973 the total was up to 169,362. At the time, critics insisted that this must mean that young women were treating abortion as merely another form of birth control, and that its popularity reflected 'an increase in promiscuity and immorality coupled with a crude, cynical, hedonistic attitude to sex', as one academic study put it in 1972. But the same study went on to debunk that argument. Most of the unmarried women who had had abortions, it emerged, were 'generally sexually inexperienced', and their plight was the result of excessive naivety rather than cynical calculation. No doubt some had been reckless or foolish, but they surely deserved pity rather than condemnation.[16]

Perhaps not surprisingly, many people were deeply disturbed at the enormous surge in legal abortions, and throughout the 1970s the Catholic Church and other conservative groups organized rallies, demonstrations and lobbying efforts, which in turn provoked feminists to set up the National Abortion Campaign to defend women's newfound rights. Yet while the great majority were essentially indifferent to the abortion controversy, it was a powerful reminder that the sexual revolution came at a price. During the late 1960s and early 1970s, there had been plenty of childish waffle about sex as liberating, radical, even subversive, inspired by the legacy of fashionable cod-Marxist thinkers such as Wilhelm Reich and Herbert Marcuse.* By the mid-1970s, however, it was already clear that there was a darker side to the sexual revolution, typified by the last scene in *The History Man*, in which, even as the predatory academic Howard is seducing a colleague at one of his debauched parties, his wife Barbara is slashing her own arm open in an apparent suicide attempt.

---

* Reich was by any standards a very strange figure. Born in the Habsburg province of Galicia, he studied under Sigmund Freud and eventually ended up in New York, where he argued that sexual urges should be indulged, not repressed, and that orgasms were the key to mental health. He later insisted that he could channel a cosmic life force called 'orgone energy' (not unlike the Force in *Star Wars*) with an 'orgone accumulator', which he could then fire at the clouds to create rain. Convinced that this was 'a fraud of the first magnitude', the Food and Drug Administration ordered Reich to stop selling the orgone accumulator. When he refused, he was imprisoned in Lewisburg, Pennsylvania, where he died in 1957. It seems likely that he was mentally ill.

Indeed, for all the talk about sex as emancipation, it was predators like Howard, who played on the insecurity, confusion and vulnerability of others, that were the real winners – in the short term at least. Women 'were so brainwashed by the desire not to appear repressed and old-fashioned', wrote Mary Ingham, that they were frightened to say no to men, even when they were recoiling inside. 'The line was, we're all friends, we all sleep with each other, and it's all fine,' another woman recalled. 'Actually, it never was fine for us girls. But you had to pretend that it was.'[17]

The irony is that within just a few years, many of the people who had initially welcomed the sexual revolution – who had, indeed, congratulated themselves at their own emancipation and looked forward eagerly to the collapse of international capitalism beneath the tide of sexual self-expression – were lamenting that it had gone badly wrong. One book published in 1978 even called it *The Illusory Freedom*. Perhaps that was going too far: the new freedoms allowing a couple to sleep together before marriage, homosexuals to lead open and unashamed lives, and women to terminate unwanted pregnancies, were real enough. Yet while people no longer chafed under the legal restraints that had survived until the late 1960s, they had arguably replaced one set of pressures with another. At the beginning of the following decade, a survey by *19* magazine found that 70 per cent of readers had lost their virginity by the time they were 17, yet 69 per cent agreed that young women came under 'too much pressure' to have sex, and two out of three admitted that they sometimes found it difficult to say no.

> What you became terribly aware of in the seventies [one woman said later] was that it wasn't free for women, it was an absolute imposition. The Pill removed your autonomy. Suddenly, you were supposed to think that it was absolutely fabulous to wave your legs in the air and get fucked . . . What did women get out of it? Lots of bad sex that they probably didn't want, men thinking that this was Christmas, and lots of sexually transmitted diseases.

The sexual revolution 'may have expanded women's access to sex', concluded the feminist Beatrix Campbell, 'but it was the same old kind of sex'.[18]

Thin, drawn and anxious, her pale face staring out under her reddish fringe, 19-year-old Janice Baildon lives at home with her parents on a nondescript suburban estate in Harlow. Her father, a stern and industrious man from Liverpool who once served in the army, works in a large store. Her mother, an overbearing woman of distinctly old-fashioned opinions, is the soul of upper-working-class conservatism. Earnest and respectable, the Baildons are baffled by their daughter's listless, disaffected behaviour: she drifts from job to job, seems unable to put down roots, and collapses on the Tube, apparently for no reason. As time goes on, Janice's condition worsens; as her parents nag and pester her, she retreats deeper into herself, ever more lethargic, ever more withdrawn. She falls pregnant by one of her student friends; her parents, horrified at the 'disgusting and unchristian' thought of an illegitimate baby, cajole her into having an abortion. Not surprisingly, her mental state worsens, and her parents take her to a sympathetic young experimental psychiatrist, complete with standard-issue black polo neck, who encourages his staff to call him Mike and gets his patients to talk through their problems in long encounter sessions. But when Mike is kicked out of the hospital by reactionary, upper-class administrators, Janice's condition takes a turn for the worse. She falls into the hands of a cold, clipped doctor who plies her with drugs and electro-convulsive treatment, and although she is briefly rescued by a scooter-riding boyfriend, another doctor forcibly retrieves her with the help of the police. Her mind collapses altogether; when we last see her, she is utterly sullen, apathetic and uncommunicative, staring blankly at an audience of uncaring, half-interested medical students while the doctor invites them to take notes. Her life has been reduced to a schizophrenic case history, her individuality crushed beneath the suffocating expectations of her family and the weight of the state machine. 'I think the clinical picture is a fairly clear one,' the doctor says dismissively. 'Any questions?'

As a portrait of the typical British family, Ken Loach's film *Family Life*, released in January 1972 and based on a script by the radical playwright David Mercer, was bleak indeed. Loach and Mercer had already worked together on a similar project for television – *In Two Minds*, which was shown in the BBC's *Wednesday Play* slot five years earlier – and like its predecessor, *Family Life* attracted praise and controversy in equal measure. Nobody questioned its disturbing power, the brilliance with which Loach had created an atmosphere of utterly convincing naturalism, or his skill at making a tiny budget stretch to capture the texture of everyday life in the early 1970s. And yet, wondered the critic John Russell Taylor in *The Times*, 'is it possible to be at once deeply moved and impressed by a film, and at the same time deeply distrustful of it?' As Taylor pointed out, it seemed at the very least highly unfair to present the first psychiatrist, played by a practising young therapist, Michael Riddall, as a straightforward 'goody', while the second, 'a professional actor doing it all crisp and thin-lipped, is presented as a baddy'. And for all its emotional punch, other reviewers found the film equally one-sided, even mendacious in its partisanship – a criticism that could, in fact, be levelled at so many of Loach's films. Contemplating 'the brutalism of electro-shock treatment in the traditional hospital; the soulless arrangement of rows of beds like a conveyor-belt set-up; the Gestapo-like dispositions of medical attendants who come to cart the girl back to the wards at the end', Alexander Walker wondered why 'people otherwise so humane and sophisticated still feel the need to allow an audience no choice but to see things their way'. Even the *Socialist Worker*'s Peter Sedgwick, who applauded Loach's left-wing commitment, thought that *Family Life* 'panders to the common prejudices which create the stigma of mental illness'. The film could not 'possibly encourage any person with serious mental trouble to seek voluntary treatment from any existing NHS facilities,' Sedgwick wrote, in a review that attracted a deluge of angry complaints. 'It can only discourage and frighten them. And it cruelly mocks (through its caricature of the family situation of a schizophrenic patient) the awful dilemmas which confront thousands of actual families in which all, perhaps, are "ill" but one particular person is actually crazy.'[19]

Like so many self-consciously progressive films and plays in the early 1970s, *Family Life* was heavily influenced by the ideas of the Scottish psychiatrist, poet and countercultural icon, R. D. Laing. A trained psychotherapist, Laing had more than a few mental issues of his own: his father was a violent and unstable man, his mother was widely regarded as virtually mad, and he was afflicted with alcoholism and clinical depression. By the mid-1960s, however, his pioneering ideas – on the 'divided self' under threat from others, or the oppressive tyranny of the 'family nexus' – were all the rage. At Kingsley Hall, in the East End of London, he set up a community for therapists and psychotic patients, encouraging the latter to regress into a kind of infantile state, from which he believed they would emerge saner and better adjusted than ever. More often than not, Laing explained madness as the alienated reaction of a confused young man or (more typically) woman to the tyrannical repression of the family. The 'mad', he argued, often had a clearer view of reality than people who thought themselves 'sane'; parents' affection for their children was really 'violence masquerading as love'; and the mental health services were running a 'police state' and a 'guerrilla war' against their patients. 'They're the violent ones,' he insisted in 1967, 'but they think they are maintaining sanity, peace, law and order.'[20]

It is hard now to reread Laing's books without shuddering at the thought of the damage they caused. No doubt traditional psychiatry had its flaws, but its practitioners were generally well-intentioned people trying to do their best for patients who were genuinely sick, and they deserved better than the crude, childish caricatures of Laing's books and Loach's film. And although some doctors listened to Laing's theories with interest and respect, many were appalled that he seemed to be trivializing, even glamorizing the serious illnesses that patients faced. Kingsley Hall, meanwhile, was not a success: local residents were horrified at reports of wild encounter sessions and patients running riot, and it closed down within five years. Yet even as Laing's medical career spun out of control, his cultural influence grew ever stronger. To a generation of writers and artists who liked nothing better than to poke fun at what they saw as bourgeois assumptions and power structures, the spectacle of an LSD-taking, poetry-writing, Buddhist-influenced 'anti-psychiatrist' was too good to resist. Laing 'made madness, alienation, hating your parents . . . all glamorous', wrote the novelist Angela Carter. 'God knows what he did for people who were *really* mad, apart from making them feel smug and self-righteous, but he certainly set the pace for the crazy hinge of the decade from 1968 on.' In the theatre, his influence was ubiquitous, from Edward Bond's shockingly violent *Lear* (1971) to Peter Shaffer's equally powerful, if didactic, *Equus* (1973), the story of a psychiatrist invited to treat a boy who has a pathological obsession with horses. Indeed, in its own way *Equus* was the perfect distillation of the fashionable themes of the period: its fascination with ritual and symbols, for example; its obsession with sex and death; its crude satirical treatment of the conservative, Christian parents; its debunking of the psychiatrist's conventional assumptions; above all, its implicit message that the mad were sane and the sane mad. All of this, like Loach and Mercer's *Family Life*, was pure Laing.[21]

Although Laing himself was in palpable decline by the beginning of the 1970s, lurching bizarrely into a nightmarish world of shamanism, robe-wearing and 'rebirthing workshops', his ideas had never been more influential in the cultural mainstream. It was not merely a question of plays and poetry: now academic experts and feminist writers alike queued up to deliver sentence on the supposedly demented, oppressive institution of the nuclear family. When, in the 1967 Reith Lectures, the eminent Cambridge anthropologist Edmund Leach insisted that 'the family, with its narrow privacy and tawdry secrets, is the source of all our discontents', he provoked a firestorm of protest, with tabloid critics fulminating against his godless moral relativism. But within a few years, such opinions were becoming almost conventional. And by the time the curtain rose on Shaffer's *Equus*, no self-respecting bohemian could fail to produce an apposite quotation from Laing or Marcuse, while premature obituaries for marriage and the family were as common as wildcat strikes. The idea of a lasting romantic union was historically 'exceptional', another anthropologist, Lucy Mair, argued in 1971. Husbands were 'not necessary' to bring up children successfully; the single-parent family was the model of the future. Monogamy was an artificial restriction on human urges, agreed Alex Comfort: sex was a natural physical pleasure, like eating, and as long as they did not hurt others, people should be able to do it when and with whom they liked. And perhaps oddly, given that these views were a standing invitation to male predators and implicitly heaped all the burden of childcare onto single mothers, they struck a chord with many feminists, for whom the traditional family was nothing but an instrument of male oppression. 'We need an ideological revolution,' wrote the feminist Ann Oakley in 1974. 'We need to abolish gender roles themselves . . . Abolish the housewife role, therefore abolish the family.'[22]

Most people, of course, had no desire to abolish the family. Indeed, by some standards the traditional family was more popular than ever. By the beginning of the decade, 95 per cent of men and 96 per cent of women under the age of 45 were married, while young couples were positively rushing to the altar: in 1970, the average age of brides at marriage fell beneath 23 for the first time since the war. Despite all the nonsense in the newspapers about the generation gap and teenage rebellion, most youngsters dreamed of getting married and settling down like their parents before them; indeed, only a tiny minority of those who came of age in the 1970s never married. It is admittedly true that women in particular had very different expectations from their mothers, placing a much higher premium on sexual satisfaction, emotional fulfilment and even achievements in the workplace. Marriage was 'increasingly required to serve the partners' own personal development,' reported a Home Office study in 1979, while a survey two years later found that people ranked love, mutual understanding and a healthy sex life as the most important ingredients of a happy union, well ahead of having children. Most people, however, still believed that marriage was the best vehicle to fulfil their dreams, and popular television shows abounded with images of lasting marriages, from the clearly loved-up Tom and Barbara in *The Good Life* to the rather more disputatious Basil and Sybil in *Fawlty Towers*. And only in a society that still valued marriage as the supreme sacrament would almost 28 million people have gathered around their televisions to watch the wedding of Princess Anne and Captain Mark Phillips in November 1973 – or would almost 21 million have tuned in four years later to watch the wedding of *Coronation Street*'s Len Fairclough and Rita Littlewood, who were even less real than the princess and her captain.[23]

Yet married bliss did not always live up to its billing. Twenty years on from his fairy-tale wedding, it emerged that Captain Mark Phillips had fathered a child with a New Zealand art teacher, while Len Fairclough's extramarital adventures only came out after his death in a car crash. And when Princess Anne and Captain Phillips were divorced in 1992, they were following in the footsteps of millions of other couples whose marriages had ended in tears and recriminations. Of course this was nothing new: in the mid-1950s there had been around 28,000 divorces a year, and there were some 40,000 in the mid-1960s. The scale, however, was different, and for that some people blamed the Divorce Reform Act of 1969, which allowed the courts to grant a divorce on the grounds of irretrievable breakdown within just two years. As with the legalization of abortion, the Act's framers never expected that it would lead to a dramatic increase: all they wanted to do was to end what Labour's Leo Abse called the 'jungle of lies, half truths, miserable stratagems and ugly publicising' that had thrived under the old system, which demanded that one party admit fault. But once the new legislation came into force, the divorce statistics went through the roof. In 1965, there had been just three divorces in Britain for every 1,000 married people. In 1970 there were almost five, by 1975 there were ten and by 1980 there were twelve. In less than two decades, in other words, the divorce rate had quadrupled, giving Britain the highest rate of marriage failure in Europe. By the end of the decade, there was one divorce for every three marriages, a statistic that filled most commentators with utter despair. What was most depressing, though, was the divorce rate among the young, which trebled in the course of the 1970s. Perhaps it was no wonder that while almost all teenagers expected they would get married, six out of ten told market researchers in 1977 that they also expected to get divorced.[24]

For a minority, there was nothing to fear in the rising divorce figures. 'The nuclear family, two adults and 2.04 children, is as artificial and unnatural and against the deepest instincts of mankind as its backlash – the attempt to do without a family at all,' wrote the *Guardian*'s house feminist Jill Tweedie in September 1975. Instead of shuddering at the thought of divorce, people should welcome it, she thought, for 'divorce creates an underground family that only needs to be stripped of its coverings, its shame, its inherent drama to produce once more a natural extended family'. This rather ludicrous rose-tinted view did not, however, chime with the views of most feminists. For decades, women's groups had actually taken a very dim view of divorce reform, arguing that it would be a 'seducers' charter' that would destroy wives' legal protections. And although by 1975 more than seven out of ten divorce petitions were filed by women, many activists insisted that the majority were wives abandoned under the new 'Casanova's charter', as they called it. For abandoned wives and mothers, argued the journalist Brenda Maddox in her book *The Half-Parent* (1975), divorce came at a heavy emotional cost: even after the marriage was over, the two parties were haunted by the ghosts of past failures and broken relationships, their children and stepchildren daily reminders of what had been lost. And even at this relatively early stage, some commentators worried that single mothers were falling into a poverty trap, caught between the demands of their children, the regulations of the welfare system and an increasingly cut-throat labour market. The charity Gingerbread, set up in 1970 after a *Sunday Times* feature about a struggling single mother, made valiant efforts to lighten the burden through babysitting, collective shopping trips and support groups. But already there were far too many lone-parent families for one charity to cope with. In 1974, a single parent headed one family in eleven; by 1980, this figure had already risen to one in eight, accounting for well over a million children – and it was still growing.[25]

And yet despite the challenges, despite the stresses and strains of a world in which husbands and wives worked long hours and struggled to reconcile the demands of offices, homes and children, the nuclear family was a much more resilient institution than its critics imagined. It is certainly true that more people got divorced than ever before, that more people broke their wedding vows, that more children grew up without two parents and that – in overwhelming numbers – more youngsters slept and lived together before or outside marriage. But although 'living in sin', as it had once been called, was now widely accepted – only 8 per cent of people aged between 15 and 24 thought it was 'wrong' in a survey in 1980 – the idea of marriage in the abstract showed little sign of losing its fairy-tale appeal. And even after undergoing the misery and trauma of the divorce courts, the overwhelming majority still believed in the institution of marriage itself. By the end of the 1970s, almost one in three marriages involved somebody who had been married before, while eight out of ten divorcees under the age of 30 subsequently remarried. They had seen the worst that marriage had to offer, but they had not lost their faith that out there somewhere was the perfect union.[26]

In December 1969, a light aircraft crashed in the Belgian village of Erpen, outside Namur. The pilot, who survived, was a 36-year-old British stuntman named John Howe, and when the Belgian police investigated the crash site, they found almost 800 pornographic films, each carefully disguised in Christmas wrapping paper. Howe had been smuggling the films on behalf of the Danish firm Original Climax, which was providing them for the London market. Instead, the films ended up in a Belgian police station and Howe in a Belgian prison. It was a satisfyingly bizarre, if trivial, story, and it caught the attention of executives at the *Sunday People*, which had recently launched a campaign against what it saw as the excesses of the permissive society. When the *People* sent two veteran reporters onto the streets of Soho to uncover the network behind the West End's booming pornography market, the trail soon led to Original Climax's local agent, a young man in his twenties called Stuart Crispie. But when the reporters set up a sting in the Hilton hotel, the tables were abruptly turned. Far from the *People* exposing the 'Blue Film Boss', as they later called him, Crispie seemed to know exactly what they were planning. He brought along a solicitor and a stills photographer of his own, and while the lawyer was threatening the *People*'s men with a writ, the photographer was taking pictures to distribute across the West End. With their photos pinned up behind the counter of every sex shop in London, the reporters' cover was well and truly blown. They had been betrayed – and the culprits, it turned out, were officers of the Metropolitan Police.[27]

Pornography was a relatively young industry in the early 1970s: although it had always been available to those with the money and contacts to import material from the Continent, it was only after the relaxation of the obscenity laws in 1959 that it could reach a big enough market to guarantee serious profits. Within a very short space of time, however, it was obvious that demand was very high indeed. The first home-grown magazine, *Penthouse*, appeared in 1964, followed by *Mayfair* and *Fiesta* two years later. By 1971, pornography was generating enough income for the entrepreneur Paul Raymond to relaunch *Men Only*, hitherto a rather dull pocket-sized magazine dedicated to cars, clothes, food and travel as well as 'glamour' pictures, as fully fledged pornography, a decision that paid handsome dividends. Naked bodies were now big business: in August 1971, the *Observer*'s business correspondent Raymond Palmer estimated that about 100 shops across the country were trading exclusively in explicit material, over half of them in London and most of those in Soho. Between them, he thought, the Soho stores had an annual turnover of at least £3 million, while the national total was probably around £10 million. But this was probably an underestimate. Most specialist sex shops charged gigantic mark-up prices on the materials they imported from Holland, Belgium and Scandinavia, and while small shops grossed about £1,000 a week, better-placed and bigger stores, like those dominating the streets of Soho, could expect to gross up to £10,000 – most of which, since they paid no tax, the retailers kept as profit.[28]

And while the performers and models themselves made very little – a participant in a blue movie might make as little as £25 – a handful of entrepreneurs did very nicely indeed. One example was the urbane Gerald Citron, the son of a washing-machine magnate, who had been educated at Repton under the headmastership of Geoffrey Fisher (later Archbishop of Canterbury) and studied law at Manchester before becoming a porn baron. By the time the police arrested him in January 1973, Citron owned a £160,000 Surrey mansion (worth at least £3 million today) with a swimming pool, an E-type Jaguar and a Rolls-Royce, had married a glamorous model, and had set up his own wine-importing business. All of this was based on the wages of sin: at his nearby farm, the police discovered 18 tons of obscene material, worth at least £500,000. But Citron was not the only man making big money from masturbation. Another Home Counties wholesaler, 'Big Jeff' Phillips, specialized in importing films from Denmark as well as making his own ('filthy of course,' he said, 'but technically very good'). Big Jeff made enough to buy a white Rolls-Royce, two blocks of flats, houses in Esher and Kingston (evidently Surrey held a weird fascination for pornography magnates), and an £80,000 country house near Reading, complete with 10 acres of land, stables and a heated swimming pool. 'Britain's first blue film millionaire', the *Sunday People* called him with pardonable exaggeration, living in a 'stately home paid for with filth'. Like Citron, however, Big Jeff came to a sticky end: exposed in February 1972 during one of the paper's periodic investigations into 'filth', he killed himself three years later.[29]

As the *People* had long since discovered, entrepreneurs like Citron and Phillips thrived not just because they exploited the fantasies of their fellow men, but because they had persuaded the Metropolitan Police's Obscene Publications Squad (the notorious 'Dirty Squad') to turn a blind eye to their enterprises. Since the late 1960s, senior officers in the Dirty Squad had been regularly accepting bribes and sweeteners from Soho pornographers. 'A police tariff operates in the West End,' one investigator told the *People* in February 1972, 'whereby certain police officers between them receive from the pornographic "kings" a sum in the region of £1,000 a week . . . paid by the "bucks" or managers of the shops either in the shop, in a club or in a pub.' So systematic were the arrangements, in fact, that Commander Wallace Virgo alone, who controlled nine Met squads including Narcotics and Obscene Publications, was paid £500 a week plus a Christmas bonus of £2,000 between January 1970 and May 1972, as well as agreeing 'rates' to sanction new shops on West End sites: £1,500 for Cranbourne Street, £1,000 for D'Arblay Street, and so on. They ran 'an evil conspiracy which turned the Obscene Publications Squad into a vast protection racket', said Mr Justice Mars-Jones when the case finally came to court in 1977. All in all, more than a dozen policemen were convicted, and Virgo himself, the most senior officer ever found guilty of corruption, was sent down for twelve years. 'Thank goodness, the Obscene Publications Squad has gone,' Mars-Jones said solemnly.

'I fear the damage you have done may be with us for a long time.'[30]

In fact the 'damage', as Mars-Jones called it, was plain for even the most casual West End visitor to see. In Soho, the obvious district for the pornographers to choose because of its cheap rents, bohemian reputation and criminal connections, it was 'impossible not to notice the porn shops', said one report. They were open seven days a week and twenty-four hours a day: 'they had large neon signs declaring that they sold "BOOKS" or "ADULT BOOKS" and their windows were filled with garish displays of generally soft-core magazines and titillating notices implying – often correctly – that the interested customer would find a wider range of merchandise inside.' Imported American magazines cost £3 each, sets of still photos £1 a pack, and 'blue movies' £15 for 200 feet in black and white, or £30 for colour. Meanwhile, as the journalist Paul Ferris noted, 'under-the-counter material covered every known sexual activity', from stories about 'women being raped, men being dominated, [and] debauched children' to images of flagellation, coprophilia and even people having enemas. And despite the destruction of the Dirty Squad, Soho continued to thrive: indeed, the sex trade seemed to be more successful and brazen than ever. With Westminster council refusing to crack down on the porn barons – not least because the Obscene Publications Act's prohibition of material that was likely to 'deprave and corrupt' was so vague as to be useless – Soho and sex became virtually synonymous. By the end of the 1970s, the district boasted 54 sex shops, 39 'cinema clubs', 16 strip and peep shows, 11 sex clubs and 12 licensed massage parlours, all packed into a tiny warren of narrow streets and run-down alleyways, and almost spilling over into more upmarket entertainment areas like Shaftesbury Avenue and Leicester Square. 'It's become increasing difficult to take a child to the London cinema,' complained the Tory MP Michael Heseltine in 1975, not without reason. 'The place is sex mad.'[31]

If the porn boom had been confined to the red-light ghetto of Soho, then it might not have been so alarming. In fact, by the time of Heseltine's complaint it had already spread into almost every corner of the country: by 1975, twelve major soft-core publishers were distributing material through 400 wholesalers and an estimated 20,000 shops, most of them newsagents and corner shops. To anyone who regularly bought anything from *The Times, The Economist* and the *Sun* to *Horse and Hound*, the *Eagle* and *Look-In*, the sight of magazines like *Mayfair, Men Only* and *Fiesta* on the top shelf was already becoming very familiar. And although very few people admitted that they read top-shelf magazines, the sales figures were extremely good. By 1975 *Men Only*'s monthly readership was an estimated 1.8 million, with *Mayfair* and *Penthouse* close behind on 1.7 million each. And when, two years later, a Home Office committee chaired by the philosopher Bernard Williams was asked to look more closely into the obscenity laws, it reported that a staggering 4 million people read one or more porn magazines every month. Most readers, it turned out, were a far cry from the dirty old men of tabloid stereotypes: the majority were men under the age of 35, many of whom were married, and readership was strongest among the skilled (i.e. supposedly respectable) working classes. Since the pornographers knew their customers, no doubt this explains why the magazines of the 1970s often had an aggressively populist feel. The sleaze baron David Sullivan, for example, specialized in selling magazines that invited readers to send in explicit pictures of their wives – a self-consciously democratic approach that saved money on models and also made him enormously rich. What Sullivan also realized, though, was that once the legal shackles were off, many readers would demand more and more hard-core material. 'Strength sells,' he told a documentary in 1977 – and curiously, it sold even better when the models literally were the girls next door.[32]

By far the most popular source of soft-core images, however, could be found on newsagents' bottom shelves, not the top ones. Ever since the *Sun* had been relaunched as an aggressively downmarket working-class tabloid under the ownership of Rupert Murdoch and the editorship of Larry Lamb, it had gone out of its way to emphasize sex. 'Sex was news. The paper did not invent it,' Lamb later insisted. 'Discussion of sexual matters had become publicly acceptable, therefore the paper had a duty to publish it, with taste, and a sense of proportion.' In many ways he was quite right: the paper's endless stream of stories about love-nests and sex romps conformed absolutely to the bawdy music-hall tradition that saw sex as both fun and funny, as long as people stuck within a conservative moral framework. The quintessential example, of course, was the Page Three topless pin-up, which first appeared in November 1970 in the form of a 'birthday suit girl' to celebrate the first anniversary of the paper's relaunch. The next Page Three girl, however, did not appear until the following March, and only in 1972 did the topless picture became a regular feature. Revealingly, however, the pictures often ran alongside stories about 'family breakdown and domestic and sexual violence': as one academic study remarks, the rather incongruous juxta-position allowed the *Sun* both to endorse permissiveness and to distance itself from it. What was also revealing was that in the early 1970s very few of the models were white British women. Many were Swedes and Germans, supposedly much more liberated where sex was concerned, and there were also plenty of black women, to whom nudity supposedly came naturally. So in July 1972, when the *Sun* decided to celebrate the fact that Britain was overcoming prejudice and 'Winning the Race War', the high point was a week of black models. 'The shape of race relations gets a real uplift from Guyana-born model Minerva Smith!' one caption claimed.[33]

Needless to say, not everyone was delighted by the appearance of girls like Minerva Smith. Even before the introduction of Page Three, in fact, the *Sun* had been banned from one Yorkshire town's public library because there was too much sex in it, prompting the paper to launch an attack on the 'Silly Burghers of Sowerby Bridge' ('We should have been thrown out of better places than this'). And although feminists made no secret of their loathing for the paper, the *Sun*'s executives were much more interested in their booming circulation figures. By 1975, when the *Mirror* felt obliged to follow suit with topless pictures of its own, the two papers were virtually neck and neck, and at the beginning of 1978 the *Sun* finally drew ahead. As the former *Sun* journalist-turned-critic Roy Greenslade puts it, this was 'an astonishing achievement: in the space of just nine years, the *Sun* had risen from almost the bottom of the tabloid heap to the top'. Topless women were not the only reason; but as the most obvious symbols of the *Sun*'s blend of sex, censoriousness, populism and permissiveness, they had a lot to do with it.[34]

The deeper importance of Page Three, though, is that it was the most obvious example of what one historian calls the 'eroticisation' of British life in the 1970s, something visible not just in the strip-clubs and sex shops of Soho, but in mainstream news reports, in cinemas, in paperback bestsellers and even on the television screens. In fashion, for example, men's trousers were often crotch-bulgingly tight, while young women now saw nothing wrong in revealing great expanses of cleavage or thigh. In advertising, too, there was now a much heavier emphasis on sexual suggestiveness. And although the blatant smut of Benny Hill's annual Thames Television spectaculars, with their apparently unvarying cast of nubile young women in bikinis and suspenders, owed something to the bawdy traditions of the music hall, it represented something new on television, something that many middle-class families had never seen before. Even mainstream sitcoms now joked openly about pornography: in the very first episode of *Whatever Happened to the Likely Lads?* (1973), Terry Collier complains that, having served in the army in West Germany, he has missed out on 'the death of censorship', 'the new morality', *Oh! Calcutta!* and 'topless waitresses in frilly knickers'. The first thing he does on being demobbed is to visit a seedy strip-club, where he almost bumps into his old friend Bob, a faithful husband-to-be who nevertheless bunks off to Soho when he gets the chance. Even ten years before, such a scene would have been unthinkable at prime time on BBC1; by 1973, however, it was nothing remarkable. Indeed, it was a measure of how far pornography had permeated the commercial main-stream that Bob and Terry might well have bumped into an up-and-coming popular detective at the Soho strip-club, for in Colin Dexter's novel *Last Seen Wearing* (1977) we discover that Inspector Morse has more than a passing acquaintance with the West End scene. In one club, he and Lewis sit through moribund performances by Fabulous Fiona, Sexy Susan and Sensational Sandra, before Voluptuous Vera and Kinky Kate manage 'to raise the general standard of the entertainment'. 'There were gimmicks aplenty,' we are told; 'fans, whips, bananas and rubber spiders', and Morse digs his colleague in the ribs as 'an extraordinarily shapely girl, dressed for a fancy-dressing ball, titillatingly and tantalizingly divested herself of all but an incongruously ugly mask.' 'Bit of class there, Lewis,' Morse says admiringly.[35]

What one cultural critic calls the spread of 'permissive populism' – 'the trickle-down of permissiveness into commodity culture' – was particularly noticeable in the film industry. The astonishing collapse of cinema-going as mass entertainment, with weekly audiences having fallen from a third of the population to just two in a hundred people between the late 1940s and the early 1970s, meant that studios were desperate for any gimmick that would drag people away from the television, and sex seemed the ideal candidate. Under the leadership of John Trevelyan, the British Board of Film Classification had moved steadily towards a position of greater permissiveness, particularly where so-called 'art' films were concerned, and the introduction of a new classification system – in particular, the AA category for those aged 14 and older, and X for those 18 and older – seemed an invitation to produce more explicit material. What was more, the system was full of loopholes. If a film was denied a BBFC certificate, it could be submitted for a licence to individual local authorities, some of which took a decidedly permissive line. In October 1970, for example, after the film version of Henry Miller's novel *Tropic of Cancer* had been rejected by the BBFC, it was promptly given a licence by the Greater London Council, much to the horror of the Conservative press. And with family audiences in deep decline, many cinemas – especially in big cities – decided that only ever more adult material would guarantee ticket sales. By April 1971, when the *Evening Standard* published a major investigation of film-going in London, no fewer than 31 out of 60 films showing in the capital had X certificates, with a further 12 being ranked as AA, 5 as A (suitable for older children) and just 12 as U. Among the X films, the paper noted, 'nudity had become commonplace, full-frontal female nudity was almost so, full-frontal male nudity becoming so'. Half of the films either depicted or referred to homosexuality, and a quarter depicted or implied masturbation. Perhaps it was no wonder that only four months before, John Trevelyan had decided to throw in the towel. 'I am simply sickened', he said, 'by having to put in days filled from dawn till dusk with the sight and sound of human copulation.'[36]

Given what happened next, Trevelyan was probably wise to get out when he did. Almost as soon as his successor, a shy, chain-smoking Scottish TV executive called Stephen Murphy, had moved in, he found himself embroiled in a blazing tabloid row about Ken Russell's wildly overwrought film *The Devils*, a story about witchcraft in seventeenth-century France, complete with enough torture, madness and sexual obsession to satisfy even the most jaded palate. After months of negotiations between the director, the studio and the BBFC, the film came out in July 1971; but although Warner Bros. had taken out scenes of nuns sexually assaulting a statue of Christ and Vanessa Redgrave masturbating with a dead priest's charred bone, what remained was bound to inflame conservative critics. 'Redgrave's perverse Mother Superior licks the stigmata of her lover who is represented as a crucified Christ figure,' wrote the *Evening Standard*'s Alexander Walker. 'Impromptu medical examinations are performed on the altar table; nude nuns massage phallic candles with lubricious relish; hot-water enemas are applied in a brutal pantomime of purgation; and the vomit of those accused of being possessed by the devil is picked through in the hope of discovering a crumb of undigested demon.' Not altogether surprisingly, seventeen local authorities banned the film, and in London the GLC committee decided against a ban, which would have destroyed the film's box-office prospects, by only three votes. But this was only the beginning of the biggest censorship row in British film history.[37]

For all its excesses, *The Devils* had been enormously unlucky. It went on general release at the exact moment that conservative moralists and Christian groups were launching a campaign against the 'ravages of permissiveness', and at a point when, with both crime and unemployment mounting, the press was becoming increasingly agitated about the moral state of the nation. What this meant was that the next major release was bound to face even more intense scrutiny, and unfortunately for Stephen Murphy the film in question was Sam Peckinpah's *Straw Dogs*, the story of a middle-class couple besieged by rapacious yokels in a Cornish cottage, and an extremely violent picture by any standards. As Walker later wrote, *Straw Dogs* was 'putting on indecent display all the nightmares that could affect the British bourgeoisie', and to many critics the scenes of sexual violence – including the savage double rape of Susan George, haplessly re-edited by the studio so that it appeared she was being buggered and, crucially, was *enjoying* it – were simply disgusting. And when Murphy defended it as 'a brilliant but brutal film that says something important', the press turned on him. On 17 December, *The Times* published an unprecedented letter from thirteen leading reviewers, including its own John Russell Taylor, Dilys Powell of the *Sunday Times*, Derek Malcolm of the *Guardian* and John Coleman of the *New Statesman*, as well as Walker himself. 'The use to which this film employs its scenes of double rape and multiple killing by a variety of hideous methods', they wrote, 'is dubious in its intention, excessive in its effect and likely to contribute to the concern expressed from time to time by many critics over films which exploit the very violence which they make a show of condemning.' For some of the critics, the decision to pass *Straw Dogs* cast a shadow not only over Murphy's survival as chief censor, but over the 'continued existence' of the BBFC itself.[38]

Although Murphy wrote a robust reply defending his censorship policy, he must have regretted that he had ever taken the job in the first place – for as he well knew, an even more contentious picture was coming in January 1972. With its shocking portrait of juvenile delinquency, rape and violence in a nightmarish future London, Stanley Kubrick's adaptation of Anthony Burgess's novella *A Clockwork Orange* would probably have stirred controversy whenever it was released. But this was the worst possible time for Murphy to have passed such a disturbing picture, since, as Alexander Walker later remarked, public opinion was 'waiting for it', with the newspapers 'ready and indeed willing to be outraged' before anyone had even seen it. Even before the film's premiere on 13 January 1972, the Home Secretary, Reginald Maudling, told the press that there was 'a new film out this week that I think I ought to go and see ... If things are being shown which one could reasonably suppose are contributing to the degree of violence, I think I ought to know.' In the event, Maudling watched the film at a special screening and then, as was his wont, did absolutely nothing about it. But his intervention had stoked the flames even higher.[39]

As a terrifying vision of utopian modernism gone wrong, teenage thugs running amok in a world of concrete tower blocks and a repressive government struggling to keep the lid on a broken society, *A Clockwork Orange* could hardly have appeared at a more appropriate moment. By the time of its premiere, the miners' strike was just days old, while the papers were full of angst at the spectacle of one million unemployed and the mounting bloodshed in Northern Ireland. In this context, Kubrick's stylized hooligans became the focus for a moral backlash of unparalleled intensity. For the *Sun*, it was the 'FILM SHOCKER TO END THEM ALL ... unparalleled in its concentrated parade of violence, viciousness and cruelty', while the *Mail*'s critic Cecil Wilson wondered 'what on earth [had] induced our censors to pass those startling scenes of rape and violence'. Even left-wing politicians joined the bandwagon: after a special screening for peers and MPs, Labour's Maurice Edelman, chairman of the all-party Film Committee, told the press that 'the film stimulates for two and a half hours an appetite for sadistic violence with the instantaneous communication which the visual arts uniquely offer'. When *A Clockwork Orange* went on general release, Edelman predicted, 'it will lead to a Clockwork cult which will magnify teenage violence'.[40]

Amid the hysteria, Stephen Murphy's argument that the film was 'in its stylised way, simply a vehicle for all kinds of speculation about the human spirit' and 'a valuable contribution to the whole debate about violence' was totally ignored. Instead, critics queued up to denounce Kubrick, Burgess and the BBFC, with *A Clockwork Orange* becoming a scapegoat for all the ills – crime, pornography, strikes, the stream of national humiliations – that seemed to be corrupting the national spirit. Across the country, local authorities delayed the film's opening, demanded more cuts or even imposed outright bans. Murphy himself was now under intense pressure to step down: he was 'out of touch with public opinion', according to the head of the Cinematograph Exhibitors Association, while an editorial in *The Times* asked 'Is Film Censorship Breaking Down?' At one stage, the pressure on the chief censor was such that, with the press camped outside his Soho Square office, he took refuge in a nearby Catholic church. In the end, he managed to tough it out: as one sympathetic journalist observed, he had 'had a most unfortunate baptism into a job which he himself has said is impossible'. But the controversy had taken its toll on a sensitive and conscientious man: at the beginning of 1975, after just four years, Murphy resigned to return to the Independent Broadcasting Authority.[41]

By the time Murphy stepped down, *A Clockwork Orange* had been withdrawn from cinemas anyway. Although Warner Bros. had restricted it to just one West End cinema for the first twelve months, an unprecedented step aimed at dampening the criticism, it had done no good. In the end, the press campaign proved too much for Stanley Kubrick: after allegations that his film had inspired the murder of a tramp in Buckinghamshire, he ordered that it be withdrawn from circulation, and it disappeared from British cinemas for the next two decades. But sex and violence did not disappear from the silver screen, for with audiences in free-fall, what remained of the British film industry had come to the conclusion that only more and more sensational material would get people back in. And by the time of Murphy's resignation, cinemas were increasingly dominated either by American imports or by perhaps the most embarrassing British cultural products of the decade – the sex comedies typified by Robin Askwith's *Confessions* films. Between 1971 and 1975, studios pumped out a staggering forty-three examples, from *Secrets of a Door-to-Door Salesman* and *Can You Keep it Up for a Week?* to *Confessions of a Driving Instructor* and *Adventures of a Plumber's Mate*. The titles were almost beyond parody, though thankfully nobody had the courage to make *Confessions of an Academic*.

Tens, even hundreds of thousands of people paid good money to see these alleged comedies: indeed, without them, the British film industry would have virtually disappeared, and many ran in provincial cinemas for months on end. The funniest thing about them was the violence of the reviews: one critic thought that *Confessions of a Window Cleaner* should be renamed *Confessions of the British: What They Don't Know about Making Films, Making Erotic Images, Making People Laugh and Making Love.* In some ways, of course, their success reflected the relative severity of the censorship regime, which was still much harsher than those on the Continent: if provincial cinemas had offered genuinely explicit fare, then people would surely not have wasted their money watching Robin Askwith leering through a suburban bedroom window. But they also tapped a rich seam of bawdy vulgarity in British working-class humour, a prurient fascination with nudity and an almost obsessive affection for jokes about breasts and bottoms. Revealingly, the publicity for the *Confessions* films insisted that they were quintessentially British, part of 'the long tradition in entertainment in this country of good, naughty laughter – from double entendres in the music hall (Max Miller is a prime example) to seaside postcards, from West End stage farces (e.g. Robertson Hare) to the "Carry On" films'. Indeed, the world of the films – a world of perky, carefree housewives and lecherous young men, of suburban sex romps and ever-available dolly birds – was instantly familiar to anybody who had ever opened a copy of the *Sun*. And Askwith himself briefly became a cult hero to *Sun* readers – 'Randy Robin', as the paper called him, an expelled public schoolboy turned bawdy working-class hero, a former Queen's Park Rangers youth footballer who now made a living 'bonking birds' – or at least pretending to.[42]

And yet for all the talk about bawdy traditions and a rich vein of naughtiness, the *Confessions* films would never have succeeded had they not seemed to offer something new. Just fifteen or even ten years earlier, a mainstream film with such explicit sexual content would have been simply unthinkable, but now they were merely part of a cultural landscape in which even the BBC, perhaps Britain's most venerated institution, the national church of the airwaves, made no apology for scenes of female nudity and utter sexual debauchery. In the justly acclaimed *I, Claudius* (1976), for example, audiences even got to watch the Emperor Caligula organizing orgies in which senators' wives are auctioned off to the highest bidder, or Claudius's wife Messalina conducting a love-making competition with the prostitute Scylla. In the same year, ITV showed *A Bouquet of Barbed Wire*, the story of incestuous passions and a taste for sado-masochism tearing a family apart, adapted from Andrea Newman's novel. By the end, as the *Observer*'s Clive James put it at the time, 'everybody had been to bed with everybody else except the baby'. Even in detective fiction, hitherto one of the most conservative of genres, there was no escape. In Ruth Rendell's *A Guilty Thing Surprised* (1970), the plot turns on an incestuous relationship; in P. D. James's *An Unsuitable Job for a Woman* (1972), a male student is found hanging by his belt, 'dressed like a woman, in a black bra and black lace panties'; in Julian Symons's *The Players and the Game* (1972), one man pays to be humiliated by prostitutes while another molests a 13-year-old girl; and in Colin Dexter's Inspector Morse novels, which began to appear in 1975, sex, pornography and general seediness are inevitably discovered beneath the veneer of Oxford gentility. As the writer Alwyn Turner remarks, the world of Hercule Poirot and Miss Marple must have seemed like ancient history.[43]

For some observers, the pornography boom of the early 1970s seemed a great and noble thing. Among the tiny handful of largely middle-class and very well-educated youngsters who made up the bohemian counter-culture, obscenity was a way of challenging the dominant assumptions of 'square' or 'bourgeois' society. Like overgrown adolescents everywhere, they were obsessed both by sex and by shocking their elders: as the playwright Joe Orton told his lover (and later murderer) Kenneth Halliwell in 1967, sex was 'the only way to smash up the wretched civilisation . . . Much more fucking and they'll be screaming hysterics in next to no time.' The same principle – which was, of course, completely misguided – informed many of the underground publications of the day, from Richard Neville's infantile and grotesquely misogynistic hippy manifesto *Play Power* (1970), in which he enthused about the benefits of a 'hurricane fuck' with a 14-year-old girl, to the equally infantile and equally misogynistic 'School Kids Issue' of the magazine *Oz*, which was published in April 1970 and became the subject of a protracted but ultimately inconsequential Old Bailey trial a year later. But although the underground rapidly imploded – indeed, virtually the only trace of it left by 1974 was the listings magazine *Time Out* – its attitudes survived, especially in sections of the academic and media worlds. When Malcolm Bradbury's loathsome protagonist Howard Kirk takes up his new job at Watermouth University, he soon falls into conversation with the vice-chancellor, a 'radical educationalist, former political scientist [and] well-known Labour voter', about a subject Howard is 'greatly interested in, the social benefits and purgative value of pornography in the cinema'.

'I've always been a serious supporter of pornography, Dr Kirk,' the vice-chancellor says earnestly – and at his words, the narrator tells us, 'Howard warmed, and felt at ease.'[44]

Most people, however, had rather more conflicted attitudes to the rise of sexual frankness and new availability of pornography. When the Tottenham football squad took the train up to Wolverhampton for the first match of the season in August 1971, their pile of magazines included a copy of *Penthouse*, from which the full back Cyril Knowles delightedly read aloud before throwing it aside with the words: 'Disgusting. They ought to ban them. I feel right degraded. Any more?' He was only joking, of course, but plenty of people *did* think that pornography was disgusting. For many feminists, for example, it represented a travesty of their faith in sexual liberation, turning women into nothing more than glorified sex objects. And although polls showed that the vast majority of the public took a remarkably liberal view of pornography – in 1973, three out of four people agreed that 'adults should be able to buy whatever indecent erotic books and magazines they like, so long as they are not on public display' – a large minority of the population, many of them older women, saw things very differently.[45]

For many people, indeed, pornography had replaced prostitution (which had been driven underground after the Wolfenden report in 1955) as the chief 'moral stain' on the national flag. Just as moral campaigners had inveighed against the vice of prostitution in the late nineteenth century or the early 1950s, now pornography was seen as the supreme symbol of Britain's ethical degeneration, 'the final desecration and commercialisation of sex . . . a manifestation of decay, a canker at the heart of respectability'. For the country's best-known moral conservative, Mary Whitehouse, who had been campaigning to 'clean up' television since the early 1960s, pornography was 'filthy', 'sinful', 'depraved' and 'perverted'. And in January 1976, contemplating the spread of violent and sadomasochistic imagery, even *The Times* reassessed its previously liberal editorial position. 'Against this pornography of cruelty we need a defence,' the paper said; 'otherwise we may be brainwashed into accepting it, not only in books and magazines, but, as already to a dangerous extent, in newspapers, films and on television . . . The pornographers are sick-minded commercial men who sell images of hatred, and particularly of hatred of women, for vast profit. We need both a law and a law-enforcement which stops them.'[46]

Oddly enough, the figure most associated with both the pornography boom and the backlash against it was not a prototypical porn star such as Fiona Richmond or Mary Millington, but an elderly peer with an unrivalled reputation as an endlessly well-meaning do-gooder of semi-comic proportions. As a veteran of both the Attlee and the Wilson governments, a crusader for unfashionable causes and a tireless campaigner for penal reform, Lord Longford was one of Britain's best-known aristocratic socialists, a passionate, deeply religious but ultimately scatty figure who seemed oblivious to the ridicule his escapades attracted from the media. He first made the issue his own in April 1971 when, having initiated a debate in the Lords about the 'incipient menace of pornography in Great Britain', he invited the press to accompany him on a tour of Soho's sleaziest establishments. These included a 'sex supermarket', various seedy cinemas and a strip-club called the Soho Stokehole, where Longford solemnly watched a girl whipping off her knickers to reveal what one reporter called 'nothing so startlingly out of the ordinary as to justify the long preliminary posturings'. Ridiculous as it was, however, Longford's Soho excursion paled by comparison with his next expedition, which saw him fly to Copenhagen on behalf of an unofficial fifty-two-member 'commission' on pornography and violence, which he saw as 'a chance to work out a coherent policy of resistance' to the tide of obscenity. To the press, however, the fact that the commission's members included Jimmy Savile and Cliff Richard, as well as Kingsley Amis, hardly a paragon of sexual sobriety, lent it an unwittingly farcical air. In his own mind, Longford was a brave crusader for decent moral values; to the *Sun*, however, he was simply 'Lord Porn.'[47]

In an era when the headlines seemed all too often to be dominated by reports of strikes, terrorism and economic disasters, Longford's expedition to Denmark in August 1971 came as welcome light relief. He was joined on the trip not only by five other commission members, most notably the former Oxford Union president and future teddy-bear collector, puzzle-book compiler and European Monopoly champion Gyles Brandreth, but by members of the press corps, who treated him with scarcely concealed hilarity. The trip kicked off with a visit to two Copenhagen sex shows, in which women were paired with men, other women and animals, but Longford found it all rather too much. He only lasted five minutes in the first club, walking out in disgust with the manager trailing behind him saying: 'But sir, you have not seen the intercourse. We have intercourse later in the programme.' The second club was even worse. Here, according to an amused reporter, 'a half naked girl thrust a whip into Lord Longford's hand and invited him to flagellate her. He declined and after she had playfully mauled him by thrusting the whip around his neck and pulling violently on it, he got up and left.' By contrast, his colleagues stuck it out rather longer, were much less shocked, and disagreed with Longford's verdict that this kind of thing was likely to encourage sexual violence. Brandreth even announced that he would like to see the Danish laws introduced at home. Not surprisingly, this all made splendid reading, but it also made it hard for people to take Longford seriously. When his report finally came out in September 1972, much of the press treated it with open disdain, while the Heath government summarily rejected his calls for a more precise definition of obscenity to include anything that outraged 'contemporary standards of decency or humanity accepted by the public at large'. In fact, Longford's recommendations were reasonably sensible and well intentioned, if rather too vague, but forever lurking at the back of readers' minds must have been the image of the elderly peer being strangled with a whip in the clubs of Copenhagen.[48]

Despite its ridiculous tone, Longford's investigation reflected a broader sense in the early years of the decade that cultural change and sexual frankness had gone too far, a gathering undercurrent of moral unease running through the heart of British society. It was at the very beginning of the 1970s, for example, that politicians and pundits alike first began to debate 'permissiveness', a word almost always used pejoratively, knitting together a host of related anxieties from pornography and promiscuity to supposedly lax sentences for criminals and falling standards in education. Permissiveness had become a 'political metaphor', and from this point on, protecting the embattled family was at the heart of conservative rhetoric. One account traces this as far back as 1966, when the newspapers were full of angst about the horrifying Moors murders. In any case, by 1970 'the language of crime, violence, chaos, anarchy' was becoming very common in the Tory press. In January 1970, for example, Edward Heath's future Lord Chancellor Quintin Hogg insisted that rising crime 'cannot be separated from private dishonesty or public demonstration in defiance of law', and warned that 'the permissive and lawless society is a by-product of Socialism'. A year later, the journal of Mary Whitehouse's National Viewers' and Listeners' Association sounded a remarkably similar theme, claiming that 'obscenity in the paperbacks and magazines and on the motion picture screen is a basic and contributing factor to violence'. 'The "Permissive Society", with its much vaunted "freedom", is now seen for what it is – a bitter and destructive thing,' insisted the Autumn 1971 issue of *Viewers and Listeners*. 'The arts are degraded, law is held in contempt and sport fouled by outbreaks of vandalism and violence. The national purse takes the strain of a health service overburdened with increasing abortion, drug addiction, mental disturbance, alcoholism and an epidemic of venereal disease.'[49]

By and large, however, most senior politicians hesitated to touch the issue of permissiveness during the Heath years. Economic affairs naturally dominated Westminster debates, and although the Wilson government had been instrumental in supporting the private members' bills that decriminalized homosexuality and legalized abortion in the late 1960s, many Labour MPs remained deeply ambivalent, even uneasy, about the so-called permissive society – which was hardly surprising given the cultural conservatism of traditional working-class Labour voters. Perhaps more surprisingly, on the right there seemed relatively little appetite for the kind of 'culture-war' politics that was becoming popular in the United States; indeed, in keeping with his buttoned-up image, Edward Heath barely mentioned cultural or moral issues at all. At the Home Office, meanwhile, Reginald Maudling seemed completely indifferent to the murmurs of discontent from the shires, striking a pose of 'civilised, tolerant weariness and cynicism'. By most standards, in fact, he was a much more liberal Home Secretary than his predecessor, Labour's bluff 'PC Jim' Callaghan. 'The object of a civilised society', he remarked in 1971, 'should be the maximum of freedom as long as the freedom of others is not infringed.' Despite all the fuss about Longford's report, for example, Maudling could not even be bothered to read it, and he showed not the slightest inclination to crack down on obscenity, writing in his memoirs that 'if one adult wishes to write a book or produce a play and show it to other adults, and they wish to see it, what right has the State to object?' Even drugs did not particularly bother him: in unguarded moments Maudling sometimes told friends that he thought cannabis ought to be legalized, while his teenage sons allegedly smoked dope at parties in his official residence, Admiralty House. If any of this had reached the Tory grass roots, of course, Maudling might well have been finished. But this was an age in which not even the Tory leader gave much thought to the anxieties of his activists, and in this respect Maudling's indifference to popular prejudice was typical not just of Heath's government, but of the liberal consensus that had dominated public affairs since the early 1960s.[50]

Ignoring the issue, however, did not make it go away, and since the politicians refused to lead, others stepped forward. In October 1969, a London doctor, Stanley Ellison, had written to *The Times* calling for a mass effort 'to resist the destructive and demoralizing trends in our present community', explaining that 'the stability of the traditional British way of life is threatened. Venereal disease is increasing. Termination of pregnancy is increasing. Drug addiction is increasing. Smoking is increasing. Gambling is increasing. All being examples of anti-social behaviour.' To Ellison, a 'tide of immorality, self-deception, and insatiable appetite for all that is worthless' was sweeping over the land, and it seemed that plenty of readers agreed: within just a few days he had received more than 200 letters of support, and in June 1971 he joined other doctors and educationalists to set up the Responsible Society. In their opening statement, they explained that while they welcomed the 'greater frankness and tolerance' that now surrounded sex, they were increasingly worried about the 'suffering and social damage which is the direct consequence of an increasingly irresponsible attitude to sex . . . encouraged by an unholy alliance of commercial sex-exploiters and "progressive" protagonists of sexual anarchy'. The Responsible Society, therefore, would 'combat the commercialization and trivialization of sex' – largely, they explained, through setting the facts before the public. 'We are not killjoys,' added Dr Anne Williams, an applied geneticist on the governing board of the society. 'I am not against sex or sex education . . . I believe sex should be part of a stable, loving society. We need, too, stable homes in which to bring up our children.'[51]

Since the Responsible Society's tone seemed so measured, it was not surprising that it immediately attracted an admiring editorial in *The Times*, which concluded, in its habitual wishy-washy style, that 'the more permissive sexual life of adults . . . has to be reconciled with the need of children for stability' (a view with which no sane person could conceivably have disagreed). The problem, though, was that a relatively measured tone was no good way to attract recruits, and within twelve months the Responsible Society's rhetoric and opposition to sex education had become notably more strident. In fact, many of the pressure groups that sprang up to fight permissiveness in the 1960s and 1970s were avowedly religious, even evangelical in spirit, appealing to middle-class churchgoers who wanted to fight the increasing secularization of society. As a wholly secular group, however, the Responsible Society was at a disadvantage, and by 1978 it had only 719 members. Revealingly, only 7 per cent of them were under 30 while no fewer than 58 per cent were in their fifties or older. Still, some groups were even smaller: the Community Standards Association, founded in Cornwall in 1974 to mobilize public opinion against 'mental and moral pollution', had just 300 members by the late 1970s. But unlike many of its competitors, the Responsible Society kept going: four decades on, it was still fighting the good fight against teenage pregnancy, sex education and morning-after pills, in the guise of the Family Education Trust.[52]

While the Responsible Society never aspired to become a mass-membership organization, another anti-permissive group formed at almost exactly the same time made a determined effort to attract thousands of recruits. In November 1970 a young couple, Peter and Janet Hill, had returned to Britain after four years abroad. Both committed Baptists, they had been working in India for an evangelical youth group, but almost as soon as they set foot on their native soil, they realized that they had been trying to spread the Gospel in the wrong country. Astounded by what he called the 'moral slide' of British society in just four years, which was characterized by the spread of pornography and the apparent media obsession with sex, Peter Hill had a vision of 'thousands of young people marching as witnesses' to the truth of the Bible's moral teachings. In early 1971, he made contact with various like-minded people, from the Clean-Up TV campaigner Mary Whitehouse and the satirist-turned-born-again-Christian Malcolm Muggeridge to the Bishop of Blackburn and the housewives' favourite, Cliff Richard. And by the summer he had established an eclectic steering committee, including a flying missionary, a shop-steward-turned-vicar and the general secretary of the Evangelical Alliance, and had also secured the support of various Anglican, Baptist and Pentecostal church groups. Both Muggeridge and Whitehouse, who were well-known television personalities with a substantial conservative following, pledged their support, and Muggeridge, with the journalist's gift for a telling phrase, came up with a name for their new movement: the Nationwide Festival of Light. In July, Hill announced plans for a rally in Trafalgar Square, a gospel festival in Hyde Park, a national day of prayer and the lighting of beacons across the country to 'alert Britain to the dangers of moral pollution which are now eroding the moral fibre of this once great nation'. The Festival would be a chance, Muggeridge added, to take back the cultural initiative from 'those who for one reason or another favour our present Gadarene slide into decadence and god-lessness. It is high time others made their voices heard.'[53]

In many ways, the involvement of Muggeridge and Whitehouse in the Festival of Light was a very mixed blessing. While it secured all the publicity the organizers could possibly want, it also gave their movement a splenetic, even cranky air, and ensured that it would face plenty of mockery in the media. The campaign's official launch in Westminster Hall on 8 September 1971, for example, was something of a disaster. Although some 4,000 people turned up, the proceedings were interrupted by at least 80 demonstrators, many of them from the Gay Liberation Front (including the young Peter Tatchell) and some of them dressed as nuns. Amid extraordinary scenes of shouting and struggling, the respected anti-apartheid activist and Bishop of Stepney, Trevor Huddleston, had to abandon his prepared remarks attacking pornography. Instead it was Muggeridge who dominated the stage, melodramatically telling the audience that the tide of permissiveness was a 'devil's arc reaching from the gutter to more rarefied and sanctimonious regions'. And this rather embarrassing beginning set the tone for the Festival's next major event, a rally in Trafalgar Square two weeks later. Muggeridge confidently predicted that 100,000 people would turn up; instead, probably less than half did so, most of them young members of Baptist and other evangelical churches. Prince Charles sent a message of good luck, but the media again concentrated on the tension between the crowd and counter-demonstrators, among them GLF members armed with stink bombs. Muggeridge was so incensed that afterwards he completely lost his temper, telling the editor of the Radio Four's *World at One* and *The World This Weekend* – an old friend and committed Catholic – that he had 'a growing feeling of revulsion for the programmes you edit'. 'In a time of moral crisis we're on different sides,' Muggeridge added, 'so much so that I consider all personal relations between us now being at an end.'[54]

In fact, despite the ludicrous scenes in central London and Muggeridge's intemperate reaction, the Festival of Light was a considerable grass-roots success. Outside London, the movement organized dozens of 'Land Aflame' rallies, attracting, they claimed, a total of 215,000 people. In

Blackburn, 10,000 people joined the local bishop and chief constable on a march for 'decency'; in Bristol, a special service in the cathedral was filled to capacity; in Sheffield, hundreds watched as none other than Cliff Richard lit a beacon, one of about 300 across the country. As far as evangelical groups were concerned, this was a moment of unprecedented unity and solidarity; indeed, it stands as a landmark in the history of inter-denominational cooperation, with Catholics and evangelical Protestants joining hands to protest against the 'corruption' of modern morals. And while the Festival of Light eventually faded from the headlines, it never went away. By the end of the decade it was still campaigning for 'love, purity and family life' and against 'destructive influences in contemporary culture', and a small team distributed 15,000 copies of a quarterly newsletter through grass-roots Christian and conservative organizations. It did not turn back the tide of pornography and permissiveness, of course. But it clearly appealed to thousands of people, predominantly middle-class churchgoers, who felt frightened and alienated by the cultural changes that were sweeping over Britain in the 1970s – people like A. R. Reynolds of Hereford, who told *The Times* that they were 'ordinary responsible people collectively calling a halt to those who are imposing on us standards of behaviour which take away dignity and decency'. 'We all know what happens to a family when self and mutual respect is lost,' he added; 'it is the crucial step towards break-up of the family. The same applies to a nation.'[55]

To people like Mr Reynolds, the true standard-bearer of the anti-permissive movement was neither Longford, the socialist peer, nor Muggeridge, the satirist-turned-moralist. It was the former senior mistress at Madeley School for Girls in Shropshire, a deeply religious woman who presented herself as an ordinary wife and mother and yet had become one of the most familiar faces in the country, her polite Midlands voice belying a passionate sense of moral mission. Ever since 1964, when she had launched the Clean-Up TV movement at a mass meeting in Birmingham Town Hall, Mary Whitehouse had come in for unrelenting mockery from her critics. The extravagantly mustachioed Conservative backbencher Sir Gerald Nabarro publicly called her a 'hypocritical old bitch'; the young *Sunday Times* columnist Jilly Cooper called her 'sinister and chilling'; the former director general of the BBC, Sir Hugh Carleton Greene, reportedly kept a nude cartoon of her with (oddly) five breasts, and used to amuse himself by throwing darts at it. In one episode of *The*

Goodies she is lampooned as Desiree Carthorse, head of the Keep Filth
Off Television Campaign, who enlists the Goodies to make a sex education
film ('How to Make Babies While Doing Dirty Things'); in *Till Death
Us Do Part*, Alf Garnett admiringly reads her book *Cleaning Up TV*,
which Mike and Rita later ceremonially burn while chanting 'Unclean,
unclean'. And all the time she was bombarded with hate mail, with
threatening telephone calls and abusive letters. She even complained that
her sons had been invited to orgies on the pretence that they were
Christmas parties.[56]

And yet even as the attacks kept on coming, Whitehouse never gave
up. In an age when female politicians were still extremely rare, with
Barbara Castle, Margaret Thatcher and Shirley Williams the only well-
known examples, she was rarely out of the headlines, 'the model of a
moral entrepreneur'. In one typical week in the mid-1970s, she spent
Monday running her pressure group, the National Viewers' and Listeners'
Association, before addressing a meeting in the Midlands. The next day
she drove to Sheffield for a debate at the university; on Wednesday she
drove down to London to appear on the BBC's *Woman's Hour*; on
Thursday she drove to South Wales for a television interview in Cardiff
and a talk at a Methodist church hall in Merthyr Tydfil; on Friday, she
had to go back down to Cardiff at short notice for yet another television
discussion. All the time she hammered home the same message that had
animated her very first manifesto back in January 1964. 'We women of
Britain believe in a Christian way of life,' it began, demanding 'the right
to bring up our own children in the truths of the Christian faith, and to
protect our homes from the exhibitions of violence'. And although her
targets included plays, newspapers, films and novels, one loomed larger
than any other: the BBC, which she accused of peddling 'the propaganda
of disbelief, doubt and dirt' and celebrating 'promiscuity, infidelity and
drinking'. People watched the BBC, Whitehouse said, 'at the risk of
serious damage to their morals, their patriotism, their discipline and their
family life'.[57]

To Whitehouse's critics, the obvious explanation for her campaign
was that she was simply a crank, a self-appointed censor who wanted
to turn back the clock to some imaginary paradise of church choirs
and happy families. And in truth she often handed the scoffers all the
ammunition they could want. Objecting to *Till Death Us Do Part*, for
example, she took issue not with Alf's racism or his reactionary opinions,

but his language, sitting with a pen and paper to note down the '121 bloodies in half an hour'. Whereas most people found the Irish comedian Dave Allen, a great BBC favourite in the 1970s, gentle and rueful, she found him 'offensive, indecent and embarrassing', largely because he poked fun at the Catholic Church. At a meeting with the BBC chairman Sir Michael Swann in January 1974 – the very existence of which testified to her impact – she singled out the inoffensive sitcoms *Some Mothers Do 'Ave 'Em* and *It Ain't Half Hot Mum*, claiming that they were guilty of repeated sexual innuendos ('It seemed that the male sex organ', she said unselfconsciously, 'was the in thing'). Not even pop music was safe from her scrutiny: when Alice Cooper's raucous 'School's Out' reached number one in August 1972, she sent a furious letter to the producer of *Top of the Pops*. 'You will hear that the lyrics contain the following chorus – "Got no principles, got no innocence; School's out for Summer, School's out for ever; School's been blown to pieces, oh! No more books, no more teachers." In our view the record is subversive. I hope you will agree and take the appropriate action. It could also amount to an incitement to violence.' Amazingly, the producers agreed to ban the video; a few days later, Cooper sent Whitehouse flowers to thank her for the publicity.[58]

Whitehouse's most famous target, however, inhabited a very different world from the theatrical violence of an Alice Cooper concert. For all her determination, stamina and articulacy, her instincts sometimes led her badly awry, and in devoting so much attention to *Doctor Who* she made herself look frankly ridiculous. Even though parents often complained that it was too frightening for very young children, few would have described the teatime show as full of 'the sickest, most horrible material . . . obscene violence and horror'. Yet to Mrs Whitehouse it was one of the most disturbing shows on television. She 'believes the Saturday serial is giving nightmares to under-sevens', explained the *Evening News* in January 1975, adding that she wanted 'to "exterminate" the zany Doctor and his unearthly foes'. After watching the third episode of 'Genesis of the Daleks' two months later, for instance, she complained to the BBC that there had been 'so much violence and sadism . . . that I believe this particular episode should not have been screened before 9 pm'. In March 1976, meanwhile, after watching Tom Baker defeat a giant man-eating plant in 'The Seeds of Doom', she solemnly denounced the programme's reliance on 'strangulation – by hand, by claw, by obscene vegetable matter'. Of course this only made her look absurd: if she wanted to maximize her public support, she would have done better to stick to genuine pornography than to worry about obscene vegetable matter. And yet the revealing thing is that for all the mockery, the BBC took her seriously. Eight months later, when the Doctor's head was violently held under water in the climax to episode three of 'The Deadly Assassin', she wrote again 'in anger and despair . . . because at a time when little children would be viewing, you showed violence of a quite unacceptable kind'. This time the BBC took note: the director general wrote her a letter of apology, while the master tape was edited to ensure that the freeze-frame cliffhanger could never be shown again.[59]

What the BBC had realized, of course, was that Whitehouse was more than an isolated crank. In March 1975, the *Sun* had mockingly wondered: 'How many of us does Mary Whitehouse really speak for?' But her support was wider than her critics often imagined. In January 1972, after the defendants in the *Oz* obscenity trial had been freed on appeal, she launched a 'Nationwide Petition for Public Decency', which called for the strengthening of the obscenity laws and might have been expected to sink without trace. Yet by the time she formally presented the petition to Edward Heath in April 1973 it had attracted a staggering 1.35 million signatures, making it by far the most successful petition since the peace campaigns of the 1930s. According to Whitehouse's own (unverifiable) figures, more than eight out of ten of people approached had agreed to sign, and there can be little doubt that it represented a genuine surge of public feeling. And then there was her pressure group, the National Viewers' and Listeners' Association, founded in 1965 as a descendant of Clean-Up TV, which by the mid-1970s boasted a membership of about 31,000 people in twenty-eight regional branches. It might well be objected that this hardly made it a mass movement in a country of almost 60 million people. Even so, this made it roughly the same size as the Communist Party and much bigger than the National Front and the Socialist Workers' Party, while there were many more NVALA members than, say, *Oz* readers. But then of course the NVALA's members were overwhelmingly female, elderly and middle-class, precisely the kind of people often overlooked not just by journalists but by historians, too. Many, perhaps most, were committed Christians; many lived in rural areas; a majority were connected to 'the older professions, small business-men, traders and shopkeepers'. These were people who lamented the abolition of the death penalty and the rise of the mugger, inveighed against the 'rent-a-crowd' agitators allegedly whipping up the unions, and struggled to contain their horror at Heath's supposed appeasement of socialism. 'I think this permissiveness comes to us through television and the newspapers,' explained a maths and scripture teacher from Lancashire. 'I'm very sympathetic to Enoch Powell . . .'[60]

From the very beginning, Whitehouse saw her movement in explicitly political terms. As a middle-class schoolteacher from the West Midlands she was a natural conservative; more importantly, however, she had for decades been a member of the evangelical Christian group Moral Re-armament, which had a fiercely anti-Communist thrust. At the root of the new permissiveness, she argued, was the 'the secular/humanist/ Marxist philosophy', and her husband Ernest even told an interviewer that they were fighting back against the 'pressure from the left-wing' to 'destroy the Christian faith'. Throughout her career, she never failed to link permissiveness and socialism, arguing – as did many like-minded people during the Wilson and Heath years – that they were part of the same campaign to subvert British democracy. 'The enemies of the West', she once explained, 'saw that Britain was the kingpin of Western civilisation; she had proved herself unbeatable on the field of battle because of her faith and her character. If Britain was to be destroyed, those things must be undercut.' Just as many grass-roots Conservatives believed that behind the industrial unrest of the 1970s was a tight-knit cabal of Communist agents, therefore, Mary Whitehouse believed, the BBC's output was inspired by Reds at Television Centre. 'They've infiltrated the trade unions,' she argued. 'Why does anyone still believe they haven't infiltrated broadcasting?' As she explained in her book *Whatever Happened to Sex?* (1977), groups as diverse as the National Council for Civil Liberties, the Albany Trust, the Campaign for Homosexual Equality and the Humanist Society all belonged to the same conspiracy, run by 'dogma-riddled lefties who see the undermining of morality as the prerequisite of take-over'. Not even the *Radio Times* was safe from subversion: after the much-loved listings magazine had run a mischievous cover montage of Christ, Tariq Ali and Coco the Clown, she warned the *Daily Telegraph* that it had fallen victim to a 'disturbing leftist trend'.[61]

In many ways, therefore, the NVALA looks like an early example of the mildly eccentric protest groups that emerged out of the ruin of the

Heath government in the mid-to-late 1970s, protesting vociferously about inflation, taxes and the impending triumph of international socialism. Like them, it appealed to provincial middle-class homeowners who felt that their values of entrepreneurship, discipline and thrift were under threat, and that they had been betrayed and abandoned by Heath's Conservative Party. And yet as Whitehouse's roots in Moral Re-armament might suggest, there was another dimension to the NVALA. By the standards of the day, she was an exceptionally pious woman: every day began with a Bible-reading in bed, and she said morning prayers before breakfast. And unlike most British women in the 1970s, she was completely convinced of the presence of the divine in her life. When her son Christopher suffered an accident and seemed likely to lose an eye, she telephoned her friends and organized prayers for him, and when the eye was unexpectedly saved, she was convinced that God had intervened. Her work, she later wrote, was about 'fulfilling God's purpose'; indeed, a detailed academic analysis of her career published in 1979 concluded that the central aim of the NVALA was 'to colonise social life for God'. There was more to Whitehouse's movement, in other words, than the economic and political anxiety of the middle classes; at a very basic level, it was a religious crusade to rescue the embattled Christian family from the 'left-wing humanists', a cry of rage by a pious minority against what they saw as the secularization and godlessness of modern British life.[62]

And this, of course, was why it failed. Despite the genuine public unease manifested in the Petition for Public Decency, there were just not enough churchgoing Christians left to support a religious revival. Even in 1960, just one in ten people had gone to church every week, and with living standards rising and so many other things to do at weekends, numbers had since continued to plummet. In total, Protestant church membership fell by almost 20 per cent in the course of the 1960s, and by the time Edward Heath became Prime Minister fewer than 2 per cent of adolescent boys were confirmed in the Church of England, while only a minority of babies were baptized. Swelled by immigration from Ireland, the Catholic Church made a better fist of keeping its members, but the Methodists and Baptists saw their congregations fall by up to a third. All in all, just 1.5 million people went to church every week in 1970, and for all Mary Whitehouse's efforts to rekindle the faith, death, disaffection and sheer indifference had whittled that down to 1.25 million by the end of the 1970s. It is true that Britain was not yet an entirely secular society: the massive sales of, for example, Malcolm Muggeridge's book on Mother Teresa in 1971 showed that many people were still fascinated by religious questions, and polls consistently showed that about three out of four people believed in God and just under half in life after death. But even if the popular fascination with spiritual questions survived, Britain in the 1970s was what the sociologist Grace Davie calls a society of 'believing without belonging', in which religious participation had fallen a long way from fashion. It was hardly surprising that when *The Times* carried out a survey on power and influence in British life, only 2 per cent of respondents thought the Church of England was 'very influential', compared with 33 per cent who named the TUC and 52 per cent who identified Mary Whitehouse's enemies at the BBC.[63]

What baffled Whitehouse, however, was that she could not even count on the support of the Anglican hierarchy. As Archbishop of Canterbury since 1961, the gentle, scholarly Michael Ramsey had steered the Church of England on a notably progressive course. He strongly supported the campaign for the legalization of homosexuality, voted for (and indeed offered to introduce in the Lords) the abolition of hanging, and encouraged the Church to take a more liberal line on divorce reform; on top of that, he vociferously opposed apartheid in South Africa and the war in Vietnam, and even argued for military intervention against the white supremacist rebels in Rhodesia. Other Churches, especially the Methodists, took a similarly liberal course: even the once austerely conservative Church of Scotland, for example, supported the decriminalization of homosexuality and the reform of the divorce laws, and in 1970 its Moral Welfare Committee even welcomed the advent of sexual permissiveness, commenting that 'the spirit of the age with its new found freedoms, and its healthy intolerance of humbug and hypocrisy, challenges Christians to re-think the implications of Christian morality – not a bad thing to have to do'. To moral conservatives like Whitehouse, all of this was bewildering and unsettling: the explanation, she thought, was that the Churches had been taken over by 'soft permissives'. Ramsey's postbag was often full of furious letters from ordinary Anglicans: his secretary never forgot one occasion when Ramsey gently put one letter aside with the words: 'I don't think that is of *much* value as it begins "You lying bastard".'[64]

But to many older parishioners who were not familiar or comfortable with the latest trends in liturgy and theology, Ramsey's leadership seemed characteristic of a religious landscape that had been infiltrated by bleeding-hearted socialists, happy-clappy weirdos and guitar-wielding hippies, in which all familiar landmarks and conventions had vanished. Even in fiction, respect for the Church seemed to be ebbing away: in television sitcoms of the early 1970s, clergymen are almost exclusively feeble, hand-wringing figures, like the incompetent clowns who run St Ogg's Cathedral in *All Gas and Gaiters*, or the ineffectual, effeminate Reverend Timothy Farthing in *Dad's Army*. And as congregations dwindled, so a sense of almost inevitable decline seemed to set in. 'Oh Christianity, Christianity, . . . are you vanishing?' asked the poet Stevie Smith, anticipating the collapse of faith into 'beliefs we do not believe in'. Other poets sounded a similar note: in the Anglican priest R. S. Thomas's 'Via Negativa' (1972), God is 'that great absence / In our lives, the empty silence / Within . . .', while in 'The Moon in Lleyn' (1975), Thomas ponders the idea that 'religion is dead'. Other churchmen were inclined to agree: at lunch with James Lees-Milne in October 1973, the Bishop of Gloucester reflected sadly on 'the loneliness and desolation of the spirit' of the modern priest. 'No clergyman in the Church of England today', he added, 'could claim spiritual success. He said that in his city eighty per cent of the inhabitants had never heard of him and didn't care tuppence for his office.' Against this background, Mary Whitehouse's dreams of a Christian renaissance were doomed from the start.[65]

In many ways Mary Whitehouse's career, like the stories of the Festival of Light, the Longford report and the Responsible Society, was a study in failure. For all the enthusiasm of her supporters, indeed for all the widespread disquiet at Britain's alleged moral decline, polls showed that most people did not want to turn back the clock. Interviewed in 1973, not only did three out of four people agree that adults should be allowed to buy indecent materials if they wanted to, but seven out of ten admitted they had never been seriously upset by an 'indecent display'. And although the Heath government introduced an Indecent Displays Bill at the end of 1973 to crack down on the visibility of pornography (including, splendidly, measures against the threat of 'indecent sounds'), it never made it onto the statute book – and the evidence of obscenity trials later in the decade suggests it might not have worked anyway. Time after time, juries acquitted proprietors and producers accused of corrupting public morals. In the most celebrated case, which came to court in 1974, a cameraman called John Lindsay was accused of making twenty-nine indecent films, which included scenes of schoolgirls pleasuring themselves with hockey sticks, nuns masturbating with crucifixes, priests debauching nuns in a convent, and what Lindsay himself called 'the worst of the lot . . . a film called *Anal Rape* in a classroom with a very young-looking blonde girl'. According to the prosecution, these films showed 'sex in the nastiest, rawest fashion, bestial and perverted, without any question of love or tenderness', while the judge, Mr Justice Wien, denounced 'the unnatural and horrible offence of sodomy', and reminded the jury what had happened to Sodom and Gomorrah. The jury failed to return a verdict, and after a retrial, Lindsay was found not guilty. So were a couple accused of running a magazine called *Libertine* from a shop in Leicester, three years later. Once again, anal rape played an oddly central role in the proceedings; once again, the verdict was not guilty. As the triumphant couple left the court, one of the female jurors cheerfully remarked: 'It's a lot of old rubbish, isn't it, my duck?'[66]

While the failure to stem the flow of pornography in the 1970s owed as much to the chaos of the obscenity laws as to the relaxation of popular attitudes, what happened to sex education was not so different. As with pornography, there was a great flurry of popular outrage in 1971–2, helping to create what one account calls a 'new discourse on sexual education' that anticipated the debates during the Thatcher years. And yet while the Family Planning Association was forced into a series of embarrassing retreats in the summer of 1971 – including the withdrawal of an explicit leaflet for teenagers entitled *Straight Facts* and the cancellation of fringe events at a 'New Frontiers of Birth Control' conference (including a bizarre wheeze to release tens of thousands of condom-themed balloons into the skies above London) – the Responsible Society and its allies never regained control of sex education. The FPA continued to offer increasingly explicit and non-judgemental advice, such as a splendid leaflet from 1973, *Too Great A Risk!*, which was modelled on a *Jackie* comic strip and featured a pretty, sexually active teenage girl learning how to avoid getting pregnant. A year later, the FPA launched a new national campaign, *Tomorrow's People Are Today's Concern*, calling for 'sex education programmes for all schools in the United Kingdom . . . to undo the layers of shame, fear, ignorance, distortion and misinformation'. Once again there were howls of protest from moral conservatives, and the protesters did win isolated victories: the cancellation of a highly explicit ITV documentary series called *Sex in Our Time* in 1976, for example, or the censorship of a new Nuffield Secondary Science textbook with explicit diagrams and references to masturbation. But while the sex education war went on, so did sex education itself, reaching an ever wider proportion of Britain's teenagers. In this respect, too, Whitehouse and her allies had lost.[67]

The fact was that, thanks to the decline of churchgoing, the erosion of collective loyalties, the advent of affluence and mass secondary education, the challenge of feminism and homosexuality and the rise of a new kind of populist individualism, there no longer existed an agreed moral consensus around which people could instinctively rally. The ideal of the stable, settled family survived, of course; so too did the ideal of the happy, enduring marriage. In their daily lives, however, growing numbers of people found these ideals impossible to live up to – perhaps partly because of their own exaggerated expectations and their obsession with self-gratification, but also surely because of the increasing economic pressures on the traditional family. As the historian Jeffrey Weeks notes, people still talked of 'love, honesty, faithfulness' as fundamental values, and in the world of the imagination the nuclear family remained the norm. Increasingly, however, events in the real world suggested otherwise. The advice columns of just one issue of *Woman's Own* from January 1975 told the wider story. A photographer had written to complain that his 16-year-old son ought to knuckle down and get a haircut; his wife, however, objected that they ought not to 'suppress' their son's personality. One woman kept her teenage daughter at home, frightened that meeting boys would lead to venereal disease, pregnancy and abortion; another, the wife of a garage mechanic, wrote that she was happy for her 15-year-old daughter to go on the Pill. There were no longer any binding rules; there were no easy answers.[68]

And yet there were limits to popular permissiveness. In 1963, the Profumo sex-and-spying scandal had almost destroyed Harold Macmillan's government, and even after a decade of social and cultural change, nobody could be certain that the public would look any more kindly on politicians' sexual failings. And as luck would have it, on 14 May 1973, just weeks before the tenth anniversary of the last great scandal, a relatively obscure government whip sent a panicky handwritten letter to the Chief Whip, Francis Pym, marked 'Private and Confidential'. In it, Sir John Stradling-Thomas reported that thanks to another Tory

MP who had been talking to one of Rupert Murdoch's PR men, he had got wind of a sensational tale that was apparently poised to destroy the government. 'Murdoch has a "Profumo" type story on the stocks *with photographs,*' he reported ominously, 'about a junior minister who is involved in sexual orgies with back benchers. The official car is involved. The story is about to break.'[69]

The junior minister at the centre of this garbled rumour was by any standards an extraordinarily colourful character. Described by a profile in *The Times* as a 'politician, journalist, aristocrat and eccentric', Antony Lambton had been MP for Berwick-upon-Tweed since 1951. Afflicted since childhood with an eye disease, he always wore dark glasses, giving him an engagingly mysterious air, and he championed an odd combination of reactionary and libertarian causes, from the revival of National Service to the reform of the obscenity laws. His lifestyle was raffish, to say the least: rated as one of the best three shots in the country, he owned two vast estates in the North of England as well as an elegant London townhouse, and was well known for his generosity, sardonic wit and appreciation of the female form. In 1970, Heath had made him Parliamentary Under-Secretary for Defence with responsibility for the RAF, but Lambton was best known for a bizarre and protracted squabble over his title. On the death of his father, the fifth Earl of Durham, in the same year, he had disclaimed his peerage so that he could stay in the Commons, but insisted that he should still be known as Lord Lambton. Most of his fellow MPs, as well as numerous constitutional experts, thought this was absurd. But Lambton took it oddly seriously. The battle over the title had 'become an obsession with him', an MI5 officer reported after Lambton's fall, 'to the extent that he was no longer able to read – and he had been a great reader – and he sought to forget his obsession in frantic activity. He had for example become an enthusiastic and vigorous gardener. Another example of this frenzied activity was his debauchery.'[70]

Whatever his motives, by the end of 1971 Lambton had become a regular client of a high-class escort agency run by London's 'leading madam', the aptly named Jean Horn. There his particular favourite was an attractive 26-year-old Irish-born prostitute called Norma, who had set herself up in an expensive Regency flat in Maida Vale and claimed to earn an astonishing £2,500 tax-free a week. By Norma's own account, the man she called 'Mr Lucas' had interesting tastes, often asking her to procure other girls or to watch him having sex with another man. His anonymity did not last long, however: with typically careless insouciance, Lambton used to pay her by personal cheque, so she soon realized that he was a government minister. What made this reckless behaviour even more dangerous, however, was the fact that in late 1972 Norma married a shady 'cab driver' (although he never seemed to drive any cabs) called Colin Levy, who was determined to make some money from his wife's connections. At the end of the following April, Levy installed a hidden camera in his wife's wardrobe and a listening device in the nose of her giant teddy bear, already a somewhat incongruous addition to the decor. On 5 May, he offered the recordings of Lambton and his wife to the *News of the World*, but the quality was deemed substandard. Instead, the newspaper installed its own equipment in the flat, with sensational results. On 9 May, they recorded Lambton asking Norma if she could get him drugs; the following day, a *News of the World* photographer hid inside the wardrobe, snapping away through a two-way mirror while Lambton enjoyed himself with Norma and a black prostitute. Inexplicably, however, executives at the *News of the World* got cold feet and decided to shelve the story. So Levy offered it instead to the *Sunday People* – who promptly passed the material to the police.[71]

This was not the first time that the police had heard about Lambton's extramarital adventures. Like Christine Keeler before her, Norma Levy found it hard to keep her mouth shut, and as early as 2 May the Home Office had asked MI5 to investigate 'security doubts' about Lambton and two other ministers rumoured to be using prostitutes. The Security Service reported back that there was 'no adverse information' about any of them in their files, but by this stage Heath and his senior ministers were becoming distinctly anxious. In this context, Stradling-Thomas's letter about the '"Profumo" type story' was deeply worrying, and on 18 May Heath himself convened a meeting of his chief aides and ordered another MI5 investigation. Three days later, Lambton was formally interviewed by the police and admitted that 'a photograph showing a man on a bed with two women was of him and that the cigarette which he was smoking in the photograph was of cannabis'. A few hours later, he went to see Francis Pym, told him the whole story and added that the police had searched his flat and found more cannabis and amphetamines. Nobody had attempted to blackmail him, he pointed out; but the drugs alone made his position untenable. That night, Lambton resigned. 'All that has happened is that some sneak pimp has seen an opportunity of making some money by the sale of the story and secret photographs to the papers at home and abroad,' read his remarkably honest statement the next day. 'I have no excuses whatsoever to make. I behaved with incredible stupidity.'[72]

Lambton's resignation was the cue for what the *Mirror* called 'a day of sensation'. Within hours of the announcement, the police had re-interviewed the fallen minister, even asking him to strip to his red flannel underwear so that they could check for heroin injection marks. Meanwhile, Heath had been handed an MI5 report identifying a second minister who regularly visited call girls: the Leader of the House of Lords, Earl Jellicoe, who had patronized Mayfair Escorts since 1970. Poor Jellicoe had no connection with either Lambton or the Levys, and MI5 thought that the 'risk of indiscretions' was 'negligible'. But Heath felt he could not afford to take chances. That evening Jellicoe was intercepted as he and his wife were leaving the Royal Opera House and whisked to Downing Street, and by the next morning he was out too. Since he was enormously popular with his fellow peers, the outcry was immediate. The Labour leader in the Lords, Lord Shackleton, declared that 'we and the country have suffered a grievous loss', while the former Labour minister Richard Crossman wrote that the government had lost 'one of [its] bravest, ablest, most decent members'. Even Lambton sardonically remarked that 'the way things were going it will soon be clear that Heath is the only member of the government who doesn't do it'. In fact, behind the bravado Lambton was devastated by the scandal. In public, however, he kept up a characteristically insouciant front. When Robin Day asked him on *Panorama* why on earth he had done it, Lambton's reaction was priceless. 'People sometimes like variety,' he remarked. 'Surely all men visit whores?'[73]

On the surface the Lambton affair – and especially the resignation of Jellicoe, who, as almost everybody recognized, had been extremely unlucky – was a testament to the lingering conservatism of popular attitudes. Lambton's fall was not merely a question of 'security', an outraged P. A. Carnwath of London W8 wrote to *The Times*, for there was 'a moral case for the resignation of a minister who is publicly known to have been involved with a call girl'. And as J. W. M. Thompson, the editor of the *Sunday Telegraph*, saw it, Lambton's fall was a sign that the baleful influence of the 1960s had penetrated far less than many conservatives feared. 'The new morality of sexual free-for-all has been assiduously propounded,' he noted, 'transforming the general idea of what is free for public consumption by way of entertainment or information.' And yet the scandal demonstrated that 'the full gale of permissiveness still belongs only in the realm of the media, or among that minority of the population who constitute the fashionable consensus. The tolerance of the majority does not imply anything approaching unqualified approval when the new morality is translated from words (or pictures) into action.'[74]

And yet what is so striking about the general reaction to the fall of Lambton and Jellicoe is that it was so unlike the censorious outrage that had greeted the Profumo scandal ten years previously. The Profumo affair, after all, had come close to destroying Macmillan's government. But although the Lambton scandal dominated tabloid front pages for days with a similar mixture of sex, sensation and security, it never posed a serious threat to Edward Heath. Inside the Commons, the mood was very different from the hysteria of the summer of 1963. 'This time', as Bernard Levin noted, 'Lord Wigg and the other leading Labour politicians who rose so enthusiastically into battle with "security" embroidered on their banners have not been heard from.' Indeed, the only Labour MP who spoke out against Lambton, James Wellbeloved, was promptly dismissed by the Liberals' John Pardoe as a 'sanctimonious creep of the first order'. And far from rounding on Lambton and Jellicoe as their predecessors had turned on Profumo, most politicians and peers struck a notably compassionate note. 'Is it not time that we grew up?' the sociologist Lady Wootton of Abinger wrote to *The Times*. 'Everyone knows that such affairs are common in all walks of life. There is no law against them and they do not by any means always result in divorces.' Lambton's critics, agreed the Labour MP Alex Lyon a few days later, were 'hypocrites and bigots'. In the Bible, he recalled, Jesus had asked an adulterous wife's accusers who would cast the first stone. 'Do you feel like aiming at Lord Lambton and Lord Jellicoe?' Lyon asked.[75]

In the editorial columns, the overwhelming tone was one of sympathy for both Lambton and Jellicoe. 'A chamber of 630 members entirely free from human frailty, or deep-dyed in the conviction that they are entirely free from human frailty, would be a hard and tyrannical House,' wrote David Wood in *The Times*. 'Politics is a trade that notoriously damages family relationships and sometimes breaks up marriages. Allowances must be made.' Even the *Daily Express*, usually one of the most strident voices of moral conservatism, lamented that 'in this modern so-called permissive age a splendid [parliamentarian] and junior minister have been cast into the wilderness . . . Can we really afford to discard men of talent, wit and patriotism because their personal lives fall short of blameless perfection?' And to the evident surprise of visiting journalists, Lambton's reputation in his rural, sleepy constituency of Berwick-upon-Tweed remained 're-markably undiminished' by the revelations. 'We still think he's a perfect gentleman,' said one of the five gamekeepers working on his estate. Among 'shoppers in the streets and the men in the pubs', wrote one reporter, 'serious feelings of outrage or even anger are hard to find'. 'Shame for his family,' was the best he could get out of female passers-by, while most of the men confined themselves to a mere 'Bad luck, mate.'[76]

While Lambton's fall superficially testified to the limits of permissive-ness, therefore, closer examination suggested a very different story. At a moment when abortion and homosexuality were legal, thousands of marriages were collapsing every year and the West End seemed awash with pornography, few people seemed genuinely shocked or even surprised by the former peer's misbehaviour. It was 'heartening to be able to say without doubt that things are better now than they were in 1963', wrote Bernard Levin in the most thoughtful contemporary analysis of the affair. In 1963, Harold Macmillan had been 'very nearly brought down, not because he was himself in any way involved, but simply because he *was* Prime Minister'. But as Levin noted, 'no "Heath must go" campaign is likely today'. The reason, he thought, was that for all the outrage of Lord Longford and Mary Whitehouse, Britain now had a 'calmer attitude' where sexual morality was concerned. Perhaps this was going a bit far: although what Levin called the 'fanaticism and intolerance' of 1963 were evaporating, the success of Whitehouse's decency petition just a few weeks earlier suggests that many people did not feel calm at all. All the same, he felt confident enough in the pace of change to risk a prediction. 'It is exactly ten years since the last political *dépit amoreux* in Britain. If another decade should elapse before the next one, the compromised minister will stay in office.' He was wrong about the details: ten years later, Cecil Parkinson failed to survive the revelation of his affair with his secretary Sara Keays, although the fact that he had fathered and abandoned a daughter made Lambton look like a pillar of moral rectitude. But in the long run, in a society in which Mary Whitehouse's dream of stemming the tide of permissiveness had long since failed, Levin was right.[77]

12

No Surrender

*The typical Protestant worker's reaction was expressed by one
labourer in a Belfast pub last week when he said, 'I wish it had
been 1,300 of the bastards.'*

         – *Time*, 14 February 1972

On 5 January 1972, BBC1 devoted three hours of evening television to
a painstaking debate about *The Question of Ulster*. In the days beforehand,
discussion of the programme had reached hysterical levels: the Home
Secretary, Reginald Maudling, had even threatened to ban it, while
Northern Ireland's Prime Minister Brian Faulkner flatly refused to take
part and urged his fellow Ulster Unionists to boycott the panel. In the
event, the programme took a serious and worthy look at the issues behind
the conflict in Northern Ireland, soliciting contributions from a range of
politicians all the way from Ian Paisley to Bernadette Devlin. Almost
two-thirds of the population of Northern Ireland were reported to have
tuned in, although half of them lost interest as midnight approached.
But the programme came up with no answers, no solutions for the
troubled province. For with communal trust destroyed and almost every
day's headlines announcing more casualties, Northern Ireland seemed
on the brink of all-out bloodshed. When a representative of its tiny
Labour Party visited Tony Benn in London, he reported that 'the Catholics
were now living in sort of tribal encampments with the barricades
removed and the houses around them burned. When the whistle blew,
the Protestants would just march in and murder them by the thousands
and there would be the most appalling civil war.'[1]

Even at Stormont, any remaining illusions had disappeared. When
Brian Faulkner flew to London to brief Edward Heath on the deteriorating

situation in October 1971, he gloomily reported that after reviewing 'the economic and social position', his officials thought that 'a breakdown in government might occur in a matter of weeks'. Heath warned him that the position was 'grave socially, economically and politically, and the British public was losing patience'. Yet still he shrank from the prospect of suspending Stormont and imposing direct rule. According to a Ministry of Defence report, 'in the event of direct rule, the co-operation to be expected from the civil service, the public utility services, et cetera, would be less than has hitherto been assumed in London. This renders the direct rule option even less palatable than we have always supposed.' Direct rule, the report gloomily concluded, might well involve the army 'fighting both sides in the middle of a civil war', which 'quite apart from its military implications, [would] be very difficult to sustain in British political terms'. It was little wonder that the Defence Secretary Lord Carrington told his staff that he was 'even more impressed than before with the importance of keeping Mr Faulkner in power as the only apparent alternative to direct rule'.[2]

The truth was that Heath had found himself trapped in a quagmire from which there was no obvious escape. Unilateral British withdrawal – the panacea often recommended by critics on the far left, as well as by ordinary people sick of seeing the conflict in the headlines – was unthinkable; quite apart from the fact that it would mean abandoning part of the United Kingdom in which a majority saw themselves as British, it would almost certainly spark massive sectarian bloodshed and full-scale civil war, sucking the Republic of Ireland into the conflict. (If the British withdrew, Irish defence chiefs reported to Dublin in the summer of 1971, the result would be 'grave peril for the country as a whole'.) From the Labour benches, Harold Wilson talked vaguely of Irish unity, but even he admitted it would take fifteen years. And although there was talk of a new power-sharing government, it ran the enormous risk of provoking a loyalist rebellion. There seemed, in short, to be no way out.

On top of all that, Northern Ireland was not even the government's main priority. Not only was Heath already overloaded by rising unemployment, strikes and the torturous progress of the Industrial Relations Act, he also had to contend with surging inflation and the parliamentary battle over Britain's entry into the EEC. Even if he had wanted to spend all day thinking about Belfast politics, he simply did not have the time. In the meantime, even senior ministers responsible for the province's security seemed to have run out of ideas. When a group of community relations advisers went to see Maudling in November 1971, they found him sprawled in an armchair by a roaring fire, apparently utterly exhausted and uninterested in what they had to say. When they met again the next morning, he asked wearily: 'What do we do? Arm the Protestants and get out?'[3]

For the ordinary soldiers struggling to keep the peace on the streets of Belfast, the conflict had taken on the proportions of a nightmare. Some could barely believe what they were seeing: when one young officer with the Royal Green Jackets flew into Belfast for the first time in August 1971, he was stunned by the sight of the entire city apparently ablaze. 'You could see roads that had been blocked and barricaded,' he recalled. 'You could see fires, from bonfires, burning cars and burning houses. I was shocked.' As he drove past the shattered shop fronts, the piles of rubble and glass, the smouldering barricades, he could hardly believe 'that all this was happening in a city of the United Kingdom', a city with 'red telephone boxes and red letter boxes'.[4]

Far from being hailed as saviours, the troops themselves, their numbers increased from 7,000 to more than 15,000, had become part of the immensely complex, tortured mosaic of sectarian politics. A heavy fog of fear had settled over Belfast's streets, and not even the army was immune. In 1971, IRA snipers shot and killed forty-two British soldiers; in 1972 they killed sixty-four. As the bounds of civility frayed and snapped, the news of each dead soldier brought cheers in nationalist pubs and homes. Visiting a grey, burned-out Belfast estate in the hot summer of 1972, Kevin Myers watched a teenage IRA gunman open fire on a British foot patrol. As one soldier bled to death in the middle of the street, Myers heard children cheering, their young voices raised in mockery of the dying man. Even those soldiers lucky enough to escape gunfire could expect a hail of missiles and abuse when they visited Catholic areas. 'They did not want to be there. They had no axe to grind,' a brigadier said later.

> Yet they were under constant verbal abuse, spat at, stoned from men, women and kids, all the time, and at risk from snipers and bombs. They saw their friends killed, shot, blown to pieces . . . and the locals gathering round to sneer or cheer when the British dead were cleared away. This was supposed to be a part of Britain but this was not how decent British people behave, or decent Irish people either, come to that.[5]

Under the circumstances, Myers – born and bred in England, but the son of Irish Catholic parents – thought that 'the forbearance and good cheer of the average squaddie, despite the direst provocation, were extraordinary'. There are plenty of underreported tales of soldiers showing astounding compassion and chivalry, for example in saving the lives of IRA men whom they themselves had wounded, or administering first aid to people who had been shooting at them only moments before. But they were not superhuman. Many soldiers were in their late teens or early twenties, the products of tough working-class backgrounds on the estates of Britain's industrial cities; turning the other cheek did not come naturally. One man, 'Jim', told the journalist Peter Taylor that most soldiers felt 'very, very close' to each other, 'and when you see these blokes being stretchered out of flats, or dying in gutters in a war which is not classed as a war, it makes you bloody bitter. It makes you angry, you know, and it fills you with hate. I hated the people in those flats and the people in those areas with an intensity that used to make me feel almost physically sick when I heard them speak.' Jim and his mates got their revenge 'by getting into their houses and breaking their telly sets and breaking their windows. If they were signalling on the ground with dustbin lids to let people know where we were, then we would break their windows, kick their doors in, and say, "you cut that out and we'll cut it out".' The inevitable result, however, was that by the end of 1971 the British army was seen as a hostile occupying force, a tool of unionist oppression. To ordinary Catholic boys on the streets, the security forces were the 'agents of a state intent on attacking their neighbourhoods'. Throughout nationalist areas, reported *The Times* in September 1971, 'the army is now regarded with corrosive hate'.[6]

Relations between the army and the local community were particularly raw in the province's second city, Londonderry, where the Catholic majority bitterly remembered their treatment at the hands of the RUC in the Battle of the Bogside two years earlier. The scars from that conflict had not yet healed: shops and offices still stood vacant and charred, while almost thirty massive barricades prevented even the army's one-tonne armoured cars from passing into nationalist 'Free Derry', which functioned as a kind of independent enclave, its entrances guarded by local vigilantes. Behind the barricades, both Provisional and Official IRA men posed for journalists wearing balaclavas and carrying guns, while gangs of unemployed teenagers, calling themselves the 'Derry Young Hooligans', used the no-go areas as bases for raids into the city centre, looting shops and carrying out nightly arson attacks against Protestant businesses.

Despite the army's attempts to keep a low profile, there was a powerful sense in the second half of 1971 that they had lost control. Londonderry's Protestant business leaders estimated that bombings and arson had cost them more than £4 million worth of damage, and were furious that British troops seemed reluctant to intervene. What seemed to sum up the situation were the daily confrontations at 'aggro corner', on the edge of the Bogside, where at teatime every afternoon local youths would hurl stones and bricks at the army patrols just outside. To more hawkish observers, it seemed unbelievable that the army never cracked down on its attackers. To Lieutenant Colonel Derek Wilford, the commanding officer of the First Battalion, the Parachute Regiment, it was totally unacceptable. 'They just stood there in the road like Aunt Sallies and never went forward,' he said later. 'It was quite horrifying . . . We did not carry shields. We did not wear cricket pads. As far as I was concerned, it was not a game of cricket that we were engaged in.'[7]

Not only did Derry's business leaders share Wilford's view, but so did Major General Robert Ford, the new commander of the British land forces in Northern Ireland. For General Ford, the black line on British military maps dividing 'Free Derry' from the rest of the city was an embarrassment to the army, while the local commanders' softly-softly policy was putting his men under intolerable pressure and risking their lives in the long run. Even for the last six months of 1971, the statistics made disheartening reading: the army in Derry had lost seven men killed and fifteen injured, while the IRA had fired almost 2,000 rounds, thrown 180 nail bombs and set off more than 200 explosions. On 14 December, Ford warned other senior officers that détente was breaking down: his men now faced perhaps 40 active IRA gunmen and 500 self-styled 'hooligans', and he thought only military action would recover the situation. The 'correct military solution', he thought, was to launch a thrust across the containment lines, root out the IRA and restore law and order to the no-go areas. Crucially, however, General Ford added that 'the drawbacks are so serious that it should not be implemented in the present circumstances'. As he explained, 'the risk of casualties is high and apart from gunmen or bombers, so-called unarmed rioters, possibly teenagers, are certain to be shot in the initial phases. Much will be made of the invasion of Derry and the slaughter of the innocent.' Instead of recommending a major offensive into the no-go areas, therefore, he suggested keeping to the status quo, albeit with a more assertive attitude.[8]

Over Christmas, the situation showed no signs of improving: indeed, two days before the end of the year another soldier, just 20 years old, was shot dead by a sniper. On 7 January, Ford wrote another report that was to become enormously controversial. Containment, he wrote, was clearly failing. Not only were the Derry Young Hooligans pushing further into the city centre, infuriating local shopkeepers, but the army had abandoned patrols outside the Bogside to protect their men from sniper fire. Even when soldiers went out in their armoured personnel carriers, they ran the risk of being surrounded and attacked by teenage 'yobbos', and then shot by snipers from the massive Rossville tower blocks when they got out of their vehicles. Law and order had degenerated to such an extent that local Protestant leaders were demanding 'curfews and shooting on sight'. The only solution, Ford believed, was to get tough:

> I am coming to the conclusion that the minimum force necessary to achieve a restoration of law and order is to shoot selected ringleaders amongst the DYH [Derry Young Hooligans], after clear warnings have been issued. I believe we would be justified in using 7.62mm but in view of the devastating effects of this weapon and the dangers of rounds killing more than one person, I believe we must consider issuing rifles adapted to fire .22 inch ammunition to sufficient members of the unit dealing with this problem to enable ringleaders to be engaged with this less lethal ammunition. If this course is implemented, as I believe it may have to be, we would have to accept the possibility that .22 rounds may be lethal. In other words, we would be reverting to the methods of internal security found successful on many occasions overseas, but would merely be trying to minimise the lethal effects by using the .22 round. I am convinced that our duty to restore law and order requires us to consider this step.

Hostile commentators have sometimes taken this passage as evidence of a supposed British army plot to murder innocent civilians; but it was clearly nothing of the kind. In any case, just four days later Heath's Cabinet committee on Northern Ireland met to discuss the situation in Londonderry and agreed that although a major military offensive 'might in time become inevitable, [it] should not be undertaken while there still remained some prospect of a successful political initiative'. Only by ignoring this wider context can anyone possibly believe that the British had a 'premeditated and well planned' operation to murder civil rights demonstrators, as Gerry Adams puts it. After all, neither the government nor the army had anything to gain from killing civilians in the full gaze of the world's media. They may have made mistakes, but they were not that stupid.[9]

It was just three weeks later that disaster struck. Since 30 January 1972, Bloody Sunday has become not merely the most controversial single incident of the entire Troubles but perhaps the most exhaustively chronicled moment in modern British and Irish history, thanks to a vast number of narrative accounts, two television films, two songs entitled 'Sunday Bloody Sunday' by John Lennon and U2 (neither of them any good), and two highly contentious public inquiries, the first a whitewash by Lord Widgery in February 1972, the second an absurdly bloated affair set up by Tony Blair at a cost of more than £200 million. So much controversy surrounds the day that eyewitnesses cannot even agree how many people went on the march that triggered the violence: while organizers claimed 30,000, Lord Widgery thought the real figure was nearer 3,000. What is clear, though, is that the march began in a festive and relaxed atmosphere. Its organizers were civil rights activists (not hardcore republicans), protesting against the internment of Catholic civilians. Prevented by army barricades from marching into the city centre, as they had planned, they walked instead to the so-called 'Free Derry Corner' where army patrols had had so much trouble from nationalist hooligans. At the barricade on William Street, however, a group of teenagers confronted the British paratroopers and started throwing stones, as had long since become routine.

It was here that the shooting started, though who fired first, or at all, is almost impossible to determine. Many historians now agree that an Official IRA sniper probably fired at least one shot, though it is not certain that he opened fire first. What is certain, though, is that the paratroopers fired five rounds, wounding a teenager and a 59-year-old man. Meanwhile, just after four o'clock, the Paras in C and Support Companies were ordered to move into the Bogside and 'scoop up' the rioters, although they were expressly ordered not to conduct a 'running battle down Rossville Street'. Only minutes later, as Support Company's armoured personnel carriers screamed into the courtyard of the towering Rossville Flats, more shooting broke out. According to the Paras, they came under heavy fire from the flats; yet no other witnesses saw gunfire, and no guns, bullets or bombs were ever recovered from the scene. What is beyond doubt, however, is that the Paras fired more than 100 rounds into the confused melee of fleeing marchers, killing thirteen unarmed civilians, seven of them teenagers. Some were trying to help the injured; others were running to safety; many were shot from behind. 'Am I going to die?' one 17-year-old boy gasped as Father Edward Daly, the Catholic priest who became for ever associated with that awful afternoon, knelt over him. 'I said no,' Daly recalled, 'but I administered the last rites. I can remember him holding my hand and squeezing it. We all wept.'[10]

By any standards it was a terrible day, a tragedy for which there could be no consolation. But it does not take £200 million to work out why Bloody Sunday happened. With armed British troops, trained to fight and kill, patrolling the streets of Northern Ireland under intense provocation from Catholics and Protestants alike and under heavy pressure from Stormont and their superiors, disaster was always a possibility. As General Ford had written in December, there was a strong likelihood that if the army went into the Bogside a 'slaughter of the innocent' would result, and he had been proved right. But the immediate context, too, was crucial. The army had been losing men almost every week to IRA snipers, and just three days before Bloody Sunday the IRA had shot dead two young Derry policemen and set off two bombs at the army's Hollywood barracks. It was hardly surprising that the army expected Sunday's civil rights march to turn violent, and Ford's officers warned him that however peaceful the marchers' intentions, 'the DYH backed up by the gunmen will undoubtedly take control at an early stage'. Above all, the Paras' operational orders on Sunday afternoon explicitly told them that they might face 'IRA terrorist activity' and 'shooting attacks against the security forces', and that 'almost certainly snipers, petrol bombers and nail bombers will support the rioters'. Since the beginning of 1971, snipers had already killed twenty-four British soldiers; news that they would be facing them that afternoon naturally made the Paras jittery. 'The one thing that stuck in my mind', Support Company's sergeant major said afterwards, 'was the fact that we were warned about sniper fire, possibly from the Rossville Flats. Sniper fire is very, very accurate . . . it's feared by soldiers . . . It's something to be very, very wary of . . . None of the people in my Company wanted to be killed by a sniper.'[11]

That said, however, the Paras were the worst people imaginable to be policing a civil rights march against such a tense, fearful background. They were intensely proud of their reputation as a highly trained, highly motivated elite: one later told Peter Taylor that their 'very hard-minded' ethos was built on 'aggression and speed of movement'. Their commanding officer, Lieutenant Colonel Wilford, was a cultured man who relaxed by reading Virgil in the original, but he insisted on a hard line and strict professionalism, with his men always blacked up and camouflaged, as though they were fighting a rival army. 'This was a war,' he said, 'so we had to behave accordingly.' In Belfast, the Paras had won a reputation for aggressive professionalism verging on outright brutality: just days before Bloody Sunday, the reporter Simon Hoggart wrote that they were the troops 'most hated by Catholics in troubled areas', and quoted one unnamed officer who said that they were 'frankly disliked' by other British officers, 'who regard some of their men as little better than thugs in uniform'.

Since Wilford had been shocked by the very idea of tolerating IRA-run no-go areas in Derry, to some extent his men were spoiling for a fight. The weekend before Bloody Sunday, C Company had already clashed with civil rights demonstrators near the internment centre at Magilligan Point, beating unarmed protesters to the ground. And on Bloody Sunday itself, other commanders were distinctly uneasy with the idea of using the Paras to 'scoop up' rioters. The colonel of the Royal Anglians begged his superiors to let his men go in instead, while another officer rang his brigadier and told him the plan was 'mad'. In the circumstances, sending in such self-consciously aggressive and gung-ho troops was asking for trouble. 'Let's teach these buggers a lesson,' one Para later remembered his officer saying the night before the march. 'We want some kills tomorrow.' He meant the IRA. Tragically, though, it was thirteen unarmed civilians who paid the price for the Paras' recklessness.[12]

Some of the Paras seem to have been wracked with guilt after their afternoon's work: the company sergeant major of Support Company, who saw no snipers or bombers that day, disbelievingly asked one soldier: 'What the hell were you doing?' But as another recalled, the general 'mood between the blokes was, not elation, but at the same time, it was a job well done'. Perhaps that is hardly surprising: these were professional killers, after all, who had little sympathy for the nationalist population and thought they were merely defending themselves. What is more striking, though, is the reaction in mainland Britain, where although there was considerable shock at the deaths of thirteen civilians, there was also strong support for the army. One paratrooper stationed in Britain recalled that when the news came through, his view was that 'the Paras had taken out the enemy . . . I am ashamed to say we cheered.' The *Daily Mail* launched a passionate defence of the army's reputation ('our troops are doing an impossible job impossibly well'); less predictably, the *Guardian* ran an editorial written by the Ulsterman John Cole that struck a similarly defiant note. 'The march was illegal,' Cole wrote. 'Warning had been given of the danger implicit in continuing with it . . . The army has an intolerably difficult time in Ireland. At times it is bound to act firmly, even severely.' And Reginald Maudling's Conservative constituency agent spoke for millions when he told the Home Secretary that although 'it is never pleasant when people are shot dead . . . I must say I am glad that, at long last, the troops have started to get tough in riot situations, and I think that this attitude will have the support of everyone interested in the preservation of law and order.'[13]

Maudling himself treated Bloody Sunday with exactly the same sensitivity and seriousness that he brought to the general subject of Northern Ireland. In a packed House of Commons the next day, he casually remarked that the march had been illegal and that the army had been returning fire at people 'attacking them with firearms and with bombs'. Not only did he not utter a single word of regret about the thirteen victims, therefore, he also contrived to smear them as IRA gunmen. Perhaps it was hardly surprising that the intemperate young Nationalist MP Bernadette Devlin launched herself across the chamber at him, pummelling the bulky Home Secretary and trying to pull his lank hair. He seemed remarkably unperturbed, though: one onlooker remarked afterwards that 'she almost woke him up'. This was hardly likely to mollify the outraged nationalist population, and they were even less impressed by the Widgery report in April, which took the Paras' self-justification at face value and issued barely a word of criticism.[14]

All in all, Bloody Sunday was a catastrophe for Britain's image abroad. In the United States, donations to NORAID went through the roof; in Dublin, a mob set fire to the British Embassy while the Irish government angrily recalled its ambassador from London. 'What swept the country', wrote the journalist and politician Conor Cruise O'Brien, 'was a great wave of emotion, compounded of grief, shock, and a sort of astonished, incredulous rage against an England which seemed to be acting in the way we often accused her of acting but of which we had not for decades really believed modern England capable'. And of course in Northern Ireland itself the Provisionals rubbed their hands with glee. The leading historian of the IRA suggests that, such was the Catholic fury after Bloody Sunday, they had 'more potential recruits than they could easily absorb'. It was not, as is often claimed, a turning point; there had been too many atrocities already, and Northern Ireland had passed the point when major sectarian strife could have been avoided. But as one leading Provo later remarked, 'events that day probably led more young nationalists to join the Provisionals than any other single action by the British'. From that day on, wrote Gerry Adams, 'money, guns and recruits flooded into the IRA'.[15]

Bloody Sunday was the death knell for Stormont. Ever since British troops had first arrived to protect Catholic neighbourhoods from Protestant mobs, direct rule had been a strong possibility. A government that could not keep order on its own streets and was heartily distrusted by a large minority of its citizens was always on borrowed time, and by the second half of 1971 there was an increasingly firm Whitehall consensus that Stormont would have to be put out of its misery. After Bloody Sunday, however, the question of Northern Ireland's constitutional future took on new urgency. It is nonsense to imagine, as republicans often do, that the British government was desperate to hang on to Northern Ireland; in fact, most ministers would gladly have been rid of it, and the public were already sick and tired of seeing it in the headlines. Indeed, it is striking how imaginative and radical Heath was prepared to be in February 1972. No option was off the table: among the alternatives his ministers discussed were a new partition of Northern Ireland allowing Catholic areas to join the Republic, a national referendum on its constitutional position, and an arrangement inviting Dublin to share the government of the troubled province. 'The long-term solution', the Cabinet minutes noted on 3 February, 'might have to involve some sort of constitutional association between the two parts of Ireland, while permitting the Six Counties of Northern Ireland to continue to form part of the United Kingdom.'

Heath's Foreign Secretary Sir Alec Douglas-Home, usually regarded as being on the right of the Tory Party, was prepared to go even further. A few weeks later, he suggested to Heath that 'the real British interest would I think be served best by pushing them towards a United Ireland rather than tying them more closely to the United Kingdom'. The problem, however, was the unionist majority; by now, any hint of a united Ireland would probably have triggered a mass armed uprising. And when Heath summoned Brian Faulkner to London to discuss the various options, he found the Stormont Prime Minister in defiant mood. Not only was Faulkner opposed to any radical solution, he even baulked at inviting moderate nationalists to join his government. The result, he said, would be a 'bedlam cabinet'; what was more, of course, it would destroy his own standing among the Unionist rank and file. As for letting Westminster take over all Northern Ireland's security arrangements, he was opposed to that, too, on the grounds that it would 'reduce our government to a mere sham'.[16]

But Faulkner's government was running out of time, for the weeks after Londonderry saw the collapse of the last vestiges of law and order. In February, the two wings of the IRA killed seventeen people, among them ten innocent civilians. In the month's most ominous incident on 23 February, the Official IRA planted a bomb near the officers' mess at the Parachute Regiment's headquarters in Aldershot, killing seven people. While the IRA boasted that their 'successful retaliatory operation' had killed 'several high-ranking officers', the victims were actually five dinner ladies, a gardener and a Catholic army chaplain. Almost two weeks later, the Provisionals followed suit by bombing the Abercorn restaurant in Belfast city centre, which was packed with women and children having a break from their afternoon's shopping. Two women in their early twenties, both Catholics, were killed; 136 men, women and children were injured, many seriously. Two sisters lost both their legs; one, who was shopping for her wedding dress, also lost an arm and an eye. Afterwards, one paramedic said, the ambulances were 'awash with blood ... It was the most distressing scene I have ever witnessed. There were bloody, mangled bodies lying everywhere.' In a nightmarish irony, the surgeon who operated on many of the wounded, Fred Bereen, discovered only later that his daughter Ann had been one of the two young women killed.[17]

By now, as the *Sunday Times* put it, 'carnage and mutilation [had become] the accompaniment of daily life'. Almost every day brought fresh reports of shootings and bombings, while the air was full of talk of pogroms and purges. There were those who still talked of peace, particularly in Belfast's leafy middle-class suburbs, a world away from the violence of the estates, but it is simply not true that the conflict was imposed on an otherwise peace-loving population. 'Hatred infected entire areas,' remembered Kevin Myers; 'it was this ruthless malignancy that gave them a common, almost reassuring identity. Politicians spoke of a "tiny minority" of terrorists: yet for every active terrorist there was probably a support group of at least fifty non-terrorist individuals.' When the BBC interviewed ordinary citizens, it found many who welcomed the prospect of a bloody reckoning. One Catholic man looked forward to the British army's withdrawal so that there could be a full-scale 'civil war', with the Republic's armed forces on the Catholics' side ('Mr Lynch won't let us down'). An elderly Protestant housewife, meanwhile, told an interviewer that when the British left, 'we'll just have to fight with our bare hands.' And on 20 March the savagery reached a new low when the Provisionals detonated their first car bomb in Belfast's busy Donegal Street. Six people were killed and some 150 injured, many of whom were actually fleeing from an earlier bomb attack in a nearby street. The scene 'looked like a battlefield', reported the *Belfast Telegraph*, with dozens of bodies 'lying in pools of blood on the roadway'. Many people were screaming in unbearable agony from the shards of glass embedded in their wounds; one old man, barely conscious on the pavement, seemed 'unaware that half his leg had been blown off in the explosion'.[18]

Heath's patience was now exhausted. Six days before, he had secretly agreed the terms of an ultimatum to Faulkner, and on 22 March he summoned Northern Ireland's Prime Minister to Downing Street and presented him with the options. Almost unbelievably, Faulkner had no idea what was coming: the day before, he had confidently told his Cabinet that Heath wanted him for 'consultation rather than announcement of decisions'. He was wrong about that: when his guest sat down in Downing Street, Heath bluntly announced that Stormont must agree to let Westminster take over the entire machinery of law and order, to scrap internment, to hold a new plebiscite on the Irish border and to invite the moderate SDLP to join a 'community government'. If not, Heath said, self-government would be suspended and direct rule imposed from London. Faulkner was stunned; as the watching Willie Whitelaw remembered, he 'really could not believe that Ted Heath was in earnest'. They argued for more than nine hours, but there was never a chance that Faulkner would agree. For one thing, he 'felt completely betrayed' that his friend could abandon him in this way; for another, he was insulted by Heath's admission that he basically saw Stormont as a glorified 'county council'. But when Faulkner flew back to Belfast late that evening, it was to news of yet another atrocity, this time a 100-pound bomb that had left the city's main railway station in ruins and injured more than seventeen people in the Europa Hotel next door. It made a suitably gloomy backdrop for the final meeting of Faulkner's last Cabinet, held the next morning in an atmosphere of outraged defiance. An hour later, he telephoned Downing Street and told Heath that he had decided to resign.[19]

On the evening of Friday, 24 March, Heath addressed the nation. After three of the most gruelling months in modern British history, after the pressure of mounting unemployment and the miners' strike, after the long battle for European entry, after the dramatic decision to change the thrust of his entire economic policy, he cut a tired figure, his face grey and weary, his voice clipped and strained. 'I am speaking to you tonight', he began, 'as Prime Minister of the United Kingdom – England, Wales, Scotland and Northern Ireland; and in particular to the people of Northern Ireland, whatever your job, your politics or your religion.' He had decided, 'after long and anxious thought', he said, 'that we must make possible a completely fresh start'. His proposals having been rejected by Stormont, the government had decided to 'take over for the time being full respon-sibility for the conduct of affairs in Northern Ireland'. Stormont was prorogued; at the end of the month, Willie Whitelaw would arrive in Belfast as the first Secretary of State for Northern Ireland, an imperial proconsul with enormously sweeping powers. And to the nationalist population, Heath made a specific appeal. 'Now is your chance,' he said earnestly. 'A chance for prosperity, a chance for peace, a chance at last to bring the bombings and killings to an end.'[20]

But his words rang hollow. In Dublin, both wings of the IRA pledged that the war would go on until they had a united Ireland. At Stormont, Brian Faulkner told an emotional press conference that many people would draw a 'sinister and depressing lesson' from the imposition of direct rule: 'that violence can pay, that violence does pay, that those who shout, lie, denigrate and even destroy earn for themselves an attention that responsible behaviour and honourable behaviour do not'. In the streets of Belfast, more than 6,000 workers from the Harland and Wolff shipyards marched in protest, their voices raised in chants against Heath, the IRA and the Catholic Church. Two days later, shops and offices closed across the province as the hard-line Ulster Vanguard movement called a national strike to protest the imposition of direct rule. In Lurgan, British troops fired rubber bullets to dispel mobs of unionist protesters; in Carrickfergus, troops had to escort Catholic workers who had refused to join the strike; in Portadown, Protestant vigilantes blocked off the centre of the town with barricades bedecked with Union Jacks while gangs of hooligans roamed the streets. At Stormont, a vast crowd, well over 100,000 people according to many estimates, assembled in front of the parliament building, a sea of Ulster flags and Orange banners as far as the eye could see. And that afternoon, two men were killed when the IRA planted a car bomb outside the RUC headquarters in Limavady, County Londonderry. Neither was a policeman; they were just ordinary people, who had the misfortune to be driving past when the bomb went off. Everything had changed; everything had stayed the same.[21]

From its position at the top of a long, narrow avenue, the white neo-classical façade of Northern Ireland's Parliament Buildings looks down over the Stormont estate with an air of regal grandeur. Built in the early 1930s, it made an incongruously magnificent setting for a legislature governing just over a million people, with its great chandeliers and marble staircases, its leather benches and glowering portraits. But at the end of March 1972, almost exactly forty years after it had been opened, Parliament Buildings fell silent. The members' library, with its collection of 27,000 books, was closed. The bar, in which journalists had swapped so many confidences and anecdotes, was shuttered up. The dispatch boxes over which so many politicians had argued, the Mace that had symbolized the Parliament's authority, were hidden away in a strong-room underneath the great white building. Now the only voices echoing down the marble corridors were the murmurs of the security guards, and the only sounds in the debating chamber were the squeaks of the cleaning ladies' shoes as they polished the benches on which nobody sat.

Half a mile to the east, Stormont Castle, a rambling Victorian baronial pile, ornamented with Gothic turrets and battlements, made a curiously appropriate new home for a man who even then seemed a throwback to a vanished age of patrician politics. To his contemporaries, Willie Whitelaw seemed the very incarnation of One Nation Conservatism: a landed gentleman by birth, an old-fashioned country squire by style, a consensus politician by trade. Born into a Scottish landowning family in the last year of the First World War, he had gone to Winchester and Cambridge, won a Blue for golf, served as a tank commander in Normandy, and became a Tory whip during the 1950s and 1960s. As Leader of the House in Heath's first two years, he cut an amiable and popular figure: when difficulties arose he resorted to self-parody, forever joking about 'my simple brain'. Critics sometimes suggested that the mask and the man were identical, and in the end Whitelaw's exaggerated performance of woolly vagueness would cost him the ultimate political prize. But he was no fool. The Stormont mandarin Sir Kenneth Bloomfield, who advised every Secretary of State until 1991, wrote that it was 'one of the great pleasures of my life to enjoy the company, and, I hope, the confidence of that large, emotional, sometimes irascible, apparently spontaneous but infinitely cunning man. His big personality lit up any room, and we were soon to become familiar with his booming cries of "Wonderful, wonderful!" . . . "Splendid, splendid!"'[22]

On his very first night in Belfast, Whitelaw tried to inspire his staff with a typically optimistic pep talk. 'Well, here we are. We've arrived,' he said breezily. 'However awful things are outside, however many bombs go off, when we're together in private we're going to enjoy ourselves. One house rule – no long faces. That won't make anything better.' It was good advice, but it was easier said than done. Across Belfast, loyalist posters read 'Outlaw Whitelaw', while one of the biggest Unionist papers erroneously reported that the new Secretary of State was a Catholic. And few people drew much reassurance from his first press conference, held in the dingy surroundings of an RAF mess just moments after he had got off the plane from London. Harried with questions about Bloody Sunday, he gave a string of increasingly vague answers before finally snapping: 'I do not intend to prejudge the past.' *The Times's* reporter Robert Fisk thought it was 'one of the most glorious sentences ever uttered by a politician in Ulster'.[23]

But to most people in Northern Ireland the past was no laughing matter. And to the crowds outside Stormont with their Ulster flags and angry placards, Whitelaw's arrival was an affront to their tradition of self-government and a craven surrender to the Provisional IRA. Even many Northern Ireland civil servants felt insulted by the presence of their new masters: one official, Joan Young, who had worked at Stormont since the days of Captain O'Neill, remembered being 'disgusted and quite seriously offended' by the attitude of the English newcomers who had been put up in the grand Culloden Hotel on the shore of Belfast Lough. The Culloden was 'for Northern Irish people, a very special place to go', she said: the place people celebrated birthdays, engagement parties and grand occasions. But when she went there for the first time under direct rule, all dressed up in her evening finery, she was stunned to see 'tables of people in casual sweaters and jeans'. To the Belfast guests, for whom it was meant to be a special place, a treat, the English visitors' casual superiority was almost heartbreaking. 'They just didn't treat the place as *we* would have liked,' she recalled.[24]

Since the politicians had manifestly failed to stem the tide of violence, many Protestants concluded that they must find their champions outside the Ulster Unionist Party. One obvious candidate was the evangelical preacher Ian Paisley, whose ferocious rhetoric had done so much to heighten the political temperature in the 1960s. As the founder of the hard-line Democratic Unionist Party and Westminster MP for North Antrim, Paisley was a central and compelling figure in Northern Irish society. Some accused him of inciting violence: since the late 1960s, there had been murmurs about his links with the terrorist Ulster Volunteer Force, although Paisley insisted that any collaboration (such as the purchase of guns and gelignite) went on entirely behind his back. But his position in the early 1970s was weaker than it would later become. Paisley seemed confused by the dramatic lurch into sectarian violence, and while his rhetoric dripped with anti-Catholic bile, his stance on specific issues often seemed oddly conciliatory. To the surprise of his supporters, he opposed internment and thought that Northern Ireland should be fully integrated into the Westminster political system. 'Stormont is a thing of the past,' he insisted, 'and there is no good use for Unionists to think that, by some way or other, Stormont shall return.' The result was that while his anti-Catholic rhetoric put off the respectable middle classes, his more moderate positions failed to win favour on Belfast's estates. For the time being, therefore, Paisley's support was limited to the Orange Order and the pious Protestants of the farms and villages in north Antrim and north Armagh. For a more defiant attitude to the new regime, unionists had to look elsewhere.[25]

The man who stepped forward as the voice of resistance was William Craig, a former Home Affairs minister who had founded the Ulster Vanguard movement in February 1972. From the outset, Vanguard was ostentatiously confrontational: at its first meeting in Lisburn, Craig warned: 'God help those who get in our way, for we mean business.' Unsympathetic observers often described it as a fascist movement, although Craig insisted that Vanguard's events were based on the Covenant rallies of Unionism's founding father, Sir Edward Carson. In fact, with their great seas of Ulster banners, their menacing UDA security staff, their strutting party officials in orange sashes, their meetings looked more like Nuremberg rallies. In other circumstances Craig would have cut a ludicrous figure, an Irish equivalent of Roderick Spode, antagonist of Bertie Wooster, proprietor of the Eulalie Soeurs underwear emporium and founder of the sinister Black Shorts. But in the spring of 1972 Craig's organization seemed genuinely frightening. He made no secret of his links to the UDA; indeed, while Paisley's rhetoric was merely inflammatory, Craig's was positively spine-chilling. Addressing a rally of 60,000 Protestants in Ormeau Park a week before direct rule, he pledged to 'build up a dossier of the men and the women who are a menace to this country, because if and when the politicians fail us, it may be our job to liquidate the enemy'. These words – 'liquidate the enemy' – were greeted at the time by an enormous bellow of approval. Even decades later, Craig refused to apologize for 'speaking in black and white'.[26]

When Heath scrapped Stormont, it seemed that Vanguard's moment had come. It was Craig who called the general strike that briefly brought the province to a standstill at the end of March 1972, and weeks later he organized a recklessly provocative march into the Derry no-go areas, which ended with street fighting on the city's Craigavon Bridge. The British government were traitors, he insisted; it was time to set Ulster free for a bloody reckoning with the IRA. Addressing a private meeting of the hard-right Monday Club in the House of Commons in October, he frankly admitted that he was 'prepared to come out and shoot and kill. Let us put the bluff aside. I am prepared to kill and those behind me will have my full support. When we say force we mean force.' That was too strong even for Ian Paisley, who thought that Craig's intemperate remarks had done 'terrible damage' to unionism's image in Britain. Even other Vanguard officials thought that the speech was 'unfortunate', and they were not reassured by reports that Craig had been 'highly emotional', 'stumbling' and 'over-tired', especially since he had been convicted of drink-driving only months before. In the long run, the speech did him enormous damage, destroying any chance of Vanguard winning middle-class support. But Craig, who had none of Paisley's cunning, refused to moderate his tone. If Britain 'betrayed' Northern Ireland, he thundered just a few days later, 'there will be a holocaust that the western world has never seen'.[27]

Unfortunately, the political context meant that it was impossible to dismiss Craig as a drunken tub-thumper. For a young Belfast man called Andy Tyrie, shortly to become the leader of the UDA, he was simply 'being honest ... the only way to beat terrorism was to terrorize the terrorist – and be better at it'. His views won considerable support on the Protestant estates, where tens of thousands of young men had rushed to join vigilante groups since the spring of 1971. As one American reporter observed, it was a little-acknowledged fact of the conflict that many recruits were bored working-class men who found life as a paramilitary more exciting and more lucrative than life on the dole. Even in the early 1970s, there was only the thinnest of lines between paramilitaries and gangsters. The UDA, for example, ran a betting business, collected protection money from local businesses and regularly hijacked lorries carrying televisions, cigarettes and alcohol. Indeed, one UDA entrepreneur did not even come from Northern Ireland. Born in Essex, Dave Fogel had been posted to Northern Ireland as a private in the army, was discharged in murky circumstances after a 'difficulty' about another soldier's radio, and settled down with a local Protestant girl. After becoming involved with his local vigilante group, he fell in with the UDA when he met their leader at, of all things, a pigeon-fanciers' club. Much in demand because of his military experience, Fogel became a major figure in the Belfast UDA, a big man and a would-be political boss. As the American reporter noted, it was a lot better 'than lying listlessly around a cramped house, watching television and waiting for the weekly dole cheque'.[28]

Indeed, despite their horrific handiwork, there was often something blackly comic about the paramilitaries' pretensions. When the reporter Peter Taylor went at Fogel's request to see a UDA unit training in a field outside Belfast, he watched amusedly as 'a series of overweight loyalists panted for breath as they "monkey-climbed" a rope suspended above the ground and went through the motions of less-than-agile hand-to-hand combat'. Kevin Myers, meanwhile, was struck by the incongruity of working-class hooligans in dark glasses and desert-warfare slouch hats pretending to be the heirs of the British army when they could not even say 'lieutenant' properly, pronouncing it 'loo-tenant' in imitation of the Americans they had seen on television. 'What other terrorist organisation in the world', he wondered mordantly, 'would have its own preposterous regimental blazer, complete with gold badge?'[29]

And yet to tens of thousands of frightened Protestants, there was nothing funny about the UDA. It was, they thought, all that stood between them and the murderous designs of the IRA and its Catholic supporters. By the spring of 1972, UDA leaders were already bragging that they had more than 20,000 members. Funds were no problem, although since they lacked the Provos' network of contacts in Ireland and the United States they found it much harder to buy weapons. But since the UDA was not technically illegal, its members had no compunction about parading openly in the streets, and throughout 1972 the sight of men in masks, dark glasses and army fatigues marching through Belfast became depressingly frequent. Its appeal reflected the sheer fear on Protestant estates, as well the collapse of their trust in the British government and the army to defend them from the IRA. By the end of the year, informed estimates placed the UDA's membership at 26,000, making it the biggest paramilitary group in the Western world.[30]

Since the UDA was supposedly a defensive organization and had no open quarrel with the British or the army, it never became as notorious as the IRA. In the autumn of 1972, a confidential Ministry of Defence memo even argued that the UDA fulfilled an 'important function', channelling 'into a constructive and disciplined direction Protestant energies which might otherwise become disruptive'. Yet it is a myth that the British regarded unionists and loyalists through rose-tinted spectacles. Lord Carrington told friends that he was 'appalled by the bigotry, drunkenness and stupidity of the Unionist Party', while after just two months Whitelaw confided that he was 'appalled by the bigotry and fear so much in evidence among the Protestants'. In any case, the criminal side of loyalist politics was hardly a secret. Once the vigilante groups lost their independent government at Stormont (which carried great symbolic importance, even if loyalists felt it was too weak), they decided to take the law into their own hands. In February, vigilantes murdered a Catholic army veteran walking along the Crumlin Road; in March, they killed a young Catholic teenager in revenge for the Abercorn bomb; in April, they shot another teenager who was walking along the Crumlin Road. Then the killings escalated. In May, loyalist gangs murdered nine

Catholics, one a 13-year-old girl walking through her nationalist estate. In June, they killed five more; in July, thirteen. These murders were born in an atmosphere of intense fear, but they also reflected the worst kind of sectarian passion, aimed at forcing Catholic residents out of Belfast. Usually fuelled by drink, they were also terrifyingly brutal: on 11 July, for example, four drunken loyalists broke into the home of a Catholic widow in the Oldpark area, shooting her mentally handicapped son before raping her and leaving her for dead. 'You may well think', the barrister told the jury at the ensuing trial, 'that in this case we have reached the lowest level of human depravity.'[31]

For the Provisional IRA, the spring and summer of 1972 represented the high point in their long campaign for Irish unity. As they saw it, direct rule was merely the first step towards British withdrawal: they were jubilant that the façade of self-government had been torn down, and looked forward to mobilizing the population against the colonial oppressor. 'Everyone felt we were very close to victory,' said one IRA man. 'Most people on the ground felt that it was only a matter of time before the British were going to finally admit defeat.' This explains why, in the summer of 1972, the IRA were keen to make contact with the British government and explore the basis on which they could be persuaded to pull out. In March, they had already held a secret meeting with Harold Wilson in Dublin, albeit to no great effect. But on 13 June, the Provisional leadership went further, holding an audacious press conference in Londonderry to announce they were ready to declare a truce if Britain would agree to peace talks. Not surprisingly, Whitelaw publicly ruled it out. Behind the scenes, however, he knew he could not afford to ignore even the slimmest hope for peace. Six days after the IRA's offer, he quietly met two of their conditions for a ceasefire, releasing Gerry Adams, the commander of the Provisionals' Ballymurphy Battalion, and granting 'special category' (that is, political) status to IRA prisoners. The next day, two men from Whitelaw's office – Frank Steele, who was also an MI6 agent, and Philip Woodfield – drove to a secret location outside Derry, and for the first time British officials sat down across the table with the IRA.[32]

Given the history of antagonism between the British and the IRA, it is striking that, as Woodfield reported, the meeting unfolded in 'an informal and relaxed atmosphere'. The IRA men, David O'Connell and Gerry Adams, were 'respectable and respectful' throughout, even addressing Woodfield as 'Sir'. 'They made no bombastic defence of their past,' he noted, 'and made no attacks on the British Government, the British Army or any other communities or bodies in Northern Ireland. Their response to every argument put to them was reasonable and moderate.' After three hours the four men had hammered out the arrangements for a short IRA ceasefire, a telephone hotline between O'Connell and Steele in case anything went wrong, and the conditions for an IRA meeting with Whitelaw himself. Woodfield thought that both O'Connell and Adams 'genuinely want a ceasefire and a permanent end to violence'. Steele, too, was impressed by what he heard. O'Connell, he recalled, 'was a very quiet, self-contained and self-disciplined man . . . I know it's an unfashionable thing to say, but I liked him.' As for Adams, who was only 23, Steele found him 'very personable, intelligent, articulate and self-disciplined'. As they were leaving, the MI6 man, almost paternally, said: 'You don't want to spend the rest of your life on the run from us British. What do you want to do?' 'I want to go to university and get a degree,' Adams replied. 'Well, we're not stopping you,' Steele said. 'All you've got to do is renounce violence and you can go to university and get a degree.' Adams thought about it. 'No,' he said, 'I've got to help to get rid of you British first.'[33]

Two days later, the Provisionals announced that a ceasefire would begin the following Monday, 26 June, to pave the way for 'meaningful talks'. But it was not until 7 July that the meeting went ahead, with the RAF secretly flying a group of IRA men from Belfast to London. As so often on such occasions, there was more than a hint of the ridiculous: on the way to the initial rendezvous, one of the IRA delegation's cars broke down, so all six of them had to cram into one small vehicle. Having been picked up by an MI6 minivan, they then contrived to get stuck behind a farmer with a herd of cows. 'I do think the British army could have given us a better escort,' remarked Seán MacStíofáin, making perhaps the only joke of his life. But the Provisionals were nervous, even refusing the apples Frank Steele had thoughtfully brought for the journey because they might be drugged. And even when they arrived at the agreed venue, an elegant house in Cheyne Walk, Chelsea, belonging to Whitelaw's junior minister Paul Channon, they remained stiff and hesitant. It was a stiflingly hot day, yet when Whitelaw offered his guests a drink, they refused – perhaps less because they were worried about poison than because they were nervous of looking weak in front of their comrades.

Compared with the meeting outside Derry, the Cheyne Walk summit was not a success. Since there were now six IRA delegates, it was hard to strike up an informal relationship, and the tone seemed stilted from the start. Whitelaw did his best to play the emollient host, congratulating the Provisionals on their observance of the ceasefire and promising that he would be a man of his word, yet his guests remained almost icily cold. It was MacStíofáin who did most of the talking. Producing a piece of paper from his pocket, he curtly read a list of demands, including complete British military withdrawal by January 1975, the release of all 'political prisoners', and an all-Ireland referendum on the border between north and south. Frank Steele thought that MacStíofáin had completely misread the situation: he saw himself as 'the representative of an army which had fought the British to a standstill', and acted 'as if we British wanted out'. Whitelaw, meanwhile, was astonished that his visitors were so inflexible. They must surely realize, he thought, that no British government could renege on its commitment to let the people of Northern Ireland decide their future on their own. But MacStíofáin showed no sign of giving way, and the meeting eventually broke up with nothing agreed. As Whitelaw put it, the historic summit had been a total 'non-event'. It had been based on a mutual misunderstanding: the British thought that the Provos would prefer talking to fighting, while the IRA thought that the British had lost their nerve. And as Steele joined the Provisionals on the flight back to Belfast, he remarked that he hoped they were not going back to their 'bloody stupid campaign of violence':

> I said if they really wanted a united Ireland, they were wasting their time shooting at British soldiers and bombing Northern Ireland into an industrial and social slum. They should be trying to persuade the Protestants and the unionists that they would have some sort of satisfactory life – jobs, housing and so on – in some sort of linkage with the South. But their basic line was, 'so long as you're there, we'll never come to a sensible agreement with the unionists . . . We've got to get rid of you British first. And the way to get rid of you British, as has been proved all over your Empire, is violence. You will get fed up and go away.'[34]

Of course it is tempting to wonder how many lives could have been saved if the Provisionals had listened to Steele's advice. But the truth is that they were nowhere near ready to renounce the gun. As they saw it, violence had brought Britain close to defeat, and they thought they had everything to gain from pressing home their advantage. As Steele reflected, 'there were too many people who could influence the continuation of the ceasefire who didn't want it', from IRA hardliners like MacStíofáin to Protestant paramilitaries who were desperate to see the IRA shot down in the streets. 'I don't think either community had suffered enough to want peace, to make peace an absolute imperative,' Steele said sadly. He was right. Two days after Cheyne Walk, fighting broke out in West Belfast, where a group of Catholic families, driven out of their homes on Protestant estates, were trying to occupy some empty houses. That Sunday night the Provisionals were eager for battle, and as the army tried to disperse the crowds, the IRA fired more than 300 rounds in anger. The next morning, Britain and Ireland awoke to the news that between them the army and the IRA had killed eleven people, six of them Catholics and five Protestants. On Wednesday, the UDA killed three more people and the IRA two. On Thursday, three British soldiers were shot in the Falls while the army killed two more Catholics in the Ardoyne. In total no fewer than forty-two people lost their lives in just nine days following the collapse of the ceasefire. Jaw-jaw had failed; it was back to war-war. 'Maybe you can't bomb a million Protestants into a united Ireland,' one IRA man remarked, 'but you could have good fun trying.'[35]

With the end of the ceasefire, Belfast returned to the cycle of sectarian bloodshed, only on a more savage scale than ever before. Repetition dulled the shock, though some atrocities were so appalling that even the most hardened cynics found themselves biting back tears. Many paramilitaries no longer made any pretence of attacking military targets; instead, they sought to cause the maximum fear and mayhem, sacrificing the lives of ordinary men, women and children to the greater good of a united Ireland or a Protestant state. So in one hour on Bloody Friday, 21 June, the Provisionals set off twenty-two bombs in the centre of Belfast after giving a series of hoax warnings. In the chaos, nine people were killed and 130 seriously injured, many of them maimed for life. The scenes of carnage defied adequate description: one police officer in Oxford Street bus station saw 'a torso of a human being lying in the middle of the street', its anatomy laid open to public view. Nearby, a soldier's arms and legs lay on the ground, the rest of the body having been blown through nearby railings. 'One of the most horrendous memories for me', the policeman said later, 'was seeing a head stuck to a wall.' Some bodies were blown apart over 30-yard areas; in the hours and days that followed, the police had the dreadful task of scooping up the human remains and shovelling them into plastic bags.

For MacStíofáin, who insisted that these were 'industrial, commercial and economic targets', the Provisionals were completely blameless. The slaughter was all the fault of the British, he said, because they had failed to act on the totally inadequate and deliberately misleading warnings. Even so, many Provisionals themselves were horrified by the slaughter. But although Bloody Friday left deep psychological scars in hundreds of families as well as physical ones in Belfast's battered cityscape, it was eventually overtaken by other atrocities and virtually forgotten. On Remembrance Sunday, the Reverend Joseph Parker, whose teenage son Stephen had been killed while trying to warn shoppers about the bombs, held a service outside City Hall, planting a white cross for every person killed in the Troubles. It was meant to be the first in an annual series, but two years later the Reverend Parker emigrated to Canada, a broken man. Eventually the services were discontinued because of lack of interest.[36]

And so the killing went on, a nightly ritual of prejudice and hatred played out against a bleak backdrop of working-class poverty and economic stagnation, what Kevin Myers calls 'a seventeenth-century religious conflict bottled in a late twentieth-century industrial decline'. In the shimmering heat of summer or the driving rains of winter, it was the same story. Teenagers were murdered because they were walking down the street at the wrong time; women and children were killed because they were in the wrong place when a bomb went off; even postmen were not safe, gunned down from the paramilitaries' cars on a clear winter's morning. By the end of 1972, the bloody rampage had accounted for 2,000 bomb explosions, 2,000 armed robberies and more than 10,000 shooting incidents, while 5,000 people had been badly injured and 479 people killed – all in just twelve months. More than half of the people killed were not soldiers or paramilitaries but ordinary members of the public, quietly going about their business until a bomb or a bullet brought the horizon crashing down. And although the army accounted for its share of the slaughter, by far the biggest killers were the paramilitaries. The IRA alone killed three times as many people as the British did – with the additional and surely crucial distinction that whereas the army never set out to hurt civilians, the Provos wanted to cause as much public suffering as possible. But they had no monopoly on savagery, as the loyalist death squads who murdered 121 people over the course of the year, often for no other reason than that they happened to be Catholics, proved only too well.[37]

For all his external exuberance, Willie Whitelaw found his mission to Belfast an emotionally punishing and physically exhausting experience. Like many who found themselves trapped in the madness of Northern Irish politics in the 1970s, he numbed the shock with alcohol: when he returned to Westminster, old friends were startled by the amount of drink he put away, including several bottles of wine merely at lunch. Meetings at Stormont were generally lubricated with vast quantities of whisky, and although Whitelaw held his drink well and never let it interfere with his job, it was hardly good for his health. And as if the pressure in Belfast was not enough, he also faced criticism from Tory activists back home. At the party conference in October 1972, speakers who defended the government's record in Ulster were booed, whereas those who demanded a harder line or mouthed trite anti-Irish rhetoric were warmly applauded. And although the army sent tanks, bulldozers and 12,000 men to dismantle the nationalist barricades and recapture the 'no-go' areas, the success of Operation Motorman did not dispel Whitelaw's doubts about his own security forces. Talking to the head of the Metropolitan Police, Sir Robert Mark, he confided that he thought the RUC badly needed reform, while even the army 'had gone a bit too far' in some of their operations. Unlike Maudling, he never took army reports at face value.[38]

In the autumn of 1972, Whitelaw published a Green Paper, *The Future of Northern Ireland*, which became the cornerstone of every future attempt to bring peace to the bleeding province. The ideal solution, he argued, was for Northern Ireland to have its own devolved government that guaranteed a role for the minority population: in other words, a power-sharing executive. Meanwhile, he acknowledged for the first time that since the problem of Ulster had a specifically Irish dimension, any settlement must 'recognise Northern Ireland's position within Ireland as a whole', and be 'acceptable to and accepted by the Republic of Ireland'. This was too much for some unionists, who condemned Britain's appeasement of Papist terrorism, yet Heath and Whitelaw were convinced it was the only possible road to peace. On 20 March 1973, just short of the first anniversary of the introduction of direct rule, Whitelaw published a White Paper setting out in more detail his plan for Northern Ireland.

Under the new scheme, Stormont would host a new seventy-eight-member legislative assembly elected by proportional representation, with an executive sharing power between the different factions and a Council of Ireland to forge links between north and south. All in all, it was an arrangement remarkably similar to the power-sharing executive agreed in the late 1990s, thousands of deaths later. But in 1973, *The Economist* called it a 'reasonable constitutional framework which could work reasonably well if it were operated by reasonable people'. For precisely that reason, the magazine observed, it was bound to fail.[39]

Whitelaw's proposals ripped the Ulster Unionist Party apart. The former Prime Minister Brian Faulkner, still nominally the driving force in unionist politics, agreed to back the scheme, even though he admitted that the White Paper was 'one of the most controversial documents ever produced by a British Government'. By contrast, both Ian Paisley and William Craig rejected it out of hand. And when the people of Northern Ireland went to the polls on 28 June, Whitelaw's birthday, to elect their representatives in the new assembly, the results were bewilderingly indecisive. With 211,000 votes and 24 seats, the Ulster Unionists were comfortably the biggest party, followed by the moderate nationalist SDLP (which also backed the deal) with 160,000 votes and 19 seats. Confusingly, however, a variety of other unionist parties, such as Craig's Vanguard Unionist Progressive Party, had won 26 seats, while some of Faulkner's own candidates made it clear they would not support the arrangement. And when experts looked at the results more closely, it became clear that perhaps 27 unionist candidates rejected the White Paper while only 22 supported it. Most of the Protestant population had voted for hardliners rather than moderates; indeed, at least half a dozen of the rebel unionists had paramilitary connections. Perhaps not surprisingly, the Assembly's opening session on 31 July was a total farce, with Ian Paisley and the other rejectionists howling down their opponents, rampaging through the chamber and even physically seizing control of the Speaker's chair, to the disbelief of watching reporters. 'To say that the first day of the assembly represented a return to the old Stormont Parliament would be too kind,' wrote Robert Fisk the next day. 'It was far worse.'[40]

Meanwhile the slaughter continued. Fewer people died in 1973 than the year before, partly because Whitelaw's initiative had reinvigorated the political process, but also because the army's renewed offensive against the IRA had damaged the Provos' organizational structure and reassured Protestants that they were not all about to be murdered by Papist maniacs. There were still plenty of moments to chill the blood, however. In March, a 19-year-old Lancashire soldier, Gary Barlow, became separated from his patrol in the Lower Falls and was surrounded by a crowd of locals. While he burst into tears with fright, some women suggested they escort him to the nearest army base. Other women, however, kept him waiting until a Provisional arrived; then, while Barlow was crying for his mother, the gunman shot him through the head. More atrocities followed. In June, an IRA bomb killed six pensioners, all in their seventies, on a day out in the County Derry countryside. Five days later, the Ulster Freedom Fighters – set up as the militant killing squad of the UDA, and made up of unemployed thugs full of drink and prejudice – took a gruesome revenge by kidnapping and murdering Paddy Wilson, a former SDLP senator in Stormont's upper house, and his friend Irene Andrews, a Protestant civil servant and one of the city's best ballroom dancers. Paddy Wilson was stabbed thirty times and had his throat cut from ear to ear. Irene Andrews suffered twenty stab wounds and had her breasts cut off in what was clearly a frenzied attack. Their killer was a man called John White, the founder of the Ulster Freedom Fighters, who was sentenced to life in prison in 1978. Two decades later, having renounced violence, he had the pleasure of walking into Downing Street as part of a loyalist delegation and shaking the Prime Minister's hand.[41]

While the killings went on, Whitelaw was desperately trying to broker a deal between Faulkner's Ulster Unionists and Gerry Fitt's SDLP on a power-sharing executive. The negotiations dragged on, and on, and on. But at last, after Whitelaw had melodramatically summoned his helicopter to wait outside Stormont Castle and threatened to fly back home, the deal was done, giving the Unionists six seats on the executive, the SDLP four, and the non-sectarian Alliance one seat. And two weeks later, at the Civil Service Staff College in Sunningdale, Berkshire, representatives of the three parties joined Heath and the Taoiseach, Liam Cosgrave, for the first full Anglo-Irish talks on Northern Ireland since the early 1920s. For Faulkner to be sitting around a table to discuss his province's future with the leader of the Republic of Ireland was an extraordinary spectacle, and the occasion was not without tension. Night after night the talks dragged into the small hours, and it took all Heath's bulldozing energy to keep them on track. But on 9 December, the conference ended in success. Cosgrave agreed that 'there could be no change in the status of

Northern Ireland until a majority of the people of Northern Ireland desired a change', while Heath promised that Britain would 'support the wishes of the majority of the people of Northern Ireland'. Meanwhile, Faulkner gave his consent to the new Council of Ireland, which had seven Northern and seven Southern ministers, a consultative body made up of thirty Irish TDs* and thirty members of Northern Ireland's assembly, and a small permanent secretariat. It had taken a lot of hard bargaining to get there, but they were there all the same. As the chief delegates assembled for the cameras, an exhausted Heath still sucking pastilles to soothe his talked-out throat, there was no mistaking the euphoria. In the House of Commons the next day, even Harold Wilson offered generous congratulations.[42]

Sunningdale was not only a testament to the vision and commitment of Heath and Whitelaw; it anticipated many of the breakthroughs of the following decades, from the Anglo-Irish Agreement and Downing Street Declaration of the 1980s and 1990s to the Belfast and St Andrews Agreements of the 2000s. The tragic irony, however, was that if anything its architects were too visionary. Sunningdale promised too much, too soon. While a more cautious approach might have yielded small but concrete results, one historian calls Sunningdale 'an unmitigated disaster for Faulkner's standing in the unionist community'. Already his power base was badly fractured: after the deal on the executive in November, five Unionist MPs at Westminster had publicly announced that they had lost confidence in him. On the very first day of the Sunningdale conference, 600 delegates from the Orange Order, the Ulster Unionist constituency associations, Craig's Vanguard movement and Paisley's Democratic Unionist Party had agreed to set up a United Ulster Unionist Council (UUUC), pledged to defeat power-sharing and the Council of Ireland. Paisley even started calling Faulkner a 'Republican Unionist', and charged that he had been 'out-flanked, out-manoeuvred and out-witted'. Even more moderate observers thought that Faulkner should have driven a harder bargain at Sunningdale, for as the unionist population saw it, he had given the Republic and the SDLP everything they wanted. To Protestants whose fears of Irish Catholicism had been whipped into a frenzy by the Provos' bombs and Paisley's bombast, the Council of Ireland was an outrageous provocation. Even at the time, Whitelaw confided to

* Members of the Irish Parliament, the Dáil.

the Irish Foreign Minister Garret FitzGerald that Brian Faulkner was 'perhaps further ahead of his party than was quite wise for him' – and so it proved.[43]

On New Year's Day 1974, buoyed by messages of goodwill from across the world, the power-sharing executive took office. The goodwill lasted just three days, long enough for the Ulster Unionists to vote by 427 to 374 to repudiate the Sunningdale agreement. For Faulkner it was a shattering blow; although he remained as head of the executive, he immediately resigned as Ulster Unionist leader to set up his own party. At the press conference afterwards, noted *The Times,* he seemed 'pale and drawn', and when he insisted that he would not alter his principles, a Unionist supporter by the door heckled: 'Then we'll alter them for you!' And when the Assembly reconvened on 23 January for the first time since Sunningdale, any pretence of serious debate soon collapsed into unimaginable chaos and absurdity. When the Speaker tried to open the session after prayers, he was shouted down by loyalist members chanting 'No, no, no', orchestrated by the hulking figure of Ian Paisley. While some loyalists clambered onto benches and desks, waving and shouting like monkeys in a zoo, the Vanguard member for South Antrim, Professor Kennedy Lindsay, rushed to the Speaker's table and tried to climb on top of it. Unfortunately (and laughably) he failed at his first attempt, sending glasses of water flying everywhere; on his second, however, he made it. 'Amid wild cries from other Assemblymen he stood up and shouted "This has gone far enough" and "The temples have been cleansed,"' reported Robert Fisk. Meanwhile, 'Mr Paisley was seen building a barricade of chairs.'

As a kind of climax, another Democratic Unionist member, North Antrim's James Craig, made a dash for the Speaker's table and grabbed the Mace, which he passed to another DUP man just as a doorman was about to collar him. Up and down the aisle the chase flowed, until finally a security guard managed to wrestle back control of the Mace. In the meantime, the police were desperately struggling to restore order, including dragging loyalist members from the Speaker's chair. Ian Paisley was 'red-faced and breathing heavily', Fisk noted, while John McQuade was dragged out shouting: 'I'll fix you, you're murdering me, you're killing me.' Even Paisley's wife Eileen got in on the act, 'insisting on her right to a frontbench seat by sitting briefly on the knee of Mr Robert Cooper, Minister for Manpower'.[44]

Behind the farcical scenes, however, was a grim political reality. Sunningdale was a noble bid to achieve consensus, but in the context of almost daily bombings and sectarian assassinations, the necessary trust and conciliation simply did not exist. 'We are opposed to a united Ireland! We will not have a united Ireland!' Ian Paisley roared to enthusiastic Belfast crowds. 'I say to the Dublin government: Mr Faulkner says that it will be hands across the border to Dublin. I say that if they do not behave themselves in the South, it will be *shots* across the border!' And although Faulkner had once commanded the loyalty of the unionist population, his failure to stem the violence and his supposed surrender to Dublin had badly corroded his support in working-class Protestant households. Like Edward Heath, he was also horribly unlucky. For when Heath called a general election a few weeks later, it came at precisely the wrong time for Faulkner, just weeks into his new Executive's tenure, when passions were running high and his political base seemed most fragile.[45]

The results on 28 February were a disaster for the cause of power-sharing. While the moderate parties – the Faulkner Unionists, the Alliance, the SDLP and Northern Ireland's Labour Party – competed against one another for votes, the loyalist UUUC parties agreed to pool their resources and run one candidate in each constituency on the simple slogan 'Dublin is Just a Sunningdale Away'. In some constituencies, the power-sharing candidates won more votes combined than their rejectionist opponent, but in a first-past-the-post system, that was no consolation. For when the votes were counted, the UUUC had swept the board, winning all but one of Northern Ireland's twelve Westminster seats. Only in West Belfast, where the SDLP's Gerry Fitt won a narow victory on the back of the heavy nationalist vote, was there a glimmer of light for the moderates. Everywhere else, the voices of consensus were blown away.[46]

The Assembly and the Executive soldiered bravely on, but as the Permanent Secretary at the Northern Ireland Office reported to London a few days later, 'Mr Faulkner was somewhat shaken and somewhat fearful.' He was right to be afraid. Three months later, a general strike organized by Protestant shipyard workers and loyalist paramilitaries brought the province to its knees and the Executive to the brink of collapse. On 28 May, less than six months after he had taken office, Faulkner resigned. By then Heath and Whitelaw were powerless by-standers, unable to intervene. But even if they had still been in power, the result would surely have been the same. The extremists had won, and the war went on. It became routine, a terrible but almost unremarkable element of daily life in Northern Ireland, where the morning papers on any day of the week might bring news of a shooting, a bomb, a family heartbroken, a community devastated. The terrible irony was that it was all for nothing.[47]

13

The Unacceptable Face
of Capitalism

PATRICK: *The pursuit of money is a force for progress.*
CURLY: *It's always been the same.*
PATRICK: *The making of money.*
CURLY: *The breaking of men.*

– David Hare, *Knuckle* (1974)

Midway between Crawley and Tunbridge Wells, the nondescript commuter town of East Grinstead, with its quiet streets of identikit inter-war
semis, is not exactly one of the world's most glamorous destinations.
When the suburban seducer Norman in Alan Ayckboun's comic trilogy
The Norman Conquests (1973) announces that he has booked a dirty
weekend in East Grinstead, the other characters' open hilarity speaks
volumes about the town's decidedly unromantic reputation. But East
Grinstead does have one small claim to fame. On the rural edge of the
town stands a squat building that for a brief moment in the early 1970s
found itself in the headlines of every major newspaper in the country.
With its brick and glass façade, its flat roofs, its stains of damp and rot,
it might be a science block in some under-funded comprehensive school.
In fact, it was a dance theatre: to be precise, the Adeline Genée dance
theatre, the pet project of the Home Secretary's wife Beryl Maudling,
and a symbol of a virulent financial and political cancer at the heart of
British public life. And as he contemplated the wreckage of his political
career, Reginald Maudling must have wished he had never heard of it.[1]

When Maudling resigned as Home Secretary in July 1972, the
consensus was that he was an honourable man brought down by sheer
bad luck. During the mid-1960s, he had agreed to serve as chairman of
an export company owned by a successful Yorkshire architect called

506

John Poulson. In return, Poulson promised to help with the financing of Beryl Maudling's beloved theatre project, a 'Little Glyndebourne for Ballet' on the edge of East Grinstead. As a teenage ballet prodigy, Beryl dreamed that the Adeline Genée theatre would help to bring dance to the masses, and she was delighted when Poulson offered a financial covenant that would bail out the troubled scheme. So work on the theatre went ahead, and in January 1967 it opened its doors with a gala performance attended by Princess Margaret, Lord Snowdon and Dame Adeline herself, a former ballet dancer now in her nineties. But then disaster struck. Despite his air of success, John Poulson was a rather less adept businessman than he seemed, and in January 1972 he was forced to declare bankruptcy. When investigators looked into his murky finances, they found some very mysterious donations to civil servants and politicians, as well as the details of the covenant to Beryl Maudling's theatre. As the Attorney General reported to the Cabinet on 13 July 1972, not only was Poulson himself possibly guilty of fraud, but at least two Members of Parliament, 'several civil servants and various individuals in public life in the north of England' might also have to face 'charges of corruption'.[2]

All of this left Maudling in a distinctly tricky spot. As Home Secretary, he would nominally be in charge of any investigation, but since he and his wife had benefited from Poulson's largesse, he could hardly claim to be unbiased. He had to leave the Cabinet Room while his colleagues were discussing the issue, which must have been excruciatingly embarrassing, and there were isolated calls from Liberal MPs for him to step down. Even so, colleagues and commentators alike were astonished when, on Tuesday, 18 July, Maudling suddenly resigned as Home Secretary. He had, he explained, done nothing wrong himself, but 'it would not be appropriate' to continue in office while the Poulson case was rumbling on. Maudling was a popular figure on both sides of the House; even as Heath was reading out his resignation letter, there were gasps of shock and cries of 'Shame!' Maudling had 'acted in the best traditions of the public service of this country', said Labour's deputy leader Ted Short, while the former Home Secretary Jim Callaghan jumped to his feet to condemn the 'witch-hunt' against his Tory successor, even adding that Heath should not have accepted his resignation – an extraordinary statement coming from the Opposition front bench. In private, Callaghan was even angrier. Grabbing one of Maudling's junior ministers by the lapels afterwards, he said: 'You've let him down. He's a good man and he shouldn't have gone.'[3]

At a time when public affairs seemed infected by greed and self-interest, the Home Secretary's self-sacrifice was a rare and inspiring moment. 'There can be little wrong with public life,' said the *Daily Express*, 'when a man in Mr Maudling's position resigns as a matter of honour.' The *Sun*'s editorial hailed 'Maudling, man of honour' and called it 'one of the most sensational personal political tragedies of the century'. The *Mirror* agreed that he 'could not have acted more honourably'. And *The Economist* even suggested that at a time when investigative journalists were uncovering corruption scandals in everything from local government to the Metropolitan Police, Maudling's resignation should mark a turning point. It was 'time now for everyone in public life, politics and journalism to consider where the line should be drawn between responsible criticism and irresponsible, even if unwitting, support to the gravediggers of parliamentary democracy'. For it had been 'a bleak week in British politics. A few MPs, and rather more Pharisees in the press, have contrived to bring down a fine politician. In doing so they have shocked the country, and some of them may even have shocked themselves.'[4]

These were fine and noble sentiments. The only problem was that Maudling was deeply, irredeemably guilty.

The roots of the Poulson scandal lay in the unprecedented moneymaking opportunities presented by the redevelopment of Britain's urban landscape. Many cities, such as London, Birmingham, Coventry and Hull, had been badly scarred by German bombing raids in the war. Some ripped out acres of slum housing and moved their inhabitants to new high-rise housing blocks; others demolished parts of their central areas to make way for brand-new motorways and dual carriageways; and still others tore down their Victorian buildings out of sheer utopian modernism, believing that only clean lines, concrete surfaces and Brutalist austerity would present an appropriately up-to-date image. Labour and Conservative local authorities alike agreed that, as *The Times* put it, 'smart typists and skilled young workers will not put up with Victorian by-law streets any longer', and by 1965 at least 500 different redevelopment schemes were being considered across the country. Since regulations were lax, however, more than a few planners and architects took the opportunity to feather their own nests. In Bradford, an investigation at the end of the 1960s uncovered an extraordinary saga of corruption, expenses-fiddling and municipal kickbacks. In Wandsworth, the police found that the head of the council's Labour group, Sidney Sporle, had pocketed thousands of pounds from developers in return for contracts to replace Victorian terraces with system-built flats. And in one of the most egregious cases, Newcastle's swashbuckling leader T. Dan Smith came up with a sweeping scheme of flyovers, shopping precincts and high-rise blocks while simultaneously acting as a paid consultant to the Crudens building company, who unsurprisingly won a lot of contracts in the North-east. He also happened to be a consultant to John Poulson, who specialized in big public commissions in the North of England.[5]

On the surface, Poulson seemed an unlikely candidate to become the incarnation of corruption. A blunt, narrow-minded, even moralistic man, the son of a Methodist preacher, Poulson never actually qualified as an architect but nevertheless set up his own Pontefract practice in 1932, when he was just 22. He was not a particularly talented architect – one of his rivals commented that he 'couldn't design a brick shithouse' – and was regarded as an impatient and unfeeling boss, once sacking an employee merely for having a beard. But he was a man of enormous ambition and enterprise, and after the war he realized that he could cut costs and attract much greater business by adopting the new concrete system-building methods and by combining architectural, surveying, engineering and valuation services under one roof, giving clients an all-in-one service. His other great insight was that not only could he cash in on the redevelopment boom in the North of England, but he could also make money abroad by winning big public contracts in the Mediterranean and Middle East. Steadily his business grew and grew, and by the late 1960s it was the biggest in the country, employing more than 700 people, most of them in Pontefract but others dispersed across the North and some even in Beirut and Lagos.

Outwardly, Poulson was a highly respectable man, a Commissioner of Taxes whose wife chaired the Yorkshire Women Conservatives, his business raking in a reported £1 million a year. But there was a dark side to his success. While some of his architects were highly talented, there were murmurs that his buildings were often cheaply and hurriedly put up. Even his best-known constructions were heartily loathed by many residents, and buildings such as London's Cannon Street station and

Leeds's International Swimming Pool and British Railways House became bywords for dreary Stalinist concrete-and-glass austerity. Critics also muttered that he won contracts only through his vast network of local politicians and council officials, among them T. Dan Smith, on whom he lavished expensive presents. Indeed, for a supposedly shrewd business-man, Poulson was remarkably cavalier with money. His employees often wondered why, given that they worked so hard and completed so many contracts, the firm always seemed to be short of cash. The explanation was that Poulson was paying out so much money in bribes, retainers and kickbacks – a total of at least £334,000, according to some estimates, although it may well have been much more.[6]

In the summer of 1966, when Reginald Maudling was feeling sorry for himself after losing out on the Tory leadership, Poulson approached him to become an international ambassador for his firm. A sharper, more scrupulous politician would have run a mile, or at least would have looked more closely into Poulson's business practices. But even at this early stage Maudling was in physical, intellectual and moral decline, his mind dulled by greed and drink. As a family friend told his biographer, Beryl Maudling had become 'insatiably greedy for the good things in life', putting her husband under 'constant pressure at home for money', and insisting that they lead a lifestyle of parties and holidays well beyond an ordinary MP's means. It was under this pressure that Maudling lent his name to the Real Estate Fund of America, an offshore invest-ment trust run by the American fraudster Jerome Hoffman. Although he resigned from the board as soon as REFA became controversial, Maudling's involvement was highly embarrassing, and his excuse – that he just wanted 'a little pot of money' for his old age – notably feeble. Yet with the honourable exception of *Private Eye*, the press gave him a free ride. He was an immensely amiable chap, as well as a former Chancellor and senior member of Heath's front bench. How could anyone suspect him of doing anything wrong?[7]

In fact, as his biographer Lewis Baston has shown, Maudling was not just quite corrupt. He was immensely corrupt. From his first meeting with Poulson, he pocked tens of thousands of pounds in gifts and retainers. In 1967 alone he accepted some £25,000, almost half a million in today's money. In return, he made some characteristically lazy efforts to suborn Tory councillors on Poulson's behalf, and, rather more seriously, intervened in the House of Commons to demand more government aid to Malta. This was a particularly unforgivable episode: Maudling knew that the money would go towards a new hospital on the island of Gozo, for which the contract had been awarded to . . . John Poulson.* Later, the House of Commons let Maudling off with a slap on the wrist, but according to the journalist who broke the story, Ray Fitzwalter, it was a clear and blatant case of parliamentary corruption. 'Poulson asks him to do underhand things to further the cause,' Fitzwalter explained. 'Maudling does it. The effect follows. Then there is reward and congratulation flowing from Poulson to Maudling' – not just the cash presents, but the covenant for Beryl's beloved theatre.

Almost incredibly, though, Maudling's greed did not end there. When he flew to the Middle East to publicize Poulson's business, the architect paid for his suit and even his luggage, claiming it as a tax-deductible expense. In return, Maudling seems to have conspired to bribe a senior Dubai official, offering him a mysterious 'favour' in return for a lucrative hotel deal. The really astonishing thing, though, is not that he was corrupt but that he was so brazen about it. On one occasion when both Maudlings were steaming with drink, the former Chancellor dug out a pile of uncut diamonds to show Poulson, explaining that they were a bribe from Dubai. Meanwhile, he thought nothing of showing off the fancy new swimming pool at his Hertfordshire home, even though it was another present from Poulson (and a characteristically botched job that always leaked). And in January 1970, Reggie and Beryl even pitched up to Antonia Fraser's Field of the Cloth of Gold Ball dressed as Arab sheikhs – a singularly inappropriate choice of costume given their relationship with the region.

Maudling's corruption did not end when he became Home Secretary. In July 1970, for example, he received a gift of £3,000 from one of Poulson's firms, for which he sent a grateful letter noting that it would 'meet all my cash requirements for the foreseeable future'. And although he no longer flew to the Middle East on missions for Poulson, he suborned his own son Martin instead, recommending him as his replacement on Poulson's board. He also encouraged his son to act as a glorified bagman for the corrupt property tycoon Eric Miller, who combined the roles of fundraiser for Harold Wilson, chairman of Peachey Properties and director of Fulham football club. Miller was so crooked he made Poulson

* The hospital seems to have been a typical Poulson masterpiece: the Maltese government later complained that it was 'the wrong design, the wrong size and in the wrong place'.

look a man of probity, and he liked to show off Martin Maudling as a kind of trophy. One lunch guest later remembered that at the end of the meal, Miller asked young Maudling to hand round the cigar box: when opened, it proved to be stuffed with £50 notes. But the links between the tycoon and the Home Secretary did not end there. Miller owned the freehold on Maudling's house, frequently invited him for dinner (baked potato with caviar, rather oddly, was a favourite dish), and in December 1970 presented Beryl Maudling with a silver chess set worth £2,750 (roughly £32,000 in today's money). At one level, it beggars belief that the minister responsible for law and order in Britain thought he could get away with this kind of behaviour. But if John Poulson had been a better businessman, then Maudling might well have got away with it.[8]

Poulson's business had been running into trouble since the late 1960s, when two large cheques to the Inland Revenue bounced. As Maudling's biographer writes, Poulson was 'leaking money all over the place', and on New Year's Eve 1969 he was forced to relinquish power over his own empire, giving way to his wife's brother-in-law John King – later the ruthless chairman of British Airways and Mrs Thatcher's favourite businessman. Disastrously, however, Poulson was still badly in debt, and in January 1972 he declared bankruptcy. Since he had always kept detailed records of his financial transactions, exposure was now inevitable. Confronted with the evidence of his wrongdoing during a tumultuous hearing in Wakefield, Poulson melodramatically collapsed under the strain, thereby guaranteeing himself a place in the headlines. By the end of July 1972, the Metropolitan Police had opened a criminal investigation, and a year later, after wading through mountains of paperwork, they charged Poulson with fraud. And when the case opened in October, it all came out: the presents, the bribes, the brown envelopes. 'It was not corruption,' Poulson said defiantly, 'because it is generally done by every building firm in this land.' There was 'so much drinking and entertaining', he insisted, that it was unfair to single him out. But it was no good: on 11 February 1974, Poulson was found guilty. Even in the depths of humiliation his self-confidence never deserted him. 'I have been a fool,' he said, 'surrounded by a pack of leeches. I took the world on its own terms, and no one can deny I once had it in my fist.' Mr Justice Waller, however, called him an 'incalculably evil' man and sent him down for five years, later increased to seven. 'To offer corrupt gifts', the judge said, 'strikes at the very heart of our government system.'[9]

As for Maudling, he never returned to government after July 1972. While Poulson's trial did not quite uncover the extent of their collaboration, it offered more than enough hints to leave the former Home Secretary looking distinctly shop-soiled. By 1974 he was under investigation by the Fraud Squad, the DTI and the Inland Revenue, although they never managed to unearth enough dirt to bring him down. When Granada's *World in Action* programme revealed the details of the Malta hospital scam in March 1974, Maudling made a personal statement in the Commons denying any impropriety – a statement that while not technically a lie, fell very short of the truth. A year later, Mrs Thatcher recalled him to the front bench as Shadow Foreign Secretary, but as she later put it, his performance was 'a source of embarrassment'. She sacked him in November 1976, and a year later, after more revelations about his association with Poulson, he suffered the indignity of being investigated, albeit very feebly, by a parliamentary Select Committee. After sinking into outright alcoholism, he died of cirrhosis of the liver in February 1979. Perhaps it was appropriate that he died at exactly the moment – the Winter of Discontent – when the post-war consensus was breaking up, for, as an unrepentant One Nation moderate, he had been its most articulate Tory champion. Even so, his passing at the age of just 61 seemed a dreadful waste. Few politicians of his generation were blessed with greater intelligence and charm, but few were cursed with such indolence and greed. He had found 'nothing more worth the wear of winning', he wrote on the final page of his memoirs, 'than laughter and the love of friends'. Except, perhaps, the love of money.[10]

Like all good scandals, the Poulson–Maudling affair captured public attention not only because it offered a compelling morality tale of individual greed and overweening ambition, but because it exposed the deep corruption beneath the surface of public life. As investigators dug deeper in the mid-1970s, they discovered that Poulson's contacts amounted to more than a handful of rogue civil servants. Subsequent trials saw officials of British Rail, the National Coal Board and even the South-Western Metropolitan Hospital Board in the dock, while an entirely unrelated investigation into local government corruption in South Wales ended with thirty people being found guilty, most of them local businessmen. And in a sensational case overshadowed by the Poulson scandal, the Birmingham city architect Alan Maudsley, who had almost

single-handedly controlled the country's biggest public housing programme outside London, was arrested in November 1973 and charged
with corruption. Maudsley had been in cahoots not just with the architectural firm of Ebery and Sharp, but with the Bryants housing giant, to
whom he had given two-thirds of all Birmingham's high-rise contracts.
Ebery and Sharp paid him £10 a house; Bryants paid for holidays,
excursions and fine living. When the case came to court in the spring of
1974, Maudsley pleaded guilty, but it did not save him from prison. He
had fallen short of the 'high standards the public of this country expect
of public servants', Mr Justice Mocatta said solemnly. But the judge was
behind the times. To anybody who read a newspaper, high standards
seemed a thing of the past. The Maudsley case, said the prosecuting
counsel George Carman, was merely 'the tip of the iceberg'.[11]

Was Britain really more corrupt than ever in the 1970s? It is certainly
true that the sweeping redevelopment of towns and cities offered unprecedented possibilities to builders, planners and councillors: as the
go-getting, Cortina-driving developer puts it in John Betjeman's poem
'Executive' (1974), all he needs is a 'luncheon and a drink or two' to 'fix
the Planning Officer, the Town Clerk and the Mayor'. It is also true that
most people genuinely believed that things had got worse. Indeed, if the
press was to be believed, the nation had sunk into an unprecedented rut
of selfishness, avarice and unashamed graft. 'Corruption runs through
all levels of British public life,' wrote the journalist Clive Irving in his
state-of-the nation survey *Pox Britannica* (also 1974), aimed at American
readers. 'Careers have been finished by the temptations of a few bottles
of whiskey, a vacation in Majorca, a swimming pool in the yard. There's
a subtle, interlocking brotherhood with connections in every town – and
there's always the man to see.'[12]

What allowed this to thrive, Irving thought, was the 'absence of any
tradition of muckraking'. But this diagnosis was out of date. The revival
of muckraking since the mid-1960s, epitomized by the success of *Private
Eye*, the *Sunday Times* Insight Team and Granada's *World in Action*,
was precisely what had convinced people that Britain had succumbed to
massive corruption. And in an intensely competitive and increasingly
populist media climate, where the irreverence of the *Eye* or the *Sun*
often set the tone, readers now looked at the shadowy world of quiet
handshakes, unspoken agreements and brown envelopes – a world that
had long existed – in a new light. In 1970 alone, *Private Eye*'s Footnotes

column ran stories about Poulson, T. Dan Smith, BP's sanctions-busting in Rhodesia and the Irish government's role in IRA gun-running, most of which the mainstream press ignored until later. Two years later, during Paul Foot's last year at the magazine, the column included stories about the corrupt Tyneside politician Andy Cunningham, the Heath government's secret talks with the IRA, Lord Carrington's land deals, Jim Slater's property deals and a pollution scandal at Rio Tinto-Zinc's Avonmouth smelter. In many respects this was the magazine's finest hour: more than any other publication, the *Eye* could claim to have punctured the bubble of self-congratulation and secrecy surrounding British public life. It might get more than a few details wrong, but, as ITV's *What the Papers Say* commented after its Poulson allegations had been vindicated, *Private Eye* was 'more important to journalism than half the Fleet Street papers'.[13]

By this point corruption had become one of the clichés of national cultural life. In Lindsay Anderson's film *O Lucky Man!*, which was shot in the summer of 1972 and released a year later, Malcolm McDowell's journey through contemporary society is the vehicle for a satire in the best picaresque tradition. Beginning the film as a young coffee salesman, he gets mixed up in everything from state-sponsored torture to the sale of chemical weapons to a crooked African dictator. As the critic Alexander Walker put it, Anderson's film presents 'the comedy of private corruption in public life', with a splendid array of character actors – Ralph Richardson, Arthur Lowe, Rachel Roberts, Graham Crowden, Dandy Nichols – playing 'ruthless tycoons, hypocritical town-hall worthies, venal policemen, perverted judges, fascist mercenaries, two-faced PR people, tyrant rulers from Black Africa [and] sin-obsessed do-gooders'. And while other British films of the era preferred to wallow in lurid escapism, the radical young playwrights of the early 1970s were quick to follow Anderson's lead. 'We thought, wrongly, as it turned out, that England was in a state of apocalyptic crisis,' recalled the dramatist David Hare. 'We had lost faith in its institutions, we thought that Britain's assumption of a non-existent world role was ludicrous, and we also thought that its economic vitality was so sapped that it wouldn't last long.'[14]

Hare's plan was to write 'short, nasty little plays which would alert an otherwise dormant population to this news', but in 1973 the new artistic director of the Nottingham Playhouse, Richard Eyre, invited him and his friend Howard Brenton to write a 'big' play diagnosing the state of the nation. The result was *Brassneck*, a sprawling satire of British life since the 1940s, told through the story of one ambitious Midlands family, the Bagleys. Hare later called it the story of the 'People's Peace . . . seen through the lives of the petty bourgeoisie, builders, solicitors, brewers, politicians, the Masonic gang who carve up provincial England'. The family wealth is based on ruthless property speculation, while both Tory and Labour politicians are suborned through bribes and blackmail. And in the architect Roderick Bagley we meet the embodiment of national corruption in the age of Poulson and Maudling. When Roderick wins the contract for a new hospital, his uncle cynically forecasts 'problems on the site, weather, that sort of thing, costs will rise during the building, we'll have to revise the estimates. Revise the profits. Slightly. Often. Upwards.' The years pass: Roderick builds tower blocks, makes money, exploits his political contacts and expands into the new markets of post-colonial Africa. The wheel of fortune turns: his tower blocks leak, his business goes bankrupt, he unwittingly admits to taking bribes and he is sent to prison. 'The Labour Party will whisper down the line,' one of his political cronies assures him. 'Builders, councils, Government departments will gloss over fat bad debts . . . Vast sums you owe will disappear in the fog. Books will be fiddled and invoices burnt the length of the land.' And in the play's supremely depressing final scene, the survivors of the Bagley network meet in a seedy strip-club in 1973 to plot their next move. One of them suggests a new venture, 'a product for our times, the perfect product, totally artificial, man-made, creating its own market, one hundred percent consumer identification': heroin from China. The deal is done: as the curtain falls, they raise their glasses 'to the last days of capitalism'.[15]

If *Brassneck* seemed rather downbeat, it was as nothing compared with Hare's next play. *Knuckle* opened in the West End in the first week of March 1974, a coincidence of timing making it the perfect theatrical epitaph for the Heath years. Again, the theme is the shabbiness and corruption of modern Britain, which we see through the eyes of Curly, a gun salesman who has returned to his native Guildford to investigate the death of his sister Sarah. And again property speculation lies at the heart of the mystery. Sarah killed herself, it turns out, after stumbling upon a gigantic scam in which an elderly woman was committed to an asylum so that developers could replace her house with 'seventeen floors of prestige offices crowned with an antique supermarket'. Even the cynical Curly is taken aback by the state of the nation after twelve years away. 'Newspapers can be bought, judges can be leant on, politicians can be stuffed with truffles and cognac,' he remarks. 'When I got back I found this country was a jampot for swindlers and cons and racketeers. Not just property. Boarding houses and bordellos and nightclubs and crooked charter flights, private clinics, horse-hair wigs and tin-can motor cars, venereal cafés with ice-cream made from whale blubber and sausages full of sawdust.' Even Guildford itself, supposedly a genteel Surrey county town, emerges as a sleazy, shabby place, a haven for property swindlers, sado-masochists and 'middle-aged voyeurs'. 'I have twice been attacked at the country club,' the club hostess Jenny tells him; 'the man in the house opposite has a telephoto lens, my breasts are often touched on commuter trains, my body is covered with random thumbprints, the doctor says he needs to undress me completely to vaccinate my arm'.[16]

At the centre of the play is the confrontation between Curly and his father Patrick, an old-fashioned gentlemanly capitalist who works in the City, reads Henry James and relaxes by playing the cello. It quickly becomes clear, though, that Patrick is even more crooked than his arms-dealer son; indeed, his corruption is all the more shocking because it is so understated, being hidden beneath the veneer of gentility that his money has bought him. Caught up in the property scam through a web of connections, he makes no apology for leaving his own daughter to kill herself on Eastbourne beach. In classic early 1970s agitprop style, Patrick is the incarnation of sexual and financial depravity, sleeping with his housekeeper and metaphorically raping the public. 'In the City,' he says complacently, 'the saying is, "The exploitation of the masses should be conducted as quietly as possible."' And although we never see the City, it is always there, looming in the background, the supreme embodiment of the abuses of capitalism. 'I told her some stories of life in the City,' muses Patrick, remembering his daughter's final moments, 'the casual cruelty of each day; take-over bids, redundancies, men ruined overnight, jobs lost, trusts betrayed, reputations smashed, life in that great trough called the City of London, sploshing about in the cash.' He justifies himself with one cliché after another: 'Somebody's bound to get hurt . . . The pursuit of money is a force for progress . . . If I didn't do it' – and on cue, his son completes the sentence: 'Somebody else would.' At the end, far from punishing his father, Curly just walks away. 'Money can be harvested like rotten fruit,' he says dismissively. 'People are just aching to be fleeced. But those of us who do it must learn the quality of self-control.'[17]

In the left-wing demonology of the early 1970s, no institution loomed larger than the City, that great financial fastness at the centre of the British establishment. To walk east from the West End, wrote Anthony Sampson in his *New Anatomy of Britain* in 1971, was to enter a different world, for 'as you pass St Paul's you can sense in the air a certain narrowing and intensifying of ambitions, like the narrowing of the street-corners themselves'. The crowds thinned, leaving only scurrying pale-faced men in dark grey suits; the colourful shop fronts gave way to 'bleak grey office blocks, frosted windows and ponderous bankers' façades'. The City of London: the last bastion of an institutional conservatism that was otherwise dying out; the last bastion of a stiff-upper-lip English-ness that was on the wane everywhere else; the last bastion, indeed, of the bowler hat. The City: 'overgrown village, rumour mill, with an atmosphere of a regimental mess and the sense of humour of an Edwardian boys' paper, full of private language, secret rituals and enough games to last a working lifetime,' as the narrator puts it in David Jordan's financial thriller *Nile Green* (1973). Nowhere better captured its values than Sweetings, the famous restaurant where 'the City man goes for lunch when he's nostalgic for his schooldays . . . Bread and butter, brown and thin and damp, a memory of cricket on the lawn before Evensong. Ginger beer and lemonade. Sherbert. Rice pudding, apple pudding, jam roly-poly and treacle tart.' The tastes and values of the English public school, preserved into the age of the IBM punch card.[18]

And yet despite the sartorial conservatism and the spotted dick, the City of London was on the brink of some of the most tumultuous changes in its history. During the 1960s, an unprecedented number of international banks had opened offices in the Square Mile: whereas there had been just 14 American banks in 1960, there were 37 ten years later, just a fraction of the 159 foreign banks that now had London branches. Thanks to low American interest rates, vast numbers of dollars were now being invested in London to take advantage of the better rate of return, and these so-called 'Eurodollars', the basic currency for international trade and multinational companies, helped the City to maintain its reputation as one of the world's greatest financial centres, even though Britain's economy had long since tumbled off the podium. But it was not only American money that made the difference. As the oil-exporting Arab members of OPEC raised their prices and began to recoup enormous rewards, so they too turned to the City of London to invest their 'petrodollar' winnings. Beneath the veneer of institutional conservatism, the City was becoming the crucible of financial globalization.

Some things remained the same: a survey of City directors in 1971 found that Eton, Oxbridge and the clubs of St James's still held sway. But even the geography of the Square Mile told a story of change that belied the City's stuffy reputation. On Old Broad Street, for example, work on Richard Seifert's NatWest Tower began in the first year of the decade: even though its fifty-two floors of steel and glass were later seen as an emblem of Thatcherism (since it opened in 1981), in commission and design it was a product of the Heath years. Further along Old Broad Street, nothing symbolized the new City better than the Stock Exchange Tower, which was formally opened by the Queen in the autumn of 1972, although trading did not start until six months later. With its Brutalist concrete façade, electronic currency displays and clocks showing the time in nine different financial centres, the new trading floor seemed light years away from the days when a waiter's rattle at a quarter past three had announced the last part of the trading day, when smoking was allowed. Even the floor itself, which was lined with rubber tiles instead of the familiar wood, represented radical change: for since cigarette butts would damage the tiles, smoking was now banned outright.[19]

The man who, more than anybody else, came to embody the new City was the son of a west London building contractor, a former grammar school boy who, like Edward Heath, became a symbol of modernization, mobility and ruthless efficiency. Jim Slater was a trained accountant who had worked for Leyland's sales division, rose to become their financial director, and wrote an acclaimed share-tipping column for Nigel Lawson's *Sunday Telegraph* City pages in the mid-1960s. In the winter of 1963, he met Peter Walker, the insurance whizz-kid turned ambitious Tory MP, and persuaded him to join forces. Slater Walker, as their new enterprise was known, became easily the most glamorous and controversial City firm of the late 1960s and early 1970s. To their admirers, Slater Walker represented a breath of fresh air and a dose of much-needed modernization; to their critics, they were nothing more than ruthless asset-strippers, buying companies of all shapes and sizes, ripping out the loss-making elements and selling them off to make a quick profit. 'While the directors were out on the grouse moors or golf courses, the gimlet eye of Slater cased the company records,' one observer wrote. 'Then the predators moved in.' The paradigmatic example was his first major takeover victim, Crittall-Hope, a family-run window-frame manufacturer. Slater told the directors that he was 'not there to make windows, but to make money', immediately sacked numerous workers, and soon sold off the profitable parts of the company. Yet as the firm's previous chairman pointed out, its performance after the takeover was not much better than it had been beforehand, while 'any activity with a speculative or long-range future was ruthlessly pruned'. Indeed, when Slater Walker finally collapsed in the mid-1970s, it became clear that Slater's castle had been built on sand. As the City's historian David Kynaston writes, he never managed to dispel the sense that he had been running 'a systematic, quite shameless insider-dealing operation'. Either way, given the endless pages of press enthusiasm, 'it was amazing how little of substance' he really achieved.[20]

In the early 1970s, however, Slater's reputation was at its peak. He was a radical hero, 'the most brilliantly successful' of 'the City's self-made men', wrote the admiring journalist Jonathan Aitken. Slater seemed to have 'found, untapped, a whole new vein of talent, particularly from the post-war grammar schools', observed the *Sunday Telegraph* in 1971, while another profile claimed that he brought 'a sense of tension, of high voltage, into the room'. Not unpredictably, one of Slater's biggest fans was another self-made grammar school boy, himself seen as the incarnation of social mobility, naked ambition and the victory of style over substance. In February 1972, Slater announced that he had bought a company called Equity Enterprises as 'a sort of investment piggy-bank' for his new best friend, David Frost. At about this point, the *Sunday Times* began running a series of articles hostile to Slater, so when Frost spotted one of the paper's executives at a garden party a few weeks later, he pounced. The newspaper should invite Slater to lunch, he gushed: 'You would be absolutely fascinated by his mind.' For dramatic effect, Frost pointed to a rosebush that stood nearby in the gathering twilight. 'I mean,' he said, 'Jim is as interested in why that rose should wither and die as he is in a balance sheet.'[21]

Even the generally sceptical journalist Anthony Sampson fell for the Slater myth. 'Still only forty-two, Jim Slater has a sense of command which quickly gives confidence to others,' he wrote in a gushing paean of praise:

> He contemplates his own motivation as if he were talking about someone else; he sees himself as a chess-player (at which he excels), extending his skills to the great game of the City, and urged on by a driving desire to prove himself right. Politically, like most self-made men, he supports Heath's views on the need for self-reliance and the dangers of cosseting; he has dined at Downing Street, and he is (like Walker) the very paragon of the new Heath-type Tory – self-made, hard-working, unsentimental, competitive. Certainly in the financial world he has stimulated a new aggressiveness, unleashing energies and money-mindedness: he loves to watch his young protégés discover their money-making potential, as he discovered his ten years before.

The link with Heath was more than merely metaphorical. Slater donated thousands of pounds to the Conservative Party, praised Heath as the 'personification of meritocracy in politics' and urged him to 'generate an atmosphere in which success and profit in business are regarded as important and in the interest of the country', while Walker became one of Heath's more effective ministers. And Slater Walker was good to Heath, who bought shares in the firm, as well as its satellite companies Ralli and Tokengate, in 1965, and sold them five years later for £21,500 – worth more than ten times that in today's money.[22]

What contemporaries often called the 'new capitalism' left a deep imprint on popular culture, manifested not just in the fawning profiles of entrepreneurs like Jim Slater, but in television series like ATV's *The Power Game* and the BBC's *The Trouble Shooters*, with their endless boardroom battles, hostile takeovers and merciless power struggles. Barely two months after the FT30 share index had reached 500 points for the first time in its history, the BBC launched perhaps the most successful series of this kind, *The Brothers* (1972–6), which chronicled the boardroom (and bedroom) intrigues behind a family haulage firm, and was mercifully a lot more glamorous than the premise sounded. If nothing else, shows like this gave the lie to the notion that the BBC merely pumped out left-wing propaganda and working-class agitprop; the critic Kenneth Tynan complained that *The Trouble Shooters* was 'naked propaganda for capitalism'. *The Brothers* even had a good claim to have produced television's first Thatcherite villain in the character of the City whiz-kid Paul Merroney (played with relish by Colin Baker, never knowingly understated). A ruthless proto-yuppie with an 'ambitious, cold personal manner and willingness to discard traditional practices', as an appalled cultural studies textbook of the day put it, Merroney would have fitted in very nicely at Slater Walker. Baker did his best to stand up for the character, insisting that he 'never told outright lies [and] never broke the law', and was merely 'ruthless in his ambition for the company'. Evidently viewers did not agree: at one point, *Sun* readers even voted him 'the 'most hated man in Britain'.[23]

As the *Sun*'s poll might suggest, the buccaneer capitalism of the 1970s was not to everybody's taste. Even during Slater's heyday, there were plenty of doubters, particularly among the City old guard who resented the meteoric rise of a self-made upstart. And with the stock and property markets booming at a time of industrial strife and mass unemployment, it was no wonder that many people saw a disturbing link between the two. When the FT30 index hit 500, many City insiders were deeply embarrassed, for on the very same day, 30 January 1972, unemployment reached the dreaded figure of one million. Even the *Financial Times* admitted that the coincidence made 'an easy anti-capitalist debating point'. And to find another uncomfortable debating point, the City's champions had only to walk half an hour west. During the previous ten years, a handful of ambitious speculators had borrowed enormous sums of money to develop space in the centres of London, Birmingham and Manchester, throwing up high-rise glass and concrete office blocks that were loved by few and hated by many. By far the most notorious was the secretive Harry Hyams, who had bought a small space beside Tottenham Court Road tube station and commissioned a thirty-two-storey skyscraper to fill it. Since the proposed building would totally dominate the area, permission would not usually have been given. But in classic David Hare-villain-style, Hyams managed to persuade the council by promising to build a transport interchange – which never quite materialized.[24]

What turned Centre Point into a national scandal, though, was the fact that when it was finished, Hyams refused to let it out. With property prices rising so quickly, he preferred to wait for a single tenant who would take the building for £1.25 million, rather than let it floor by floor, as the council repeatedly requested. London was therefore left with the embarrassing spectacle of a 385-foot concrete tower at the end of its most famous thoroughfare, finished but completely vacant, at a time of mass unemployment and rising public concern about homelessness. By June 1972, it had been empty for almost eight years, yet still Hyams showed no signs of finding a tenant; indeed, because of the tax laws on capital gains, he was probably making more money by keeping it empty than if he had rented it out. At one stage, the borough of Camden threatened to apply for a compulsory purchase order, while Peter Walker even threatened to use public money to nationalize it. A year later, a group of Labour MPs organized a public protest on the steps outside the unoccupied building, and in January 1974 more than a hundred demonstrators managed to get into it. Still Hyams refused to budge. Indeed, by the time Heath faced the voters, Centre Point had become a nationwide symbol of the excesses of property speculation and the apparent callousness of the new capitalism.[25]

For a government keen to encourage enterprise and entrepreneurship, Centre Point was a painful embarrassment. Heath's administration, said a stern leader in *The Times*, had been 'too soft in its attitude towards property development', encouraging the widespread feeling that 'the Conservatives are to a considerable extent to blame for it'. Writing in May 1972, as the railwaymen prepared to join the dockers on strike for a better wage, the paper's star columnist Bernard Levin wondered if Heath realized the resentment that was building among the low-paid. 'Has he any idea what a man earning £20 a week feels when he sees speculators about to make untold millions by befouling Piccadilly Circus and Covent Garden and indeed any other bits of any other city that they can get their hands on?' Levin wrote. 'What sort of a society is it that says dockers are holding the country to ransom by striking but does not say that developers are doing so by keeping office blocks empty until the rent has risen high enough to satisfy their greed?' And it was a sign of the times that the piece next to Levin's column took a similar line. Written as an open letter from a company director who had lost his job, his Jaguar and his £5,000 annual salary, it warned the Prime Minister that working-class people had lost all faith in his sense of fairness. 'You may sincerely believe it when you talk about "one nation" and conquering inflation for the common good but they frankly don't believe it,' the former director wrote. 'To them you are a plummy-voiced, granite-hearted lot of bastards who are out to kill the unions and grind them down. And everything you say about inflated wage demands confirms it.'[26]

Given that Heath's ministers spent more money on social services than any of their predecessors, planned to expand the NHS and state education, pumped millions into Upper Clyde Shipbuilders and Rolls-Royce, and rapidly abandoned their early economic rigour in an attempt to get people back to work, it is ironic that they were perceived as granite-hearted bastards. The problem for Heath, though, was that he could never shake off the albatross of Selsdon Man. By talking so much about competition, enterprise and meritocracy, he had earned the reputation of a ruthless modernizer, the political equivalent of Jim Slater, slashing through the red tape of the welfare state. Even though the union leaders knew that this image was a myth, their members were convinced it was true. On top of that, Heath had become the symbol of a deeper change sweeping through British society: the rise of the 'self-made men', ambitious and assertive grammar school boys like Slater and Merroney, impatient with tradition, determined to wring every possible penny from a society ripe for development. Ten years later they would be called Thatcherites; now they were the 'new capitalists', the young meteors of a society in which, as the researcher Mark Abrams wrote in October 1974, 'more money has become almost a terminal value'. And it was not only left-wing idealists who found them deeply unsettling. Plenty of Tory voters shared the sentiments of the ex-serviceman Turner in David Edgar's play *Destiny* (1976), who is dumbfounded when his beloved antique shop is ripped down by developers. 'You bastard,' he tells the long-haired, denim-jacketed Monty, the incarnation of the new capitalism. 'No, not bastard,' Monty says. 'Selsdon Man . . . We make money out of money. We covet on a global scale. We got cupidity beyond your wildest dreams of avarice.' Despite his years of service, his love of country, Turner is out of date; it is Monty who represents the future. 'Once we stood for patriotism, Empire,' laments an old-fashioned middle-class Conservative lady in the same play. 'Now it's all sharp young men with coloured shirts and Cockney accents, reading the *Economist*.'[27]

But it was Heath himself who coined the phrase that defined the excesses of the era. Amid all the rumours and revelations of financial corruption that dominated headlines in the early 1970s, one name cropped up again and again: Lonrho. Founded at the start of the century as the London and Rhodesian Mining Company, it had fallen in the early 1960s into the hands of an Anglo-German financial adventurer, 'Tiny' Rowland, who drank and gambled with, among others, Jim Slater and

James Goldsmith at the Clermont Club in Mayfair. Like his gambling partners, Rowland called himself a 'revolutionary capitalist'. A tall, charismatic man, he cultivated the image of an imperial adventurer, jetting ceaselessly around Africa, charming the black leaders of the newly independent states, and gradually acquiring a vast portfolio of concessions, mining and trading rights, newspapers and even a Malawian railway. 'He was brought up against a background of restless danger,' an aide reverentially explained, 'so his mind never worked in conventional ways.' By the early 1970s, Rowland had become one of Britain's best-known and most flamboyant entrepreneurs, having bought the Hadfields steelworks, the distillers Whyte and Mackay, the Volkswagen agency and a string of casinos. He also seemed determined to buy his way into the British establishment, having recruited the former Conservative Defence Secretary Duncan Sandys, the former Labour Attorney General Lord Shawcross, and the chairman of the backbench 1922 Committee Edward du Cann to act as his advisers.[28]

Rowland's methods made him plenty of enemies. As early as 1971, his banker Sir Siegmund Warburg, no shrinking violet himself, had decided that he could no longer represent Lonrho. Meanwhile some of the firm's older directors were getting cold feet about Rowland's buccaneering, autocratic style. At last, led by the former BOAC chairman Sir Basil Smallpeice, they tried to have him dismissed as Lonrho's chief executive. The ensuing scandal dominated press headlines in May 1973, as Rowland first tried to get the High Court to restrain his adversaries, and then decided to take his case to a full shareholders' meeting, hoping that Lonrho's small shareholders, who had made large amounts of money under his guidance, would stay loyal. Since it was clear that Rowland had not only bribed African officials and defied international sanctions against Rhodesia, but had systematically hidden from his own board various other activities, including an annual $100,000 tax-free bribe to Duncan Sandys, the press was unanimous. 'Mr Rowland Must Go,' insisted a long *Times* leader just before the shareholders' meeting, explaining that he could not be allowed 'to run a major British public company as if it was still a personal fief'.[29]

For Heath, the Lonrho affair was yet another embarrassment. The problem was not just that it involved two well-known Conservatives in Sandys and du Cann, for the affair had come to symbolize a broader financial culture of irresponsibility, ruthlessness and greed, which the government itself was supposed to have encouraged. In the House of Commons on 15 May, the Labour backbencher Jack Ashley pointedly asked how Heath could 'justify the double standard of constantly refusing to intervene in the great national scandals of big business . . . while he constantly intervenes and moralises about the legitimate wage claims of trade unions?' Would he accept, added the Liberals' Jo Grimond, that excesses on Lonrho's scale were 'fatal to the counter-inflationary policy', and that 'greed does not now seem to be a monopoly of the trade unions'? The questions gave Heath no choice, for as he later explained, Lonrho had 'presented socialists with a marvellous propaganda coup. To have defended such behaviour would have been a disgraceful own goal.' And what he said next guaranteed his place in the dictionary of quotations. Lonrho, he gloomily told the House, represented 'the unpleasant and unacceptable face of capitalism'.[30]

It has since been suggested that Heath's best-known saying was actually a mistake, and that his notes called for him to say 'facet' rather than 'face', which, if true, speaks volumes about his insensitivity to language. In his memoirs, however, he stuck by the famous formula. He never understood why the remark was seen as a mistake: it was 'sheer stupidity', he thought,

"Is there a Conservative in the House?"

To many Tory activists, Heath's government seemed to be losing conviction. On the left, Sir Gerald Nabarro leads a rebellion against the Maplin airport scheme. In the centre, Enoch Powell makes a typically lonely stand against the EEC. On the right, Heath himself denounces the 'unacceptable face of capitalism'. Cummings in the *Daily Express*, 15 June 1973.

for Conservatives to 'fall into the trap of reflexively defending' the excesses and defects of capitalism, and 'no true friend of free enterprise could have said less'. But even he was taken aback by the way in which the phrase stuck, being brandished time and again by Labour MPs like some badge of victory. At a time when sub-Marxist ideas were proving enormously popular in academia and the arts, when the headlines were full of the 'class war' between the government and the unions, and when the property boom had drawn fresh attention to the economic inequalities in British society, Heath seemed to have scored a dreadful own goal. Even capitalism's most eminent champion, it seemed, could not deny its 'unpleasant and unacceptable' face. Perhaps the remark would soon have been forgotten. But on the right of the Conservative Party, there was a growing sense that it was a Freudian slip, a mistake that revealed the crypto-socialist behind the mask of the self-made man. For by this stage Heath had left the 'quiet revolution' long behind, and to his Conservative critics, he was fast becoming more socialist than the socialists themselves.[31]

On New Year's Day 1973, Britain finally became a member of the European Economic Community, fulfilling Edward Heath's dearest dream. For the United Kingdom's 55 million people, however, little seemed to have changed. On the front page of *The Times*, the main headline reported that Heath and Wilson had clashed over Britain's future in Europe, the latter claiming that the government had accepted 'utterly crippling' terms in defiance of public opinion. Elsewhere, headlines announced that the Irish police had arrested 'one of the most wanted men in Northern Ireland,' the Provisional IRA's Londonderry commander Martin McGuinness; that London's gas workers were on an unofficial overtime ban, endangering gas supplies to almost a million people in the South-east; and that the Ugandan president Idi Amin had accused Britain of interfering in his plans for economic renewal. In other news, Jimmy Savile had been awarded the Variety Club's award for showbusiness personality of the year, while Peter Cormack's goal against Crystal Palace had taken Liverpool clear at the top of the First Division. On the letters page, the controversy over the Post Office's admission that it had made a mess of Christmas deliveries still rumbled on. In the Women's Advertisements, there were appeals for travel representatives in Majorca and Torremolinos, for 'young ladies with personality' to work as general assistants at the Richmond Arms Hotel, Goodwood, and for a 'young attractive receptionist' to work for a Chelsea estate agent. On Radio One, Tony Blackburn was in Luxembourg, of all places, to mark the big European day, while Jimmy Young was in Brussels and Dave Lee Travis in Cologne. That evening, television viewers could look forward to *The Generation Game, Tarbuck's Follies, Opportunity Knocks* and *Coronation Street*. And in the charts, little Jimmy Osmond still held sway over the hearts and minds of Britain's teenagers, thanks to his merciless rendition of 'Long-Haired Lover From Liverpool'.[32]

Even as he celebrated Britain's accession to the Common Market, Heath's mind was on the next stage of his pay policy. On 17 January, flanked by Anthony Barber and Sir William Armstrong in the gilded splendour of Lancaster House, he unveiled Stage Two, which was scheduled to begin on the first day of April. Under the new regime, pay rises were to be limited to a flat £1 a week plus 4 per cent, with nobody's annual increase allowed to exceed £250. There were strict controls on rents and dividends, and companies' profits were not allowed to exceed the average of their best two years out of the last five. Meanwhile, there were two new government bodies to police the new arrangements: a Pay Board to examine all settlements involving more than 1,000 employees; and a Price Commission to scrutinize retail, wholesale and manufacturers' prices, with manufacturers allowed to raise prices only in exceptional circumstances, as defined by a new Prices and Pay Code. All of this seemed a long way from Selsdon Man, and Heath insisted that it was merely a cruel necessity before the government could return to voluntary arrangements. But a strategy paper prepared for the Tory high command a few weeks later told a different story. 'Few people are in the long term going to be prepared to leave it to the government to decide the remuneration appropriate to their work,' the paper correctly noted, while a 'large section of the middle class' was bound to resent 'the prodigious extension of the powers of the state'. But it was 'unlikely', the authors concluded, that Britain could return to free pay bargaining until there had been 'some fundamental change in the techniques of economic management' as well as a 'completely new solution to the problem of cost-push inflation' – and neither seemed likely to materialize any time soon.[33]

Not unpredictably, union leaders reacted furiously to the news of Stage Two. The general secretary of NUPE, Alan Fisher, colourfully claimed that Heath's concern for the low paid had been exposed as 'political pornography; it stimulates the desire but does not relieve the need', a slightly strange formula given that, with the pornography trade booming, thousands of men clearly thought it did offer relief of a kind. In the weeks after the announcement, individual unions rushed to try to impose more generous settlements; by February, gasmen, teachers, hospital staff, train drivers and Ford car workers had all walked out, with the Civil Service staging its first ever one-day strike on 27 February. By the standards of the previous year, however, this was all fairly small-scale stuff. The NUM, for example, was divided, and in a strike ballot on 13 April the miners voted by almost two to one against striking for higher pay. This took much of the sting out of the TUC's planned resistance, and although the unions called for a 'day of national protest' on 1 May, the result was a damp squib. While the railways, engineering firms and car factories suffered severe disruption, hundreds of thousands of workers defied their unions' instructions. At British Leyland, eight out of ten workers reported for duty, more than a hundred NUM pits carried on as usual, and in London, most buses and tube trains ran as normal. Heath's pay policy, it seemed, might just work: even the hawkish *Economist* predicted that inflation for 1973 should be around 8 per cent, less than half the figure for 1972. The government was well on the way, it said, to a 'historic, if temporary, victory'.[34]

If Stage Two had genuinely worked to keep inflation down, then perhaps it would have been worth the gargantuan bureaucracy of Pay Boards and Price Commissions, which smacked of some Eastern European Ministry of Tractors rather than a government that talked endlessly about dynamism and competition. But although Heath had brought a temporary end to inflationary wage claims, rising prices meant that workers were bound to demand a pay rise eventually – and when that happened, the logic of the incomes policy meant that the government was legally bound to confront them. As the *Financial Times*'s columnist Samuel Brittan, an early cheerleader for monetarism, never ceased to point out, the only way to avoid a fight was to institute 'a permanent system of [wage] regulation', which rather defeated the point of a free economy. The real problem, though, was that the world economy was rapidly sliding into a new age of inflation, recession and instability. Across the industrialized world, productivity and output were slowing down after years of massive growth. Automation and computers were throwing millions out of work, and yet consumers' enlarged expectations meant that inflationary pressures were greater than ever. Meanwhile, the end of the old colonial empires and the rise of the developing nations meant that world commodity prices were sharply increasing, most famously oil, which had begun to climb even before the emblematic shock of late 1973. The truth was that although many politicians – especially on the Labour benches – refused to face it, Britain was now part of a globalized economic system, and not even the most powerful Pay Board or Price Commission could hold back the tide of world inflation.[35]

It is often thought, quite wrongly, that the oil shock of late 1973 changed everything. In fact, global commodity prices were already rising by terrifying margins. According to *The Economist*'s authoritative indices, the cost of materials used in manufacturing almost doubled between September 1972 and September 1973, with the price of copper going up by 115 per cent, cotton by 127 per cent, cocoa by 173 per cent and zinc by a staggering 308 per cent. What was particularly bad news for Britain was that prices were going up at precisely the moment when the government had launched a domestic boom, so demand not just for commodities but also for imported consumer goods like cars and colour televisions was unusually high. With import prices up by 26 per cent, Britain spent an extra £2 billion on imports during 1973, plunging the balance of payments deep into the red. It was no wonder that the pound continued to drop on the international exchange markets (thereby making imports even more expensive); little wonder, either, that the markets were becoming seriously worried about the long-term prospects of the British economy. Within the walls of the City of London, panic was quietly setting in. Not even the most prestigious institutions were immune: when Cazenove's, brokers to the Royal Family, sent a circular to its clients in February 1973 condemning 'the general lack of respect for important values (ignored murders in Ulster, indiscipline and public exhibitions of filth)', it was hard to miss the whiff of hysteria.[36]

As Heath was often the first to point out, there was not much he could do about the rise in global commodity prices, short of closing Britain's borders to imports. But the Barber boom made a bad situation much worse. Not only did it stimulate demand for imports at the worst possible moment, it also sent the money supply rocketing far beyond the limits of good sense. With broad money (M3) growing at more than 25 per cent for two successive years, it did not take a dogmatic monetarist to see that there was an enormous risk of the economy tipping into rampant

of Stage Three, Egyptian and Syrian troops crossed the ceasefire lines in the Sinai desert and the Golan Heights, launching a coordinated offensive that took Israel almost completely by surprise. Six days later, American planes began airlifting supplies to Israel – a decision that President Nixon and his Secretary of State, Henry Kissinger, had already been warned might provoke severe economic repercussions from the Arab nations who dominated OPEC, the oil-producers' cartel. And vengeance came swiftly. On 16 October, the delegates of OPEC's six Gulf states released their first bombshell: a 70 per cent increase in the posted price of oil, which now reached a record $5.11 a barrel. It was the first time they had set the price without bothering to consult the world's major oil companies, among them the part-British firms BP and Shell. 'The moment has come,' remarked the Saudi oil minister. 'We are masters of our own commodity.'[43]

It is a complete myth that the oil shock of late 1973 was a surprise, breaking like thunder in an untroubled blue sky. In fact, the papers had been predicting it for months, even years, and the OPEC nations had actually secured their first price increase two years before, reflecting not only the new self-assertion of the post-colonial Arab world, but the fact that greedy Western consumers were guzzling more oil than ever before – 44 million barrels a day by 1970 – while trying to sell the Arabs manufactured goods at rapidly rising prices. What is more, the notion that the Arabs kept their monopoly of oil hidden up their capacious sleeves as a kind of secret weapon is utter nonsense. As early as 1971, Heath himself had told the West German Chancellor Willy Brandt that if there was another war between Israel and the Arabs, then OPEC might cut oil supplies to the West. A year later, officials at the Department of Trade and Industry predicted that a steep increase in the price of oil was bound to happen soon, and in June 1973 Reginald Maudling warned the readers of the *Sunday Express* that conflict in the Middle East was bound to trigger a sharp increase in the near future. Indeed, the Arabs hardly made a secret of their intentions. In May 1973, Saudi Arabia's King Faisal publicly declared that the West must 'do something to change the direction that events were taking in the Middle East', or they would have to pay the price. And as late as September, he told American television that 'America's continued support of Zionism against the Arabs makes it extremely difficult for us to continue to supply the United States with oil'. The West could hardly say it had not been warned.[44]

What few had anticipated, however, was how savage the blow would be. Since Heath's government was regarded as friendly by the Arab world, Britain was spared a full embargo. Even so, the impact of the price hike as well as severe production cutbacks meant that the price of a barrel of oil surged from $2.40 in early 1973 to a staggering $11.65 by the end of the year – and this compared with just $1.80 at the turn of the decade. But Heath believed, with characteristic stubbornness, that Britain could escape the storm because of its connections to Shell and BP, of which it owned 40 per cent and 51 per cent respectively. A few weeks after the crisis began, he summoned Sir Frank McFadzean, the chairman of Shell, and Sir Eric Drake, his counterpart at BP, to a secret meeting at Chequers, and told them that they must not cut their supply to Britain, as they were doing elsewhere in the world. McFadzean pointed out that since Shell was 60 per cent owned by the Dutch, he could hardly give Britain preferential treatment. So Heath focused on Sir Eric Drake, not asking him but ordering him, as his majority shareholder, to do as he was told. Not for the first time, though, Heath had chosen his adversaries badly. A tough and blunt man, Drake had once been threatened with death in Iran, and had no intention of letting Heath 'destroy my company'. As he aggressively pointed out, if Britain insisted on preferential treatment, not only would BP's smaller shareholders sue the government, but its subsidiaries in France, West Germany and elsewhere would almost certainly be nationalized in retaliation. If Heath insisted, Drake said, 'then I must tell you that I must have it in writing. Then we can plead *force majeure* to the other governments because I'm under government instructions.' Heath hesitated: such a document, he knew, would destroy his relationship with his new European partners. 'You know perfectly well I can't put it in writing,' he snapped. 'Then I won't do it,' Drake said calmly.[45]

Heath's fury was understandable, because the oil crisis had the potential to destroy his economic ambitions; but it was impotent fury all the same. In the long run, the crisis was a watershed not just in British but in world history, the moment when globalization made itself felt, when the Western industrial powers realized that they could not have everything their own way, and when millions of ordinary families felt the shuddering impact of distant events hundreds and thousands of miles away. As a result of the price rise, the industrialized world faced a bill for more than $70 billion a year on top of what they were paying already.

And with oil at almost $12 a barrel, the Western economy plunged almost overnight into a nightmarish combination of recession and inflation, 'stagflation', amounting to the worst global downturn since the Second World War. For Heath, it was the worst possible news, and there was no silver lining. *The Economist* estimated that the cost in imports would add an extra £1.8 billion to the balance of payments deficit in the next twelve months, while the inflationary effect would be as if the entire country had awarded itself a pay rise of 15 to 20 per cent. And with prices increasing, Heath's own policies guaranteed that wages would rise too, thanks to Stage Three's threshold payments, which were triggered eleven times in the next few months. 'I realised very quickly', said Anthony Barber, 'that all we'd been trying to achieve was really coming to an end.'[46]

But it is also a myth that the oil shock was always bound to bring doom and disaster in its wake. In the United States – which was punished even more severely than Britain, because of its support for Israel – the Nixon and Ford administrations managed to weather the economic blizzard without plunging the economy into a devastating bout of inflation, and although there was a prolonged and painful recession, the American economy was in recovery by early 1976. But coming after three draining years of industrial conflict, pay restraint and rhetorical class warfare, the oil shock brought out the very worst in British politics. What was more, it exposed all the weaknesses of Heath's economic policies: the wishful thinking, the reckless spending, the naive faith in rational bureaucratic solutions. And it handed power to the one group of workers that Heath most dreaded seeing again in the headlines: the miners. Only months earlier, Joe Gormley had promised the NUM conference that 'never again will we say we shall be more loyal to the country than to our members'. With the country desperate for energy, the miners found themselves in a position of unprecedented power – and they intended to use it.[47]

14

We Hate Humans

Wednesday, 17 October 1973: a cool, damp evening in north-west London as the players of England and Poland lined up in the tunnel for their decisive World Cup qualifier. In an era when few football matches were shown on television, it was a testament to the importance of the game that not only were the BBC broadcasting it live to millions of nail-chewing English fans, but a global audience potentially reaching 200 million people was expected to tune in. Wembley had been sold out for weeks, and as the players' studs clattered in the stadium tunnel they could already hear the mighty roar of the crowd, the needy, surging chants of '*England, England*'. The camera panned across the gum-chewing faces as the line of blue tracksuits began the long march out into the arena, their features taut with tension: Martin Peters, the captain and hero of 1966; Peter Shilton, the impossibly athletic young goalkeeper; Roy McFarland, the cultured centre back who had replaced Bobby Moore as leader of the back line; the dynamic combination of Allan Clarke,

Mick Channon and Martin Chivers in attack, a riot of sideburns and goals. In the corner of the screen, a grey-haired man in a fawn raincoat slipped past almost unnoticed, impassive and self-contained. Some said Sir Alf Ramsey, the mastermind behind England's World Cup victory seven years before, was behind the times. But Ramsey needed only this victory to take his country to the World Cup finals in West Germany.

As England dominated the early minutes, urged on by the roar of 100,000 fans, Ramsey sat motionless on the team bench, his face barely betraying a flicker of emotion as Mick Channon smacked the ball against the Polish post, or as Tony Currie thundered in a shot that seemed destined for the net until the Polish goalkeeper, Jan Tomaszewski, pawed it aside. On television beforehand, the outspoken Brian Clough – who had sensationally resigned only days before from Derby County – had told viewers that Tomaszewski was a 'clown'. But Ramsey, who had managed England for eleven years and knew better than to underestimate unknown foreign opponents, was not laughing. Nor were Ramsey's players as the Polish goalkeeper pulled off save after save, shrugging aside the congratulations of his defenders as though it were merely another day at the office. The pressure continued – by the end, England would have 26 corners to Poland's 2 – and still no goal came. Channon had a shot cleared off the line, a header clawed away; Clarke headed over; Colin Bell cracked in a shot that somehow, diving from nowhere, Tomaszewski touched wide. 'The night wore its jagged path away,' wrote the veteran football correspondent Geoffrey Green, one of a dying breed of highly literate sportswriters, 'amidst a wall of sound rising in layers from the 100,000 crowd while nervous cigarettes darted like fireflies in the night.'

There was just half an hour left when, at last, a goal came. Poland were packed into their own half, England pressing yet again, when Currie lost the ball on the right and it was swept on towards Gadocha on the Poles' left wing. 'Hunter's got to make that,' the BBC's commentator Barry Davies said, a hint of urgency in his voice as the Leeds defender moved to intercept – and then, suddenly: 'He's lost it! Gadocha is inside McFarland, Hughes trying to get back goal-side' – and as red Polish shirts flooded towards England's goal – 'Domarski coming up square, number ten' – and at that moment the Polish forward hit a low, scuffed shot that slipped through Shilton's despairing fingers, and in the blink of an eye England were behind. '*And it's there!*' yelled Davies, his voice shrill with horror. '*Hunter had to make that challenge, and he didn't succeed!*' On the pitch, the white-shirted players stared at the ground in disbelief. On the bench, Ramsey sat impassive, his face carved from stone. He made no move to change tactics, to bring on fresh legs, to gee up his players. He just sat there, calmly and quietly, as he always had.

England drew level six minutes later, Clarke coolly converting a penalty after Martin Peters had been pushed in the penalty area. But although shots continued to rain down on Tomaszewski's goal, the clock was ticking remorselessly down. Hunter had a fabulous chance when the ball broke to him on the edge of the Polish area, but again Tomaszewski was there to palm the ball away. With just two minutes left, Ramsey made his move, bringing on Derby's Kevin Hector for the misfiring Chivers. But it was surely too late. 'We move into injury and stoppage time,' exclaimed Davies above the din of the crowd. England threw in one last corner; Tomaszewski flailed desperately; the ball ricocheted towards the net, came back off a Polish defender, and at the back post Hector stretched – and poked it wide. And then, seconds later, the referee blew his whistle, and it was all over. As red shirts streamed towards the Polish bench in celebration, a photographer captured Norman Hunter, his face crumpled with disappointment, his eyes turned to the ground, his shoulders slumped in despair. 'We all sat in the dressing room afterwards and not a word was said,' Tony Currie recalled afterwards. 'Everyone was in shock.'[1]

Even in an autumn of inflation, bombings and strikes, there were few more compelling symbols of national decline than England's failure against Poland. Just seven years after the golden victory that had supposedly capped the youthful optimism of Harold Wilson's swinging Britain, England had failed even to reach the final stage of sport's most lucrative tournament. When Alf Garnett contemplated the disaster a few weeks later on *Till Death Us Do Part*, he was still trembling with anger at the base ingratitude of Britain's wartime allies. The World Cup, he spat bitterly, would be 'a laughing stock without England'. The press, meanwhile, was unforgiving. 'WE'VE HAD IT!' screamed the back page of the *Sun*, pointing the finger squarely at the manager. On television, Brian Clough held up a nail and quipped that he would like to hammer it into Ramsey's coffin. 'For Sir Alf I can find no excuse,' wrote Geoffrey Green in *The Times*; for 'as the minutes unwound, seemingly faster and faster, there he sat with his substitutes on the sidelines . . . immobile while his men on the field drained themselves of their last ounce of energy', like some sporting equivalent of the politicians who had fiddled as Britain's economic reputation went up in smoke. And like so many commentators in the decades to come, Green diagnosed a chronic failure of the English game, crippled by 'fear of defeat', a 'stagnant defence' and a fatal addiction to 'head-ball', and typified by 'the hoisting of high lobs into a penalty area' that resembled 'Piccadilly during the evening rush hour'. As the *Daily Telegraph* grimly put it, England had been 'relegated to a place among soccer's second-class powers'.[2]

The axe fell on Sir Alf Ramsey in April 1974. He had never been popular with senior officials in the Football Association, who treated him as little more than a hired servant, mocked his half-suppressed Dagenham vowels, and resented his popularity with the sporting public. 'He always referred to me, even to my face, as Ramsey, which I found insulting,' Sir Alf said later of Sir Harold Thompson, the notoriously autocratic Oxford chemist who dominated the FA's international committee. Despite his knighthood, Ramsey had been paid just £7,200 a year, less than some Third Division managers. That his pay-off was a derisory £8,000, with an annual pension of £1,200, was an indictment of the FA's snobbery and indifference. Even within the wider game, the conqueror of 1966 was seen as a remote, outdated figure; the only job offer immediately after his dismissal came from a boys' team in Leek, Staffordshire, which admitted it could afford neither pay nor expenses. By the 1980s, Ramsey had been condemned to the sporting equivalent of internal exile, spending his days in obscurity in suburban Ipswich, far from the football pitch or the television studio. It was a sad end to a career that had once epitomized the optimism of the affluent society, and that had seemed to run in parallel with Harold Wilson's rise to national fame. 'He should have resigned at the top,' the Labour leader's aide Bernard Donoughue remarked when they heard the news of Ramsey's dismissal. 'We all find that difficult to do,' Wilson said quietly.[3]

At a time when the headlines were dominated by reports of economic decline, social fragmentation and moral collapse, and when Britain seemed to be sinking beneath the tides of historical change, sport could often seem like the most trivial of distractions. Yet as the government itself put it when announcing new funding for elite athletes in 1975, 'success in international competition has an important part to play in national morale'. What it had recognized, and what would become even clearer in later years, was that almost nothing expressed a sense of national identity and common endeavour better than international sporting achievements. Thanks to television, not even the most stubborn sports-hater could ignore the annual ritual of the FA Cup Final, with its two-channel, all-day coverage, or the Derby, or the Five Nations, or the Boat Race, events that were woven into the nation's cultural fabric as deeply as *Coronation Street* and *Morecambe and Wise*. It was sport that helped to sell the *Mirror* and the *Sun*, sport that occupied the imaginations of millions of schoolboys, and sport that dominated conversation in pubs across the land.

Paradoxically, sporting attendances were in free fall, with crowds for football, county cricket and rugby league in deep decline since their heyday in the late 1940s – a result, above all, of the decline of Britain's collective working-class culture and the vast expansion of other leisure opportunities. But while television certainly had a deleterious effect on some sports – county cricket being an obvious example – it transformed others such as showjumping, snooker and darts, which proved un-expectedly successful on the small screen. And public interest, certainly in terms of television coverage and newsprint, remained enormous. The winners of the BBC's Sports Personality of the Year award, such as Jackie Stewart (1973), Virginia Wade (1977) and Sebastian Coe (1979), were immediately familiar and beloved figures; more controversial characters such as George Best, Geoffrey Boycott and Daley Thompson gave the tabloids plenty of material; and, thanks to television, overseas stars such as Pelé and Muhammad Ali loomed large in the popular consciousness. By some measures, indeed, this was a golden age for sport. Many of the leading lights came from outside England: in Billy Bremner, Danny McGrain and Kenny Dalglish, Scotland had footballers that their neigh-bours could only envy, while the Edinburgh swimmer David Wilkie not only won gold but broke the 200-metres world record at the Montreal Olympics. And in Wales, Carwyn James's gloriously flamboyant rugby side not only set standards that have never been bettered, but became the supreme expression of Welsh pride in an era of growing national self-consciousness. Thanks to Barry John, Gareth Edwards, Phil Bennett and J. P. R. Williams, the red-shirted warriors could plausibly claim to be the pre-eminent British sporting team of the decade – although the footballers of Liverpool and Nottingham Forest, who won back-to-back

European Cups between 1976 and 1980, might have disagreed.[4]

By now football had definitively displaced cricket as Britain's national sport, its place entrenched in the television schedules by *Match of the Day* and *The Big Match* and in the newsagents by *Football Monthly, Shoot* and *Match*. Although it had originally been the game of the working-class North and Midlands, its popularity had long since filtered through class and regional barriers. Within political circles, Harold Wilson was a keen Huddersfield Town fan, Anthony Crosland never missed a Saturday edition of *Match of the Day*, and Edward Heath had supported Arsenal since boyhood, later recording his pride that their manager Arsène Wenger based his transfer policy on 'my own principles of wide international co-operation'. He missed Arsenal's victory in the FA Cup final of 1971, which secured their first domestic Double, because he was sailing *Morning Cloud* in the Seine Bay race – but he did secure Wembley tickets for his father and stepmother to watch Charlie George's Double-winning rocket at first hand. 'Unlike Harold Wilson five years earlier, when England won the World Cup,' Heath rather tartly remarked in his memoirs, 'I saw no justification for claiming the credit.'[5]

In 1966, Wilson's keenness to associate himself with Ramsey's World Cup-winning side had reached ludicrous proportions. Before the World Cup final, he had even asked the BBC if he could appear at half-time to deliver his expert analysis, and after the game he milked the applause at the post-match banquet. Four years later, Wilson took the World Cup in Mexico so seriously that it became a genuine consideration in his election planning: during a Cabinet strategy meeting, he even told his ministers that he 'was now trying to find out at what time of day the match was played, because he thought that was a determining factor'. As Roy Jenkins later put it, Wilson had 'a theory of almost mystical symbiosis between the fortunes of the Labour Party and the England football eleven'. And when England's collapse against West Germany was followed a few days later by Labour's election disappointment, Wilson's theory seemed to be confirmed. The parallels were irresistible: the champions of 1966, apparently comfortably ahead, basking in sunny over-confidence, brought down at the last by the underestimated rivals they had beaten four years before. And just as many fans thought that England would have won if only their goalkeeper Gordon Banks had been fit, or if only Ramsey had not taken off Bobby Charlton, so many Labour supporters thought that Wilson would still be in Number 10 if only the election had been held a week earlier, or if only the economic picture had not been distorted by freakishly bad trade figures. In fact, the biggest factor was probably the revolt of the housewives, who cared more about rising prices than goal-line scrambles. But England's defeat, like Wilson's, had deeper roots than many supporters realized at the time – as became clear in the miserable years that followed.[6]

Not even a Prime Minister with Heath's abysmal presentation skills would have wanted to associate himself with the England team during the early 1970s. Loyal to a fault, Sir Alf Ramsey preferred to rely on the players who had served him in the past rather than introduce new blood, and refused to alter his cautious, compact tactics. When England ran out in April 1972 for the first leg of their European Championship quarter-final against (yet again) West Germany, eight of Ramsey's team had played in Mexico and five were survivors from 1966. Expectation turned to disaster, however, when the visitors recorded a comfortable 3–1 victory – a scoreline that actually flattered England. And perhaps more than any other sporting moment of the decade, it was this swaggering German victory on the sacred Wembley turf that summed up Britain's wider economic and political decline. In football as in economic management and labour relations, it seemed, the old country had fallen behind its Continental rivals. The West Germans had reinvented their game since 1966, wrote Brian Glanville in the *Sunday Times*, adopting 'a wonderfully flexible formation' with 'a high level of technique . . . flair and imagination'. But England had 'never taken that leap forward' – a diagnosis that might have been borrowed from an article comparing the two countries' public transport systems, car industries or trade unions. The English players had been outclassed, agreed the *Observer*, their 'cautious, joyless football' years behind the times. 'As is so often the case,' wrote Peter Wilson in the *Mirror*, 'we have been content to dwell in the past and rest complacently on past triumphs until events – and other nations – overtake and surpass us.'[7]

What really summed up the negative, introverted flavour of English football, however, was the second leg, played in West Berlin two weeks later. This time, Ramsey packed his team with defensive ball-winners and watched with grim satisfaction as they ground out a nil–nil draw. Played in driving rain, interrupted twenty-seven times by violent English fouls, the game seemed indelibly stamped with the spirit of national life in the strike-torn spring of 1972. Afterwards Ramsey's players dismissed their opponents as 'cry-babies', but most observers were appalled by England's brutal negativity. For the German media, England had betrayed their national reputation for fair play, while the British press was even more damning. England had played 'cynically and, at times, viciously', wrote a sorrowful Peter Batt in the *Sun*, while the *Telegraph*'s Donald Saunders recorded his admiration for the Germans' self-control in taking 'so much illegal punishment without retaliation'. 'I felt embarrassed and ashamed by the Englishmen's violent ugly methods,' wrote Alan Hoby in the *Sunday Express*. And to Ramsey's critics the game captured everything that was wrong with his approach to football. If England 'should suddenly "come good"', the result would be 'disastrous . . . because it would once again assert Ramsey's values as the ideal', argued *Foul!*, the first football fanzine, produced at the end of 1972 by two Cambridge students. 'The whole underlying philosophy of Ramseyism must go when its founder does: the sooner the better.'[8]

But the rot went much deeper than the insecurities of Sir Alf Ramsey, as the Centenary FA Cup Final, scheduled between England's two games against West Germany, proved only too well. Taking place exactly a hundred years after the Wanderers had beaten the Royal Engineers, it was supposed to be a celebration of English football, with representatives of past winners set to parade around Wembley and the Queen on hand to present the trophy. On paper, the match seemed a mouth-watering clash pitting the previous year's Double-winners, Arsenal, against Don Revie's Leeds United, the most consistently successful team in the land. In reality, it began with a bad foul after just five seconds, was marred by violent tackles throughout, and was a thoroughly drab and miserable occasion. Yet it could hardly have come as a surprise to anyone who regularly watched the national game. Despite the allure of the BBC's highlights show *Match of the Day*, the everyday reality was often negative, crude, over-aggressive football. In 1962, Alf Ramsey's supposedly dour Ipswich Town had won the First Division by scoring 93 goals in 42 games. Yet in 1972 Brian Clough's supposedly attacking Derby County won the title with just 69 goals. And Derby's triumph was symptomatic of a game in which goals were ever more scarce. Between 1964 and 1974, as managers adopted increasingly defensive tactics, the average number of goals scored in Division One fell by 30 per cent. 'In England,' the former Manchester City striker Rodney Marsh told an American audience in 1979, 'soccer is a grey game played by grey people on grey days.'[9]

English football in the 1970s was not all doom and gloom. For one thing, it was intensely, unpredictably competitive: between 1970 and 1981, seven different clubs won the league title, while ten different clubs won the FA Cup. That Sunderland, Southampton and West Ham won the Cup from the Second Division speaks volumes about the relative egalitarianism of English football in an age before gigantic television revenues. Meanwhile, English clubs were extraordinarily successful in Europe, their power and physicality proving too much for Continental opponents. Between 1968 and 1973, English teams won the UEFA Cup (or the Fairs Cup, as it was originally known) six years in a row, while between 1977 and 1984 they brought home the European Cup seven times in eight years. Scottish clubs were less successful: Celtic reached the European Cup final in 1970, losing to Feyenoord, while Rangers won the Cup Winners' Cup in 1972. But as many Scottish fans were quick to point out, most of their best players plied their trade south of the border: indeed, without the contributions of Billy Bremner, Peter Lorimer, Kenny Dalglish, Graeme Souness, John Robertson and Archie Gemmill, Leeds, Liverpool and Nottingham Forest would never have enjoyed such outstanding success.

For the young men who made their living playing football, the rewards were greater than ever. Thanks to Jimmy Hill and the Professional Footballers' Association, the maximum wage had been outlawed in 1961, and since then footballers' wages had steadily risen to match their celebrity status. When Hunter Davies spent the 1971–2 season with Tottenham Hotspur, he estimated that an established first-team player earned about £10,000 a year (perhaps £100,000 in today's money). Tottenham, however, were a notably rich and glamorous club, and most footballers earned rather less. The journalist Duncan Hamilton, who followed Nottingham Forest during their Clough years, reckoned that a typical footballer in the late 1970s earned £135 a week, almost double the average working man's wage. It was not enough to catapult them into the ranks of the super-rich, but it did mean that footballers enjoyed comforts their working-class parents could barely have imagined. And when the Tottenham players filled in Davies's questionnaires, the results were highly illuminating. Many already had business interests outside the game, owning pubs and garages, and they drove expensive cars: Martin Peters a Jaguar, Martin Chivers a Zodiac, Mike England a Capri, Joe Kinnear an MGB GT. They lived in large new mock-Georgian houses in Surrey and Hertfordshire, took their holidays in Majorca, Malta and Portugal, and spent their free time playing middle-class games like golf and tennis. Asked how they voted, eight said Conservative and only three Labour, with six not interested. Footballers were clearly proud of their newfound wealth and status, and in magazines like *Shoot* they were held up as exemplars of the new world of working-class affluence. So youthful readers were treated to photo-spreads of Mick Mills in tight tartan shorts mowing his suburban lawn, Geoff Hurst posing in a floral shirt 'on the terrace of his luxurious home in Chigwell, Essex', Jimmy Greenhoff cleaning 'the family's gleaming four-door Rover saloon', or an extravagantly permed Kevin Keegan showing off his 'country retreat' in North Wales. At times these articles seemed more interested in the appliances than their owners: a shot of Keegan mowing the lawn, for example, boasted a caption – 'Keeping my lawn in trim is dead easy, thanks to my high-speed motor mower' – that might have been an advertising man's dream. Beneath the consumerist pornography, however, old attitudes died hard: a picture of Keegan embracing his future wife carried the caption: 'A special hug for girlfriend Jean, who's made curtains and helped decorate the place. She's also cooked some smashing meals.'[10]

No club captured the tension between old and new better than the winners of the Centenary Cup Final and champions of 1969 and 1974, Leeds United. Once an obscure Second Division side, the team of Bremner, Lorimer, Giles and Hunter dominated English football like no other team in the early 1970s. Almost every season ended with them in pursuit of honours, yet they suffered from incredible bad luck, exacerbated, some said, by their over-competitiveness and insecurity. Between 1965 and 1975, Leeds were First Division runners-up five times, lost three FA Cup finals and two semi-finals, and lost a Fairs Cup final, a Cup Winners' Cup final and a European Cup final. Sometimes they were the victims of incompetent or crooked refereeing: in the 1972 Cup Winners' Cup final, for example, the Greek referee turned down several obvious penalties and was later alleged to have taken money from Leeds's opponents, AC Milan, while the referee in the 1975 European Cup final turned down yet another clear penalty and disallowed a perfectly good goal. But Leeds were also the victims of their own success. In the late spring of 1970, they were heavily favoured to secure an unprecedented treble of League, Cup and European Cup, yet were forced to play an exhausting nine games in twenty-two days and lost all three. Like Sisyphus, wrote

Geoffrey Green, they had 'pushed three boulders almost to the top of three mountains, and are now left to see them all back in the dark of the valley'. A year later, two points clear with four games left, they controversially lost at home to West Bromwich Albion after the referee allowed a blatantly offside goal, and promptly collapsed in the title race. And in 1972, having already won the Cup, their shattered players were forced to play their final league game just two days later. Victory would have secured the Double; once again, they managed to lose to Wolves, again in controversial circumstances. 'In this case injustice was not only done but seen to be done by everyone in a 53,000 gathering except the referee and the linesman,' Green wrote. 'Leeds are clearly not the darlings of the gods.'[11]

Since the fates so clearly had it in for Leeds's players, they might have been expected to benefit from a tide of public sympathy. Yet most football supporters outside Yorkshire loathed them. Even in an age of brutal tackling and posturing hard-men, Don Revie's side were regarded as ruthlessly unsporting, their sheer will to win often taking them over the boundaries recognized by fellow professionals. 'Don Revie's so-called family had more in keeping with the Mafia than Mothercare,' his rival Brian Clough once remarked. The veteran forward Jimmy Greaves recalled that he had 'the bruises on my memory' to remind him that playing Leeds was like trying to cross a minefield, and in the summer of 1973 the Football Association threatened them with a suspended £3,000 fine for 'persistent misconduct on the field of play'. Clough even claimed that Leeds should be relegated as a punishment for being the 'dirtiest club in Britain', a remark that would return to haunt him when he briefly succeeded Revie at Elland Road a year later. And although Revie's players cleaned up their act and played with greater freedom in their 1973–4 title-winning campaign, they never captured the neutrals' hearts. Even Revie admitted that his early success had been based on 'a rather defensive, physical style which made us probably the hardest team to beat in the League ... Once we got a goal I would light a cigar, sit back on the trainers' bench and enjoy the rest of the game, secure in the knowledge that it would need a minor miracle for the other side to equalise.' Perhaps, he went on, 'we did not exactly endear ourselves to the soccer purists ... but I had to be realistic'.[12]

Revie called it realism; others, however, saw it as a kind of neurotic insecurity, rooted in the Leeds manager's introverted psyche. In his classic book *The Football Man* (1968), Arthur Hopcraft described Revie as 'a big, flat-fronted man with an outdoors face as though he lives permanently in a keen wind'. It was a face that seemed to be wearing a permanent frown, as if Revie were constantly contemplating his own misfortune. When television pictures caught the Leeds manager glowering from the dugout in his supposedly lucky blue suit and sheepskin jacket, he looked like a man out of time, crippled by self-doubt, unable to shake off the fear of defeat. His superstitions were legendary. Not only did he pray on his knees every night, he arranged for a minister from Knaresborough to visit the players every week, carried a little statue of St John of the Cross in his blue suit pocket, took a rabbit's foot into the dugout, and made exactly the same walk to a nearby set of traffic lights before every home game, convinced that this would guarantee good luck. On the other hand, he regarded all feathered creatures as unlucky, banishing the club's peacock emblem from his players' shirts. Even as manager of England in the mid-1970s, he took football's spiritual side – such as it was – painfully seriously. 'I believe it will help you if you pray every night before you go to sleep,' he told his charges during an early meeting, 'and ask God to help you become better players.'[13]

Revie's fear of failure was rooted in the difficult circumstances of his boyhood. To the young footballers plying their trade in the mid-1970s, with their expensive cars parked outside their neat suburban homes, the Hungry Thirties seemed like ancient history. For Revie, however, they had left a mark that would never fade. Born in 1927 and brought up in a little terraced house in working-class Middlesbrough, he vividly remembered the privations of the Depression, when his father, a joiner, had spent years out of work. Middlesbrough in the 1930s was not a particularly happy place to grow up: J. B. Priestley memorably called it 'a dismal town, even with beer and football', the twin obsessions of many local men. And Revie's childhood was hardly the warm working-class upbringing of nostalgic stereotypes. When he was 12, his mother died of cancer, and four years later he moved to Leicester as an apprentice footballer. There he was known as a reserved, serious lad who never drank, never smoked and worked tirelessly to better himself. As a teenager, he had effectively missed out on family life; as a manager decades later, he was obsessed with turning Leeds into a surrogate family, where his players could feel loved. The players 'were his children ... and their children his grandchildren', one friend said later. 'Junior players are taught carefully about bank accounts, table manners and sex,' reported Arthur Hopcraft. 'There are regular homilies about keeping their hair short and their clothes smart and not getting caught up with loose girls.' Many other managers did the same thing; none, however, did it more passionately than Revie. He even called himself 'the head of the family', inadvertently earning the nickname 'The Godfather'.[14]

In his cultural conservatism, his fear of poverty, his respect for family values and his obsession with providing for his 'children', Revie reflected the values of a generation who could never quite bring themselves to trust in the abundance of the affluent society. Determined to re-create the family life he had never had, he invited his wife's mother, uncles and aunts to live in their large house, Three Chimneys, in middle-class north Leeds, while his son Duncan was sent to boarding school at Repton, something that would have seemed impossible when Revie was growing up. At the time, his obsession with money earned him the nickname 'Don Readies', while wags pointed out that his name was an anagram of the phrase *envie d'or*, the love of gold. Even when Revie was a player, friends had remarked on his financial ambition: the sign of success, he allegedly told one teammate, was 'how much you have got in the bank'. In the late 1970s, old enemies condemned him as greedy. But the key factor was surely not avarice but anxiety. Like many people who had known genuine poverty, Revie never felt satisfied, even once he had become a relatively rich man. And in many ways, despite his obvious conservatism, he was a pioneer. In the early 1970s his innovations at Leeds, from the players' choreographed salute to their personalized tracksuits and numbered sock-tags, were derided as mercenary gimmicks. Thirty years later, however, it was clear that they were simply ahead of their time.[15]

By an uncanny coincidence, Revie's fiercest rival and successor as Leeds manager was another Middlesbrough boy, born a few streets away in a nondescript council house in 1935, who had also played for Sunderland and England. Brian Clough's confidant Duncan Hamilton recorded that he 'hated Revie', and their animosity lit up television screens and tabloid back pages throughout the first half of the 1970s. Yet although they were often seen as direct opposites – Clough the flamboyant manager of upstart Derby, Revie the grim mastermind behind ruthless Leeds – they had a great deal in common. Clough was just eight years younger than Revie, although his rebellious temperament, such a stark contrast with the older man's conservatism, made the gap seem much wider. Like Revie, he had grown up in poverty. Like Revie, he was constantly agitating for pay rises. Like Revie, he was ultimately accused of crossing the line between financial shrewdness and outright corruption. Clough 'was obsessed with money', Duncan Hamilton wrote, 'as if he feared he might wake up one morning and find himself a pauper again ... He would read out to me the salaries of other people – players, managers, pop and film stars, politicians – if he came across them in a newspaper.' This was not 'purely greed', Hamilton thought, but 'a form of self-protection'. For as Clough once told him, 'the only people who aren't obsessed with money are those who have got more than enough of it'. These were the values not only of football managers born in the 1920s and 1930s, but of millions of newly affluent Britons who had broken out of working-class poverty in the decades after the war. They were values that helped to drive the new conservatism from the mid-1970s onwards, but they also inspired much of the trade union militancy of the period: the desperate desire to fight off the encroaching forces of inflation and unemployment, to cling on to the hard-won indicators of status, in a never-ending struggle against social and economic insecurity.[16]

In many ways, Clough's public persona, like Revie's, was a way of banishing the anxieties rooted in their shared background. The difference was that Clough's personality – boastful, bombastic, witty and loquacious – was far better suited to the populist cultural climate of the 1970s, which is why he became such a star on television. At the time, many chose to overlook his more conservative opinions: his highly autocratic approach to management, his obsession with players' discipline, even his contempt for long hair, sportswomen and foreigners. What shone through was his sheer rebelliousness, from his outspoken attack on Juventus after they fraudulently knocked Derby out of Europe in 1973 ('cheating fucking Italian bastards') to his impulsive resignation later that year – a mistake, he later admitted, provoked by Derby's efforts to stop him hurling opinions around on television.[17]

In this respect, Clough was the managerial equivalent of that other football folk hero of the early 1970s, Manchester United's Northern Irish winger George Best, loved as much for his impish misbehaviour as for his good looks and stunning skill. Best, however, was clearly past his prime, having spectacularly failed to handle his sudden ascent to stardom. In 1968, Arthur Hopcraft had acutely observed that he was 'not fundamentally ostentatious; he is merely young, popular and rich by lower-middle-class standards'. It was only because footballers had until recently been paid like 'factory helots', Hopcraft thought, 'that Best and his contemporaries look so excessively and immodestly affluent'. But when he revised his book three years later, his verdict had changed. Best's name, he wrote in the updated edition, was now synonymous with 'contempt for authority and heedless petulance'. His problem was not money; it was a terrible combination of celebrity, alcoholism and sheer self-indulgence, through which Best had 'come to represent almost every extreme in the modern footballer's lifestyle'.[18]

Although Best lived in a house worth £30,000 and made at least £25,000 a year, stratospheric earnings even by professional sportsmen's standards, his effectiveness and application were in rapid decline. In January 1972, after he had disappeared from Manchester United's training ground for an entire week, he was dropped from the team for the first time anyone could remember. The fact that the news made the front page of *The Times* spoke volumes about Best's celebrity status; a few days later, when the club ordered him to move back into digs with his boyhood landlady, the story again made the front page. With grim inevitability the decline continued. In May 1972, dropped by Northern Ireland after missing training (front-page news again), Best fled to Marbella and sold the story of his 'retirement' to the *Mirror* for £5,000, which he promptly invested in brandy-and-cokes for himself and his cronies. Although he subsequently returned to Old Trafford, he was manifestly out of control, and on New Year's Day 1974 he played his final game for Manchester United. When he turned up for the next game, said the club's manager Tommy Docherty, 'he was standing there pissed out of his mind and with a young lady'. That was the end: told he was no longer wanted, Best remained in the players' lounge, drinking tea and watching the horseracing on television. At the end of the season, United were relegated. England's most famous club would recover, but for the man once known as the Fifth Beatle, an embodiment of the youth and swagger of the 1960s, there remained only the sad decline into drunkenness, disease and degradation.[19]

The extraordinarily public nature of Best's collapse would have been inconceivable a few years before, when the game was still governed by the maximum wage and footballers were not yet treated like teenage pop idols. But while Best's talent and fame set him apart from his contemporaries, his was not an especially unusual story. Footballers had always drunk heavily, reflecting broader working-class habits. What was different in the early 1970s was not just the obsessive interest of the media, but the opportunities open to footballers thanks to their vastly increased spending power. To young men brought up in a world of increasing affluence, irreverence and individualism, the cautious, deferential values of Alf Ramsey and Don Revie seemed laughably old-fashioned. Attempting to motivate the talented but inconsistent Rodney Marsh before an England game in 1973, Ramsey warned him that he had 'to work harder', and that 'if you don't, I'm going to pull you off at half-time'. 'Christ,' Marsh replied under his breath. 'At Manchester City all we get at half-time is a cup of tea and an orange.' It was a story he told and retold in later years with deepening relish, but as the critic D. J. Taylor remarks, it marked a wide 'symbolic divide' between the serious-minded, intensely patriotic Ramsey 'and a new breed of mavericks more interested in soccer's rewards than some of its obligations'. It is almost impossible to imagine any of the players of the 1950s and 1960s speaking to Ramsey in such a way. But then it is also impossible to imagine them earning £15,000 a year in wages and another £15,000 in boot endorsements, deodorant adverts and personal appearance fees, as Marsh did in the early 1970s, or driving a Lotus Europa whose number plate appropriately contained the letters E, G and O.[20]

Best and Marsh were typical examples of a new breed of football stars in the early 1970s, self-styled entertainers who seemed more interested in making money and modelling clothes than in knuckling down, playing for their country and winning trophies. It is a myth that they were persistently overlooked by the England management: Sheffield United's playmaker Tony Currie, for example, won seventeen caps, played in the dramatic draw with Poland in October 1973, and might have won more caps had he not been crippled by injuries. But the careers of other talented players – not just Marsh, but Stan Bowles, Peter Osgood, Alan Hudson, Charlie George and Frank Worthington – were conspicuous for their sense of waste and disappointment. In an era when young men were much less likely to take orders from their seniors, they were unable to cope with the temptations of affluence and the pressures of celebrity. Alan Hudson, for example, broke into the England team in March 1975, played superbly against West Germany, and then pressed the self-destruct button by drinking heavily after an Under-23 game in Hungary, defying a direct warning from the England manager. But Hudson's intake of vodka, brandy and beer was just as illustrative of football's new affluence as was Frank Worthington's *Jason King*-style outfit when he arrived for his first trip abroad with England: a lime-green velvet jacket, a red silk shirt, leather trousers and high-heeled cowboy boots. When Ramsey caught sight of him, he turned pale with shock. His assistant Harold Shepherdson insisted that the young man walking towards them could not possibly be Worthington, because no young England player would ever turn up in such garish attire. But Shepherdson had been born during the First World War. Like many of his generation, he no longer understood how affluent young men thought and behaved.[21]

During the 1960s, Manchester United had been the most glamorous sporting institution in the country, its romantic appeal strengthened by the terrible Munich air disaster and the heart-warming story of Sir Matt Busby's long march from the brink of death to capture the European Cup. By the summer of 1974, however, Britain's best-supported club found itself in desperate straits. Since Busby's retirement, United had already sacked two promising young managers, and although the voluble Scot Tommy Docherty promised to restore the club's fortunes, George Best's outrageous misbehaviour had left a devastating hole in the team's morale. With two games of the season left, United teetered on the brink of the unthinkable: relegation to the Second Division. And as luck would have it, their last home game, on 27 April, was against their high-flying neighbours, Manchester City – their attack now led by the Scottish striker Denis Law, formerly the embodiment of United's attacking flair during the Busby years.

That it was Law who effectively condemned United to relegation, his back-heeled finish trickling into the net with only minutes remaining, seemed almost predictable. But it was what happened next that crowned Old Trafford's day of shame. 'Immediately the crowd were on the pitch,' wrote Tom Freeman in *The Times*, 'not from the Stretford End, where the United supporters were tightly packed, but from the more thinly populated opposite end. Seconds later they were joined by the crowds flooding on from the Stretford End.' With the players dashing for the safety of the tunnel, the game was halted; then, a few minutes later, after the pitch had been cleared, it restarted. But within moments the referee stopped it again, 'with the crowds once more surging onto the field, fights breaking out all over the terraces, and one goal partly obscured by smoke from a fire'.

Then came what Freeman described as 'the saddest moment' of the debacle, as the amplified voice of Sir Matt Busby echoed across the pitch, begging the invaders to disperse. 'For the sake of the club,' he said desperately, but they took no notice. 'Here was a man who had made Manchester United one of the greatest club sides in the world, and who had led them to a series of unprecedented triumphs', Freeman wrote sadly. 'Now, his team already doomed to second division football, he was faced with the additional ignominy of appealing to thousands of hooligans to avoid the disgrace of having the match abandoned and the ground closed for a long period next season.' But it was no good; in the end, the match was abandoned. 'Most of us left Old Trafford', Freeman concluded, 'with a feeling of despair, not only for the future of Manchester United, but the future of football itself. For let us face it. The abandonment at Old Trafford was just another example of the way the mobs can influence the outcome of matches these days.'[22]

One of the most depressing things about what had happened at Old Trafford was that nobody was surprised. Unlike many clubs, Manchester United commanded a considerable travelling following, nicknamed the 'Red Army' or 'Stretford Enders', including hundreds of young working-class fans from small towns and suburbs whose own local teams could not compete with United's prestige. 'They are mainly unskilled or unemployed and migrant young workers, social misfits, and plain soccer fanatics,' two academics wrote rather dismissively in the early 1970s, noting that they were 'as proud of the image they have foisted on the rest of youth as being "the best fighters in the land" as they are of following a famous team'. By this point the Red Army already had an unenviable reputation for causing trouble, especially when they visited the capital. When United played Arsenal in the spring of 1972, a thousand fans with red scarves marched north from Kings Cross and 'broke windows, smashed up cars, threw rocks and swore at passers-by'. By nightfall, the academics wrote, 'the Stretford End had not only "taken" the North Bank, but the whole of this part of North London', an achievement that won them yet more admiration from disaffected youngsters on London's estates.[23]

As the team's fortunes deteriorated, so did the behaviour of its fans. By May 1974 the *Mirror* had placed the Stretford Enders at the top of its 'League of Violence', naming United as 'the team whose visit is most dreaded'. After the pitch invasion that greeted the team's relegation, the club erected a massive steel fence across the Stretford End; unfortunately, this only added to the 'prestige' of United's hooligans. The fence had made the Stretford End 'a kind of academy of violence, where promising young fans can study the arts of intimidation', reported the *Observer* in December 1974. 'It resembles the sort of cage, formidable and expensive, that is put up by a zoo to contain the animals it needs but slightly fears. Its effect has been to make the Stretford terraces even more exclusive and to turn the occupants into an elite.'[24]

The comparison with a zoo was not unfair: the fans themselves used to chant 'We Hate Humans'. And a year later, as Tommy Docherty's revitalized side took the Second Division by storm, so the Stretford Enders conducted a campaign of terror across provincial England and Wales. In September, hundreds of extra policemen had to be drafted in to keep the peace when United visited Cardiff. In January 1975, enraged supporters smashed shop windows and overturned cars after their team's defeat to Norwich; in April, they caused yet more trouble during a game away at Notts County. And after Manchester United won promotion to the First Division, the fans celebrated in predictable style. In their very first match, away at Wolverhampton, fourteen people were stabbed, local businesses suffered thousands of pounds' worth of damage, and eighty-six United supporters were arrested after an afternoon of mayhem. 'We have seen nothing quite like it,' a West Midlands police spokesman said sadly. 'It must have been bottling up inside them all through the long, hot summer.'[25]

Football grounds were far from pleasant places to be in the 1970s. 'They are hideously uncomfortable,' wrote Arthur Hopcraft. 'The steps are as greasy as a school playground lavatory in the rain. The air is rancid with beer and onions and belching and worse. The language is a gross purple of obscenity.' When the crowd surged after a shot, he noted, 'a man or boy, and sometimes a girl, can be lifted off the ground in the crush . . . and dangled about for minutes on end, perhaps never getting back to within four or five steps of the spot from which the monster made its bite'. In these conditions, it was a miracle that more people were not badly injured or killed. But disaster was always lurking in the shadows. At Ibrox in January 1971, sixty-six Rangers fans, many of them children, were crushed to death when barriers collapsed after the Old Firm derby. At the time there were plenty of fine words from FA officials and Cabinet ministers about the need for more safety measures. But as the decade progressed, with clubs' revenue threatened by inflation and falling attendances, it became clear that this was just talk. Most grounds were grim, dilapidated places, the paint peeling, the stands rusting, the terraces stained with urine, rainwater and even the blood of those supporters caught up in the game's growing culture of violence. When Reginald Maudling told clubs that they had a 'right and duty' to keep troublemakers out of their grounds, it was symptomatic of the general defeatism that the Arsenal secretary claimed it would be 'quite impracticable' to do so. 'Football wasn't just out of kilter with fashion,' the journalist Duncan Hamilton wrote later. 'It was regarded as faintly repellent, like a sour smell,' a crude, primitive pastime played by long-haired yobs and watched by the dregs of society, a game whose supporters were more likely to end up with a knife between the ribs than to see a genuinely exciting sporting occasion.[26]

In later years, football hooliganism was sometimes associated, quite wrongly, with Thatcherism. In fact, it had first become a major public concern during the 1960s, the last years of buoyant growth and full employment. Even before the 1966 World Cup there were fears of crowd trouble, with stories describing Saturday afternoons 'somewhere between the storming of the Bastille and a civil rights march in Alabama', and accounts of court cases in which skinny youths from Liverpool or Manchester pleaded guilty to possession of flick-knives or kicking policemen. Violence was particularly common at games in London, partly because the capital had eleven league clubs, but also because its transport links made it easy for visiting fans to attend games but hard for the authorities to police them. And by the end of the 1960s many of the familiar ingredients of football hooliganism were already present, including the phenomenon of end-taking, which involved visiting fans fighting for control of the ends usually reserved for the keenest home supporters. In January 1970, for example, sixty-one people ended up in hospital, fourteen of them with serious injuries, when Leeds fans 'took' Stoke City, and a few months later the FA advised clubs to install small fenced 'pens' to control visiting fans.[27]

Perhaps the decisive moment in public perceptions of football violence came in September 1969. Returning from Derby, where their team had been thrashed 5–0, five hundred Tottenham fans ran amok on their special train, smashing up fixtures and fittings, hurling furniture out of the windows and repeatedly pulling on the emergency cord, which automatically triggered the brake and risked causing a crash. By the time the train had reached Bedfordshire, the driver had had enough. Passing through the village of Flitwick, he slowed the train to a halt and refused to move until the fans were kicked off. Scores of local police rushed to the scene and managed to force the fans out of the carriages, but then they somehow lost control. The next thing anybody knew, hundreds of fans were off on what a reporter called 'a stone-throwing spree, terrorizing villages, smashing windows, and attacking cars', as though the Visigoths had descended on rural Bedfordshire. As luck would have it, many residents were at a wine-and-cheese party in Flitwick's village hall; alarmed by the noise, they rushed out to find themselves in a re-enactment of the sack of Rome. Some took refuge in the local pub while the battle raged outside; others tried to defend their homes, not unlike Dustin Hoffman's character in the film *Straw Dogs*. Although the police finally regained control, the evening sent a powerful message that 'hooliganism was quite capable of moving into anyone's back garden'. The government immediately announced new measures to fight disorder, and one newspaper even ran the headline 'Home Office Acts To End Football Hooliganism'. But hooliganism was far from beaten, and the Battle of Flitwick was just a taste of the horrors to come.[28]

In the 1970s and 1980s, football hooliganism became a staple topic of Sunday supplement journalism and second-rate sociological studies. Some writers, treating football fans like some bizarre Amazonian tribe, devised elaborate anthropological classifications, tracing the hooligan's 'career development' from 11-year-old 'Novice' to adolescent 'Rowdy' and hard-case 'Nutter'. In fact, even during the worst years of hooliganism the common stereotypes were misleading: most fans were not hooligans, while most violence was disorganized, drunken and largely symbolic. And yet, behind all the sociological waffle about rituals and subcultures, hundreds of people were seriously hurt and some lost their lives. The disasters at Heysel and Hillsborough in the 1980s were often blamed on police and officials, but they would never have happened without the climate of fear and violence created by hooliganism. Indeed, the surprising thing is that more people were not killed, especially given the kinds of weapons being taken to games. On Arsenal's North Bank, some fans carried a terrifying array of hardware, 'from meat-cleavers and sharpened combs to knuckle-dusters studded with broken razor blades'. And during Hunter Davies's season with Tottenham, one game was nearly abandoned when steel staples were fired at a visiting goal-keeper from a catapult.[29]

Indeed, these weapons were not just for show. On Saturday, 24 August 1974, English football recorded its first murder, when 18-year-old Kevin Olsson was stabbed to death during Blackpool's clash with Bolton. At the same game, two Bolton fans – neither the killer – were arrested for carrying knives, while another was fined for carrying a 4-foot sharpened wooden stake. In Manchester, another fan was arrested for wielding a carving knife during a fight at Piccadilly station. Yet there was no shortage of commentators who insisted that hooligans should be pitied rather than punished. 'The malaise is not in the adolescent, whose male aggression is innate and biologically healthy, but in our urban society which fails to provide a socially advantageous outlet for a natural force,' one John Cole of Oxford wrote to *The Times*. Hooligans would be forced to misbehave, he explained, until society met 'their innate biological needs for a gang, a territory and a goal that they can achieve'. Not unpredictably, he was an Anglican vicar.[30]

For observers on the political right, football hooliganism, like other social ills, was ultimately a product of the permissive society, its perpetrators mollycoddled by liberal parents, progressive teachers and profligate politicians. Football violence, Norman Tebbit once said, was a result of 'the era and attitudes of post-war funk'. But this explanation had serious problems. Since most hooligans were unskilled or unemployed manual workers – labourers, bouncers, bricklayers, factory workers and so on – they were precisely those people *least* likely to have grown up with liberal, indulgent parents, while their own values were decidedly non-permissive. What was more, hooliganism had a very long history. 'Across the centuries,' wrote the historian Geoffrey Pearson in 1983, 'we have seen the same rituals of territorial dominance, trials of strength, gang fights, mockery towards elders and authorities, and antagonism towards "outsiders" as typical focuses for youthful energy and aggressive mischief.' The 'modern football rowdy', he thought, was simply 'a reincarnation of the unruly apprentice, or the late Victorian "Hooligan"', or even the 'hostile factions at the theatres and hippodromes in Byzantine Rome and Constantinople'. Even in the supposedly staid and orderly 1950s, football violence was not unknown. 'Trains, carrying rampaging young fans, would end their journeys with windows broken, upholstery smashed, lavatory fittings broken, the carriages running with beer and crunching underfoot with broken glass like gravel,' wrote Arthur Hopcraft – a vision of Harold Macmillan's Britain very different from the cosy caricatures becoming popular two decades later.[31]

On the left and in academic circles, a popular explanation was that football hooliganism was a moral panic fuelled by the press, who had 'invented hooliganism as a "social problem"' by drawing attention to 'relatively minor acts of rowdyism'. It is certainly true that from about 1967 onwards, the popular newspapers, fighting desperately for circulation in an increasingly competitive market, adopted a much more sensationalist attitude to football violence, with the *Sun* and *Mirror* leading the way in banner headlines and military metaphors. 'Thugs' and 'louts' were regularly 'marching to war', 'on the warpath' or 'preparing for battle', while potentially troublesome matches were previewed with almost gleeful pessimism. Before one game in November 1967, for example, the *Mirror* reported that 'Oldham's young fans have already been told to stand by for major trouble from Stockport supporters when the clubs meet' – which inevitably meant that fans arrived at the game spoiling for a fight. And by September 1974 the *Mail*, like the *Mirror*, was running a 'Thugs' League', which was supposed to shame clubs into cleaning up their act but probably had the opposite effect. 'Chelsea, London's soccer violence champions for two years running, are in line to land the hat-trick,' one report began, noting that they 'share the lead with West Ham in Scotland Yard's league of violence'. On occasions the press even reported hooligan clashes as though they, not the action on the pitch, were the real sporting story: when Manchester United visited Cardiff in September 1974, previews of 'Cardiff v United' referred to the violence, not the football. Papers even had their favourite villains, with the hated Stretford Enders at the foot of the list. When fighting broke out at the West Ham–Manchester United game in October 1975, the press cast West Ham's hooligans as 'avenging angels' dealing out a hard lesson. 'The Day The Terrace Terrors Were Hunted Like Animals and *Hammered*!' roared the *Sun*'s triumphant headline.[32]

Blaming the press for 'inventing' hooliganism, though, is not very convincing. As the historian Richard Holt points out, interviews with hooligans provided no evidence that they had learned 'how to behave from the papers'. And the common academic claim that 'alarmist' columnists 'distorted the scale and seriousness of the incidents' seems downright deluded given how many people were seriously hurt at football matches. The anthropologist Desmond Morris even insisted that hooliganism was nothing more than 'ritual rudeness' with 'little or no bloodletting', which would have come as scant consolation to the families of those injured, blinded or killed, or to the innocent passers-by caught up in the fighting. And the other fashionable explanations of the 1970s and 1980s are equally unsatisfying. Left-wing commentators often liked to quote the FA secretary Ted Croker's remark that the troublemakers were not football's hooligans, but Mrs Thatcher's hooligans, the implication being that their violence flowed from working-class unemployment and inner-city decline. But this is clearly nonsense. Many hooligans came from small towns and suburbs, not big cities, while violence first became a major social problem during an era of almost full employment. Even in the Thatcher years, many hooligans came from the booming Southeast of England and had steady jobs: a Thames Television survey of 140 members of West Ham's 'Inter City Firm' found four chefs, three electricians, three clothes-makers, six motor mechanics, two solicitors' clerks, a landscape gardener and an insurance underwriter – people for whom violence was hardly some kind of protest against modern economic conditions.

Hooligans themselves often reacted with horror and contempt when they came across academic arguments that their actions were a form of insurgency against bourgeois ideology. 'All we are going for is a good game of football; a good punch up and a good kick up,' one bemused fan told an interviewer from the BBC's *Panorama*. And after watching a panel of self-styled experts on a television show in the early 1970s, one young Arsenal fan put it very nicely. 'Well, there was this geezer sitting there who thought he knew all about it, but he didn't know nothing if you ask me,' he said (and it would be fun to know which academic expert he had in mind). 'He was going on about soccer hooligans and how they carry on down the ends, and he says, well, it's all because they don't like the middle classes taking over the game.' But the Arsenal fan was having none of it. 'Anybody who ever been down the North Bank'll tell you they don't give a sod for all the students and all the other wankers and pooftas that turn up,' he said. 'They never go down the end anyway, they're too scared. All the North Bank care about is their team and the other end and that's all there is to it.'[33]

The obvious explanation for the surge in football hooliganism in the early 1970s is very simple. As the heirs to a long tradition of adolescent gangs, tribal aggression and general mischief-making, football crowds had always had the potential for violence. Until the 1960s, however, this potential was contained by the fact that there were very few away fans and, crucially, that football crowds contained thousands of older men, including the fathers and grandfathers of the youngsters present. Fans went to games in family, neighbourhood or factory groups, standing beside people they knew, with youthful high jinks effectively controlled by married men who had no desire to get involved in a mass punch-up. Interviewed in the 1980s, fans who remembered those days often pointed out that while there was plenty of banter and bad language, teenagers who stepped out of line were given 'a bloody good hiding' by their fathers. But once working-class supporters began to share in the fruits of affluence, the composition of the crowds changed. Married men stayed at home, tinkering with their cars, taking their wives shopping, or going out for drives and day-trips, instead of automatically going to the match. Between the early 1950s and the early 1980s, football attendances fell by half, mirroring similar declines in pubs, churches, music halls and cinemas. Remaining older fans moved to the seats, leaving the cheaper terraces – the 'ends' – to young, unskilled manual workers who had nobody to supervise them. And as more fans travelled to away games, the process of segregation became self-reinforcing. Older men stayed away from areas where there might be trouble; young men took over and began to enjoy the violence for its own sake, a ritualized display of masculine aggression that began to eat into the game like a cancer. It was not poverty that opened the door to hooliganism; it was affluence.[34]

By 1975 it was obvious to all but a handful of sociologists that football hooliganism was out of control. Copying the Stretford Enders, other fans were now treating away games as an opportunity to run amok in railway stations, town centres and motorway service stations. Even the Cup Final was no longer sacred: after West Ham's victory over Fulham, celebrating fans invaded the pitch and tried to taunt their disappointed rivals into a fight. But worse was to come a few months later, when the 1975–6 season opened amid scenes of medieval savagery. The opening day alone saw Manchester United fans clashing with police in Wolverhampton, Nottingham Forest and Plymouth Argyle fans fighting on the pitch (undeterred by Brian Clough, who ran on to restrain them), and Sheffield United fans rampaging down the Southend seafront. But it was the last Saturday of August that marked the nadir. When Chelsea went three goals down in their Second Division game at Luton, enraged fans invaded the pitch, attacking players and officials, punching the Luton goalkeeper to the ground, and leaving one steward with a broken nose and another nursing stab wounds. After the final whistle, they ran wild in the streets, vandalizing cars and shops; on the journey home to St Pancras, they burned out one railway carriage, threw seats and toilet fittings out onto the track, and forced the guard to lock himself in to protect the mail. On the same day, fifty Manchester United fans were arrested after fighting broke out in Stoke, sixty Rangers fans were arrested outside Ibrox, and dozens of Liverpool supporters – giving the lie to their tiresome claim that they were only ever the victims of football disorder, never the perpetrators – set fire to the train carrying them home from Leicester, causing £70,000 worth of damage.[35]

'To travel to and from matches', lamented *The Times* two days later, 'is to run the gauntlet with these packs of marauding fiends as they terrorize the community at large.' Some observers called for drastic measures, emulating Brentford's chairman, who had carried out a citizen's arrest on one troublemaker during one of his team's home matches. British Rail scrapped their 'football specials' and withdrew their cheap long-distance tickets for Saturday travel, the Police Superintendents' Association suggested that fans under the age of 16 be banned from 'X-rated' games unless they were accompanied by an adult, and a judge told a dock full of QPR hooligans that he wished he could put them in the stocks. Meanwhile the government, as usual, announced its determination to beat the 'pathological thugs'; and, as usual, the disorder continued. In September, London's Tube and bus drivers even staged an unofficial strike merely to avoid carrying Manchester United fans to their game at QPR. And by the end of the following season, nobody was surprised by the violent pitch invasion that greeted Tottenham's relegation to the Second Division, the 'screaming young mob, several thousand strong, swarming like bees' into the main stand, the press room and the directors' box. By now, the movement towards caging fans like wild animals was irresistible. Officials had been talking of installing steel fences for years, but hesitated because of safety, cost and image concerns. Manchester United, though, had been ordered to install fences in the summer of 1974, and where they led others followed.[36]

As a purely domestic problem, hooliganism was bad enough. But what was even more disturbing was that it was beginning to spill over into

Europe. The potential for trouble had been obvious since 1967, when thousands of good-natured Celtic fans had descended on Lisbon for the European Cup final. As it happened, the match was a joyous occasion (although the Portuguese police were taken aback by the Scottish supporters' pitch invasion), but what it showed was that thousands of working-class fans now had the money and the means to follow their teams abroad. Five years later, when Rangers won their first European trophy against Dynamo Moscow in Barcelona, the scenes were rather less festive. Three times drunken fans invaded the field, and at the final whistle a pitched battle broke out between the Rangers supporters, wielding bottles and pieces of wood torn from the stadium, and the baton-wielding Spanish police, with 150 people being injured and one killed. The Rangers fans claimed they had been provoked; the president of UEFA, however, described them as 'savages', and the Lord Provost of Glasgow called them a disgrace to the city.[37]

But Scottish supporters certainly did not have a monopoly on violence overseas. When Tottenham arrived in Rotterdam for the second leg of their UEFA Cup final against Feyenoord in May 1974, some of the city's residents claimed they had seen nothing like it since the German occupation. The afternoon before the match, twenty-one English fans were arrested for looting a clothing shop and an off-licence, and even before kick-off the Tottenham chairman made a public appeal for supporters to behave. But it did no good. As soon as Feyenoord scored, the English fans 'erupted in hideous battle', ripping out their wooden seats and throwing them onto the field. The ensuing riot went on for some twenty minutes, quelled only by the intervention of more than 100 Dutch policemen, while over the public address system Tottenham's manager Bill Nicholson vainly appealed for calm. Afterwards, the scene was like some medieval battlefield; reports estimated that 200 people had been hurt, fifty were treated for wounds, several were in hospital with serious injuries, and one policeman was in a critical condition after being beaten with an iron bar. 'We were ashamed of our fans,' said Mike England, the Spurs captain, calling them 'disgraceful and disgusting'. The entire nation, said *The Times*, 'cannot but feel a sense of shame that the Dutch hosts were given such a bad example of British youth. It calls for something more than an apology.' The paper suggested that a group of Tottenham supporters might like to 'go over to Rotterdam to help clear up some of the mess at the stadium'. But of course that never happened.[38]

Working-class Middlesbrough boys, national icons and deadly rivals: Brian Clough prepares for an appearance on ITV's *The Big Match*, while Don Revie enjoys Leeds United's victory in the FA Cup semi-final, April 1972.

At a moment of supreme economic crisis, the miners' strike of February 1974 ripped the heart out of Heath's government.

Left, miners show off their completed strike ballots.

Below, the National Union of Students rallies in support of the NUM.

With Heath declaring a three-day week, Britain seemed on the verge of economic anarchy. Above, clerical workers at the Slumberdown firm wrap themselves in 'continental quilts' to keep warm. Below, commuters at Benfleet station in Essex find that their trains have been cancelled.

Forced into calling a general election, Heath asked the electorate to decide 'who governs'. Above, he addresses the nation for the final time in a party political broadcast. But the verdict was not what he expected: by 2 March 1974, a world-weary Harold Wilson was back as Prime Minister.

And so the awful saga went on. A year later, when Leeds controversially lost the European Cup final in Paris, their fans greeted each Bayern Munich goal with a hail of missiles. Before the game, German supporters had been attacked in the streets and a supermarket looted; now, as metal seats cascaded onto the field, a French policeman and a ball-boy were knocked unconscious, a photographer had his arm broken, and a German cameraman was blinded in one eye. The final whistle was the cue for more carnage; one of the troublemakers turned out to be a junior official at the British Embassy, who was sent home for throwing a moped through a chemist's window. In the circumstances, it was hardly surprising that UEFA banned Leeds from European competition for four years. It was 'the end of a decade of glory and greatness', said the *Sun* sententiously.[39]

But this was by no means the end of the cycle of violence. Disorder had now become an inevitable part of the fabric of the game, no longer making the headlines unless it was particularly brutal. When Liverpool reached the European Cup final in Rome in 1977, for example, it was as though the Vandals had returned to the Eternal City. 'Noisy, aggressive, arrogant and drunk, swarming all day through the streets of the city centre, the Liverpool fans stopped cars, molested girls, commandeered the Trevi Fountain and the Piazza di Spagna, swept through the city with bottles of wine or beer glued to their lips, defecated in the gardens, urinated in the streets,' reported *La Repubblica*. But the British press barely seemed to notice, and the disorder had no major consequences. In an age when attendances were falling and the middle classes remained wary of the self-styled people's game, there was little scope for the kind of radical modernization that eliminated hooliganism twenty years later.[40]

No doubt very few of the French and Dutch shopkeepers who suffered at the hands of British hooligans would have agreed that they represented a radical subculture, a healthy challenge to the bourgeois order, or the latest flowering of a hilariously mischievous Hogarthian tradition. Instead, they represented perhaps the darkest blot on the national escutcheon in a decade when Britain's image abroad had rarely been worse, and yet another symbol of the growing coarseness, disorder and violence that many felt had overtaken everyday national life. To horrified observers both at home and abroad, it was as though some corruption had infected the very soul of the national game – a disease from which, it turned out, not even England's football figurehead was immune.

*

When Sir Alf Ramsey was sacked as manager of England in April 1974, *The Times* predicted that his replacement would be found among the younger managers 'of the modern track suit set'. But on the fourth day of July the front pages broke the astonishing news that Don Revie – unquestionably the most qualified manager in the land – had been lured from Leeds by a record salary of £20,000 a year, more than twice Ramsey's earnings. In a statement, Revie characteristically remarked that he had 'tried to build the club into a family, and there must be sadness when anybody leaves a family'. The allure of managing his country, though, was impossible to resist, and like Edward Heath, Revie presented himself as a dynamic new broom, bringing the bracing smack of modernity after years of stagnation. In typical fashion, the first thing he did as England's manager was to negotiate improved bonuses for the players. Next, he announced that the rousing 'Land of Hope and Glory' would replace 'God Save the Queen' as the team's anthem, a populist touch designed to inspire the gloomy Wembley crowd. And in his first match against Czechoslovakia in October 1974 – football's equivalent of Heath's 'quiet revolution' – the fans duly responded, roaring out the words from their printed song-sheets as Revie's boys recorded a 3–0 victory.[41]

Revie's innovations did not end there. Reporters were wooed with drinks and sandwiches, a padded trainers' bench was installed at Wembley, and the FA arranged a groundbreaking new kit deal with Admiral, which later, quite unfairly, became a symbol of Revie's obsession with money. Yet within just a few months the clouds had begun to gather. Revie had set out to turn England into a club side, re-creating the family atmosphere that had worked so well at Leeds. But the enforced sessions of bingo and carpet bowls, as well as the ten o'clock curfew and detailed dossiers on forthcoming opponents, went down badly with established players used to more permissive regimes. Crucially, he could not decide on a settled side, partly because of his restless insistence on tinkering with the line-up, but also because key players such as Roy McFarland, Colin Bell and Gerry Francis suffered horrendous luck with injuries. In just twenty-nine games Revie used no fewer than fifty-two different players, some of whom – Phil Boyer, Tony Towers, Ian Gillard, Steve Whitworth – were decidedly obscure. He could not even decide on a captain, switching almost at random between Emlyn Hughes, Alan Ball, Gerry Francis, Kevin Keegan and Mick Channon. Yet the truth was that his indecision was largely forced on him. He dispensed with Ball, for example, only after the player's club, Arsenal, had already dropped him as punishment for insubordination – a sadly typical story of the mid-1970s.[42]

By the autumn of 1976 Revie's dream of modernization, like those of Wilson and Heath before him, was turning sour. With England's participation in the next World Cup hanging on a good result against Italy in Rome, he horrified commentators by making six changes to his team, including playing the defenders Brian Greenhoff and Trevor Cherry in central midfield. They promptly lost 2–0, making qualification highly unlikely. Revie's players were 'the worst England side I have ever seen,' said the Italian captain Giacinto Facchetti, noting that 'most surprising of all for a team for England, they seemed to have little heart for the battle'. As was becoming traditional on these occasions, the tabloids took the opportunity to lament the decline of the national game: the debacle was a 'failure of English football as a whole', said the *Mirror*, explaining that 'we have men who can run and chase, battle and work . . . but the Italians have men who can PLAY'. It was an impression confirmed by England's next game in February 1977, a friendly against Holland, who won even more comfortably than the 2–0 score suggested. More debacles followed: in May, England lost at home to Wales; in June, they lost at home to Scotland. With the pressure building, Revie seemed almost paralysed with indecision. 'You sensed his frustration,' Channon recalled. 'He would sweat through nerves. I don't think he could trust anyone . . . he thought everybody was going to do him.'[43]

As Henry Kissinger once remarked of Richard Nixon – whom Revie increasingly resembled – even the paranoid do have enemies. Like Ramsey before him, the England manager had incurred the displeasure of the acerbic FA chairman Sir Harold Thompson, who regarded him as little more than a jumped-up lackey. 'When I get to know you better, Revie, I shall call you Don,' Thompson once remarked at a dinner. 'And when I get to know you better, Thompson, I shall call you Sir Harold,' Revie replied, a rare flash of wit that was neither forgotten nor forgiven. Even before the defeats to Wales and Scotland, his head was on the block. On 30 May 1977, the day before England played Wales, Bernard Donoughue, a keen amateur footballer, had drinks with Ted Croker, the secretary of the Football Association. 'They are clearly thinking of sacking Don Revie,' Donoughue recorded afterwards. But Revie was no fool. A few weeks later, on tour with England in South America, he told Dick Wragg, the head of the FA international committee, that the job was bringing 'heartache' to his wife, and that he was certain he was about to be sacked. If the FA paid up the last two years on his contract, Revie said, he would quietly walk away. Stunned, Wragg insisted that there were no plans to sack him, while Ted Croker promised that he would be allowed to see out his contract. But Revie had long since lost faith in his employers. Unknown to them, he had made other plans.[44]

'Revie Quits Over "Aggro"', screamed an enormous headline on the front page of the *Daily Mail* on 12 July, unveiling the most sensational sporting exclusive of the decade. Inside, Revie announced that he was resigning as England's manager, a decision he had not yet shared with his employers at the FA. 'I sat down with Elsie one night and we agreed that the job was no longer worth the aggravation,' he explained. 'It was bringing too much heartache to those nearest to us . . . Nearly everyone in the country seems to want me out. So I am giving them what they want. I know people will accuse me of running away and it does sicken me that I cannot finish the job by taking England to the World Cup finals in Argentina next year. But the situation has become impossible.'

That Revie had chosen to reveal his decision through the *Daily Mail*, which paid a rumoured £20,000 for the exclusive, was shocking enough. But it was as nothing compared with the news that broke the following day. Revie was not walking away to join Manchester United, as some had suspected. Instead, he had already signed a gigantic £340,000 tax-free four-year contract to manage the United Arab Emirates. What was worse, he had negotiated the deal weeks before. Supposed to be watching Italy and Finland play in Helsinki, he had actually flown to Dubai, accompanied by the *Mail*'s Jeff Powell, to agree the new contract. The symbolism was unmistakable: just four years after the OPEC oil shock, the grainy photographs of the England manager, smiling awkwardly in his powder-blue suit beside the sheikhs in their dishdashas, hammered home the stunning reality of Arab wealth and British humiliation. Perhaps only if the Prime Minister had packed his bags, scribbled out his resignation and flown off to run the Saudi economy would the shock have been greater. 'It is impossible to escape the irony', said *The Times*, 'of the man who encouraged crowds to sing Land of Hope and Glory turning to seek his deserts in the desert.'[45]

As it happened, *The Times* was one of the few papers to show any sympathy for Revie. His task had been made impossible by a 'mediocre' crop of players and incredibly bad luck with injuries, wrote Gerald Sinstadt, while his apparent indecision 'in reality reflected the paucity of really outstanding individuals'. At a time of 'mounting disenchantment among critics, paid and unpaid', Revie had been offered 'a job which would guarantee in four years security for life. Which of us can say that, in that position, we would have made a different decision?' For a man who had known poverty on the streets of Middlesbrough and was obsessed with providing for his wife and children, the chance to become extremely rich almost overnight was simply too good to resist. The sheikhs' offer was 'an unbelievable opportunity to secure my family's future', Revie told the *Mail*, adding that the British 'tax structure, let alone the salaries available, makes it impossible to earn this kind of money at home'. These were not necessarily base or sordid motives. In any case, the FA were merely reaping what they had sown. Barely three years before, they had discarded Sir Alf Ramsey, the man who had won the World Cup, with the haughty cruelty of aristocrats dismissing a disgraced parlourmaid. They could hardly complain when his successor drew the obvious lesson.[46]

What Revie did not expect, however, was a chorus of execration based on the notion that he had 'betrayed' his country for 'a handful of shekels', as the tabloids insisted on putting it. 'Don Revie's decision doesn't surprise me in the slightest,' said his old enemy Alan Hardaker, the secretary of the Football League. 'I only hope he can quickly learn to call out bingo numbers in Arabic.' His defection was 'a pathetic capitulation to Mammon', wrote the *Daily Express*'s David Miller, while Revie's old rival Bob Stokoe, once the manager of Sunderland, claimed that he 'should have been castrated for the way he left England'. Above all, Sir Harold Thompson was furious at having been humiliated by a man so far beneath him that he did not even merit being addressed by his Christian name. On 28 July, the FA formally charged Revie with bringing the game into disrepute.

The case dragged on until December 1978 but was grotesquely biased, with Thompson, who had already savaged Revie in the press, serving simultaneously as witness, judge and prosecuting counsel. His decision – a ten-year suspension from English football – was predictably absurd, and Revie's solicitors promptly applied for justice to the High Court, the case being settled by Mr Justice Cantley in December 1979. But although Cantley had no choice but to throw out Thompson's verdict, he missed no opportunity to besmirch Revie's reputation. Ludicrously, he insisted that Thompson had showed himself an 'honourable man' (a view that even the FA's Ted Croker thought was 'very wrong') while Revie had 'presented to the public a sensational and notorious example of disloyalty, breach of duty, discourtesy and selfishness'. It was a verdict that chimed with the views of many tabloid commentators, but Revie's friends thought it spectacularly unfair. Cantley's opinion was 'one of the craziest things I have ever read', said Lord Harewood, the president of Leeds United and former president of the FA, who had testified on Revie's behalf. 'If he really thought that Sir Harold had behaved admirably and Don hadn't, then he is a very, very poor judge of character . . . He plainly disbelieved every word I said, but I don't give a bugger what he thought.'[47]

By this time, however, Revie's reputation had suffered a blow from which it never recovered. In September 1977, two months after he had walked out to join the UAE, the *Mirror* alleged that he had been fixing matches for years. It was not the first time there had been rumours of underhand dealings: in 1972, the *Sunday People* had claimed that Revie had offered three Wolves players £1,000 each to 'take it easy' in their title decider against Leeds. At the time, neither the FA nor the police had found any evidence of corruption, but the *Mirror* now claimed that Revie had used Mike O'Grady, a former Leeds player on Wolves' books, as a go-between. And there was more: the Wolves match, the *Mirror* insisted, was merely part of a broader pattern. 'Don Revie planned and schemed and offered bribes, leaving as little as possible to chance,' wrote the paper's chief reporter, Richard Stott. 'He relied on the loyalty of those he took into his confidence not to talk, and it nearly worked.'

Bob Stokoe claimed that in 1962 Revie ('an evil man') had asked him to forfeit a Second Division game when he was managing Bury. 'He offered me £500 to take it easy,' Stokoe said. 'There were no witnesses. I said no. And when I said no, he asked me if he could approach my players. I said under no circumstances.' And there were other shocking revelations. The former Manchester City manager Malcolm Allison claimed that Revie 'used to leave three hundred or four hundred quid in the referees' room, in an envelope', while Alan Ball claimed that during the 1960s Revie had sent him weekly £100 bribes, hoping to persuade him to move from Blackpool to Leeds. Most damaging of all, Revie's former goalkeeper Gary Sprake claimed that he had been a go-between in match-fixing operations against Wolves and Nottingham Forest. Since

Sprake had been paid £15,000 by the *Mirror* and later retracted his story after being ostracized by his old teammates, some dismissed his allegations. But years later, Sprake not only retracted his retraction, but made fresh accusations, claiming that in 1965 Revie had tried to get him to 'tap up' two fellow Welsh players before a crucial match with Birmingham on the last day of the season.

Revie's former players were unsurprisingly furious at the allegations that their beloved mentor had been cheating throughout his managerial career. When the *Sunday People* claimed that Revie had used his captain Billy Bremner as a go-between, Bremner sued and won £100,000. The winger Peter Lorimer, who remained devoted to Revie, insisted that 'if the boss tried to fix anything, we never saw it', and pointed out that the Wolves match at the centre of the storm had ended with a beaten Leeds missing out on the championship. As Revie's son Duncan later remarked, it was 'ludicrous' to imagine that Leeds triumphed by cheating, 'because they won for at least ten years'. The irony is that if Revie did cheat, he was not very good at it. After all, Leeds were notorious for narrowly missing out on glory, and the quality of his team was such that he hardly needed to fix games anyway. When the police and the FA investigated the *Mirror*'s story, neither found a case to answer, while Mike O'Grady claimed he had been misquoted and not one referee came forward to corroborate Malcolm Allison's bribery claims.

The truth is that, in the absence of hard evidence, it is simply impossible to know whether Revie was genuinely corrupt, or whether the stories were concocted by his enemies amid the hysteria that greeted his defection to the UAE. Only two things are clear. One is that Revie, cheat or no cheat, was a superb manager who built a magnificent team, suffered from extraordinarily bad luck and was unfairly pilloried for leaving a job from which he was probably going to be sacked anyway. The other is that plenty of people at the time *did* think he was corrupt. Malcolm Allison was not the only man in football convinced that Revie was 'crooked'. In September 1977, even before the *Mirror*'s allegations, Bernard Donoughue recorded having 'dinner with Ted Croker of the FA, who told me some alarming corruption stories about Don Revie, England team manager'. A month later, at a Downing Street lunch for the Prime Minister of Spain, Donoughue found himself sitting beside the former Manchester United manager Sir Matt Busby. 'More terrible stories about Don Revie', he noted afterwards. Of course this hardly proves the allegations – and yet it is surely revealing that both Croker and Busby believed them.[48]

No doubt many people would shudder at the thought of Don Revie as a symbol of British sport in the 1970s. It was, after all, a decade of heroes as well as villains: the figure skaters John Curry and Robin Cousins; the middle-distance arch-rivals Steve Ovett and Sebastian Coe; the tennis star Virginia Wade, whose Wimbledon victory in 1977 was the perfect curtain-raiser for the Queen's Silver Jubilee. But the fact is that, thanks largely to football hooliganism, sport was increasingly seen in terms of failure and corruption. This was, after all, a decade in which two of the country's most celebrated footballers, Billy Bremner and Kevin Keegan, were expelled from the Charity Shield match for fighting, and in which Manchester United sacked Tommy Docherty for an adulterous affair with the club physiotherapist's wife. It was also a decade of sensationally incompetent Olympic performances, the nadir coming in 1976, when Britain won a grand total of thirteen medals, finishing behind the likes of Poland, Bulgaria and Romania. In track and field, Britain won just one medal (a bronze), while David Jenkins, who went to Montreal as the world's number one 400-metre runner, contrived to finish seventh. His was merely one among many failures that made the 1970s, by and large, a decade of sporting disappointment. 'When a fifteen is selected to represent England at Rugby football, we are defeated by all and sundry,' lamented Air Chief Marshal Sir Christopher Foxley-Morris in 1975. 'When an eleven is selected to play cricket against Australia, it is not just beaten but humiliatingly thrashed . . . On the playing fields of the world, we appear to have become the perennial losers, the predictable holders of all the wooden spoons.'[49]

Even cricket, the game of village greens and summer shadows, of pristine whites and gracious losers, seemed to have succumbed to the prevailing malaise. For the first time in fifty years, England lost Test matches at home to India and away to New Zealand, while a string of defeats to the West Indies and Australia included the calamitous 4–1 Ashes fiasco in 1974–5, generally regarded as a low point in the national team's fortunes. By this point, England had been deprived of arguably their best batsman, Geoff Boycott, who had gone into self-imposed exile in 1974, supposedly because he had lost his appetite for Test cricket, but more plausibly because he was aggrieved not to have been made captain.

The selectors had their reasons, though, because Boycott was not only the most controversial cricketer in the country, but one of the most divisive sportsmen in any discipline, notorious for his single-minded self-centredness and dour, defensive presence at the crease. A coal miner's son with fierce opinions and an extremely healthy ego, he had been appointed captain of Yorkshire in 1971 but was fiercely hated by many of his fellow players. Committee members and former players regularly called for his head, and five years later a dressing-room poll found that more than nine out of ten players wanted him to be sacked. It was somehow symptomatic of Boycott's career – as well as the general flavour of cricket in the 1970s – that the club committee waited until just after his mother had died of cancer to dismiss him; it was also characteristic that he immediately went on the *Parkinson* show to denounce them as 'small-minded people', who 'could have allowed my mother to be buried in peace' but 'could not wait'.[50]

The Boycott saga was only one of a number of controversies that dominated the sporting pages in the 1970s. In previous decades, sport had offered a sense of escapism and reassurance in hard times, allowing people to take refuge from the rigours of unemployment and austerity in their appreciation of Jack Hobbs, Denis Compton, Billy Wright and Stanley Matthews. To be sure, sport in the 1970s offered plenty of pleasures – the sight of Gareth Edwards in full flow, of Kenny Dalglish banging in the goals, of Jackie Stewart closing in on the chequered flag, of Mary Peters nearing the finish line, even of Big Daddy and Giant Haystacks locked in bone-shuddering combat. Yet all too often it seemed to be infected by the same aggression, materialism and self-interest that had seeped into so many other corners of national life. Major events were often starkly politicized: the 1972 Five Nations championship was abandoned after Scotland and Wales refused to travel to Dublin for fear of IRA reprisals, the Olympic Games later that year were blighted by the murder of eleven Israeli athletes by Palestinian gunmen, and enormous controversy surrounded the so-called private cricket tours of South Africa organized by the promoter Derrick Robins, who attracted top-class English players such as Brian Close, Bob Willis and Tony Greig. In this context, not even the most politically indifferent spectator could keep up the illusion that sport was pure escapism, immune to the pressures of the modern world. When the Olympic organizers at Munich decided to continue with the Games after the murders of the Israeli athletes, *The*

Times thought the decision was thoroughly 'distasteful'. 'What taste can be satisfied', it asked, 'with the significance of competitive sports when a tragedy at once personal, shameful and symbolic, has occurred?'[51]

The show went on, of course. But there was more suffering, more disappointment, more disgrace to come. And if there was one moment that summed up the disillusionment of British sport – and of so much beyond that – it came on 4 June 1977, when England and Scotland, the world's oldest international football teams, met at Wembley to decide the Home Nations Championship. The atmosphere in the famous old stadium, now visibly crumbling and dilapidated, was very different from the buoyant enthusiasm that had greeted England's World Cup triumph eleven years before. The atmosphere, one reporter wrote, 'was overwhelmingly influenced by Scotland, and Scotch. It was at once powerful and obscene, and gave no comfort to England who might have been on Scottish soil.' Only weeks earlier, the Scottish National Party – driven by bitter frustration with the major national parties and excitement at the potential benefits of North Sea oil – had made sweeping gains in the council elections. Now, as goals by Gordon McQueen and Kenny Dalglish confirmed the visitors' superiority over Revie's constipated England, Wembley seemed awash with Celtic triumphalism. That the quality of the football was generally poor – it was yet another match crippled by defensive tactics and endless fouls – bothered the visitors not at all. Even before the final whistle, said *The Times*, 'thousands of Scots were struggling to be first onto the pitch'.

Several months earlier, the Football Association had announced plans to install 8-foot-high metal fences around the Wembley perimeter, hoping to deter the pitch invasions that had spoiled so many major sporting occasions. But in a story that spoke volumes about British efficiency in the mid-1970s, the plan had been delayed. And as the final whistle blew that hot June afternoon, thousands of visiting supporters streamed drunkenly onto the pitch, and as one Scottish writer later put it, 'began clawing at it with the relish of battle-high warriors picking over the booty on the bodies of the dead enemy on some ancient battlefield'. With their long hair lank and greasy with sweat under their tartan caps, their T-shirts sodden with beer, their flared jeans ripped and grass-stained, they looked like some invading barbarian horde. As they ripped and tore at the turf, as they clambered onto the goal-frames until the posts finally gave way and the goals symbolically collapsed beneath the jeering mob, the

Corinthian spirit seemed a long way away. For the nation that had given organized sport and fair play to the world, it was a supremely humiliating moment. 'There is only one consolation,' said the *Daily Mirror* afterwards. 'It won't happen again. By the next time the Scottish hordes descend on Wembley the crowd will be caged in. In the long history of battles between the two countries the Wembley fences will be the football equivalent of Hadrian's Wall.' It was an ominous prediction, for, as events were to prove, metal fences brought terrible dangers of their own. But as reporters looked down from the press box and surveyed the scarred and battered sporting turf, the shattered goalposts, the field littered with beer cans and broken bottles, there seemed no alternative. As one of them quietly remarked, it had been 'another afternoon of British rubbish'.[52]

15

The Last Days of Pompeii

*Heard that the government is to introduce a 3 day working week
in order to meet the fuel crisis! Apparently everyone will lose wages
in the process! And it applies to everything!*
   – Kenneth Williams's diary, 13 December 1973

*The whole country was in turmoil. That's why I came up with the
line* 'Look to the future now / It's only just begun.' *That's what
everybody had to do. The country couldn't have been at a lower
ebb. In times like that, people always turn to showbiz.*
   – Noddy Holder in *Mojo*, November 2006

One fine day in July 1973, Joe Gormley, the president of the National
Union of Mineworkers, came to see Edward Heath at Number 10. It
was a secret meeting: as the two old antagonists sat in the garden and
chatted amiably, only Heath's diligent mandarin, Sir William Armstrong,
knew that Gormley was there. Despite their bitter struggle the previous
year, Gormley liked Heath and found him serious and approachable: a
better listener, he thought, than Harold Wilson. And although Gormley
made no secret of his ambitions for his men – his dream, he said, was
for every miner to have 'a good education for the children, a Jaguar at
the front, a Mini at the back to take the wife shopping' – he was no left-
wing firebrand. Ever since he had first gone down the pit at the age of
14, Gormley had been steadfastly opposed to Communism, and for all
his gruff, pugnacious style, he was a moderate, not a militant. Even as
he was telling television viewers that the miners deserved more and were
determined to get it, he was secretly passing information to Special

Branch about his own union. As his handler later put it, 'he was a patriot and he was very wary about the growth of militancy'.[1]

By the summer of 1973, Gormley was seriously concerned about the ambitions of some of his colleagues on the NUM executive, which had shifted well to the left since the miners' great victory a year earlier. Even though the government had poured more than £1 billion into the coal industry, reversing the policy of closing pits, the militants wanted blood. At the miners' annual conference at the beginning of July, Mick McGahey said that he wanted to see 'agitation in the streets of this country to remove the government', while Arthur Scargill won cheers of approval when he pledged to destroy 'the most immoral, the most corrupt government in living memory'. Ominously, the conference then voted to demand a massive 35 per cent wage increase, in clear defiance of Heath's pay policy. But neither Heath nor Gormley wanted another fight to the death; the former could not afford another winter of power cuts, while the NUM leader had no desire to be outflanked by the militants. So when Heath secretly invited Gormley to Downing Street, he came willingly. And as they talked, Gormley explained that, although he was obliged to follow his conference's instructions and to seek a 35 per cent deal, there might be a way out. What Heath should do, he implied, was to make a special arrangement for 'unsocial hours', so that the miners could have extra payments on top of the forthcoming Stage Three pay deal. That way, Heath could claim he had stuck to the pay policy, while Gormley could tell his members they had got a special deal. And as Gormley finished, he was pleased to see that Heath and Armstrong seemed to have taken the hint. 'We never thought of that,' he remembered them saying. 'We never thought of that at all!'[2]

It was not until three months later, when Heath unveiled Stage Three to the press, that Gormley realized they had totally misunderstood his meaning. Instead of the 'unsocial hours' loophole being reserved for the miners alone, which would allow the NUM to claim a great victory, it was potentially open to all shift workers. 'I must say that I wasn't best pleased,' Gormley wrote. 'I had gone there to try to solve our problem, not to help them run the country as a whole.' And two days later, on 10 October, came an even bigger blunder. Gormley was in a difficult position: he did not really want a strike, but he needed to show his members that he was squeezing every last penny out of the government. But when the

National Coal Board announced its answer to the miners' pay claim, the terms were much more generous than many people had expected. Instead of trying to bargain with the miners – which would have given Gormley room to extract a few concessions and then claim victory – the Coal Board offered as much as they possibly could under the terms of Stage Three. Coming to a hefty 16.5 per cent, their offer was potentially the biggest increase the NUM had ever had without a strike. As the Coal Board saw it, this was the best way to avoid another battle: by putting all their cards on the table, right at the beginning, they would leave the miners with no choice but to accept. But as *The Economist* pointed out, offering such a 'horrifying pay rise' would only encourage the militants to demand even more concessions. The Coal Board had 'left no room for negotiation and bargaining', admitted Robert Carr, even though the time-honoured rituals of pay talks meant that the miners were bound to ask for more. Indeed, even if Gormley had wanted to accept the deal, the NUM executive would never have let him. So even as the Coal Board bosses were congratulating themselves on their generous offer, Heath's ministers were reeling in horror. Carr recalled that he felt a 'sense of doom, as though a Greek tragedy was about to be acted out'. The government was 'being manoeuvred again towards the same fatal field', wrote Douglas Hurd, 'still littered with relics of the last defeat'.[3]

It is a myth – although an enduring one on the left – that Heath welcomed the thought of a return bout with the miners because he wanted revenge for 1972. In fact, he had done all in his power to mollify the NUM, and he was in no position to invite a return to hostilities. For while the events of 1972 had amply demonstrated the miners' economic muscle, the Arab attack on Israel, launched just four days before the Coal Board's offer, played right into the miners' hands. The NUM was still considering the Coal Board's offer when, on 16 October, OPEC broke the devastating news of their oil price rise, which changed the game completely. Not only did the oil shock put Heath's counter-inflation policy under intense pressure, it left the miners in an even stronger position. Britain depended heavily on imported oil to meet its energy requirements; indeed, since 1972 the government had been quietly building up coal stocks by burning more oil instead. Thanks to the oil shock, however, the government could hardly rely on imported oil if negotiations with the miners broke down; indeed, with North Sea oil yet to come on stream, OPEC's blackmail had left Britain more dependent on coal than ever. The miners had a knife to the government's throat, and after years of redundancies they felt little compunction about using it. On 23 October, in a desperate but probably misguided attempt to handle the situation personally, Heath invited the miners' leaders to Downing Street and begged them to put the national interest first. But he was wasting his time. After lunch, Gormley, looking 'pale and drawn', visited Heath's study and told him that they had voted to reject the deal. Two days later the NUM executive called for industrial action.[4]

That the country could be lurching towards another confrontation between the state and the miners, so soon after the government's humiliation in 1972, seemed almost beyond belief. Yet in the face of the miners' intransigence, Heath seemed close to powerless. Having put his faith in Gormley's ability to hold his men back from the brink, the embattled Prime Minister now had no answer to their demands for special treatment. And when the overtime ban came into effect on Monday, 12 November, the situation seemed bleaker than ever. Although the government had stockpiled a record 18 million tons of coal at power stations across the country, the Arab oil cutbacks meant that there were real fears of shortages over the winter. By an extraordinarily unlucky coincidence, not only were the power workers on strike too, but the weather forecasters were predicting a sudden cold snap. In Monday evening's papers the Electricity Board warned that two-hour power cuts were likely over the next few nights. And when the Cabinet met the next morning, Peter Walker grimly told his colleagues that coal production was expected to fall by as much as 40 per cent during the first week of the overtime ban.[5]

On Tuesday afternoon, Robert Carr announced in the Commons that the government had no choice but to declare its fifth state of emergency in three years. Electric advertising and floodlighting were banned, while public offices were directed to cut their power consumption by one-tenth. In the next day's papers, there were reports that the government was ready to introduce petrol rationing. 'The ration cards', reported *The Times*, 'are already in post offices.' But the bad news did not end there. For even as the government was preparing to unveil the state of emergency, the Department of Trade and Industry announced a set of trade figures that, as Peter Jay put it, were simply 'epithet-defying'. Exports had fallen, but thanks to the Barber boom imports had reached a record high, sending Britain's monthly trade deficit to a record £298 million. That afternoon, in a desperate bid to reassure the world markets that Britain's economy was still a going concern, the Bank of England announced the biggest credit squeeze in living memory. Minimum lending rate went up to a record 13 per cent, banks were ordered to hand over a further 2 per cent in special deposits, and overdraft interest rates were forecast to rise to an excruciating 18 per cent.[6]

The next day was a national holiday, proclaimed to mark the wedding of Princess Anne and Captain Mark Phillips. But in Westminster and Whitehall, few people felt in the mood to celebrate. Douglas Hurd, never far from his master's side during this latest crisis, nipped out to the Horse Guards to watch the royal carriages rattling towards Westminster Abbey. 'Leaves and breastplates and a smiling Queen,' he recorded in his diary. 'After all the carping the magic works.' But then it was back to Downing Street, where he was drafting a new prime ministerial address to the nation. And Hurd was not the only observer to note the incongruity of so much pageantry at a moment of supreme national crisis. Amid the faded grandeur of his St James's club, James Lees-Milne watched the wedding on a television that staff had installed in the members' bar. Yet he could not forget the newspaper hoardings outside, which contained 'the gloomiest portents in their headings, fuel crises, more strikes, Bank Rate rising to unprecedented heights'. As Auberon Waugh put it, 'the show goes on, but now it is played as farce'.[7]

Heath never gave up trying to find a compromise that would end the crisis. But since there was no question of him abandoning Stage Three, a deal never seemed likely. When the miners' leaders returned to Downing Street on 28 November, Heath's entreaties that they remember the national interest fell on deaf ears. 'Prime Minister, what I can't understand is this,' said a little man perched at 'the very back, almost out of the window'. 'You have told us that we have no option but to pay the Arabs the price they're demanding for the oil. Now, as far as I know, the Arabs never helped us in World War I, and in World War II, and we flogged our guts out in all of that. Why can't you pay us for coal what you are willing to pay the Arabs for oil?' A cannier, less scrupulous politician, more interested in personal self-preservation than in economic discipline, might have taken the hint. Certainly Harold Wilson – and probably Margaret Thatcher – would have used the same argument to the nation to justify giving the miners a raise and scrapping Stage Three. But that was never Heath's style; determined to stick to his pay policy, he 'had no answer', recalled William Armstrong, to the miner's question.

And by the end of the meeting, his patience had run out. 'What is it that you want, Mr McGahey?' Heath asked, almost in desperation. McGahey stared back at him. 'I want to see the end of your government,' he said finally, in his distinctive gravelly voice. There was a long silence. 'Come on lads,' said Joe Gormley finally, 'let's go.'[8]

By the end of November, the news seemed almost unremittingly depressing. The combination of the oil shock and the miners' dispute, Heath grimly told a public meeting in Nelson, Lancashire, was 'now threatening to create serious difficulty for every factory, for every office, for every farm, and for every family in this country'. In London, schools were reportedly sending children home because of heating problems; in Lincolnshire, policemen were abandoning their cars and returning to the beat to cut their petrol consumption; in West Sussex, 10,000 street lights had been turned off to save power. 'FUEL AND POWER EMERGENCY: LEAVE YOUR CAR AT HOME THIS WEEKEND' read stark government advertisements in the national papers, begging drivers to cut out 'weekend motoring', to organize rotas and car pools, and to keep below 50 mph at all times. 'The choice is stark,' the deputy chairman of the Electricity Council explained to the American magazine *Time*. 'Either the public cooperates or complete cities could lose their supply of electricity at a stroke. It could even happen before Christmas.'[9]

Since there seemed no respite from the bad news, Heath's advisers made no attempt to lighten the mood. When, on the last weekend of the month, Douglas Hurd drove up to Oxfordshire to address the rather early Christmas dinner of one little Conservative branch, he gave them a 'short speech of unexampled gloom. Everything was going wrong. The prospect had never been darker. Great sacrifice would be required by all.' Oddly, he recorded, 'this went extremely well, and seemed to cheer them immensely'. And as Hurd drove back to London, he began to wonder whether, instead of trying to play down the threat to the nation, Heath should instead do just the opposite. 'The Government should seek to *emphasize* the gravity of the crisis,' he wrote to Heath on the night of 6 December, introducing a paper he had drafted with his young colleague William Waldegrave. Settling with the miners, they argued, would be a mistake: 'it would destroy [your] authority and break the morale of the Conservative Party beyond hope of restoration.' Instead, Heath should hold firm. Indeed, he should consider an early general election, 'soon after the immediate crisis had passed', inviting the public to rally behind the government at a time of supreme economic danger. It would be 'a highly charged and violent Election', they conceded. But they thought he would win it.[10]

But while Heath's young advisers appeared almost gung-ho in their enthusiasm for the battle, many older observers thought, like Falstaff, that the better part of valour was discretion. Perhaps the outstanding example was Ronald McIntosh, who had become the director general of the National Economic Development Council (the NEDC, or 'Neddy', a forum for ministers, trade unionists and businessmen) in the middle of 1973. McIntosh was a classic pillar of the old establishment, a sympathetic, thoughtful man, whose diaries not only provide an illuminatingly detailed view of the crisis, but are steeped in the civilized, consensual and faintly ineffectual values of a generation of Whitehall mandarins.* On 4 December, for example, he recorded that it was 'imperative to work again for a consensus between the government, the employers and the unions'. Confronting the unions struck him as madness: when one of the directors of the Pearson media group suggested that the only solution was a 'right-wing regime with "tanks in the streets"', McIntosh argued for 'recognising where industrial power lay and coming to terms with it rather than confronting it – even if this meant big changes in our ideas about relative rewards etc., which many of the better off would find distasteful and hard to accept'. In a similar argument with a Tory MP in December, McIntosh was even more explicit, insisting that 'the best way to protect democracy was to recognise the willingness of those who had industrial power to use it and to avoid outright conflict'. His old Balliol friend Roy Jenkins, already drifting apart from the Labour Party, tried to persuade him that the government simply could not 'give way' to the miners, for 'if we did we would soon have domestic inflation of 25 per cent or more' (an uncannily accurate prediction, as it turned out). But McIntosh thought 'we needed to stop using terms like "give way". I understood the dangers of inflation but I was convinced that the disruption we were going to suffer was too high a price to pay.'[11]

For McIntosh, giving in to the miners' economic power was simply being 'sensible and balanced' – a way of thinking that would later

---

* It also speaks volumes about the nature of power in Britain at the time that he had attended the same Oxford college as Ted Heath, Roy Jenkins and Denis Healey: it is faintly bizarre to find, in June 1974, McIntosh, Heath and Jenkins having a private chat about the state of the nation at the Balliol College Gaudy.

strike Mrs Thatcher and her admirers as spineless appeasement. He was certainly not alone: at least two members of Heath's Think Tank, Dick Ross and Adam Ridley, thought that the Prime Minister should play the 'Arab card', tell the public that the oil crisis had created a set of exceptional circumstances, and make the miners a special case. But even at the time there were plenty of people, like Roy Jenkins, who thought that Heath had no choice but to stand up to such an inflationary pay demand, not least because the government could not afford to be seen appeasing sheer industrial muscle. Later in December, McIntosh's next-door neighbour, the Conservative MP Piers Dixon, told him that 'the threat to democracy posed by the miners outweighs the dislocation which the three-day week will cause', and said that if Heath surrendered, 'the Tory Party would disintegrate and Enoch Powell will take over'. The editor of the *Financial Times*, Fredy Fisher, agreed that there was a 'real risk of a right-wing authoritarian government next year'. Yet he, too, told McIntosh that he was 'against giving in to the miners because it would result in an inflation rate of anywhere between 20 and 25 per cent'. Crucially, the general public seemed to share Fisher's views: in early December, a survey for ITN found that most disapproved of the miners' action, and a majority thought that the government should hold firm to its pay policy. Indeed, the crisis actually seemed to have done Heath some good. Although a staggering 82 per cent said they were 'not happy with the way things are going in Britain', Heath now held a narrow 3 per cent lead over Wilson, and more than 53 per cent thought he was doing a good job as Prime Minister. 'The Government must on no account give in to the NUM,' reported the Tory party chairman Lord Carrington; 'this time the Conservative party expected to see the miners smashed'.[12]

Yet Heath himself seemed oddly cautious, passive, even hesitant. It was not just, as his biographer suggests, that he felt trapped between the need to stick to his pay policy and his fear of losing a second round with the miners. After three years rushing from one problem to another like a firemen surrounded by arsonists, he was physically, morally and intellectually exhausted. It was little wonder he was so tired: not only did he have to deal with the miners' dispute, but he also had to handle the oil crisis, the trade deficit and the emergency economic measures that were clearly necessary, as well as the desperately tricky Sunningdale talks on power-sharing in Northern Ireland. Senior colleagues, too, were moving through what Hurd called 'a fog of tiredness'. Barber appeared physically overwhelmed by the economic blizzard, Carr seemed about to keel over from exhaustion, and Victor Rothschild suffered a serious heart attack in the middle of December. In the past, the Prime Minister, unflagging and indomitable, had been the rock on whom they all depended. But now even he seemed to have lost his way. Ronald McIntosh, who saw a fair bit of Heath that winter, recorded on 12 December that 'overwork and fatigue were sapping the Prime Minister's energies'. A few days later Vic Feather confided that he 'thought Ted was suffering from overwork and strain'. It later transpired that Heath's increasingly glacial silences, his apparent indecision, his intellectual ponderousness and even his alarming recent weight gain were all linked to a thyroid disorder, which was not diagnosed until two years later. But at the time the word in the Commons was that the Prime Minister had been broken by fatigue. Enoch Powell told a businessmen's lunch at the end of November that he could not 'but entertain fears for [Heath's] mental and emotional stability'. Even hardbitten journalists thought that was below the belt, and nothing did more to distance Powell from ordinary Tories in his Wolverhampton constituency, horrified by what the *Telegraph* called 'a premeditated insult, carefully calculated to cause maximum offence'.[13]

Unfortunately for Heath, the worsening energy situation offered no pause for breath. On 3 December, a secret report by the DTI not only forecast an oil shortfall of up to 20 per cent over the next month, but advised ministers that coal production had fallen by 24, 28 and 30 per cent over the last three weeks. If the overtime ban continued into January, Peter Walker wrote, the weekly shortfall might reach 40 per cent, and if the miners called a full-scale strike, stocks would probably run out in February. By that point, there would only be enough power for 'essential services and domestic lighting, and very little for non-essential industry, shops and offices, or for domestic space and water heating'. Unpalatable as this might sound, the government might 'very soon' have to put industry on a three-day or even two-day week, merely 'to scrape through the winter without major disruption'. Not surprisingly, the following morning's Cabinet was a distinctly gloomy affair, dominated by discussions of oil shortages, the possibility of fuel rationing over Christmas and the devastating news that ASLEF, the railwaymen's union, had voted to join the miners in an overtime ban for higher pay. As yet the Cabinet shrank from the prospect of a three-day week. But when the Central

Electricity Generating Board reported three days later that supplies were now in 'grave danger', with power stations likely to run out of fuel before the end of the winter, the options narrowed. Ominously, the Cabinet Office's Civil Contingencies Unit was already working on a worst-case scenario, including drastic plans for regional government if energy supplies broke down completely. There was even talk of the army stepping in to safeguard hospitals and to forestall the possible riots and anarchy if the lights went out for good.[14]

By Wednesday, 12 December, the situation had reached breaking point. At five that afternoon the Cabinet met in a mood of funereal gloom. Night was drawing in, literally and metaphorically. The only solution, the minutes recorded, was to 'shock' the unions 'by stressing the risk of reduced employment, while at the same time increasing our capacity for endurance to the maximum possible extent'. As Walker explained, the railwaymen's dispute meant that it was increasingly difficult to move even the dwindling supplies of coal that remained. Just to maintain 'essential services' and to 'get through the winter without major disruption', he said, the government would have to cut power demand by as much as 20 per cent. They had to face facts: industry must be put onto a three-day week. The next morning, they met again to confirm the details. Already, offices had been ordered to keep their temperatures below 63 °F, and street lighting had been cut by 50 per cent. Now the use of floodlights for sport was outlawed (prompting the Football League to defy one of its oldest taboos by giving reluctant approval to games on Sunday afternoons), while both the BBC and ITV were ordered to cut off television broadcasts at 10.30 on weekdays. There was even talk of banning the use of electricity to heat more than one room in each house, but as Jim Prior pointed out, this would be both 'harsh' and 'unenforceable'. On the broad outlines, however, there was general agreement. A few hours later Heath rose ponderously from his seat in the Commons and grimly announced that from New Year's Eve, Britain would be on a three-day week.[15]

That night Heath addressed the nation on television. Thanks to a schedule of almost unparalleled intensity, whisking him from the delicate Sunningdale negotiations to a succession of formal banquets for visiting statesmen, briefings on the oil crisis, meetings on the miners' dispute and preparations for the forthcoming EEC summit, he was physically and mentally shattered. He had barely slept for four days, and the pressure of events was such that there was no time even to go through the script his advisers had drafted for him. Even as the camera light blinked on and the words 'The Rt. Hon. Edward Heath, MP. The Prime Minister' appeared on millions of television screens across the country, he still looked exhausted, his heavy features ashen with tiredness, his eyes narrowed almost to slits, his dark blue suit and tie appropriately funereal. Yet this was arguably the most momentous ministerial broadcast since the Second World War, and Heath made no effort to disguise the severity of the moment.

'As Prime Minister,' he began simply, 'I want to talk to you about the grave emergency facing our country.' He explained the background: the oil crisis, the miners' dispute, the appalling balance of payments situation, the looming shortages at the power stations. But where some of his younger advisers would have preferred him to mobilize public opinion against the miners, most of the speech was devoted to a wooden ex-planation of the government's emergency measures. 'We shall have a harder Christmas than we have known since the war,' Heath said gloomily. 'We shall have to postpone some of the hopes and aims we have set ourselves for expansion and for our standard of living.' And in his final lines, where many Tories would have liked a blistering denunci-ation of the miners' cynical self-aggrandizement at a time of national crisis, he fell back on the One Nation rhetoric he had learned as a young man. 'At times like these,' he said with desperate earnestness, 'there is deep in all of us an instinct which tells us we must abandon disputes among ourselves. We must close our ranks so that we can deal together with the difficulties which come to us whether from within or from beyond our own shores. That has been our way in the past, and it is a good way.' It was meant to sound like Winston Churchill. But to many Tories it sounded more like Neville Chamberlain.[16]

There was, of course, a basic inconsistency in Heath's approach. On the one hand, he refused to heed the advice of those who thought he should give in to the miners, arguing that it would be madness to sacrifice the counter-inflationary rigour of Stage Three. Yet on the other, he refused to listen to advisers like Hurd and Waldegrave who urged him to whip up national outrage at the selfishness of the miners' leaders, preferring the rhetoric of compromise and consensus. As even his sympathetic biographer puts it, 'Heath's words signalled that he did not have the stomach for a fight.' For all his talk of radical modernization, he remained at heart a One Nation politician: although he earnestly wanted change, he shrank from the confrontation necessary to bring it about.[17]

Even close aides found it hard to work out Heath's strategy. On 2 December, he had recalled Willie Whitelaw – then by far the government's most popular minister – from Northern Ireland, making him Secretary of State for Employment with special responsibility for fighting inflation. Given Whitelaw's reputation as the supreme negotiator, the press saw it as a stroke of genius. In fact, Whitelaw was shattered by his experience in Belfast and out of touch with what was going on in London. 'I was totally exhausted,' he said later. 'I was emotionally affected by all I had been involved with in Ireland. I was not mentally conditioned for home politics.' Above all, though, his chief never gave him a clear sense of direction. After just a few days, Whitelaw discovered that Heath had been holding strategy meetings behind his back with his civil servants – another sign of the Prime Minister's increasing isolation. He immediately rang Downing Street in sheer frustration. 'Tell me what you want me to do with this department,' he begged. 'Do you want me to settle, or do you want war?' But from Heath, he remembered, there came 'no reply of any clarity'.[18]

Working almost as a freelance mediator between Heath and the miners, Whitelaw briefly came tantalizingly close to finding a way forward. On 20 December, after an IRA bomb scare had forced him and the miners' leaders to take temporary refuge in an Italian restaurant, where they reassured themselves with bottles of beer, Gormley suggested that the miners might be a special case after all, because unlike other workers they not only had to change and wait for the lift at the start of each shift, but had to scrub themselves clean of coal dust afterwards. If the government could justify extra pay for 'waiting and bathing time', Gormley hinted, then a deal might be possible. Whitelaw seemed interested, and Gormley thought they had a real chance of a breakthrough. The next day, however, he made the mistake of mentioning it to Harold Wilson, who immediately complained that he was 'pulling the Tory Government's irons out of the fire for them', and rushed to the Commons to unveil the idea as his own. This was clever but supremely cynical politics from Wilson, making it much more difficult for the government to accept the deal while ensuring that Labour would get the credit if they did. Gormley and Whitelaw were furious: years later, the miners' leader wrote that he 'would never forgive Harold Wilson' for sabotaging the last chance for peace.[19]

But the truth is that 'waiting and bathing' never offered a realistic solution. Over Christmas, the Pay Board examined the idea and found that it would justify much less extra pay than Gormley thought. In any case, since neither Heath nor the NUM militants were prepared to blink first, any compromise was distinctly unlikely. Heath seemed determined to stick to 'a fairly hard line, making it clear that the three-day week was all the miners' fault', recorded Ronald McIntosh after an NEDC meeting on 21 December. At lunch, McIntosh took Heath aside and implored him to 'reach an accommodation' for the good of the country, giving the miners concessions in return for a TUC statement 'on the need to control wage inflation'. But since such a statement would have been worthless, Heath treated the idea with barely concealed contempt. 'I felt tired and unutterably depressed,' McIntosh recorded afterwards. He thought Heath was behaving 'irresponsibly' because the miners were bound 'to get a settlement outside Phase 3 in the end' – a classic case of Whitehall defeatism. 'It is a dreadful thing to sit and watch a country slide into chaos, through the obstinacy of a few individuals,' he wrote. 'I am sure that the three-day week will bring greater chaos more quickly than ministers realise. It will also cause great bitterness and will mean that we face the tremendous problems which the oil crisis will bring as a deeply divided country.'[20]

This was more than the apocalyptic pessimism of some gentlemen's-club reactionary. The director general of the NEDC had the ear of some of Whitehall's most influential economic experts, and what they were telling him was deeply disturbing. At a meeting on 6 December, the head of British Rail, Richard Marsh, confided that 'we faced the most dangerous situation we have had since the 1930s'. Two weeks later, the Permanent Secretary to the Treasury, Sir Douglas Allen – a man with almost un-paralleled clout in Whitehall – was even more pessimistic. 'He took a very gloomy line about the future,' McIntosh noted after they had talked for more than an hour, 'and said that the Treasury predicted GDP would fall next year. This would lead to high unemployment (perhaps a million at the end of 1974) and hence a drop in the standard of living. He talked about the possibility of our moving into a siege economy with rationing on the wartime model.'[21]

This might sound absurdly alarmist, yet to those in the know, the return of rationing and the advent of a new dark age, an era of recession and austerity on a scale that might eclipse even the Great Depression, seemed a strong possibility. 'We are heading for a major slump,' the deputy chairman of Rio Tinto-Zinc, one of Britain's biggest conglomerates, told Tony Benn at lunch on 29 November. 'We shall have to have direction of labour and wartime rationing.' A few weeks later, the *Guardian*'s Peter Jenkins warned that Treasury sources were predicting 'nil growth' in 1974 at best, and 'a 5 per cent recession' at worst, as well as 'a 15–20 per cent rate of inflation and a balance of payments deficit in the region of £4,000 millions this year'. At almost exactly the same time, Labour's Shadow Chancellor, Denis Healey, told his colleagues that Britain faced an 'economic holocaust'. Meanwhile, the historian A. J. P. Taylor was sending a series of increasingly gloomy letters to his Hungarian wife Éva. He was 'terrified' by the 'approaching hurricane', he wrote, predicting shortages of oil and coal, the absence of heat and light, and millions thrown out of work. 'I have been expecting the collapse of capitalism all my life,' he remarked with gallows humour. 'Now that it comes I am rather annoyed.'[22]

At the root of the economic panic was the collapse of the Barber boom. Even without the oil shock, the government's dash for growth would probably have ended in tears. But the crisis had come at precisely the worst possible time: after months of reckless monetary expansion, surging world commodity prices and terrible trade figures, the economy was trembling on the brink of disaster. 'The country is now facing the gravest economic crisis since the end of the war,' Anthony Barber told his Cabinet colleagues on 12 December, in a secret report of unparalleled pessimism. With oil and coal supplies running out and overall production bound to fall in 1974, the only way to 'make some impact on a worsening balance of payments situation' and to 'restore confidence in sterling' was to 'take immediate steps to reduce demand'. The Chancellor admitted that his proposals would 'bear very heavily on certain programmes', but they had no choice: new orders must be postponed or cancelled, subsidies must be slashed, and in the long run the government might have to cut spending by as much as £3 billion. The plans for Concorde, one of the last major prestige projects left over from the 1960s, must be scaled back; the plan for a new London airport at Maplin Sands must be delayed. But the situation was so desperate, Barber admitted, that 'even with the most severe measures, the impact on the forecast balance of payments deficit would only be marginal. It would be necessary to borrow abroad for some considerable time before a turn around could be achieved.' There was no disguising the underlying message. The dream of economic expansion lay in ruins. The good times were over.[23]

Barber revealed the extent of the crisis to the Commons on 17 December. 'Over the past week or so, many have described the situation which we as a nation now face as by far the gravest since the end of the war,' he began ominously. 'They do not exaggerate. The duty of the Government is to take whatever action the national interest requires, however severe.' So his Christmas present to the nation was an emergency mini-budget, slashing public expenditure by some £1,200 million (roughly 4 per cent), the biggest spending cut in modern history. There were cuts of £178 million in defence and £182 million in the education budget, destroying Margaret Thatcher's ambitious plans for nursery schools and university expansion. There were stringent new controls on hire-purchase credit, bank lending was subject to a 'corset' to prevent the money supply growing too quickly, and holders of Barclaycard and Access cards were compelled to pay back at least 15 per cent of their balance a month. 'It was a swing of the axe that was meant to hurt,' one reporter wrote the next day. But this was more than the usual stop-go economics to which the country had become accustomed over the previous twenty years. It was the death knell for an era of economic optimism, the end of a consensus based on ever-growing public spending and ambitious Whitehall-driven empire-building. The Barber boom had been a last attempt to reaffirm growth as the motor of social and economic change, with the government cast as a masterful driver steering the welfare state towards the sunlit uplands of wealth and security. But now the wheels had fallen off, and the driver found himself lost in a forbidding global landscape he no longer recognized. For the welfare state, for the post-war consensus and for Heath himself, it would be never glad confident morning again.[24]

For millions of children, Christmas in 1973 was as exciting as ever. 'I've only got a few presents!' wrote the 12-year-old Essex diarist, whose haul included talcum powder, two bottles of nail varnish, a lock-up diary, a nightdress, the board game Cluedo, a Leo Sayer record and a 'David Cassidy life story book', as well as £20 to buy clothes. It was a sign of how affluent Britain had become that even her friends gave her 'lots of presents like bath cubes, bubble bath & bath salts'. Ten or twenty years before, such gifts would have been well beyond the reach of ordinary 12-year-old girls, but now most took them for granted. For some of their parents, too, the economic crisis barely impinged at all. Fortnum & Mason reported booming sales of smoked salmon, caviar, game pies, *foie gras* and peaches in brandy, while one American correspondent told his readers that the Christmas shopping spree had been 'as intense as ever' as 'Londoners stocked up heavily on turkey, ham, sausage, wine, cake, candy and everything else that goes on the holiday table'.[25]

Even for families that had deliberately tightened their belts, the festive season was not all doom and gloom. In the charts, Slade's 'Merry Xmas Everybody', conceived by Noddy Holder as a 'working-class British Christmas song', ruled unchallenged, cheerfully urging listeners to 'look to the future now / It's only just begun'. And the television schedules could hardly have been better designed to distract viewers from the looming prospect of the three-day week, from the Christmas Day specials of *The Generation Game*, *The Mike Yarwood Show* and *Morecambe and Wise* to Boxing Day's diet of Les Dawson, Ken Dodd, Dick Emery and *The Two Ronnies*. Escapism was the order of the day: when Downing Street caught sight of the Queen's proposed Christmas message, in which she expressed 'deep concern' at the 'special difficulties Britain is now facing', Heath vetoed it outright. Nothing must alarm the nation on Christmas Day, he insisted: even her second draft ('Christmas is so much a family occasion that you would not wish me to harp on these difficulties') was too much. In the end, the Queen showed viewers a selection of Princess Anne's wedding pictures instead.[26]

Not even the pleasures of Leo Sayer, Bruce Forsyth and Princess Anne, however, could banish the glowering reality of the crisis. The news was unremittingly bad: just seven days before Christmas, the IRA set off a string of car and parcel bombs in Westminster, Pentonville and Hampstead that injured sixty people, many of them women on their way to work. Almost every day brought more bomb scares, and the air seemed heavy with anxiety and suspicion. 'Bad news all the time,' recorded the National Theatre's director Peter Hall on Christmas Eve. 'An economic slump threatens. The bomb scares go on. The miners continue their go-slow. The trains are in chaos. Meantime, the nation is on a prodigal pre-Christmas spending spree.' Other diarists were in similarly gloomy form, exacerbated, no doubt, by the fact that many shops had inconveniently run out of toilet paper after a surge of panic buying. 'The news becomes more depressing every day,' wrote Kenneth Williams, 'as we watch democracy simper itself off the bill.' James Lees-Milne, meanwhile, could barely contain his horror at the flood of bad news. 'The morale of the British Mr Average has never been lower, his values more debased, his covetousness, greed and lack of self-respect more conspicuous,' he recorded at the end of the year. Earlier, after Barber's broadcast on the emergency spending cuts, he had shuddered with horror at the 'simultaneous news of the Arabs shooting and killing over thirty innocent travellers in Rome airport, the three bombs in London planted by the IRA, the squabbles of the European Community meeting'. Everything was 'so atrocious and evil', he thought, 'that it is a wonder we do not all go raving mad, or commit suicide'.[27]

In the press the mood could hardly have been grimmer. On 23 December, the *Sunday Times* predicted massive random power cuts and public 'chaos' by the end of January. The next day, Christmas Eve, an extraordinarily sweeping *Times* leader predicted global shortages of 'food and raw materials' and diagnosed 'a crisis in the culture and values of modern industrial society'. On page three, a full-page government advertisement, headlined in thick black type 'The Three Day Order', summarized the emergency provisions that would come into effect on 31 December. On the Continent, where the oil crisis was creating severe economic problems but nothing to rival the political crisis across the Channel, commentators gazed with horror on Britain's apparent self-immolation. In Europe, wrote one Brussels correspondent, the 'apparent fecklessness of the British worker and his delight in wringing the once golden goose's neck is matched in continental eyes by the reluctance of British Management to get to work first [and] roll up its sleeves'. Britain was now admired 'only for its ability to stagger along on its knees', especially as the last remnants of Beatlemania had long since blown away. 'The swinging London of the '60s has given way to a London as gloomy as the city described by Charles Dickens', remarked the German magazine *Der Spiegel*, with 'the once imperial streets of the capital' now 'sparsely lighted like the slummy streets of a former British imperial township'. Most Britons, reported the *New York Times*, were alarmed less by the prospect of 'prolonged poverty' and 'drastic inflation' than by fears that 'the fabric of British society is about to be ripped up'. This kind of reporting infuriated Edward Heath, who gave a splendidly grumpy interview to the American paper in January, insisting that their portrait of Britain in a state of 'perpetual crisis' did not 'bear any relationship to the facts' – although his claim that, until the end of 1973, Britain had enjoyed 'a period of very great industrial peace' strained credulity too far.[28]

Around the world, Britain was becoming a byword for industrial unrest and economic collapse. One humiliation was particularly painful, although it must have represented sweet revenge for one of the empire's former subjects. The people of Uganda, Idi Amin wrote to Heath in December 1973, were 'following with sorrow the alarming economic crisis befalling on Britain', and were keen to offer their 'abundant food-stuffs' to help their old friends in their hour of need. 'I have decided to contribute 10,000 Ugandan shillings from my savings,' Amin added, 'and I am convinced that many Ugandans will donate generously to rescue their innocent friends who are becoming victims of sharp tax increases, tighter credit squeeze and a possible pay squeeze.' The Foreign Office advised that no reply be sent, so as not to encourage the African dictator's 'delusions of statesmanship'. But five weeks later Amin wrote again to report that his 'Save Britain Fund', established to 'save and assist our former colonial masters from economic catastrophe', was a great success. The response had been 'so good', he added, 'that today, 21 January 1974, the people of Kigezi district donated one lorry load of vegetables and wheat. I am now requesting you to send an aircraft to collect this donation urgently before it goes bad'. When no reply was forthcoming, Amin tried to send a telegram to the Queen, but to no avail. Eventually the British High Commissioner was detailed to decline the offer as politely as possible. It was a ludicrous moment, and yet it spoke volumes about Britain's declining position in world affairs. Only eleven years before, Uganda had been a British colony. Now its leader, a man regarded in Britain as a murderous buffoon, was offering to help the mother country through its economic travails. How the mighty had fallen.[29]

For most people, however, the prospect of crippling inflation, millions out of work and a fight to the death between the government and the unions was no laughing matter. What was more, thanks to the IRA's bombing offensive against central London, the conflict in Northern Ireland now seemed likely to engulf the mainland. In conservative circles, there were genuine fears of total political and social breakdown. In December, one of the art critic Sacheverell Sitwell's City friends told him that they had 'only three months to clear out of England'; another advised him 'to hoard his cartridges, for there will be shooting within that time'.

Even more moderate observers shared their fears. In December, Peter Hall recorded his fears that 'out of the chaos we are going into, some simple and extremist group of the far right or the far left may very well break up our society and take over,' while the NEDC's new 'sociological adviser', Professor Oliver McGregor, told Ronald McIntosh that there was 'now a real risk that political democracy will not survive in Britain'. And in February 1974, James Lees-Milne's stockbroker friend Lord Roger Manners told him that the City expected 'a complete economic collapse any day, when we shall be in the same condition as Germany in 1923. We must expect chaos, the £ to be worth 1 penny, if we are lucky, and the oil sheiks buying up our industries. A jolly prospect.'[30]

At one level, the popularity of the Weimar parallel was a classic illustration of the contemporary obsession with the Second World War, which dominated the British imagination like no other historical event. By the end of 1973, indeed, it seemed that almost no economic setback went by without observers reaching for their textbooks on the German hyperinflation of the 1920s, the collapse of Weimar democracy and the rise of National Socialism. As Sir Alec Guinness, who wore the dictator's uniform for the wildly sensationalist film *Hitler: The Last Ten Days* (1973), told *Time* magazine, 'the situation in England strikes every month a decadent, yes *decadent* note. All these depressing things. People say, why not get someone else to sort it all out for them . . . a strong man.' Some even welcomed the prospect: David Bowie, then at the height of his fame, told the *NME* that Britain needed 'an extreme right front [to] come up and sweep everything off its feet and tidy everything up'. In 1976, he was even photographed giving what appeared to be a Nazi salute at Victoria station, although he insisted he was only waving to his fans.[31]

Most people, however, shuddered at the very notion – but that did not mean they did not take it seriously. Even the Secretary of State for the Environment, Geoffrey Rippon, reportedly told friends at a dinner party in December 1973 that Britain was 'on the same course as the Weimar government, with runaway inflation and ultra-high unemployment at the end'. That a Cabinet minister could seriously liken the situation to the last days of Weimar democracy spoke volumes about the mood of barely suppressed hysteria. And when the government sent tanks and armed police to Heathrow on 6 January for an exercise in protecting planes from terrorist attack – not such an outlandish idea, given that Palestinian terrorists had killed thirty people in Rome airport two weeks before – some observers on the left were convinced that this was actually a dry run for a military coup. 'My suspicious mind led me to the possibility that Carrington wanted to get people used to tanks and armed patrols in the streets of London,' wrote Tony Benn excitably. He almost seemed disappointed when Labour's defence spokesman Fred Peart wearily told him that it was indeed just an exercise, 'and anyway it will get the troops off their bottoms'. 'A most cynical view,' recorded an outraged Benn.[32]

It was against this background that at midnight on New Year's Eve the three-day week finally came into operation. Factories and businesses were limited to just three days of electricity – either Monday, Tuesday and Wednesday, or Thursday, Friday and Saturday – while shops, unless they were considered essential, were limited to either mornings or afternoons. Nothing like it had ever been seen before in Britain in peacetime, and life during the last days of 1973 had a faint, domesticated whiff of the last days of Pompeii about it, with reports of people queuing outside shops for bread, candles, paraffin, toilet paper and cans of soup. In many towns there had already been minor petrol panics as motorists, terrified by reports that petrol coupons had been printed and sent to post offices across the country, besieged the pumps to fill their tanks. Some garages closed down entirely; others tried to limit the demand, such as the Colchester garage that served only 'regular clients' and turned away 'casuals'. With rail services disrupted by the ASLEF dispute, commuters shivered on platforms for trains that never arrived, and with more people shopping locally for Christmas presents, some shops even ran out of toys. And nobody liked the prospect of a three-day week: in Essex, a rural vicar earned brief notoriety by telling his local paper that thanks to the unions' selfishness, the old and infirm might be 'dying of starvation within the next year or two'. The union militants, he suggested, might have to be gaoled or even shot if they 'persist in fomenting strikes', a rather unchristian view that earned him a spot on Radio Four's *The World at One*.[33]

In general, however, blame was fairly evenly divided. On Christmas Eve, a Marplan poll found that 54 per cent blamed the unions and 40 per cent the government. And although most of the press sided with the government, dissenting voices were not hard to find. The three-day week was 'the peacetime equivalent of a scorched-earth policy', insisted the

New Statesman, which predicted that 'many firms soon will go out of business, unemployment will soar, and the critical balance of payments situation will become a nightmare'. Even a few business leaders came out against the government. 'I've been down three coal mines in my life, and each time I've said, "If I had to work there, I'd want paying to go to work and paying again when I'd done it,"' said Sir Raymond Brooke, chairman of the engineering firm GKN. And all the time, letters poured in to newspapers heaping abuse on Heath's supposed stubbornness and cruelty. 'Dictator Heath and his £10,000-plus a year henchmen have imposed a three-day working week. Why? Because this yacht owner claims the miners/electricians are causing such severe damage to the nation that it is essential,' a self-described 'working class engineering employee' called Roderick Colyer wrote to *The Times*. He was a 'floating voter', he added, but his loathing for Heath, his outrage at the effects of inflation and his sheer class-consciousness smouldered from every line:

> If I sound bitter, it is because I am. I am bitter because I have to work continuous nights to earn a gross wage of £35 and a take home pay of £29. I am bitter because I can no longer meet mortgage payments and other financial expenses. I am bitter because my marriage has broken under financial strain. I am bitter because of the fortunes being made and lost by the upper and middle classes over the backs of the workers. I am bitter because the same people – the so-called industrialists and ruling classes – stop a worker having a couple of pounds extra whilst they line their pockets with rises of £315 a week plus, or the Government give them salaries of £10,000 to £20,000 a year. What on earth do they do with that type of money? I am bitter because pensioners, like my Mum and Dad, cannot get £480 a year, yet it was they that brought us through the last two world wars that the Government and others keep referring to. Unite us, Heath? Not me.[34]

On the left, scorn for the three-day week was almost universal. The radical artist Jamie Reid, later notorious as the designer of the Sex Pistols' record covers, designed a poster to be put on shop windows with the legend: 'Last Days: Buy Now While Stocks Last: This store will be closing soon owing to the pending collapse of monopoly capitalism.' Other stickers advised motorists to 'Save Petrol: Burn Cars', or to 'Keep Warm: Make Trouble'. Another told shoppers: 'Special offer . . . this store welcomes shoplifters.' For young radicals, it became a point of pride to waste power by leaving lights on, and the Labour councillors of Clay Cross, Derbyshire deliberately left their street lights on full power to show their support for 'men who deserve a better deal'. And in the *Till Death Us Do Part* episodes 'Strikes and Blackouts' and 'Three Day Week', written by the left-wing Johnny Speight and broadcast at the end of January, Alf Garnett's daughter Rita and her radical husband Mike scurry around the house turning on every appliance they can find. 'Don't Save Fuel – Use It Up!' is their slogan. Alf, of course, is horrified: conservative as ever, he blames the crisis on the ungrateful 'wogs' who are 'acting like world powers and expecting us to pay for it' and the 'Mick Commies' who write for Mike's beloved *Militant* paper. 'Mr Heath', Alf insists, is going to 'put the economy of this country right'. When Mike taunts him about unemployment, Alf angrily replies that Heath needs to 'create some unemployment'. (Perhaps Alf had been going to the Institute of Economic Affairs' lunchtime briefings.) But not even Alf can stick the three-day week for long, especially when his wife Else, who supports the miners, goes on a three-day week herself and refuses to cook his dinner. Outraged, Alf tours the shops, only to find none open. In any case, the housekeeping money has long since run out, eroded by weeks of price rises. The others, needless to say, are delighted at his discomfiture: unlike Alf, they hold Heath in total contempt. 'Everyone wants to get back on the job, everyone,' Rita bursts out bitterly. 'And everyone wants to pay the miners. But old Fatso won't, oh no. He makes me sick, every time I see him on there with his great porky face wobbling with fat.'[35]

The Garnett household's experience of the three-day week conforms absolutely to many people's recollections of the era. The lights are low, the cupboards are bare, the house is cold and the streets are empty. Since both the BBC and ITV close down at 10.30, Alf cannot even console himself with late-night television, and when the family try to play Monopoly, they are promptly struck by an apparent power cut. And of course this is how the three-day week is usually remembered: literally a murky moment in the nation's history. It was a time when newspaper advertisements ordered households to 'switch off something'; when clergymen took to the airwaves to debate the morality of family members sharing baths to save hot water; when the High Commissions of Australia and New Zealand were bombarded with enquiries about emigration; and when a government energy minister – the hapless Patrick Jenkin – urged people to 'clean their teeth in the dark', only to become a figure of public ridicule when the press found five lights blazing in his north London house first thing in the morning. Popular history has enthroned it as the defining moment of the entire 1970s and a landmark in the modern British experience, the point 'when the lights went out', when people lived by the flickering glow of candlelight, when they dug paraffin lamps out of the attic, nursed their dwindling food supplies and shivered in the freezing darkness.[36]

Ironically, though, the conventional wisdom that the three-day week saw 'the lights go out' owes more to garbled memories than to hard facts. It is true that street lamps were extinguished, many people dutifully switched off unnecessary lights and heaters, and the nation's television screens fell dark at half past ten. But contrary to popular belief, the three-day regime did *not* see widespread power cuts. The whole point of the exercise, after all, was to stop power cuts from happening. And although demand for candles went through the roof – one Battersea manufacturer turned out a million a day, the most popular coming in the shape of the Prime Minister – most people barely needed them. Later, when they remembered hosting dinner parties by candlelight or playing board games beside a guttering paraffin lamp, people were actually recalling the last weeks of 1970 or the early months of 1972, not (as they thought) the first weeks of 1974. It was not even particularly cold: as luck would have it, the weather took a turn for the better in the New Year, and the temperatures in January and February were almost twice as high as usual. Indeed, the weather was so mild that after less than three weeks, it was already clear that the predictions of blackouts and anarchy had been wildly exaggerated. Fuel stocks were much 'higher than had been expected', Peter Walker told the Cabinet on 17 January, 'because of warm weather and because of the satisfactory response to Ministerial appeals for savings in domestic consumption'. It was now likely that 'the coal stocks by the end of March would still amount to 11 million tons', something few had imagined possible just weeks before. And even at this early stage Walker thought there was 'room for cautious relaxation of the three-day week'. Backed by the CBI and the Electricity Board, some ministers were even pressing for a transition to a four-day week, which would 'help to maintain overseas confidence in the pound'. Indeed, instead of preparing to put troops on the streets to fight off revolution, the government was now thinking up ways to defend itself from accusations that it had overreacted. They should tell people, Heath said, that 'common prudence had required them to plan for the worst' – and thankfully the worst had not happened.[37]

For many people, of course, the three-day week was not only inconvenient but deeply alarming. Many small businesses, forced to become part-time enterprises overnight, found it impossible to pay bills left over from their five-day operations. Hundreds of thousands of people lost their jobs – albeit only temporarily – because there was not enough work for them to do, and on 13 January LWT's current affairs show *Weekend World* claimed that national income had fallen by up to 15 per cent, a bigger drop than in the General Strike or the worst year of the Great Depression. And yet the truth is that the economic impact of the three-day week was much smaller than anyone had imagined. Since many companies offered their men longer hours on their three working days, average weekly take-home pay actually fell by just £2 from £37.69 in December to £35.71 in January. The rise in unemployment, too, was much less drastic than expected, the figures rising from 2.1 per cent in December to 2.4 per cent in February, by which time only 600,000 workers were still on short time. Perhaps most strikingly, though, the three-day week caused much less damage to production than had been anticipated, not least because many firms responded with energy and ingenuity, using battered old screwdrivers and spanners to keep working even when the power had been turned off. In Nottingham, clerical staff at Raleigh Industries worked without heat or light so that all power could be switched to the production line; in Sheffield, a snuff-making firm reverted to using a waterwheel that had last seen action in 1737; on the King's Road, Chelsea, a furrier's shop displayed the sign 'OPEN SIX DAYS A WEEK – BY CANDLE POWER, BATTERY POWER AND WILL POWER'. And in the Berkshire New Town of Bracknell, production levels fell by less than a tenth – which spoke volumes for the energy with which firms approached the three-day week, but did not exactly say much for their efficiency beforehand. Indeed, even though many firms lost 40 per cent of their working hours, they still maintained production at 75 to 80 per cent, and by the end of February output was virtually back to normal. British industry had handled the crisis with 'something approaching gusto', enthused the *Sunday Times*, hailing its 'impressive powers of improvisation' and 'imaginative derring-do' – but rather glossing over the implication that firms could not be working very hard over five days if they found the transition so easy.[38]

The irony of all this was that it worked against the government. Heath's advisers had banked on the three-day week stoking a crisis atmosphere that would mobilize people behind a brave, Churchillian Prime Minister, but the anticipated sense of outrage never materialized. Indeed, some people seemed almost to enjoy the experience, rediscovering habits they had lost since the advent of television, from reading and playing board games to pursuing hobbies and diversions outside the home. Audiences trebled for late-night radio shows hosted by John Peel and 'Whispering' Bob Harris, who liked to torment night owls with interminable progressive rock. Fishing-tackle shops reported booming sales, golf courses were deluged with aspiring Tony Jacklins, and the introduction of earlier kick-off times and Sunday games allowed the Football League to continue as normal, with Don Revie's Leeds United setting a record of twenty-nine matches without defeat. The average worker's loss of £10 a week (an estimate that later proved wildly exaggerated), the actor Robert Morley helpfully suggested in *The Times*, was surely worth 'freedom, happiness, getting to know the neighbours, even one's own kids. Discovering literature and theatre, discovering art and life. Ten pounds a week – it's cheap at the price.' 'Now, at last, we've time to do all those lazy – and free – things we always wanted,' agreed the *Daily Mail*'s Jane Gaskell, suggesting that 'the 1974 crisis could, surprisingly, be good for us'. Given the materialism of modern society, it was no bad thing to return to an 'almost peasant state', and people ought to relish 're-reading an old book or digging a garden'. She even found a psychiatrist who thought, in classic early 1970s style, that the three-day week was a chance for husbands and wives 'to be more spontaneous, to experiment more in their sex lives while the children are doing a five-day week at school'.*39

The obvious problem for Heath was that in the absence of any sense of crisis or Dunkirk spirit, people were bound to turn against the government who had inflicted the three-day week on them. As Alan Watkins remarked in the *New Statesman*, there seemed to be no sense of personal involvement in the crisis, since most people knew 'perfectly well that switching off the odd electric light bulb here and there is going to have about as much effect on the power situation as collecting Lord Beaverbrook's ludicrous aluminium saucepans had on the course of the Battle of Britain' – the wartime analogy again. And as Watkins predicted, unless the government quickly resolved the situation, there was a strong chance the voters would elect another to do it for them. Polls found

---

* It evidently worked for some couples. I was born almost exactly nine months after the beginning of the three-day week.

support for the emergency measures steadily declining, and even many Conservative supporters concluded that the government had overreacted. In Downing Street, Douglas Hurd became seriously worried that the miners were winning the propaganda war. And on 10 January, Kenneth Williams found himself on a commuter train 'packed with vexed & irritated passengers' whose services had been disrupted in the ongoing ASLEF dispute. 'We all seem to be taking these ridiculous measures like a load of sheep,' one passenger from Lancashire remarked. 'Nobody is protesting . . . no coal, no transport, nothing.' 'And you feel this in all conversation,' Williams recorded later, 'that it has gone too far . . . that the 3 day week etc. is all rubbish and the miners should be paid. Oh, it's ghastly.' Even *Doctor Who* came out for the NUM, albeit a few months late. When the Doctor makes a new expedition to the planet Peladon, where miners are striking for better conditions and against modern working methods, he advises the Queen to send for their moderate leader Gebek (but not his hot-headed deputy Ettis, an intergalactic Mick McGahey to Gebek's Joe Gormley). 'Promise him a better way of life for his miners, and see that they get it,' the Doctor suggests. 'You've got to convince your people that the Federation means a better way of life for everybody, not just for a few nobles at court.'[40]

At the court of King Ted, the mood was bleak. 'They were all very tired men,' recalled the Cabinet Secretary, Sir John Hunt, later. 'It struck me that the smell of death was around.' For three and a half years, ministers and officials had taken their lead from their captain, yet Heath now cut a curiously indecisive figure, listless and lethargic where he had once been curt and decisive. Some aides worried that, as a lonely man with nobody to comfort him in the midnight hour, he had succumbed to depression. No doubt his thyroid condition also played its part. And for a man who only a few years before had prided himself on his sporting hinterland, he was also suddenly and very noticeably overweight. When the *Daily Express*'s formidable columnist Jean Rook wondered if he was getting a bit fat, Heath blamed the three-day week. 'Yes, I must say I am,' he said mournfully. 'The trouble is I don't get any swimming now. We had to turn off the pool heating at Chequers – it's oil.'[41]

Heath's indecisiveness was particularly marked over the question of an early election to take advantage of the crisis. The idea had been floating around for a long time: as early as November 1972, *Private Eye* had reported 'considerable agitation in the Tory ranks for a spring election on the simple issue of bashing the unions'. The following February, the Conservative Research Department was already making contingency plans for a 'snap' election fought on a single issue, and by the summer of 1973 Central Office already had a draft manifesto and a list of possible dates. The biggest champion of an early election, though, was the young journalist Nigel Lawson, who was recruited to the Conservative Research Department in October 1973 and argued tirelessly for Heath to seek a new mandate based on the oil crisis and the transition to an age of austerity. It was Lawson who persuaded Douglas Hurd – his future Cabinet colleague – that an early election was a good idea, and they were supported by the party chairman and deputy chairman, Lord Carrington and Jim Prior, who reported that local activists were itching for a fight to the death with the unions. Persuading the Prime Minister, however, was rather more difficult. 'Slowly the band waggon for an early General Election is beginning to roll,' Hurd noted in his diary on 18 December – 'but EH, so far as one can gather, still unconvinced.'[42]

Choosing the day he will face the voters is probably the single most important decision any Prime Minister has to make, and not one to be taken lightly. But there were obvious advantages to an early election. The miners' dispute had not done Heath's popularity any harm: indeed, on 7 December an ORC poll put the Tories ahead of Labour for only the second time in two years. In the press, speculation mounted that Heath might take advantage of the apparent spirit of national unity at a time of crisis: *The Times* ran a front-page story on the possibility five days later, and on 17 December the paper's political correspondent David Wood devoted his column to discussing the pros and cons. And even after the three-day week began, the polls remained promising. At the beginning of January, both ORC and Gallup still had the Conservatives narrowly ahead – and this, of course, after two years in which they had been consistently lagging – and on 10 January NOP reported that the Tory lead had stretched to 4 per cent. The Conservative Party seemed robust, united, hungry for the battle; by contrast, the Liberals were still desperately trying to find candidates for many seats, while Labour were arguing among themselves about the right way to handle the miners' dispute. And as everyone knew, a new electoral register was due to come in on 15 February – and it would suit the government to fight under the old one.[43]

Yet Heath was uneasy at the thought of an early election. His mandate still had eighteen months to run: if he wanted, he could wait until June 1975 before he faced the voters. Crucially, almost all of his senior ministers, many of whom had waited years to get their hands on the levers of power, disapproved of the idea. Willie Whitelaw, now effectively deputy Prime Minister, was dead against it, partly because he still hoped to settle the miners' dispute, but also because he dreaded its effect on the delicate power-sharing arrangement in Northern Ireland. The former Chief Whip Francis Pym, now moved to replace Whitelaw at Stormont, agreed with him; so did the Home Secretary, Robert Carr. Even Heath's most influential mandarin, Sir William Armstrong, thought it was a bad idea: it would look as if the government was 'running away' from its problems, he said. And above all, it offended all of Heath's political instincts. To him it smacked of cynical self-interest: going for a quick victory on the back of an international crisis and an old electoral register was just the kind of thing that Harold Wilson would do. And while his grass-roots activists and younger aides wanted him to rally the nation against the miners, he shrank from the idea. On the steps of Number 10, after all, he had promised 'to create one nation'. He wanted the unions beside him as his partners, not against him as his enemies. And when Heath went to South Worcestershire on New Year's Eve, addressing a Tory rally on the eve of a crucial by-election (and the eve of the three-day week), Douglas Hurd was struck by his refusal to exploit the situation. 'He could have worked that audience to a pitch of fiery loyalty,' Hurd wrote. 'He could have whipped them up against the miners. He could have sent them excited and enthusiastic into the streets. It did not occur him to do so . . . He saw it as his duty to educate and inform, not to inflame one part of the country against another.'[44]

Deep down, Heath had never quite given up hope that if he held firm, if the country rallied and the three-day week worked, then the miners would see sense. 'Heath believes that if the miners can be convinced that they have no chance of getting an increase beyond Phase 3,' his energy minister Patrick Jenkin told Ronald McIntosh, 'they will cut their losses and agree to talk about pensions, a long-term review of the coal industry, etc.' What Heath was not prepared to accept, however, was a deal that went beyond Stage Three – as became clear when, on Wednesday, 9 January, the unions came up with what seemed to be an honourable compromise. The TUC's new general secretary Len Murray had no desire to begin his tenure with a titanic battle against the government. He was keen to see the end of the three-day week, which was damaging his members' earnings, and he was worried that the longer the dispute went on, the more it would destroy the relationship between Downing Street and the unions. Other union leaders, too, including Jack Jones and Hugh Scanlon, were similarly anxious to bring the crisis to an end. And when the NEDC met at Millbank on 9 January, bringing together union leaders, ministers and business leaders, the railwaymen's leader Sidney Greene – regarded as one of the most moderate union bosses – produced the text of a compromise. 'The General Council accept that there is a distinctive and exceptional situation in the mining industry,' he read aloud. 'If the Government are prepared to give an assurance that they will make possible a settlement between the miners and the National Coal Board, other unions will not use this as an argument in negotiations in their own settlements.' When he had finished, the other union leaders murmured their agreement. Even Jones and Scanlon, Len Murray told Ronald McIntosh, 'were completely committed to it'.[45]

The TUC's offer seemed the perfect opportunity for the government to strike a deal with the miners without sacrificing Stage Three – the perfect opportunity to have peace with honour. So McIntosh was all the more astonished when Anthony Barber immediately said no. The Chancellor 'said several times that HMG could not in any circumstances contemplate any settlement outside Phase 3', McIntosh recorded. The Treasury mandarin Sir Douglas Allen, who was in the middle of writing Barber a note urging him to 'keep talking', was stunned when his boss said curtly: 'It's not good enough.' Even the union leaders were taken aback by his 'negative and hostile' tone, and Greene read the statement again in case Barber had misunderstood it. There is some disagreement whether Barber bothered to consult Heath: the Chancellor later claimed he slipped out to ring him from a payphone, while McIntosh and Jack Jones insisted that he never moved. Some onlookers even claim that if Heath had been there instead of Barber, he might have accepted the deal, changing the entire course of British political history. But this seems very unlikely. Sir John Hunt remembered Barber coming round to Number 10 later that afternoon to tell Heath what had happened. Their discussion, Hunt recalled, was 'very short' indeed: it was clear that Heath agreed with his Chancellor's position.[46]

As the point at which the miners' strike and general election of

February 1974 might have been averted, Barber's rejection of the TUC's offer is one of the most intriguing what-ifs of modern political history. McIntosh thought Barber was mad to reject such a 'serious and well-considered' offer, while even Mick McGahey, whose priorities were rather different, thought that the miners would have accepted the deal, and was delighted that Barber turned it down. But the truth is that Heath and Barber never believed it could work. As Barber pointed out, the TUC had always refused to promise that other unions 'would not do this, that or the other', so he never believed that they could 'bring home the bacon'. Neither he nor Heath had much faith in Len Murray, a quiet, mild man who had only just taken over at the top of the TUC. If Murray had been serious, they thought, he would have come to them privately beforehand instead of grandstanding in front of the union bosses. Above all, they had no confidence in the TUC's ability to enforce what was basically a toothless agreement. It was all very well for the TUC to pledge that the miners were an exceptional case, Heath said later. 'But I said, does this mean that there'll be no other special cases? You see, you can say the miners have special circumstances, therefore they are a special case – now suppose special circumstances of a different kind come along, will you . . . agree that that is not a special case?' In particular, he was worried about the electricians, whose leader Frank Chapple had already announced that if the miners got a deal outside Stage Three, he would demand one too. Could the TUC really keep him in line? And for that matter, could the union leaders really be trusted to restrain their own members?[47]

Of course, a more cynical politician would have taken the deal even though he knew it might fail. Jim Prior, for instance, thought that 'it would have got us off the hook, and put the unions on their best behaviour. Had their self-restraint failed, we would then have been in a much stronger position to take whatever steps might then have been necessary.' Even Len Murray made the same argument. 'If [Heath] had taken the offer and it had failed to work,' he said later, 'he would have been home and dry with all his anti-union policies – Industrial Relations Act and incomes policy. If it had worked, it would have been his great political triumph, showing he could bring the unions to heel.' But it was not Heath's style to accept a bargain knowing that it might break down. By now his political instincts, never very strong anyway, had been dulled by three years in office: he saw himself as a national statesman, an honest broker, not a man who struck grubby deals for personal advantage, as Harold Wilson did. And at the point when a more cunning, supple politician might have taken the deal, presenting it as a victory while quietly preparing the ground for an offensive against the unions if they failed to honour their side of the bargain, Heath obstinately stuck to his guns. It was Stage Three or nothing, he said. So he got nothing.[48]

If the union leaders were astonished at Heath's stubborn refusal to countenance a deal, they were even more struck by his uncharacteristic behaviour as the three-day week wore on. Once so proud and self-assured, the Conradian captain on the bridge of his ship, he now seemed more like a sullen, self-pitying schoolboy. Murray recalled that at their meetings 'there were very long silences. Ted would sit for what seemed like minutes with his head sunk deep on his chest, pondering.' But for many observers, the most revealing moment came during talks on 21 January, when the Prime Minister seemed more taciturn and miserable than ever. At last, after the meeting had got nowhere, Hugh Scanlon turned to Heath and asked directly: 'Is there anything, anything at all, that we can say or do that will satisfy you?' As Murray recalled, 'Heath remained silent: his head sunk into his shoulders: wanting to say something but unable to do so.' Yet missing from the union leaders' account was another exchange that told the other side of the story and made the stalemate painfully clear. Later in the same meeting, Heath roused himself from his gloom, 'turned across the table to the TUC', and said bluntly: 'But if an exceptional settlement were conceded to the miners, you know you couldn't hold the line, could you?' 'That too was followed by silence,' a watching civil servant recalled. 'It seems to me that represented the distance between the two positions.'[49]

In the meantime, the pressure on Heath to take his case to the voters was becoming virtually irresistible. 'Election rumours continue to grow at a fantastic rate,' recorded Tony Benn on 12 January. By now, Tory party officials were working on the assumption that an election was coming, and Lord Carrington's soundings among local activists found a strong consensus for going to the country in early February. On 11 January, Heath reluctantly authorized Central Office to begin its election countdown; three days later, *The Times* declared that there was 'ample constitutional justification for an immediate election', while its political correspondent David Wood wrote that unless there was an unexpected and immediate breakthrough, Heath had 'no choice but to decide on an early election or make himself a hostage to fortune until spring'. This was Heath's moment: by now, almost everybody expected that he would go to the country on 7 February and ask for a mandate to lead Britain through the economic crisis.[50]

Yet even now Heath shrank from the crucial decision. Even now an election campaign pitting the government against the unions was the last thing he wanted. And when he summoned his chief advisers to Chequers to discuss the election, it was clear his heart was not in it. 'Everything was geared up for 7 February,' recalled Nigel Lawson. Then: '13 January. Chequers. Sunday . . . for the first time Ted actually *expressed* scepticism about an election.' Instead of giving his men the green light, Heath told Lawson to redraft the proposed manifesto – a sign, some thought, that he was losing his nerve. 'Unhappy evening. We are in a desperate plight. I long to get the election behind us,' wrote Douglas Hurd, one of the young hawks. Two days later, Lawson reported back. But by this stage the momentum seemed to be evaporating. When they met to review Lawson's draft, Hurd noted, 'the Prime Minister was slack in the chair, and we made slow progress'. He felt like one of Elizabeth I's courtiers arguing for the execution of Mary Queen of Scots, trying to wear down the monarch's instinctive resistance. The difference, however, was that Heath was up against a tight deadline. If he wanted an election on 7 February, he had to call it by 17 January. The day before the deadline, he seemed to be leaning towards an election at last: Carrington and Hurd thought their pressure had done the trick. But at the crucial moment they dropped their guard. Late that night, Willie Whitelaw invited his chief for a private dinner, just the two of them, and it was then that he persuaded him that the risks were too great. The next day, no announcement came. Heath had changed his mind.[51]

Many Tories were furious at Heath's reluctance to call a contest. The aspiring politician Alan Clark, who had been adopted as the Conservative candidate for Plymouth Sutton, had been 'in tremendous form' at the prospect of fighting on an 'anti-union platform'. 'Now total reversal,' he recorded. 'Heath lost his nerve at the last moment that afternoon, morale shattered.' Jim Prior, meanwhile, was aghast: in the Commons that afternoon he angrily told his leader that he had made a terrible mistake. 'We had already marched the Party's troops up the hill, ready for combat,' he warned, 'and then had to march them down again; it would be much harder to march them up a second time.' By contrast, the Opposition were delighted, crowing that the Tories had lost their nerve. 'The Labour Party and the people in the Tea Room are raising their hats to you this afternoon,' Prior snapped, 'and saying you let them off the hook.'[52]

But not everybody thought Heath had made a mistake. A week later, Alan Clark, afflicted with atrocious toothache, was sitting in his dentist's waiting room when he noticed 'an old gentleman wearing a mac' loudly rustling a copy of *The Times* 'in a rather ego, demonstrative manner'. After a moment, Clark realized who it was – '*Uncle Harold!*' – and when the aspiring MP went over, he found the former Prime Minister in fine and talkative form. An election, Macmillan said, 'would be a disaster', because the working classes 'would see it as a loyalty vote'. He thought 'that the miners had to be bought off until North Sea oil came on stream', Clark recorded; 'that it should not be difficult to outmanoeuvre Len Murray; that McGahey wasn't popular in the TUC; that the real agitator was (*Scrimgeour** was it? – the words came thick and fast and I was transfixed); that it was urgent to find some way of reassuring the middle classes who were puzzled and that we ought now to be talking to the Liberal Party.' All good advice, as it turned out. Perhaps it was a shame for the Conservatives that Heath's teeth were in good condition.[53]

But by this stage Heath was being swept along by events like a drowning man in a roiling sea. On 23 January, the miners' executive voted by a narrow majority to hold a pithead ballot on an all-out strike. 'With fuel stocks holding out and spring around the corner,' Joe Gormley wrote, 'our final card had to be played now or never.' Heath's advisers were in despair: as Hurd remarked, 'it was clear that reason was not going to prevail.' But the Prime Minister had not given up hope: in one last desperate effort, he had a patriotic appeal photocopied and sent to every member of the NUM executive, reminding them that the oil crisis had plunged Britain into the worst economic emergency since 1945, and promising that if they settled within Stage Three, they would get a sweeping re-evaluation of pay and conditions later. It did no good: in Gormley's view, 'it was obviously designed for the public's ears, as much as for ours'. In any case, many miners had long since made up their minds that they wanted a fight. 'We've poleaxed Ted Heath before, an' we shall do it again,' one young miner told a television interviewer. 'Heath's

---

* Presumably Arthur Scargill; if so, a remarkably perceptive remark, given that Scargill had only just become president of the Yorkshire miners.

decided he's going to have the miners going back on their bellies,' agreed the NUM's spokesman in Mansfield. 'I've got news for him. We crawl on our bellies all day long and we're sick of it. When we're done with Heath, he'll be the one on his belly.' But it was a miner from the Rhondda who best expressed the spirit of defiance:

> If Ted Heath would come to our colliery, I would take him by the arm and show him how we work. We would go down the pit and walk two miles to the coal face, crouching because of the low roof. His eyes would sting with the dust and he would think his brain was coming loose with the noise of the drills. He would see us eat sandwiches with filthy hands and hear about roof falls and he would get tired just watching us dig coal for seven hours a day in all that din and muck. Then I would say, 'Would you do it – the stinkingest job in Britain – for thirty-one quid take-home?' And while he was pondering I would tell him the day of the cheap miner is over.[54]

On Monday, 4 February, the NUM announced that an overwhelming 81 per cent of miners had voted for an all-out strike to begin at midnight on Sunday. For Heath, it was a dreadful moment. Despite all his efforts, the miners had declared war on the government for the second time in three years. There was talk of trying to arrange a new bargain under the aegis of the Pay Board, which had just issued a report on the problem of pay relativities. But both the TUC and the NUM had lost patience with the government; indeed, Gormley refused point-blank even to meet Willie Whitelaw without an offer of more money on the table. As David Wood grimly but presciently wrote in *The Times*, there were now only three possible outcomes: 'surrender by the government, in circumstances that would make further surrenders inevitable; a fight to the finish in which the British economy would be devastated; or a general election decided in conditions of bitterness and perhaps violence that would make Conservative Government nearly impossible and the return of a Labour Government the signal for runaway inflation'. But even Heath now saw no alternative: if the miners and the government could not settle their differences, then the people must decide. The following evening, he dined with his closest advisers at Prunier's, his favourite restaurant. Hurd joined them 'for a glass after dinner' and found them in gloomy form. 'Mr Heath explained more clearly than ever before his desperate worry about the size of the stake on the table,' he recorded. 'Everything which he had tried to do seemed at risk. No one pressed him that evening. Events had already taken over the argument.'[55]

Not only had events overtaken the argument, but an extraordinarily febrile, almost hysterical mood had enveloped the highest ranks of government. In the Commons the next day, Anthony Barber – who had endured perhaps the roughest, worst-judged and unluckiest ride of any Chancellor since the war – was on astonishingly strident form, telling the House that the blame for the crisis lay with Labour, who had been deliberately stirring up 'envy and hatred' across the land. 'The issue at stake', he insisted, 'is whether our affairs are to be governed by the rule of reason, by the rule of Parliament and by the rule of democracy. The vast majority of people in Britain detest the alternative, which ultimately can only be chaos, anarchy and a totalitarian or Communist regime.' This was strong stuff, but Barber was not the only senior figure feeling the pressure. Only a few days before, Heath's indispensable right-hand man, his ever-reliable mandarin Sir William Armstrong, had finally cracked under the strain. As the architect of Stage Three and the most intense and uncompromising of all the counter-inflation hawks, Armstrong had long since lost sight of his role as a supposedly neutral civil servant. Over Christmas and the New Year he had consistently urged Heath to take a hard line against the miners, even talking of the crisis as an apocalyptic clash between the state and the unions, between democracy and Communism. Many ministers worried that Armstrong was losing his mind: Prior thought he now saw himself as a 'messianic' figure.[56]

On the last weekend of January, attending an Anglo-American conference at Ditchley Park, Oxfordshire, Armstrong was in particularly strange, domineering form. Showing an appropriately diplomatic touch, Hurd wrote later that 'the atmosphere was Chekhovian. We sat on sofas in front of great log fires and discussed first principles while the rain lashed the windows. Sir William was full of notions, ordinary and extraordinary.' Other participants remembered that Armstrong seemed obsessed with coups and coalitions, subjects much in the air at the time: that very week, the *Spectator*'s editorial had claimed: 'Britain is on a Chilean brink.' One of Armstrong's more extraordinary notions, recalled the CBI's Campbell Adamson, was that 'the Communists were infiltrating everything. They might even be infiltrating, he said, the room he was in. It was quite clear that the immense strain and overwork was taking its toll.' And when Armstrong returned to London the following Monday it was obvious that he was seriously unwell. 'He really did go mad,' Heath's young aide William Waldegrave confided to the journalist Hugo Young. 'He used to talk about the phoenix rising from the ashes . . . He really believed in the ruination of Britain, to be followed by the resurrection. He talked about things like "I'll move my red army this way and the blue army that way."' This was a bit much, even by the standards of the early 1970s: when a delegation from the CBI visited Armstrong on 31 January, they were horrified to find him 'under great strain and almost mentally ill'. One account has Sir William haranguing a meeting of stunned ministers about the need to resist a Communist coup; another has him locking a group of Permanent Secretaries in a room before lecturing them about 'the Bible and sex'. The climax seems to have come when, waiting for an appointment with the Prime Minister, Armstrong lay full length on the floor of Number 10 while lecturing the visiting head of the Institute of Chartered Accountants. Another version has him removing his clothes and haranguing the Governor of the Bank of England, though this is probably a bit of an exaggeration. In any case, this clearly could not go on: later that afternoon Armstrong was at last persuaded to see Victor Rothschild, who 'diagnosed insanity' and sent him off to his villa in Barbados to recuperate.[57]

Even if Armstrong had still been on the scene in early February, it is unlikely he could have dissuaded Heath from going to the country. The pressure from his own party was now overwhelming: in the Commons on 6 February, Denis Healey memorably gibed that his old friend had been 'manipulated into this dead end by an oddly assorted quartet of his colleagues, who are now trundling him like a great marble statue towards the precipice'. The polls were mixed: the latest Harris poll had the government 4 per cent ahead, but Gallup put them 3 per cent behind. But as David Wood explained in that morning's *Times*, 'the Conservative Party sees itself facing a choice of blind alleys and dead ends unless a general election brings in a government with refreshed authority and a renewed lease'. Better an election, most Tories thought, than another gruelling war of attrition against an enemy who had already beaten them once. And Heath himself, his reserves of energy and intellect utterly spent, no longer had the patience to stand in their way. Just after half past twelve on Thursday, 7 February – ironically, the very day that the hawks had originally wanted for an early election – Radio Two broke into the *Jimmy Young Show* with a news flash that Heath had asked the Queen for a dissolution of Parliament and an election in three weeks' time. 'In the House it was like the end of term,' noted Tony Benn, 'with cheering and counter cheering and shouting and so on.' But not everyone was quite so excited. 'Some Tories are obviously distressed,' recorded Barbara Castle. '"No one wants this election," one of them told me.'[58]

That evening, Heath addressed the nation for the final time as Prime Minister. Even now he refused to take on the miners directly, talking only in vague but painfully sincere terms about the importance of Stage Three and the threat of inflation; indeed, he emphasized that he was happy to refer the miners' claim to the Pay Board and would abide by its recommendation. But he insisted that an election would give ordinary people a chance to say to the unions: 'Times are hard, we are all in the same boat, and if you sink us now we will all drown.' Looking earnestly into the camera, he explained:

> The issue before you is a simple one. As a country we face grave problems at home and abroad. Do you want a strong Government which has clear authority for the future to take the decisions which will be needed?
>
> Do you want Parliament and the elected Government to continue to fight strenuously against inflation?
>
> Or do you want them to abandon the struggle against rising prices under pressure from one particularly powerful group of workers? . . .
>
> This time the strife has got to stop. Only you can stop it. It's time for you to speak – with your vote.
>
> It's time for your voice to be heard – the voice of the moderate and reasonable people of Britain: the voice of the majority.
>
> It's time for you to say to the extremists, the militants, and the plain and simply misguided: we've had enough. There's a lot to be done. For heaven's sake, let's get on with it.

It was an appeal summed up in a simple two-word phrase – a phrase that became a symbol of the decade. 'Who governs?' But the answer was not what Heath was expecting.[59]

16

The Crisis Election

These are the greatest days England's ever gone through. The people are rising at last!
  – Mike Rawlins in *Till Death Us Do Part*, 30 January 1974

Went to bed & dreamed that I was attending a political meeting addressed by Harold Wilson. I was talking to him & he was complaining of the sparse attendance, and I saw Heath in the front row smiling and wearing a ridiculous square shouldered ladies' musquash coat. It was absurd.
  – Kenneth Williams's diary, 9 March 1974

The coach left from Chorlton Street, Manchester just after eleven on Sunday evening, picking up speed as it reached the M62. It was packed with servicemen and their families – young men telling jokes under their breath, young wives trying to get some sleep, children snoring or staring out of the window – who had spent the weekend with friends and relatives in Manchester, and were now heading back to their barracks in Catterick and Darlington. Normally they would have taken the train, but of course there were no trains, because of the ASLEF dispute that had crippled the railway network since December. So the army had booked a North Yorkshire coach company to pick them up. As it happened, the driver, Rowland Handley, was a director of the firm, and knew the route well. After twenty minutes he stopped in Oldham to pick up a second group of passengers, and half an hour later in Huddersfield he collected some more. By midnight he had almost reached Leeds, making excellent time along the motorway, and behind him many of the passengers were fast asleep. And then it happened.

One moment the coach was cruising smoothly and effortlessly through the night. The next there was an almighty, heart-stopping bang, as 25 pounds of high explosive went off in one of the luggage lockers. In that instant, the entire back of the coach was torn apart, the force of the blast sending pieces of twisted, blackened metal spinning across the carriageway. At the front, Rowland Handley, who had no idea what was happening, struggled to keep his grip on the wheel as shards of the shattered windscreen flew into his face and the vehicle lurched across the road. Somehow – he never knew how – he managed to steer what remained of the coach towards the side of the road, braking desperately, blood pouring from his forehead. He turned off the engine, fumbled for a torch, and heaved himself trembling from the cab. Mr Handley could hardly have realized it in those desperate, frantic moments, but by keeping the coach on the road so long he had probably saved dozens of lives. But what he saw next would live with him for ever. He had served in Cyprus with the RAF, but he had never seen anything like it. The entire back section of the coach had simply been shredded. As he disbelievingly moved his torch over the wreckage, he saw 'a young child of two or three lying in the road. It was dead. There were bodies all over.'

The explosion was so great that it shook buildings half a mile away. But to many of the survivors it seemed like a terrible nightmare from which they would soon awake. 'I just thought it was a dream, I just thought I'd fallen asleep into a bad dream and I just kept on shaking my head and trying to come round,' said David Dendeck. 'Then I found out it was real. I was just under all this metal. There was blood coming in my eye . . . It was dark and there were people screaming and running up the verge on the grass. I could hear my sister on the other side of the coach shouting for me.' Another passenger, 20-year-old Trooper Michael Ashton, had been sitting behind the driver when the bomb went off. Now, staggering around the side of the vehicle, he came across 'a girl about 17', who had been thrown '200 yards back up the road'. She was hysterical, he remembered; her legs were crumpled and useless. Around her lay more bodies, motionless, bloody, some of them women and children. 'It was just absolutely unbelievable,' said John Clark, a passing motorist who stopped to help. 'The smell was what upset me really. It was dark so you couldn't see how bad the injuries really were, but it was the smell of it. It was absolutely total carnage.'

Eleven people died that night, Sunday, 4 February 1974, victims of the Provisional IRA. Eight of them were soldiers in their late teens or early twenties. One of the dead soldiers, 23-year-old Corporal Clifford Houghton, had been travelling with his wife Linda and their two children, 5-year-old Robert and 2-year-old Lee. All three were killed alongside him, an entire family wiped out in the blink of an eye. Fifty people were injured, many of them seriously; one, a 6-year-old boy, was so badly burned that doctors feared for his life. For years afterwards, the survivors had to cope with nightmares, trauma and disability: as one Oldham lad, just 18 when the bomb went off, remarked at the unveiling of a memorial thirty-five years later, it was a moment that, try as he might, he could 'never forget'. But of course he was one of the lucky ones; four days after the atrocity, a twelfth victim died of his injuries, his death casting a dark shadow over the first day of the general election campaign.[1]

It was not the first time the Provisionals had launched attacks on the mainland. In March 1973 they had set off bombs at the Old Bailey, while in August and September they had planted explosives at Harrods, King's Cross and Euston, as well as in Birmingham, where a soldier had been killed trying to defuse the bomb. But this was something new: a devastating, indiscriminate atrocity, extinguishing the lives of a dozen people. In the next few days, newspaper columnists and politicians clamoured for the reintroduction of the death penalty for terrorists. And in the panicked rush to judgement, a mentally ill but entirely innocent woman, Judith Ward, was eventually sent to prison – the first in a series of miscarriages of justice born out of the intense pressure to find scapegoats for the murderous handiwork of the IRA.

The horror on the M62 seemed yet another indication of a society in which the veneer of consensus had cracked, a society lurching into violence and disorder. And although the election campaign meant that the coach bombing quickly disappeared from the headlines, it was far from the last attack on British soil. On 13 February a second bomb ripped through the National Defence College in the sleepy village of Latimer, Buckinghamshire. Ten people were badly hurt; no one, miraculously, was killed. But by now terrorism seemed to be the stuff of everyday life. Quite apart from the slaughter in Northern Ireland, the previous six months had seen a hijacking in Austria, an embassy bombing in Marseilles, a massacre at Rome airport, the assassination of the Spanish Prime Minister, and the kidnapping of the American heiress Patty Hearst. Not even the Royal Family, 'the symbol of the nation and of the standards which

Britain has lived by', was immune. On the evening of 20 March, as Princess Anne and Captain Mark Phillips were returning from a charity event for disabled children, an armed madman held up the Princess's car in the Mall and told her to get out. 'Not bloody likely!' she snapped, and in the ensuing melee she managed to get away. But it was yet another sign, said *The Times*, that 'acts of casual terrorism' had become 'part of the texture of our lives in the 1970s'. 'There is no pause in violence,' it lamented; it was 'as though the vanguard of anarchy were at loose in the world . . . We do not suffer this pressure of anarchy more than other countries, but we do not suffer it less either. It is a sign of a civilization in regression, turning back from achievement to a neobarbarism.'[2]

It was against this dark and bloody backdrop that Edward Heath launched his great election gamble. It was, the press agreed, an election without precedent in modern British history. Both the *Sun* and the *Mirror* called it the 'Crisis Election': every morning the slogan adorned their front pages. What was at stake, said *The Times*, was 'more than one strike: it is the future of the country'. Nobody could remember an election in grimmer circumstances. The Harris poll found that nine out of ten people thought 'things are going very badly for Britain', while only two out of ten expected the desperate economic situation to improve over the next twelve months. And while the politicians warned darkly of bitterness and extremism, and exchanged accusations that their opponents were dividing the country, perhaps the really depressing thing was the sheer passivity, the gloom and apathy that seemed to have enveloped the general public. The experience of the last ten years, wrote the *Guardian*'s perceptive columnist Peter Jenkins the day after the election was declared, proved only that 'neither party' could handle Britain's problems. As the authoritative Nuffield study of the election put it a few months later, 'it was an unpopularity contest between two contenders widely seen as incompetent on the major issues'.[3]

Heath set out his case for re-election in the first Conservative election broadcast, three days into the campaign. The theme was Heath as the man of destiny, the strong leader guiding the nation through stormy waters. At the beginning, supposedly ordinary voters told the camera that he had 'done all that is expected of a Prime Minister', and would 'get England back on its feet'. Then Heath himself told the audience that his quarrel was not with the broad union movement but with 'a small group of extremists'. It was 'time to take a firm line', he said, 'because only by being firm can we hope to be fair'. This was the theme of the manifesto, too, which was entitled *Firm Action for a Fair Britain*. Some readers were shocked by the manifesto's strident rhetoric: not only did it claim that the Opposition had been taken over by 'a small group of power-hungry trade union leaders' who were 'committed to a left-wing programme more dangerous and more extreme than ever before in its history', it warned that a Labour victory would be a 'major national disaster'. In fact, even this was only a watered-down version of Nigel Lawson's original draft, which had claimed that 'the very fabric of our society is at risk', only to be rejected by Tory colleagues who thought it was too 'hard and anti-union'.[4]

Beneath the surface of the Conservative campaign, which was spear-headed by Heath at his most presidential, there ran an undercurrent of deep anxiety, even paranoia, about the consequences of defeat. The long months of tension had taken their toll, and on 19 February the Tories' advertising team overstepped the mark with a particularly embarrassing example of hysterical scaremongering. On screen, pictures of Harold Wilson and James Callaghan dissolved to show the terrifying features of Michael Foot and Tony Benn, while a narrator warned that Labour would confiscate 'your bank account, your mortgage and your wage packet'. 'It wouldn't take much more of a move to the Left,' the commentary went on, 'and you could find yourself not even owning your own home.' On screen, a young couple's house obligingly vanished. Not surprisingly, Wilson was furious, playing back the tape at his morning press conference to show how low the Tories had sunk. And not un-reasonably the Nuffield study later called it 'a sorry broadcast in its ethical blindness, its clumsy cascade of visual gimmicks, and its abysmal view of the electorate's intelligence'. Even the Tory high command was embarrassed, and Wilson was only slightly mollified when Lord Carrington offered a formal apology.[5]

Oddly, however, the great flaw in the Conservative campaign was that in general it was not strident *enough*. When Carrington asked Nigel Lawson to redraft the manifesto and produce something 'more One-Nation', he was echoing the views of Heath himself, who was determined not to make the election a confrontation between the government and the miners. But this was a very strange position to take, because clearly at one level the election *was* a contest between the government and the

NUM. The result was that apart from its anti-Labour conclusion, the Tory manifesto was a very vague and woolly production indeed, with plenty of bluster about firmness and fairness but no detailed policies or sense of direction. As so often, Heath ended up falling between two stools, trapped between the need to mobilize opinion against the unions on the one hand, and his One Nation instincts on the other. If he wanted a sweeping new mandate, he needed to whip up public outrage against the miners, to emphasize the desperate urgency of the situation, to hammer home the themes of crisis and betrayal. Instead, he talked of fairness and moderation: ideal themes for the Labour leader, perhaps, but surely not the Conservative one. Even his best speech of the campaign – a resounding reassertion of One Nation principles in Manchester's Free Trade Hall, presenting the Tories as 'the union for the unemployed and the low paid ... for those in poverty and for the hard pressed' – sounded like the kind of thing Harold Wilson should be saying. It was one of the supreme ironies of Heath's career that when it mattered most, a politician often caricatured as a callous reactionary could not bring himself to live up to his billing.[6]

But while Heath's campaign was at least slick and confident, his Labour opponents seemed to be in a very feeble state. Not only were senior figures still nursing their wounds after their battle over Europe, but many were deeply unhappy with their own manifesto, which promised the most radical programme since the 1930s. The product of months of infighting, it reflected a leftward tilt at the Labour grass roots and was heavily influenced by the ideas of the economist Stuart Holland, then a great favourite of the Shadow Industry Secretary, Tony Benn. Gone was the talk of science and technology, the rhetoric of 'planned, purposive growth', the pledges of dynamic modernization that had marked Labour manifestos in the 1960s. In their place, the new manifesto promised 'a fundamental and irreversible shift in the balance of power and wealth in favour of working people and their families' as well as 'greater economic equality in income, wealth and living standards', and measures 'to make power in industry genuinely accountable to the workers and the community'. It committed the next Labour government to 'a fundamental renegotiation of the terms of [EEC] entry' and a national referendum on British membership. And despite the nation's parlous economic condition, the manifesto promised a range of new wealth and property taxes, the abolition of Heath's industrial relations apparatus, and extensive new spending plans for health, education and pensions – even though it was far from clear that there would be enough money to pay for them.[7]

Potentially the most radical commitment, though, was the promise to set up compulsory planning agreements with industry and a National Enterprise Board (NEB) to take over firms 'where a public holding is essential to enable the Government to control prices, stimulate investment, encourage exports, create employment, protect workers and consumers from the activities of irresponsible multi-national companies, and to plan the national economy in the national interest'. These were words that gladdened the hearts of radical Labour activists, but they horrified most businessmen. And more than any other part of the programme, they reflected the ideas of Tony Benn and his intellectual circle. Having 'reincarnated' himself (as Michael Foot scathingly put it) from the former Viscount Stansgate into plain Tony, the tribune of the plebs, Benn now believed that only massive state intervention could make Britain both egalitarian and competitive. His diaries brimmed with messianic expectation, and he eagerly looked forward to the 'great crisis of capitalism' when a 'popular front' including Marxist and far-left groups could take power. 'I think we would need the Emergency Powers Act and an emergency Industrial Act,' he noted, 'which would give the Minister absolute power to deal with the situation.'[8]

To all but those on the far left, talk of 'emergency powers' was potentially terrifying stuff. Even Benn's own mentors often shuddered at his radical intransigence. Stuart Holland, the intellectual godfather of the state holding company scheme, wrote later of his horror at Benn's 'dogmatic' and wildly unrealistic vision of a socialist Little England sealed off from the world economy. And on the right, where Benn had once been seen as an amusing, eccentric but ultimately harmless figure, he now loomed as the incarnation of socialist devilry, the Red Menace made flesh. By September 1972, Radio Four's *Today* programme had dubbed him 'the most hated man in Britain'; in the *Sunday Express* a month later, Michael Cummings portrayed him in full Nazi stormtrooper regalia. *The Times* accused him of stirring up class warfare; the *Sunday Telegraph* called him 'Bolshevik Benn'; even the *Observer* thought that he was 'hysterical'. But the more the press demonized him, the more Harold Wilson tried to ignore him, the more Shadow Cabinet colleagues like Denis Healey and Anthony Crosland openly laughed at him, the more

Benn knew he was right. Even the history books he read in his spare time fuelled his sense of mission: after working his way through a pile of books on the Levellers, he lamented that 'the Levellers lost and Cromwell won, and Harold Wilson or Denis Healey is the Cromwell of our day, not me'. And yet as 'Chairman Tony' built up support among Labour's disillusioned grass-roots activists, he seemed to be destined for a much more successful career than his radical heroes. In preparation for taking power, he even drafted a plan for the NEB to take over 'twenty-five of our largest manufacturers' – a tremendous first step, as he saw it, towards an economy liberated from the multinational corporations, and based on the principles of public ownership and workers' control.⁹

In the City, once the supreme symbol of Heath's new capitalism, the Labour manifesto felt like a declaration of war. In almost every section of society, complained the *Banker*, could be heard 'the pure emotional assertion that the City is no more than a band of robbers, who contribute little to the country whilst making fortunes for themselves'. This was not just confined to the far left: it was 'probably what most people in Britain believe, either half-heartedly or completely'. How many commuters could be 'sure that the wives they leave behind each morning do not secretly think so themselves?' But the *Banker*'s greatest ire was reserved, not for the BBC scriptwriters, pulp-novel authors and saloon-bar pundits who popularized the idea of the Square Mile as rapacious and corrupt, but for Her Majesty's Opposition. 'To people in the City itself,' it explained, 'the Labour Party and many other critics appear strictly mad. What on earth can be the national interest in destroying or sniping at one of the few really efficient and competitive sectors of its economy?' The City could hardly be blamed 'if it just decided to pack its bag and go somewhere where the sky is blue, the natives friendly and where a man's money is his own. Just possibly, that is what may happen. Messrs Wilson, Benn *et al* would then find themselves barking at an empty fortress.'¹⁰

Behind the City's fury lay not just the predictable self-interest of the wealthy and well connected, but a growing sense of panic about the nation's economic future. By February 1974, the days when the City had been the go-ahead incarnation of Edward Heath's new Britain seemed a very distant memory. And for all the gleaming modernity of the new Stock Exchange Tower, images of the Great Depression now loomed larger than exhilarating visions of future prosperity. Since November, the City had been engulfed in a perfect storm, its confidence shattered by a plunging property market, soaring oil prices and the biggest credit squeeze anyone could remember. Nobody doubted that Anthony Barber had been right to put the brakes on: the alternative would have been inflation of South American proportions. But for the so-called 'secondary' banks that had lent so much money to developers during the Barber boom, the implications of his credit controls were simply devastating. Not for the first time, and certainly not for the last, many banks had over-extended themselves in the pursuit of profit, blind to the reality that one day boom would turn to bust. But now the great property bubble had burst, and nemesis had caught up with them. 'We used to go to visit the Governor of the Bank of England every Wednesday,' the deputy chairman of the Stock Exchange later recalled, 'and listen to the appalling news of one bank after another closing its doors.'[11]

This was no exaggeration. By Christmas, the value of many fringe banks had dropped by as much as a third, and there were genuine fears that the entire structure might topple like a house of cards. And as oil prices mounted, as Britain went on a three-day week, as talks between the government and the miners dragged on, anxiety turned to panic. House prices were plummeting; land values dropped by about half in barely a year; even the markets in vintage cars, in antiques, in works of fine art, burst like popped balloons. Between mid-November and mid-December, the FT30 share index lost a quarter of its value. By 28 January, four days after the NUM executive had voted to hold its national strike ballot, the index had fallen to just 301.6 – a drop of almost half since its peak in May 1972. It was the worst bear market in history. Britain must be prepared, declared the Governor of the Bank of England, for a decade of austerity in order to settle the yawning budget deficit. Even Jim Slater, once the incarnation of buccaneer capitalism, now cut a distinctly gloomy figure. 'There's a hurricane blowing through the financial world,' he told one reporter. 'You must put your head down and wait for the hurricane to finish blowing.'[12]

Ten years earlier, Harold Wilson might have been sympathetic to the City's plight. But the mood inside the Labour Party was now very different from the technocratic pro-growth ethos of the early 1960s. With its local branches increasingly dominated by the middle-class 'polyocracy' and its leadership ageing and passive, Labour had swung further to the left than at any time since the 1930s. Even relatively centrist politicians like the Shadow Chancellor, Denis Healey, now played to the radical gallery. In his reply to Anthony Barber's austerity measures, Healey had called for 'increased taxes on luxuries such as fur coats, wines and brandy' to pay for food subsidies, which, as even he admitted later, was a totally 'inadequate' response to the crisis. Now he boasted that he would levy whopping new taxes on 'food manufacturers and retailers' and would 'squeeze the property speculators until the pips squeak'. To Healey this was just good knockabout electioneering stuff. But to the Conservative middle classes it seemed a bone-chilling warning, a sign that the 'socialists' were hell-bent on class warfare. The details of Healey's remarks were lost amid the hysteria; people told one another that he had pledged to squeeze 'the rich' until the pips squeaked. Newspaper cartoonists showed Labour's leaders as beetle-browed Bolsheviks, their hands reaching out to grasp the levers of power and the wealth of the middle classes. In the *Express*, Cummings drew Wilson and his colleagues as French revolutionaries encouraging Joe Gormley to bring down the guillotine on Ted Heath; in the *Mail*, Emmwood showed Wilson tucked up in bed beside a very dodgy-looking character in dark glasses. 'LEFT-WING EXTREMISTS' reads the sign on the latter's placard. In case there was any doubt, his pyjamas are patterned with the hammer and sickle.[13]

Quite apart from the problem of finding the money to pay for more nationalization, the obvious problem with the Labour manifesto was that not even its own supporters believed in it. Although committed activists loved Tony Benn's proposals, the great mass of relatively apathetic Labour voters did not. The party's private polls found that only 37 per cent of Labour supporters wanted to see more public ownership, with 44 per cent against. Only 30 per cent of Labour voters agreed with the nationalization of North Sea Oil, only 26 per cent supported the nationalization of land, and just 12 per cent agreed with the commitments to nationalize the ports, aircraft industries and shipbuilding. The proposed National Enterprise Board, meanwhile, was overwhelmingly unpopular: for all Tony Benn's passionate salesmanship (or perhaps because of it), only a pitiful 6 per cent of Labour voters and 7 per cent of trade unionists thought it was a good idea. And on top of that, almost none of the party's senior figures believed in their own commitments. In the Shadow Cabinet, Benn's NEB scheme was particularly unpopular. 'Why don't we nationalise Marks and Spencer to make it as efficient as the Co-op?' Healey asked sarcastically, while Tony Crosland and Edmund Dell made no secret of their belief that the nationalization programme was total madness ('half-baked' and 'idiotic' were Crosland's characteristically trenchant words).* Even left-wingers were uneasy with Benn's utopian plans. Michael Foot told Benn that 'the twenty-five companies proposal was crazy' and asked in disbelief: 'Do you think we could win the Election? Do you *want* to win the Election? What are you up to? What are you saying?' And Jack Jones, the old Communist warrior, warned Benn that the working classes 'didn't want airy-fairy stuff. Nationalisation was unpopular; it failed.' 'Why don't you make a speech on pensions instead of all this airy-fairy stuff?' Jones asked him. But Benn knew what was going on: the TGWU boss had 'completely abandoned his serious left-wing programme'. Like Foot, like Healey, like Wilson, like all the rest of them, the Emperor Jones was just another right-wing sell-out.[14]

In many ways it was a sign of Harold Wilson's declining authority that he was saddled with a manifesto he patently did not want. But it was also a sign of his growing detachment from domestic politics: his physical and intellectual weariness, his declining ambition, his sheer lack of hunger. In the 1960s he had placed himself at centre stage, hogging the limelight like an American presidential candidate. But now he presented himself as merely part of a team, allowing Callaghan and Healey to dominate the daily press conferences and his latest protégée, Shirley Williams, to become the star of the television broadcasts. They were 'the wise old firm', ran the message, 'who could get on with the unions and get the country back to work'. Meanwhile, the extravagant promises of the manifesto were quietly forgotten. Even the word 'socialism' seemed to have disappeared, Wilson using it only twice in his speeches, and then only in the vaguest terms. Although he had clung on to the party leadership with the tenacity of a limpet, he had long since given up being the candidate of change, the modernizer who would lead Britain into a brave new world of progress and equality. Now he was content to play the trusted old family doctor, the voice of reason, the pipe-smoking reincarnation of Stanley Baldwin. Tony Benn was disgusted, recording that 'all this "national interest", "working together", "keep calm and keep cool", and "a Labour Government will knit the nation" seems absolute rubbish'. But even Labour right-wingers felt a twinge of unease at what seemed a highly disingenuous campaign. David Owen

---

* Some sources attribute the Marks & Spencer line to Crosland, too, but Michael Hatfield's definitive account gives it to Healey, and it certainly sounds like the kind of thing he would say.

later called it the 'shabbiest' campaign he had ever been involved in. And Roy Jenkins, now even more detached than his leader, thought that they deserved to lose, and hoped that they would.[15]

No election campaign had been attended by more publicity than the contest in February 1974. Both the BBC and ITV ran 'Election 74' bulletins several times a day, while the newspapers were dominated by campaign stories. But what was also unprecedented, at least since the war, was the level of sheer partisanship. Only the *Guardian* refused to commit itself, calling rather limply for a 'three-way balance'. The *Mirror*, as usual, backed Labour, but Rupert Murdoch's *Sun*, hitherto a Labour paper, urged its readers to re-elect Heath. What was really striking, though, was the sheer intensity of the Conservative papers' rhetoric, which reawakened memories of the Zinoviev letter and the anti-socialist scares of the 1920s. A Labour government would be 'complete chaos: ruin public and private', said the *Telegraph*, which thought that their manifesto illustrated Wilson's 'craven subservience to trade union power'. If he won, agreed the *Sun*, the result would be 'galloping inflation and the sinister and ever-growing power of a small band of anarchists, bully-boys and professional class-war warriors'.[16]

By contrast, the *Daily Mail* – which had prepared but did not run a story about Wilson's murky finances – directed much of its fire at the miners, blaming them for 'producing the worst inflation in our history'. But it reserved some of its ammunition for Tony Benn, who for the right had become the ultimate demonic stage villain. One *Mail* cartoon showed Benn as a Gauleiter ordering Joe Gormley to torture the British public with the words 've haf vays off makink you suffer!' Another showed him as a blacksmith, setting about the pound with a hammer and sickle while hot air pours out of his forehead. And other Tory papers were hardly more generous: on the last day of the campaign, the *Evening Standard* ran a piece by Kingsley Amis explaining why Benn was 'the most dangerous man in Britain'. The *Evening News*, meanwhile, ran an extraordinary article by the retired MI6 officer and hard-right Tory candidate George Young, who claimed that there were '40 or 50 Labour MPs for whom the Labour label is cover for more sinister roles'. They formed, he said, a 'Black Hand Gang', working alongside the 'Red Hand Gang' in the unions.[17]

Yet whether commentators favoured Heath or Wilson, almost none

COLDITZ '74

The second series of the BBC's hugely popular *Colditz* was just starting when Emmwood drew this cartoon for the *Daily Mail* (7 January 1974). The miners' president Joe Gormley and the railwaymen's leader Ray Buckton wield the cudgels, 'Adolf Benn' gives the orders, and the public quails in terror.

doubted that the Prime Minister would win; indeed, many expected a landslide. Bookmakers had the Tories favourites at 2–1 on, a stark contrast with their underdog status back in 1970, and by the end of the first week Harris, NOP, ORC and Marplan all gave them a lead of between 6 and 9 per cent. Now that battle had been joined, Heath seemed unusually relaxed and confident, enjoying the liberation of campaigning rather than governing. 'Presidential' was the word that often sprang to mind: one profile even called him 'the iron man', stern and authoritative. And as poll after poll forecast a clear Tory lead, a sense of inevitability began to take hold. Irrespective of how they planned to vote themselves, no fewer than six out of ten voters thought that Heath would win the election, compared with just two who expected Wilson to win. 'The present one-sided picture of a relaxed and "statesmanlike" Prime Minster chastising the militants on behalf of the nation and a rather tired and rattled Labour Party swinging wildly,' wrote David Watt in the *Financial Times*, 'can only produce one result.'[18]

In the Labour ranks, all was despondency. Only three days into the campaign, the political scientist David Butler, who co-edited the Nuffield election studies and had been an on-screen expert for the BBC since 1950, warned Tony Benn that he 'foresaw a Tory landslide [and] was afraid that the Labour Party couldn't survive'. The next evening, after spending the day touring a Bristol housing estate in the wind and rain, Benn noted that even Labour housewives had been 'impressed by [Heath's] arguments about the unions, about the miners, about Communists, about Militants, about strikes and about being fair but firm'. He felt 'tired, exhausted and rather depressed'. So did Harold Wilson, whose aides worried that at heart he had already given up. In the old days Wilson had loved campaigning, but now Joe Haines, his faithful but acerbic press secretary, thought that his performances were 'abysmal', his speeches falling 'from tired lips on to a leaden audience'. The *Sunday Times* thought he seemed 'withdrawn, nervous, tentative, apprehensive, not to say distinctly bored with the whole affair'. He seemed 'exhausted by the relentless treadmill of the campaign', wrote his young policy adviser Bernard Donoughue, 'his voice croaking and his eyes puffy and red-rimmed'. And every night, as Wilson relaxed with a large glass of whisky, he seemed older and more deflated, his faint hopes of victory slipping further away. It was like watching a condemned man, making the last inevitable journey to the scaffold. When Benn accompanied his leader to a rally with only six days to go, he was struck by the fact that Wilson seemed uncharacteristically nervous. 'I think he does realise', Benn wrote, 'that he is perhaps within a week of the end of his political career.'[19]

There were, however, two chinks of light for Wilson. The first was the performance of the Liberal Party, whose popularity had been gradually rising since the leadership of Jo Grimond back in the late 1950s and early 1960s. In 1970 the Liberals had won less than 8 per cent of the vote, but since then they had enjoyed considerable success picking up disaffected Tory voters, especially after the Heath government ran into trouble in 1972. Almost beneath the surface of political events, the two-party system, based on class, regional, religious and family loyalties, was beginning to collapse under the impact of affluence and social change, and the Liberals' reputation as 'amiable, moderate and relatively harmless' made them the ideal party of protest. Their by-election victories in late 1972 and mid-1973 confirmed them as a genuine force in British politics: indeed, Liberal candidates won more votes in 1973 than those of any other party, and by August they had broken through the 20 per cent barrier for the first time in polling history. Many observers expected their support to evaporate under the pressure of a general election, especially as their campaign was such a shoestring effort. But far from collapsing, the Liberals seemed more buoyant than ever. Their manifesto, with its promises of devolution and political reform and its impossibly vague economic agenda, evidently appealed to middle-class voters sick of the mudslinging of the other parties and nostalgic for a lost golden age of quiet moderation. And in their debonair leader, Jeremy Thorpe, they had the star of the campaign, a wry, charming television presence who took questions down a closed-circuit link from Barnstaple, making him seem somehow above the fray. In fact, Thorpe had a dark side that would have been entirely unimaginable in his rivals. But nobody knew that then.[20]

The other good news for Wilson was that despite the papers' melo-dramatic talk of the 'crisis election', any sense of crisis seemed to be ebbing away. Although the miners had walked out on 10 February, the NUM shrewdly discouraged mass picketing and there were none of the violent clashes that had horrified the public two years before. Throughout the campaign, the miners kept a low profile, with only six men on each picket: Jim Prior wrote afterwards that they had been 'as quiet and well-behaved as mice'. The anticipated power emergency, too, failed to materialize. The weather continued to be unseasonably warm, the three-day week seemed to be working, and power stations reported no shortages of fuel. Above all, Heath lifted the late-night television curfew on 7 February so that the election could get proper coverage. But with the schedules having returned to normal, many people took the attitude that the crisis was basically over.[21]

As the sense of urgency disappeared, so polls began to show that the miners' dispute was fading as an election issue. By 15 February, when the latest Retail Price Index showed that prices had increased by a staggering 20 per cent in just twelve months, inflation was beginning to take over as the electorate's chief anxiety. Concern about the unions began to recede: whereas 40 per cent had named strikes as a major issue on 8 February, only 24 per cent thought the same on 23 February – while twice as many were worried about high food prices. One by one, the newspapers that had originally claimed that this was a single-issue, government-versus-miners election changed their tune. From *The Times* on 12 February and the *Telegraph* on 18 February to the *Sun* on 21 February and the *Mail* on 27 February, they all decided that the 'real issue' was inflation after all.* This was good news for Wilson, who urged the voters to kick out 'Mr Rising Price', and promised that through a vague and undefined 'Social Contract' with the unions, he would be able to end the industrial unrest while still keeping prices down. But it was a disaster for Heath. He had set out to fight a 'Who Governs' election, not a referendum on his economic record – which by any standards, whether it was his fault or not, was frankly abysmal. Partly because of his own passivity, partly because of sheer bad luck, he had lost control of the election narrative.[22]

On Thursday, 21 February, a week before polling day, there was more bad news for Heath. Just after six that evening, the Pay Board issued its long-awaited report on the miners' relativities, and it contained a bombshell. Far from being paid more than most manufacturing workers, as the Coal Board had claimed, it seemed that most miners were actually paid 8 per cent less – which obviously strengthened their case for a raise. Heath was furious, Wilson delighted, and the next day's papers had a field day. 'THE GREAT PIT BLUNDER', roared the *Mail*. As Heath pointed out, the story was not quite as it seemed: it was really all a question of different statistical tables. But the damage was done. At that moment, many Tories later recalled, there was a tiny but palpable sense of the momentum shifting. What was more, some of Heath's advisers were becoming distinctly alarmed by the Liberal surge, not least because nobody knew how it would affect the electoral map. Indeed, the Liberals' rise defied all conventional wisdom: having been on just 12 per cent in Marplan's poll on 10 February, they had surged to a stunning 28 per cent by the final Sunday of the campaign. Many people, it seemed, shared the views of Ronald McIntosh, who recorded that he and his wife had decided to vote Liberal for the first time because 'if Heath gets back he will draw the moral that he was right all along and that would be quite

* By contrast, issues such as devolution, feminism, crime and immigration barely featured at all. Even Europe was not really an election issue in 1974 – a sign of how little the electorate cared about it.

disastrous . . . The Liberals have a good manifesto, they are sound on Europe and they are preaching moderation so they seem to us to be well worth voting for.' Indeed, almost incredibly, four out of ten people now told pollsters that they would vote Liberal if Thorpe had a chance of holding the balance of power, and 48 per cent said they would vote for them if they could be the next government. At the very least, this was a resounding vote of no confidence in the two main parties. 'Are you voting Liberal to get rid of Mr Heath or Mr Wilson?' one voter asks another in a *Times* cartoon published two days later.[23]

With the polls still putting him around 5 per cent clear, Heath remained outwardly buoyant. Mulling over the figures at Chequers with his aides on the last Sunday of the campaign, he was reportedly 'in a mood of high confidence', the only doubt being 'the magnitude of his victory'. Wilson, by contrast, seemed to have sunk into total despair. Seeing him in Birmingham that Sunday for a big meeting in the town hall, Roy Jenkins thought that his leader seemed 'tired, depressed and expecting defeat, keeping going with some difficulty and gallantry until by the Thursday night he would have completed his final throw in politics'. Already Jenkins's supporters were discussing the possibility of a leadership challenge: with Wilson bound to resign, it would surely mean a fight to the death against Callaghan, Foot and Benn. And on the Monday morning the mood was worse than ever, with a private poll suggesting that Labour were even further behind than they thought, and rumours circulating that the *Daily Mail* was about to produce its dossier on Wilson's finances, his political secretary Marcia Williams, and their involvement in a strange land deal in the North of England. That night, Donoughue recalled, 'the atmosphere was very bad . . . Wilson sat slumped, tired, sour, scowling, his eyes dead like a fish. He snarled at Joe about his speeches being "too sophisticated". He drank brandy heavily.' The next day, Wilson was scheduled to give his last major address in the Fairfield Halls, Croydon, and his aides were delighted to find a huge crowd outside. Only when Wilson walked in to a less than packed house did they realize that only 400 people had been queuing for the Labour leader. The other 1,700 had been waiting to see the film *Trams, Trams, Trams* in the hall next door.[24]

Yet it was not all dark clouds for Wilson. Over the last weekend a long-planned clandestine operation had been put into effect, and at its centre was perhaps the least likely man in Britain to lend his support to the Labour cause. Enoch Powell's disaffection with his party leadership had been on record for years, but what few people realized was that he had been coming under intense pressure from middle-class Tories in his Wolverhampton constituency. During the fevered early weeks of 1974, his breach with both the leadership and his local association had widened even further. On 15 January, he had even declared that 'it would be fraudulent – or worse' for Heath to call an early election when neither the unions nor the miners had broken the law, and when the root of the crisis (as he thought) lay in Heath's foolish incomes policy. And when Heath did call an election, Powell wasted no time in issuing a statement that sent shock waves through Conservative ranks. The election was 'essentially fraudulent', he declared, and 'an act of gross irresponsibility'. Heath was trying 'to steal success by telling the public one thing during an election and doing the opposite afterwards'. Powell could not 'ask electors to vote for policies which are directly opposite to those we stood for in 1970' – when Heath had, of course, ruled out any kind of incomes policy – 'and which I have myself consistently condemned as being inherently impracticable and bound to create the very difficulties in which the nation now finds itself'. With regret, therefore, he would not be standing for re-election as a Conservative in Wolverhampton. For Powell, it was a searing emotional moment: he reportedly had tears in his eyes when he went into the Commons that evening. His friend Michael Foot rang and begged him to reconsider, calling his decision 'courageous, brilliant – but reckless'. But when Powell's mind was made up, there was no changing it.[25]

If Powell's decision not to stand was a surprise, what followed was one of the biggest political shocks of the decade. Such was his contempt for Heath that party loyalty counted for little: all that mattered was to kick the erring helmsman out of Downing Street and replace him with somebody who might pull Britain out of Europe. A few days later, Powell's friend Andrew Alexander, a columnist for the *Daily Mail*, contacted Wilson's press secretary Joe Haines and told him that Powell wanted to issue a broadside against Heath: what would be the best timing for the Labour campaign? And on Sunday, 23 February, when Powell addressed an audience in the forbidding surroundings of the Mecca Dance Hall at the Bull Ring, Birmingham, even experienced commentators were left dumbstruck by his words. The overriding issue in this campaign, Powell said, was whether Britain was to 'remain a democratic nation, governed by the will of its own electorate expressed in its own parliament, or whether it will become one province in a new Europe super-state under institutions which know nothing of political rights and liberties which we have so long taken for granted'. Under these circumstances, the 'national duty' must be to replace the man who had deprived Parliament of 'its sole right to make the laws and impose the taxes of the country'. Powell never used the words 'Vote Labour'. He did not have to. But when one of his listeners asked how they could be rid of 'that confidence trickster, Heath', he said calmly: 'If you want to do it, you can.'[26]

Powell's speech was a sensation. 'ENOCH PUTS THE BOOT IN', screamed the *Sun;* 'THEY WEPT FOR ENOCH', countered the *Express*. It is true that Europe was hardly the most rousing issue; until then it had barely featured in the campaign at all, and most people remained as confused and apathetic as ever. But Powell was still the most admired politician in the country, with an unparalleled ability to make headlines. And two days later at Shipley, where the hall was packed with 1,000 people and a further 3,000 were waiting outside, he was even more explicit. 'I was born a Tory, am a Tory and shall die a Tory,' he said, but he nevertheless hoped for a victory by 'the party which is committed to fundamental renegotiation of the Treaty of Brussels and to submitting to the British people thereafter, for their final yea or nay, the outcome of that renegotiation' – in other words, Labour. For Heath he had the deadliest insult of all, commenting that where U-turns were concerned 'Harold Wilson, for all his nimbleness and skill, is simply no match for the breathtaking, thoroughgoing efficiency of the present Prime Minister'. At that, amid the shouting and applause, a heckler yelled: 'Judas!' Suddenly it was as though Powell had been connected to an electric current. His eyes blazing, his voice burning with conviction, his finger stabbing the air, he shot back: 'Judas was paid! *Judas was paid!* I am making a sacrifice!'[27]

For Powell to be making the headlines just days before the election was the last thing Heath wanted. In the *Express*, Cummings portrayed the Prime Minister as a shipwrecked mariner, desperately scrabbling across a desert island towards the sanctuary of Number 10, while a gigantic black vulture in the shape of Enoch Powell moves in for the kill. But the shocks did not end there. Thinking that he was speaking off the record, the CBI's secretary general Campbell Adamson told an audience that the Industrial Relations Act was now 'so surrounded by hatred' that the next government ought to repeal it and start all over again. Heath was furious and Adamson offered to resign, but the damage was done. More serious still was the news on Monday, 25 February, when the DTI's latest batch of trade figures made for appalling reading. Back in 1970, a bad set of trade figures, showing a monthly deficit of £32 million, had helped to swing the election to Heath. But how times had changed! Now the figures showed an eye-watering £383 million deficit, the worst in history, thanks above all to the soaring price of oil. Heath insisted that the figures merely confirmed 'the gravity of the situation' and the need for a new mandate. But Wilson pounced. 'On every count,' he said, 'the handling of the nation's economy by this Conservative Government has been a disaster. Today's devastating trade figures underline their incompetence. No excuse, no defence, no pretence can now hide from the country the fact that the economic crisis is deeper and more funda-mental than the Conservatives have ever admitted.' And as Roy Jenkins wryly remarked, it was very odd for Heath to claim that the atrocious figures somehow strengthened his case: 'He presumably thinks a still worse result would have given him a still stronger claim.'[28]

On Monday night, Labour made its final televised appeal. As always, the broadcast emphasized the theme of teamwork, with one shadow minister after another – Michael Foot, Denis Healey, Shirley Williams – explaining how they would put Britain 'on the road to recovery', before Harold Wilson made some characteristically anodyne remarks about national unity: 'Trades unionists are people. Employers are people. We can't go on setting one against the other except at the cost of damage to the nation itself.' By contrast, the Conservative broadcast on Tuesday evening was classic man-of-destiny stuff, opening with a montage of film clips and photographs while a narrator described Heath as 'an extraordinary man. A private man. A solitary man. Perhaps single-minded sums it up . . . This is a man the world respects. A man who has done so much and yet a man who has so much left to do.' Speaking woodenly but earnestly into the camera, Heath addressed the charge that he was too stubborn:

> Is it stubborn to fight and fight hard to stop the country you love from tearing itself apart? Is it stubborn to insist that everyone in that country should have the choice and the chance to take his life and make of it what he can? Is it stubborn to want to see this country take back the place that history means us to have?
>
> If it is – then, yes, I most certainly am stubborn . . .

I love this country. I'll do all that I can for this country. And isn't that what you want too? We've started a job together. With your will, we shall go on and finish the job.[29]

It was the same kind of patriotic appeal he had made in his final broadcast almost four years before, when he had been facing apparently certain defeat. Then, the polls had been wrong. This time, Heath had to hope they were right.

The Election Day headlines made encouraging reading for Conservative supporters. 'It's Heath By 5%', said the *Express*, while the *Mail* predicted 'A Handsome Win For Heath'. Neither paper mentioned that the polls had been quietly narrowing over the last few days, or that the Tory lead was now within the margin of error. In any case, all the major polling groups had Heath ahead by between 2 and 5 per cent. Among Tory insiders, the real question was not whether they would win, but the size of the victory, which would be crucial in claiming a new mandate: most reckoned they might get a 40- to 50-seat majority. Among Wilson's aides, meanwhile, the great hope was that somehow they might deny Heath an overall majority, allowing them to claim a moral victory against the odds. Their mood was 'sombre', Bernard Donoughue remembered. Wilson himself seemed decidedly pessimistic: even as people were streaming out to vote, he told Donoughue that after his own Huyton constituency count he would tell the press that he was going back to the Adelphi Hotel, his traditional haunt on election night, but would in fact slip away to the Golden Eagle in Kirkby. There, Wilson said, he would watch the results. Then, early in the morning, he would leave by plane for London but secretly land at an airfield in Bedfordshire, from where he would drive to his Buckinghamshire farmhouse or some other rural retreat. Donoughue listened in total bewilderment, and then the penny dropped. 'I suddenly realised what was behind all these bizarre plans,' he recorded in his diary. 'HW was preparing to lose! He was preparing his getaway plans. Unwilling to face the press, as anybody when beaten.'[30]

Election Day had dawned clear and bright, but by midday the weather was already changing, the dark clouds drawing in, the first drops of rain beginning to fall. At Conservative Central Office in London, the mood was nervous but still optimistic; in Liverpool, Donoughue walked with Marcia Williams along the Mersey waterfront, watching worriedly as the fog rolled in, looking at his watch and praying that the rain held off. 'Every half-hour matters,' he thought. Williams was so nervous that she had developed blisters, but Mary Wilson, never a great fan of politics, seemed completely unperturbed and spent the afternoon calmly reading the new *Oxford Book of Poetry* at their hotel. Heavy winds and snow were forecast in the north, yet reports indicated turnout was high: well up, indeed, on 1970.

In the Adelphi, the Labour team ate an early dinner of steak and chips, and Wilson again brought up his elaborate escape plan, which was now 'too complicated to follow', with 'trains and diversionary cars as well as the airplane'. Donoughue was so confused that he lost track of 'which hotel I am staying in or how I am going back to London if at all'. Wilson seemed a bit chirpier, however, and at 8.30 his young aide accompanied him on a last tour of his Huyton constituency. It was a grim, dreary scene. For two hours, Donoughue recorded, they trudged the streets, 'in rain and sleet, very dark, totally lost in miles of council house estates'. The party offices and clubs were deserted: most Labour activists were still out canvassing. Reporters and police followed at a distance, but seemed barely interested. Wilson was yesterday's man. 'I sensed that everybody saw him as a loser, finished, who could soon be just an old back-bench MP,' Donoughue noted. 'At times we walked in the rain, just the two of us, HW and myself, rather lonely figures lost in anonymous wet streets.' Trying to cheer them both up, Donoughue suggested that it was going to be like the election of 1964, Wilson's first victory, 'when we just scraped home. He agreed.'[31]

At ten the polls closed. Heath was now in Bexley, his constituency for so many years, waiting for the count with his closest allies. In Liverpool, Wilson and his team were huddled around the television in his hotel suite, clutching large glasses of whisky. Marcia Williams was 'trembling with nerves'; Joe Haines was 'tense and silent'. Donoughue detected their 'concern, almost terror, that this will be a repeat of last time'. And then, one by one, the results started coming in. Guildford: a comfortable Tory win. Salford: a boost to Labour's majority. Wolverhampton North East – Powell country – a swing of 10 per cent to Labour. Just as they had done four years before, the first results were turning all the predictions on their heads. 'We can't lose now,' Donoughue murmured, as though willing himself to believe it. 'It may be very close, but we won't lose.'

Close was hardly the word: by midnight, the BBC's computers were predicting a dead heat. When Wilson left his suite there were suddenly hordes of policemen around him, holding the doors, watching the stairs, ushering him into the lift. Downstairs, Donoughue noted, 'the press is bubbling and crowd around him and wish him good luck. They know he might win and suddenly the police care and the press change sides.' At the count, Mary Wilson and Marcia Williams uncorked a bottle of champagne. And at Huyton Labour Club afterwards, the room erupted with screams of delight when Wilson walked in. 'Everybody singing and chanting,' Donoughue wrote. 'Packed. Woman next to me had tears streaming down her face and was shouting, "I love him, I love him."'[32]

Hundreds of miles to the south, the mood was very different. When Heath arrived for his Bexley count just after midnight, his face seemed pale and taut, his smile forced, his eyes glassy. After his result had been confirmed, he confined himself to a few bland remarks of thanks and was then whisked away to his car. Back in Downing Street, he stared at the television in silent disbelief as the results continued to flow in, like a man in deep shock. He had got it all wrong, he told his friend Lord Aldington, and silently the tears of self-pity streamed down his face. But not all Conservatives felt similarly heartbroken. Enoch Powell declined to watch the results, but spent the evening at his London home with his wife and children. The next morning, when he went down at seven o'clock to collect *The Times* from the letterbox, the headline stared up at him: 'Mr Heath's General Election Gamble Fails'. For Powell, it was the sweetest of moments. He went straight back upstairs, ran himself a bath and loudly sang the 'Te Deum'. 'I had had my revenge', he said later, 'on the man who had destroyed the self-government of the United Kingdom.'[33]

The result of the election was both extraordinarily close and bewilderingly inconclusive. In terms of the total vote, the Conservatives had won 37.9 per cent, Labour had won 37.2 per cent, the Liberals won 19.3 per cent and the various nationalist parties won the remaining 5 per cent. But the picture in terms of seats was much more complicated. Labour was the biggest party, with 301 seats but no overall majority, the Tories had 297 seats, and the Liberals, punished by the electoral system, had just 14. In Wales, Plaid Cymru did less well than they had hoped, their share falling to just over 10 per cent even though they won two seats. In Scotland, however, the Scottish Nationalists were delighted with their haul, picking up 22 per cent of the vote and six new seats to add to the one they already had. And in Northern Ireland, the results were a devastating blow not just to the cause of power sharing but to Heath's chances of holding onto power, as the pro-government Unionists were completely blown away and replaced by anti-Heath hardliners under the aegis of the United Ulster Unionist Council. And if anyone doubted that the old two-party system was in deep decay, here was the proof. Both the Conservatives and Labour had suffered blows unprecedented in their history, the Tory vote collapsing by 8 per cent and Labour's by 6 per cent. Never again would the two major parties command nine-tenths of the vote; from February 1974 onwards, at least one in four people would choose to cast their votes elsewhere.[34]

For the Conservatives, the results naturally seemed a disaster. No government had suffered a bigger electoral collapse since 1945, and what was particularly disturbing was that the party seemed to have lost touch with its core affluent middle-class voters, 16 per cent of whom had defected to the Liberals. The biggest regional collapse, predictably enough, had come in the Black Country, where the Powell effect saw a swing to Labour of between 5 and 10 per cent, well above the national average. (In Wolverhampton, the swing was even bigger, a massive 12 per cent.) Yet there was an obvious silver lining for Tory supporters. Although Labour crowed that they had won the election, their electoral performance had been almost as poor. Their biggest gains had come among the middle classes – teachers, lecturers, clerical workers and so on – but they had lost votes among manual workers and even trade union households. Indeed, far from improving since 1970, Labour had actually lost half a million votes, the worst performance by an opposition party in modern times. There was certainly no mandate for Labour's policies: exit polls showed that only a minority of the electorate supported its commitments to more nationalization, the repeal of the incomes policy and the abolition of the industrial relations apparatus. Indeed, 71 per cent told pollsters that they were disappointed with the election results, and only 34 per cent had any faith that a Labour government could succeed. It was hardly a vote of confidence. Yet one of the biggest mistakes Labour ever made was to treat the February 1974 election as a great victory, and to ignore the deeper reality that it was steadily haemorrhaging support.[35]

The day after the election, Heath cut a very disconsolate figure. With the results so close, he still had a tiny chance of remaining as Prime Minister, but as he dined with friends on Friday night he seemed 'shell-shocked', barely seeming to notice as he shovelled down two dozen

oysters they had ordered from his beloved Prunier's. Many people thought
he had only himself to blame: Douglas Hurd believed that if Heath had
only called the election earlier, for 7 February rather than 28 February,
then they would have won. But there is no evidence that any date would
have given him the majority he needed, and even if he had scraped home
on the 7th, a narrow victory would have solved nothing. Looking back,
many senior Conservatives thought that they should have settled with
the miners after all, taking the TUC's offer and pleading exceptional
circumstances to the public. Months later, Willie Whitelaw told Ronald
McIntosh that his great regret was not settling with the miners before
Christmas. Even Margaret Thatcher told ITV's Brian Walden in 1977
that she was 'sorry' the government had not followed up the TUC's 'very
responsible proposal' on 9 January. Given her legendary loathing for
Heathite appeasement, it is surprising to think that she would have taken
the deal and ducked the confrontation. But then Mrs Thatcher was always
much more flexible than her reputation suggests – and unlike Heath, she
never lost sight of her political self-interest.[36]

For Harold Wilson, the night of 28 February should have been one
to remember, a night of champagne, laughter and sweet satisfaction. In
fact, he spent the hours after his count scuttling off to his bolt-hole
in Kirkby: 'a small, miserable hotel', Donoughue recalled, 'with poky
modern rooms and no atmosphere whatsoever'. Even the receptionist
was surly and unfriendly: 'clearly Tory', Donoughue thought, although
given the standards of hotel service in the mid-1970s, she probably
thought she was treating them like honoured guests. In any case, since
Wilson had defied the odds, the fact that he was still going through with
his convoluted escape plan seemed utterly preposterous, especially as the
press soon found out where he was and started shouting and clamouring
downstairs. 'What are we doing here?' Donoughue wondered. 'We are
winning, not losing . . . Unhappy to be at this dismal hotel. No place to
celebrate a marvellous victory. We should be at the Adelphi, with the
Labour crowds celebrating, putting up two fingers to the press. This is
wrong.' But as even he admitted, they could hardly go back there now:
'That would be too bizarre, to run away from two hotels in one night.'

On Friday morning, Wilson's party flew back to London. Rain and
sleet were pouring down, but Donoughue felt that they all shared 'the
feeling of a job well done'. Only Mary Wilson seemed less than delighted:
as the plane descended towards the capital, she remarked that she was

not looking forward to life back in Number 10, and would have preferred a quiet retirement with the family. When they landed, however, it was still not clear that she was going to Downing Street. Nobody seemed to have the latest results, and when Donoughue rang Transport House from Heathrow, he was amazed to find that 'nobody there seemed to know, or was particularly interested to help their party leader find out'. In the end, he had to get the results by phoning the *Daily Mirror*, who told him that Labour were clearly going to be the biggest single party, but that an overall majority was touch and go. There was nothing to do but wait; if Heath could stitch together a coalition, they might yet be denied the prize. And so they waited, killing time at Wilson's house in Lord North Street, their elation turning into tiredness and irritability. Morning became afternoon; afternoon stretched into evening. In public, Wilson presented a calm, unruffled front. In private, he was weary and ill-tempered, snapping at his aides, even ringing Jim Callaghan and asking him to issue a statement that they were being cheated. Callaghan refused. 'We are all tired,' said Marcia Williams, announcing that she was off to bed.[37]

The constitutional picture was intensely complicated. Was the Queen morally obliged to invite Wilson, as the leader of the single biggest party, to form the next government? Or should she allow Heath, as the incumbent Prime Minister, to try to form a government with the Liberals, sending for somebody else only if he failed? 'The Queen could only await events,' was the message from her Private Secretary, Sir Martin Charteris, on Friday morning. 'She would not be called upon to take action unless and until Mr Heath tendered his resignation, and if and when he did so it would then be her duty to send for Mr Wilson.' This gave Heath one last chance to hang on to office. As he admitted to his Principal Private Secretary, Robert Armstrong, it was bound to invite accusations that he was a bad loser, clinging on to power by his fingertips. But Heath was nothing if not stubborn, and, as he saw it, there was a happy coincidence between his personal self-interest and the well-being of the nation. A Labour government, Armstrong recorded, would be committed to such big spending increases that it would put the nation's economic recovery in severe jeopardy, and it was much 'less likely to command the degree of confidence overseas which would be required if the sterling exchange rate was to be held and the expected balance of payments deficit financed'. And when Heath's Cabinet met at six on Friday afternoon, tired and miserable after the shock of the night's results, they agreed that they should at least try to strike a deal with the Liberals, on the grounds that 'there was a large anti-Socialist majority which supported both an incomes policy and Britain's continued membership of the European Community'. Late that night, Armstrong telephoned Jeremy Thorpe and asked him to come to London.[38]

Britain awoke on Saturday morning to a situation of utter deadlock and confusion. Outside Downing Street, radical demonstrators gathered to chant for Heath's resignation, led by a group of International Socialists and the freelance protester Tariq Ali. A few minutes' walk away, Wilson's Georgian terraced house on Lord North Street stood silent and empty. Yielding to his advisers' suggestions, the Labour leader had decamped to his farmhouse at Great Missenden, Buckinghamshire, where he presented a typically confident and jaunty image, kicking a ball about in the cool spring sunshine with Paddy, his gigantic Labrador. Behind the scenes, however, Wilson was not relaxed at all: indeed, he phoned Bernard Donoughue several times to vent his fury that the Liberals were going to snatch victory away from him. In his darker moments, he even fantasized about striking directly at Jeremy Thorpe, whose murky involvement with the stable boy Norman Scott had come to the attention of MI5 – and therefore to the government – during the 1960s. Wisely, however, Wilson held back from using this ultimate weapon, and simply waited for events to play themselves out. And by the time Barbara Castle rang for a chat on Sunday morning, he was in much better spirits, joking about the strange situation and mulling over his plans for the new Cabinet. There would be 'no more of those off the record discussions of what the Government is going to do', he told her; he wanted a calmer, wiser, less hysterical government this time. 'Some of his old spirit seems to have come back,' she noted afterwards. 'Certainly Harold is the only man for this tricky hour. It could be that he has really learned the lessons of last time.'[39]

Behind Wilson's good cheer lay the fact that a Conservative–Liberal coalition was now looking distinctly unlikely. Early on Saturday morning, Thorpe had slipped out of his North Devon home, wearing a country coat and wellington boots over his characteristically dapper dark suit. He trudged across three damp fields to a neighbouring farm, and from there drove to Taunton station, hoping to escape press scrutiny. He did not make it to Downing Street until four that afternoon, when Armstrong smuggled him past the demonstrators through the Foreign Office and the steps from St James's Park. But while Thorpe's talks with Heath were 'friendly and easy', Armstrong recorded, there was no great breakthrough. Although Heath was willing to contemplate a 'high level inquiry' on electoral reform, Thorpe pointed out that Liberal activists would want something rather more concrete – especially as they were seething at the injustice of having won almost 20 per cent of the vote but only fourteen seats. And although Thorpe was naturally excited at the thought of becoming a political kingmaker and perhaps even sitting in the Cabinet as Home Secretary, he was well aware that many Liberals loathed Heath and would be furious at the prospect of saving his bacon. Indeed, within hours of Thorpe leaving Downing Street, he rang his friend Nigel Fisher, a Tory MP, and told him that he was already 'encountering a rather embarrassing problem with his colleagues about the Prime Minister personally. They feel they could not agree to serve as long as he is the Prime Minister.' On top of that, 'there could be no deal' without a commitment to electoral reform within six months, which Heath could never give without alienating his own backbenchers. And that, in essence, was the end of that.[40]

Thorpe did not put Heath out of his misery until Monday afternoon, when he had finished his soundings among his Liberal colleagues. 'I am sorry, this is obviously hell – a nightmare on stilts for you,' Thorpe told him on the phone on Sunday night, adding that if it were left to him, he would love to 'work something out'. But when Heath summoned his Cabinet on Monday morning, it was painfully obvious that there was nothing to discuss. As they all agreed, the economic situation was so desperate that only a secure, stable government could sort it out – which meant a formal coalition with the Liberals, and that was clearly not on the agenda. In any case, ministers reported that Tory backbenchers were 'increasingly worried by talk of a deal with the Liberals over proportional representation'. To all intents and purposes, the game was up. 'From now on,' Robert Armstrong recorded, 'it was probably only a matter of hours before the Prime Minister resigned.' In the Cabinet Room he organized an impromptu champagne farewell for Heath's chief civil servants, including the now recovered Sir William Armstrong, but the Prime Minister was in no mood for sentimental partings. 'It was not a cheerful occasion,' Armstrong noted, and a few hours later Heath confessed that 'he felt worn out'. Late that afternoon, the Liberals definitively rejected his offer. His premiership was over.[41]

Heath had been Prime Minister for three years and 259 days, although his period in office was packed with so many crises that he seemed to have been there for a decade. By conventional standards, his government had been a total failure. When elected, he had promised to revive the British economy, yet unemployment broke through the one million mark for the first time since the 1930s, inflation began to surge into double figures, the money supply ran disastrously out of control, government borrowing rose to record levels and the balance of payments deficit – which had played a key part in his rise to power – reached an unprecedented £380 million. He had promised to revitalize the nation's industry, yet by 1974 Britain was mocked abroad as the Sick Man of Europe, its travails epitomized by the humiliating collapse of Rolls-Royce. He had promised to rekindle the values of competition and free enterprise, yet he threw millions of pounds of taxpayers' money not only at Rolls-Royce but also at Upper Clyde Shipbuilders, in clear defiance of his experts' advice. He had promised to let the free market govern wages and prices, yet he left office having set up a gargantuan apparatus of Pay Boards and Price Commissions that appalled many of his own supporters. He had promised to reform industrial relations on clean, rational lines, yet he presided over the most debilitating industrial conflicts in living memory and saw his government twice humiliated by the miners. He had promised 'not to divide but to unite', yet he left office loathed by many of his own people, who saw him as a cruel, confrontational reactionary. And he had promised 'to create one nation', yet he presided over some of the most savage civil conflict in the history of the United Kingdom, with blood on the streets of Belfast and bombs in the streets of London.

Yet much of the conventional wisdom about the Heath government is simply wrong. It is not true, as critics on the left claim, that he was bent on confrontation with the unions. In fact, he wanted nothing more than to work in partnership with them, tried to bring them into economic decision-making, and did all he could (as he saw it) to avoid the miners' dispute that brought him down. And it is not true, as his Thatcherite adversaries insist, that he cravenly abandoned his free-market 'Selsdon Man' commitments when the going got tough. It is true that in some ways he anticipated Mrs Thatcher – in his provincial grammar school background, in his emphasis on entrepreneurship, in his impatience with tradition. But he was too much a creature of the system, too deeply marked by the experiences of the Depression and the war, to be a true proto-Thatcherite. His friends Denis Healey and Douglas Hurd – one Labour, one Tory – agreed that the politician he most resembled was Sir Robert Peel, who smashed his own party with the repeal of the Corn Laws in 1846. Like Peel, Heath was an industrious, earnest, terse and repressed man from outside the magic circle. Like Peel, he was a modernizer, a reformer, a pragmatist who believed that every problem had a rational solution and that reasoned argument could reconcile competing interests to the greater good. Like Peel, he saw further than many of his colleagues: in his case, his European enthusiasm marked him out as a much more visionary politician than most of his contemporaries. But like Peel, he lacked the communication skills, the deftness of touch, the political dexterity and personal charisma to win the nation to his standard and to unite his party around him.[42]

That Heath had serious flaws as a national leader is surely not in doubt. He was a terrible speaker; he was preposterously rude and grumpy; he was far too impatient; he tried to do too much too quickly; and he was insensitive to the values and pressures that drove other people. It is worth pointing out, however, that he was also incredibly unlucky. No Prime Minister since Ramsay MacDonald had been dealt such a terrible hand: in June 1970, not even the most pessimistic forecaster could possibly have predicted the collapse of the global financial system, the rise of worldwide inflation, the oil shock, the escalation of violence in Northern Ireland, and the wider sense of social breakdown that flowed from the rise in street crime, the explosion of football hooliganism and the controversies over permissiveness, immigration and delinquency. As his friend Jim Prior later wrote, Heath, his government and the institutions of Britain were like a 'captain, his crew and an ageing ship setting out with new charts on a voyage during which he planned to introduce new disciplines and to refurbish the engine and hull. But what neither Ted nor any of his officers could know was that we were heading for heavy seas.' It was the worst possible context in which to attempt such a brusque and rapid programme of modernization, and it was Heath who paid the price.[43]

If his administration was a failure, though, it was not an ignoble one. And although Heath got the date of his re-election bid badly wrong, the fact remains that on many of the big questions he was absolutely right. He was right, for example, to see that Britain's future as a trading nation lay within the European Community. He was right in his prescription for Northern Ireland; there is a peculiar injustice that his regime is remembered for Bloody Sunday when the Sunningdale agreement so closely anticipated the peace process of the 1990s. He was right to see that Britain's industrial relations were an anarchic shambles, right to see that its public institutions were complacent and sclerotic, right to see the dangers of rampant wage inflation, and right to see that British industry needed drastic modernization to compete in a globalized world. The irony, though, is that he paid a heavy penalty for being right on so many issues and for his impatience to tackle them all at once. As his biographer remarks, the truth is that the British electorate, fattened by decades of affluence, shrank from the painful changes Heath was offering. When they were offered the chance of a quieter life under good old Mr Wilson, they took it. As Bernard Donoughue, of all people, later admitted, 'the electorate realised that Heath was right and one day there had to be a battle with the unions to curb their irresponsibilities. But the public was not quite ready for it yet. They were tempted by Wilson's Labour as the fudge to put off the evil day of battle.' But that day was coming, all the same.[44]

Early on the morning of Monday, 4 March, Heath held one last, rather pointless Cabinet meeting, a bleak occasion at which most of his ministers were too tired and depressed even for the usual farewell compliments. Only Margaret Thatcher roused herself to offer an emotional tribute, praising the 'wonderful experience of team loyalty' she had shared since 1970 – an extraordinarily ironic moment, given what was to come. Just before six, the Prime Minister bade farewell to the Downing Street staff, having told Robert Armstrong that he did not want to endure the humiliation of returning to collect his grand piano and his manuscripts of music scores after he had formally resigned. It was Armstrong, the fellow musical enthusiast, who replied on behalf of the staff, wishing him 'good health and better luck'. Upstairs, his aides were frantically stuffing piles of paper into boxes and bin liners, rushing to evacuate the building before their replacements arrived.

And then it was all over, and the two men left for Buckingham Palace. 'On the drive we neither of us said a word,' Armstrong recalled. 'There was so much, or nothing, left to say.' Even at this last, supremely emotional moment, Heath remained impassive, masking his shock and disappointment behind the familiar granite mask. But for Armstrong, who had become so close to his chief, it was all too much to bear. After Heath had disappeared to see the Queen, Sir Martin Charteris took the young Private Secretary aside and murmured a few words of sympathy. 'I do not remember what he said,' Armstrong wrote later, 'but I remember that I nearly broke into tears when he said it.'[45]

In Lord North Street, where Harold Wilson was waiting for the call to kiss hands as Prime Minister, there was a sense of relief and jubilation at his second coming – something many had thought impossible only weeks before. From the brink of annihilation, Wilson now found himself once more the master of British politics, as well as the first Labour leader in history to win three general elections. But some things had not changed. While Wilson was upstairs shaving for his meeting with the monarch, his aides were arguing about the shape of his new Cabinet. Since his last administration had been blighted by an extraordinary amount of factionalism and disloyalty, his colleagues might have been expected to have learned their lesson. But even before he had gone to the Palace, the bickering had started. At lunchtime, Wilson had sent Bernard Donoughue to the Commons to tell Roy Jenkins that he was not going to be the new Chancellor, as promised, but would have to be content with the Home Office. It was typical Wilson: he hated giving people bad news, so he asked his aides to do it instead. And Jenkins's reaction, too, brought back memories of the 1960s. 'You tell Harold Wilson he must bloody well come to see me,' he exploded, 'and if he doesn't watch out, I won't join his bloody government!' Since they were standing on a public staircase, Donoughue found the whole scene excruciatingly embarrassing, but Jenkins seemed undeterred by the attention. 'This is typical of the bloody awful way Harold Wilson does things!' he shouted, as if he wanted everybody to hear him. It was not an ideal start.[46]

Just after seven that evening, Wilson's car left for Buckingham Palace and his audience with the Queen. Behind him, crammed into a rented Daimler, followed his closest aides, and as Wilson and his wife went in to see the monarch, they sat downstairs in an unheated palace room and complained about the lack of drinks. An hour later, after the new Prime Minister had emerged, they drove on to Downing Street. It was almost exactly fifty years since Wilson, a cheeky little boy in an oversized cap and knee-length shorts, had been photographed by his father on the steps of Number 10. Now, as he trudged almost disconsolately to the familiar spot, his shoulders hunched, his smile thin, his eyes weary, he looked older than his 57 years, a white-haired little man in a crumpled suit. And this time, as the photographers' flashbulbs popped in the evening air, there were no fine words. 'We've got a job to do,' he said slowly, his flat Yorkshire voice barely audible above the mingled cheers and boos of the crowd. 'We can only do that job as one people, and I'm going right in to start that job now.'

As the heavy black door swung shut, there was silence in the Number 10 hallway. 'It was eerily quiet,' remembered Bernard Donoughue, who stood behind his leader, barely able to believe his good fortune. Along the walls the staff stood and waited: policy advisers and press officers, civil servants and messengers, security officers and secretaries. 'They were totally silent,' Donoughue wrote, 'and appeared apprehensive, as if we were a threatening force of alien occupation. The tension was tangible.' Only a few hours before, they had stood in exactly the same spot to bid farewell to Edward Heath. Many of them, Donoughue noticed, had been crying. For a brief moment, nobody spoke. Nobody moved. And then from among the rows of men in dark suits Robert Armstrong stepped forward and began to clap, and suddenly the applause and the cheers rang around the hallway, and Harold Wilson stepped forward and began shaking the outstretched hands.[47]

Acknowledgements

Glancing through a selection of history books written in the 1970s, I could not help noticing that their acknowledgements were a lot shorter and less effusive than their twenty-first-century equivalents. So I will keep this brief and to the point. My thanks go first to my splendid editor Simon Winder, who combines the stoicism of Ted Heath, the cunning of Harold Wilson, the enthusiasm of Tony Benn and the charisma of Jason King. Working with Simon and his colleagues at Penguin has been an absolute pleasure: among others, I would like to thank Stefan McGrath, Nicola Hill, Natalie Ramm, Jenny Fry, Mari Yamazaki and Caroline Elliker. My copy-editor, the brilliant Elizabeth Stratford, saved me from more mistakes than I could have imagined. At the Wylie Agency, I am grateful to Andrew Wylie, Scott Moyers and James Pullen. I am grateful, too, to the various literary and features editors who kept me supplied with distracting but hugely enjoyable commissions, especially Andy Neather, Sam Leith, Brian MacArthur, Andrew Holgate, Matt Warren and Dave Musgrove, and particularly Jason Cowley, who allowed me to float some initial thoughts about Thatcherism, Don Revie and the politics of the 1970s in the *New Statesman*. For the initial inspiration, my thanks go to Roy Allen, Joe Gauci and above all Tim Whiting. For ideas and encouragement, my thanks to Simon Hooper, Martin O'Neill, Ted Vallance, Andrew Preston, Simon Hall and Tom Holland. I am especially grateful to Professor Iwan Morgan of the University of London for a preview of his paper on the life and death of the post-war Keynesian consensus, to Professor Sue Harper of the University of Portsmouth for inviting me to talk through my early thoughts on the 1970s, and to Rachel Morley for her strange but oddly contagious enthusiasm for all things 1973. My greatest and most heartfelt thanks, though, are to my brother Alex Sandbrook, my parents Rhys and Hilary Sandbrook, and above all my beloved wife Catherine Morley. She deserved a lot better than to spend the first years of her married life listening to me talking about Ted Heath, and in a just world she would now get a break. Even as you read this, however, I am probably talking to her about Jim Callaghan – and she is almost certainly listening with the kindness, patience and good humour I scarcely deserve.

Notes

Documents designated PRO can be found in the National Archives (formerly the Public Record Office); those marked CAB can also be found online at http://www. nationalarchives.gov.uk/cabinetpapers/.

PREFACE: A STATE OF EMERGENCY

1. *The Times*, 12 November 1973, 13 November 1973, 15 November 1973; James Lees-Milne, *Diaries, 1971–1983* (London, 2008), p. 118.
2. *The Times*, 15 November 1973.
3. *The Times*, 14 November 1973, 15 November 1973; *New York Times*, 15 November 1973.
4. *The Times*, 12 November 1973; *Radio Times*, 10–16 November 1973.
5. Lees-Milne, *Diaries*, p. 118; *Time*, 26 November 1973.
6. *The Times*, 12 November 1973, 13 November 1973; Hansard, 13 November 1973.
7. *The Times*, 14 November 1973.
8. Hansard, 21 January 1997, 23 January 1997; *Daily Telegraph*, 6 July 2008; *Daily Mail*, 15 September 2009.
9. Richard Clutterbuck, *Britain in Agony: The Growth of Political Violence* (London, 1978), p. 255; 'The Diaries of Smurfette', 28 February 1974, 4 March 1974, http://www.escape-to-the-seventies.com/diaries/february_1974.php.
10. Clutterbuck, *Britain in Agony*, p. 20; *New Statesman*, 2 April 2009.

CHAPTER 1. A BETTER TOMORROW

1. *The Times*, 19 June 1970.
2. *The Times*, 17 June 1970, 19 June 1970; John Campbell, *Edward Heath: A Biography* (London, 1993), p. 273; D. R. Thorpe, *Alec Douglas-Home* (London, 1996), pp. 402–3; Mark Garnett and Ian Aitken, *Splendid! Splendid! The Authorized Biography of Willie Whitelaw* (London, 2003), p. 85; Edward Heath, *The Course of My Life* (London, 1998), p. 307.
3. *Time*, 29 June 1970; Marcia Williams, *Inside Number 10* (London, 1975), p. 10.

4. Heath, *The Course of My Life*, pp. 307–8; Campbell, *Edward Heath*, p. 284; *The Times*, 20 June 1970.

5. Campbell, *Edward Heath*, p. 18; Anthony Sampson, *The New Anatomy of Britain* (London, 1971), p. 660.

6. *Daily Mirror*, 28 July 1965; *Sunday Times*, 1 August 1965; Campbell, *Edward Heath*, pp. 3–6, 18–19, 183.

7. See ibid., p. 60.

8. Michael Young and Peter Willmott, *The Symmetrical Family: A Study of Work and Leisure in the London Region* (London, 1973), pp. 29–30, 48; Arthur Marwick, *British Society Since 1945* (Harmondsworth, 1982), p. 121; Ken Coates and Richard Silburn, *Poverty: The Forgotten Englishmen* (Harmondsworth, 1970), p. 60; Piers Paul Read, *A Married Man* (London, 1979), p. 42.

9. Dominic Sandbrook, *Never Had It So Good: A History of Britain from Suez to the Beatles* (London, 2005), p. 101; Richard Hoggart, *The Uses of Literacy* (Harmondsworth, 1958), p. 240; Margaret Drabble, *The Ice Age* (London, 1977), p. 55.

10. David Butler and Dennis Kavanagh, *The British General Election of February 1974* (London, 1974), p. 17.

11. Denis Healey, *The Time of My Life* (London, 1989), pp. 136–40.

12. Ibid., p. 136; Kester Aspden, *The Hounding of David Oluwale* (London, 2008), pp. 84–5; Michael Bilton, *Wicked Beyond Belief: The Hunt for the Yorkshire Ripper* (London, 2003), p. 145; *Guardian*, 18 February 2009; Rob Bagchi and Paul Rogerson, *The Unforgiven: The Story of Don Revie's Leeds United* (London, 2003), pp. 11–12.

13. On tea and coffee, see John Burnett, *Liquid Pleasures: A Social History of Drinks in Modern Britain* (London, 1999), pp. 47, 67; on Bingley, see Gordon Burn, *Somebody's Husband, Somebody's Son: The Story of Peter Sutcliffe* (London, 1984), pp. 4–5.

14. Jeremy Seabrook, *City Close-Up* (Harmondsworth, 1973), pp. 11–12, 43.

15. Jeremy Seabrook, *What Went Wrong? Working People and the Ideals of the Labour Movement* (London, 1978), pp. 38 ff. See also Andy Beckett, *When the Lights Went Out: Britain in the Seventies* (London, 2009), pp. 418–19.

16. Adrian Hastings, *A History of English Christianity 1920–1985* (London, 1985), pp. 602–3.

17. Campbell, *Edward Heath*, p. 380; Stuart Ball, 'The Conservative Party and the Heath Government', in Stuart Ball and Anthony Seldon (eds.), *The Heath Government, 1970–1974: A Reappraisal* (Harlow, 1996), p. 325; *The Times*, 15 February 1971, 16 February 1971; *Daily Mail*, 15 February 1971; Richard Weight, *Patriots: National Identity in Britain 1940–2000* (London, 2002), p. 487.

18. 'D-Day delivers new UK currency,' BBC News, 15 February 1971, http://news.bbc.co.uk/onthisday; Robert J. Wybrow, *Britain Speaks Out, 1937–87: A Social History as Seen Through the Gallup Data* (London, 1989), p. 96; *The Times*, 16 February 1971.

19. *Daily Mail*, 15 February 1971; Ball, 'The Conservative Party and the Heath Government', p. 325; Brian Miller, 'Peter Nichols', in George W. Brandt (ed.), *British Television Drama* (Cambridge, 1981), p. 133.

20. Seabrook, *City Close-Up*, pp. 35–7.

21. Steve Chibnall, *Get Carter* (London, 2003), pp. 10, 39–41, 90–92; Michael Caine, *What's It All About? The Autobiography* (London, 1992), p. 159.

22. Alwyn W. Turner, *Crisis? What Crisis? Britain in the 1970s* (London, 2008), p. 60; Miriam Akhtar and Steve Humphries, *The Fifties and Sixties: A Lifestyle Revolution* (London, 2001), pp. 110–11; Roger Protz, *Pulling a Fast One: What Your Brewers Have Done to Your Beer* (London, 1978), p. 14.

23. Coates and Silburn, *Poverty*, p. 142; Seabrook, *City Close-Up*, p. 154; Colin Dexter, *Last Seen Wearing* (London, 1977), p. 125.

24. Coates and Silburn, *Poverty*, pp. 67–8, 73, 80–81; Burn, *Somebody's Husband, Somebody's Son*, p. 54; Peter Calvocoressi, *The British Experience 1945–75* (Harmondsworth, 1978), p. 140; Clive Irving, *Pox Britannica: The Unmaking of the British* (New York, 1974), p. 168.

25. Young and Willmott, *The Symmetrical Family*, pp. 212, 216; Marwick, *British Society Since 1945*, pp. 250–51.

26. Brian Harrison and Josephine Webb, 'Volunteers and Voluntarism', in A. H. Halsey and Josephine Webb (eds.), *Twentieth-Century Social Trends* (Basingstoke, 2000), pp. 589–90, 600–602; George L. Bernstein, *The Myth of Decline: The Rise of Britain Since 1945* (London, 2004), pp. 453–5.

27. Jeffrey Hill, *Sport, Leisure and Culture in Twentieth-Century Britain* (Basingstoke, 2002), pp. 134–5; Brian Jackson, *Working-Class Community* (Harmondsworth, 1968), pp. 41, 48, 64, 70, 106.

28. See James Lees-Milne, *Diaries, 1971–1983* (London, 2008), pp. 17, 26; Wybrow, *Britain Speaks Out*, pp. 102, 104.

29. Ibid., p. 96; Ben Pimlott, *The Queen: A Biography of Elizabeth II* (London, 1996), p. 412; Marwick, *British Society Since 1945*, p. 254; Nick Tiratsoo, 'The Seventies', in Folio Society, *England 1945–2000* (London, 2001), p. 296.

30. *The Times*, 2 January 1973.

31. Tiratsoo, 'The Seventies', pp. 298–9; *New Society*, 29 May 1975, 20 July 1978.

32. Bernard D. Nossiter, *Britain: A Future That Works* (London, 1978), pp. 90–91, 93.

33. Shawn Levy, *Ready, Steady, Go! Swinging London and the Invention of Cool* (London, 2002), p. 66; Jonathan Aitken, *The Young Meteors* (London, 1967), pp. 272–3; David Frost and Antony Jay, *To England with Love* (London, 1967), p. 85.

34. Campbell, *Edward Heath*, p. 199.

35. Jilly Cooper, *Class: A View from Middle England* (London, 1979), p. 13; Sandbrook, *Never Had It So Good*, pp. 38–40; John Benson, *The Rise of Consumer Society in Britain, 1880–1980* (Harlow, 1994), p. 100; David Cannadine, *Class in Britain* (London, 2000), p. 147; Patrick Hutber, *The Decline*

and Fall of the Middle Class – and How It Can Fight Back (Harmondsworth, 1977), p. 20.

36. Hunter Davies, *The Glory Game* (London, 1972), p. 230; Mary Abbott, *Family Affairs: A History of the Family in Twentieth-Century England* (London, 2003), p. 134; Lees-Milne, *Diaries*, p. 38.

37. A. H. Halsey, *Change in British Society* (Oxford, 1981); Sampson, *The New Anatomy of Britain*, pp. 134–5, 158–60.

38. Jackson, *Working-Class Community*, p. 159; Young and Willmott, *The Symmetrical Family*, p. 217; Joe Rogaly, *Grunwick* (Harmondsworth, 1977), pp. 111–12; Abbott, *Family Affairs*, p. 130.

39. Hoggart, *The Uses of Literacy*, p. 62: David Marquand, *The Progressive Dilemma: From Lloyd George to Blair* (London, 1999), pp. 221–2.

40. *The Times*, 15 December 1976.

41. *Time*, 15 September 1975.

42. David Butler and Michael Pinto-Duschinsky, *The British General Election of 1970* (London, 1971), pp. 232–3; Roy Greenslade, *Press Gang: How Newspapers Make Profits from Propaganda* (London, 2004), pp. 207–8, 271–3.

43. Larry Lamb, *Sunrise: The Remarkable Rise and Rise of the Bestselling Soaraway Sun* (London, 1989), pp. 26–7, 158; Greenslade, *Press Gang*, pp. 213–16, 250–51; Stuart Laing, 'The Politics of Culture: Institutional Change in the 1970s', in Bart Moore-Gilbert (ed.), *The Arts in the 1970s: Cultural Closure?* (London, 1994), pp. 36, 54.

44. *Bookseller*, 4 February 1978, 25 February 1978; Bart Moore-Gilbert, 'Cultural Closure or Post-Avantgardism?', in Moore-Gilbert (ed.), *The Arts in the 1970s*, pp. 12–14.

45. Randall Stevenson, *The Oxford English Literary History*, volume 12: *1960–2000: The Last of England?* (Oxford, 2004), pp. 127–8, 132, 137; John Sutherland, *Bestsellers: Popular Fiction of the 1970s* (London, 1981), p. 28.

46. *New Review*, 5:1 (Summer 1978), pp. 16, 37; Patricia Waugh, *Harvest of the Sixties: English Literature and its Background, 1960 to 1990* (Oxford, 1995), p. 70; Bernard Bergonzi, *The Situation of the Novel* (London, 1970), p. 57; Bart Moore-Gilbert, 'Apocalypse Now? The Novel in the 1970s', in Moore-Gilbert (ed.), *The Arts in the 1970s*, pp. 152–3.

47. David Lodge, 'The Novelist at the Crossroads,' in Malcolm Bradbury (ed.), *The Novel Today: Contemporary Writers on Modern Fiction* (London, 1977), p. 100; Robert Sheppard, 'Artifice and the Everyday World: Poetry in the 1970s,' in Moore-Gilbert (ed.), *The Arts in the 1970s*, pp. 130–31; Gilbert Phelps, 'Literature and Drama', in Boris Ford (ed.), *The Cambridge Cultural History of Britain*, vol. 9: *Modern Britain* (Cambridge, 1992), p. 209.

48. Sutherland, *Bestsellers*, pp. 85, 96–7; and see the same author's *Reading the Decades: Fifty Years of British History Through the Nation's Bestsellers* (London, 2002), pp. 83–112.

49. Christopher Booker, *The Seventies: Portrait of a Decade* (London, 1980),

pp. 259–61; Campbell, *Edward Heath*, pp. 390–91; Stuart Sillars, 'Visual Art in the 1970s', in Moore-Gilbert (ed.), *The Arts in the 1970s*, p. 273; *The Times*, 1 April 1972, 15 April 1972, 4 April 1972.

50. *Observer*, 2 September 1975; Moore-Gilbert, 'Cultural Closure or Post-Avantgardism?', pp. 14–19; Laing, 'The Politics of Culture', p. 43; Robert Hewison, *Too Much: Art and Society in the Sixties, 1960–75* (London, 1986), pp. 269–71.

51. Edward Heath, *Music: A Joy for Life* (London, 1976), pp. 176–9; Campbell, *Edward Heath*, pp. 496–7; *Daily Telegraph*, 7 June 2008, 8 April 2008.

52. Dominic Shellard, *British Theatre Since the War* (New Haven, 2000), pp. 180, 183–5; Michael Billington, *State of the Nation: British Theatre Since 1945* (London, 2007), pp. 208, 234–5, 242, 246, 266; Hewison, *Too Much*, p. 189; *The Times*, 19 February 1973, 20 September 1978; John Goodwin (ed.), *Peter Hall's Diaries: The Story of a Dramatic Battle* (London, 1983), pp. 378–9.

53. Alexander Walker, *Hollywood England: The British Film Industry in the Sixties* (London, 1974), pp. 441–3; Justin Smith, 'Glam, Spam and Uncle Sam: Funding Diversity in 1970s British Film Production', in Robert Shail (ed.), *Seventies British Cinema* (London, 2008), p. 70.

54. Alexander Walker, *National Heroes: British Cinema in the Seventies and Eighties* (London, 1985), pp. 15, 113; Wheeler Winston Dixon, 'The End of Hammer', in Shail (ed.), *Seventies British Cinema*, pp. 14–23; Ian Conrich, 'The Divergence and Mutation of British Horror Cinema', in Shail (ed.), *Seventies British Cinema*, pp. 25–34.

55. I. Q. Hunter, 'Take an Easy Ride: Sexploitation in the 1970s', in Shail (ed.), *Seventies British Cinema*, pp. 3–11; Leon Hunt, *British Low Culture: From Safari Suits to Sexploitation* (London, 1998), pp. 112–41; Richard Webber, *Fifty Years of Carry On* (London, 2008), pp. 143, 152–3; *Daily Mirror*, 29 October 1976.

56. Laing, 'The Politics of Culture', p. 34; Andrew Higson, 'Renewing British Cinema in the 1970s', in Moore-Gilbert (ed.), *The Arts in the 1970s*, pp. 218–20; Smith, 'Glam, Spam and Uncle Sam', pp. 67–9.

57. Higson, 'Renewing British Cinema in the 1970s', p. 222; Hunt, *British Low Culture*, pp. 31–2.

58. Young and Willmott, *The Symmetrical Family*, pp. 215, 211–13; Sampson, *The New Anatomy of Britain*, p. 442; Asa Briggs, *The History of Broadcasting in the United Kingdom*, vol. 5: *Competition* (Oxford, 1995), p. 959; Krishan Kumar, 'The Social and Cultural Setting', in Boris Ford (ed.), *The New Pelican Guide to English Literature*, volume 8: *From Orwell to Naipaul* (London, 1998), p. 28; Joe Moran, *Queuing for Beginners: The Story of Daily Life from Breakfast to Bedtime* (London, 2007), p. 180.

59. Laing, 'The Politics of Culture', pp. 31–4; Briggs, *Competition*, pp. 848–9.

60. Michael Tracey and David Morrison, *Whitehouse* (London, 1979), p. 59; Max Caulfield, *Mary Whitehouse* (London, 1975), pp. 83, 140, 170; Russell Davies (ed.), *The Kenneth Williams Diaries* (London, 1993), p. 414.

61. Caulfield, *Mary Whitehouse*, p. 83; Richard Clutterbuck, *Britain in Agony: The Growth of Political Violence* (London, 1978), pp. 236–7; Humphrey Carpenter, *Dennis Potter: A Biography* (London, 1998), pp. 328–9; Turner, *Crisis? What Crisis?*, pp. 233–4; *The Best of Private Eye 1974* (London, 1974). On *Play for Today*, see Brandt (ed.), *British Television Drama*; Irene Shubik, *Play for Today: The Evolution of Television Drama* (London, 2002); and the excellent sites at http://tv.cream.org/lookin/playfortoday and www.playfortoday.co.uk.

62. *Daily Telegraph*, 14 November 1972, 1 November 1972; Briggs, *Competition*, pp. 958–9; *The Times*, 21 January 1975; Carpenter, *Dennis Potter*, pp. 368–71.

63. Briggs, *Competition*, pp. 948–9; Louis Barfe, *Turned Out Nice Again: The Story of British Light Entertainment* (London, 2008), pp. 1, 146, 234–7, 253, 279–81.

64. Davies (ed.), *The Kenneth Williams Diaries*, p. 505; *The Times*, 5 April 1973; on the sitcom landscape in the early 1970s, see Hunt, *British Low Culture*, pp. 28–9; Graham McCann, *Fawlty Towers: The Story of Britain's Favourite Sitcom* (London, 2007), p. 43.

65. Hunt, *British Low Culture*, pp. 40–41; Phil Wickham, 'Steptoe and Son', http://www.screenonline.org.uk/tv/id/467085/index.html.

66. Phil Wickham, *The Likely Lads* (Basingstoke, 2008), pp. 39–43, 49.

67. Graham McCann, *Dad's Army: The Story of a Classic Television Show* (London, 2001), pp. 116, 135.

68. *Evening Standard*, 22 September 1975; *Listener*, 9 October 1975; *Daily Mirror*, 26 September 1975; McCann, *Fawlty Towers*, pp. 57, 75–6, 119–21, 139; John Cleese and Connie Booth, *The Complete Fawlty Towers* (London, 1989), p. 150.

69. Ibid., pp. 139, 225, 87; McCann, *Fawlty Towers*, pp. 3–4, 10–17; John le Carré, *Tinker Tailor Soldier Spy* (London, 1974), pp. 111–12, 239; Kingsley Amis, *Jake's Thing* (London, 1978), pp. 123, 230.

70. Campbell, *Edward Heath*, p. 295.

71. Douglas Hurd, *An End to Promises* (London, 1978), p. 31; Heath, *The Course of My Life*, pp. 308–9.

72. Peter Hennessy, *The Prime Minister: The Office and its Holders Since 1945* (London 2000), p. 340.

CHAPTER 2. HEATHCO

1. Mark Garnett and Ian Aitken, *Splendid! Splendid! The Authorized Biography of Willie Whitelaw* (London, 2003), p. 88; Anthony Sampson, *The New Anatomy of Britain* (London, 1971), p. 80; Marcia Falkender, *Downing Street in Perspective* (London 1983), pp. 104–5; Barbara Castle, *The Castle Diaries 1974–76*, (London, 1980), p. 35; John Campbell, *Edward Heath: A Biography* (London, 1993), pp. 292–3.

2. John Cole, *As It Seemed To Me: Political Memoirs* (London, 1995), p. 80; John

Ramsden, 'The Prime Minister and the Making of Policy,' in Stuart Ball and Anthony Seldon (eds.), *The Heath Government, 1970–1974: A Reappraisal* (Harlow, 1996), pp. 21, 35; Peter Hennessy, *Muddling Through: Power, Politics and the Quality of Government in Postwar Britain* (London, 1997), p. 270; Peter Hennessy, *The Prime Minister: The Office and its Holders Since 1945* (London, 2000), pp. 336, 342; PRO CAB 128/47, CM (70) 1, 22 June 1970.

3. Sampson, *The New Anatomy of Britain*, p. 99; Kevin Theakston, 'The Heath Government, Whitehall and the Civil Service', in Ball and Seldon (eds.), *The Heath Government*, p. 75; Hennessy, *The Prime Minister*, pp. 337, 344; Edward Heath, *The Course of My Life* (London, 1998), pp. 318–19; Douglas Hurd, *An End to Promises* (London, 1978), p. 92.

4. PRO CAB 128/47, CM (70) 1, 22 June 1970.

5. Campbell, *Edward Heath*, pp. 178, 264–7; Philip Whitehead, *The Writing on the Wall: Britain in the Seventies* (London, 1985), p. 40; *The Economist*, 7 February 1970; *Spectator*, 7 February 1970; John Ramsden, *An Appetite for Power: A History of the Conservative Party Since 1830* (London, 1999), pp. 398–400; E. H. H. Green, *Ideologies of Conservatism: Conservative Political Ideas in the Twentieth Century* (Oxford, 2002), pp. 231–2.

6. See Dennis Kavanagh, *Thatcherism and British Politics: The End of Consensus?* (Oxford, 1987), pp. 6–8, 26–60; David Butler and Michael Pinto-Duschinsky, *The British General Election of 1970* (London, 1971), p. 24; Ivor Crewe and Anthony King, *SDP: The Birth, Life and Death of the Social Democratic Party* (Oxford, 1995), pp. 3–4; David Marquand, *The Progressive Dilemma: From Lloyd George to Blair* (London, 1999), p. 155.

7. Jim Tomlinson, 'Inventing "Decline": The Falling Behind of the British Economy in the Post-War Years', *Economic History Review*, 49:4 (1996), pp. 731–57; Jim Tomlinson, *The Politics of Decline: Understanding Post-war Britain* (London, 2000); Jim Tomlinson, 'Thrice Denied: "Declinism" as a Recurrent Theme in British History in the Long Twentieth Century', *Twentieth Century British History*, 20:2 (2009), pp. 227–51; Andrew Gamble, *Britain in Decline: Economic Policy, Political Strategy and the British State* (Basingstoke, 1994), pp. xv, 15, 17; Catherine R. Schenk, 'Britain and the Common Market', in Richard Coopey and Nicholas Woodward (eds.), *Britain in the 1970s: The Troubled Economy* (London, 1996), p. 193; *The Times*, 16 July 1970.

8. Gamble, *Britain in Decline*, pp. 105, 109, 115; Richard Coopey and Nicholas Woodward, 'The British Economy in the 1970s', in Coopey and Woodward (eds.), *Britain in the 1970s*, pp. 8–9; Nicholas Crafts, 'Economic Growth in the 1970s', in Coopey and Woodward (eds.), *Britain in the 1970s*, p. 102; Terry Gourvish, 'Beyond the Merger Mania: Merger and De-Merger Activity', in Coopey and Woodward (eds.), *Britain in the 1970s*, pp. 236–7; Geoffrey Owen, *From Empire to Europe: The Decline and Revival of British Industry Since the Second World War* (London, 1999), pp. 3, 5, 9–29, 422–3, 439–41, 447–61.

9. *The Times*, 29 June 1970; Sir Alec Cairncross, 'The Heath Government and the

British Economy', in Ball and Seldon (eds.), *The Heath Government*, pp. 109–10; Ramsden, 'The Prime Minister and the Making of Policy', pp. 26–7; Whitehead, *The Writing on the Wall*, p. 54.

10. Campbell, *Edward Heath*, pp. 230, 232–3, 272; Ramsden, 'The Prime Minister and the Making of Policy', pp. 28–30; Ramsden, *An Appetite for Power*, pp. 396–8; Peter Walker, *Staying Power: An Autobiography* (London, 1991), p. 52.

11. Robert Shepherd, *Iain Macleod: A Biography* (London, 1994), pp. 431, 440–41, 446–7, 462–3.

12. Ibid., pp. 534–5, 538–9; Heath, *The Course of My Life*, p. 320; Whitehead, *The Writing on the Wall*, p. 54; Campbell, *Edward Heath*, pp. 302–3; Edmund Dell, *The Chancellors: A History of the Chancellors of the Exchequer, 1945–90* (London, 1996), pp. 374–5.

13. Campbell, *Edward Heath*, p. 297; Cecil King, *The Cecil King Diary 1965–70* (London, 1972), p. 286; Lewis Baston, *Reggie: The Life of Reginald Maudling* (Stroud, 2004), pp. 264–5, 350, 391.

14. Lewis Baston and Anthony Seldon, 'Number 10 under Edward Heath', in Ball and Seldon (eds.), *The Heath Government*, pp. 53–62; Ramsden, 'The Prime Minister and the Making of Policy', p. 36; Campbell, *Edward Heath*, pp. 298–9, 377–8; Sampson, *The New Anatomy of Britain*, pp. 105–6, 126–7, 108–9; Whitehead, *The Writing on the Wall*, p. 31.

15. *Daily Telegraph*, 8 April 2008, 7 June 2008; Campbell, *Edward Heath*, pp. 7–8, 10, 52, 258; Ramsden, *An Appetite for Power*, p. 388; Baston and Seldon, 'Number 10 under Edward Heath', pp. 51–2; Hurd, *An End to Promises*, p. 137.

16. Hennessy, *The Prime Minister*, p. 341; Jim Prior, *A Balance of Power* (London, 1986), pp. 38, 101; Campbell, *Edward Heath*, p. 259; *Evening Standard*, 12 October 1970.

17. *The Times*, 19 June 1970; Campbell, *Edward Heath*, pp. 285–6, 289; Ramsden, *An Appetite for Power*, pp. 389, 401; Michael Cockerell, *Live from Number Ten: The Inside Story of Prime Ministers and Television* (London, 1989), pp. 170–71; Baston and Seldon, 'Number 10 under Edward Heath', pp. 49–50.

18. Hansard, 2 July 1970; Campbell, *Edward Heath*, pp. 300–301, 310–12.

19. *Evening Standard*, 12 October 1970; *New Statesman*, 8 December 1970; Campbell, *Edward Heath*, pp. 314, 317–27; Baston and Seldon, 'Number 10 under Edward Heath', pp. 67–9; Theakston, 'The Heath Government, Whitehall and the Civil Service', pp. 94–8.

20. *The Times*, 21 December 1970, 29 January 1971, 24 June 1971, 9 August 1972; Robert Taylor, 'The Heath Government, Industrial Policy and the "New Capitalism"', in Ball and Seldon (eds.), *The Heath Government*, pp. 148–9; Campbell, *Edward Heath*, pp. 331, 378–9.

21. *The Times*, 12 June 1969, 17 February 1971, 17 October 1972, 28 March 1973, 13 August 1973, 1 April 1973, 5 June 1974; PRO CAB 128/47, CM (71)

8, 4 February 1971; Campbell, *Edward Heath*, pp. 379–80; Ball, 'The Conservative Party and the Heath Government,' p. 325.

22. Prior, *A Balance of Power*, p. 71; Rodney Lowe, 'The Social Policy of the Heath Government', in Ball and Seldon, *The Heath Government*, pp. 191, 199; Campbell, *Edward Heath*, p. 376; Nicholas Timmins, *The Five Giants: A Biography of the Welfare State* (London, 1996), p. 280.

23. Andrew Denham and Mark Garnett, *Keith Joseph* (Chesham, 2002), pp. 14, 24, 48–50, 55, 219; Hansard, 28 November 1972; Lowe, 'The Social Policy of the Heath Government', pp. 205–7, 210–13; Timmins, *The Five Giants*, pp. 287–8, 292–7, 301–3.

24. John Campbell, *Margaret Thatcher*, vol. 1: *The Grocer's Daughter* (London, 2000), pp. 228–42; *Guardian*, 14 January 1974.

25. PRO CAB 129/150, CP (70) 24, 'The Economic Outlook', 21 July 1970; *The Times*, 15 April 1970, 21 April 1970, 30 April 1970; Coopey and Woodward, 'The British Economy in the 1970s', pp. 4–5; Max-Stephan Schulze and Nicholas Woodward, 'The Emergence of Rapid Inflation', in Coopey and Woodward (eds.), *Britain in the 1970s*, pp. 109–12; Cairncross, 'The Heath Government and the British Economy', pp. 111–12; Sir Alec Cairncross, *The British Economy Since 1945: Economic Policy and Performance, 1945–1990* (Oxford, 1992), pp. 164–7, 189–90.

26. PRO CAB 129/150, CP (70) 24, 'The Economic Outlook', 21 July 1970; Hansard, 27 October 1970; Campbell, *Edward Heath*, pp. 327–8; Dell, *The Chancellors*, pp. 378–9; PRO CAB 128/47, CM (70) 12, 3 September 1970.

27. *The Times*, 12 August 1970; Gerald A. Dorfman, *Government versus Trade Unionism in British Politics Since 1968* (London, 1979), pp. 67–9; Campbell, *Edward Heath*, pp. 309, 328–9.

28. PRO CAB 128/47, CM (70) 12, 3 September 1970.

29. PRO CAB 128/47, CM (70) 36, 26 October 1970; PRO CAB 128/47, CM (70) 34, 29 October 1970; *The Times*, 3 October 1970, 5 October 1970, 6 October 1970, 7 October 1970, 2 November 1970; Alwyn W. Turner, *Crisis? What Crisis? Britain in the 1970s* (London, 2008), p. 10.

30. PRO CAB 129/53, CP (70) 82, 'Local Government: Manual Workers' Dispute', 12 October 1970; PRO CAB 128/47, CM (70) 30, 15 October 1970; *The Times*, 6 November 1970, 7 November 1970; Campbell, *Edward Heath*, pp. 328–9.

31. Cockerell, *Live from Number Ten*, p. 172; Campbell, *Edward Heath*, pp. 329, 373; Ramsden, *An Appetite for Power*, p. 394.

32. *The Times*, 12 November 1970, 7 December 1970, 8 December 1970; Campbell, *Edward Heath*, pp. 329–30; Tony Benn, *Office Without Power: Diaries 1968–72* (London, 1988), p. 318; Hurd, *An End to Promises*, p. 99.

33. *The Times*, 9 December 1970, 10 December 1970.

34. *The Times*, 10 December 1970; Norman Tebbit, *Upwardly Mobile* (London, 1988), p. 102.

35. *The Times*, 12 December 1970, 14 December 1970, 19 January 1971; PRO

CAB 128/47, CM (70) 44, 8 December 1970; PRO CAB 128/47, CM (70) 46, 12 December 1970; Christopher Andrew, *The Defence of the Realm: The Authorized History of MI5* (London, 2009), pp. 589–90; PRO CAB 128/47, CM (70) 47, 14 December 1970.

36. PRO CAB 129/55, CP (71) 19, 'The Wilberforce Report', 8 February 1971; *The Times*, 11 February 1971; *The Economist*, 13 February 1971: Richard Clutterbuck, *Britain in Agony: The Growth of Political Violence* (London, 1978), p. 43; Campbell, *Edward Heath*, p. 330.

37. Sampson, *The New Anatomy of Britain*, p. 79; *Private Eye*, 15 July 1971; Campbell, *Edward Heath*, pp. 333, 501–2.

38. PRO CAB 128/47 CM (71) 6, 2 February 1971; PRO CAB 128/47, CM (71) 7, 3 February 1971; PRO CAB 128/47, CM (71) 8, 4 February 1971; *The Times*, 5 February 1971.

39. PRO CAB 128/47 CM (71) 6, 2 February 1971; Taylor, 'The Heath Government, Industrial Policy and the "New Capitalism"', pp. 140, 146–8; Hansard, 4 November 1970.

40. Ramsden, 'The Prime Minister and the Making of Policy', pp. 32–3; Taylor, 'The Heath Government, Industrial Policy and the "New Capitalism"', pp. 139, 141, 144, 146; Nicholas Ridley, *My Style of Government: The Thatcher Years* (London, 1992), p. 4; Dell, *The Chancellors*, p. 379.

41. *The Times*, 8 February 1971; PRO CAB 128/47 CM (71) 6, 2 February 1971; PRO CAB 128/47, CM (71) 7, 3 February 1971; PRO CAB 128/47 CM (71) 9, 9 February 1971; Heath, *The Course of My Life*, p. 340; Tebbit, *Upwardly Mobile*, p. 103; Taylor, 'The Heath Government, Industrial Policy and the "New Capitalism"', p. 150; Campbell, *Edward Heath*, p. 330; Simon Heffer, *Like the Roman: The Life of Enoch Powell* (London, 1998), pp. 575, 583.

42. Hansard, 14 June 1971, 21 June 1971; *The Times*, 14 June 1971, 15 June 1971, 25 June 1971, 30 July 1971; PRO CAB 129/158, CP 71 (95), 'Shipbuilding on the Upper Clyde', 27 July 1971; John Foster and Charles Woolfson, *The Politics of the UCS Work-In: Class Alliances and the Right to Work* (London, 1986), pp. 192, 328; Taylor, 'The Heath Government, Industrial Policy and the "New Capitalism"', p. 151.

43. PRO CAB 129/158, CP 71 (95), 'Shipbuilding on the Upper Clyde', 27 July 1971; Hansard, 29 July 1971; *The Times*, 30 July 1971.

44. *The Times*, 17 June 1971.

45. *The Times*, 10 October 1972; Whitehead, *The Writing on the Wall*, pp. 80–81; Campbell, *Edward Heath*, p. 371; Benn, *Office Without Power*, p. 363.

46. Ibid., pp. 349–50, 364, 366; *The Times*, 24 June 1971, 3 August 1971, 19 August 1971.

47. *The Times*, 12 August 1971; Heath, *The Course of My Life*, p. 367; Campbell, *Edward Heath*, pp. 499–500.

48. Cairncross, 'The Heath Government and the British Economy', p. 113; *The Times*, 19 June 1971; Campbell, *Edward Heath*, pp. 369–70.

49. Hansard, 30 March 1971; Campbell, *Edward Heath*, pp. 369–70, 408; Timmins, *The Five Giants*, p. 306; Dell, *The Chancellors*, pp. 380–82, 391.

50. *The Times*, 20 July 1971, 22 November 1971; Cairncross, 'The Heath Government and the British Economy', pp. 115–16; Dell, *The Chancellors*, p. 383; Campbell, *Edward Heath*, pp. 374–5.

51. *Guardian*, 25 November 1971; *The Times*, 19 November 1971, 25 November 1971.

52. *The Economist*, 27 November 1971; N. F. R. Crafts, 'Economic Growth in the 1970s', in Coopey and Woodward (eds.), *Britain in the 1970s*, p. 102; Schulze and Woodward, 'The Emergence of Rapid Inflation', pp. 121, 132; Nicholas Woodward, 'The Retreat from Full Employment', in Coopey and Woodward (eds.), *Britain in the 1970s*, pp. 136–62; Campbell, *Edward Heath*, pp. 409–11; Dell, *The Chancellors*, p. 391; Prior, *A Balance of Power*, p. 74.

53. PRO CAB 128/50, CM (72) 3, 20 January 1972; Hansard, 20 January 1972; *The Times*, 21 January 1972; *Daily Mirror*, 21 January 1972.

54. Hansard, 24 January 1972; *The Times*, 26 January 1972; *Daily Telegraph*, 26 January 1972; Whitehead, *The Writing on the Wall*, p. 82; Campbell, *Edward Heath*, pp. 408, 411.

CHAPTER 3. GHOSTS OF 1926

1. Tony Lane and Kenneth Roberts, *Strike at Pilkingtons* (London, 1971), pp. 31–2.
2. Ibid., pp. 11–12, 64–76; *Daily Express*, 6 May 1970; *Financial Times*, 6 May 1970.
3. Lane and Roberts, *Strike at Pilkingtons*, pp. 67, 124–5, 176–7.
4. Ibid., pp. 86–8, 95, 103–7, 124–5, 180.
5. Paul Ferris, *The New Militants: Crisis in the Trade Unions* (Harmondsworth, 1972), p. 7; Alwyn W. Turner, *Crisis? What Crisis? Britain in the 1970s* (London, 2008), p. 82; Raphael Samuel, *The Lost World of British Communism* (London, 2006), pp. 210–11.
6. Anthony Sampson, *The New Anatomy of Britain* (London, 1971), pp. 626, 630; Stephen Milligan, *The New Barons: Union Power in the 1970s* (London, 1976), pp. 80–81; Geoffrey Owen, *From Empire to Europe: The Decline and Revival of British Industry Since the Second World War* (London, 1999), p. 431.
7. Sampson, *The New Anatomy of Britain*, pp. 636–7; Ferris, *The New Militants*, pp. 66–8; Milligan, *The New Barons*, p. 164; Chris Wrigley, 'Trade Unions, Strikes and the Government', in Richard Coopey and Nicholas Woodward (eds.), *Britain in the 1970s: The Troubled Economy* (London, 1996), pp. 274–5.
8. John McIlroy and Alan Campbell, 'The High Tide of Trade Unionism: Mapping Industrial Politics, 1964–79', in John McIlroy, Nina Fishman and Alan Campbell (eds.), *The High Tide of British Trade Unionism: Trade Unions and Industrial Politics, 1964–1979* (Monmouth, 2007), p.99; Milligan, *The New Barons*, pp. 23, 39–40.
9. Richard Clutterbuck, *Britain in Agony: The Growth of Political Violence*

61. *The Times*, 18 February 1972, 19 February 1972; PRO COAL 26/1110, 'Report on the Miners' Wage Claim,' 18 February 1972; Campbell, *Edward Heath*, p. 418.
62. *The Times*, 19 February 1972; PRO CAB 128/50, 72 (8), 18 February 1972; Joe Gormley, *Battered Cherub* (London, 1982), pp. 113–14; *Sunday Times*, 20 February 1972; Routledge, *Scargill*, p. 82; Heath, *The Course of My Life*, p. 353.
63. *The Times*, 22 February 1972; *Sheffield Star*, 28 February 1972; Routledge, *Scargill*, p. 80.
64. *The Times*, 28 February 1972; Heath, *The Course of My Life*, p. 353; Campbell, *Edward Heath*, pp. 420–21.
65. *Guardian*, 18 January 1974; *The Times*, 21 February 1972, 8 March 1972; Campbell, *Edward Heath*, pp. 420, 422; Robert J. Wybrow, *Britain Speaks Out, 1937–87: A Social History as Seen Through the Gallup Data* (London, 1989), p. 100; Greenslade, *Press Gang*, p. 288; Benn, *Office Without Power*, p. 405; *Sunday Express*, 6 February 1972; Stuart Hall et al., *Policing the Crisis: Mugging, the State, and Law and Order* (Basingstoke, 1978), p. 300.
66. *New Statesman*, 24 February 1972; Lees-Milne, *Diaries*, p. 71; Ferris, *The New Militants*, pp. 10, 43; PRO PREM 15/986, note signed 'E,' 23 February 1972; Richard Vinen, *Thatcher's Britain: The Politics and Social Upheaval of the 1980s* (London, 2009), p. 39.

CHAPTER 4. FANFARE FOR EUROPE

1. See the town council's history page at http//www.broadstairs.gov.uk/Core/Broadstairs/Pages/History_1.aspx.
2. Edward Heath, *Travels: People and Places in My Life* (London, 1977), p. 10; Edward Heath, *The Course of My Life* (London, 1998), p. 14.
3. Ibid., pp. 40–44, 68–71, 100–106.
4. Hansard, 26 June 1950; John Campbell, *Edward Heath: A Biography* (London, 1993), pp, 121–2, 130–31; Heath, *The Course of My Life*, pp. 147, 234–5.
5. Dominic Sandbrook, *White Heat: A History of Britain in the Swinging Sixties* (London, 2006), pp. 387–91; *Private Eye*, 12 May 1967; David Smith, *From Boom to Bust: Trial and Error in British Economic Policy* (Harmondsworth, 1992), p. 8; J. F. Wright, *Britain in the Age of Economic Management: An Economic History Since 1939* (Oxford, 1979), pp. 21–2; Andrew Gamble, *Britain in Decline: Economic Policy, Political Strategy and the British State* (Basingstoke, 1994), pp. 17–19.
6. John W. Young, 'The Heath Government and British Entry into the European Community', in Stuart Ball and Anthony Seldon (eds.), *The Heath Government, 1970–1974: A Reappraisal* (Harlow, 1996), pp. 261–2; Campbell, *Edward Heath*, pp. 352–3; *Time*, 8 November 1971; Hugo Young, *This Blessed Plot: Britain and Europe from Churchill to Blair* (London, 1998), pp. 223–5.
7. Ben Pimlott, *Harold Wilson* (London, 1992), p. 659; Bernard Donoughue, 'Harold Wilson and the Renegotiation of the EEC Terms of Membership,

1974–5: A Witness Account', in Brian Brivati and Harriet Jones (eds.), *From Reconstruction to Integration: Britain and Europe Since 1945* (Leicester, 1993), p. 204; Bernard Donoughue, *Downing Street Diary: With Harold Wilson in No. 10* (London, 2005), p. 60.

8. Campbell, *Edward Heath*, pp. 336–7, 342; Henry Kissinger, *Years of Upheaval* (London, 1982), pp. 140–41; Peter Hennessy, *The Prime Minister: The Office and its Holders Since 1945* (London, 2000), pp. 350–51.

9. See John Kennedy O'Connor, *The Eurovision Song Contest: The Official History* (London, 2006).

10. Alwyn W. Turner, *Crisis? What Crisis? Britain in the 1970s* (London, 2008), p. 164.

11. Miriam Akhtar and Steve Humphries, *Some Liked It Hot: The British on Holiday at Home and Abroad* (London, 2000), pp. 33–6, 73, 76; Edward Heath, 'Introduction', in Anthony Gishford and Victor Caudery (eds.), *Fanfare for Europe: Official Programme Book* (London, 1973), p. 23; Steve Gerrard, 'What a Carry On!', in Robert Shail (ed.), *Seventies British Cinema* (London, 2008), p. 39.

12. Alan Clark, *Diaries: Into Politics 1972–1982*, ed. Ion Trewin (London, 2001). p. 33; Akhtar and Humphries, *Some Liked It Hot*, p. 113.

13. Roger Bray and Vladimir Raitz, *Flight to the Sun: The Story of the Holiday Revolution* (London, 2001); *Independent*, 10 January 2004; Akhtar and Humphries, *Some Liked It Hot*, pp. 102, 105–9, 115; *Daily Mirror*, 1 June 1970, 5 June 1970: Turner, *Crisis? What Crisis?*, p. 165.

14. Paul Routledge, *Arthur Scargill: The Unauthorized Biography* (London, 1993), p. 96; Akhtar and Humphries, *Some Liked It Hot*, pp. 115–7; Richard Webber, *Fifty Years of Carry On* (London, 2008), p. 125.

15. Akhtar and Humphries, *Some Liked It Hot*, pp. 121–4; Turner, *Crisis? What Crisis?*, p. 174; John Benson, *The Rise of Consumer Society in Britain 1880–1980* (Harlow, 1994), pp. 100–101; Louis Turner and John Ash, *The Golden Hordes: International Tourism and the Pleasure Periphery* (London, 1975); the *Monty Python* sketch, first broadcast on 16 November 1972, is now all over the Internet.

16. Akhtar and Humphries, *Some Liked It Hot*, pp. 124–5; Hunter Davies, *The Glory Game* (London, 1972), p. 141.

17. Lawrence James, *The Middle Class: A History* (London, 2006), p. 436; Jonathan Raban, *Soft City* (London, 1975), p. 35. The MacDonald interview is reprinted in Barney Ronay (ed.), *Studs!: The Greatest Retro Football Annual the World Has Ever Seen* (London, 2006); the Vesta advert is in Alison Pressley, *The Seventies: Good Times, Bad Taste* (London, 2002), p. 69.

18. Davies, *The Glory Game*, p. 78; John Burnett, *Liquid Pleasures: A Social History of Drinks in Modern Britain* (London, 1999), pp. 154–5; Gishford and Caudery (eds.), *Fanfare for Europe*, pp. 152–3; John Cleese and Connie Booth, *The Complete Fawlty Towers* (London, 1989), p. 97.

19. Young, 'The Heath Government and British Entry into the European

Community', pp. 266–74; Campbell, *Edward Heath*, pp. 354–5, 361; Hugo Young, *This Blessed Plot: Britain and Europe from Churchill to Blair* (London, 1998), pp. 226–9, 232.

20. Douglas Hurd, *An End to Promises* (London, 1978), p. 58; Young, *This Blessed Plot*, pp. 235–6.

21. Hurd, *An End to Promises*, pp. 62–3; *The Times*, 18 May 1971, 20 May 1971; Campbell, *Edward Heath*, p. 358; Phillip Whitehead, *The Writing on the Wall: Britain in the Seventies* (London, 1985), p. 61.

22. *The Times*, 20 May 1971, 21 May 1971; Hurd, *An End to Promises*, pp. 63–4; Campbell, *Edward Heath*, pp. 359–60; Young, *This Blessed Plot*, pp. 237–8; Heath, *The Course of My Life*, pp. 371–2.

23. *The Times*, 23 June 1971, 24 June 1971, 8 July 1971, 9 July 1971; PRO CAB 128/49, CM (71) 33, 24 June 1971; PRO CAB 129/158, CP (71) 76, 'European Economic Communities: Draft White Paper', 29 June 1971; and see Whitehead, *The Writing on the Wall*, pp. 62–3; Campbell, *Edward Heath*, pp. 361–2, 397–8.

24. *The Times*, 9 July 1971; Campbell *Edward Heath*, pp. 334–5, 401; Young, *This Blessed Plot*, pp. 246–7, 251–2; Young, 'The Heath Government and British Entry into the European Community', p. 274; Richard Weight, *Patriots: National Identity in Britain 1940–2000* (London, 2002), pp. 482–3.

25. Pimlott, *Harold Wilson*, pp. 568, 577; Philip Ziegler, *Wilson: The Authorized Life* (London, 1993), pp. 355–6, 369, 370, 372; Anthony Sampson, *The New Anatomy of Britain* (London, 1971), p. 46.

26. Sandbrook, *White Heat*, pp. 641–2; Pimlott, *Harold Wilson*, p. 574; David Butler and Dennis Kavanagh, *The British General Election of October 1974* (London, 1975), pp. 214–16.

27. Tony Benn, *Office Without Power* (London, 1988), pp. 295–459, esp. p. 443; on Benn, see Michael Hatfield, *The House the Left Built: Inside Labour Party Policy Making 1970–1975* (London, 1978), pp. 67–90; Kenneth O. Morgan, *Labour People: Leaders and Lieutenants, Hardie to Kinnock* (Oxford, 1992), pp. 301–13; Turner, *Crisis? What Crisis?*, p. 39.

28. Pimlott, *Harold Wilson*, p. 575; Ziegler, *Wilson*, p. 375; Sampson, *The New Anatomy of Britain*, p. 42; Ronald McIntosh, *Challenge to Democracy: Politics, Trade Union Power and Economic Failure in the 1970s* (London, 2006), p. 58.

29. Young, *This Blessed Plot*, pp. 260–61; Edmund Dell, *A Strange Eventful History: Democratic Socialism in Britain* (London, 2000), pp. 420–21; Mervyn Jones, *Michael Foot* (London, 1995), p. 330; Martin Westlake, *Kinnock: The Biography* (London, 2001), pp. 87–8.

30. Pimlott, *Harold Wilson*, p. 581; Kenneth O. Morgan, *Callaghan: A Life* (Oxford, 1997), pp. 394–61.

31. Benn, *Office Without Power*, pp. 352, 356; *The Times*, 19 July 1971; Pimlott, *Harold Wilson*, pp. 583–5.

32. Roy Jenkins, *A Life at the Centre* (London, 1991), pp. 319–20; Pimlott, *Harold Wilson*, p. 582; Sampson, *The New Anatomy of Britain*, pp. 50, 52; David

Marquand, '"The Welsh Wrecker"', in Andrew Adonis and Keith Thomas (eds.), *Roy Jenkins: A Retrospective* (Oxford, 2004), p. 120.

33. *The Times*, 20 July 1971; Benn, *Office Without Power*, pp. 357–9, 382; John Campbell, *Roy Jenkins: A Biography* (London, 1983), pp. 140–41; Jenkins, *A Life at the Centre*, pp. 322–3, 329; Pimlott, *Harold Wilson*, pp. 585–7.

34. Benn, *Office Without Power*, pp. 313–14, 316, 421; Pimlott, *Harold Wilson*, pp. 592, 595, 598; Ziegler, *Wilson*, p. 386; Jenkins, *A Life at the Centre*, pp. 342–9; Marquand, '"The Welsh Wrecker"', p. 124; *Daily Express*, 2 October 1972.

35. Roy Hattersley, *Who Goes Home? Scenes from a Political Life* (London, 1996), p. 109; *Daily Telegraph*, 24 April 1972; Denis Healey, *The Time of My Life* (London, 1989), p. 360; Pimlott, *Harold Wilson*, pp. 590, 597; *New Statesman*, 30 June 1972.

36. Healey, *The Time of My Life*, p. 359; Pimlott, *Harold Wilson*, pp. 600–601; Young, *This Blessed Plot*, p. 271.

37. Ibid., p. 239; Robert J. Wybrow, *Britain Speaks Out, 1937–87: A Social History as Seen Through the Gallup Data* (London, 1989), pp. 95, 98; Campbell, *Edward Heath*, p. 356; Weight, *Patriots*, pp. 477–8.

38. Ibid., pp. 477–8, 481–2; Hansard, 21 July 1971; *The Times*, 13 July 1971.

39. *Daily Telegraph*, 16 August 1971; *Daily Mirror*, 8 July 1971, 22 July, 1971; *Daily Express*, 14 May 1971, 22 May 1971, 22 July 1971; *Sun*, 23 July 1971; Roy Greenslade, *Press Gang: How Newspapers Make Profits from Propaganda* (London, 2004), pp. 292–4.

40. *Encounter*, June 1971, July 1971; *Time*, 8 November 1971; *The Times*, 27 July 1971; Weight, *Patriots*, p. 479; John Lahr (ed.), *The Diaries of Kenneth Tynan* (London 2001), pp. 52, 59; Russell Davies (ed.), *The Kenneth Williams Diaries* (London, 1993), p. 402; James Chapman, *Inside the TARDIS: The Worlds of Doctor Who* (London, 2006), p. 93.

41. Campbell, *Edward Heath*, p. 397; Stuart Ball, 'The Conservative Party and the Heath Government', in Ball and Seldon (eds.), *The Heath Government*, p. 317; Weight, *Patriots*, p. 485.

42. Simon Heffer, *Like the Roman: The Life of Enoch Powell* (London, 1998), pp. 517–18, 547, 579–80, 622–3.

43. Campbell, *Edward Heath*, pp. 400–402; Heath, *The Course of My Life*, pp. 379–80.

44. Hansard, 28 October 1971; *The Times*, 28 October 1971, 29 October 1971; Bernard D. Nossiter, *Britain: A Future That Works* (London, 1978), pp. 94–5, 97; Campbell, *Edward Heath*, pp. 403–4.

45. *The Times*, 29 October 1971; Jenkins, *A Life at the Centre*, pp. 330–31; Benn, *Office Without Power*, p. 382; Heffer, *Like the Roman*, p. 607.

46. *The Times*, 29 October 1971; *Time*, 8 November 1971.

47. Heath, *The Course of My Life*, p. 381; Campbell, *Edward Heath*, pp. 404–5.

48. *Sunday Times*, 23 January 1972; Heath, *The Course of My Life*, pp. 381–2.

49. *The Times*, 17 February 1972, 18 February 1972, 3 May 1972; Campbell, *Edward Heath*, pp. 437–41; Young, 'The Heath Government and British Entry into the European Community', pp. 277–8; Jim Prior, *A Balance of Power* (London, 1986), p. 86.

50. *The Times*, 1 January 1973, 2 January 1973; David Butler and Uwe Kitzinger, *The 1975 Referendum* (London, 1976), p. 21.

51. *Daily Mirror*, 1 January 1973; *The Times*, 1 January 1973, 2 January 1973; *Daily Express*, 1 January 1973.

52. Hansard, 9 November 1972; Weight, *Patriots*, p. 498.

53. *The Times*, 4 January 1973; *Sunday Times*, 7 January 1973; Heath, *The Course of My Life*, p. 394; Weight, *Patriots*, p. 500.

54. *The Times*, 3 January 1973, 4 January 1973; *Guardian*, 4 January 1973; Christopher Booker, *The Seventies: Portrait of a Decade* (London, 1980), p. 127; Weight, *Patriots*, p. 499–500; Andy Beckett, *When the Lights Went Out: Britain in the Seventies* (London, 2009), pp. 93–4.

55. Campbell, *Edward Heath*, pp. 352–3; Young, *This Blessed Plot*, pp. 215–16.

56. Young, 'The Heath Government and British Entry into the European Community', p. 281; Neill Nugent, 'British Public Opinion and the European Community', in Stephen George (ed.), *Britain and the European Community: The Politics of Semi-Detachment* (Oxford, 1992), p. 181; *Observer*, 6 October 1974; Weight, *Patriots*, pp. 494–6; *Encounter*, January 1963. On au pairs and town-twinning, see Weight, *Patriots*, pp. 488–9; on the rise of the duvet, see Joe Moran, *Queuing for Beginners: The Story of Daily Life from Breakfast to Bedtime* (London, 2007), pp. 206–7.

57. Cleese and Booth, *The Complete Fawlty Towers*, pp. 140, 154–7.

58. Weight, *Patriots*, p. 492; John Ramsden, *Don't Mention the War: The British and the Germans Since 1890* (London, 2006), pp. 363, 386–7, 389; John Mander, *Our German Cousins* (London, 1974), pp. 3, 5, 26–34.

59. Campbell, *Edward Heath*, p. 381; Weight, *Patriots*, p. 491; Barbara Castle, *The Castle Diaries 1974–76* (London, 1980), p. 281; Bernard Donoughue, *Downing Street Diary*, vol. 2: *With James Callaghan in No. 10* (London, 2008), p. 216; Clark, *Diaries*, p. 64.

CHAPTER 5. THE GREEN DEATH

1. Malcolm Bradbury, *The History Man* (London, 1977), pp. 3, 4–5, 16, 50–51, 70, 73.

2. Marnie Fogg, *Boutique: A '60s Cultural Phenomenon* (London, 2003), pp. 178–80; Robert Hewison, *Too Much: Art and Culture in the Sixties, 1960–75* (London, 1986), pp. 165–6, 172–3; Dave Haslam, *Not Abba: The Real Story of the 1970s* (London, 2005), pp. 45, 67; Jonathon Green, *All Dressed Up: The Sixties and the Counterculture* (London, 1998), pp. 277–81, 367–72, 397; Jann Wenner (ed.), *Lennon Remembers: The Rolling Stone Interviews* (Harmondsworth, 1972).

3. Hewison, *Too Much*, pp. 175–6; Jon Savage, *England's Dreaming: Sex Pistols and Punk Rock* (London, 2005), p. 43; 'Rock Fans Clash with Police at Festival', BBC News, 29 August 1974, at http://news.bbc.co.uk/onthisday; *Observer*, 1 September 1974.

4. Hewison, *Too Much*, pp. 211–12, Michael Billington, *State of the Nation: British Theatre Since 1945* (London, 2007), pp. 210–13, 215, 232, 259; Patricia Waugh, *Harvest of the Sixties: English Literature and its Background, 1960 to 1990* (Oxford, 1995), pp. 16–17, 176; Richard Boon, *Brenton the Playwright* (London, 1991), p. 63.

5. Mary Ingham, *Now We Are Thirty: Women of the Breakthrough Generation* (London, 1982), pp. 16–17.

6. Jonathan Raban, *Soft City* (London, 1975), pp. 60, 88, 175, 190; Roy Greenslade, *Press Gang: How Newspapers Make Profits from Propaganda* (London, 2004), p. 337; Lawrence James, *The Middle Class: A History* (London 2006), pp. 575–7.

7. Margaret Drabble, *The Middle Ground* (Harmondsworth, 1980), p. 207; Michael Frayn, 'Festival', in Michael Sissons and Philip French (eds.), *Age of Austerity* (Oxford, 1963), pp. 307–8.

8. Gordon Rattray Taylor, *The Doomsday Book: Can the World Survive?* (London, 1970), pp. 13–14, 17, 52–3, 59–61, 229, 275.

9. Philip Lowe and Jane Goyder, *Environmental Groups in Politics* (London, 1983), pp. 16–17; Edward M. Nicholson, *The Environmental Revolution* (Harmondsworth, 1972), pp. 158–60; S. K. Brooks *et al.*, 'The Growth of the Environment as a Political Issue in Britain', *British Journal of Political Science*, 6 (April 1976), pp. 245–55; Meredith Veldman, *Fantasy, the Bomb and the Greening of Britain: Romantic Protest, 1945–1980* (Cambridge, 1994), pp. 208–10.

10. Martin Weiner, *English Culture and the Decline of the Industrial Spirit, 1850–1980* (Cambridge, 1981); Peter Laslett, *The World We Have Lost: England Before the Industrial Age* (New York, 1965), p. 22; E. J. Mishan, *The Costs of Economic Growth* (London, 1967), pp. 161, 166, 171; Barbara Ward, *Spaceship Earth* (London, 1966), pp. 1, 15; and see Veldman, *Fantasy, the Bomb and the Greening of Britain*, pp. 211–12, 252–8; Robert M. Collins, *More: The Politics of Economic Growth in Postwar America* (Oxford, 2000), p. 133.

11. *The Times*, 6 September 1977; Veldman, *Fantasy, the Bomb and the Greening of Britain* pp. 273–7.

12. E. F. Schumacher, *Small is Beautiful: Economics as if People Mattered* (New York, 1973), pp. 159, 55, 17, 297; Veldman, *Fantasy, the Bomb and the Greening of Britain*, pp. 277–8, 286–95.

13. Anthony Sampson, *The New Anatomy of Britain* (London, 1971), pp. 559–60, 564; Anthony Sampson, *The Changing Anatomy of Britain* (London 1983), pp. 339–40; Phillip Whitehead, *The Writing on the Wall: Britain in the Seventies* (London, 1985), pp. 251–2, 394.

14. Robert Colls, *Identity of England* (Oxford, 2002), p. 350; Taylor, *The Doomsday Book*, p. 49; Des Wilson, *The Environmental Crisis* (London, 1984),

pp. 41, 43; James, *The Middle Class*, p. 485; Whitehead, *The Writing on the Wall*, p. 252; Marion Shoard, *The Theft of the Countryside* (London, 1980), p. 16.

15. Geoffrey Moorhouse, *Britain in the Sixties: The Other England* (Harmondsworth, 1964), pp. 95, 97; *The Times*, 8 June 1972.

16. Margaret Drabble, *The Ice Age* (London, 1977), pp. 168–9, 30, 51–2.

17. Raban, *Soft City*, p. 28; Gordon E. Cherry, *Town Planning in Britain Since 1900: The Rise and Fall of the Planning Ideal* (Oxford, 1996), p. 184; David Eversley, *The Planner in Society: The Changing Role of a Profession* (London, 1973), p. 14; Douglas Adams, *The Hitchhiker's Guide to the Galaxy* (London, 1982), p. 53.

18. Patrick Dunleavy, *The Politics of Mass Housing in Britain, 1945–1975* (Oxford, 1981), pp. 36, 41, 44–8, 259; Patrick Nuttgens, *The Home Front: Housing the People 1840–1990* (London, 1989), p. 86; Jerry White, *London in the Twentieth Century* (London, 2001), p. 55; and see Dominic Sandbrook, *White Heat: A History of Britain in the Swinging Sixties* (London, 2006), pp. 627–34.

19. Barbara Adams and Jean Conway, *The Social Effects of Living off the Ground* (London, 1973), p. 8; Elizabeth Gittus, *Flats, Families and the Under Fives* (London, 1976); Sutherland Lyall, *The State of British Architecture* (London, 1980), pp. 33, 42–3, 45–50; *Building Design*, 5 January 1979; Dunleavy, *The Politics of Mass Housing in Britain*, pp. 70, 94–9.

20. Peter Hall, *Cities of Tomorrow: An Intellectual History of Urban Planning in the Twentieth Century* (Oxford, 1996), pp. 226–7; Cherry, *Town Planning in Britain Since 1900*, p. 185; Raban, *Soft City*, pp. 26–7; J. G. Ballard, *High Rise* (London, 1975).

21. Christopher Booker, *The Seventies: Portrait of a Decade* (London, 1980), p. 300; White, *London in the Twentieth Century*, p. 83; Alice Coleman, *Utopia on Trial: Vision and Reality in Planned Housing* (London, 1985), p. 180.

22. James Lees-Milne, *Diaries, 1971–1983* (London, 2008), pp. 67, 81–2.

23. Ibid., pp. 84–5; Bevis Hillier, *John Betjeman: The Biography* (London, 2002), pp. 506–8.

24. Cherry, *Town Planning in Britain Since 1900*, p. 163; White, *London in the Twentieth Century*, pp. 67–71; Simon Jenkins, *A City at Risk: A Contemporary Look at London's Streets* (London, 1970); Terry Christensen, *Neighbourhood Survival: The Struggle for Covent Garden's Future* (Dorchester, 1979); Nick Wates, *The Battle for Tolmers Square* (London, 1976).

25. *The Times*, 23 February 1971, 5 April 1971, 27 April 1971, 3 February 1972, 3 May 1972, 6 February 1973, 1 February 1974, 21 March 1974, 12 June 1974; Noel Annan, *Our Age: The Generation That Made Post-War Britain* (London, 1991), pp. 465–6; Andy Beckett, *When the Lights Went Out: Britain in the Seventies* (London, 2009), pp. 37–45.

26. *Scotsman*, 7 November 1970, 29 November 1972; James, *The Middle Class*, pp. 479, 484; *The Times*, 4 December 1974, 5 December 1974, 5 November

1975, 8 November 1975, 4 February 1976, 5 February 1976. 14 February 1976.

27. *The Times*, 30 June 1976, 1 July 1976, 14 July 1976; Tom Sharpe, *Blott on the Landscape* (London, 1975).

28. Whitehead, *The Writing on the Wall*, pp. 244, 250; Deborah S. Ryan, *The Ideal Home Through the Twentieth Century* (London, 1997), p. 145.

29. White, *London in the Twentieth Century*, p. 68; Richard Weight, *Patriots: National Identity in Britain 1940–2000* (London, 2002), p. 578; James, *The Middle Class*, p. 534; David Cannadine, 'The National Trust and the National Heritage', in David Cannadine, *In Churchill's Shadow: Confronting the Past in Modern Britain* (London, 2002), pp. 240, 238; Patrick Cormack, *Heritage in Danger* (London, 1978), p. 10.

30. John Sutherland, *Reading the Decades: Fifty Years of British History Through the Nation's Bestsellers* (London, 2002), pp. 88–9; Alwyn W. Turner, *Crisis? What Crisis? Britain in the 1970s* (London, 2008), pp. 150–51; Walker, *Hollywood, England*, p. 432; Ruth Barton, 'When the Chickens Came Home to Roost: British Thrillers of the 1970s', in Robert Shail (ed.), *Seventies British Cinema* (London, 2008), p. 48; Alexander Walker, *National Heroes: British Cinema in the Seventies and Eighties* (London, 1985), pp. 129, 227–8; John Leggott, 'Nothing To Do Around Here: British Realist Cinema in the 1970s', in Shail (ed.), *Seventies British Cinema*, p.100; John Goodwin (ed.), *Peter Hall's Diaries: The Story of a Dramatic Battle* (London, 1983), pp. 227–8.

31. Asa Briggs, *The History of Broadcasting in the United Kingdom*, vol. 5: *Competition* (Oxford, 1995), pp. 944–6; Weight, *Patriots*, pp. 543–4; Sergio Angelini, 'Upstairs, Downstairs', http://www.screenonline.org.uk/tv/id/473764/.

32. Turner, *Crisis? What Crisis?*, pp. 48, 67; Elizabeth Wilson, *Adorned in Dreams: Fashion and Modernity* (London 1985), pp. 114, 177; *The Times*, 11 September 1973, 22 August 1972.

33. Veldman, *Fantasy, the Bomb and the Greening of Britain*, pp. 98–101; *Evening News*, 2 July 1979; *Sunday Times Magazine*, 2 January 1972.

34. *The Times*, 3 September 1973; Veldman, *Fantasy, the Bomb and the Greening of Britain*, pp. 83, 87, 108–10; Patrick Curry, *Defending Middle-earth: Tolkien, Myth and Modernity* (London, 1998), pp. 59–97; Colin Wilson, *'Tree' by Tolkien* (London, 1973), pp. 28–9.

35. *Independent*, 8 June 1996; *New Statesman*, 22 December 1972; *The Economist*, 23 December 1972; Booker, *The Seventies*, p. 251; Sutherland, *Reading the Decades*, p. 88.

36. Booker, *The Seventies*, pp. 255–6; John Sutherland, *Bestsellers: Popular Fiction of the 1970s* (London, 1981), pp. 112, 114; Walker, *National Heroes*, p. 176; Barbara Castle, *The Castle Diaries 1974–76* (London, 1980), p. 145.

37. Turner, *Crisis? What Crisis?*, pp. 43–5, 54; Walter Harris, *The Fifth Horseman* (London, 1976), p. 48; PRO CAB 128/47, CM (70) 34, 29 October 1970; *The Times*, 3 October 1970, 5 October 1970, 6 October 1970, 7 October 1970, 2 November 1970; *Daily Mail*, 11 March 1975.

38. *Radio Times*, 5 February 1970; Briggs, *Competition*, p. 946; Anthony Clark, 'Doomwatch', http://www.screenonline.org.uk/tv/id/442747/index.html; for background and synopses, see the excellent website http://www.doomwatch. org/.

39. James Chapman, *Inside the TARDIS: The Worlds of Doctor Who* (London, 2006), pp. 76, 77–83, 85–6, 108–9.

40. Ibid., pp. 89–91; Turner, *Crisis? What Crisis?*, pp. 54–5.

41. John Christopher, *The Prince in Waiting* (pbk., Harmondsworth, 1973), pp. 10, 19, 39, 58, 148–50.

42. See another fine website, http://www.thechestnut.com/changes.htm.

43. Rich Cross and Andy Priestner, *The End of the World: The Unofficial and Unauthorised Guide to Survivors* (London, 2005); Turner, *Crisis? What Crisis?*, pp. 202–3; and see the splendid episode guides at http://www.survivorstvseries. com/index2.htm and http://www.survivors-mad-dog.org.uk/a-world-away/index. shtml.

44. *Radio Times*, 10 April 1975; John and Sally Seymour, *Self-Sufficiency* (London, 1970); John Seymour, *The Complete Book of Self-Sufficiency* (London, 1976); 'How CAT Started', http://www.cat.org.uk/information/aboutcatx.tmpl?init=4; Gwilym Thear, 'The Self-Sufficiency Movement and the Apocalyptic Image in 1970s British Culture', http://www.1970sproject.co.uk/events/papers/ gwilym-thear.pdf.

45. Raban, *Soft City*, p. 118; Russell Davies (ed.), *The Kenneth Williams Diaries* (London, 1993), p. 492.

46. Ryan, *The Ideal Home Through the Twentieth Century*, p. 154; *Observer*, 11 October 1964; Lowe and Goyder, *Environmental Groups in Politics*, p. 78; Veldman, *Fantasy, the Bomb and the Greening of Britain*, pp. 218–19, 221–2.

47. *The Times*, 19 February 1971, 10 May 1971, 11 May 1971; Veldman, *Fantasy, the Bomb and the Greening of Britain*, pp. 222–4.

48. *The Times*, 7 March, 1972, 27 March 1972, 9 June 1975; Veldman, *Fantasy, the Bomb and the Greening of Britain*, pp. 224–6.

49. Frank Chapple, *Sparks Fly! A Trade Union Life* (London, 1984), p. 158; Turner, *Crisis? What Crisis?*, p. 50; Susan Crosland, *Tony Crosland* (London, 1982), pp. 254, 256–7.

50. *The Ecologist*, March 1971; James, *The Middle Class*, pp. 473, 478–80; Val Stevens, 'The Importance of the Environmental Movement', in John Minnion and Philip Bolsover (eds.), *The CND Story* (London, 1983), pp. 77–9; Veldman, *Fantasy, the Bomb and the Greening of Britain*, pp. 244, 305–10; Tony Benn, *Conflicts of Interest: Diaries 1977–80* (London, 1990), p. 259.

51. *The Ecologist*, July 1970; Veldman, *Fantasy, the Bomb and the Greening of Britain*, pp. 227–8; Beckett, *When the Lights Went Out*, pp. 235–6. For back issues and articles from *The Ecologist*, see http://www.theecologist.info/pageo. html and http://www.edwardgoldsmith.org/.

52. *The Ecologist*, July 1975, November 1975; Edward Goldsmith, *Can Britain*

Survive? (London, 1971), pp. 44–55, 227–30; Veldman, *Fantasy, the Bomb and the Greening of Britain*, pp. 227–30, 267, 269–70; Beckett, *When the Lights Went Out*, p. 238.

53. *The Ecologist*, January 1972, reprinted as *A Blueprint for Survival* (Harmondsworth, 1972). The entire Blueprint is online at http://www.theecologist.info/key27.html.

54. *Guardian*, 14 January 1972; *The Times*, 14 January 1972, 25 January 1972; *Sunday Times*, 16 January 1972; *Daily Mail*, 14 January 1972; Lees-Milne, *Diaries*, p. 40.

55. Hansard, 28 April 1972; *The Times*, 1 March 1972; Veldman, *Fantasy, the Bomb and the Greening of Britain*, pp. 234–5; *Guardian*, 15 January 1972.

56. *Coventry Evening Telegraph*, 21 January 1973; Veldman, *Fantasy, the Bomb and the Greening of Britain*, pp. 240–43; *Independent*, 17 May 2009; Beckett, *When the Lights Went Out*, pp. 240–41.

57. *The Ecologist*, March 1974; Whitehead, *The Writing on the Wall*, p. 242.

58. Stevens, 'The Importance of the Environmental Movement', pp. 77–8; Cherry, *Town Planning in Britain Since 1900*, pp. 208–9; Whitehead, *The Writing on the Wall*, p. 250; *The Times*, 5 August 1975.

59. Christopher Frayling, 'The Crafts', in Boris Ford (ed.), *The Cambridge Cultural History of Britain*, vol. 9: *Modern Britain* (Cambridge, 1992), pp. 173, 186–7; Sampson, *The Changing Anatomy of Britain*, pp. 343–4; Whitehead, *The Writing on the Wall*, pp. 253–4; Joe Moran, *Queuing for Beginners: The Story of Daily Life from Breakfast to Bedtime* (London, 2007), pp. 14, 18, 138–40.

CHAPTER 6. A BLOODY AWFUL COUNTRY

1. *The Times*, 4 July 1970, 6 July 1970; *Sunday Times*, 5 July 1970; *Sunday Times* Insight Team, *Ulster* (Harmondsworth, 1972), pp. 214–21; Peter Taylor, *Provos: The IRA and Sinn Fein* (London, 1998), pp. 78–83; Gerry Adams, *Before the Dawn: An Autobiography* (London, 1996), p. 142.

2. Peter Taylor, *Brits: The War Against the IRA* (London, 2002), pp. 25, 29, 32; for good summaries of the origins of the Troubles, see David McKittrick and David McVea, *Making Sense of the Troubles* (London, 2001), pp. 1–61; Henry Patterson, *Ireland Since 1939: The Persistence of Conflict* (London, 2007), pp. 180–217.

3. Taylor, *Provos*, pp. 72–4; PRO PREM 15/100, 'Background Brief for PM by Burke Trend', 21 June 1970.

4. PRO PREM, 15/100, 'Meeting of the Special N.I. Cabinet Ministers', 22 June 1970; Jeremy Smith, 'Walking a Real Tight-rope of Difficulties: Sir Edward Heath and the Search for Stability in Northern Ireland, June 1970–March 1971', *Twentieth Century British History*, 18:2 (2007), pp. 223–5; Lewis Baston, *Reggie: The Life of Reginald Maudling* (Stroud 2004), pp. 367–8; Taylor, *Provos*, pp. 75–7; *Sunday Times* Insight Team, *Ulster*, p. 212.

5. Richard English, *Armed Struggle: The History of the IRA* (London, 2003), pp. 128–9, 147; John Campbell, *Edward Heath: A Biography* (London, 1993), p. 179; Clive Irving, *Pox Britannica: The Unmaking of the British* (New York, 1974), p. 177; Baston, *Reggie*, p. 364; *Sunday Times* Insight Team, *Ulster*, pp. 212–13.

6. McKittrick and McVea, *Making Sense of the Troubles*, pp. 53, 57, 63–4; Patterson, *Ireland Since 1939*, pp. 213, 218; PRO CAB 129/141, C (69) 45, 'Northern Ireland', 5 May 1969; PRO CAB 128/44, CC (69) 21, 7 May 1969; PRO PREM 15/101, Trend to Heath, 9 July 1970; and see Smith, 'Walking a Real Tight-rope of Difficulties', pp. 233–5.

7. Taylor, *Provos*, pp. 60–61, 64–7; English, *Armed Struggle*, pp. 104–8.

8. Ibid., pp. 109–12, 125, 128, 120–21.

9. Taylor, *Provos*, p. 70; English, *Armed Struggle*, pp. 123–6, 131; Kevin Myers, *Watching the Door: Cheating Death in 1970s Belfast* (London, 2008), pp. 91, 115; *Guardian*, 20 May 2001.

10. Taylor, *Provos*, pp. 72, 84–5, 108; Taylor, *Brits*, p. 57; English, *Armed Struggle*, pp. 113–14, 116–18; Patterson, *Ireland Since 1939*, pp. 173–5, 216.

11. Ibid., p. 217; English, *Armed Struggle*, pp. 136, 146; Tim Pat Coogan, *The IRA* (London, 1995), p. 552; McKittrick and McVea, *Making Sense of the Troubles*, p. 62.

12. Myers, *Watching the Door*, pp. 19, 25; PRO DEFE 5/186, Chiefs of Staff Committee, Memorandum 61, 11 September 1970.

13. *Sunday Times* Insight Team, *Ulster*, p. 237; Taylor, *Provos*, pp. 87–8.

14. *The Times*, 6 February 1971, 8 February 1971; *Belfast Telegraph*, 8 February 1971; Taylor, *Provos*, p. 89.

15. PRO CAB 128/49, CM (71) 9, 9 February 1971.

16. Smith, 'Walking a Real Tight-rope of Difficulties', pp. 252–3; for a similar conclusion, see Thomas Hennessey, *Northern Ireland: The Origins of the Troubles* (Dublin, 2005), pp. 394–5.

17. *The Times*, 11 March 1971, 12 March 1971; Taylor, *Provos*, p. 91; Taylor, *Brits*, p. 59; McKittrick and McVea, *Making Sense of the Troubles*, p. 65; Myers, *Watching the Door*, pp. 15, 19; Harry McCallion, *Killing Zone: A Life in the Paras, the Recces, the SAS and the RUC* (London, 1996), p. 30.

18. Peter Taylor, *Loyalists* (London, 2000), pp. 76–8.

19. Ibid., pp. 81, 83–4; *Daily Telegraph*, 23 October 2007.

20. Taylor, *Brits*, pp. 59–60, 62–3; Baston, *Reggie*, pp. 369–70; PRO PREM 15/476, Cable from UKREP NI, 2 March 1971; Patterson, *Ireland Since 1939*, pp. 177–8; *The Times*, 5 December 1970, 7 December 1970, 11 March 1971, 12 March 1971.

21. PRO CAB 128/49, CM (71) 9, 9 February 1971; PRO PREM 15/476, Note of Meeting, 16 March 1971.

22. Baston, *Reggie*, p. 371; PRO PREM 15/476, 'Record of Conversation between the Prime Minister and Major Chichester-Clark', 19 March 1971.

23. *Sunday Times* Insight Team, *Ulster*, p. 252; McKittrick and McVea, *Making*

Sense of the Troubles, p. 65; PRO CAB 128/48, CM (71) 15, Confidential Annex, 18 March 1971; *The Times*, 24 March 1971.

24. *Sunday Times* Insight Team, *Ulster*, p. 260; Taylor, *Loyalists*, p. 85; McKittrick and McVea, *Making Sense of the Troubles*, p. 67; *The Times*, 2 August 1971.

25. PRO PREM 15/476, Cable from UKREP NI, 13 March 1971; PRO PREM 15/475, Note of Meeting, 13 February 1971; PRO CAB 164/878, Tony Stephens to Peter Gregson, 21 July 1971; *Sunday Times* Insight Team, *Ulster*, pp. 265 ff.; Baston, *Reggie*, pp. 370, 372–3; PRO PREM 15/478, Cable from Sir John Peck, 30 July 1971.

26. PRO PREM 15/478, Note of Meeting, 5 August 1971; Reginald Maudling, *Memoirs* (London, 1978), pp. 184–5.

27. Taylor, *Provos*, p. 102.

28. *The Times*, 10 August 1971; Taylor, *Provos*, pp. 92–3: Taylor, *Brits*, pp. 63–4, 69.

29. *Sunday Times* Insight Team, *Ulster*, pp. 270–71.

30. *The Times*, 11 August 1971, 12 August 1971; *Time*, 23 August 1971; McKittrick and McVea, *Making Sense of the Troubles*, p. 69; Myers, *Watching the Door*, pp. 28–35.

31. Baston, *Reggie*, pp. 374–5, 377; Taylor, *Brits*, p. 67; McKittrick and McVea, *Making Sense of the Troubles*, p. 69; English, *Armed Struggle*, pp. 140–41.

32. *Sunday Times* Insight Team, *Ulster*, pp. 289–90; Taylor, *Provos*, pp. 94–6; Taylor, *Brits*, pp. 65, 70; PRO CAB 130/522, GEN (71) 47, 6th meeting, 18 October 1971.

33. Taylor, *Provos*, pp. 94–5; English, *Armed Struggle*, p. 142; *Sunday Times*, 17 October 1971; PRO CAB 130/522, GEN (71) 47, 6th meeting, 18 October 1971; Taylor, *Brits*, pp. 71–3; *The Times*, 12 December 1971, 3 March 1972. Compton's report (Cmnd. 4823) is reproduced online at http://cain.ulst.ac.uk/hmso/compton.htm.

34. *Republican News*, 18 August 1999; Richard Clutterbuck, *Britain in Agony: The Growth of Political Violence* (London, 1978), p. 146; Andy Beckett, *When the Lights Went Out: Britain in the Seventies* (London, 2009), p. 121.

35. Liz Curtis, *Ireland, the Propaganda War: The Battle for Hearts and Minds* (London, 1984), pp. 119, 121; John Cleese and Connie Booth, *The Complete Fawlty Towers* (London, 1989), p. 44; Beckett, *When the Lights Went Out*, p. 124; Richard Weight, *Patriots: National Identity in Britain 1940–2000* (London, 2002), p. 534.

36. Beckett, *When the Lights Went out*, pp. 117–18; Michael Cockerell, *Live from Number Ten: The Inside Story of Prime Ministers and Television* (London, 1989), pp. 181–3; Bernard D. Nossiter, *Britain: A Future That Works* (London, 1978), p. 130.

37. PRO CAB 128/49, CM (71) 9, 9 February 1971; Beckett, *When the Lights Went Out*, p. 121; James Lees-Milne, *Diaries, 1971–1983* (London, 2008), p. 3; *Evening Standard*, 6 October 1974.

38. *The Times*, 30 September 1971, 6 December 1971; *Sunday Times*, 12 December 1971; Taylor, *Loyalists*, pp. 87–8, 90–91.

CHAPTER 7. LOVE THY NEIGHBOUR

1. *The Times*, 19 January 1971, 20 January 1971; Denis Judd, *Empire: The British Imperial Experience, from 1765 to the Present* (London, 1997), pp. 385, 390; Pat Hutton and Jonathan Bloch, 'The Making of Idi Amin', *New African* (February 2001), http://www.hartford-hwp.com/archives/36/502.html.

2. *The Times*, 26 January 1971, 29 January 1971, 7 August 1972; *Guardian*, 26 January 1971; Hutton and Bloch, 'The Making of Idi Amin'; *Scotsman*, 17 August 2003.

3. Robert Winder, *Bloody Foreigners: The Story of Immigration to Britain* (London, 2004), p. 292; Francis Wheen, *Strange Days Indeed: The Golden Age of Paranoia* (London, 2009), p. 235; *Independent*, 5 August 2002; *The Times*, 5 August 1972, 7 August 1972.

4. PRO CAB 128/50, CM (72) 40, 8 August 1972; Zig Layton-Henry, 'Immigration and the Heath Government', in Stuart Ball and Anthony Seldon (eds.), *The Heath Government 1970–1974: A Reappraisal* (Harlow, 1996), pp. 223–5; PRO CAB 128/47, CM (71) 1/3; PRO CAB 129/157, CP (71) 58, 'Immigration Policy', 10 May 1971; Lewis Baston, *Reggie: The Life of Reginald Maudling* (Stroud, 2004), p. 400; Harry Goulbourne, *Race Relations in Britain Since 1945* (Basingstoke, 1998), p. 53; John Campbell, *Edward Heath: A Biography* (London, 1993), p. 392.

5. *The Times*, 7 August 1972, 11 August 1972, 12 August 1972, 18 August 1972; Baston, *Reggie*, p. 401; Winder, *Bloody Foreigners*, p. 293.

6. *The Times*, 7 August 1972, 8 August 1972, 14 August 1972, 25 August 1972, 5 September 1972; Winder, *Bloody Foreigners*, p. 292; Stuart Hall *et al.*, *Policing the Crisis: Mugging, the State and Law and Order* (Basingstoke, 1978), p. 299.

7. *The Times*, 7 August 1972, 17 August 1972; Martin Walker, *The National Front* (London, 1977). p. 127; Simon Heffer, *Like the Roman: The Life of Enoch Powell* (London, 1998), p. 643.

8. *The Times*, 13 September 1972; Heffer, *Like the Roman*, p. 643.

9. *Sunday Express*, 4 April 1965; *Guardian*, 13 June 1969; Heffer, *Like the Roman*, pp. 462–8, 514, 567–8, 657, 690 and *passim*.

10. Ibid., pp. 253–5, 380; *The Times*, 1 May 1968; Walker, *The National Front*, p. 115.

11. Jeremy Seabrook, *City Close-Up* (Harmondsworth, 1973), pp. 58–9; Alwyn W. Turner, *Crisis? What Crisis? Britain in the 1970s* (London, 2008), pp. 35–6.

12. *The Times*, 25 August 1972, 8 September 1972, 11 September 1972, 13 September 1972.

13. *The Times*, 7 September 1972, 15 September 1972, 16 September 1972; *The Economist*, 19 August 1972; Winder, *Bloody Foreigners*, p. 293.

14. PRO CAB 129/164, CP (72) 91, 'United Kingdom Passport Holders in Uganda', 6 September 1972; PRO CAB 128/50, CM (72) 41, 7 September 1972.
15. PRO CAB 128/50, CM (72) 42, 27 September 1972; *The Times*, 1 December 1972; Campbell, *Edward Heath*, pp. 393–4.
16. *The Times*, 19 August 1972, 1 September 1972.
17. Shamit Saggar, *Race and Politics in Britain* (Hemel Hempstead, 1992), pp. 41, 45, 53; Peter Clarke, *Hope and Glory: Britain 1900–1990* (London, 1996), p. 327; Jerry White, *London in the Twentieth Century* (London, 2001), p. 133; Winder, *Bloody Foreigners*, pp. 297–8, 311.
18. White, *London in the Twentieth Century*, pp. 137, 140; Winder, *Bloody Foreigners*, pp. 303–5.
19. Nicholas Deakin, *Colour, Citizenship and British Society* (London, 1970), ch. 4; Hall *et al.*, *Policing the Crisis*, pp. 342–3; Colin Brown, *Black and White Britain* (London, 1984), p. 157; Goulbourne, *Race Relations in Britain Since 1945*; White, *London in the Twentieth Century*, pp. 163–4.
20. Daniel Lawrence, *Black Migrants: White Natives. A Study of Race Relations in Nottingham* (Cambridge, 1974), pp. 10, 75, 93, 32, 118, 39–42.
21. Ibid., pp. 93, 114.
22. Seabrook, *City Close-Up*, pp. 39, 40, 43–4, 50–52, 54.
23. Ibid., pp. 53, 57.
24. *Daily Mirror*, 22 April 1968, 3 July 1969; Richard Weight. *Patriots: National Identity in Britain 1940–2000* (London, 2002), pp. 436–7.
25. James Lees-Milne, *Diaries, 1971–1985* (London, 2008), p. 243; Andrew Motion, *Philip Larkin: A Writer's Life* (London, 1994), p. 410; Colin Dexter, *Last Seen Wearing* (London, 1977), p. 56.
26. *Sunday Times*, 30 September 1973; Gordon Burn, *Somebody's Husband, Somebody's Son: The Story of Peter Sutcliffe* (London, 1984), p. 127; Trevor Griffiths, *Comedians* (London, 1976), pp. 42, 44, 56.
27. *The Times*, 2 September 2006; *Daily Telegraph*, 4 September 2006; *Guardian*, 4 September 2006; Mike Phillips and Trevor Phillips, *Windrush: The Irresistible Rise of Multi-Racial Britain* (London, 1999), pp. 314–15.
28. Ibid., pp. 311–12, 315; *Guardian*, 7 February 2009.
29. *The Times*, 19 May 1967; Louis Barfe, *Turned Out Nice Again: The Story of British Light Entertainment* (London, 2008), pp. 122–3, 289–90; Turner, *Crisis? What Crisis?*, p. 207; and see the excellent BBC Four documentary *Black and White Minstrel Show: Revisited* (2004).
30. Simon Winder, *The Man Who Saved Britain: A Personal Journey into the Disturbing World of James Bond* (London, 2006), pp. 1, 52; for a more sober analysis, see James Chapman, *Licence to Thrill: A Cultural History of the James Bond Films* (London, 1999), pp. 166–8.
31. Turner, *Crisis? What Crisis?*, pp. 205–6; Mark Duguid, 'Race and the Sitcom', http://www.screenonline.org.uk/tv/id/1108234/index.html.
32. Leon Hunt, *British Low Culture: From Safari Suits to Sexploitation* (London,

1998), pp. 52–4; Vic Pratt, 'Love Thy Neighbour', http://www.screenonline.org.uk/tv/id/501026/index.html.

33. *Daily Telegraph*, 18 April 1972; *Observer*, 16 April 1972; *The Times*, 21 April 1972, 18 September 1972; *New Society*, 31 July 1975; *Daily Express*, 9 May 1975; Hunt, *British Low Culture*, pp. 54–5.

34. *The Times*, 7 April 1970, 8 April 1970, 9 April 1970, 14 April 1970, 20 April 1970; White, *London in the Twentieth Century*, pp. 151–2; Winder, *Bloody Foreigners*, p. 300.

35. *The Times*, 27 April 1970, 25 May 1970, 28 May 1970; John Davis, *Youth and the Condition of Britain: Images of Adolescent Conflict* (London, 1990), p. 212; Eric Dunning, Patrick Murphy and John M. Williams, *The Roots of Football Hooliganism: A Historical and Sociological Study* (London, 1988), pp. 169–71; Turner, *Crisis? What Crisis?*, pp. 62–3; Pat Doyle, Pete McGuire and Susie Daniel, *The Paint House: Words from an East End Gang* (Harmondsworth, 1972), p. 79.

36. Pete Fowler, 'Skins Rule', in Charlie Gillett (ed.), *Rock File* (London, 1972), p. 20; Turner, *Crisis? What Crisis?*, p. 63; Richard Holt, *Sport and the British: A Modern History* (Oxford, 1990), p. 339; White, *London in the Twentieth Century*, p. 151.

37. *The Times*, 14 April 1970, 19 November 1970; *Daily Telegraph*, 7 January 1977; Turner, *Crisis? What Crisis?*, pp. 215–16; Zig Layton-Henry, *The Politics of Immigration: Immigration, Race and Race Relations in Post-War Britain* (Oxford, 1992), p. 126; Lawrence, *Black Migrants: White Natives*, p. 207; Maureen Cain, *Society and the Policeman's Role* (London, 1973), p. 117.

38. Lawrence, *Black Migrants: White Natives*, pp. 206–8; Layton-Henry, *The Politics of Immigration*, p. 127; Phillips and Phillips, *Windrush*, pp. 301–2.

39. *Guardian*, 28 January 1972, 11 February 1972, 9 March 1972; Hall *et al.*, *Policing the Crisis*, pp. 44, 47, 329; Goulbourne, *Race Relations in Britain Since 1945*, p. 68; Phillips and Phillips, *Windrush*, p. 281; White, *London in the Twentieth Century*, p. 297; *The Times*, 19 March 1974.

40. *Sunday Times*, 5 August 1973; *Daily Mirror*, 14 June 1973; Hall *et al.*, *Policing the Crisis*, pp. 43–4, 290–93, 300; White, *London in the Twentieth Century*, pp. 279, 283.

41. *The Times*, 30 December 1972; Lees-Milne, *Diaries*, p. 14.

42. *Daily Mirror*, 17 August 1972; *The Times*, 20 October 1972; Hall *et al.*, *Policing the Crisis*, pp. 3–5, 18–28.

43. Ibid., pp. 7–8, 17, 75; *Sunday Mirror*, 22 October 1972; *Sun*, 13 October 1972; *Daily Mail*, 26 October 1972; *The Times*, 1 November 1972, 2 November 1972.

44. Hall *et al.*, *Policing the Crisis*, pp. vii–viii, 33–8, 163, 183, 250, 323 and *passim*.

45. Ibid., pp. 10, 14, quoting data from the *Annual Reports* of the Commissioner of the Metropolitan Police and the Chief Inspector of Constabulary; George L. Bernstein, *The Myth of Decline: The Rise of Britain Since 1945* (London, 2004), p. 437; Alan Sked and Chris Cook, *Post-War Britain: A Political History* (London,

1988), p. 354; Turner, *Crisis? What Crisis?*, pp. 258–9; *Daily Mirror*, 14 January 1978.

46. Layton-Henry, 'Immigration and the Heath Government', p. 234; Saggar, *Race and Politics in Britain*, pp. 110, 116.

47. Ibid., p. 180; Walker, *The National Front*, pp. 67–70; John Tomlinson, *Left, Right: The March of Political Extremism in Britain* (London, 1981), p. 30; *Daily Telegraph*, 25 September 1997; Weight, *Patriots*, p. 539.

48. Walker, *The National Front*, pp. 90–91; David Robins and Philip Cohen, *Knuckle Sandwich: Growing Up in the Working-Class City* (Harmondsworth 1978), pp. 199, 202, 168.

49. Walker, *The National Front*, p. 217; Saggar, *Race and Politics in Britain*, p. 181; Richard Clutterbuck, *Britain in Agony: The Growth of Political Violence* (London, 1978), pp. 238–9; Jeremy Seabrook, *What Went Wrong? Working People and the Ideals of the Labour Movement* (London, 1978), p. 93.

50. Tomlinson, *Left, Right*, pp. 43, 49, 54–5, 57–8; *The Times*, 17 May 1975.

51. *The Times*, 23 August 1972, 25 August 1972; Walker, *The National Front*, pp. 135–6.

52. *The Times*, 25 May 1973, 26 May 1973, 31 May 1973; Walker, *The National Front*, pp. 133–9, 142–3.

53. *The Times*, 9 June 1973.

54. David Butler and Dennis Kavanagh, *The British General Election of February 1974* (London, 1974), p. 336; Walker, *The National Front*, pp. 9, 149–51, 166.

55. *The Times*, 31 August 1972, 1 September 1972, 19 September 1972, 26 September 1972.

56. Winder, *Bloody Foreigners*, pp. 293–4; *The Times*, 2 October 1972, 16 October 1972.

CHAPTER 8. THE LIMITS TO GROWTH

1. Donella Meadows *et al.*, *The Limits to Growth: A Report for the Club of Rome* (New York, 1972), p. 29; Robert M. Collins, *More: The Politics of Economic Growth in Postwar America* (Oxford, 2000), pp. 139–45.

2. *The Times*, 31 May 1972, 1 April 1972; Collins, *More*, p. 141.

3. John Campbell, *Edward Heath: A Biography* (London, 1993), p. 406; James Margach, *The Abuse of Power* (London, 1978), p. 160; Michael Cockerell, *Live from Number Ten: The Inside Story of Prime Ministers and Television* (London, 1989), p. 190; John Ramsden, 'The Prime Minister and the Making of Policy', in Stuart Ball and Anthony Seldon (eds.), *The Heath Government, 1970–1974: A Reappraisal* (Harlow, 1996), pp. 40–41; Lewis Baston and Anthony Seldon, 'Number 10 under Edward Heath', in Ball and Seldon (eds.), *The Heath Government*, pp. 66–7; Kevin Theakston, 'The Heath Government, Whitehall and the Civil Service', in Ball and Seldon (eds.), *The Heath Government*, pp. 88–9; Ion Trewin (ed.), *The Hugo Young Papers: Thirty Years of British*

Politics – Off the Record (London, 2008), pp. 78, 82, and see also pp. 72–3, 76–80, 82–3, 86–7.

4. *The Times*, 8 March 1972; Taylor, 'The Heath Government, Industrial Policy and the "New Capitalism"', in Ball and Seldon (eds.), *The Heath Government*, pp. 141–2; Campbell, *Edward Heath*, pp. 451–2; Donald MacDougall, *Don and Mandarin: Memoirs of an Economist* (London, 1987), pp. 188–9.

5. PRO CAB 128/50, CM (72) 10, 24 February 1972.

6. Hansard, 28 February 1972; *The Times*, 29 February 1972; *The Economist*, 4 April 1972, 24 June 1972; Taylor, 'The Heath Government, Industrial Policy and the "New Capitalism"', pp. 151–2; Campbell, *Edward Heath* pp. 443–4.

7. Edward Heath, *The Course of My Life* (London, 1998), p. 348; Edmund Dell, *The Chancellors: A History of the Chancellors of the Exchequer, 1945–90* (London, 1996), p. 385; Douglas Hurd, *An End to Promises* (London, 1978), pp. 86–7, 90; Campbell, *Edward Heath*, pp. 411–12, 442.

8. Hansard, 21 March 1972; Dell, *The Chancellors*, pp. 387–8; Sir Alec Cairncross, 'The Heath Government and the British Economy', in Ball and Seldon (eds.), *The Heath Government*, p. 117.

9. Campbell, *Edward Heath*, p. 444; Hansard, 21 March 1972; Dilwyn Porter, 'Government and the Economy', in Richard Coopey and Nicholas Woodward (eds.), *Britain in the 1970s: The Troubled Economy* (London, 1996), p. 38; *The Times*, 21 March 1972, 22 March 1972.

10. Phillip Whitehead, *The Writing on the Wall: Britain in the Seventies* (London, 1985), pp. 84–5; Campbell, *Edward Heath*, p. 445; Richard Coopey and Nicholas Woodward, 'The British Economy in the 1970s', in Coopey and Woodward (eds.), *Britain in the 1970s*, p. 14; Max-Stephen Schulze and Nicholas Woodward, 'The Emergence of Rapid Inflation', in Coopey and Woodward (eds.), *Britain in the 1970s*, p. 113; Dell, *The Chancellors*, pp. 385–7.

11. David Smith, *The Rise and Fall of Monetarism: The Theory and Politics of an Economic Experiment* (London, 1991), pp. 31–4; Cairncross, 'The Heath Government and the British Economy', pp. 130–33; Coopey and Woodward, 'The British Economy in the 1970s', pp. 4–5; Campbell, *Edward Heath*, pp. 454–5; *The Times*, 24 June 1972; Dell, *The Chancellors*, p. 90.

12. *The Times*, 13 September 1971; Sir Alec Cairncross, *The British Economy Since 1945: Economic Policy and Performance, 1945–1990* (Oxford, 1992), pp. 190–91; Smith, *The Rise and Fall of Monetarism*, pp. 39–40; David Kynaston, *The City of London*, vol. 4: *A Club No More, 1945–2000*, pp. 436–40.

13. Smith, *The Rise and Fall of Monetarism*, p. 41; Kynaston, *A Club No More*, p. 451; Schulze and Woodward, 'The Emergence of Rapid Inflation', p. 113; Peter Clarke, *Hope and Glory: Britain 1900–1990* (London, 1996), p. 336.

14. Whitehead, *The Writing on the Wall*, pp. 94–5; Clive Irving, *Pox Britannica: The Unmaking of the British* (New York, 1974), p. 161; Christopher Booker, *The Seventies: Portrait of a Decade* (London 1980), pp. 105, 108; Jerry White,

London in the Twentieth Century (London, 2001), pp. 65–6; Jonathan Raban, *Soft City* (London, 1975), pp. 187–8.

15. Taylor, 'The Heath Government, Industrial Policy and the "New Capitalism"', pp. 141–2; Campbell, *Edward Heath*, pp. 451–2; MacDougall, *Don and Mandarin*, pp. 188–9; Heath, *The Course of My Life*, p. 400; *Evening Standard*, 1–2 June 1972.

16. Campbell, *Edward Heath*, pp. 446–8; Taylor, 'The Heath Government, Industrial Policy and the "New Capitalism"', pp. 152–3; Hansard, 22 March 1972.

17. Tony Benn, *Office Without Power: Diaries 1968–72* (London, 1988), p. 417; Hansard, 22 May 1972, 28 July 1972; Campbell, *Edward Heath*, pp. 449–50, 453.

18. *The Economist*, 13 May 1972; Taylor, 'The Heath Government, Industrial Policy and the "New Capitalism"', pp 154–6; Campbell, *Edward Heath*, p. 453; Peter Walker, *Staying Power: An Autobiography* (London, 1991), p. 99.

19. Taylor, 'The Heath Government, Industrial Policy and the "New Capitalism"', pp. 154–60; Campbell, *Edward Heath*, pp. 452, 454.

20. Ibid., pp. 421, 469–70; *The Times*, 10 March 1972; Robert Taylor, 'The Heath Government and Industrial Relations', in Ball and Seldon (eds.), *The Heath Government*, pp. 178–9; Whitehead, *The Writing on the Wall*, p. 87.

21. Robert J. Wybrow, *Britain Speaks Out, 1937–87: A Social History as Seen Through the Gallup Data* (London, 1989), p. 100; Robert Harris, *The Making of Neil Kinnock* (London, 1984), pp. 66–8; Stephen Haseler, *The Death of British Democracy* (London, 1976), pp. 103–4; Eric Heffer, *The Class Struggle in Parliament* (London, 1973); Anthony Barnett, 'Class Struggle and the Heath Government', *New Left Review*, 77 (January–February 1973), pp. 3–41; Campbell, *Edward Heath*, p. 502; *New Statesman*, 18 February 1972.

22. *The Times*, 21 April 1972; Paul Ferris, *The New Militants: Crisis in the Trade Unions* (Harmondsworth, 1972), pp. 102–3; Richard Clutterbuck *Britain in Agony: The Growth of Political Violence* (London, 1978), pp. 49–50; Dave Lyddon, '"Glorious Summer", 1972', in John McIlroy, Nina Fishman and Alan Campbell (eds.), *The High Tide of British Trade Unionism: Trade Unions and Industrial Politics, 1964–1979* (Monmouth, 2007), pp. 334–5.

23. On the dockers: *The Times*, 22 April 1972, 24 April 1972, 25 April 1972; on the railwaymen: *The Times*, 13 April 1972, 14 April 1972, 19 April 1972, 13 May 1972, 20 May 1972, 13 June 1972, 14 June 1972; and see Campbell, *Edward Heath*, pp. 458–9.

24. *The Times*, 14 June 1972; Campbell, *Edward Heath*, pp. 459–60; Whitehead, *The Writing on the Wall*, p. 78; Heath, *The Course of My Life*, p. 406.

25. Ferris, *The New Militants*, pp. 103–5; Whitehead, *The Writing on the Wall*, p. 78; Clutterbuck, *Britain in Agony*, pp. 50–51; *The Times*, 14 June 1972, 16 June 1972; Cecil King, *The Cecil King Diary, 1970–1974* (London, 1975), p. 210.

26. *The Times*, 17 June 1972; Whitehead, *The Writing on the Wall*, pp. 78–9.

27. *The Times*, 21 July 1972, 22 July 1972; Hansard, 25 July 1972; *Time*, 14 August 1972; Ferris, *The New Militants*, p. 105; Clutterbuck, *Britain in Agony*, p. 51; Campbell, *Edward Heath*, pp. 460–61; Lyddon, '"Glorious Summer", 1972', pp. 336–7.

28. *The Economist*, 29 July 1972; *Guardian*, 28 July 1972; *The Times*, 28 July 1972; PRO CAB 128/50, CM (72) 38, 27 July 1972; Lyddon '"Glorious Summer", 1972', pp. 338–9; Gerald A. Dorfman, *Government versus Trade Unionism in British Politics Since 1968* (London, 1979), pp. 63–4; Campbell, *Edward Heath*, pp. 461–2.

29. *The Times*, 4 August 1972, 17 August 1972; Ferris, *The New Militants*, pp. 106–7; Campbell, *Edward Heath*, p. 462.

30. Campbell, *Edward Heath*, pp. 463–6; Clutterbuck, *Britain in Agony*, p. 54; Andrew Taylor, 'The Conservative Party and the Trade Unions', in McIlroy, Fishman and Campbell (eds.), *The High Tide of British Trade Unionism*, pp. 165–6; Stephen Milligan, *The New Barons: Union Power in the 1970s* (London, 1976), p. 7; Porter, 'Government and the Economy', p. 40.

31. King, *The Cecil King Diary 1970–1974*, p. 223; Campbell, *Edward Heath*, pp. 467, 471; Heath, *The Course of My Life*, p. 412; Dorfman, *Government versus Trade Unionism*, pp. 79–81; Trewin (ed.), *The Hugo Young Papers*, p. 108.

32. Heath, *The Course of My Life*, p. 413; Whitehead, *The Writing on the Wall*, p. 87; and see Taylor, 'The Heath Government and Industrial Relations', p. 189; Vernon Bogdanor, 'The Fall of Heath and the End of the Postwar Settlement', in Ball and Seldon (eds.), *The Heath Government*, pp. 379–80.

33. PRO CAB 129/164, CP (72) 93, 26 September 1972; PRO CAB 129/164, CP (72) 99, 27 September 1972; *The Times*, 27 September 1972, 28 September 1972; Taylor, 'The Heath Government and Industrial Relations', pp. 179–80; Campbell, *Edward Heath*, pp. 472–3.

34. PRO CAB 128/50, CM (72) 46, 25 October 1972; Heath, *The Course of My Life*, p. 414; Campbell, *Edward Heath*, pp. 474–6; Hurd, *An End to Promises*, p. 40.

35. PRO CAB 128/50, CM (72) 48, 2 November 1972; PRO CAB 128/50, CM (72) 49, 3 November 1972; *The Times*, 4 November 1972; Heath, *The Course of My Life*, p. 415.

36. Hansard, 6 November 1972; *The Times*, 7 November 1972; Simon Heffer, *Like the Roman: The Life of Enoch Powell* (London, 1998), pp. 654–5.

37. Hansard, 5 April 1971, 28 June 1971, 11 October 1973, 23 July 1973: Heffer, *Like the Roman*, pp. 590–91, 597, 645, 658–9, 672, 678; Tony Benn, *Against the Tide: Diaries 1973–1976* (London, 1989), p. 55.

38. E. H. H. Green, *Ideologies of Conservatism: Conservative Political Ideas in the Twentieth Century* (Oxford, 2002), pp. 232–4; Trewin (ed.), *The Hugo Young Papers*, p. 12; Richard Cockett, *Thinking the Unthinkable: Think-Tanks and the*

Economic Counter-Revolution, 1931–1983 (London, 1995), pp. 203–4, 209–10; John Ranelagh, *Thatcher's People* (London, 1992), pp. 115–16; Smith, *The Rise and Fall of Monetarism*, p. 50.

39. See Campbell, *Edward Heath*, pp. 456, 471.

40. Cockett, *Thinking the Unthinkable*, p. 212; Anthony Seldon, 'The Heath Government in History', in Ball and Seldon (eds.), *The Heath Government*, pp. 6–7, 9, 13; Taylor, 'The Heath Government, Industrial Policy and the "New Capitalism"', p. 141; Anthony Seldon, 'The Heathman: An Interview with John Campbell', *Contemporary Record*, 7:3 (Winter 1993), p. 589; Whitehead, *The Writing on the Wall*, p. 89; Ramsden, 'The Prime Minister and the Making of Policy', p. 41.

41. See Seldon, 'The Heath Government in History', pp. 14–15; John Ramsden, *An Appetite for Power: A History of the Conservative Party Since 1830* (London, 1999), pp. 401–2.

42. Campbell, *Edward Heath*, pp. 470–71; *The Times*. 16 June 1972, 12 September 1972; Reginald Maudling, *Memoirs* (London 1978), pp. 263–5; *The Economist*, 28 October 1972.

43. Heffer, *Like the Roman*, p. 657; Campbell, *Edward Heath*, pp. 509–11; John Ramsden, 'The Conservative Party and the Heath Government', in Ball and Seldon (eds.), *The Heath Government*, pp. 323–4, 326–7, 334–5.

44. Norman Tebbit, *Upwardly Mobile* (London, 1988), p. 123; Ramsden, 'The Prime Minister and the Making of Policy', pp. 44–6; Ramsden, *An Appetite for Power*, p. 408; *Spectator*, 2 December 1972; Campbell, *Edward Heath*, pp. 515–20; Heffer, *Like the Roman*, p. 615.

CHAPTER 9. METRO-LAND

1. *The Times*, 26 February 1973, 28 February 1973, 1 March 1973; *Evening Standard*, 26 February 1973, 1 March 1973.

2. Bevis Hillier, *John Betjeman: The Biography* (London, 2007), pp. 464–73; Michael Brooke, 'Metro-Land', http://www.screenonline.org.uk/tv/id/1259604/index.html.

3. John Carey, *The Intellectuals and the Masses: Pride and Prejudice among the Literary Intelligentsia, 1880–1939* (London, 1992), pp. 50–51, and see pp. 47–70 in general; George Orwell, *Coming Up for Air* (Harmondsworth, 1962), pp. 13–14.

4. D. J. Taylor, *After the War: The Novel and England Since 1945* (London, 1993), p. 45; Dominic Sandbrook, *Never Had It So Good: A History of Britain from Suez to the Beatles* (London, 2005), pp. 122–3; Mark Clapson, *Invincible Green Suburbs, Brave New Towns* (Manchester, 1998), p. 12; Jon Savage, *England's Dreaming: Sex Pistols and Punk Rock* (London, 2005), pp. 146, 241.

5. Clapson, *Invincible Green Suburbs, Brave New Towns*, pp. 10–11; Leon Hunt,

British Low Culture: From Safari Suits to Sexploitation (London, 1998), pp. 103–5.

6. Lawrence James, *The Middle Class: A History* (London, 2006), p. 525; Alwyn W. Turner, *Crisis? What Crisis?: Britain in the 1970s* (London, 2008), p. 198; Mark Duguid, 'The Good Life', http://www.screenonline.org.uk/tv/id/579110/index.html; Mike Sutton, 'The Fall and Rise of Reginald Perrin', http://www.screenonline.org.uk/tv/id/534926/index.html.

7. Simon Gunn and Rachel Bell, *Middle Classes: Their Rise and Sprawl* (London, 2003), pp. 193–4.

8. *Radio Times*, 4 February 1968; James, *The Middle Class*, pp. 512–13; John Betjeman, 'Executive', in John Betjeman, *Collected Poems* (London, 2001), pp. 312–13; Michael Billington, *State of the Nation: British Theatre Since 1945* (London, 2007), pp. 233–4; Martin Amis, *Success* (London, 1985), pp. 184, 217–18.

9. *Encounter*, October 1974; Deborah S. Ryan, *The Ideal Home Through the Twentieth Century* (London, 1997), p. 157.

10. Phil Wickham, *The Likely Lads* (Basingstoke, 2008), p. 46; *The Times*, 12 February 1968; *Daily Mirror*, 10 March 1978; Joe Moran, *Queuing for Beginners: The Story of Daily Life from Breakfast to Bedtime* (London, 2007), pp. 51, 77; John Burnett, *Liquid Pleasures: A Social History of Drinks in Modern Britain* (London, 1999), pp. 90–91; Gunn and Bell, *Middle Classes*, p. 201.

11. Michael Young and Peter Willmott, *The Symmetrical Family: A Study of Work and Leisure in the London Region* (London, 1973), pp. 166–7, 278–80.

12. Arthur M. Edwards, *The Design of Suburbia* (London, 1981), pp. 243–4; James, *The Middle Class*, pp. 522–3; Wickham, *The Likely Lads*, pp. 16, 34.

13. Young and Willmott, *The Symmetrical Family*, pp. 29–30, 48.

14. Paul Oliver, 'A Lighthouse on the Mantlepiece: Symbolism in the Home', in Paul Oliver, Ian Davis and Ian Bentley (eds.), *Dunroamin: The Suburban Semi and Its Enemies* (London, 1981), pp. 179, 181–2; Piers Paul Read, *A Married Man* (London, 1979), pp. 157–8.

15. *Sunday Times*, 24 April 1977; James, *The Middle Class*, pp. 533–4; Jonathan Raban, *Soft City* (London, 1975), p. 89; Alison Pressley, *The Seventies: Good Times, Bad Taste* (London, 2002), p. 71.

16. Richard Weight, *Patriots: National Identity in Britain 1940–2000* (London, 2002), pp. 323–4; Ryan, *The Ideal Home Through the Twentieth Century*, pp. 145, 151.

17. James, *The Middle Class*, pp. 536, 568–9; Young and Willmott, *The Symmetrical Family*, pp. 212, 216, 247; Hunter Davies, *The Glory Game* (London, 1972), pp. 310–12; Anthony Sampson, *The New Anatomy of Britain* (London, 1971), p. 427.

18. John Benson, *The Rise of Consumer Society in Britain, 1880–1980* (Harlow, 1994), p. 69; Roger Cox, 'Carrefour at Caerphilly: The Shoppers and the Competition', *International Journal of Retail and Distribution Management*,

3:3 (1975), pp. 39–41; *The Times*, 13 September 1972, 23 September 1972, 13 April 1973, 10 September 1973, 30 April 1974.

19. Ann Oakley, *Housewife* (London, 1974), p. 131; Benson, *The Rise of Consumer Society*, pp. 70–71.

20. Arthur Marwick, *British Society Since 1945* (Harmondsworth, 1982), pp. 242–3; Benson, *The Rise of Consumer Society*, p. 72; *Screen Digest*, April 1979; Justin Smith, 'Glam, Spam and Uncle Sam: Funding Diversity in 1970s British Film Production', in Robert Shail (ed.), *Seventies British Cinema* (London, 2008), p. 68.

21. Marwick, *British Society Since 1945*, p. 242; Kate Colquhoun, *Taste: The Story of Britain Through Its Cooking* (London, 2007), p. 353; Moran, *Queuing for Beginners*, pp. 153–4; *The Times*, 5 February 1972, 17 January 1983, 12 April 1983.

22. Colquhoun, *Taste*, p. 365; Moran, *Queuing for Beginners*, pp. 154, 17; Turner, *Crisis? What Crisis?*, p. 46; Mary Abbott, *Family Affairs: A History of the Family in Twentieth-Century England* (London, 2003), p. 138.

23. Ken Coates and Richard Silburn, *Poverty: The Forgotten Englishmen* (Harmondsworth, 1970), pp. 95–6; Read, *A Married Man*, p. 67; Kingsley Amis, *Jake's Thing* (London, 1978), p. 38; Margaret Drabble, *The Ice Age* (London, 1977), p. 84; John Burnett, 'The Way We Lived Then: Homes and Families, 1945–2000', in Folio Society, *England 1945–2000* (London, 2001), p. 142.

24. James, *The Middle Class*, p. 537; Colquhoun, *Taste*, pp. 350–53.

25. Nick Clarke, *The Shadow of a Nation: The Changing Face of Britain* (London, 2003), pp. 129–30, 143; John Sutherland, *Reading the Decades: Fifty Years of British History Through the Nation's Bestsellers* (London, 2002), p. 133.

26. Clarke, *The Shadow of a Nation*, pp. 127–8; Colquhoun, *Taste*, pp. 366–7; *The Times*, 4 September 1973, 15 March 1980.

27. Mike Leigh, *Abigail's Party* (London, 1979); *Sunday Times*, 24 April 1977, 1 May 1977; and see Billington, *State of the Nation*, pp. 279–81.

28. Alan Ayckbourn, *The Norman Conquests* (London, 1973), p. 55; and see Dominic Shellard, *British Theatre Since the War* (New Haven, 2000), pp. 170–72; Randall Stevenson, *The Oxford English Literary History*, vol. 12: *1960–2000: The Last of England?* (Oxford, 2004), p. 358; Billington, *State of the Nation*. p. 201.

29. June Norris, *Human Aspects of Redevelopment* (Birmingham, 1962), pp. 11, 27–8; Peter Willmott and Michael Young, *Family and Class in a London Suburb* (London, 1960), pp. 91, 112; Clapson, *Invincible New Suburbs, Brave New Towns*, pp. 45–7; *The Times*, 10 September 1968; and see Sandbrook, *Never Had It So Good*, pp. 124–6, and Dominic Sandbrook, *White Heat: A History of Britain in the Swinging Sixties* (London, 2006), pp. 190–91.

30. Richard Clutterbuck, *Britain in Agony: The Growth of Political Violence* (London, 1978), p. 20; William B. Gwyn, 'Jeremiahs and Pragmatists: Perceptions of British Decline', in William B. Gwyn and Richard Rose, (eds.), *Britain: Progress and Decline* (London, 1980), p. 25; Kenneth O. Morgan, *The People's*

Peace: British History Since 1945 (Oxford, 1999), pp. 395, 424–5, 432.

31. Simon Winder, *The Man Who Saved Britain: A Personal Journey into the Disturbing World of James Bond* (London, 2006), p. 254; 'The Diaries of Smurfette', 1 January 1974, 21 February 1974, www.escape-to-the-seventies. com/Diaries/January_1974.php.

32. Hunter Davies, *The Creighton Report* (London, 1977), pp. 278–9; 'The Diaries of Smurfette', 2 February 1974, 15 February 1974.

33. *The Times*, 28 April 1975, 27 January 1972, 29 January 1972; James Chapman, *Inside the TARDIS: The Worlds of Doctor Who* (London, 2006), pp. 111–14.

34. *The Times*, 8 February 1978, 21 January 1975; Stevenson, *The Last of England?*, p. 138; Elaine Moss, 'The Seventies in British Children's Books', in Nancy Chambers (ed.), *The Signal Approach to Children's Books* (Harmondsworth, 1980), pp. 48–80.

35. Ibid., pp. 63–4; Bernard T. Harrison, 'Books for Younger Readers', in Boris Ford (ed.), *The New Pelican Guide to English Literature*, vol. 8: *From Orwell to Naipaul* (London, 1998), p. 363; *The Times*, 6 October 1972; Frank Whitehead et al., *Children and Their Books: Final Report of the Schools Council Research Project on Children's Reading Habits, 10–15* (London, 1977), pp. 131–2.

36. J. B. Priestley, *The English* (London, 1973), p. 245; Jeremy Seabrook, *City Close-Up* (Harmondsworth, 1973), pp. 150, 155, 159–62.

37. George Bernstein, *The Myth of Decline: The Rise of Britain Since 1945* (London, 2004), pp. 453–5; Irene Rauta and Audrey Hunt, *Fifth Form Girls: Their Hopes for the Future* (London, 1975); Nick Tiratsoo, 'The Seventies', in Folio Society, *England 1945–2000*, pp. 296–7; David Butler and Dennis Kavanagh, *The British General Election of 1979* (London, 1980), p. 343.

38. Dave Harker, 'Blood on the Tracks: Popular Music in the 1970s', in Bart Moore-Gilbert (ed.), *The Arts in the 1970s: Cultural Closure?* (London, 1994), pp. 251–2; Dave Laing, *One Chord Wonders: Power and Meaning in Punk Rock* (Milton Keynes, 1985), pp. 1–4; 'The Diaries of Smurfette', 18 April 1974, 9 May 1974.

39. Ian MacDonald, *Revolution in the Head: The Beatles' Records and the Sixties* (London, 1997), p. 340; Ian MacDonald, *The People's Music* (London, 2003), pp. viii–ix; Philip Norman, *The Stones* (London, 1993), p. 284; and see Charlie Gillett, *The Sound of the City: The Rise of Rock and Roll* (London, 1983), pp. 375–7; Iain Chambers, *Urban Rhythms: Pop Music and Popular Culture* (Basingstoke, 1985), pp. 84–5, 111–15.

40. *NME*, 19 February 1972, 14 July 1973, 16 September 1972, 15 April 1972.

41. *Melody Maker*, 20 November 1971, 22 January 1972; *NME*, 24 September 1977; Barney Hoskyns, *Glam! Bowie, Bolan and the Glitter Rock Revolution* (London, 1998), pp. 15–19, 40–41, 52.

42. *Melody Maker*, 9 November 1974, 19 April 1975.

43. *NME*, 17 July 1971; *Melody Maker*, 16 September 1972; Tony Palmer, *All You Need Is Love: The Story of Popular Music* (London, 1977), pp. 261–2.

44. *Melody Maker*, 29 September 1973; *The Times*, 21 November 1973.

45. *Melody Maker*, 9 February 1974.

46. *The Times*, 2 September 1970, 11 February 1970, 7 September 1970, 23 January 1971; Abbott, *Family Affairs*, pp. 130–31; on Maria Colwell, see *The Times*, 10, 11, 13, 16 and 17 October 1973.

47. David Robins and Philip Cohen, *Knuckle Sandwich: Growing Up in the Working-Class City* (Harmondsworth, 1978), pp. 17–18, 22, 35–6, 115–18, 123–4, 203.

48. Jerry White, *London in the Twentieth Century* (London, 2001), p. 73; Seabrook, *City Close-Up*, p. 14.

49. C. Lesley Andrews, *Tenants and Town Hall* (London, 1979), pp. 53, 59; Tony Parker, *The People of Providence: A Housing Estate and Some of Its Inhabitants* (London, 1983); Paul Harrison, *Inside the Inner City: Life under the Cutting Edge* (London, 1983), pp. 229–30, 382; White, *London in the Twentieth Century*, pp. 163–4.

50. Ibid., pp. 204–6, 72–3; on the dockers, see also Paul Ferris, *The New Militants: Crisis in the Trade Unions* (Harmondsworth, 1972), pp. 17, 102, 108.

51. *The Times*, 14 March 1975, 19 April 1975, 5 June 1976; Russell Davies (ed.), *The Kenneth Williams Diaries* (London, 1993), p. 409; David Wilcox and David Richards, *London: The Heartless City* (London, 1977), p. 11; Clive Irving, *Pox Britannica: The Unmaking of the British* (New York, 1974), p. 159; Raban, *Soft City*, pp. 169–70.

52. Dave Haslam, *Not Abba: The Real Story of the 1970s* (London, 2005), p. 237; James Herbert, *The Rats* (London, 1974), p. 59; Turner, *Crisis? What Crisis?*, p. 45; Alexander Walker, *National Heroes: British Cinema in the Seventies and Eighties* (London, 1985), pp. 16–17; Amis, *Success*, p. 118; Margaret Drabble, *The Middle Ground* (Harmondsworth, 1980), p. 111.

53. Haslam, *Not Abba*, p. 178; Phillip Whitehead, *The Writing on the Wall: Britain in the Seventies* (London, 1989), p. 246; *The Times*, 13 June 1978.

54. Haslam, *Not Abba*, pp. 139–40; *Time*, 15 September 1975; Whitehead, *The Writing on the Wall*, pp. 394–6; Gordon Burn, *Somebody's Husband, Somebody's Son: The Story of Peter Sutcliffe* (London, 1984), p. 74; Seabrook, *City Close-Up*, pp. 12, 14.

55. Robert Colls, *Identity of England* (Oxford, 2002), p. 341; Bernstein, *The Myth of Decline*, pp. 419–20; Wickham, *The Likely Lads*, pp. 25–6.

56. David Marquand, *The Progressive Dilemma: From Lloyd George to Blair* (London, 1999), pp. 170–71, 191–2, 212; Ben Pimlott, *Harold Wilson* (London, 1992), pp. 577–8.

57. Morgan, *The People's Peace*, p. 394; *The Times*, 4 July 1975; 'The Science Park Story', www.cambridgesciencepark.co.uk/about/9/history-early-years; Whitehead, *The Writing on the Wall*, pp. 392–3; *The Times*, 11 September 1970; White, *London in the Twentieth Century*, p. 58.

58. *The Times*, 18 March 1970, 24 March 1972; Mark Clapson, *A Social History*

of Milton Keynes: Middle England/Edge City (London, 2004), pp. 45–6, 54, 58, 65.

59. Clapson, *A Social History of Milton Keynes*, pp. 111–12; *Daily Telegraph*, 6 July 1974; Christopher Booker, *The Seventies: Portrait of a Decade* (London, 1980), pp. 145–8.

60. *The Times*, 17 May 1973, 23 October 1976; Andy Beckett, *When the Lights Went Out: Britain in the Seventies* (London, 2009), p. 430; Clapson, *A Social History of Milton Keynes*, pp. 112, 168.

61. *The Times*, 28 August 1975, 23 October 1976, 20 August 1980.

CHAPTER 10. WHO NEEDS MEN?

1. See James Chapman, *Inside the TARDIS: The Worlds of Doctor Who* (London, 2006), pp. 79–80.

2. *The Times*, 21 June 1965, 8 October 1971; John Campbell, *Margaret Thatcher*, vol. 1: *The Grocer's Daughter* (London, 2000), p. 210.

3. Brian Jackson, *Working-Class Community* (Harmondsworth, 1968), pp. 11, 172.

4. Mary Ingham, *Now We Are Thirty: Women of the Breakthrough Generation* (London, 1982), pp. 15, 18; Sheila Rowbotham, *A Century of Women: The History of Women in Britain and the United States* (London, 1999), p. 398.

5. Steven Fielding, *The Labour Governments, 1964–1970*, vol. 1: *Labour and Cultural Change* (Manchester, 2003), p. 127; Barbara Castle, *The Castle Diaries, 1964–70* (London, 1984), p. 373; Elizabeth Wilson, *Only Halfway to Paradise: Women in Postwar Britain. 1945–1968* (London, 1980), pp. 184–5; Sheila Rowbotham, *Women, Resistance and Revolution* (Harmondsworth, 1973), p. 12.

6. Jonathon Green, *Days in the Life: Voices from the English Underground, 1961–1971* (London, 1998), pp. 418–19; Miriam Akhtar and Steve Humphries, *The Fifties and Sixties: A Lifestyle Revolution* (London, 2001), p. 181.

7. Green, *Days in the Life*, p. 401; Sheila Rowbotham, *Promise of a Dream: Remembering the Sixties* (London, 2000), pp. 208–11; *Idiot International*, October 1970.

8. *The Times*, 3 February 1968, 4 February 1968 (on Hull); 10 June 1968, 15 June 1968, 18 June 1968 (on Dagenham); Sheila Rowbotham, *Dreams and Dilemmas: Collected Writings* (London, 1983), pp. 33–4; Rowbotham, *A Century of Women*, pp. 347–9.

9. *The Times*, 19 May 1969; *Black Dwarf*, 1 June 1969; Rowbotham, *Dreams and Dilemmas*, pp. 54–5; Rowbotham, *Promise of a Dream*, pp. 234–5.

10. *The Times*, 6 May 1968, 29 January 1970, 14 February 1970, 12 May 1970; Fielding, *Labour and Cultural Change*, pp. 131–2.

11. *The Times*, 21 November 1970; Green, *Days in the Life*, p. 412; Jonathon

Green, *All Dressed Up: The Sixties and the Counterculture* (London, 1998), pp. 407–8; Paul Ferris, *Sex and the British: A Twentieth-Century History* (London, 1993), p. 219.

12. *The Times*, 2 March 1970; Rowbotham, *Dreams and Dilemmas*, p. 39; Rowbotham, *A Century of Women*, p. 401; Green, *Days in the Life*, pp. 405–6; Green, *All Dressed Up*, pp. 403–6.

13. Rowbotham, *Dreams and Dilemmas*, pp. 87–9; Green, *All Dressed Up*, p. 406; Eve Setch, 'The Face of Metropolitan Feminism: The London Women's Liberation Workshop, 1969–79', *Twentieth Century British History*, 13:2 (2002), pp. 171–90.

14. *Guardian*, 7 March 1971; Setch, 'The Face of Metropolitan Feminism', p. 185; Rowbotham, *A Century of Women*, p. 402; *Evening Standard*, 7 March 1971; *Daily Telegraph*, 6 March 1971.

15. Zelda Curtis, 'Older Women and Feminism: Don't Say Sorry', *Feminist Review*, 31 (28 February 1989), p. 144; Sue O'Sullivan, 'Passionate Beginnings: Ideological Politics 1969–72', *Feminist Review*, 11 (30 June 1982), pp. 82–3; Elaine Aston, 'Finding a Voice: Feminism and Theatre in the 1970s', in Bart Moore-Gilbert (ed.), *The Arts in the 1970s: Cultural Closure?* (London, 1994), p. 104.

16. Cate Haste, *Rules of Desire: Sex in Britain, World War I to the Present* (London, 1994), pp. 235, 243; Rowbotham, *A Century of Women*, pp. 402, 404, 419; Rowbotham, *Dreams and Dilemmas*, p. 40; Jenny Diski, *The Sixties* (London, 2009), pp. 51–2.

17. Elizabeth Wilson, *What Is To Be Done About Violence Against Women?* (Harmondsworth, 1983), p. 84; *Sun*, 9 July 1970; Rowbotham, *A Century of Women*, p. 420; Haste, *Rules of Desire*, pp. 239–40; Mary Abbott, *Family Affairs: A History of the Family in Twentieth-Century England* (London, 2003), p. 140; *Daily Mail*, 22 January 2007; Hansard, 11 July 1975.

18. Abbott, *Family Affairs*, p. 140: Mark Garnett, *From Anger to Apathy: The British Experience Since 1975* (London, 2007), p. 55; *The Times*, 28 June 1975, 21 June 1975, 18 June 1977, 20 June 1977, 21 June 1977, 22 June 1977.

19. Haste, *Rules of Desire*, p. 241; Rowbotham, *A Century of Women*, p. 407; and see http://www.corrie.net/updates/classic/1977.html and http://coronation street.wikia.com/wiki/Coronation_Street_in_1977.

20. Rosie Boycott, *A Nice Girl Like Me: A Story of the Seventies* (London, 1984), pp. 66 ff.; Green, *Days in the Life*, pp. 412–17; Andy Beckett, *When the Lights Went Out: Britain in the Seventies* (London, 2009), pp. 225–8; Ingham, *Now We Are Thirty*, p. 140; and see Marsha Rowe, *The Spare Rib Reader* (London, 1982).

21. On the history of Virago, see 'About Virago', http://www.virago.co.uk/; the Callil quotations are from Alison Pressley, *The Seventies: Good Times, Bad Taste* (London, 2002), p. 48.

22. Wilson, *Only Halfway to Paradise*, pp. 146–61; A. S. Byatt, *The Game* (London,

1968), p. 115; D. J. Taylor, *After the War: The Novel and England Since 1945* (London, 1993), pp. 255–7.

23. Mandy Koonen, 'Undesirable Desires: Sexuality as Subjectivity in Angela Carter's *The Infernal Desire Machines of Doctor Hoffman*', *Women's Studies*, 36:6 (September 2007), pp. 399–416; Angela Carter, *The Passion of New Eve* (London, 1977); Aidan Day, *Angela Carter: The Rational Glass* (Manchester, 1998), pp. 55–131.

24. *Guardian*, 7 March 1991, 31 May 2007; Green, *All Dressed Up*, pp. 329–30.

25. Germaine Greer, *The Female Eunuch* (London, 1970), p. 325; *New York Times*, 22 March 1971.

26. *Listener*, 22 October 1970; *New Society*, 22 October 1970; *Observer*, 11 October 1970; John Sutherland, *Reading the Decades: Fifty Years of British History Through the Nation's Bestsellers* (London, 2002), pp. 109–10; Green, *All Dressed Up*, pp. 410–11.

27. Green, *Days in the Life*, p. 411; Green, *All Dressed Up*, pp. 411–13; Wilson, *Only Halfway to Paradise*, pp. 194–203.

28. Roy Greenslade, *Press Gang: How Newspapers Make Profits from Propaganda* (London, 2004), pp. 262, 273; Larry Lamb, *Sunrise: The Remarkable Rise and Rise of the Bestselling Soaraway Sun* (London, 1989), pp. 56–7; Patricia Holland, 'The Politics of the Smile: "Soft News" and the Sexualisation of the Popular Press', in Cynthia Carter, Gill Branston and Stuart Allan (eds.), *News, Gender and Power* (London, 1998), p. 24.

29. *The Times*, 16 February 1972; *Cosmopolitan*, March 1972; Rowbotham, *A Century of Women*, pp. 417, 428.

30. Alwyn W. Turner, *Crisis? What Crisis? Britain in the 1970s* (London, 2008), p. 114; Chapman, *Inside the TARDIS*, pp. 80, 114–15; John Tulloch and Manuel Alvarado, *Doctor Who: The Unfolding Text* (London, 1983), pp. 212–13; *The Times*, 10 October 1977.

31. Alexander Walker, *National Heroes: British Cinema in the Seventies and Eighties* (London, 1985), pp. 19–21; James Chapman, *Licence to Thrill: A Cultural History of the James Bond Films* (London, 1999), pp. 118–19; *People* [US], 18 July 1983.

32. Richard Webber, *Fifty Years of Carry On* (London, 2008), pp. 129–32; Leon Hunt, *British Low Culture: From Safari Suits to Sexploitation* (London, 1998), pp. 39–40.

33. Ann Oakley, *Housewife* (London, 1974), pp. 143–4.

34. Ibid., pp. 238–40; Michael Young and Peter Willmott, *The Symmetrical Family: A Study of Work and Leisure in the London Region* (London, 1973), p. 113; Jane Lewis, *Women in Britain Since 1945* (Oxford, 1992), p. 88; Peter Clarke, *Hope and Glory: Britain 1900–1990* (London, 1996), p. 365.

35. Oakley, *Housewife*, pp. 99–101, 144–5, 147–8, 150–52.

36. Ibid., pp. 142, 153–5.

37. Ibid., pp. 108–9, 111, 113; Ingham, *Now We Are Thirty*, pp. 136–7, 139.

38. Ina Zweiniger-Bargielowska, 'Housewifery', in Ina Zweiniger-Bargielowska (ed.), *Women in Twentieth-Century Britain* (Harlow, 2001), p. 153; Wilson, *Only Halfway to Paradise*, p. 40; Hera Cook, *The Long Sexual Revolution: English Women, Sex and Contraception 1800–1975* (Oxford, 2005), p. 336.

39. Joe Moran, *Queuing for Beginners: The Story of Daily Life from Breakfast to Bedtime* (London, 2007), p. 39; *Daily Mirror*, 12 August 1965; Jackson, *Working-Class Community*, pp. 86–8.

40. *Daily Mirror*, 5 June 1970; Turner, *Crisis? What Crisis?*, p. 112; Sandra Stanley Holton, 'The Women's Movement, Politics and Citizenship, 1960s-2000', in Zweiniger-Bargielowska (ed.), *Women in Twentieth-Century Britain*, pp. 282–3; *Time*, 2 February 1976; *New Society*, 23 August 1979; Rowbotham, *A Century of Women*, pp. 404–6, 413–14; Chris Wrigley, 'Women in the Labour Market and in the Unions', in John McIlroy, Nina Campbell and Alan Fishman (eds.), *The High Tide of British Trade Unionism: Trade Unions and Industrial Politics, 1964–1979* (Monmouth, 2007), p. 56; *Sunday Times*, 1 February 1970.

41. Tony Benn, *Office Without Power: Diaries 1968–72* (London, 1988), p. 427; Wrigley, 'Women in the Labour Market and in the Unions', pp. 56–7, 59–60, 66; Rowbotham, *A Century of Women*, pp. 414–18.

42. David Childs, *Britain Since 1945: A Political History* (London, 1979), pp. 276–7; *Time*, 2 February 1976; *The Times*, 3 May 1972, 6 May 1972, 9 May 1972, 27 March 1973, 16 June 1973; Christopher Andrew, *The Defence of the Realm: The Authorized History of MI5* (London, 2009), pp. 550–51; David Kynaston, *The City of London*, vol. 4: *A Club No More, 1945–2000* (London, 2001), p. 420.

43. *Cosmopolitan*, February 1978; Lawrence James, *The Middle Class: A History* (London, 2006), p. 554; Christopher Booker, *The Seventies: Portrait of a Decade* (London, 1980), pp. 136–41.

44. Jackson, *Working-Class Community*, p. 167; Young and Willmott, *The Symmetrical Family*, pp. 95, 115; Oakley, *Housewife*, p. 93.

45. Kate Colquhoun, *Taste: The Story of Britain Through Its Cooking* (London, 2007), pp. 354–5; various *Shoot* articles reprinted in Barney Ronay (ed.), *Studs!: The Greatest Retro Football Annual The World Has Ever Seen* (London, 2006); Hunter Davies, *The Glory Game* (London, 1972), pp. 96, 325–9.

46. Ibid., p. 248; Marnie Fogg, *Boutique: A '60s Cultural Phenomenon* (London, 2003), pp. 74–5; Howard Sounes, *Seventies: The Sights, Sounds and Ideas of a Brilliant Decade* (London, 2006), pp. 18, 27; Hunt, *British Low Culture*, pp. 60–63, 66.

47. James Chapman, *Saints and Avengers: British Adventure Series of the 1960s* (London, 2002), pp. 214–15; Davies, *The Glory Game*, p. 114.

48. Ibid., pp. 25, 27; Phil Wickham, *The Likely Lads* (Basingstoke, 2008), pp. 54–5; Graham McCann, *Fawlty Towers: The Story of Britain's Favourite Sitcom* (London, 2007), p. 179.

49. *NME*, 26 August 1972; *Plays and Players*, November 1972; Sounes, *Seventies*,

pp. 145–6, 156; James Miller, *Flowers in the Dustbin: The Rise of Rock and Roll, 1947–1977* (New York, 1999), pp. 298–9.

50. Barney Hoskyns, *Glam! Bowie, Bolan and the Glitter Rock Revolution* (London, 1998), pp. 10–14; Sounes, *Seventies*, pp. 140, 146–7; Hunt, *British Low Culture*, pp. 4, 11, 58; Dave Haslam, *Not Abba: The Real Story of the 1970s* (London, 2005), pp. 30–31.

51. *NME*, 3 April 1971, 27 January 1973; *Melody Maker*, 22 January 1972, 12 March 1973; *Rolling Stone*, 1 April 1971. Bowie in 1993 is quoted at http://www.5years.com/shape.htm.

52. *Melody Maker*, 20 November 1971, 1 July 1972, 14 July 1973; George Tremlett, *The Slade Story* (London, 1975), p. 49; Haslam, *Not Abba*, p. 132; David Robins and Philip Cohen, *Knuckle Sandwich: Growing Up in the Working-class City* (Harmondsworth, 1978), p. 81.

53. Dominic Sandbrook, *White Heat: A History of Britain in the Swinging Sixties* (London, 2006), pp. 495–6; Jeffrey Weeks, *Sex, Politics and Society: The Regulation of Society Since 1800* (Harlow, 1989), pp. 285–6; Green, *Days in the Life*, pp. 378–9; Beckett, *When the Lights Went Out*, pp. 210–12, 215.

54. 'Poove Power', in *Private Eyesores* (London, 1970).

55. Green, *All Dressed Up*, pp. 393–4; Beckett, *When the Lights Went Out*, pp. 219–20; Weeks, *Sex, Politics and Society*, p. 286; Raban, *Soft City*, pp. 200–201.

56. Margaret Drabble, *Angus Wilson, A Biography* (London, 1995), pp. 415–17; Turner, *Crisis? What Crisis?*, p. 244; Nigel Nicolson, *Portrait of a Marriage* (London, 1973); Michael Tracey and David Morrison, *Whitehouse* (London, 1979), p. 173.

57. Turner, *Crisis? What Crisis?*, pp. 243–4; *Sunday Telegraph*, 24 June 1979.

58. Stephen Poliakoff, *Strawberry Fields* (London, 1977), p. 25; *Gay News*, 20 November 1975; Robert J. Wybrow, *Britain Speaks Out, 1937–87: A Social History as Seen Through the Gallup Data* (London, 1989), p. 116; Drabble, *Angus Wilson*, pp. 482, 486; Weeks, *Sex, Politics and Society*, p. 275; *The Times*, 20 January 1970, 5 February 1970, 26 January 1978.

59. Eric Dunning, Patrick Murphy and John M. Williams, *The Roots of Football Hooliganism: A Historical and Sociological Study* (London, 1988), pp. 169–71, 187; Richard Holt, *Sport and the British: A Modern History* (Oxford, 1990), pp. 330, 337, 339.

60. Peter Everett, *You'll Never Be 16 Again: An Illustrated History of the British Teenager* (London, 1986), p. 104; Pete Fowler, 'Skins Rule', in Charlie Gillett (ed.), *Rock File* (London, 1972), p. 15; Turner, *Crisis? What Crisis?*, pp. 62–3.

61. Trevor Griffiths, *Comedians* (London, 1976), p. 41; Kynaston, *A Club No More*, p. 425; Castle, *The Castle Diaries, 1964–70*, p. 486.

62. Phillip Whitehead, *The Writing on the Wall: Britain in the Seventies* (London, 1985), p. 223 (photograph facing page); Elizabeth Wilson, *Adorned in Dreams: Fashion and Modernity* (London, 1985), p. 241; *Guardian*, 7 February 1973.

63. Angela McRobbie, *Feminism and Youth Culture: From Jackie to Just Seventeen* (Basingstoke, 1991), pp. 67–115; Pressley, *The Seventies*, p. 49. The *Shoot* story from 1970 is reprinted in the *Studs!* anthology.

64. Hunt, *British Low Culture*, pp. 41–3, 46–7.

65. Chapman, *Saints and Avengers*, pp. 235–6; Hunt, *British Low Culture*, pp. 71–2.

66. Humphrey Carpenter, *Dennis Potter: A Biography* (London, 1998), pp. 309–17.

67. Hunt, *British Low Culture*, pp. 44, 154; Pamela Church Gibson and Andrew Hill, '"Tutto e Marchio!": Excess, Masquerade and Performativity in 70s Cinema', in Robert Murphy (ed.), *The British Cinema Book* (London, 2001), pp. 263–4.

68. Zachary Leader, *The Life of Kingsley Amis* (London, 2006), pp. 666–7, 670–83; Neil Powell, *Amis and Son* (London, 2009), pp. 195–201; Kingsley Amis, *Jake's Thing* (London, 1978), pp. 197–8, 269.

69. Leader, *The Life of Kingsley Amis*, pp. 725–33; Powell, *Amis and Son*, p. 220; Zachary Leader (ed.), *The Letters of Kingsley Amis* (London, 2000), p. 955.

70. Pamela Kettle, *The Day of the Women* (London, 1970); *Science Fiction Monthly*, 2:4 (1975), transcript online at http://www.bondle.co.uk/edmund_cooper/misc_files/interview.pdf.

71. Edmund Cooper, *Five to Twelve* (London, 1969); Edmund Cooper, *Who Needs Men?* (London, 1973); Turner, *Crisis? What Crisis?*, p. 114; and see Turner's entertaining pulp fiction website, http://www.trashfiction.co.uk/index2.

72. Setch, 'The Face of Metropolitan Feminism', pp. 184–5, 188; Rowbotham, *A Century of Women*, pp. 404, 407, 431; Curtis, 'Older Women and Feminism', pp. 144–5.

73. Oakley, *Housewife*, p. 141.

74. Pressley, *The Seventies*, p. 100; Ingham, *Now We Are Thirty*, pp. 132, 134; Hunter Davies, *The Creighton Report* (London, 1977), p. 95.

75. *The Times*, 23 December 1981; Rowbotham, *A Century of Women*, pp. 399–400, 413–14; Wrigley, 'Women in the Labour Market and in the Unions', p. 56; Whitehead, *The Writing on the Wall*, p. 313; Ingham, *Now We Are Thirty*, p. 136; Rowbotham, *Dreams and Dilemmas*, p. 93.

76. *The Times*, 10 November 1978; Hannah Hamad, 'Butterflies', http://www.screenonline.org.uk/tv/id/1180242/.

77. Beatrix Campbell, *The Iron Ladies: Why Do Women Vote Tory?* (London, 1987), pp. 160–61; Patrick Cosgrave, *Margaret Thatcher* (London, 1978), p. 14.

78. Margaret Thatcher Foundation [MTF] online archive, Document 103662, Thatcher interview for *Hornsey Journal*, 21 April 1978.

79. MTF 100936, *Sunday Graphic*, 17 February 1952; Campbell, *The Grocer's Daughter*, p. 96; MTF 100939, *Onward*, April 1954.

80. E. H. H. Green, *Thatcher* (London, 2006) pp. 13–15.

81. MTF 103725, Speech on the fiftieth anniversary of equal female suffrage, 3 July 1978.

CHAPTER 11. THE RAVAGES OF PERMISSIVENESS

1. *The Times*, 17 April 1971; *Guardian*, 17 April 1971.

2. *Guardian*, 1 May 1971; *The Times*, 5 June 1971; *Time*, 10 September 1973; *Independent*, 28 July 1993; Elizabeth Wilson, *Only Halfway to Paradise: Women in Postwar Britain: 1945–1968* (London, 1980), pp. 105–6; David Limond, '"I Never Imagined That the Time Would Come": Martin Cole, the *Growing Up* Controversy and the Limits of School Sex Education in 1970s England', *History of Education*, 37:3 (May 2008), pp. 411–13.

3. Hansard, 21 April 1971; *The Times*, 29 April 1971, 25 April 1972; *Cherwell*, 31 October 1975; Limond, '"I Never Imagined That the Time Would Come"', pp. 417–21.

4. James Hampshire and Jane Lewis, '"The Ravages of Permissiveness": Sex Education and the Permissive Society', *Twentieth Century British History*, 15:3 (2004), pp. 291, 295–7, 303; Michael Schofield, *The Sexual Behaviour of Young People* (London, 1965), pp. 84–5; Hansard, 6 May 1971.

5. Hampshire and Lewis, '"The Ravages of Permissiveness"', pp. 292, 300; Larry Lamb, *Sunrise: The Remarkable Rise and Rise of the Bestselling Soaraway Sun* (London, 1989), p. 142; *Nova*, June 1972.

6. Jeffrey Weeks, *Sex, Politics and Society: The Regulation of Sexuality Since 1800* (Harlow, 1989), pp. 249–52; *Guardian*, 11 October 1967.

7. *New Society*, 27 November 1969; Weeks, *Sex, Politics and Society*, pp. 252–4; Schofield, *The Sexual Behaviour of Young People*, pp. 78, 99–102, 231; Geoffrey Gorer, *Sex and Marriage in England Today* (London, 1971), pp. 30, 44–5; and see Dominic Sandbrook, *White Heat: A History of Britain in the Swinging Sixties* (London, 2006), pp. 477–500.

8. Hera Cook, *The Long Sexual Revolution: English Women, Sex and Contraception 1800–1975* (Oxford, 2005), pp. 274–82, 290, 298; Paul Ferris, *Sex and the British: A Twentieth-Century History* (London, 1993), pp. 204–7; Gorer, *Sex and Marriage in England Today*, pp. 131–3, 216; Weeks, *Sex, Politics and Society*, p. 260; Christie Davies, *Permissive Britain: Social Change in the Sixties and Seventies* (London, 1975), p. 74; *Evening Standard*, 10 August 1971.

9. Weeks, *Sex, Politics and Society*, p. 260; Cate Haste, *Rules of Desire: Sex in Britain, World War I to the Present* (London, 1994), pp. 205–6, 237–8; Ferris, *Sex and the British*, pp. 207, 209; Cook, *The Long Sexual Revolution*, pp. 289–90, 335; Wilson, *Only Halfway to Paradise*, p. 97; 'Jane', 'Unwomanly and Unnatural: Some Thoughts on the Pill', in Sara Maitland (ed.), *Very Heaven: Looking Back at the 1960s* (London, 1988), p. 152.

10. *Sunday Times*, 27 February 1972; Ann Cartwright, *Parents and Family Planning Services* (London, 1970), p. 245; Wilson, *Only Halfway to Paradise*, p. 98; Cook, *The Long Sexual Revolution*, pp. 294, 337–8.

11. Ibid., pp. 318, 339; Haste, *Rules of Desire*, pp. 222, 186; Jeremy Seabrook, *City Close-Up* (Harmondsworth, 1973), p. 151.

12. Celia Haddon, *The Limits of Sex* (London, 1982), p. 84; John Sutherland, *Reading the Decades: Fifty Years of British History Through the Nation's Bestsellers* (London, 2002), pp. 10–12; Cook, *The Long Sexual Revolution*, p. 226; Alex Comfort, *The Joy of Sex: A Cordon Bleu Guide to Lovemaking* (New York, 1972), pp. 158, 248.

13. *Cosmopolitan*, March 1972, December 1978; Haste, *Rules of Desire*, p. 228; Lawrence James, *The Middle Class: A History* (London, 2006), p. 554.

14. Ferris, *Sex and the British*, p. 241; Kaye Wellings *et al.*, *Sexual Attitudes and Lifestyles* (Oxford, 1994), pp. 70, 115, 235; Cook, *The Long Sexual Revolution*, pp. 320, 327, 335; Mary Ingham, *Now We Are Thirty: Women of the Break-through Generation* (London, 1982), p. 133.

15. Jane Lewis, 'Marriage', in Ina Zweiniger-Bargielowska (ed.), *Women in Twentieth-Century Britain* (Harlow, 2001), p. 73; Peter Hitchens, *The Abolition of Britain: The British Cultural Revolution from Lady Chatterley to Tony Blair* (London, 2000), p. 189.

16. Ferris, *Sex and the British*, p. 189; Davies, *Permissive Britain*, pp. 26, 68, 72–3; Jean Morton Williams and Keith Hindell, *Abortion and Contraception: A Study of Patients' Attitudes* (London, 1972), pp. 55–6.

17. Weeks, *Sex, Politics and Society*, p. 276; Sheila Rowbotham, *A Century of Women: The History of Women in Britain and the United States* (London, 1999), pp. 428–9; Ingham, *Now We Are Thirty*, p. 179; Alison Pressley, *The Seventies: Good Times, Bad Taste* (London, 2002), pp. 74–5.

18. Graham Heath, *The Illusory Freedom: The Intellectual Origins and Social Consequences of the Sexual Revolution* (London, 1978); *19*, April 1982; Haste, *Rules of Desire*, p. 229; Pressley, *The Seventies*, pp. 74–5; Phillip Whitehead, *The Writing on The Wall: Britain in the Seventies* (London, 1985), p. 310.

19. Anthony Hayward, *Which Side Are You On? Ken Loach and his Films* (London, 2005), pp. 70–74, 123–8; *The Times*, 14 January 1972; Alexander Walker, *Hollywood, England: The British Film Industry in the Sixties* (London, 1974), pp. 381–3; *Socialist Worker*, 5 February 1972.

20. Gavin Miller, *R. D. Laing* (Edinburgh, 2005), pp. 7–64; R. D. Laing, *The Politics of Experience and the Bird of Paradise* (Harmondsworth, 1967); Robert Hewison, *Too Much: Art and Society in the Sixties, 1960–75* (London, 1986), p. 134.

21. Angela Carter, 'Truly, It Felt Like Year One', in Maitland (ed.), *Very Heaven*, p. 215; Jonathon Green, *All Dressed Up: The Sixties and the Counterculture* (London, 1998), pp. 202–5; and see Patricia Waugh, *Harvest of the Sixties: English Literature and its Background, 1960–1990* (Oxford, 1995), p. 6; Randall Stevenson, *The Oxford Literary History*, vol. 12: *1960–2000: The Last of England?*, p. 375.

22. *The Times*, 2 January 1968; Hitchens, *The Abolition of Britain*, pp. 224–5;

Lucy Mair, *Marriage* (Harmondsworth, 1971), p. 19; Mary Abbott, *Family Affairs: A History of the Family in Twentieth-Century England* (London, 2003), p. 124; Cook, *The Long Sexual Revolution*, pp. 286–7; Whitehead, *The Writing on the Wall*, p. 318; Ann Oakley, *Housewife* (London, 1974), p. 238.

23. Lewis, 'Marriage', pp. 71–5; Weeks, *Sex, Politics and Society*, p. 252; Haste, *Rules of Desire*, pp. 223–4; George L. Bernstein, *The Myth of Decline: The Rise of Britain Since 1945* (London, 2004), p. 303; Home Office, *Marriage Matters: A Consultative Document by the Working Party on Marriage Guidance* (London, 1979), p. 21; *Sunday Times*, 2 May 1982.

24. Wilson, *Only Halfway to Paradise*, p. 77; Hansard, 17 December 1968; Lewis, 'Marriage', p. 73; *Guardian*, 24 September 1979, 19 December 1979; Weeks, *Sex, Politics and Society*, p. 274; Haste, *Rules of Desire*, pp. 215, 226.

25. *Guardian*, 8 September 1975; Wilson, *Only Halfway to Paradise*, p. 75; Haste, *Rules of Desire*, pp. 286, 288; Ingham, *Now We Are Thirty*, p. 152; Abbott, *Family Affairs*, p. 141.

26. *Sunday Times*, 2 March 1980; Haste, *Rules of Desire*, pp. 226, 234–5, 287; Weeks, *Sex, Politics and Society*, p. 274.

27. *The Times*, 11 December 1969, 10 February 1970; Barry Cox, John Shirley and Martin Short, *The Fall of Scotland Yard* (Harmondsworth, 1977), pp. 143–4.

28. *Observer*, 15 August 1971; Cox, Shirley and Short, *The Fall of Scotland Yard*, pp. 160–61, 165.

29. *The Times*, 31 January 1973, 22 May 1974; *Sunday People*, 6 February 1972; Cox, Shirley and Short, *The Fall of Scotland Yard*, pp. 181–2, 184–5.

30. *The Times*, 23 December 1976, 12 May 1977, 14 May 1977; Cox, Shirley and Short, *The Fall of Scotland Yard*, pp. 158–9, 207–9.

31. Ibid., p. 162; Ferris, *Sex and the British*, p. 231; Bill Thompson, *Softcore* (London, 1994), p. 44; *Screen International*, 3 (1975); Leon Hunt, *British Low Culture: From Safari Suits to Sexploitation* (London, 1998), pp. 23–51.

32. Cox, Shirley and Short, *The Fall of Scotland Yard*, p. 163; *New Statesman*, 30 May 1975; *Report of the Committee on Obscenity and Film Censorship*, Cmnd. 7772 (London, 1979), pp. 44–5; Haste, *Rules of Desire*, p. 256; Mark Killick, *The Sultan of Sleaze: The Story of David Sullivan's Sex and Media Empire* (London, 1994), p. 23; Hunt, *British Low Culture*, pp. 129–30.

33. Lamb, *Sunrise*, pp. 140–41; Rebecca Loncraine, 'Bosom of the Nation: Page Three in the 1970s and 1980s', in Mina Gorji (ed.), *Rude Britannia* (London, 2007), pp. 96–103.

34. Ibid., p. 105; Roy Greenslade, *Press Gang: How Newspapers Make Profits from Propaganda* (London, 2004), pp. 258, 337.

35. Weeks, *Sex, Politics and Society*, p. 251; Hunt, *British Low Culture*, pp. 19–20, 24, 46–7; Colin Dexter, *Last Seen Wearing* (London, 1977), pp. 56–7.

36. Hunt, *British Low Culture*, p. 2; Stuart Laing, 'The Politics of Culture: Institutional Change in the 1970s', in Bart Moore-Gilbert (ed.), *The Arts in the 1970s: Cultural*

Closure? (London, 1994) p. 34; Alexander Walker, *National Heroes: British Cinema in the Seventies and Eighties* (London, 1985), pp. 30–32, 35; Haste, *Rules of Desire*, pp. 198–9; *Evening Standard*, 9 December 1970, 29 April 1971.

37. *The Times*, 23 July 1971; Walker, *National Heroes*, pp. 41–2; Pamela Church Gibson and Andrew Hill, '"Tutto e Marchio!": Excess, Masquerade and Performativity in 70s Cinema', in Robert Murphy (ed.), *The British Cinema Book* (London, 2001), p. 268.

38. Walker, *National Heroes*, pp. 42–3; Sheldon Hall, 'Under Siege: The Double Rape of *Straw Dogs*', in Robert Shail (ed.), *Seventies British Cinema* (London, 2008), pp. 130–32; *The Times*, 17 December 1971.

39. Walker, *National Heroes*, pp. 43–4, 48; *Sun*, 10 January 1972; *The Times*, 18 January 1972; Lewis Baston, *Reggie: The Life of Reginald Maudling* (Stroud, 2004), p. 395; and see Christian Bugge, 'The *Clockwork* Controversy', http://www.visual-memory.co.uk/amk/doc/0012.html.

40. Ali Catterall and Simon Wells, *Your Face Here: British Cult Movies Since the Sixties* (London, 2002), pp. 127–8; *Sun*, 6 January 1972; *Evening News*, 27 January 1972.

41. Catterall and Wells, *Your Face Here*, p. 128; Walker, *National Heroes*, pp. 48–9; *The Times*, 9 March 1972, 10 March 1972, 16 March 1972, 4 January 1975.

42. I. Q. Hunter, 'Take an Easy Ride: Sexploitation in the 1970s', in Shail (ed.), *Seventies British Cinema*, pp. 3, 5–7; *Films and Filming*, September 1974; Hunt, *British Low Culture*, pp. 112, 117–18, 120; and see the very funny account of these films in Matthew Sweet, *Shepperton Babylon: The Lost Worlds of British Cinema* (London, 2005), pp. 287–317.

43. *Guardian*, 21 September 2009; P. D. James, *An Unsuitable Job for a Woman* (Harmondsworth, 1974), p. 136; Alwyn W. Turner, *Crisis? What Crisis?: Britain in the 1970s* (London, 2008), pp. 250–52.

44. John Lahr, *Prick Up Your Ears: The Biography of Joe Orton* (Berkeley, 2000), p. 114; Richard Neville, *Play Power* (London, 1970), p. 74: Malcolm Bradbury, *The History Man* (London, 1977), pp. 46–7.

45. Hunter Davies, *The Glory Game* (London, 1972), p. 57; Haste, *Rules of Desire*, pp. 252, 255–6; Rowbotham, *A Century of Women*, p. 429; *Sunday Times*, 30 December 1973.

46. Ferris, *Sex and the British*, p. 246; Weeks, *Sex, Politics and Society*, p. 280; Michael Tracey and David Morrison, *Whitehouse* (London, 1979), p. 181; *The Times*, 30 January 1976.

47. *The Times*, 12 April 1971, 21 May 1971; and see Paul Johnson's entry on Longford in the *Oxford Dictionary of National Biography*.

48. *The Times*, 25 April 1971, 26 April 1971, 27 April 1971, 20 September 1972; Longford Committee Investigating Pornography, *Pornography: The Longford Report* (London, 1972).

49. Haste, *Rules of Desire*, p. 217; Weeks, *Sex, Politics and Society*, pp. 249, 279;

Sunday Express, 22 February 1970; Stuart Hall *et al.*, *Policing the Crisis: Mugging, the State and Law and Order* (Basingstoke, 1978), pp. 239–40, 250, 275, 287.

50. Weeks, *Sex, Politics and Society*, pp. 266–7; Baston, *Reggie*, pp. 390, 393–4, 396; *New Statesman*, 20 August 1971; Reginald Maudling, *Memoirs* (London, 1978), pp. 170–72.

51. *The Times*, 11 October 1969, 14 June 1971, 16 June 1971.

52. *The Times*, 16 June 1971; Dallas Cliff, 'Religion, Morality and the Middle Class', in Roger King and Neill Nugent (eds.), *Respectable Rebels: Middle Class Campaigns in Britain in the 1970s* (London, 1979), pp. 129, 130, 141, 148; Hampshire and Lewis, '"The Ravages of Permissiveness"', pp. 29–300; and see http://www.famyouth.org.uk/.

53. *The Times*, 12 July 1971, 10 September 1971; Max Caulfield, *Mary Whitehouse* (London, 1975), p. 182; Richard Ingrams, *Muggeridge: The Biography* (London, 1996), p. 217; Green, *All Dressed Up*, p. 348.

54. *The Times*, 10 September 1971; Ingrams, *Muggeridge*, pp. 217–18.

55. Hall *et al.*, *Policing the Crisis*, p. 286; Cliff, 'Religion, Morality and the Middle Class', p. 128; *The Times*, 28 September 1971.

56. Caulfield, *Mary Whitehouse*, pp. 45–6, 110, 127; *Daily Telegraph*, 24 November 2001; *Guardian*, 21 July 2006; and see Mary Warnock's excellent entry on Whitehouse in the *Oxford Dictionary of National Biography*.

57. Weeks, *Sex, Politics and Society*, p. 277; Caulfield, *Mary Whitehouse*, p. 142; Tracey and Morrison, *Whitehouse*, pp. 42–4.

58. *Independent*, 24 November 2001; Tracey and Morrison, *Whitehouse*, pp. 88–9; *The Times*, 24 May 2008.

59. *Independent*, 24 November 2001; *The Times*, 24 May 2008; Caulfield, *Mary Whitehouse*, p. 152; Tracey and Morrison, *Whitehouse*, p. 85; James Chapman, *Inside the TARDIS: The Worlds of Doctor Who* (London, 2006), pp. 112–14.

60. *Sun*, 26 March 1975; *The Times*, 18 April 1973; Caulfield, *Mary Whitehouse*, pp. 120, 170; Tracey and Morrison, *Whitehouse*, p. 145; Cliff, 'Religion, Morality and the Middle Class', pp. 128, 140; Seabrook, *City Close-Up*, pp. 98–9.

61. Mary Whitehouse, *Whatever Happened to Sex?* (London, 1977), pp. 71–2, 243; Cliff, 'Religion, Morality and the Middle Class', p. 136; Tracey and Morrison, *Whitehouse*, pp. 49, 64; *Daily Telegraph*, 19 September 1969.

62. Weeks, *Sex, Politics and Society*, pp. 277–9; Caulfield, *Mary Whitehouse*, pp. 4–5, 40; Tracey and Morrison, *Whitehouse*, pp. 55, 188–9, 198; Cliff, 'Religion, Morality and the Middle Class', pp. 129–30; Mary Whitehouse, *Who Does She Think She Is?* (London, 1972), p. 15. On the middle-class groups of the later 1970s, see the various essays in King and Nugent (eds.), *Respectable Rebels*.

63. Mark Garnett, *From Anger to Apathy: The British Experience Since 1975* (London, 2007), p. 183; Ingrams, *Muggeridge*, p. 213; Grace Davie, *Religion in Britain Since 1945: Believing Without Belonging* (Oxford, 1994), pp. 52, 61, 78–9; *The Times*, 1 October 1971.

64. Callum Brown, *The Death of Christian Britain* (London, 2001), pp. 179–80; Whitehouse, *Who Does She Think She Is?*, p. 11; Owen Chadwick, *Michael Ramsey: A Life* (London, 1990), p. 114.

65. Stevenson, *The Last of England*, pp. 239–40; C. B. Cox, 'Welsh Bards in Hard Times: Dylan Thomas and R. S. Thomas', in Boris Ford (ed.), *The New Pelican Guide to English Literature*, vol. 8: *From Orwell to Naipaul* (London, 1998), pp. 208–10; James Lees-Milne, *Diaries, 1971–1985* (London, 2008), pp. 114–15.

66. *Sunday Times*, 30 December 1973; James, *The Middle Class*, pp. 444–5; *The Times*, 19 October 1974, 23 October 1974; Ferris, *Sex and the British*, pp. 232–5.

67. Hampshire and Lewis, '"The Ravages of Permissiveness"', pp. 301, 307–9; Ferris, *Sex and the British*, pp. 208–9, 238, 243; Family Planning Association, *Too Great a Risk!* (1973), reprinted in Zweiniger-Bargielowska (ed.), *Women in Twentieth-Century Britain*, pp. 62–5.

68. Weeks, *Sex, Politics and Society*, pp. 273, 288, 296; James, *The Middle Class*, pp. 553–4; *Woman's Own*, 4 January 1975.

69. PRO PREM 15/1904, Sir John Stradling-Thomas to Francis Pym, 14 May 1973; the letter is also reproduced online at http://www.nationalarchives.gov. uk/releases/2004/nyo/scandal.htm.

70. *The Times*, 24 May 1973; 'Sex scandal Tory blamed pressure', http://news. bbc.co.uk/1/hi/uk/3360629.stm; *Daily Telegraph*, 2 January 2007.

71. *Daily Mail*, 26 January 2007: Matthew Parris, *Great Parliamentary Scandals: Four Centuries of Calumny, Smear and Innuendo* (London, 1995), pp. 170–72; Christopher Andrew, *The Defence of the Realm: The Authorized History of MI5* (London, 2009), p. 575.

72. PRO PREM 15/1904, Record of Meeting Chaired by Prime Minister, 18 May 1973; Parris, *Great Parliamentary Scandals*, p. 172; Andrew, *The Defence of the Realm*, pp. 575–6.

73. *Daily Mirror*, 24 May 1973; *The Times*, 25 May 1973, 30 May 1973; Hansard, 5 June 1973; 'Sex scandal Tory blamed pressure', http://news.bbc.co.uk/1/hi/ uk/3360629.stm; *Daily Telegraph*, 1 January 2004, 2 January 2007.

74. *The Times*, 26 May 1973; *Sunday Telegraph*, 27 May 1973.

75. *The Times*, 26 May 1973, 28 May 1973, 29 May 1973.

76. *The Times*, 25 May 1973, 28 May 1973; Parris, *Great Parliamentary Scandals*, p. 174.

77. *The Times*, 29 May 1973.

CHAPTER 12. NO SURRENDER

1. *The Times*, 5 January 1972, 6 January 1972; Tony Benn, *Office Without Power: Diaries 1968–72* (London, 1988), p. 366.

2. David McKittrick and David McVea, *Making Sense of the Troubles* (London, 2001), pp. 74–5.

3. Ibid., pp. 73–4; Richard English, *Armed Struggle: The History of the IRA* (London, 2003), p. 144; Lewis Baston, *Reggie: The Life of Reginald Maudling* (Stroud, 2004), pp. 389, 379.

4. Peter Taylor, *Brits: The War Against the IRA* (London, 2002), p. 75.

5. Peter Taylor, *Provos: The IRA and Sinn Fein* (London, 1998), p. 109; Kevin Myers, *Watching the Door: Cheating Death in 1970s Belfast* (London, 2008), p. x; Robin Neillands, *A Fighting Retreat: The British Empire 1947–1997* (London, 1997), p. 497.

6. Myers, *Watching the Door* p. 140; Taylor, *Provos*, pp. 96–7, 99; McKittrick and McVea, *Making Sense of the Troubles*, pp. 70–71; *The Times*, 2 September 1971.

7. Taylor, *Brits*, pp. 82–3; Taylor, *Provos*, pp. 114–15.

8. Ibid., p. 115; Taylor, *Brits*, pp. 84–6.

9. Ibid., pp. 87–8; *Guardian*, 13 March 2000, 29 March 2000; English, *Armed Struggle*, p. 154.

10. There are hundreds of narratives of Bloody Sunday. For good, balanced summaries, see Taylor, *Provos*, pp. 119–27; Taylor, *Brits*, pp. 95–108; and http://cain.ulst.ac.uk/events/bsunday/index.html, which has a detailed chronology and links to sources, eyewitness accounts and the special BBC, *Guardian* and Saville Inquiry websites. Father Daly is quoted in McKittrick and McVea, *Making Sense of the Troubles*, p. 77.

11. Taylor, *Provos*, pp. 116–18; Taylor, *Brits*, pp. 88–90.

12. Taylor, *Provos*, pp. 114–16, 118; Taylor, *Brits*, pp. 77–8, 89, 91–3, 105; *Irish News*, 26 January 1972.

13. Taylor, *Brits*, p. 101; Michael Asher, *Shoot to Kill: A Soldier's Journey Through Violence* (London, 1990), p. 65; *Daily Mail*, 20 April 1972; Liz Curtis, *Ireland, The Propaganda War: The Battle for Hearts and Minds* (London, 1984), p. 44; Baston, *Reggie*, p. 384.

14. Hansard, 31 January 1972; Baston, *Reggie*, pp. 384–5.

15. Conor Cruise O'Brien, *Memoir: My Life and Themes* (London, 1998), p. 335; English, *Armed Struggle*, p. 151; McKittrick and McVea, *Making Sense of the Troubles*, p. 771.

16. PRO CAB 128/48, CM (72) 5, Confidential Annex, 3 February 1972; PRO CAB 130/560, GEN 72 (47), 9 February 1972; PRO PREM 15/1004, Douglas-Home to Heath, 13 March 1972; Henry Patterson, *Ireland Since 1939: The Persistence of Conflict* (London, 2007), p. 221; McKittrick and McVea, *Making Sense of the Troubles*, pp. 79, 82–3; Baston, *Reggie*, p. 386.

17. *The Times*, 23 February 1972, 6 March 1972; Taylor, *Provos*, pp. 131, 136; English, *Armed Struggle*, p. 156.

18. *Sunday Times* Insight Team, *Ulster* (Harmondsworth, 1972), p. 305; Myers, *Watching the Door*, p. 166; BBC interviews, 5 October 1971, on the CD *BBC Eyewitness: 1970–1979* (2005); *The Times*, 21 March 1972; *Belfast Telegraph*, 21 March 1972; Taylor, *Provos*, p. 134; McKittrick and McVea, *Making Sense of the Troubles*, p. 78.

19. PRO CAB 128/48, CM (72) 18, Confidential Annex, 23 March 1972; William Whitelaw, *The Whitelaw Memoirs* (London, 1989), p. 80; text of speech by Brian Faulkner, 24 March 1972, at http://cain.ulst.ac.uk/events/directrule/faulkner 240372.htm; John Campbell, *Edward Heath: A Biography* (London, 1993), pp. 431–2; Patterson, *Ireland Since 1939*, pp. 224–5.

20. *The Times*, 25 March 1972.

21. *The Times*, 28 March 1972, 29 March 1972; Peter Taylor, *Loyalists* (London, 2000), pp. 98–9.

22. Ibid., p. 119; Mark Garnett and Ian Aitken, *Splendid! Splendid!: The Authorized Biography of Willie Whitelaw* (London, 2003), pp. 9, 91, 115; Ken Bloomfield, *Stormont in Crisis: A Memoir* (Belfast, 1994), p. 173.

23. Garnett and Aitken, *Splendid! Splendid!*, pp. 116–17; *The Times*, 3 December 1973.

24. Taylor, *Brits*, p. 113.

25. McKittrick and McVea, *Making Sense of the Troubles*, p. 89; Patterson, *Ireland Since 1939*, pp. 228–9.

26. *The Times*, 14 February 1972, 20 March 1972; Taylor, *Loyalists*, pp. 95–6; Patterson, *Ireland Since 1939*, p. 226.

27. *The Times*, 25 March 1972, 28 March 1972, 20 October 1972, 21 October 1972, 25 October 1972; and see Patterson, *Ireland Since 1939*, pp. 229–30.

28. McKittrick and McVea, *Making Sense of the Troubles*, p. 86; Bernard D. Nossiter, *Britain: A Future that Works* (London, 1978), pp. 159–60.

29. Taylor, *Loyalists*, pp. 100–101, 103; Myers, *Watching the Door*, pp. 87, 119.

30. Steve Bruce, *The Red Hand: Protestant Paramilitaries in Northern Ireland* (Oxford, 1991), p. 59.

31. PRO PREM 15/1016, Ronnie Custis to Christopher Roberts, 29 November 1972; Cecil King, *The Cecil King Diary 1970–1974* (London, 1975), pp. 99, 207; Taylor, *Loyalists*, p. 105; Tim Pat Coogan, *The Troubles: Ireland's Ordeal 1966–1996 and the Search for Peace* (London, 1996), p. 183; McKittrick and McVea, *Making Sense of the Troubles*, pp. 86–7.

32. Taylor, *Provos*, pp. 132, 135–8; Ben Pimlott, *Harold Wilson* (London, 1992), p. 593; *The Times*, 14 June 1972; Garnett and Aitken, *Splendid! Splendid!*, pp. 133–4; Taylor, *Brits*, pp. 119–21.

33. PRO PREM 15/1009, 'Note of a Meeting with Representatives of the Provisional IRA', 21 June 1972; Taylor, *Provos*, pp. 138–9.

34. Ibid., pp. 139–43; Garnett and Aitken, *Splendid! Splendid!*, pp. 136–8.

35. Taylor, *Provos*, p. 146; *The Times*, 10 July 1972; Taylor, *Loyalists*, pp. 106–7; Garnett and Aitken, *Splendid! Splendid!*, pp. 139–41.

36. Taylor, *Provos*, pp. 149–51; *The Times*, 22 July 1971.

37. Myers, *Watching the Door*, p. 65; English, *Armed Struggle*, p. 160; on the death toll, see the definitive index of casualties at http://cain.ulst.ac.uk/sutton/index.html.

38. Garnett and Aitken, *Splendid! Splendid!*, pp. 146–7, 152.

39. *The Times*, 21 March 1973; *The Economist*, 24 March 1973; Garnett and Aitken, *Splendid! Splendid!*, pp. 153–4; 'Northern Ireland Constitutional Proposals', Cmnd. 5259, at http://cain.ulst.ac.uk/hmso/cmd5259.htm.

40. *The Times*, 30 June 1973, 2 July 1973, 1 August 1973; McKittrick and McVea, *Making Sense of the Troubles*, pp. 92–4; Garnett and Aitken, *Splendid! Splendid!*, pp. 155–6; and for a detailed statistical breakdown of the Assembly election results, see http://cain.ulst.ac.uk/issues/politics/election/ra1973.htm.

41. Taylor, *Provos*, pp. 110–11; Myers, *Watching the Door*, p. 141; Patterson, *Ireland Since 1939*, pp. 227–8; Taylor, *Loyalists*, pp. 116, 118.

42. *The Times*, 22 November 1973, 23 November 1973, 10 December 1973, 11 December 1973; McKittrick and McVea, *Making Sense of the Troubles*, pp. 95–7; Garnett and Aitken, *Splendid! Splendid!*, pp. 158–63; text of the Sunningdale Agreement, 9 December 1973, at http://cain.ulst.ac.uk/events/sunningdale/agreement.htm.

43. Paul Arthur, 'The Heath Government and Northern Ireland', in Stuart Ball and Anthony Seldon (eds.), *The Heath Government, 1970–1974: A Reappraisal* (Harlow, 1996), pp. 236–7, 254–8; Patterson, *Ireland Since 1939*, pp. 240–41; Taylor, *Provos*, p. 160; Taylor, *Loyalists*, p. 121; *Irish Times*, 2 January 2004.

44. *The Times*, 5 January 1974, 23 January 1974; Taylor, *Loyalists*, p. 121.

45. For the Paisley quotation, see episode two of Peter Taylor's documentary series *Loyalists* (BBC, 1999).

46. *The Times*, 2 March 1974, 5 March 1974; McKittrick and McVea, *Making Sense of the Troubles*, pp. 100–101; Patterson, *Ireland Since 1939*, p. 242.

47. PRO FCO 87/334, 'Confidential Note for the Record', 5 March 1974.

CHAPTER 13. THE UNACCEPTABLE FACE OF CAPITALISM

1. Alan Ayckbourn, *Round and Round the Garden* (London, 1975), p. 7.

2. *The Times*, 4 July 1972; PRO CAB 128/50, CM (72) 36, 13 July 1972; Lewis Baston, *Reggie: The Life of Reginald Maudling* (Stroud, 2004), pp. 23–4, 176–7, 275–6, 284–6.

3. Hansard, 18 July 1972; *The Times*, 19 July 1972; Baston, *Reggie*, pp. 425–8.

4. *Daily Express*, *Sun* and *Mirror*, all 19 July 1972; *The Economist*, 22 July 1972; Baston, *Reggie*, pp. 428–9.

5. *The Times*, 14 June 1960; Peter Mandler, 'New Towns for Old: The Fate of the Town Centre', in Becky E. Conekin, Frank Mort and Chris Waters (eds.), *Moments of Modernity: Reconstructing Britain 1945–1964* (London, 1999), pp. 219–21; Baston, *Reggie*, p. 345; and see Dominic Sandbrook, *White Heat: A History of Britain in the Swinging Sixties* (London, 2006), pp. 624–5, 628–9.

6. See Ray Fitzwalter and Daniel Taylor, *Web of Corruption: The Full Story of John Poulson and T. Dan Smith* (London, 1981); Michael Gillard and Martin Tomkinson, *Nothing to Declare: The Political Corruptions of John Poulson* (London, 1981);

and see also Owen Luder's entry on Poulson in the *Oxford Dictionary of National Biography* and the summary in Baston, *Reggie*, pp. 272–5.

7. Ibid., pp. 264–5, 330–36.

8. Ibid., pp. 276–83, 286, 289, 297, 304–16, 327, 343, 415–16 and *passim*.

9. *The Times*, 8 January 1974, 12 February 1974, 4 February 1993.

10. Baston, *Reggie*, pp. 456, 494–5, 504–5; Margaret Thatcher, *The Path to Power* (London, 1995), p. 319; Reginald Maudling, *Memoirs* (London, 1978), p. 256.

11. *Sunday Times*, 4 December 1977; *The Times*, 22 November 1973, 19 June 1974, 22 June 1974; Patrick Dunleavy, *The Politics of Mass Housing in Britain, 1945–1975* (Oxford, 1981), pp. 292–4.

12. John Betjeman, 'Executive', in *Collected Poems* (London, 2001), p. 312; Clive Irving, *Pox Britannica: The Unmaking of the British* (New York, 1974), p. 9.

13. Patrick Marnham, *The Private Eye Story* (London, 1982), pp. 132–4.

14. Alexander Walker, *National Heroes: British Cinema in the Seventies and Eighties* (London, 1985), p. 52; Patricia Waugh, *Harvest of the Sixties: English Literature and its Background, 1960 to 1990* (Oxford, 1995), pp. 176–7; Michael Billington, *State of the Nation: British Theatre Since 1945* (London, 2007), pp. 217–18; Georg Gaston, 'Interview with David Hare', *Theatre Journal*, 45:2 (May 1993), p. 214.

15. Howard Brenton and David Hare, *Brassneck* (London, 1975), pp. 43, 92, 99; and see Adam Knowles, 'Memories of England: British Identity and the Rhetoric of Decline in Postwar British Drama, 1956–1982', unpublished Ph.D. dissertation, University of Texas at Austin, pp. 273–304.

16. David Hare, *Plays I* (London, 1996), pp. 234, 273–4, 291, 294; Billington, *State of the Nation*, pp. 218–19.

17. Hare, *Plays I*, pp. 274, 308–11; and see the discussion in Scott Fraser, *A Politic Theatre: The Plays of David Hare* (Amsterdam, 1996), pp. 112–23.

18. Anthony Sampson, *The New Anatomy of Britain* (London, 1971), p. 471; David Jordan, *Nile Green* (London, 1973), pp. 9, 91–3; David Kynaston, *The City of London*, vol. 4: *A Club No More, 1945–2000* (London, 2001), p. 416.

19. Jerry White, *London in the Twentieth Century* (London, 2001), pp. 209–10; Kynaston, *A Club No More*, pp. 401, 417–18, 422, 447.

20. Sampson, *The New Anatomy of Britain*, pp. 498–9; Irving, *Pox Britannica*, p. 115; Kynaston, *A Club No More*, pp. 350–53, 455; Michael Hope, 'On Being Taken Over By Slater Walker', *Journal of Industrial Economics*, 24:3 (March 1976), pp. 163–78; Charles Raw, *Slater Walker: An Investigation of a Financial Phenomenon* (London, 1977), pp. 222–42, 307.

21. Jonathan Aitken, *The Young Meteors* (New York, 1967), p. 183; *Sunday Telegraph*, 12 December 1971, 23 January 1972, 30 January 1972; Kynaston, *A Club No More*, pp. 453–4; Christopher Booker, *The Seventies: Portrait of a Decade* (London, 1980), p. 206.

22. Sampson, *The New Anatomy of Britain*, pp. 500–501; Irving, *Pox Britannica*, p. 120; Raw, *Slater Walker*, pp. 256, 260.

23. Sampson, *The New Anatomy of Britain*, p. 527; Alwyn W. Turner, *Crisis? What Crisis? Britain in the 1970s* (London, 2008), pp. 127–8; John Fiske and John Hartley, *Reading Television* (London, 1978), pp. 107–8. For Baker on Merroney, see http://www.freewebs.com/colinbaker/paulmerroneyqa.htm.

24. Kynaston, *A Club No More*, p. 452; *Financial Times*, 21 January 1972.

25. *The Times*, 23 February 1971, 28 June 1972, 29 June 1972, 25 June 1973, 19 January 1974, 12 February 1974.

26. *The Times*, 30 May 1972.

27. *Encounter*, October 1974; Walker, *National Heroes*, pp. 26, 75; David Edgar, *Destiny* (London, 1976), pp. 19, 31–2.

28. Marnham, *The Private Eye Story*, pp. 132–6; Anthony Sampson, *The Changing Anatomy of Britain* (London, 1983), pp. 367–9.

29. Ibid., pp. 369–71; *The Times*, 9 May 1973, 15 May 1973.

30. Hansard, 15 May 1973; Edward Heath, *The Course of my Life* (London, 1998), p. 418.

31. John Campbell, *Edward Heath: A Biography* (London, 1993), p. 528; Heath, *The Course of My Life*, p. 418.

32. *The Times*, 1 January 1973.

33. PRO CAB 128/51, CM (73) 2, 15 January 1973; PRO CAB 129/167, CP (73) 5, 'Prices and Pay – The Next Phase', 16 January 1973; *The Times*, 18 January 1973, 26 March 1973; Campbell, *Edward Heath*, pp. 531–2; Robert Taylor, 'The Heath Government and Industrial Relations', in Stuart Ball and Anthony Seldon (eds.), *The Heath Government, 1970–1974: A Reappraisal* (Harlow, 1996), pp. 182–3.

34. *The Times*, 18 January 1973, 2 May 1973; Richard Clutterbuck, *Britain in Agony: The Growth of Political Violence* (London, 1978), p. 93; Campbell, *Edward Heath*, pp. 532–3; *The Economist*, 31 March 1973.

35. Campbell, *Edward Heath*, pp. 535–6; Samuel Brittan, *The Economic Consequences of Democracy* (London, 1977), p. 59; Sir Alec Cairncross, 'The Heath Government and the British Economy', in Ball and Seldon (eds.), *The Heath Government*, p. 107; Richard Coopey and Nicholas Woodward, 'The British Economy in the 1970s', in Richard Coopey and Nicholas Woodward (eds.), *Britain in the 1970s: The Troubled Economy* (London, 1996), pp. 4–6; Max-Stephan Schulze and Nicholas Woodward, 'The Emergence of Rapid Inflation', in Coopey and Woodward (eds.), *Britain in the 1970s*, pp. 112–14.

36. Coopey and Woodward, 'The British Economy in the 1970s', p. 6; Schulze and Woodward, 'The Emergence of Rapid Inflation', p. 112; Alan Sked and Chris Cook, *Post-War Britain: A Political History* (London, 1988), pp. 257–8, 260; *The Times*, 19 April 1973; Kynaston, *A Club No More*, pp. 470–71.

37. Cairncross, 'The Heath Government and the British Economy', pp. 118, 121, 125–6; David Smith, *The Rise and Fall of Monetarism: The Theory and Politics of an Economic Experiment* (London, 1991), pp. 40–41, 60; Schulze and Woodward, 'The Emergence of Rapid Inflation', pp. 112, 116–19; *Banker*,

September 1972; Kynaston, *A Club No More*, p. 460; David Smith, *From Boom to Bust: Trial and Error in British Economic Policy* (Harmondsworth, 1992), p. 14; *The Times*, 3 May 1973, 11 July 1973.

38. Campbell, *Edward Heath*, pp. 523–4, 530; Edmund Dell, *The Chancellors: A History of the Chancellors of the Exchequer, 1945–90* (London, 1996), p. 396; *The Times*, 7 March 1973, 7 May 1973, 28 July 1973; *Spectator*, 10 March 1973; *The Economist*, 1 September 1973.

39. Smith, *The Rise and Fall of Monetarism*, p. 59; *The Times*, 12 September 1973, 14 November 1973, 1 December 1973; Kynaston, *A Club No More*, pp. 484–5.

40. Douglas Hurd, *An End to Promises* (London, 1978), p. 112.

41. PRO CAB 128/153, CM (73) 45, 5 October 1973; PRO CAB 129/172, CP (73) 97, 'The Programme for Controlling Inflation – Consultative Document', 8 October 1973; PRO CAB 129/172, CP (73) 114, 'Price and Pay Code for Stage 3', 24 October 1973; *The Times*, 9 October 1973; *The Economist*, 13 October 1973; and see Clutterbuck, *Britain in Agony*, pp. 95–6.

42. *The Times*, 6 October 1973; *New Statesman*, 12 October 1973; Campbell, *Edward Heath*, pp. 537–8; Dilwyn Porter, 'Government and the Economy', in Coopey and Woodward (eds.), *Britain in the 1970s*, pp. 41–2; Dell, *The Chancellors*, p. 398.

43. *New York Times*, 16 October 1973, 17 October 1973; Daniel Yergin, *The Prize: The Epic Quest for Oil, Money, and Power* (New York, 1992), pp. 597, 601, 603–6.

44. *New York Times*, 20 May 1973, 8 July 1973, 4 September 1973, 23 September 1973; Yergin, *The Prize*, pp. 595–6, 598–9; Willy Brandt, *People and Politics: 1960–75* (London, 1978), pp. 466–7; Dell, *The Chancellors*, p. 397; *Sunday Express*, 3 June 1973; Baston, *Reggie*, p. 446.

45. Yergin, *The Prize*, pp. 623–4.

46. Smith, *The Rise and Fall of Monetarism*, p. 57; Coopey and Woodward, 'The British Economy in the 1970s', pp. 6–7; Clutterbuck, *Britain in Agony*, pp. 101–2; Phillip Whitehead, *The Writing on the Wall: Britain in the Seventies* (London, 1985), p. 105.

47. Paul Routledge, *Scargill: The Unauthorized Biography* (London, 1993), p. 89.

CHAPTER 14. WE HATE HUMANS

1. Rob Steen, *The Mavericks: English Football When Flair Wore Flares* (Edinburgh, 1995), p. 164.

2. *The Times*, 8 October 1973, 16 October 1973, 17 October 1973, 16 November 1973; *Sun*, 17 October 1973; David Winner, *Those Feet: An Intimate History of English Football* (London, 2006), pp. 138–9.

3. *The Times*, 1 May 1974, 2 May 1974, 9 May 1974; *Guardian*, 21 May 2009;

Leo McKinstry, *Sir Alf: A Major Reappraisal of the Life and Times of England's Greatest Football Manager* (London, 2007); Bernard Donoughue, *Downing Street Diary: With Harold Wilson in No. 10* (London, 2005), p. 112.

4. John Benson, *The Rise of Consumer Society in Britain, 1880–1980* (Harlow, 1994), p. 151; Martin Polley, *Moving the Goalposts: A History of Sport and Society since 1945* (London, 1998), pp. 71–2; Richard Holt, *Sport and the British: A Modern History* (Oxford, 1990), pp. 252–3.

5. Edward Heath, *The Course of My Life* (London, 1998), p. 10.

6. *Observer*, 31 July 1966; Roy Jenkins, *A Life at the Centre* (London, 1991), p. 301; Dominic Sandbrook, *White Heat: A History of Britain in the Swinging Sixties* (London, 2006), pp. 769–84.

7. David Downing, *The Best of Enemies: England v Germany, A Century of Footballing Rivalry* (London, 2000), pp. 133–6, 141–3; Winner, *Those Feet*, p. 138.

8. Downing, *The Best of Enemies*, pp. 144–5; Winner, *Those Feet*, p. 163.

9. *The Times*, 6 May 1972, 8 May 1972; Steen, *The Mavericks*, pp. 30, 32.

10. Hunter Davies, *The Glory Game* (London, 1972), pp. 15, 23, 310–12, 325–9; Duncan Hamilton, *Provided You Don't Kiss Me: 20 Years with Brian Clough* (London, 2008), p. 24; the *Shoot* features are reprinted in the amusing Barney Ronay (ed.), *Studs!* (London, 2006).

11. *The Times*, 30 April 1970, 10 May 1972, 17 May 1973; Rob Bagchi and Paul Rogerson, *The Unforgiven: The Story of Don Revie's Leeds United* (London, 2003).

12. *Observer*, 25 November 2007; Jimmy Greaves and Norman Giller, *Don't Shoot the Manager: The Revealing Story of England's Soccer Bosses* (London, 1994), p. 84; *The Times*, 26 July 1973; Bagchi and Rogerson, *The Unforgiven*, p. 194.

13. Arthur Hopcraft, *The Football Man: People and Passions in Soccer* (Harmondsworth, 1971), p. 90; Bagchi and Rogerson, *The Unforgiven*, p. 3; Andrew Mourant, *Don Revie: Portrait of a Footballing Enigma* (Edinburgh, 1990), pp. 43, 209; Greaves and Giller, *Don't Shoot the Manager*, p. 90.

14. Mourant, *Don Revie*, pp. 13, 19–20, 111, 208–9; Hopcraft, *The Football Man*, p. 89.

15. Mourant, *Don Revie*, pp. 12, 112, 28, 51; Bagchi and Rogerson, *The Unforgiven*, p. 152.

16. Hamilton, *Provided You Don't Kiss Me*, pp. 31, 35.

17. Brian Clough and John Sadler, *Clough: The Autobiography* (London, 1995), p. 95; *The Times*, 28 September 2004.

18. Hopcraft, *The Football Man*, pp. 19–21.

19. *The Times*, 8 January 1972, 11 January 1972, 20 May 1972, 22 May 1972; Gordon Burn, *Best and Edwards: Football, Fame and Oblivion* (London, 2006), pp. 80–82, 174, 181.

20. *Spectator*, 17 May 2006; *Guardian*, 21 May 2009; Steen, *The Mavericks*, p. 141.

21. Steen, *The Mavericks*, pp. 111, 119–20, 177; Winner, *Those Feet*, p. 33.

22. *The Times*, 29 April 1974.

23. Eric Dunning, Patrick Murphy and John M. Williams, *The Roots of Football Hooliganism: A Historical and Sociological Study* (London, 1988), pp. 174–5; David Robins and Philip Cohen, *Knuckle Sandwich: Growing Up in the Working-Class City* (Harmondsworth, 1978), pp. 150–51.

24. Dunning, Murphy and Williams, *The Roots of Football Hooliganism*, pp. 153, 174–5; *Observer*, 1 December 1974.

25. *The Times*, 23 January 1975, 22 April 1975, 18 August 1975; Mark Garnett, *From Anger to Apathy: The British Experience Since 1975* (London, 2007), p. 169.

26. Hopcraft, *The Football Man*, pp. 162–3; *Observer*, 3 January 1971; *The Times*, 4 January 1971, 6 January 1971; Hamilton, *Provided You Don't Kiss Me*, pp. 13–14.

27. Hopcraft, *The Football Man*, pp. 151–2, 154; Dunning, Murphy and Williams, *The Roots of Football Hooliganism*, pp. 17, 168–71, 173.

28. *The Times*, 22 September 1969, 25 September 1969, 27 September 1969; Dunning, Murphy and Williams, *The Roots of Football Hooliganism*, p. 173.

29. Peter Marsh, 'Life and Careers on the Soccer Terraces', in Roger Ingham *et al.*, *Football Hooliganism: The Wider Context* (London, 1978), pp. 61–82; Holt, *Sport and the British*, p. 340; Robins and Cohen, *Knuckle Sandwich*, p. 141; Davies, *The Glory Game*, p. 90.

30. *The Times*, 27 August 1974, 2 September 1974.

31. Dunning, Murphy and Williams, *The Roots of Football Hooliganism*, pp. 18, 186–9; Geoffrey Pearson, *Hooligan: A History of Respectable Fears* (London, 1983), pp. 220–21; Holt, *Sport and the British*, pp. 327–8; Hopcraft, *The Football Man*, pp. 156–7.

32. Holt, *Sport and the British*, p. 326; Dunning, Murphy and Williams, *The Roots of Football Hooliganism*, pp. 152–3, 176–7; *Daily Mirror*, 26 September 1967; *Daily Mail*, 12 September 1974; *Sun*, 27 October 1975.

33. Holt, *Sport and the British*, pp. 329, 336; *Time*, 17 April 1978; Dunning, Murphy and Williams, *The Roots of Football Hooliganism*, pp. 17, 155; Bernard D. Nossiter, *Britain: A Future that Works* (London, 1978), p. 177; Robins and Cohen, *Knuckle Sandwich*, pp. 102–3. For a splendidly dated view of hooliganism as working-class rebellion, see John Clarke, 'Football and Working-Class Fans: Tradition and Change', in Ingham *et al.*, *Football Hooliganism*, pp. 37–60.

34. Holt, *Sport and the British*, pp. 334–5, 342–3; Dunning, Murphy and Williams, *The Roots of Football Hooliganism*, p. 132; George L. Bernstein, *The Myth of Decline: The Rise of Britain Since 1945* (London, 2004), pp. 443–4.

35. Dave Haslam, *Not Abba: The Real Story of the 1970s* (London, 2005), pp. 167–9; *Daily Telegraph*, 5 May 1975; *The Times*, 1 September 1975, 2 September 1975.

36. *The Times*, 9 August 1975, 1 September 1975, 13 September 1975, 20 February 1976, 16 May 1977; *Sunday Times*, 31 August 1975; Haslam, *Not Abba*, pp. 170, 193; on fences, see *The Times*, 24 May 1974, 13 June 1974, 3 September 1976, 6 June 1977.

37. *Daily Telegraph*, 26 May 1972; *The Times*, 26 May 1972, 27 May 1972.

38. *The Times*, 29 May 1974, 30 May 1974, 31 May 1974.

39. Downing, *The Best of Enemies*, pp. 153–5; *The Times*, 30 May 1975, 31 May 1975.

40. *Spectator*, 11 June 1977.

41. *The Times*, 2 May 1974, 4 July 1974, 5 July 1974; Mourant, *Don Revie*, pp. 152–3, 157–9.

42. *The Times*, 5 February 1975, 21 August 1975; Mourant, *Don Revie*, pp. 157, 160, 163–4; Greaves and Giller, *Don't Shoot the Manager*, pp. 88–90, 95–7.

43. *The Times*, 18 November 1976; Mourant, *Don Revie*, pp. 171, 173; Steen, *The Mavericks*, pp. 39–40; Winner, *Those Feet*, p. 219.

44. Mourant, *Don Revie*, pp. 168, 174–5; Donoughue, *Downing Street Diary*, vol. 2: *With James Callaghan in No. 10* (London, 2008), p. 193.

45. *Daily Mail*, 12 July 1977, 13 July 1977; Mourant, *Don Revie*, pp. 176–7; *The Times*, 15 July 1977.

46. *Daily Mail*, 13 July 1977; *The Times*, 13 July 1977, 15 July 1977.

47. Steen, *The Mavericks*, p. 43; Mourant, *Don Revie*, pp. 178–86; *The Times*, 14 December 1979.

48. Mourant, *Don Revie*, pp. 64–5, 133–4, 204–5; Bagchi and Rogerson, *The Unforgiven*, pp. 166–7; Steen, *The Mavericks*, p. 44; *Observer*, 25 November 2007; Donoughue, *Downing Street Diary*, vol. 2, pp. 238, 249.

49. Winner, *Those Feet*, p. 148; *Sun*, 4 July 1977, 5 July 1977; Alwyn W. Turner, *Crisis? What Crisis?: Britain in the 1970s* (London, 2008), p. 190; *The Times*, 4 February 1975.

50. Leo McKinstry, *Geoff Boycott: A Cricketing Hero* (London, 2005), pp. 128, 141, 179–82.

51. *The Times*, 7 September 1976.

52. *Daily Mirror*, 6 June 1977; *The Times*, 6 June 1977; Graham McColl, '78: *How a Nation Lost the World Cup* (London, 2006), pp. 25–6, 198; Richard Weight, *Patriots: National Identity in Britain 1940–2000* (London, 2002), pp. 556–7; Norman Barrett, *The Daily Telegraph Football Chronicle* (London, 1993), p. 169.

CHAPTER 15. THE LAST DAYS OF POMPEII

1. Stephen Milligan, *The New Barons: Union Power in the 1970s* (London, 1976), pp. 116–18; Kenneth O. Morgan, *Labour People: Leaders and Lieutenants, Hardie to Kinnock* (Oxford, 1992), pp. 291–2; Nick Clarke, *The Shadow of a Nation: The Changing Face of Britain* (London, 2003), p. 168.

2. Michael Crick, *Scargill and the Miners*, (Harmondsworth, 1985), pp. 64–5; Richard Clutterbuck, *Britain in Agony: The Growth of Political Violence* (London, 1978), p. 96; Paul Routledge, *Scargill: The Unauthorized Biography* (London, 1993), p. 89; John Campbell, *Edward Heath: A Biography* (London, 1993), pp. 561–2; Joe Gormley, *Battered Cherub* (London, 1982), p. 124; Phillip Whitehead, *The Writing on the Wall: Britain in the Seventies* (London, 1985) p. 100.

3. Gormley, *Battered Cherub*, p. 127; Whitehead, *The Writing on the Wall*, pp. 101–2; *The Economist*, 13 October 1973; Campbell, *Edward Heath*, p. 564; Douglas Hurd, *An End to Promises* (London, 1978), p. 115.

4. Campbell, *Edward Heath*, pp. 561, 563, 565; Edward Heath, *The Course of My Life* (London, 1998), p. 503; *The Times*, 24 October 1973, 25 October 1973.

5. Clutterbuck, *Britain in Agony*, pp. 104–5; *The Times*, 12 November 1973, 13 November 1973; PRO CAB 128/53, CM (73) 55, 13 November 1973.

6. Hansard, 13 November 1973; *The Times*, 14 November 1973.

7. Hurd, *An End to Promises*, pp. 116–17; James Lees-Milne, *Diaries, 1971–1983* (London, 2008), p. 118; *Time*, 26 November 1973.

8. Whitehead, *The Writing on the Wall*, p. 104; Campbell, *Edward Heath*, p. 567.

9. *The Times*, 23 November 1973; Francis Wheen, *Strange Days Indeed: The Golden Age of Paranoia* (London, 2009), p. 185; David Butler and Dennis Kavanagh, *The British General Election of February 1974* (London, 1974), pp. 30–31; Clutterbuck, *Britain in Agony*, p. 105; *Time*, 24 December 1973.

10. Hurd, *An End to Promises*, pp. 118–20.

11. Ronald McIntosh, *Challenge to Democracy: Politics, Trade Union Power and Economic Failure in the 1970s* (London, 2006), pp. 5, 6, 22–3.

12. Ibid., pp. 6, 23, 24; *The Times*, 7 December 1973, 8 December 1973; Campbell, *Edward Heath*, pp. 568–9.

13. Ibid., pp. 569–70, 576–7; McIntosh, *Challenge to Democracy*, pp. 16, 25; Hurd, *An End to Promises*, p. 121; Simon Heffer, *Like the Roman: The Life of Enoch Powell* (London, 1998), p. 683; *Daily Telegraph*, 30 November 1973.

14. PRO CAB 129/173, CP (73) 136, 'Fuel and Electricity Supplies: Note by the Secretary of State for Trade and Industry', 3 December 1973; PRO CAB 128/53, CM (73) 59, 4 December 1973; Clutterbuck, *Britain in Agony*, p. 108; Campbell, *Edward Heath*, p. 571.

15. PRO CAB 128/53, CM (73) 60, 12 December 1973; PRO CAB 128/53, CM (73) 61, 13 December 1973; Hansard, 13 December 1973; *The Times*, 14 December 1973; Tony Benn, *Against the Tide: Diaries 1973–1976* (London, 1989), p. 77.

16. *The Times*, 14 December 1974; Hurd, *An End to Promises*, pp. 121–2; Michael Cockerell, *Live from Number Ten: The Inside Story of Prime Ministers and Television*, p. 193; Campbell, *Edward Heath*, pp. 572–3.

17. Ibid., p. 573.

18. Clutterbuck, *Britain in Agony*, p. 107; Ion Trewin (ed.), *The Hugo Young Papers: Thirty Years of British Politics – Off the Record* (London, 2008),

p.O68; Mark Garnett and Ian Aitken, *Splendid! Splendid! The Authorized Biography of Willie Whitelaw* (London, 2003), pp. 170–72.

19. Gormley, *Battered Cherub*, pp. 132–3, 135; Garnett and Aitken, *Sptendid! Splendid!*, pp. 174–5.

20. McIntosh, *Challenge to Democracy*, pp. 30–34.

21. Ibid., pp. 8, 19.

22. Benn, *Against the Tide*, p. 75; *Guardian*, 18 January 1974; Barbara Castle, *The Castle Diaries 1974–76* (London, 1980), p. 23; Adam Sisman, *A. J. P. Taylor: A Biography* (London, 1994), p. 369.

23. PRO CAB 129/173, CP (73) 139, 'Energy Situation: Public Expenditure Measures: A Note by the Chancellor of the Exchequer', 12 December 1973; PRO CAB 128/53, CP (73) 60, 12 December 1973.

24. Hansard, 17 December 1973; *The Times*, 18 December 1973; Edmun Dell, *The Chancellors: A History of the Chancellors of the Exchequer 1945–90* (London, 1996), p. 398; Nicholas Timmins, *The Five Giants: A Biography of the Welfare State* (London 1996), p. 308.

25. 'The Diaries of Smurfette', 25 December 1973, www.escape-to-the-seventies.com/Diaries; Clive Irving, *Pox Britannica: The Unmaking of the British* (New York, 1974), p. 238.

26. Wheen, *Strange Days Indeed*, p. 54; *The Times*, 24 December 1973; *Mojo*, November 2006; *Daily Telegraph*, 1 January 2004.

27. *The Times*, 19 December 1973; John Goodwin (ed.), *Peter Hall's Diaries: The Story of a Dramatic Battle* (London, 1983), p. 70; Russell Davies (ed.), *The Kenneth Williams Diaries* (London, 1993), p.77; Lees-Milne, *Diaries*, pp. 129, 124.

28. *Sunday Times* 23 December 1973; 20 January 1974; *The Times*, 24 December 1973, 26 September 1974; Wheen, *Strange Days Indeed*, pp. 201–2, 205.

29. *The Times*, 31 December 1973, 1 January 2005; *Time*, 21 January 1974; *Scotsman*, 17 August 2003.

30. Lees-Milne, *Diaries*, pp. 122, 135; Goodwin (ed.), *Peter Hall's Diaries*, p. 69; McIntosh, *Challenge to Democracy*, p. 61.

31. *Time*, 28 August 1972; *NME*, 4 October 1975; Ian MacDonald, *The People's Music* (London, 2003), pp. 142–3.

32. Cecil King, *The Cecil King Diary 1970–1974* (London, 1975), p. 332; Benn, *Against the Tide*, p. 87.

33. Andy Beckett, *When the Lights Went Out: Britain in the Seventies* (London, 2009), pp. 125–6, 139, 140; Butler and Kavanagh, *The British General Election of February 1974*, p. 33.

34. *The Times*, 24 December 1973, 21 December 1973; *Time*, 21 January 1974, 25 February 1974.

35. John A. Walker, *Left Shift: Radical Art in 1970s Britain* (London, 2002), p. 42; *Daily Mail*, 19 December 1973; Alwyn W. Turner, *Crisis? What Crisis? Britain in the 1970s* (London, 2008), pp. 21–2, 90.

36. Ibid., p. 21; Beckett, *When the Lights Went Out*, pp. 134–5; Daniel Yergin,

The Prize: The Epic Quest for Oil, Money, and Power (New York, 1992), p. 630; Campbell, *Edward Heath*, p. 574.

37. Campbell, *Edward Heath*, pp. 574–5; *Time*, 21 January 1974; PRO CAB 128/53, CM (74) 3, 17 January 1974.

38. *New Society*, 31 December 1974; Beckett, *When the Lights Went Out*, p. 145; Clutterbuck, *Britain in Agony*, p. 110; *Time*, 21 January 1974; *The Economist*, 12 January 1974, 2 February 1974; *Sunday Times*, 6 January 1974.

39. *The Times*, 4 January 1974; *Daily Mail*, 21 January 1974; Beckett, *When the Lights Went Out*, pp. 142–4.

40. *New Statesman*, 4 January 1974; Campbell, *Edward Heath*, p. 575; Hurd, *An End to Promises*, p. 80; Davies (ed.), *The Kenneth Williams Diaries*, pp. 465–6; James Chapman, *Inside the TARDIS: The Worlds of Doctor Who* (London, 2006), pp. 94–5.

41. Campbell, *Edward Heath*, pp. 576–7; Wheen, *Strange Days Indeed*, p. 48.

42. *Private Eye*, 3 November 1972; Dennis Kavanagh, 'The Fatal Choice: The Calling of the February 1974 Election', in Stuart Ball and Anthony Seldon (eds.), *The Heath Government 1970–1974: A Reappraisal* (Harlow, 1996), pp. 355–7; Hurd, *An End to Promises*, pp. 119–20, 122; Campbell, *Edward Heath*, p. 577.

43. *The Times*, 7 December 1973, 12 December 1973, 17 December 1973; Butler and Kavanagh, *The British General Election of February 1974*, pp. 28–9; Campbell, *Edward Heath*, pp. 577–8.

44. Ibid., pp. 578–9; Hurd, *An End to Promises*, pp. 123–4.

45. McIntosh, *Challenge to Democracy*, pp. 42–5, 52; Gerald A. Dorfman, *Government versus Trade Unionism in British Politics Since 1968* (London 1979), p. 98; Stephen Fay and Hugo Young, *The Fall of Heath* (London, 1976), p. 20; Campbell, *Edward Heath*, p. 580.

46. McIntosh, *Challenge to Democracy*, p. 45; *The Times*, 10 January 1974; Whitehead, *The Writing on the Wall*, p. 107; Campbell, *Edward Heath*, p. 581.

47. Whitehead, *The Writing on the Wall*, p. 107; Robert Taylor, 'The Heath Government and Industrial Relations', in Ball and Seldon (eds.), *The Heath Government*, pp. 186–7; Campbell, *Edward Heath*, pp. 580–84; Fay and Young, *The Fall of Heath*, p. 22.

48. Ibid., p. 22; Jim Prior, *A Balance of Power* (London, 1986), p. 92; Campbell, *Edward Heath*, pp. 583–4.

49. Trewin (ed.), *The Hugo Young Papers*, pp. 30–31, 82; Taylor, 'The Heath Government and Industrial Relations', p. 186; Fay and Young, *The Fall of Heath*, p. 22; Campbell, *Edward Heath*, pp. 584–5.

50. Benn, *Against the Tide*, p. 90; Kavanagh, 'The Fatal Choice', p. 360; Campbell, *Edward Heath*, pp. 585–6; *The Times*, 14 January 1974.

51. Kavanagh, 'The Fatal Choice', p. 364; Trewin (ed.), *The Hugo Young Papers*, pp. 61–2; Hurd, *An End to Promises*, pp. 126–7; Garnett and Aitken, *Splendid! Splendid!*, p. 178.

52. Prior, *A Balance of Power*, p. 92; Trewin (ed.), *The Hugo Young Papers*, p. 63; Whitehead. *The Writing on the Wall*, p. 109.

53. Alan Clark, *Diaries: Into Politics*, ed. Ion Trewin (London, 2001), pp. 39–40.

54. Gormley, *Battered Cherub*, p. 139; *The Times*, 24 January 1974, 25 January 1974; Campbell, *Edward Heath*, p. 588; Whitehead, *The Writing on the Wall*, p. 109; Kevin Jefferys, *Finest and Darkest Hours: The Decisive Events in British Politics from Churchill to Blair* (London, 2002), p. 175; *Time*, 11 February 1974; *The Times*, 10 January 1974.

55. *The Times*, 28 January 1974, 5 February 1974; Campbell, *Edward Heath*, pp. 592–3; Hurd, *An End to Promises*, p. 132.

56. Hansard, 6 February 1974; Prior, *A Balance of Power*, p. 90; Trewin (ed.), *The Hugo Young Papers*, p. 78.

57. Hurd, *An End to Promises*, p. 131; *Spectator*, 31 January 1974; Whitehead, *The Writing on the Wall*, p. 110; Wheen, *Strange Days Indeed*, pp. 61–2; Trewin (ed.), *The Hugo Young Papers*, pp. 76, 78, 79, 82–3; McIntosh, *Challenge to Democracy*, pp. 68, 71.

58. Hansard, 6 February 1974; *The Times*, 6 February 1974, 7 February 1974, 8 February 1974; Butler and Kavanagh, *The British General Election of February 1974*, pp. 43, 146; Benn, *Against the Tide*, p. 105; Castle, *The Castle Diaries 1974–76*, p. 28.

59. *The Times*, 8 February 1974; Butler and Kavanagh, *The British General Election of February 1974*, p. 73; Campbell, *Edward Heath*, pp. 595–6.

CHAPTER 16. THE CRISIS ELECTION

1. *The Times*, 5 February 1974, 6 February 1974; 'Tragedy on the M62', http://www.bbc.co.uk/bradford/content/articles/2006/11/29/m62_bombing_feature.shtml; 'M62 bomb blast memorial unveiled', BBC News, 4 February 2009, http://news.bbc.co.uk/1/hi/england/bradford/7869077.stm.

2. *The Times*, 13 February 1974, 21 March 1974.

3. *The Times*, 8 February 1974; John Campbell, *Edward Heath: A Biography* (London, 1993), p. 595; David Butler and Dennis Kavanagh, *The British General Election of February 1974* (London, 1974), pp. 145, 140–41; Anthony King and Robert J. Wybrow (eds.), *British Political Opinion: 1937–2000* (London, 2001), p. 312; *Guardian*, 8 February 1974.

4. *The Times*, 11 February 1974, 12 February 1974; Michael Cockerell, *Live from Number Ten: The Inside Story of Prime Ministers and Television* (London, 1989), p. 195; Stuart Ball, 'The Conservative Party and the Heath Government', in Stuart Ball and Anthony Seldon (eds.), *The Heath Government, 1970–1974: A Reappraisal* (Harlow, 1996), p. 346; Dennis Kavanagh, 'The Fatal Choice', in Ball and Seldon (eds.), *The Heath Government* p. 358.

5. Cockerell, *Live from Number Ten*, p. 199; Butler and Kavanagh, *The British General Election of February 1974*, p. 160.

6. Kavanagh, 'The Fatal Choice', p. 358; Campbell, *Edward Heath*, pp. 598, 600–601, 603, 605; *The Times*, 21 February 1974; John Ramsden, *An Appetite for Power: The History of the Conservative Party Since 1830* (London, 1999), p. 412.

7. Butler and Kavanagh, *The British General Election of February 1974*, pp. 50–51. The text of the manifesto is reproduced in *The Times*, 9 February 1974, and at http://www.labour-party.org.uk/manifestos/1974/feb/.

8. Michael Hatfield, *The House the Left Built: Inside Labour Policy Making 1970–1975* (London, 1978), esp. pp. 171–229; Tony Benn, *Against the Tide: Diaries 1973–1976* (London, 1989), pp. 11, 15, 23–4, 26, 56.

9. Stuart Holland, 'The Industrial Strategy', in Anthony Seldon and Kevin Hickson (eds.), *New Labour, Old Labour: The Wilson and Callaghan Governments, 1974–1979* (London, 2004), pp. 297–9; Tony Benn, *Office Without Power: Diaries 1968–72* (London, 1988), pp. 448–9, 457; *Sunday Express*, 8 October 1972; *The Times*, 14 February 1973; *Observer*, 18 February 1973; *Sunday Telegraph*, 13 May 1973; Benn, *Against the Tide*, pp. 6–7, 32, 42, 50, 54.

10. *Banker*, February 1974, quoted in David Kynaston, *The City of London*, vol. 4: *A Club No More, 1945–2000* (London, 2001), pp. 490–91.

11. Ibid., pp. 483–5; Simon Gunn and Rachel Bell, *Middle Classes: Their Rise and Sprawl* (London, 2003), p. 208.

12. Kynaston, *A Club No More*, pp. 488–90; Keith Middlemas, *Power, Competition and the State*, vol. 3: *The End of the Postwar Era: Britain Since 1974* (Basingstoke, 1991), pp. 10, 14, 30, 33; *The Times*, 16 January 1974, 25 March 1974.

13. Hansard, 19 December 1973; *The Times*, 19 February 1974; Edward Pearce, *Denis Healey: A Life in Our Times* (London, 2002), pp. 403, 406; *Daily Express*, 23 January 1974; *Daily Mail*, 25 February 1974.

14. Hatfield, *The House the Left Built*, pp. 193, 197, 207, 228–9; Benn, *Against the Tide*, pp. 46–9, 62.

15. Philip Ziegler, *Wilson: The Authorized Life* (London, 1993), pp. 401–2; Ben Pimlott, *Harold Wilson* (London, 1992), p. 610; Butler and Kavanagh, *The British General Election of February 1974*, pp. 125, 161–2; Campbell, *Edward Heath*, p. 609; Benn, *Against the Tide*, p. 97; David Owen, *Time to Declare* (London, 1992), p. 224; Roy Jenkins, *A Life at the Centre* (London, 1991), p. 364.

16. Butler and Kavanagh, *The British General Election of February 1974*, pp. 147, 172, 174; Larry Lamb, *Sunrise: The Remarkable Rise and Rise of the Bestselling Soaraway Sun* (London, 1989), p. 172; Roy Greenslade, *Press Gang: How Newspapers Make Profits from Propaganda* (London, 2004), pp. 289–90.

17. *Daily Mail*, 4 January 1974, 7 January 1974, 28 February 1974; Benn, *Against the Tide*, pp. 87, 109; *Evening Standard*, 27 February 1974; *Evening News*, 20 February 1974; and see Stephen Dorril and Robin Ramsay, *Smear! Wilson and the Secret State* (London, 1992), p. 231.

18. Campbell, *Edward Heath*, pp. 598, 604; Butler and Kavanagh, *The British General Election of February 1974*, pp. 93, 83; *The Times*, 23 February 1974; King and Wybrow (eds.), *British Political Opinion*, p. 28; *Financial Times*, 15 February 1974.

19. Benn, *Against the Tide*, pp. 106, 109; Cockerell, *Live from Number Ten*, p. 198; Bernard Donoughue, *The Heat of the Kitchen: An Autobiography* (London, 2003), pp. 109, 115; and see Pimlott, *Harold Wilson*, pp. 608–9; Ziegler, *Wilson*, pp. 404–5.

20. Ivor Crewe and Anthony King, *SDP: The Birth, Life and Death of the Social Democratic Party* (Oxford, 1995), pp. 10–11; Butler and Kavanagh, *The British General Election of February 1974*, pp. 26, 53, 80, 130; Cockerell, *Live from Number Ten*, p. 200.

21. Richard Clutterbuck, *Britain in Agony: The Growth of Political Violence* (London, 1978), p. 112; Jim Prior, *A Balance of Power* (London, 1986), p. 93; Butler and Kavanagh, *The British General Election of February 1974*, pp. 67, 72.

22. *The Times*, 16 February 1974; Campbell, *Edward Heath*, p. 606; Butler and Kavanagh, *The British General Election of February 1974*, pp. 97, 139, 186; Ramsden, *An Appetite for Power*, p. 412.

23. *The Times*, 22 February 1974, 26 February 1974; *Daily Mail*, 22 February 1974; Butler and Kavanagh, *The British General Election of February 1974*, pp. 100–101, 91, 108–9; Campbell, *Edward Heath*, pp. 607, 610; Ronald McIntosh, *Challenge to Democracy: Politics, Trade Union Power and Economic Failure in the 1970s* (London, 2006), pp. 85–6.

24. *The Times*, 25 February 1974; Campbell, *Edward Heath*, p. 611; Jenkins, *A Life at the Centre*, p. 365; Donoughue, *The Heat of the Kitchen*, p. 112; *Daily Mirror*, 1 March 1974; Alwyn W. Turner, *Crisis? What Crisis? Britain in the 1970s* (London, 2008), p. 95.

25. Simon Heffer, *Like the Roman: The Life of Enoch Powell* (London, 1998), pp. 684, 693–4, 699–701; *The Times*, 16 January 1974, 8 February 1974.

26. Heffer, *Like the Roman*, pp. 701, 705–7; Pimlott, *Harold Wilson*, p. 611; *Daily Telegraph*, 24 February 1974.

27. Butler and Kavanagh, *The British General Election of February 1974*, pp. 194, 104; Heffer, *Like the Roman*, pp. 708–9; *The Times*, 26 February 1974.

28. *Sunday Express*, 24 February 1974; *The Times*, 26 February 1974, 27 February 1974; Campbell, *Edward Heath*, pp. 606, 608–9.

29. *The Times*, 26 February 1974, 27 February 1974; Cockerell, *Live from Number Ten*, pp. 202–3.

30. *Daily Express*, 28 February 1974; *Daily Mail*, 28 February 1974; Butler and Kavanagh, *The British General Election of February 1974*, pp. 110, 179; Greenslade, *Press Gang*, p. 290; Donoughue, *The Heat of the Kitchen*, p. 112; Bernard Donoughue, *Downing Street Diary: With Harold Wilson in No. 10* (London, 2005), pp. 41–2.

31. Ibid., pp. 41–3.

32. Ibid., p. 44; Donoughue, *The Heat of the Kitchen*, p. 114.

33. Campbell, *Edward Heath*, pp. 613–14; McIntosh, *Challenge to Democracy*, p. 151; Heffer, *Like the Roman*, pp. 710–11.

34. Butler and Kavanagh, *The British General Election of February 1974*, pp. 258–73.

35. Ball, 'The Conservative Party and the Heath Government,' p. 348; Butler and Kavanagh, *The British General Election of February 1974*, pp. 141, 259, 263–4, 271, 278, 280; Pimlott, *Harold Wilson*, p. 613; Vernon Bogdanor, 'The Fall of Heath and the End of the Postwar Settlement', in Ball and Seldon (eds.), *The Heath Government*, p. 378.

36. Prior, *A Balance of Power*, p. 95; Douglas Hurd, *An End to Promises* (London, 1978), p. 128; Kavanagh, 'The Fatal Choice', pp. 368, 370; McIntosh, *Challenge to Democracy*, pp. 166, 362.

37. Donoughue, *Downing Street Diary*, pp. 45–8; Donoughue, *The Heat of the Kitchen*, pp. 114, 117.

38. PRO PREM 16/231, 'Note for the Record: Events Leading to Mr Heath's Resignation on 4 March 1974', 16 March 1974; PRO CAB 128/53, CM (74) 9, 1 March 1974.

39. Donoughue, *Downing Street Diary*, p. 49; Pimlott, *Harold Wilson*, pp. 614–15; Joe Haines, *Glimmers of Twilight: Harold Wilson in Decline* (London, 1993), pp. 81–2; Barbara Castle, *The Castle Diaries 1974–76* (London, 1980), pp. 32–3.

40. PRO PREM 16/231, 'Note for the Record', 16 March 1974; PRO PREM 15/2069, '1974 Elections', Aide Memoire for Meeting with Mr Thorpe, 2 March 1974; PRO PREM 15/2069, '1974 Elections', Note of Meeting with Mr Thorpe, 2 March 1974; PRO PREM 15/2069, '1974 Elections', Armstrong to Heath, 2 March 1974.

41. PRO PREM 15/2069, '1974 Elections', Telephone Conversation between the Prime Minister and Mr Thorpe, 3 March 1974; PRO CAB 128/53, CM (74) 10, 3 March 1974; PRO PREM 16/231, 'Note for the Record', 16 March 1974.

42. See Denis Healey, *The Time of My Life* (London, 1989), p. 354; Douglas Hurd, *Robert Peel: A Biography* (London, 2007).

43. Prior, *A Balance of Power*, p. 72; and see Campbell, *Edward Heath*, p. xix.

44. Ibid., p. 619; Donoughue, *The Heat of the Kitchen*, p. 115.

45. Campbell, *Edward Heath*, p. 618; John Campbell, *Margaret Thatcher*, vol. 1: *The Grocer's Daughter* (London, 2000), p. 255; Hurd, *An End to Promises*, p. 137; PRO PREM 16/231, 'Note for the Record', 16 March 1974.

46. Donoughue, *Downing Street Diary*, pp. 52–3; and see Donoughue, *The Heat of the Kitchen*, p. 119; Jenkins, *A Life at the Centre*, pp. 369–70.

47. *The Times*, 5 March 1974; *Time*, 18 March 1974; Donoughue, *Downing Street Diary*, pp. 53–4; Donoughue, *The Heat of the Kitchen*, pp. 120–22.

Further Reading

The advantage of writing about very recent history – as well as the great disadvantage – is that so much material is immediately available on the Internet. In the 1970s, a historian writing about events four decades earlier would have been compelled to make endless long trips to research libraries, cranking through the rolls of microfilmed newspapers until he was driven almost mad with boredom and frustration. These days, however, the online archives of *The Times*, the *Guardian* and the *Observer* are available to subscribers at the click of a mouse, as are the archives of the American magazine *Time*, which gives a fascinating outsider's view of British affairs. For the ultimate insider's view, though, there is no better source than the National Archives, whose website now has plenty of digitized material, including the minutes of all Cabinet meetings (http://www.nationalarchives.gov.uk/cabinetpapers/) as well as a selection of particularly significant government documents from year to year – although of course most documents need to be consulted at the archives in Kew.

All the parliamentary debates from the decade can be consulted at the terrific Hansard site (http://hansard.millbanksystems.com/sittings/1970s), while the BBC site's *On this Day* feature carries reports and brief clips relating to many major news stories of the time. The Margaret Thatcher Foundation (http://www.margaretthatcher.org/archive) has a stupendous range of documents, speeches, minutes and articles covering the whole of her career over half a century, including dozens of documents on the Heath government. But by far the most impressive online resource is the University of Ulster's CAIN archive (http://cain.ulst.ac.uk/) on the conflict in Northern Ireland since 1968, which has a vast wealth of chronologies, statistics, documents and eyewitness accounts – more than enough, in fact, for even the most assiduous researcher.

Although the 1970s have not had the same scholarly attention as earlier decades, this book necessarily draws on the research of other historians. I have tried to acknowledge all my debts in the Notes, but it is worth repeating that, as with my previous books, writing *State of Emergency* would have been impossible, or at least a lot more difficult, had it not been for the hugely rich work of all those scholars who have already crossed some of this ground. Books about the period are now coming out every year, most recently Andy Beckett's journalistic account *When the Lights Went Out: Britain in the Seventies* and Francis Wheen's hilarious *Strange Days Indeed: The Golden Age of Paranoia* (both 2009). The best place to start, though, is still Phillip Whitehead, *The Writing on the Wall: Britain in the Seventies* (1985), an evocative account by a former Labour MP who interviewed many of the key players for a Channel 4 documentary series. For general accounts of the culture of the period, meanwhile, see Robert Hewison, *Too Much: Art and Culture in the Sixties, 1960–75* (1986), Dave Haslam, *Not Abba: The Real Story of the 1970s* (2005), and Howard Sounes, *Seventies: The Sights, Sounds and Ideas of a Brilliant Decade* (2006). And for a highly impressive attempt to bring all this material together, see Alwyn W. Turner, *Crisis? What Crisis? Britain in the 1970s* (2008), which has some terrific material about television, pop music and pulp bestsellers, among other things.

On the politics of the era, the obvious starting point is John Campbell's masterful biography of *Edward Heath* (1993), a classic of the genre and far more informative than Heath's stodgy memoirs. The only scholarly account of the government itself is Stuart Ball and Anthony Seldon (eds.), *The Heath Government, 1970–1974: A Reappraisal* (1996), a fine collection of detailed essays on everything from economic policy to Northern Ireland. Douglas Hurd's *An End to Promises* (1978) is a thoughtful and colourful insider's memoir. The most useful biographies of other key figures are Simon Heffer, *Like the Roman: The Life of Enoch Powell* (1998), John Campbell, *Margaret Thatcher*, vol. 1: *The Grocer's Daughter* (2000), Mark Garnett and Ian Aitken, *Splendid! Splendid! The Authorized Biography of Willie Whitelaw* (2003), and Lewis Baston, *Reggie: The Life of Reginald Maudling* (2004), all of which are superb. On the Labour side, Ben Pimlott's *Harold Wilson* (1992) and Philip Ziegler's *Wilson: The Authorized Life* (1993) do their best to lighten the gloom with moments of wry humour, while Kenneth O. Morgan's *Callaghan: A Life* (1997) is an excellent read. But the real pleasure lies in reading what Wilson's colleagues wrote about themselves and each other: for example, in Denis Healey's boisterous *The Time of My Life* (1989) and Roy Jenkins's stylish *A Life at the Centre* (1991), and above all in the relevant volumes of Tony Benn's diaries, *Office Without Power: Diaries 1968–72* (1988) and *Against the Tide: Diaries 1973–1976* (1989). And among a host of books on the political turmoil of the early 1970s, I would single out Richard Clutterbuck, *Britain in Agony: The Growth of Political Violence* (1978), Michael Hatfield, *The House the Left Built: Inside Labour Policy Making 1970–1975* (1978) and especially David Butler and Dennis Kavanagh, *The British General Election of February 1974* (1974).

For more on the British economy, the reader is spoilt for choice. The scholarly essays in Richard Coopey and Nicholas Woodward (eds.), *Britain in the 1970s: The Troubled Economy* (1996) are absolutely indispensable for specialists but perhaps a bit hard going for the lay reader. Edmund Dell's hilariously waspish *The Chancellors: A History of the Chancellors of the Exchequer, 1945–90* (1996) is a more obvious place to start. Geoffrey Owen, *From Empire to Europe: The Decline and Revival of British Industry Since the Second World War* (1999) is quite outstanding, and I also recommend David Smith's insightful *The Rise and Fall of Monetarism: The Theory and Politics of an Economic Experiment* (1991) and David Kynaston's characteristically brilliant *The City of London*, vol. 4: *A Club No More, 1945–2000* (2001). On the unions, I learned a lot from the essays in John McIlroy, Nina Fishman and Alan Campbell (eds.), *The High Tide of British Trade Unionism: Trade Unions and Industrial Politics, 1964–1979* (2007), as well as from older books such as Paul Ferris, *The New Militants: Crisis in the Trade Unions* (1972) and Stephen Milligan, *The New Barons: Union Power in the 1970s* (1976). On Northern Ireland, meanwhile, I relied heavily on Peter Taylor's trilogy *Provos* (1997, pbk. 1998), *Loyalists* (1999, pbk. 2000) and *Brits* (2001, pbk. 2002), Richard English's thoughtful *Armed Struggle: The History of the IRA* (2003), and Kevin Myers's colourful, hilarious and justly acclaimed *Watching the Door: Cheating Death in 1970s Belfast* (2008).

For the sections on Europe, I found Hugo Young, *This Blessed Plot: Britain and Europe from Churchill to Blair* (1998) enormously useful. For holidays, I relied on Miriam Akhtar and Steve Humphries, *Some Liked It Hot: The British on Holiday at Home and Abroad* (2000); on environmentalism, I found Meredith Veldman, *Fantasy, the Bomb and the Greening of Britain: Romantic Protest, 1945–1980* (1994) very helpful. Among a host of excellent books on women and feminism, meanwhile, I recommend Mary Ingham, *Now We Are Thirty: Women of the Breakthrough Generation* (1982), Sheila Rowbotham, *A Century of Women: The History of Women in Britain and the United States* (1999) and the essays in Ina Zweiniger-Bargielowska (ed.), *Women in Twentieth-Century Britain* (2001). For more on race and immigration, see Mike Phillips and Trevor Phillips, *Windrush: The Irresistible Rise of Multi-Racial Britain* (1999), Shamit Saggar, *Race and Politics in Britain* (1992) and Robert Winder, *Bloody Foreigners: The Story of Immigration to Britain* (2004). And despite the swathes of amusingly dated Marxist cultural analysis, Stuart Hall *et al.*, *Policing the Crisis: Mugging, the State and Law and Order* (1978) remains well worth a look, while Martin Walker, *The National Front* (1977) is the best book on a distinctly unpleasant subject.

On a happier note, Paul Ferris, *Sex and the British: A Twentieth-Century History* (1993), Cate Haste, *Rules of Desire: Sex in Britain, World War I to the Present* (1994) and Hera Cook, *The Long Sexual Revolution: English Women, Sex and Contraception 1800–1975* (2005) all make much more cheerful reading. The most useful book on London is Jerry White's masterful *London in the Twentieth Century* (2001), while Mark Clapson's books *Invincible Green Suburbs, Brave New Towns* (1998) and *A Social History of Milton Keynes: Middle England/Edge City* (2004) are terrific on suburbia. On pop music, see Barney Hoskyns, *Glam! Bowie, Bolan and the Glitter Rock Revolution* (1998), as well as Dave Harker's indispensable essay 'Blood on the Tracks: Popular Music in the 1970s', in Bart Moore-Gilbert (ed.), *The Arts in the 1970s: Cultural Closure?* (1994). On football, Hunter Davies, *The Glory Game* (1972), is a classic, while I also relied on Eric Dunning, Patrick Murphy and John M. Williams, *The Roots of Football Hooliganism: A Historical and Sociological Study* (1988), Richard Holt, *Sport and the British: A Modern History* (1990) and Andrew Mourant, *Don Revie: Portrait of a Footballing Enigma* (1990).

Perhaps the most enjoyable books on the 1970s, though, fall into none of these categories. Among contemporary works of non-fiction, few books are more moving than Ken Coates and Richard Silburn, *Poverty: The Forgotten Englishmen* (1970), while Jeremy Seabrook's evocative

City Close-Up (1973) overflows with the voices of the people of Black-burn, Jonathan Raban's elegant *Soft City* (1974, pbk. 1975) is terrific on bohemian London, and Ann Oakley's passionate *Housewife* (1974) brings to life a group of women usually ignored by historians. For splendidly dark recreations of the grittier side of life in the 1970s, see Gordon Burn, *Somebody's Husband, Somebody's Son: The Story of Peter Sutcliffe* (1984) and Kester Aspden, *The Hounding of David Oluwale* (2008). And while there are plenty of published diaries relating to the period, I found the most illuminating to be Ronald McIntosh, *Challenge to Democracy: Politics, Trade Union Power and Economic Failure in the 1970s* (2006), James Lees-Milne, *Diaries, 1971–1983* (2008) and Russell Davies (ed.), *The Kenneth Williams Diaries* (1993) – this last both hilarious and unbearably sad.

In fiction, the seventies offer plenty of unexpected pleasures: among the most atmospheric and revealing are Kingsley Amis, *Girl, 20* (1971); Martin Amis, *The Rachel Papers* (1973); John le Carré, *Tinker Tailor Soldier Spy* (1974); Margaret Drabble's *The Ice Age* (1977) and *The Middle Ground* (1980); and Piers Paul Read's *A Married Man* (1979, but set five years earlier). Above all, of course, there is Malcolm Bradbury's coruscating *The History Man* (1975, pbk. 1977), dated in parts, dis-turbingly relevant in others. This was a golden age of the theatre, too: for savage dissections of the Heath years, see Howard Brenton and David Hare, *Brassneck* (performed 1974) and David Hare, *Knuckle* (performed 1974), although the best drama of the decade was surely Alan Ayckbourn's uproarious and tragic trilogy *The Norman Conquests* (1973). For guidance through the literary and dramatic worlds, incidentally, I relied on two outstanding works: D. J. Taylor, *After the War: The Novel and England Since 1945* (1993) and Michael Billington, *State of the Nation: British Theatre Since 1945* (2007).

Among films, *A Clockwork Orange* (1971), *Carry On at Your Con-venience* (1971) and *Live and Let Die* (1973) stand out for sheer entertainment, as well as for some unintentional insights. Alexander Walker, *National Heroes: British Cinema in the Seventies and Eighties* (1985) remains a splendidly entertaining survey, while Robert Shail (ed.), *Seventies British Cinema* (2008) has essays on virtually every aspect of the domestic film industry at its lowest point. Leon Hunt, *British Low Culture: From Safari Suits to Sexploitation* (1998) is surely the last word on sex comedies. Television in the early seventies, meanwhile, was in a class of its own: for a good survey, see Asa Briggs, *The History of Broadcasting in the United Kingdom*, vol. 5: *Competition* (1995). On DVD the list of delights is endless, from *Upstairs, Downstairs* to *Fawlty Towers* and from *The Onedin Line* to *Whatever Happened to the Likely Lads?* A brave man might start with the adventures of *Jason King*, while the best and most revealing stories of *Doctor Who* from this period are probably 'Inferno' (1970) and 'The Green Death' (1973). Almost unbelievably, you can even buy boxed sets of *Love Thy Neighbour*, but it is probably best not to leave them lying around.

Index

miners 7, 14, 21, 90, 91, 113, 117,
    529, 595
  wage demands 113, 114, 115,
    127, 577–9
  wages 113, 114, 127, 130–31,
    577–9, 628
  working conditions 116–17
miners' strike, 1972 113–33, 298,
    310, 578
  media coverage 115, 117–18,
    125–6, 127
  National Coal Board and 115,
    116, 118, 121, 125, 126
  NUM and 113–26, 130–31, 578;
    Arthur Scargill and 118–19,
    122–6, 131
  opinion polls on/support for 117–
    19, 125, 132
  picketing 118–19, 120–25
  police action during 122, 123,
    124, 125, 126
miners' strike, 1973/4 579–87, 595–
    601, 608–10, 612, 617–18,
    621, 627–8, 637
  opinion polls on 583
  TUC negotiations with
    government over 603–6
Mirzoeff, Edward 329–30
Mishan, E. J: *The Cost of Economic
    Growth* 183
Mitchell, Juliet: *Women in Society*
    385–6
Mocatta, Mr Justice 514
Moffatt, James *see* Allen, Richard
    (pseud.)
Monday Club 258–9, 491
Monnet, Jean 165, 167
Moore, Marie 224–5
Moore, Roger 275, 388, 398, 410
  questionable dress sense 398
Moorhouse, Geoffrey 186
Moral Re-armament 463, 464
Morecambe and Wise 48–9, 591

Morgan-Giles, Rear Admiral Morgan
    194–5
Morley, Robert 600
Morning Star 107
Morris, Desmond 561
Morrison, Sara 66
Mortimer, Penelope 385
Mosley, Sir Oswald 287, 292
Moss, Elaine 350
Movement for Survival 219
Muggeridge, Malcolm 457, 458,
    459, 465
mugging 282, 283–6, 359, 362
Mullery, Alan 398
multinational corporations *see*
    globalization
Mulvey, Laura 375
Murdoch, Rupert 38, 443
Murphy, Stephen 446, 447, 448–9
Murray, James 278
Murray, Len 102, 603–4, 605, 606
Murray, Dame Rosemary 395
Murrell, Wally 262–3
Muscutt, Jennifer 422
museums/galleries 41–2, 196
  entrance charges 41, 73, 196
music *see* classical music; popular
    music
Myers, Kevin 231, 233, 236–7, 245,
    476–7, 486, 492–3, 498

Nabarro, Sir Gerald 459, 526
The Naked Civil Servant 404–5
Nation, Terry 210
National Abortion Campaign 431
National Coal Board (NCB) 113,
    183, 578
  in 1972 miners' strike 115, 116,
    118, 121, 125, 126
  Derek Ezra as chairman 115,
    118
  Lord Robens as chairman 113
National Council of Women 374

Tebbit, Norman 78, 82, 327–8, 559
teenagers *see* young people
television 6, 10, 14, 30, 45–52, 47n,
174, 433–4, 528, 585, 591
for children/young people 348–9,
352, 354
criticism of 47–8, 49, 348–9; *see
also* Whitehouse, Mary
numbers of sets 5, 19, 20, 21, 46
Play for Today 311, 345, 346
subject matter: capitalism 521–2;
cookery 344; environmental
issues 197–8, 203–7, 208,
211–12; feminism 387–8,
410–12, 416–17; football
coverage 543, 545; homo-
sexuality 404–5; racial issues,
religion 466; social issues 311
viewing figures 4–5, 28, 46
violence on 350
see also individual programmes
Tennant, Emma 39
terrorism/terrorists 9, 140, 282–3,
347, 394–5, 615–16
see also IRA; violence
Thatcher, Margaret 10, 28, 51, 300,
413, 418–19, 460, 637, 643
as Education Secretary 65, 71–2,
369, 422–3
on feminism 417–18
on masturbation 422
as Prime Minister 89, 110, 126,
148, 309, 324, 325, 326, 351–
2, 395, 513
Thear, David and Katie 211
theatre 42–3, 178–9, 515–18
see also individual playwrights
Thomas, R. S.
'The Moon in Lleyn' 466
'Via Negativa' 466
Thompson, J. W. M. 471–2
Thompson, Sir Harold 541, 567,
569, 570

Thomson, George 154–5, 159, 168
Thorn, John 195
Thorpe, Jeremy 6, 165, 167, 405,
532, 627, 639–40
three-day week, 1973 584, 585–6,
595–601, 603–6
Thrower, Percy 336
Thwaite, Anthony 271
Till Death Us Do Part 174, 250, 262,
269, 276, 311, 460–61, 540, 597
Time 7, 36, 316, 581, 594
Time Out 451
The Times 4, 8, 124, 147, 182, 186,
194, 195, 212, 213, 217, 220,
282–3, 313, 339, 346, 369, 465,
469, 508, 527, 616, 619, 635
in 1974 general election 606–7,
609, 611, 616, 628
on Common Market 30, 151,
162, 169, 170
critics writing in 43, 49, 277, 344,
349, 356, 434, 447
on economic conditions 24, 75,
79, 87, 88, 115, 117, 298, 299,
303, 326, 531, 532, 579, 592,
600, 602, 628
editorials/leaders 218, 294, 299,
320, 326, 374, 379, 449, 472,
523, 525, 532, 564, 566, 568–
9, 573–4, 579, 592, 606–7,
609, 616
on football 540–41, 552, 563,
564, 566, 568, 573–4
on Edward Heath 16, 17, 42, 61,
67, 72, 304, 314, 559, 602, 606
on immigration 254, 257, 258,
265, 271, 274, 277, 278, 362
letters to 106, 131, 218, 248,
258, 447, 456, 459, 471, 472,
527, 559, 596
on the miners 121, 127, 130, 132,
609
news photographs 128, 129, 315